"This Systematic Theology volume has been an excellent and honest read, taking great pains to evaluate the early beliefs of the first-century Church, without the unnecessary interpretations and additions of later church councils and creeds. In addition to being theologically accurate, it is also extremely practical, a quality often lacking in many works of systematic theology. As a pastor, I have found it difficult to introduce the average layperson to deeper theological works, as many other works fail to communicate the application of such findings with regular day-to-day life: this volume has succeeded in addressing that 'gap' between the scholar and the layperson. You simply will not find a more theologically honest, accurate, and applicable systematic theology than this present volume."

— Talon Paul
Senior Pastor
Maple Grove Community Church

"Dustin Smith has produced a methodical work of reconstructing first-century theology by uncovering the beliefs and practices of some of the earliest Christians. This book serves both the serious scholar and the everyday Christian who wants to go deeper into biblical studies. Smith consistently provides daily and practical application drawn directly from the theology itself. It encourages us to live out the command from James to "be doers of the word, and not hearers only" (James 1:22). Correct doctrine leads to correct living, and the subjects in this book are treated with care and depth. If you've ever had questions about the nature of God, how sin affects human beings, what happens when we die, or how we are called to live within the church, you'll find thoughtful, biblically grounded responses to these crucial doctrines, and more."

— Nathan Massie
Associate Pastor
Oregon Church of God

"Dustin Smith, together with his co-authors and editors, has delivered a systematic theology that is both richly biblical and refreshingly clear. This volume combines theological depth with an accessible format, offering practical wisdom for today's believer. For anyone seeking a well-organized resource that presents key doctrines from a first-century, restorationist perspective, this work is a must-have. This book is an incredible gift to the church. Clear, well-sourced, and deeply instructive, it is a resource the Body of Christ will treasure for years to come."

— William Barlow
Head Pastor
Compass Christian Church

"Dustin Smith is to be commended for his prodigious work on Systematic Theology. He has produced a volume that surveys many of the cardinal doctrines of theology in an orderly and detailed way. His helpful introductions will serve students of the Bible to get the lay of the theological land. Though there are drawbacks to this approach, the advantage is that Smith has produced in one text a comprehensive articulation that allows the reader to observe connections between doctrines and contemplate the system as a whole."

— Sean Finnegan
President
Living Hope International Ministries

"I've read systematic theology books before, but I've never encountered anything like this... until now! Dustin Smith endeavors to take us back to the foundations of Christianity and the early church as he explores what Jesus' original disciples believed and why, way before flawed councils and erroneous creeds that punished dissenters got involved. Dustin will take you on an exciting journey with rich Jewish context and a comprehensive background to paint a beautiful picture of a deeply robust history, but not at the expense of being accessible to the average person. His clarity, wisdom, and encouragement from Genesis to Revelation and most everywhere in between will help all readers understand who God truly is, what he's done, and what he's promised he will do. I'm grateful to Dr. Smith for bringing the timeless and tremendous truth of the most powerful redemption story in the history of the universe to a new audience in a fresh way. May all readers of these pages be filled with scriptural hope and joy as they surrender the rest of their lives to following the Messiah who saves!"

— Dan Cain
Pastor
Troy View Church of God

"To anyone wondering, 'Do we need another systematic theology?' the answer is unequivocally yes. This work fills a long-standing gap by proposing a theology shaped exclusively by the earliest Christians. The language is highly accessible, the scope is broad, and yet it remains thorough enough to leave few stones unturned. Dr. Smith and other contributors make a compelling case for a systematic theology grounded not in later credal formulations, but in the convictions of the biblical authors. *A Systematic Theology of the Early Church* will challenge even the most seasoned and confident students of Scripture to re-evaluate their beliefs in light of the early church's theology."

— Levi Salyers
Lead Pastor
Lakeshore Bible Church

A Systematic Theology of the Early Church

†

Dustin R. Smith

Edited by J. Jeffery Fletcher and Scott A. Deane

Integrity Syndicate
Boise, ID

A SYSTEMATIC THEOLOGY OF THE EARLY CHURCH

Copyright © 2025 Dustin R. Smith. All rights reserved. Except for brief quotations in publications or reviews, no part of this book may be reproduced in any manner without prior written permission from the publisher. Write: Permissions, Integrity Syndicate LLC, 10673 W Lake Hazel Road #64, Boise, ID 83709.

Published by Integrity Syndicate
Boise, ID
info@integritysyndicate.com
Integrity Syndicate publishes critical resources at the core of the New Testament.

HARDCOVER ISBN: 978-1-969070-21-1
PAPERBACK ISBN: 978-1-969070-22-8
EBOOK ISBN: 978-1-969070-23-5

Print LCCN: 2025912358

Classification: LCC BT75 .S11 2025

Scripture quotations are from the New Revised Standard Version Bible, copyright © 1989 National Council of the Churches of Christ in the United States of America; the New American Standard Bible, copyright © 1995 the Lockman Foundation; and the English Standard Version Bible, copyright © 2001 Crossway, a publishing ministry of Good News Publishers. Used with permission. All rights reserved worldwide.

Cover design by Aubrey L. Partain.

To Alexander and Micah.

Contents

Author's Preface	1
Chapter 1: What is Systematic Theology?	5

Part One: Theology — 9
- Chapter 2: The Only True God — 10
- Chapter 3: God is One Person — 18
- Chapter 4: The Natural Attributes of God — 30
- Chapter 5: The Moral Attributes of God — 39
- Chapter 6: God's Agents — 54
- Chapter 7: Applying Theology Today — 74

Part Two: Anthropology — 77
- Chapter 8: Humanity and the Image of God — 78
- Chapter 9: The Mortality of Humanity — 88
- Chapter 10: The Destination of the Dying — 97
- Chapter 11: The Condition of the Dead — 108
- Chapter 12: The Hope of Resurrection — 120
- Chapter 13: The Annihilation of the Wicked — 131
- Chapter 14: Applying Anthropology Today — 142

Part Three: Hamartiology — 145
- Chapter 15: Humanity's Sin and God's Solution — 146
- Chapter 16: The Mosaic Covenant — 157
- Chapter 17: The New Covenant — 169
- Chapter 18: The Universal Effects of Sin — 179
- Chapter 19: Creation in Rebellion — 187
- Chapter 20: Applying Hamartiology Today — 206

Part Four: Christology — 209
- Chapter 21: The Messianic Expectations from the Old Testament — 210
- Chapter 22: The Birth of Jesus — 221
- Chapter 23: Jesus' Messianic Roles — 233
- Chapter 24: Jesus as God's Agent — 251
- Chapter 25: Wisdom Christology and Logos Christology — 263
- Chapter 26: The Death, Resurrection, and Exaltation of Jesus — 278
- Chapter 27: Applying Christology Today — 289

Part Five: Pneumatology — 292
- Chapter 28: Holy Spirit as God's Power and Presence — 293
- Chapter 29: How The Spirit Relates to the Father and the Son — 303
- Chapter 30: The Spirit's Role in the New Covenant — 312
- Chapter 31: Walking By the Spirit — 321
- Chapter 32: Applying Pneumatology Today — 329

Part Six: Soteriology — 332
- Chapter 33: The Gospel of the Kingdom of God — 333
- Chapter 34: Faith and Believing — 342
- Chapter 35: What Conversion Looked Like — 352
- Chapter 36: Salvation and the In-Breaking of the Kingdom — 367
- Chapter 37: Righteousness and Justification in the New Covenant — 379
- Chapter 38: Applying Soteriology Today — 390

Part Seven: Ecclesiology — 393
- Chapter 39: The Church as the Renewed People of God — 394
- Chapter 40: The Church as the New Temple — 403
- Chapter 41: Baptism and the Lord's Supper — 412
- Chapter 42: The Church's Approach to the Law of Moses — 423
- Chapter 43: The Church as Bride and New Jerusalem — 436
- Chapter 44: Applying Ecclesiology Today — 446

Part Eight: Eschatology — 449
- Chapter 45: Old Testament Promises of Restoration — 450
- Chapter 46: The Future Hope of the Kingdom of God — 462
- Chapter 47: The Present Experience of the Kingdom of God — 474
- Chapter 48: The Second Coming of Christ — 483
- Chapter 49: The Millennial Reign — 496
- Chapter 50: Applying Eschatology Today — 508

Bibliography — 511
Scriptural Index — 530

Author's Preface

Writing a systematic theology is a difficult endeavor. Good authors will always write with their intended audience in mind, and this goal motivated the composition of this volume. However, systematizing all of the central doctrines of the Early Church was no simple task. I knew that I needed to discuss God, humanity, sin, Christ, the Spirit, salvation, the church, and the kingdom of God. These are self-evident beliefs that have so much material that I was forced to summarize even the most important points. Furthermore, attaining a mastery of the biblical material, which is vast and deep, would be impossible with even an entire lifetime of study. Moreover, keeping up with the scholarly literature pertaining to all of these key doctrines is a never-ending (and expensive) task. In light of all of these admitted difficulties, I'm fully aware that I have undoubtedly made mistakes; therefore, I hope that this volume serves as a conversation with my readers, rather than unquestionable dogma that should never be interrogated. Truth has nothing to fear from inquiry, and I would be grateful to learn more effective ways to communicate these essential truths that the Early Church held so dear. In other words, I am certainly not above correction, and I have undoubtedly been mistaken in the past.

Another difficulty lies in determining how to fairly handle doctrines that appear only in a single passage. Technically, they do belong in a volume dedicated to the beliefs and teachings of the Early Church. However, it can be reasonably asked whether every Christian community in the first century AD practiced baptism on behalf of the dead, something that is only mentioned in a single verse (1 Cor 15:29). Although it is clear that love undergirded the regular practices of the churches, which included the motivation behind giving financial support to widows over the age of sixty (1 Tim 5:9), only one verse mentions this rule. Unfortunately, we simply have no evidence that this rule governed the policies in any other church at that time. What about the detail mentioned by Paul concerning the living believers who will be caught up (commonly known as the "rapture") at the second coming of Christ, which is mentioned only in 1 Thessalonians 4:17? To include comments on and the incorporation of all of these single-verse nuances of early Christian theology would result in an impossible volume to compose. As such, I had to be selective, choosing to focus on the doctrines that are widely attested and shared by multiple authors of the biblical texts.

One of the key motivators for this volume was Alva G. Huffer's 1960 work, *Systematic Theology*. Dr. Huffer's book on systematic theology was noteworthy for its treatment of the doctrines of God and Christ that closely mirrored the beliefs of early Christians. While other systematic theologies written in the twentieth and twenty-first centuries have organized their doctrines under the presuppositions of denominational decisions made hundreds of years after the New Testament was written, Huffer attempted to focus on doctrines held by the earliest communities of Christian faith. I had the great honor and privilege of taking several courses with Dr. Huffer in my undergraduate theological training, and I was deeply impacted by his passion for teaching these simple truths. His volume on systematic theology utilized the popular translation of his day, the King James Version, a translation that served his initial readers very well in their theological formation. Since the churches in the twenty-first century have gravitated towards modern versions of the Bible, it was decided that a new volume of systematic theology should be made available for the contemporary generation. As such, I decided to draw upon my familiarity with the three biblical languages and employ modern translations (i.e., NASB, NRSV, ESV) in order to more accurately convey the precise meaning of the texts of Scripture to my target audience.

Another consideration that went into the composition of this present volume is the need to offer readers clarity on the identity of God. While several modern worship songs offer praise to "the Lord," it is often difficult to discern who this intended object is, whether the *Lord* God or our *lord* Jesus Christ. The biblical authors, however, never confused these two figures or collapsed them into a single being defined as "the Lord." Further confusion sometimes occurs when people read the designation that frequently appears in the pages of the Old Testament, LORD, which is an editorial substitute for the personal name of the only true God, *Yahweh*. In an attempt to offer clarity on God's identity and to avoid confusing the LORD with Jesus Christ, our lord, I have made the decision to use the personal name of God, Yahweh, when it appears in quotations of the Old Testament. Several modern English translations of the Bible have made the same decision to include Yahweh in their Old Testaments (e.g., Holman Christian Standard Bible, Lexham English Bible, Legacy Standard Bible). I hope that the decision to include Yahweh will assist in bringing clarity to the readers and their understanding of the Early Church's theology.

Furthermore, I have made a concerted effort to minimize the use of key original biblical language vocabulary to avoid unnecessarily distancing myself from my target audience. Occasionally, as the reader will encounter in this volume, consulting the original languages is necessary in order to convey a key interpretive point in a passage or a central doctrine. Discussion of these Hebrew, Aramaic, and Greek words is written in a manner that is accessible to readers. No previous training in biblical languages is necessary to follow the discussion surrounding the meaning of these noteworthy words. Moreover, I have attempted to use passages that are textually secure, meaning they are not plagued with variants in the manuscript traditions that might call into question their legitimacy. To the best of my knowledge, I have not used any passage from either the Old or New Testaments that has been seriously called into question by textual critics (e.g., Mark 16:9–20; John 7:53–8:11).

A volume of this undertaking would be impossible without the support of several people. I'm grateful to my family, especially my wife, Valerie, for being a helpful sounding board as I try to convey the concepts in my head clearly. I would also like to express my sincere appreciation to the Wednesday night adult Bible study class at Guthrie Grove Church of God, which listened to abbreviated drafts of several chapters and offered helpful comments. Special thanks to several pastors who provided invaluable feedback during the composition of this volume, including Talon Paul, Nathan Massie, and Jake Ballard. I want to express my appreciation to Aubrey Partain for her talented and graceful cover design. I'm grateful for the helpful suggestions offered by Dennis Sharp, who read through several drafts of this manuscript. Moreover, the wise, sage advice from J. Jeffery Fletcher proved invaluable as I wrote the individual chapters. "Jeff," as most know him, provided helpful insights and feedback on tone, as well as wise editorial advice on what content to include. Jeff authored the practical applications within Chapter 7: Applying Theology Today. I would also like to extend my sincere appreciation to my other editor, Scott A. Deane, for his valuable assistance, vital comments, and gracious spirit. Both of my editors were a pleasure to work with, and this present volume owes considerable credit to their involvement.

I pray that this book encourages and equips its readers to love God and live as citizens of his kingdom, which will be fully realized at the return of his son, Jesus Christ.

Dustin R. Smith

October 8, 2025

1
WHAT IS SYSTEMATIC THEOLOGY?

Systematic theology is a part of religious studies that aims to present an organized, coherent, and comprehensive account of the doctrines of the Christian faith. It seeks to summarize and explain Christian teachings systematically by integrating various aspects of theology. The goal of this process is to provide a unified understanding of the doctrines, beliefs, and practices of the Christian faith. The present volume will draw solely on the Protestant Christian Bible, comprising the Old Testament (also known as the Hebrew Bible) and the New Testament as its primary source of material.

It may be beneficial to distinguish *systematic theology* from other theological works, such as *New Testament theology* and *biblical theology*. New Testament theology concentrates solely on the teachings, themes, and theological beliefs presented by the authors of the New Testament documents alone. Biblical theology, on the other hand, is far wider in scope, covering both testaments contained within the Bible. The focus of biblical theology is squarely on the development of theological themes from Genesis to Revelation. A systematic theology, however, presents the major doctrines thematically. It presents each doctrine logically, showing its presence across the entire Bible. While this particular volume focuses on the systematic theology of the Early Church, it should rightly be distinguished from a New Testament theology. Along the same lines, the present volume will offer an organized account of each of the major doctrines from the entire biblical record, but it should not be confused with a work on biblical theology.

Readers familiar with the never-ending production of books in the field of biblical studies will know that there are already several systematic theologies available. One might be tempted to ask why another contribution is even necessary. It is important on this occasion to offer the reader justification for this present volume. First, many popular books on systematic theology openly admit that their approach combines biblical texts with doctrines developed centuries after the completion of the New Testament. This blending of the Bible and post-biblical doctrines results in these systematic theologies becoming flawed in their conclusions. For example, James O. Buswell Jr.'s volume of Presbyterian systematic theology openly admits in its introduction that it presupposes "the sovereign Triune God" in its presentation of the Christian religion.[1] Before Louis Berkhof attempts, unsuccessfully in my opinion, to demonstrate the doctrine from the texts of Scripture in his Reformed systematic theology, he acknowledges that the Church

---

[1] Buswell, *A Systematic Theology of the Christian Religion*, 15.

"began to formulate the doctrine of the Trinity in the fourth century."[2] Similarly, the first volume of Charles Hodge's *Systematic Theology* admits that the Trinity cannot be proved by any scriptural citation and that it was progressively revealed over time.[3] More recently, the 2020 edition of Wayne Grudem's Baptist-leaning *Systematic Theology* encourages the use of church history, the creeds, and philosophy to help readers understand what the entire Bible teaches on various subjects.[4] These books claim to offer systematic treatments of the doctrines and teachings contained within the Bible, but they are guilty of mingling post-biblical doctrines with scriptural doctrines, resulting in a version of the Christian faith that would have been unrecognizable to Jesus Christ and the Early Church.

The present volume expressly aims to present a systematic theology of the Early Church that is derived from the biblical texts alone. There are several noteworthy developments of doctrine that took place in the centuries following the completion of the New Testament documents, including the immortality of the soul, veneration of deceased saints, apostolic succession, eternal torment, the two natures of Christ, and the famous doctrine of the Trinity. This volume will not consider these developments in its systematic treatment of the Bible's theology. As such, the scope of our study is more precise and careful than the previously mentioned attempts at creating a systematic theology, resulting in a far more accurate portrayal of what the earliest followers of Christ believed and taught in their communities of faith. Readers interested in the theology held by the first-century Christians, rather than the diverse theological perspectives of the fourth and fifth centuries, will find this volume useful.

Throughout this book, I will introduce and systematically explore eight of the most important biblical doctrines of the Early Church. These doctrines are theology, anthropology, hamartiology, christology, pneumatology, soteriology, ecclesiology, and eschatology. These are elaborate terms that biblical scholars use to distinguish these essential works of theological study from one another, and as such, the terminology may be foreign to some readers. I will briefly introduce the terms here, while they will receive a fuller treatment in the parts of this volume dedicated to them. *Theology* refers to the study of the one true God, the Creator, whose personal name is Yahweh. The study of God is the obvious starting place for any systematic theology. *Anthropology* discusses the study of humanity, the crowning accomplishment of the Creator's good creation. Since the Bible tells the story of how God works with human beings throughout their fall and redemption, anthropology is certainly worthy of our study. *Hamartiology* is the next major doctrine, focusing on the study of sin and its effects on all creation. As such, this doctrine will cover how God's creation has sinned against his purposes and the ensuing results of that rebellion. *Christology* is the study of the person of Jesus Christ, the promised Jewish

---

[2] Berkhof, *Systematic Theology*, 82.
[3] Hodge, *Systematic Theology*, 1:446.
[4] Grudem, *Systematic Theology*, 1.

messiah. This doctrine will explore Jesus' origins, titles, relationship to the God of Israel, humanity, and questions surrounding the nature of his preexistence. *Pneumatology* refers to the study of the Holy Spirit. We will give attention to the many ways in which the Spirit of God interacts with God's creation, both in the past and in the present. *Soteriology* is the study of salvation, deliverance, and redemption. In this study, we will concentrate on the gospel of the kingdom of God, the work of the cross, and the significance of the new covenant. *Ecclesiology* comes next, which means the study of the church. This doctrine gives us the opportunity to look closely at how the renewed people of God are located in Christ, the head of the body of believers. *Eschatology* is appropriately the final doctrine in our systematic theology, as it pertains to the study of the last things. The Early Church set its hope on the return of Jesus to consummate his kingdom, judge the living and the dead, and rule on the throne of David. These eight doctrines summarize the major beliefs and teachings of early Christians.

On a much more practical note, each of these eight doctrines will conclude with a chapter dedicated to how Christians in the twenty-first century might choose to apply these important truths to their lives. Following the lead of Kevin Vanhoozer, who argues persuasively that "Any adequate account of the role of systematic theology in the interpretation of Scripture must address . . . how theology best serves the church,"[5] this present volume will operate under the conviction that sound doctrine and obedient Christian living must coalesce. Simply *knowing* the beliefs and truths that early Christians held is not enough to be a follower of Christ. Doctrinal truth must motivate godly living. To this effect, this volume will endeavor to provide several life applications for each of the eight doctrines in order to encourage the reader to continue the work of the Early Church of making disciples and teaching these converts to observe all that Jesus taught (Matt 28:19–20). This allows the vital work of systematic theology to contribute to the crucial formation of Christian character, discipleship, and righteous living. I will consider my literary efforts successful if readers are inspired to become more informed, Christ-like, holy, and obedient to the terms of the new covenant.

---

[5] Vanhoozer, "Systematic Theology," 774.

PART ONE: THEOLOGY

†

2
THE ONLY TRUE GOD

Theology is the study of God, whom Jesus Christ defined as "the only true God" (John 17:3). Since God is the Creator, redeemer, and sustainer of all that exists, the doctrine that seeks to define, understand, and know him better is the self-evident place to begin any systematic treatment of theology. All life comes from God, which naturally makes him the source. Of equal importance is Paul's insistence that the Christian life should be oriented towards bringing glory to God, whom Paul repeatedly defined as the Father alone (Phil 2:11). As such, the only true God is both the *beginning* and also the *goal* of all theological reflection.

This chapter will initiate our in-depth exploration of theology by examining the most prominent designations of the one and only true God. First, we will explore the personal name of the only true God, which is the most common way that the biblical authors who wrote the Old Testament scriptures referred to Israel's God. Second, we will examine the Hebrew designation *Adonai*, a noteworthy Hebrew title that characterizes God as the supreme Lord. Third, we will turn our attention to the common noun *elohim*, the basic Hebrew designation that translates to "God." Fourth, we will look closely at the Greek equivalent of *elohim*, the noun *theos*, in order to determine how the early Christians defined the person of Israel's Creator. Lastly, we will focus on the familiar designation "Father" that the authors of both testaments employed to illustrate the true God. Once we have laid the necessary groundwork by adequately defining these key designations for the only true God, we will be on a more reliable footing to continue our study of theology with further explorations of his identity, oneness, attributes, and relationship with his creation.

The Name *Yahweh*

The God of Israel has a personal name. English editions of the Bible, out of reverence and respect for God, replace the personal name of God with the designation LORD. What lies behind these capitalized letters are four Hebrew consonants: *yod, he, vav,* and *he*. These four letters are known as the Tetragrammaton (which means "the four letters"). Some readers prefer to say the name of God instead of saying "LORD," and Hebrew specialists and grammarians have good reasons for thinking that the pronunciation of the tetragrammaton is *Yahweh*.[1] Yahweh, the personal name for the God of Israel, appears over 6,800 times in the Old Testament, making it the most frequent way the biblical authors referred to the Creator of heaven and earth. Many modern readers find it beneficial to say "Yahweh" when they see the Tetragrammaton (LORD) printed in the Old Testament.[2]

The pronunciation of the name of God as "Yahweh" can be made with a measure of confidence due to several strands of evidence.[3] The first half of this name ("Yah") is a frequently used shorthand for God, a fact that English Bibles often indicate in the footnotes in order to avoid confusion.[4] The most memorable occurrence of Yah appears in the Psalms, where it serves as the object of the verb "to praise," *Hallelu-Yah* (Pss 135:21; 146:1; 147:1).[5] The Early Church continued to use this Hebrew phrase, maintaining it even in the Greek text of the Book of Revelation, where it appears four times (Rev 19:1, 3, 4, 6).[6] Furthermore, "Yah" is a common ending in theophoric Hebrew names, that is, names that refer to the individual's God, such as Josiah (*"Yosiyah"*) and Zechariah (*"Zechariyah"*).

Three of the Church Fathers, important Christian writers living in the few centuries following the completion of the New Testament documents, provide significant assistance in verifying the pronunciation of the name of Israel's God. Clement of Alexandria, writing in Greek around the year AD 180, recounts how he overheard the name of God pronounced: "Further, the mystic name of the four letters which was affixed to those alone to whom the inner sanctuary was accessible, is called 'Iaoue.'"[7] This rendering in Greek closely resembles the pronunciation "Yahweh," especially when each letter is pronounced individually. Epiphanius of Salamis, who lived in the fourth century AD, relates the pronunciation of the divine name in Greek as "Iabe."[8] Similarly, Theodoret of Cyrus recounts how the Samaritans of his time in the fifth century articulated the Tetragrammaton as "Iabe."[9] When we consider that the Greek *beta* has a "v" sound, the name bears a remarkable resemblance to the Hebrew pronunciation "Yahweh." When we consider all this evidence, we can be reasonably confident that the personal name of the God of Israel, the only true God, is none other than *Yahweh*.

---

[1] Alter, *The Hebrew Bible*, 1:xxxix. It will be the regular practice of this volume to use the name Yahweh when it appears in quotations of the Old Testament.
[2] Eichrodt, *Theology of the Old Testament*, 1:207, rightly observes that "he feels no need to keep his Name a secret, but rather expressly communicates it to his worshippers to be used freely."
[3] Thompson, "Yahweh," 1011.
[4] E.g., Exod 15:2; Ps 68:18; Isa 12:2.
[5] Goldingay, *Old Testament Theology*, 3:174.
[6] Aune, *Revelation 17–22*, 1024.
[7] Clement of Alexandria, *Stromata*, V. 6.
[8] Epiphanius of Salamis, *The Panarion*, Book 1, chapter 50, section 5.8–10.
[9] Theodoret of Cyrus, *Questions on Exodus*, 15.4–10.

The Title *Adonai*

During the time of Jesus and his earliest followers, pious Jews did not utter the personal name of God out of respect and reverence. When they read the Hebrew text and came across the Tetragrammaton, they would substitute a different word instead: *Adonai*. This exalted title means "my Lord" or simply "Lord" (not to be confused with the Tetragrammaton in all caps, LORD). The noun *Adonai* appears 449 times in the Hebrew Bible, with almost every occurrence referring to the God of Israel. Consider this example from 2 Samuel 7:22: "For this reason, You are great, O *Adonai Yahweh*, for there is none like You, and there is no God besides You." The title *Adonai* suggests the incomparable status that Yahweh, the God of Israel, naturally possesses. A similar passage can be observed in Psalm 16:2: "I said to Yahweh, 'You are my Lord (*Adonai*); I have no good besides You.'" In both passages, *Adonai* is clearly another designation that refers to Yahweh, the only true God. The Hebrew grammar of the noun *Adonai* indicates that the title is what linguists refer to as a "plural of majesty," or an intensive Hebrew plural.[10] The plural of majesty occurs when a plural word is used honorifically for a single person.[11] In the case of *Adonai*, its form is the result of adding the first-person suffix ("my") onto the majestically plural noun *adonim*.[12] As we can observe in the passages above, *Adonai* clearly refers to a single person, to Yahweh himself, a fact that is easily verifiable by noticing the singular pronouns.

The Noun *Elohim*

The next noteworthy designation, *elohim*, is one of the most frequently appearing nouns in the Old Testament, appearing over 2,750 times, and it translates into the noun "God." Sometimes, the Hebrew text describes Yahweh with *elohim* in a way that suggests that it functions as a title, indicated by the definite article "the" (i.e., "the God").[13] More often than not, the noun *elohim* serves as a casual reference for Yahweh, referring to him simply as "God." In essence, the noun "God" acts as a proper name for Yahweh himself. Consider the following examples:

> In the beginning God created the heavens and the earth. (Gen 1:1)

> Then God said, "Let there be light"; and there was light. (Gen 1:3)

> Then Yahweh said to Moses, "Go to Pharaoh and speak to him, 'Thus says Yahweh, the God of the Hebrews, "Let My people go, that they may serve me."'" (Exod 9:1)

---

[10] Köhler, *Old Testament Theology*, 30.
[11] Beckman, "Pluralis Majestatis: Biblical Hebrew," 145–46; Williams, *Williams' Hebrew Syntax*, 2.
[12] Köhler et al., *Hebrew and Aramaic Lexicon*, 13; Waltke and O'Connor, *Biblical Hebrew Syntax*, 122–23.
[13] E.g., Gen 6:9; Exod 3:11; Deut 4:35.

> Arise, O Yahweh; save me, O my God! (Ps 3:7)

> "I am a Hebrew," he replied. "I worship Yahweh, the God of heaven, who made the sea and the dry land." (Jonah 1:9)

Without a doubt, *elohim* is the most prominent designation for Yahweh in the Old Testament.

In the past, interpreters have pointed out that *elohim* is grammatically plural in form, being the plural of the Hebrew noun *eloah*, which is also translated as "God." Readers used to speculate about whether the grammatically plural *elohim* hinted or suggested that God is actually more than one person. More recently, however, these speculations have been abandoned by scholars due to several convincing reasons. First, it is now widely acknowledged that *elohim*, like *Adonai*, is a plural of majesty, an intensive Hebrew plural.[14] This means that *elohim* is plural in form but singular in meaning. Second, the standard practice of the authors of the Old Testament was to govern *elohim* with singular verbs and singular adjectives, demonstrating that these ancient authors clearly understood *elohim* to refer to a single person when used to describe the God of Israel.[15] The following examples illustrate the care with which the biblical authors handled portrayals of the single personhood of Yahweh as *elohim*:

> Know therefore today, and take it to your heart, that Yahweh, He is God in heaven above and on earth below; there is no other. (Deut 4:39)

> Do not fear, for I am with you. Do not anxiously look about you, for I am your God. I will strengthen you, surely I will help you. Surely I will uphold you with My righteous right hand. (Isa 41:10)

> You will live in the land that I gave to your forefathers; so you will be My people, and I will be your God. (Ezek 36:28)

Since the biblical authors intentionally portrayed the God of Israel with the plurally majestic noun *elohim* over 2,000 times, we can safely conclude that this reflects a deeply felt conviction that Yahweh is the most outstanding, most excellent, and only true God.[16]

The Noun *Theos*

Following the conquest of Alexander the Great, which ushered in the Hellenistic period in the fourth century BC, the Jewish people required a version of the Scriptures in the

---

[14] Joüon and Muraoka, *A Grammar of Biblical Hebrew*, 469–70; Fretheim, "אֱלֹהִים," 405; Köhler et al., *Hebrew and Aramaic Lexicon*, 53, 122.
[15] Ringgren, "אֱלֹהִים," 272–73.
[16] Seow, *A Grammar for Biblical Hebrew*, 19, 96.

common language of the time. Beginning in the mid-third century BC, Jewish scribes began translating the Hebrew Bible into Greek (a translation known as the Septuagint), which enabled Greek-speaking Jews to access the Scriptures in their own language. As such, the Hebrew noun for God (*elohim*) was translated into its Greek equivalent, *theos*, the noun from which we get the word *theology*, the study of God. By the first century AD, Greek was the dominant language in the Eastern Mediterranean and in much of the Western Roman Empire. As such, all twenty-seven New Testament documents were originally written in the Greek language.[17] When the New Testament authors referred to the only true God, they naturally employed the Greek noun theos approximately 1,300 times. This frequency makes *theos* the most common designation that the writers of the New Testament used to illustrate the only true God.

On several occasions, we find *theos* paired with the definite article in Greek, which translates into "the God." Consider the following evidence from the New Testament:

> The God of Abraham, Isaac, and Jacob, the God of our fathers, has glorified His child Jesus (Acts 3:13)

> Blessed be the God and Father of our Lord Jesus Christ, the Father of mercies and God of all comfort (2 Cor 1:3)

> The God and Father of the Lord Jesus, He who is blessed forever, knows that I am not lying. (2 Cor 11:31)

> Now may the God of peace Himself sanctify you entirely (1 Thes 5:23)

As we can observe, "the God" is regularly characterized by singular references and pronouns. Furthermore, he is defined as *the Father* and as *the God* of the patriarchs Abraham, Isaac, and Jacob.[18] Noteworthy is the detail that this God is the God of our Lord Jesus. Yes, the Early Church believed that Jesus has a God.[19]

The True God as Father

The final designation for the only true God to discuss in this chapter is that God is *the Father*, and his people are *his children*. The fatherhood of God is expressed in several Old Testament passages:

---

[17] Mussies, "Languages (Greek)," 202; Wallace, *Greek Grammar*, 26.
[18] Bauer et al., *Greek-English Lexicon*, 451.
[19] The Early Church frequently portrayed the fact that Jesus had a God above him. See Matt 27:46; Mark 15:34; John 20:17; Rom 15:6; 2 Cor 1:3; 11:31; Eph 1:17; Heb 1:9; 1 Pet 1:3; Rev 1:6; 3:2, 12.

> Do you thus repay Yahweh, you foolish and senseless people? Is not He your father, who created you, who made you and established you? (Deut 32:6)
>
> You, O Yahweh, are our Father, our Redeemer from of old is Your name. (Isa 63:16)
>
> But now, O Yahweh, You are our Father, we are the clay and You our potter; and all of us are the work of Your hand. (Isa 64:8)
>
> Then I said, "How I would set you among My sons and give you a pleasant land, the most beautiful inheritance of the nations!" And I said, "You shall call Me, My Father, and not turn away from following Me." (Jer 3:19)
>
> Do we not all have one Father? Has not one God created us? (Mal 2:10)

The God of Israel's role as a father is indicative of him being the Creator and maker of all things.[20] Additionally, it firmly sets him in an intimate relationship with his covenant people, who are identified as his children.[21] When we reach the New Testament, these emphases on the Father's role as Creator and covenant God, who is in relationship with his sons and daughters, continue to appear. Observe how the true God is illustrated as the Father alone:

> "Pray, then, in this way: 'Our Father who is in heaven, hallowed be Your name.'" (Matt 6:9)
>
> Yet for us there is one God the Father, from whom are all things, and we for Him (1 Cor 8:6)
>
> "And I will be a Father to you, and you shall be sons and daughters to Me," says the Lord Almighty. (2 Cor 6:18)

The New Testament authors did not see fit to reproduce the personal name of the only true God, Yahweh, in Greek (with the lone exceptions being the four references to *Hallelujah* in Revelation 19). Instead, the writers used "Father" as the most common title for God in the New Testament. Even Jesus Christ was remembered as describing God as the Father more than any other title (Matt 6:1; John 14:28; 20:17).[22] When Jesus prayed to the Father, he addressed him as the only true God: "This is eternal life, that they may know You, the only true God" (John 17:3).

For the Jewish Christians, understanding God as the Father would be recognizable from the inherited teachings of Judaism and the familiar portrayals within the Hebrew Scriptures.[23] But what about Gentiles who converted to becoming Christ-followers? How did they come to speak of and identify the God of their newfound

---

[20] Baker, "God," 365.
[21] Oswalt, "God," 291.
[22] Hurtado, "God," 271, 275–76.
[23] Bassler, "God (NT)," 1054–55; Bright, *The Authority of the Old Testament*, 186.

monotheistic faith? When we examine the preaching of Paul, the apostle to the Gentiles, an answer becomes readily available. To become a believer in Christ, pagans needed to abandon their polytheism and embrace Jewish monotheism, which included the understanding that the only true God is the Father. We may easily observe how Paul taught the identity of God to his Gentile converts:

> For you have not received a spirit of slavery leading to fear again, but you have received a spirit of adoption as sons by which we cry out, "Abba! Father!" (Rom 8:15)

> So that with one accord you may with one voice glorify the God and Father of our Lord Jesus Christ (Rom 15:6)

> Grace to you and peace from God our Father and the Lord Jesus Christ (Gal 1:3)

We may gather some additional data from the opening chapter of Paul's first letter to the Thessalonians. Paul reminds his readers of their conversion experience in which they "turned to God from idols to serve a living and true God, and to wait for His Son from heaven" (1 Thes 1:9–10). The Thessalonian Christians served the true God, and they waited for the true God's son, Jesus, to return. If the living and true God has a son, then the true God must be *the Father* of that son. In this way, we can confirm that Paul summoned his Gentile converts to abandon their idols and to serve the Father as the one and only true God.[24]

While Jesus and Paul are surely the most influential teachers of the Early Church's theology, they were not alone in defining the only true God as the Father. The portrayal of God as the Father alone is the consistent witness of the rest of the authors of the New Testament. For example:

> It is for discipline that you endure; God deals with you as with sons; for what son is there whom his father does not discipline? (Heb 12:7)

> Every good thing given and every perfect gift is from above, coming down from the Father of lights, with whom there is no variation or shifting shadow. (James 1:17)

> If you address as Father the One who impartially judges according to each one's work, conduct yourselves in fear during the time of your stay (1 Pet 1:17)

> See how great a love the Father has bestowed on us, that we would be called children of God (1 John 3:1)

> Grace, mercy, and peace will be with us from God the Father and from Jesus Christ, the Father's son, in truth and love. (2 John 1:3)

---

[24] Dunn, *Theology of Paul*, 31–37; Kim and Bruce, *1 & 2 Thessalonians*, 170–72.

And [Jesus] has made us a kingdom, priests to his God and Father—to him be the glory and the dominion forever and ever. Amen. (Rev 1:6)

Conclusion

To summarize, the study of *theology* involves the examination of God, the rightful and self-evident subject of theological reflection. The authors of the biblical texts portrayed the only true God with several vital titles and designations. We first examined God's personal and proper name, *Yahweh*, which is designated in our English versions of the Old Testament as LORD. Then, we drew attention to the exalted title describing the God of Israel, *Adonai*. This title, commonly rendered as "my Lord," served as a substitute designation when pious readers wanted to avoid pronouncing the divine name "Yahweh" out of respect and reverence for him. We also examined the common Hebrew noun referring to God, *elohim*. We noted its plural form while also giving attention to its singular meaning when referencing the God of Israel. Then we examined the Greek noun for God, *theos*. This common New Testament noun, often emphasized with the definite article ("the God"), defined the object of early Christian monotheistic faith. Lastly, we explored the familial title of "Father," which was the customary way the Early Church referred to the only true God. Emphasizing God's role as the Creator, the maker of the covenant relationship with his people, and his relationship with the son, Jesus Christ, the understanding that the true God was *the Father alone* was firmly entrenched among the earliest Christians.

Having given adequate attention to the most common designations and titles that the authors of the biblical texts used to illustrate the only true God, we can now turn our attention to a topic that is both deeply meaningful to the Jewish people and controversial in the history of Christian attempts to define God over the last 1,700 years. The oneness of the God of Israel was creedally essential to Jesus Christ, while also being theologically divisive in the centuries of theological speculation that continues even today. As we will soon see, however, the doctrine of the oneness of God is simple, straightforward, and frequently displayed in the teachings of the biblical record, both in the Old and New Testaments. It is to the important question of how Yahweh, our God, is "one" that we will now direct our attention.

3
GOD IS ONE PERSON

The most central tenet of the Jewish religion is that the God of Israel, maker of heaven and earth, is one.[1] Jesus, the Jewish messiah, naturally taught his followers that the God of Israel is one. The Apostle Paul, who preached the gospel to Gentiles and converted them to become Christ-followers, also taught that the monotheistic God of early Christianity was one. The oneness and unity of God, therefore, was a foundational conviction of the Early Church, which had its roots in the Jewish teachings it inherited from Judaism. Unfortunately, this conviction has been abandoned by many churches today, insisting instead that God is triune, three distinct persons that make up the one God.[2]

This chapter will explore the various ways in which the writers of both the Old and New Testaments portrayed the God of Israel as one person. The aim is to gain a comprehensive understanding of who Yahweh is by examining closely how he is revealed in Scripture by the biblical authors. First, we will take stock of how the writers of Scripture portrayed God with singular references (and how frequently this grammatical emphasis appears in our data). Second, we will draw attention to the various ways in which the one God is distinguished from others. Third, we will examine how the titles conferred upon Yahweh by the biblical authors demonstrate his oneness. Fourth, we will give attention to the creed of Israel, the *Shema*, by examining its meaning and importance. We will observe how the early Christian movement continued to believe and teach the *Shema* in their communities of faith. Lastly, we will explore the conviction of the Early Church that the Father alone was the one true God. To fully appreciate the portrayal of the one God, we must consider the totality of evidence presented in Scripture, not just a few isolated texts.

Singular References for the Only True God

When we take the time to account for the sheer amount of language dedicated by the biblical authors to carefully characterize Yahweh, the God of Israel, the argument for the

---

[1] Sanders, *Judaism*, 195–96; Levenson, *Sinai & Zion*, 82–84.
[2] Nemes, *Trinity & Incarnation*, 36–63, offers much clarity on this issue. Guthrie, *Christian Doctrine*, 76, admits, "The Bible does not teach the doctrine of the Trinity. Neither the word 'trinity' itself nor such language as 'one-in-three,' 'three-in-one,' one 'essence' (or 'substance'), and three 'persons' is biblical language."

oneness of God really begins to come in full force. Grammatically, the number of singular pronouns and singular verbs that illustrate Yahweh as one person in Scripture is in the tens of thousands. These pronouns include instances where Yahweh speaks in the first person (e.g., I, me, myself) and when others refer to Yahweh in the second and third person (e.g., you, yourself, he, him, himself). This inference is self-evident based on the following sample of the biblical data:

> "Sojourn in this land and I will be with you and I will bless you, for to you and to your descendants I will give all these lands, and I will establish the oath which I swore to your father Abraham." (Gen 26:3)

> He said, "O Yahweh, the God of Israel, there is no God like You in heaven above or on earth beneath, keeping covenant and faithfulness to Your servant who walk before You with all their heart" (1 Kgs 8:23)

> Know that Yahweh Himself is God; it is He who has made us, and not we ourselves; we are His people and the sheep of His pasture. (Ps 100:3)

In all three biblical languages—Hebrew, Aramaic, and Greek—the verbs are parsed as having either singular or plural subjects performing the action in question. The biblical authors employed thousands of singular verbs to illustrate the numerous acts of the God of Israel, indicating that this God is a singular person.[3] If the writers of Scripture were convinced that Yahweh is comprised of multiple persons, one would expect several thousand plural pronouns and plural verbs, but this is simply not what the data indicate. Instead, we have the repeated and unrelenting insistence that Yahweh, the only true God, is one person, and the grammar supports this conclusion tens of thousands of times.[4]

Within the Greek language, there is an emphatic way in which a writer can use the third-person singular reflexive pronoun ("himself") in order to highlight the subject meaningfully.[5] As it happens, this grammatical point occurs in several descriptions of the God of Israel. Consider these examples from the New Testament in which the third-person pronoun is utilized intensively:

> Nor is He served by human hands, as though He needed anything, since He Himself gives to all people life and breath and all things (Acts 17:25)

> Now may the God of peace Himself sanctify you entirely (1 Thes 5:23)

---

[3] Neusner, *Judaism When Christianity Began*, 38.
[4] Goldingay, *Biblical Theology*, 33, admits, "It is the biblical portrait of Yahweh as the one God and as the God who has a name, which reflects his being not an idea but a person."
[5] Bauer et al., *Greek-English Lexicon*, 152; Moulton and Porter, *Moulton's Grammar of New Testament Greek: Vol. 1*, 85–86; Black, *New Testament Greek*, 68–69.

> Make sure that your character is free from the love of money, being content with what you have; for He Himself has said, "I will never desert you, nor will I ever forsake you" (Heb 13:5)
>
> God cannot be tempted by evil, and He Himself does not tempt anyone. (James 1:13)
>
> After you have suffered for a little while, the God of all grace, who called you to His eternal glory in Christ, will Himself perfect, confirm, strengthen and establish you. (1 Pet 5:10)
>
> "Behold, the tabernacle of God is among men, and He will dwell among them, and they shall be His people, and God Himself will be among them" (Rev 21:3)

The intensive use of the third-person Greek pronoun for the only true God demonstrates an awareness among these New Testament authors that God was a single person.

In addition to the plethora of singular pronouns and verbs that characterize Yahweh, the biblical authors utilize singular adjectives to further emphasize God's oneness and singularity of person. Again, all three biblical languages possess singular and plural forms for their respective adjectives, and the scriptural data indicate that Yahweh, the God of Israel, was illustrated with singular adjectives hundreds of times. Of particular note are Yahweh's titles "the Holy One" (Ps 71:22; Isa 1:4; Ezek 39:7; Hos 11:9),[6] "the Righteous One" (Exod 9:27; Isa 24:16), "the only wise God" (Rom 16:27), and the "only God" (Jude 1:25). These singular adjectives describing the true God further demonstrate that the authors of the biblical texts believed that he was only one person. As such, these convictions were passed along to their readers and embraced by the Early Church.

One of the distinctive features of Hebrew and Aramaic is the way in which these languages demonstrate possession of nouns. In order to convey that a particular noun belongs to someone or something, a pronominal suffix is added to the end of the noun in both of these languages.[7] For example, the English phrase "his sheep" appears in Hebrew and Aramaic as the noun "sheep" with a suffix at the end of that noun, indicating that it belongs to a third-person masculine singular subject. In an overly literal translation, the translator may render the entire phrase as "sheep of him," but modern translations of the Bible smooth this out for a less clunky rendering, "his sheep." What this means for our current study is that we can examine the various nouns attributed to God and discern quite clearly whether the biblical authors of the Old Testament regarded God as being one person (by using a singular suffix) or multiple persons (by using a plural suffix). The data indicate that there are several thousand instances where singular pronominal suffixes describe Yahweh as possessing a given noun. Some of the more frequently occurring examples include "My people" (Exod 3:7; 1 Sam 9:16; Ezek 36:28), "His people"

---

[6] Köhler, *Old Testament Theology*, 51–53.
[7] Waltke and O'Connor, *Biblical Hebrew Syntax*, 302–5.

(Exod 18:1; Deut 32:9; Ruth 1:6), "His name" (Exod 3:13; Ezra 6:12; Zech 14:9); "My servant" (Gen 26:24; 2 Sam 3:18; Isa 53:11), and "His anointed one" (1 Sam 2:10; 2 Sam 22:51; Ps 2:2). These singular pronominal suffixes give further clarity to how the biblical authors understood the oneness of the God of Israel.

Distinguishing the Only True God from All Others

We can find additional evidence of the concept of God's oneness in the scriptural characterizations of him being numerically distinguished from others in an exclusive way. Several writers of the biblical texts emphasize Yahweh's premier position by contrasting him with all others.[8] Take, for example, the following passages where the figure of Yahweh is distinguished from other figures:

> To you it was shown that you might know Yahweh, He is God; there is no other besides Him. (Deut 4:35)

> Know therefore today, and take it to your heart, that Yahweh, He is God in heaven above and on the earth below; there is no other. (Deut 4:39)

> "Who has long since declared it? Is it not I, Yahweh? And there is no God besides Me, a righteous God and a Savior; there is none except Me." (Isa 45:21)

> "That they may know from the rising to the setting of the sun that there is no one besides Me. I am Yahweh, and there is no other" (Isa 45:6)

> "Remember the former things long past, for I am God, and there is no other; I am God, and there is no one like Me" (Isa 46:9)

> "Thus you will know that I am in the midst of Israel, and that I am Yahweh your God, and there is no other" (Joel 2:27)

Two important facts emerge in these Old Testament passages. First, Yahweh is portrayed as having no one else alongside him ("there is no other").[9] This truth will change after Jesus is born and eventually exalted to sit at God's right hand. However, in the Old Testament portrayal of Yahweh, no one else is with him.[10] No figure sits at Yahweh's right hand in the Old Testament prophetic visions of the heavenly throne room (1 Kgs 22:19; Isa 6:1; Ezek 1:26–28). The second key fact that we may observe from these passages is that when Yahweh is numerically distinguished from all others, he is displayed with singular references. There is no other besides *him*, there is no God besides *me*, there

---

[8] Brueggemann, *Theology of the Old Testament*, 228.
[9] Westermann, *Elements of Old Testament Theology*, 33.
[10] Dyrness, *Themes in Old Testament Theology*, 48.

is none except *me*. These emphases further demonstrate how the biblical authors understood the oneness of God.[11]

Additionally, the biblical authors characterized the only true God as performing actions by himself or all alone. This portrayal sheds further light on the doctrine of the oneness of God. Consider carefully the following examples with this particular language that the writers of Scripture employ:

> "O Yahweh, the God of Israel, who are enthroned above the cherubim, You are the God, You alone, of all the kingdoms of the earth. You have made heaven and earth." (2 Kings 19:15)
>
> Who alone stretches out the heavens and tramples down the waves of the sea (Job 9:8)
>
> Blessed be Yahweh God, the God of Israel, who alone works wonders. (Ps 72:18)
>
> Let them praise the name of Yahweh, for His name alone is exalted; His glory is above earth and heaven. (Ps 148:13)
>
> Thus says Yahweh, the one who redeemed you, and the one who formed you from the womb, "I, Yahweh, am the maker of all things, stretching out the heavens by Myself and spreading out the earth all alone" (Isa 44:24)

Even the New Testament authors use the adjectives "alone" or "only" to describe the one and only true God on several occasions.[12] Take, for example, these verses:

> "How can you believe, when you receive glory from one another and you do not seek the glory that is from the one who alone is God?" (John 5:44)
>
> "This is eternal life, that they may know You, the only true God, and Jesus Christ whom You have sent." (John 17:3)
>
> Now to the King eternal, immortal, invisible, the only God, be honor and glory forever and ever. Amen. (1 Tim 1:17)
>
> Who will not fear, O Lord, and glorify Your name? For You alone are holy; for all the nations will come and worship before You, for Your righteous acts have been revealed. (Rev 15:4)

Observe carefully how these New Testament texts describe God as *the only God*, or the *one who alone is God*, while also using singular references to describe him as only one person.[13]

---

[11] Routledge, *Old Testament Theology*, 99–100.
[12] Schneider, "God," 73, describes the Father of Jesus by drawing attention to the exclusive terminology employed by the authors of the New Testament: "The one God is the living and only true God."
[13] Smith, *Wisdom Christology*, 90–91.

This scriptural evidence affirms the conclusion that the Early Church adopted the Jewish doctrine of the oneness of God, likely due to the influence of Jesus' teachings.

Singular Titles Belonging to the Only True God

Several texts attribute titles and roles to the God of Israel, and upon examining these titles, we can glean further evidence to consider in our study of God's oneness. One important example is God's role as the Creator and maker of all things. In English, we render these titles as nouns, but when they appear in the original languages, they are verbs. When we parse these important verbs (e.g., "the one who creates," "the one who makes"), we find, yet again, further evidence that God is one person. The Old Testament authors expressed the only true God as the Creator and maker with singular verbs in several instances (Job 4:17; Ps 95:6; Isa 27:11; 40:28; Jer 10:16; Hos 8:14). The New Testament writers, composing in Greek, continued this characterization by using a singular verb to illustrate God as the one who creates. The Gospel of Matthew records Jesus describing the Creator God as "He who created" the original man and woman (Matt 19:4).[14] Similarly, the Apostle Paul illustrates he who is blessed forever as "the one who creates" (Rom 1:25). Christians are to put on the new self, which is being renewed in the knowledge of the image of "the one who created" him (Col 3:10). Consistently in the New Testament writings the verb "to create" is singular, indicating a widespread belief and acceptance that the Creator is only one person.

Another noteworthy title that demonstrates the only true God's strength and power is "the Almighty." The New Testament authors reliably reserve this title for God alone, and the Greek behind this title indicates a single almighty person. Therefore, it naturally follows that whoever bears this title is recognized by the writers of the New Testament as only one person. The Apostle Paul attributes this title to the figure of the Father in 2 Corinthians 6:18: "'And I will be a Father to you, and you shall be sons and daughters to Me,' says the Lord Almighty." John of Patmos attributes the title "Almighty" to the one God in several instances. In doing so, John exemplifies the Almighty God as a single person (Rev 1:8), as the Creator (Rev 4:8–11), king of the nations (Rev 11:17; 15:3; 19:6), and faithful judge (Rev 16:7; 19:15). The Book of Revelation carefully distinguishes the Almighty from the figure of the Lamb, which is a common symbolic title for the person of Christ. By referring to God as "the Almighty," these authors emphasize the oneness of that strong, powerful God.

---

[14] Hagner, *Matthew 14–28*, 548; Davies and Allison, *Matthew*, 3:9; Nolland, *Matthew*, 770.

The *Shema*

Probably the most impactful text on the religious understanding of the Jewish people is Deuteronomy 6:4–5, known as the *Shema* due to the first Hebrew word in the passage, which summons people to hear/listen.[15] The passage states: "Hear, O Israel. Yahweh our God, Yahweh is one. You shall love Yahweh your God with all your heart and with all your soul and with all your might." The *Shema* identified who the true God is for the people of Israel, offering his personal name and defining him as one.[16] Then, the *Shema* summons the followers of the one true God to faithfully love him with their entire being, their full devotion. By the time of the inception of the early Christian movement, there is evidence strongly suggesting that Jews were reciting the *Shema* as a creed twice a day, in the morning and in the evening.[17] This practice drew its inspiration from the verses that directly follow the *Shema*, which instructs Israel to recite "these words" when you lie down and when you rise (Deut 6:6–7). Over time, the *Shema* became the standard Jewish expression of their monotheistic faith, which firmly maintained that the Creator God is only one person.[18] As we will soon observe, Jewish monotheism continued to be cherished, believed, and taught among the Early Church.

At some point during the ministry of Jesus Christ, a Jewish scribe approached him and asked which commandment was the most important of all (Mark 12:28). Out of the hundreds of possible choices available, Jesus selected the *Shema* from Deuteronomy 6:4–5, answering the scribe with a recitation of that passage:

> Jesus answered, "The most important is, 'Hear, O Israel! The Lord our God, the Lord is one. And you shall love the Lord your God with all your heart and with all your soul and with all your mind and with all your strength.'" (Mark 12:29–30)

In addition to citing the *Shema*, Jesus offered an additional commandment from Leviticus 19:18, which summons God's people to love their neighbor as themselves. What we can observe from this exchange is that Jesus taught that the greatest teaching from the Scriptures is that God is one, and that one should love this God with all that they have and love their neighbor as themselves. The scribe who initially asked Jesus the question about the most essential commandment expresses his agreement with Jesus' selection of passages, "You are right, Teacher. You have truly said that He is one, and there is no other besides Him" (Mark 12:32). In the scribe's reply, he especially draws attention to the oneness of God expressed in Jesus' recitation of the *Shema*. The scribe, however, introduces another passage into the conversation, Deuteronomy 4:35, which identifies

---

[15] Brueggemann, *Introduction to the Old Testament*, 87.
[16] Fretheim, "God," 610.
[17] Sanders, *Judaism*, 196.
[18] Eichrodt, *Theology of the Old Testament*, 1:226; Dunn, *New Testament Theology*, 45. Sanders, *Judaism*, 242, summarizes the data well: "The Shema' specifies that the Lord God is *one*, which in the first century implied strict monotheism: the one Lord is the *only* Lord. Jewish sensitivity to these commandments was high."

Yahweh as a singular person while also emphasizing that no one else is alongside him. For the scribe, Deuteronomy 4:35 serves as a natural complement to Jesus' insistence that God is one. The narrator informs the reader that Jesus found the scribe's response to be intelligent and that Jesus tells him, "You are not far from the kingdom of God" (Mark 12:34), actions that indicate Jesus' agreement with the scribe's assessment of the oneness of God.[19] This important exchange between Jesus and the Jewish scribe underscores a key point for early Christianity: Jesus Christ believed, affirmed, and taught the Jewish doctrine of the oneness of God.[20]

When we examine how the Early Church continued to spread Jesus' teaching that the Jewish God is one person, we find that the *Shema* continued to be recited. The Apostle Paul, who wrote letters to churches consisting of both Jewish Christians and Gentile Christians, united these two groups under the umbrella of the one true God. Note how Paul weaves in the *Shema* in his correspondence with the Romans and the Galatians:[21]

> Or is God the God of Jews only? Is he not the God of Gentiles also? Yes, of Gentiles also, since God is one—who will justify the circumcised by faith and the uncircumcised through faith. (Rom 3:29–30)

> Why then the law? It was added because of transgressions, until the offspring should come to whom the promise had been made, and it was put in place through angels by an intermediary. Now an intermediary implies more than one, but God is one. (Gal 3:19–20)

As we can observe, Paul did not abandon his commitment to the *Shema* upon joining the early Christians. In fact, Paul taught his converts the truth of the only true God. Even the Epistle of James acknowledges the belief that "God is one" is a doctrine already firmly possessed by his readers: "You believe that God is one; you do well. Even the demons believe—and shudder" (James 2:19). James compliments his readers on doing well in their belief that God is one. He also informs the readers that demons believe the truth of the oneness of God, and they are fearful of this fundamental truth.[22] We can safely conclude that the oneness of God was a foundational Jewish confession that Jesus believed and taught widely among the early Christian communities. The Early Church did not modify the oneness of God or expand the belief that "God is one" to include multiple persons. Jesus and his followers were unitary monotheists in direct continuity with the Judaism of their time.[23]

---

[19] Carter, *Mark*, 342; Perkins, "The Gospel of Mark," 678.
[20] Brueggemann, *Old Testament Theology: An Introduction*, 121.
[21] De Boer, *Galatians*, 228; Dunn, *Galatians*, 191; Longenecker, *Romans*, 448–49.
[22] Allison, *The Epistle of James*, 473–78.
[23] Dunn, *New Testament Theology*, 45–46.

The Christian Understanding of the True God as the Father Alone

Finally, we have reached a point where we can examine how the Early Church understood and defined the one true God, particularly in relation to God's oneness. The identification of Yahweh as the Father continued in early Christian teachings, which insisted that there is only one God, and that this God is *the Father alone*. If God is one person, then that person just is the Father. The understanding that the one true God of the Early Church is the Father alone is easily discernible in the greetings that appear at the head of the epistles contained within the New Testament. In the Pauline letters, God and Christ send greetings to the intended recipients. In these greetings, however, God is always defined as only one person, the Father alone. Jesus Christ is consistently distinguished from God in these epistolary greetings. Observe how Paul clearly identifies "God" as the Father alone while also differentiating Christ from God:

> Grace to you and peace from God our Father and the Lord Jesus Christ. (Rom 1:7)

> Grace to you and peace from God our Father and the Lord Jesus Christ. (1 Cor 1:3)

> Grace to you and peace from God our Father and the Lord Jesus Christ. Blessed be the God and Father of our Lord Jesus Christ, the Father of mercies and God of all comfort (2 Cor 1:2–3)

> Grace to you and peace from God our Father and the Lord Jesus Christ, who gave Himself for our sins so that He might rescue us from this present evil age, according to the will of our God and Father (Gal 1:3–4)

> Grace to you and peace from God our Father and the Lord Jesus Christ. (Phil 1:2)

> Paul and Silvanus and Timothy, to the church of the Thessalonians in God the Father and the Lord Jesus Christ: Grace to you and peace. We give thanks to God always for all of you, making mention of you in our prayers; constantly bearing in mind your work of faith and labor of love and steadfastness of hope in our Lord Jesus Christ in the presence of our God and Father (1 Thes 1:1–3)

> Grace to you and peace from God our Father and the Lord Jesus Christ. (Phlm 1:3)

Paul was not alone in sharing greetings with his churches that identified "God" as the Father while also distinguishing Christ from God. The same understanding of the oneness of God, defined as the Father alone, appears in the other New Testament epistles:

> Blessed be the God and Father of our Lord Jesus Christ (1 Pet 1:3)

> Grace, mercy, and peace will be with us from God the Father and from Jesus Christ, the Father's Son, in truth and love. (2 John 1:3)

> To those who are the called, beloved in God the Father, and kept for Jesus Christ (Jude 1:1)

This survey, which could be expanded to include all of the New Testament letters, demonstrates the widespread belief among the Early Church that the only true God was known simply as the Father.

When we examine the New Testament documents more closely, we can observe how casually the Father is presented as the one God. There are no attempts to redefine the only true God to refer to anyone other than the Father alone. For these early Christians, the oneness of God is expressed in the firm commitment to the belief that the Father is Jesus Christ's God. The *God of Jesus* is defined as the Father alone in several passages (Rom 15:6; 2 Cor 1:3; 11:31; Eph 1:3; 1 Pet 1:3),[24] and it is even a belief that Jesus himself held deeply and taught to his disciples (John 20:17).[25] Jesus expressed agreement with his Jewish opponents when they confessed, "We have one Father: God" (John 8:41–42).[26] Ephesians carefully defines the one God who is over all, through all, and in all, as none other than the Father (Eph 4:6).[27]

Another important way the New Testament authors expressed the oneness of God is seen in the way that they numerically distinguished the one God and Jesus, the son of God. In several instances, Jesus is illustrated in his relationship to the one God as "His son," that is, *God's own son*. The use of the singular masculine pronoun in the phrase "His son" indicates a firm commitment to God as only one person. It also expresses the logical conclusion that one person who is grammatically masculine and who has a son must be the Father. Observe carefully the common practice in which the writers of the New Testament differentiate God and Jesus while also emphasizing Jesus as "His son":

> For God so loved the world, that he gave his only Son, that whoever believes in him should not perish but have eternal life. (John 3:16)

> For God, whom I serve in my spirit in the preaching of the gospel of His son, is my witness (Rom 1:9)

> For if while we were enemies we were reconciled to God through the death of His son (Rom 5:10)

> God is faithful, through whom you were called into fellowship with His son, Jesus Christ our Lord (1 Cor 1:9)

> But when God, who had set me apart from my mother's womb and called me through His grace, was pleased to reveal His son in me (Gal 1:15–16)

> But when the fullness of the time came, God sent forth His son (Gal 4:4)

---

[24] Dunn, *Did the First Christians Worship Jesus?* 3.
[25] Irons et al., *The Son of God*, 142.
[26] McGrath, *The Only True God*, 60.
[27] Best, *Ephesians*, 370–71; Schüssler Fiorenza, *Ephesians*, 51–52; Lincoln, *Ephesians*, 240–41.

In this is love, not that we loved God, but that He loved us and sent His son to be the propitiation for our sins. (1 John 4:10)

The examples of this understanding that God is one person, *the Father of Jesus*, can be multiplied (Rom 1:1–3; Gal 4:6; 1 Thes 1:9–10; 1 John 3:21–23; 5:9, 10, 11; 5:20), but this sampling should be sufficient for observing this crucial theological conviction of the Early Church.

The care and attention that the New Testament writers gave to the pronouns describing the one true God confirms their conviction of God's oneness. Another noteworthy example that demonstrates the belief that God is one can be seen in the frequent citation of the most common passage from the Old Testament by the authors of the New Testament: Psalm 110:1 ("Yahweh says to my lord: 'Sit at My right hand until I make your enemies a footstool for your feet'"). In this passage, Yahweh, the God of Israel, summons a second figure to an exalted position, that is, to sit enthroned at the right hand of Yahweh. In this privileged invitation, the early Christians understood that its fulfillment was found in the resurrected Jesus being highly exalted to heaven to sit at the right hand of God, where he would patiently wait until the time of the consummation of his rule over his enemies. In Psalm 110:1, the exalted lord who sits at the right hand of Yahweh is self-evidently distinguished from Yahweh. The two figures are never confused or collapsed into a single being.[28] Furthermore, when Yahweh speaks forth his summons to the second figure, he refers to himself with singular references ("*my* right hand," "*I* make your enemies"). In other words, Psalm 110:1 defines Yahweh as a single person who is differentiated from a second figure, whom Christians regarded as the risen Jesus, invited to sit at Yahweh's right hand.[29]

As we mentioned, Psalm 110:1 is the most frequently quoted passage from the Old Testament in the New Testament, indicating a widespread belief among the Early Church that the true God is one person and that he has highly exalted Jesus to sit at his right hand. The New Testament gospel accounts portray Jesus citing Psalm 110:1 (Matt 22:44; Mark 12:36; Luke 20:42) and the Book of Acts quotes or alludes to it in Peter's sermons (Acts 2:34; 5:31).[30] The passage frequently appears throughout the Epistle to the Hebrews (e.g., Heb 1:3, 13; 8:1; 10:12).[31] The God of Jesus, the Father of glory, has seated Jesus at his right hand, according to Ephesians 1:17–20.[32] By drawing upon Psalm 110:1, the Early Church acknowledged its adamant conviction of Jesus' post-resurrection exaltation to the right hand of God, who is himself portrayed as one person.

---

[28] Dunn, *Unity and Diversity*, 56.
[29] McIntosh, *One God, Three Persons*, 92, 98; Irons et al., *The Son of God*, 143.
[30] Gaston, *Dynamic Monarchianism*, 269–70
[31] Johnson, *Hebrews*, 71–73.
[32] Lincoln, *Ephesians*, 56, 61–62.

Conclusion

In summary, we have observed that the biblical authors overwhelmingly portrayed Yahweh, the only true God, as a single person. When we total the number of singular references attributed to illustrating God, the number exceeds twenty thousand instances, which is the most voluminous statistic that can arguably be compiled for any biblical doctrine. We drew attention to the thousands of singular pronouns and verbs illustrating the oneness of God in each of the biblical languages, Greek, Hebrew, and Aramaic. We also observed thousands of singular adjectives within the data that describe God as one, especially in titles such as "the Holy One" and "the Righteous One." Additionally, we drew attention to the Hebrew and Aramaic suffixes that indicate a widespread acceptance of the notion that God is a single person. The Old Testament authors insisted that Yahweh has no one besides him, while both Testaments use the adjective "alone" to describe the workings of the true God. Even the role of Creator/maker and the title "Almighty" indicate that God is one person. The creed of Israel, the *Shema*, underscored the importance of the oneness of Yahweh, and we took special note of how Jesus and the early Christians continued to cherish and teach the *Shema*. Finally, we closely examined how the earliest followers of Jesus numerically distinguished God and Christ in a manner that pointed to their conviction that God is only one person, the Father alone. At no point in our examination of the grammar describing the true God is there any hint that Yahweh is three persons, and he is never identified with the number three in any passage.[33] In sum, the Early Church was fiercely monotheistic, describing the Jewish God as the Father of the risen Jesus and affirming God's oneness in continuity with the Judaism of the first century AD.

What did the biblical authors think God was like? What sort of attributes did the writers of Scripture ascribe to the only true God? In other words, what makes Yahweh, the God of Israel, the greatest conceivable being? Our next chapter will explore the attributes of God in order that we may better understand who he is and what makes him different from the rest of his creation.

---

[33] Schneider, "God," 84, arrives at the same conclusion: "The NT does not contain the developed doctrine of the Trinity . . . primitive Christianity did not have an explicit doctrine of the Trinity such as was subsequently elaborated in the creeds of the early church."

4
THE NATURAL ATTRIBUTES OF GOD

Yahweh, the God of Israel, the Father of Jesus, reveals himself as a personal, loving, forgiving, and faithful God. When the psalmist insists, "The heavens declare the glory of God, and the sky above proclaims the work of his hands" (Ps 19:1), the reader gets the clear impression that the Creator God is not distant or aloof, but recognizable through the brilliance of creation itself.[1] Similarly, Paul impresses upon his Roman recipients that God's attributes can be clearly discerned through what is made, resulting in a God who can be known, understood, and believed in (Rom 1:20).

This chapter will explore the natural attributes of the only true God as they are revealed in Scripture, namely, those characteristics that are innate to God's very being. First, we will examine the omnipotence of Yahweh, which serves to define him as all-powerful. Second, we will give attention to his omniscience, the attribute that refers to God's ability to know all things. Third, we will focus on God's immutability, that is, his inability to change his perfect nature and person. Fourth, we will turn to examine a lesser-known but equally important attribute of Yahweh, his impassibility. This attribute illustrates how an all-powerful and perfect God cannot suffer, experience pain, or get tired. Related to the impassibility of God is the crucial attribute of his immortality, or his inability to die, which will be our fifth area of concentration. Finally, we will take a close look at the important fact that the Creator is himself uncreated, in contrast with his creation that he brings into existence. These explorations will help us better understand what makes Yahweh who he is and why the biblical authors acknowledged that there is no one like him. We will reserve an examination of the noteworthy moral attributes of Yahweh for the following chapter.

God is Omnipotent

We may begin our study of the natural attributes of the only true God by drawing attention to his *omnipotence*, which refers to God being all-powerful. As the Creator, Yahweh naturally has the capacity to bring all things into existence. Several texts demonstrate the ease with which Yahweh made all things, particularly by speaking them into existence with his creative and powerful utterance (Gen 1:3; Ps 33:6; Heb 11:3). The

---

[1] Routledge, *Old Testament Theology*, 100.

prophet Jeremiah acknowledges God's omnipotence in his prayer, "Ah, *Adonai* Yahweh! It is you who made the heavens and the earth by Your great power and by Your outstretched arm! Nothing is too difficult for you" (Jer 32:17). In one of the visions in the Book of Revelation, the twenty-four elders worship the one seated on the throne, "Worthy are You, our Lord and our God, to receive glory and honor and power; because You created all things, and because of Your will they were, and they were created" (Rev 4:11). The all-powerful God, the one seated upon the throne, is the sole Creator of all things, and he brought them into existence because of his will and desire. Truly, he who made all things possesses omnipotence, and the readers of Revelation are encouraged to participate in the worship that acknowledges the true God as this powerful Creator.[2]

The biblical authors frequently recognize that the only true God possesses the capacity to do all things, which further supports the conclusion that God is omnipotent. Jesus taught his disciples that some things are impossible for humans to perform, but with God, all things are possible (Matt 19:26; Mark 10:27; Luke 18:27). Jesus likely learned this truth from God himself, who told Abraham rhetorically, "Is anything too difficult for Yahweh?" (Gen 18:14). The psalmist writes that our God does whatever he pleases (Ps 115:3), and the angel Gabriel confirms this point, "Nothing will be impossible with God" (Luke 1:37). We have already observed in chapter three that one of God's titles is "the Almighty," which underscores his unrivaled strength and power. There are, however, a few things that the Almighty God admits he cannot do, likely due to his moral character. For one, God is incapable of being tempted by evil (James 1:13).[3] Second, God cannot possibly tell a lie (Heb 6:18), being what Titus 1:2 calls the God "who never lies."[4] And third, God cannot die, for he is innately immortal (1 Tim 1:17; 6:16).[5] As such, God's omnipotence is closely associated with his character.

God is Omniscient

The next attribute that we need to explore is God's *omniscience*, which denotes his ability to know all things. On the surface, this may seem to be a reasonably straightforward doctrine. However, the topic is a bit more complex, based on the biblical data. On the one hand, several texts indicate that God's knowledge is complete. Consider the following sampling of passages:

> O Yahweh, You have searched me and known me. You know when I sit down and when I rise up; You understand my thought from afar. You scrutinize my path and my lying

---

[2] Mulholland, "Revelation," 463; Aune, *Revelation 1–5*, 315–17; Koester, *Revelation*, 371.
[3] Martin, *James*, 35; Blomberg and Kamell, *James*, 70–71; Bauer et al., *Greek-English Lexicon*, 100.
[4] Lane, *Hebrews 1–8*, 152; Koester, *Hebrews*, 334; Marshall, *The Pastoral Epistles*, 126.
[5] Marshall, *The Pastoral Epistles*, 404–5; Johnson, *The First and Second Letters to Timothy*, 182; Mounce, *Pastoral Epistles*, 361–62.

down, and are intimately acquainted with all my ways. Even before there is a word on my tongue, behold, O Yahweh, You know it all. (Ps 139:1–4)

"I am God, and there is no one like Me, declaring the end from the beginning, and from ancient times things which have not been done, saying, 'My counsel will be established, and I will accomplish all My good pleasure'" (Isa 46:9–10)

God is greater than our heart, and He knows all things (1 John 3:20)

The Early Church remembered Jesus' teaching that the Father knows the number of hairs on one's head (Matt 10:30). Regarding the day and hour of the second coming, Jesus taught that no one knows, not even the heavenly angels or Jesus himself. Only the Father possesses this knowledge (Matt 24:36; Mark 13:32).[6] When teaching his disciples how to pray, Jesus acknowledges that the "Father knows what you need before you ask Him" (Matt 6:8). Clearly, Jesus believed and taught that the Father, the only true God, possesses extensive knowledge of humanity and his plans for Christ's return.

On the other hand, many texts suggest that, because human beings possess free will and the ability to make choices as moral agents, God does not have exhaustive knowledge of the future. Since the future is open and contingent on human decisions, the definition of God's omniscience would need to be nuanced to include the fact that he knows all that can be known, but this does not include the open future.[7] This can be observed in passages that indicate that God planned to perform an action, but due to the actions of humans exercising free will, God has a change of heart.[8] Take a look at these texts where it appears that God changes his mind from what he had formerly purposed to accomplish:

So Yahweh changed His mind about the harm that He said He would do to His people. (Exod 32:14)

If at any time I declare concerning a nation or a kingdom, that I will pluck up and break down and destroy it, and if that nation, concerning which I have spoken, turns from its evil, I will relent of the disaster that I intended to do to it. (Jer 18:7–8)

"Yet even now," declares Yahweh, "Return to Me with all your heart, and with fasting, weeping and mourning; and rend your heart and not your garments." Now return to Yahweh your God, for He is gracious and compassionate, slow to anger, abounding in covenant love and relenting of evil. Who knows whether He will not turn and relent, and leave a blessing behind Him" (Joel 2:12–14)

---

[6] Perkins, "The Gospel of Mark," 694.
[7] Pinnock et al., *The Openness of God*, 18.
[8] See especially Goldingay, *Old Testament Theology*, 2:89–91.

> When God saw their deeds, that they turned from their wicked way, then God changed his mind concerning the calamity which He had declared He would bring upon them, and He did not do it. (Jonah 3:10)

In a fascinating story that is preserved in 2 Kings 20:1–6 and in Isaiah 38:1–5, God tells King Hezekiah to set his house in order "for you will die and you will not live." Hezekiah responded to this horrifying news by turning towards the wall, praying, and bitterly weeping. The prophet Isaiah, who delivered the bad news to the king, received a word from Yahweh before he left the middle court of the temple that said, "I have heard your prayer, I have seen your tears; behold, I will heal you" (2 Kgs 20:5). God added fifteen years to Hezekiah's life, which is a remarkable turn of events from his promise that the king would die and not live. It is difficult to ignore the conclusion that God changed what he planned to do because of Hezekiah's pious behavior.[9]

The openness of the omniscient God is evident when we consider the choice laid out before humanity to repent and believe the gospel.[10] John 3:16 famously states that "whoever" believes will not perish, suggesting to many that eternal life is contingent on one's choice to respond appropriately to the gospel. Similarly, God is described in 2 Peter 3:9 as being patient, not desiring that anyone should perish, but that all would come to repentance. God's patience in this passage is illustrated in a way that indicates that the future is open for people to change their behavior. Furthermore, the early Christians firmly believed that prayer could move God to perform several actions that would not otherwise take place without petitioning him. These include asking God to bless, forgive trespasses, heal, open doors for evangelism, send out laborers into the harvest, give good health, and bring separated believers together. The Early Church, it seems, was comfortable with the tension that God knows all things, including the intentions of our hearts, while God also responds to human choices, often in ways that are the opposite of what he had planned. If the writers of the New Testament believed that both of these tenets of God's omniscience were true, then we ought also to regard them as compatible, not contradictory.

God is Immutable

Another noteworthy attribute of Yahweh is that he is *immutable*. The immutability of God refers to his nature that does not change, particularly as it relates to his being, attributes, and perfection. A related term to God's immutability is *aseity*, which describes his self-existence and independence. Aseity comes from the Latin *"a se,"* which means "from himself." Since Yahweh is eternal and self-existent, he is immutable, meaning that his

---

[9] Boyd, *God of the Possible*, 7–8; Seow, "The First and Second Books of Kings," 271; Watts, *Isaiah 34–66*, 51.
[10] Shank, *Elect in the Son*, 161–218.

person does not change. We should not confuse the immutability of God with his willingness to respond positively to prayer, show patience, and change his mind. The openness of God is not the same as his unchanging nature, his eternality, and his perfect attributes.

Abraham was convinced that Yahweh was the everlasting God (Gen 21:33). Similarly, Isaiah 40:28 illustrates the Creator of the ends of the earth as "the everlasting God." Several texts help develop the conviction that the only true God possesses immutability. Consider the following passages:

> Before the mountains were born or You gave birth to the earth and the world, even from everlasting to everlasting, You are God. (Ps 90:2)
>
> Even they will perish, but You endure; and all of them will wear out like a garment; like clothing You will change them and they will be changed. But You are the same, and Your years will not come to an end. (Ps 102:26–27)
>
> "For I, Yahweh, do not change" (Mal 3:6)
>
> Every good gift and every perfect gift is from above, coming down from the Father of lights with whom there is no variation or shadow due to change. (James 1:17)

The New Testament authors continued to attribute immutable characteristics to the Father. Jesus taught that the Father has life in himself and that the Father has shared that life with Jesus (John 5:26). Luke summarizes Paul's preaching in which the true God is portrayed as not needing anything, "The God who made the world and all things in it, since He is Lord of heaven and earth, does not dwell in temples made with hands; nor is He served by human hands, as though He needed anything, since He Himself gives to all people life and breath and all things" (Acts 17:24–25). Furthermore, the Almighty sends greetings in the Book of Revelation by referring to himself as "Him who is and who was and who is to come," which strongly suggests his eternality (Rev 1:4).[11] We have already observed that God cannot be tempted (James 1:13), a conclusion that naturally follows from the realization that he is immutable. The resulting portrayal that the authors of the New Testament offer illustrates the Father as self-sufficient and everlasting.

God is Impassible

Having discussed the immutability of God, we can take the opportunity to briefly introduce the attribute of *impassibility*, which refers to God's inability to suffer or experience pain. As the everlasting God, Yahweh does not faint or grow weary

---

[11] Koester, *Revelation*, 226.

(Isa 40:28).[12] In other words, God cannot get tired, become exhausted, or succumb to weakness due to his immutable nature. No one can physically harm God or bring him pain, for he is everlasting and immortal (1 Tim 6:16). As the maker of heaven and earth, God is praised as one who will not slumber nor sleep (Ps 121:2–4).[13] Although it has become customary for translations to suggest that God "rested" on the seventh day of creation, giving the impression that the all-powerful Creator was tired after six days of making the heavens and the earth, the Hebrew verb *shabat* that appears in Genesis 2:2–3 means "to cease."[14] In other words, God did not rest from a state of weariness and fatigue; he simply ceased from the act of creation.[15]

It is essential to acknowledge that biblical authors often attributed human qualities, feelings, and characteristics to God. This literary device is commonly referred to as *anthropomorphism*, and its function in Scripture is to convey truths about God in ways that are accessible to human thought patterns.[16] God is anthropomorphically illustrated as possessing a mouth (Jer 9:12), lips and a tongue (Isa 30:27), a head (Ps 60:7), a face (Num 6:25), eyes (Amos 9:4), hands (Ezek 13:9), fingers (Deut 9:10), an arm (Jer 27:5), a back (Exod 33:23), a heart (Gen 6:6), ears (Num 11:18), feet (Nah 1:3), and even a footstool for his feet (Isa 66:1).[17] The Early Church continued to apply anthropomorphisms to the person of the Father. Jesus was remembered as teaching that the Father has a hand (John 10:29), a face (Matt 18:10), a body that sits on a throne (Matt 23:22), and feet for his footstool (Matt 5:35). Furthermore, 1 Peter 3:12 illustrates God as having eyes, ears, and a face. However, these anthropomorphisms are merely literary devices that attribute human qualities to a God who is invisible (Col 1:15; 1 Tim 1:17; 6:16) and, according to Jesus, without form (John 5:37).

Related to the regular and consistent portrayal by the biblical authors of Yahweh with anthropomorphisms is his depiction as having human emotions, feelings, and passions. This illustration of God is called *anthropopathism*, and the writers of the biblical texts frequently used these human-like emotions to explain God's dealings and experiences with humanity in ways that are more relatable. For example, God rejoices (Zeph 3:17), feels delighted (Jer 9:24), can be pleased with human actions (1 Kgs 3:10), gets angry (Ps 7:11), is very jealous (Exod 20:5), is compassionate (Exod 34:6), experiences grief (Ps 78:40), shows hate (Deut 12:31), and pity (Ps 103:13).[18] Early Christians continued to understand the only true God in anthropopathic ways. The Father is portrayed by Jesus as compassionate (Luke 15:20) and one who rejoices when his

---

[12] Goldingay and Payne, *Isaiah 40–55*, 1:127–28; Paul, *Isaiah 40–66*, 154–55.
[13] Allen, *Psalms 101–150*, 154; deClaissé-Walford et al., *Psalms*, 896–97; Hossfeld and Zenger, *Psalms 3*, 324–26.
[14] Köhler et al., *Hebrew and Aramaic Lexicon*, 1407.
[15] Goldingay, *Old Testament Theology*, 1:127; Kaiser, *Toward an Old Testament Theology*, 76.
[16] Howe, "Anthropomorphism," 174.
[17] Köhler, *Old Testament Theology*, 22–23.
[18] Köhler, *Old Testament Theology*, 23.

wayward people repent (Luke 15:32). Paul was convinced that God could be pleased when Christians faithfully preach the gospel (1 Thes 2:4). Failing to respond appropriately to God's summons, however, makes him angry (Luke 14:21) and wrathful (Rom 1:18). Furthermore, God continues to jealously desire his people's full commitment (James 4:5), showing patience towards sinners (2 Peter 3:9). These depictions of God helped the Early Church better understand the Father and how he relates to his covenant people.

God is Immortal

As an all-powerful and unchanging Creator who innately possesses life, we can logically conclude that the only true God is *immortal*, which means that he cannot die by any method possible. For one to possess immortality is the direct opposite of being mortal, that is, possessing the capacity to die. The biblical authors freely acknowledge that Yahweh is an eternal being who has always existed.[19] God's existence cannot come to an end; he cannot cease to be, nor can he perish.

The writers of the Old Testament frequently attested to God's existence as without beginning or end. In the Song of Moses, God himself possesses eternity, "As I live forever" (Deut 32:40). Along the same lines, Isaiah 57:15 illustrates Yahweh as the one "who inhabits eternity." The Book of Daniel presents a prayer offered by Nebuchadnezzar, who praised the Most High as "Him who lives forever" (Dan 4:34). Several other Old Testament authors corroborate this vital attribute:

> God also said to Moses, "Say this to the people of Israel, 'Yahweh, the God of your fathers, the God of Abraham, the God of Isaac, and the God of Jacob, has sent me to you.' This is My name forever" (Exod 3:15)

> But Yahweh sits enthroned forever; he has established his throne for justice (Ps 9:7)

> Blessed be Yahweh, the God of Israel, from everlasting to everlasting. (Ps 41:13)

> You, O Yahweh, rule forever; Your throne is from generation to generation. (Lam 5:19)

> I heard the man dressed in linen, who was above the waters of the river, as he raised his right hand and his left toward heaven, and swore by Him who lives forever (Dan 12:7)

> Are You not from everlasting, O Yahweh, my God, my Holy One? (Hab 1:12)

As we can observe, Yahweh has always existed, and he will remain forever. He is from everlasting, and his reign will continue for all generations to come.

---

[19] Goldingay, *Old Testament Theology*, 1:63.

The writers of the New Testament demonstrate that the Early Church continued to attribute immortality and eternality to God, whom they regarded as the Father alone. The true God is characterized as immortal (Rom 1:23; 1 Tim 1:17; 6:16). As the one who alone possesses immortality, he can grant eternal life to anyone he chooses.[20] In fact, Jesus Christ taught his followers that the Father innately has life in himself and that he has shared that life with his agent, Jesus (John 5:26). As the Almighty God, he is the one who is, who was, and who is to come—a designation indicating that he is without beginning or end (Rev 1:8). Furthermore, the living creatures in one of Revelation's visions worship the one seated upon the throne who lives "forever and ever" (Rev 4:8–9). In fact, the description "he who lives forever and ever" is repeatedly applied to God in the Book of Revelation (4:10; 10:6; 15:7). The Early Church believed and taught that the only true God is eternal, possesses immortality, and has life in himself.

God is Uncreated

As a natural corollary to Yahweh's eternality and immortality, he is an *uncreated* person. As the Creator and maker of all things, it is self-evident that Yahweh is uncreated. The authors of the Old Testament often distinguished Yahweh, the Creator, from his creation, demonstrating an awareness that God is obviously uncreated. Consider the following passages where the maker and his creation are differentiated:

> Can mankind be just before God? Can a man be pure before his Maker? (Job 4:17)
>
> Come, let us worship and bow down, let us kneel before Yahweh our Maker. For He is our God, and we are the people of His pasture and the sheep of His hand. (Ps 95:6–7)
>
> The rich and the poor have a common bond, Yahweh is the Maker of them all. (Prov 22:2)
>
> Shall the potter be considered as equal with the clay, that what is created would say to its Creator, "He did not create me;" or what is made say to him who is its Maker, "He has no understanding"? (Isa 29:16)
>
> Thus says Yahweh, the Holy One of Israel, and his Maker: "Ask Me about the things to come concerning My sons, and you shall commit to Me the work of My hands. It is I who made the earth, and I created man upon it. I stretched out the heavens with My hands and I ordained all their host." (Isa 45:11–12)

The New Testament authors likewise recognized the difference between the uncreated Creator and all his creation. The Apostle Paul shows evidence of this understanding when he explicitly contrasts the creature and the Creator—the one who is blessed forever

---

[20] Brown, "Resurrection," 304.

(Rom 1:25).[21] We observed in chapter three that the English noun "creator" is actually a verb in Greek, literally "the one who creates," which helpfully offers the reminder that the Creator is only one person. Fortunately for us who are interested in discerning Paul's theology of the Creator, Paul clearly tells his readers who is the maker of all things. In 1 Corinthians, Paul defines the one true God in contrast to the many so-called gods and so-called lords, "Yet for us there is one God, the Father, out of whom are all things, and we for him" (1 Cor 8:6). We can find confirmation of this identification of the Father as the sole Creator of all creation in Ephesians, "one God and Father of all, who is over all and through all and in all" (Eph 4:6). While there is some ambiguity in the Greek adjectives "all" in this passage as to whether they refer to all people or to all things, what remains clear is that the Father is the sole Creator of his creation. In short, it seems pretty apparent that the Early Church regarded the Father, the Creator of all things, as he who alone is categorically distinct from creation itself. The Father, therefore, is uncreated.

Conclusion

We may conclude this chapter by summarizing our findings and contrasting Yahweh's natural attributes with those of human beings.[22] As we have observed, the only true God is omnipotent, but human beings live in weakness (2 Cor 13:4). The Father is omniscient, knowing all that can be known. Still, human beings have learned only a small portion of knowledge (Heb 5:2). The only true God is immutable in his very being. At the same time, humanity develops from childhood to adolescence and then to adulthood (Judges 13:24). The Almighty is impassible, being incapable of experiencing pain, suffering, or fatigue. However, human beings feel pain, undergo suffering, and get tired (Matt 16:21). The immortal God is incapable of dying. In contrast, every single human being is mortal and is thus susceptible to death, corruption, and the loss of life (Rom 5:12). Lastly, the Creator is self-evidently an uncreated person. In contrast, every human man, woman, and child is part of God's good creation (Gen 1:31). There is no question that God and humanity are very different, and the two should never be confused.[23]

We can now devote our attention to the only true God's moral attributes. These essential characteristics, which illustrate how God interacts with his people, will be thoroughly explored in the following chapter.

---

[21] Gaventa, *Romans*, 66; Keck, *Romans*, 64.
[22] Readers may also find it beneficial to perform this contrast between these six natural attributes of God and the attributes of Jesus Christ. The son of God was not omnipotent, omniscient, immutable, impassible, innately immortal, nor uncreated. The Early Church, self-evidently, did not regard Christ as the only true God.
[23] Soulen, *The God of Israel and Christian Theology*, 122.

5
THE MORAL ATTRIBUTES OF GOD

God's moral attributes shed light on God's character and the way in which he enters into relationship with his people. In the ancient world, there were various and diverse understandings of the gods and how they interacted with those who claimed them. These pagan conceptions of the gods portrayed them as sometimes wholly absent; other times, they were angry, or they might bless you and curse your enemies in exchange for certain sacrifices. For the children of Israel and the early Christians alike, there was only one God, the Father, and as the all-powerful Creator, he cares for his good creation. Yahweh is a personal God who loved the world by giving his unique son, Jesus Christ (John 3:16).

This chapter will focus our attention on the particular attributes of the only true God that illustrate his morality, particularly those qualities experienced by human beings who enter into a relationship with him. Many readers will undoubtedly find this chapter more practical than our previous chapter, which explored the natural attributes of Yahweh. While it is possible to supply numerous words to describe God, such as we find in Exodus 34:6–7, these can be appropriately summarized into three primary qualities. First, we will look closely at the biblical portrayals of Yahweh as a *gracious* God, a God who loves, forgives, and is merciful towards his covenant people. Second, we will explore the ways in which God expresses his *faithfulness*, particularly in his commitment to keep his promises, despite human disobedience. Finally, we will examine the *just* attribute of God, which reflects his role as the impartial cosmic judge who will defeat evil and bring redemption to his people on the Day of Judgment.

God is Gracious

The first of these moral attributes is that Yahweh is *gracious*. The biblical record is filled with instances of God showing grace, mercy, goodness, and forgiveness towards his people. In fact, the petition "Be gracious to me" is such a common refrain (Pss 4:1; 6:2; 9:13; 30:10; 41:4; 86:3; 119:58) that the reader gets the impression that the biblical authors take for granted that God is one known for his abundant grace.[1] Some readers have mistakenly concluded that the God depicted in the Old Testament is a God of wrath,

---

[1] McCann, "The Book of Psalms," 697.

while the God portrayed in the New Testament is a *God of grace*. This representation tells only one side of the story, ignoring the overwhelming illustration of Yahweh as a gracious God by the authors of the Old Testament.[2] Consider the following description of God's choosing of the children of Israel and the motivation behind it:

> "Yahweh did not set His love on you nor choose you because you were more in number than any of the peoples, for you were the fewest of all peoples, but because Yahweh loved you and kept the oath which He swore to your forefathers, Yahweh brought you out by a mighty hand and redeemed you from the house of slavery, from the hand of Pharaoh king of Egypt." (Deut 7:7–8)

Yahweh, the gracious God, was moved by his love and his commitment to his promises in his dealings with Israel.[3] Similarly, Nehemiah points to the grace of God as the reason why he did not forsake his people when they were disobedient in the wilderness:[4]

> They refused to listen, and did not remember Your wondrous deeds which You had performed among them; so they became stubborn and appointed a leader to return to their slavery in Egypt. But You are a God of forgiveness, gracious and compassionate, slow to anger and abounding in covenant love; and You did not forsake them. (Neh 9:17)

When the prophet Joel wanted his listeners to rend their hearts and return to Yahweh their God, he pointed first to God's graciousness as the primary means of motivation (Joel 2:13). There were several instances where people requested that God show himself to be gracious in a given situation of need:

> "May God be gracious to you, my son!" (Gen 43:29)

> Yahweh bless you, and keep you; Yahweh make His face shine on you, and be gracious to you (Num 6:24–25)

> God be gracious to us and bless us, cause His face to shine upon us—Selah. (Ps 67:1)

The belief that Yahweh is a God of grace, love, mercy, and goodness fueled the hope for redemption and deliverance. Psalm 130:7–8 is a prime example: "O Israel, hope in Yahweh; for with Yahweh there is covenant love, and with Him is abundant redemption. And He will redeem Israel from all his iniquities." At this point, we can confidently conclude that the God of the Old Testament is overwhelmingly gracious in character and deed.

Since Yahweh, the gracious God of the Old Testament, is recognized as the Father who sends his grace (Rom 1:7; 1 Cor 1:3; 2 Cor 1:2), it is not surprising that the

---

[2] Westerholm, "Grace," 655–56.
[3] Christensen, *Deuteronomy 1:1–21:9*, 156; Tigay, *Deuteronomy*, 87; Clements, "The Book of Deuteronomy," 350.
[4] Williamson, *Ezra, Nehemiah*, 319.

Early Church continued to portray the true God as himself gracious.[5] Jesus, the unique son of the Father, embodies the Father's grace and truth (John 1:14, 17). The proclamation of the gospel message is displayed as a message of grace.[6] Paul's preaching of the kingdom of God is summarized as the gospel of grace (Acts 20:24–25). It is only by the grace of God that the unsaved come to place their faith in the gospel (Acts 18:27), and after believing the gospel, these people begin to experience grace in their lives (Acts 11:23). Several texts can be shown indicating an awareness among the Early Church that God regularly demonstrated his graciousness in the lives of the earliest followers of Christ:

> Now when the meeting of the synagogue had broken up, many of the Jews and of the God-fearing proselytes followed Paul and Barnabas, who, speaking to them, were urging them to continue in the grace of God. (Acts 13:43)

> From there they sailed to Antioch, from which they had been commended to the grace of God for the work that they had accomplished. (Acts 14:26)

> But Paul chose Silas and left, being committed by the brethren to the grace of the Lord. (Acts 15:40)

> And now I commend you to God and to the word of His grace, which is able to build you up and to give you the inheritance among all those who are sanctified. (Acts 20:32)

The gracious involvement of God is continually experienced in the local churches, where God pours out his grace through his risen son, Jesus Christ. For example, Paul indicates that the enrichment and gifting of believers is precisely due to the grace of God that was given to them in Christ Jesus (1 Cor 1:4–6). Similarly, Christian faith leads to the grace upon which believers stand, all of which is made possible by having peace with God through Christ (Rom 5:1–2). Paul expects members of the body of Christ to exercise their differing gifts "according to the grace given to us" (Rom 12:6). In fact, Paul recounts his own calling in terms of God calling him through his grace to reveal his son to Paul (Gal 1:15–16).[7]

It is no surprise that the early Christians attributed their own conversion experience to the gracious act of a loving God who works through the death and resurrection of Christ.[8] Forgiveness from our trespasses and redemption are all made possible by the riches of the grace of God (Eph 1:7). Christians have been saved by grace (Eph 2:5, 8; 2 Tim 1:9), justified by grace (Rom 3:24; Titus 3:7), and are summoned to grow in grace (2 Pet 3:18). When Paul makes the critical argument that the obedience of Christ offsets the disobedience of Adam (Rom 5:12–21), he contrasts the former reign of personified Sin with the present reign and rule of personified Grace, "as sin reigned in

---

[5] Esser, "Grace," 118–23.
[6] Jeremias, *New Testament Theology*, 122.
[7] Hays, "The Letter to the Galatians," 215.
[8] Casurella, "Grace," 433–35.

death, even so grace would reign through righteousness to eternal life through Jesus Christ our Lord" (Rom 5:21).[9] In summary, the Early Church's entire religious experience centered on the goodness and mercy of a loving God who embodied the attribute of grace.

God is Faithful

The second moral attribute of God is his *faithfulness*. The faithfulness of God refers to his unwavering commitment to upholding all that he promised to do.[10] Since Yahweh is "the faithful God" (Deut 7:9; Ps 31:5; Hos 11:12), he can be relied upon as the object of one's trust, obedience, and loyalty. The authors of the Old Testament regularly ascribe to God the moral attribute of faithfulness, often using the important Hebrew noun *chesed*, which refers to God's loving acts within the covenant agreement (or more simply, "covenant love"). For example, Psalm 25:10 celebrates the reality that "All the paths of Yahweh are covenant love (*chesed*) and faithfulness, for those who keep His covenant and His testimonies." Everything that God does, that is, all of his works, "are faithful and just; all His precepts are trustworthy" (Ps 111:7). As the Creator of heaven, earth, the sea, and all that is in them, Yahweh is one "who keeps faith forever" (Ps 146:6).[11] The prophet Micah concludes his literary work by reminding God (and Micah's readers) that "You will show faithfulness to Jacob and covenant love (*chesed*) to Abraham, as you have sworn to our fathers from the days of old" (Mic 7:20).

Micah raises an important point that continues to give hope to the people of God even to this day, namely, that God will be absolutely faithful to the promises he made to the patriarchs. Although we will go deeper into the significance of God's faithful promises made to Abraham in Chapter 45, we can briefly introduce the topic here as it pertains to the moral attribute of faithfulness. After human beings sinned and the image of God became tarnished, the reader of Genesis is given eight chapters (Gen 4–11) that overwhelmingly illustrate just how far humanity has fallen. Then, at the beginning of Genesis chapter twelve, a figure named Abram appears, and God selects him to be the means through whom God will restore humanity to its rightful position:

> Now Yahweh said to Abram, "Go forth from your country, and from your relatives and from your father's house, to the land which I will show you; and I will make you a great nation, and I will bless you, and make your name great; and so you shall be a blessing; and I will bless those who bless you, and the one who curses you I will curse. And in you all the families of the earth will be blessed." (Gen 12:1–3)

---

[9] Gaventa, *Romans*, 162–65.
[10] Soulen, *The God of Israel and Christian Theology*, 114.
[11] Goldingay, *Old Testament Theology*, 1:89.

This is the first of many instances in which Yahweh makes several promises to Abram, who later changes his name to Abraham. In this passage, however, we can summarize the promises into three main points.[12] First, God promises Abram *the land*. This promise is crucial because humanity in the Garden of Eden was created to rule over the land and to subdue it (Gen 1:28), but humanity was exiled in light of their disobedience. Second, Abram is given the promise that he will have many *descendants*, including the formation of a great nation, and that this will have a positive effect on all the families of the earth. This promise also recalls humanity in the Garden of Eden, who was given the mandate to be fruitful, multiply, and fill the earth (Gen 1:27–28). Third, Yahweh promises that Abram will be a *blessing* to others. This blessing might appear to the unmindful reader to be a generic piece of good fortune, but in the unfolding theology of Genesis, a blessing to all the families of the earth undoes the curse of humanity that was a result of disobedience (Gen 3:17–19). In short, the promises that God made to Abraham—the land, multiple descendants, and a blessing—will result in the redemption of the entire human race, restoring humanity to its rightful place as rulers and stewards of God's creation.[13]

It is no wonder that the biblical authors continued to rely upon Yahweh's faithfulness. God has committed to unwavering fidelity in his promise to renew humanity through Abraham, who is also a member of the human race.[14] In several instances, the authors of the Old Testament characterize Yahweh as remembering the promises he made to Abraham (and his offspring, Isaac and Jacob), and responding faithfully in connection with those promises:

> So God heard their groaning; and God remembered His covenant with Abraham, Isaac, and Jacob. (Exod 2:24)
>
> "I will bring you to the land which I swore to give to Abraham, Isaac, and Jacob, and I will give it to you for a possession; I am Yahweh." (Exod 6:8)
>
> "Remember Abraham, Isaac, and Israel, Your servants to whom You swore by Yourself, and said to them, 'I will multiply your descendants as the stars of the heavens, and all this land of which I have spoken I will give to your descendants, and they shall inherit it forever.'" (Exod 32:13)
>
> "I call heaven and earth to witness against you today, that I have set before you life and death, the blessing and the curse. So choose life in order that you may live, you and your descendants, by loving Yahweh your God, by obeying His voice, and by holding fast to Him; for this is your life and the length of your days, that you may live in the land which Yahweh swore to your fathers, to Abraham, Isaac, and Jacob, to give them." (Deut 30:19–20)

---

[12] Brueggemann, *Old Testament Theology: An Introduction*, 269–71.
[13] Goldingay, *Old Testament Theology*, 1:205–24.
[14] Goldingay, *Old Testament Theology*, 1:194–201.

Throughout the Old Testament narrative, Yahweh establishes and upholds the moral reputation of being faithful to his covenant people. Jacob, the grandson of Abraham, admits that "I am unworthy of all the covenant love (*chesed*) and all the faithfulness which you have shown Your servant" (Gen 32:10).[15] Deuteronomy 7:9 describes God's attribute in this manner, "Know therefore that Yahweh your God, He is God, the faithful God, who keeps His covenant and His covenant love (*chesed*) to a thousandth generation with those who love Him and keep His commandments." The narrator of Joshua confidently assures his readers that "Not one of the good promises which Yahweh had made to the house of Israel failed; all came to pass" (Josh 21:45). Even during the Babylonian exile, when God's people were removed from the land, Yahweh is praised for his faithful commitment:

> This I recall to my mind, therefore I have hope. Yahweh's covenant love (*chesed*) indeed never ceases, for His compassions never fail. They are new every morning; great is Your faithfulness. (Lam 3:21–23)

Notable also is the covenant that God enters into with King David, as this encompasses several promises to which God faithfully commits. Just as Yahweh demonstrates his faithfulness to the promises he made to Abraham, the authors of the Old Testament frequently stress the commitment Yahweh made to David. The terms of the agreement are recorded in 2 Samuel 7:12–16 and 1 Chronicles 17:11–14, and they are worth examining here:

> "When your days are fulfilled that you must go to be with your fathers, that I will set up one of your descendants after you, who will be of your sons; and I will establish his kingdom. He shall build for Me a house, and I will establish his throne forever. I will be his Father and he shall be My son; and I will not take My covenant love (*chesed*) away from him, as I took it from him who was before you. But I will settle him in My house and in My kingdom forever, and his throne shall be established forever." (1 Chron 17:11–14)

The importance of this passage will be explored in more detail in Chapter 21, which examines the promises of the Messiah in the Old Testament. For now, we can make some general observations. Yahweh, who identifies himself as the "Father" in this passage, makes three crucial promises to David the king. First, God promises David that his sons will possess a *house* forever. This "house" refers to a temple dwelling in this passage, and it may also have dynasty overtones in the version preserved in 2 Samuel 7:12–16.[16] Either way, it won't be David building a house for God but God providing a house for David's royal descendants. Second, David's *throne* will be established forever. This throne, of course, refers to the kingly chair that is geographically tied to Jerusalem, the capital city, and the rightful seat of the Israelite human king. Third, Yahweh promises that the Davidic

---

[15] Hamilton, *Genesis 18–50*, 323.
[16] Birch, "The First and Second Books of Samuel," 1257.

kingdom will endure forever. This indicates that a lineal descendant of David will reign as king, and his rule will never come to an end. Effectively, Yahweh faithfully commits to providing the sons of King David an enduring house, throne, and kingdom.[17] Yahweh's pact with David is appropriately referred to as the *Davidic covenant*.

The Old Testament authors frequently celebrate Yahweh's faithfulness to his promises made to David, specifically the stipulations outlined in the Davidic covenant. Consider the following passages where God is illustrated as faithful:

> He gives great deliverance to His king, and shows covenant love (*chesed*) to His anointed, to David and his descendants forever. (Ps 18:50)

> I will sing of the covenant love (*chesed*) of Yahweh forever; to all generations I will make known Your faithfulness with my mouth. For I have said, "Covenant love (*chesed*) will be built up forever; in the heavens You will establish Your faithfulness. I have made a covenant with My chosen; I have sworn to David My servant, I will establish your seed forever and build up your throne to all generations." (Ps 89:1–4)

> He will cry to Me, "You are my Father, My God, and the rock of my salvation." I also shall make him firstborn, the highest of the kings of the earth. My covenant love (*chesed*) I will keep for him forever, and My covenant shall be confirmed to him." (Ps 89:26–28)

> "My covenant I will not violate, nor will I alter the utterance of My lips. Once I have sworn by My holiness; I will not lie to David. His descendants shall endure forever and his throne as the sun before Me. It shall be established forever like the moon, and the witness in the sky is faithful." (Ps 89:34–37)

> For the sake of David Your servant, do not turn away the face of Your anointed. Yahweh has sworn to David a truth from which He will not turn back: "Of the fruit of your body I will set upon your throne." (Ps 132:10–11)

As we can observe, Yahweh's faithful commitment to the Davidic covenant is woven into the psalms of praise.[18] We can find further instances of God's commitment to his promise to establish a human descendant of David upon his throne in the prophetic literature (Isa 16:5; Jer 23:5; 30:9; 33:15–17; Ezek 34:23–24), but the above sampling of passages is sufficient to demonstrate that the authors of the Old Testament depicted the true God as utterly faithful to his pledged covenant obligations.

When we examine how the Early Church wrote about and placed their trust in the faithfulness of God, we are in an advantageous position, for several of the authors of the New Testament celebrate the Father's ongoing faithful commitment to his people. In fact, the faithfulness of God is regularly tied to the covenant behavior that is expected of

---

[17] Goldingay, *Old Testament Theology*, 1:559–60; Allen, "The First and Second Books of Chronicles," 407.
[18] Guinan, "Davidic Covenant," 70; Kraus, *Theology of the Psalms*, 109.

the New Testament people of God. Take into consideration the following texts that emphasize the faithful moral attribute of God:

> God is faithful, through whom you were called into fellowship with His Son, Jesus Christ our Lord. (1 Cor 1:9)
>
> But as God is faithful, our word to you is not yes and no. (2 Cor 1:18)
>
> Now may the God of peace Himself sanctify you entirely; and may your spirit and soul and body be preserved complete, without blame at the coming of our Lord Jesus Christ. Faithful is He who calls you, and He also will bring it to pass. (1 Thes 5:23–24)
>
> Let us hold fast the confession of our hope without wavering, for He who promised is faithful (Heb 10:23)
>
> Therefore, those also who suffer according to the will of God shall entrust their souls to a faithful Creator in doing what is right. (1 Pet 4:19)

Within Paul's Epistle to the Romans, there are some lengthy expositions of the faithfulness of God. For example, Romans 3:1–4 begins by talking about the Jewish people's advantage, namely the fact that God entrusted them with his oracles. However, the history of Israel reveals that they were unfaithful to this entrusted vocation, which may lead some to question if this presents God also as unfaithful since he initially gave the mission to Israel. Paul responds to this question by arguing that Israel's disobedience does not nullify God's faithful commitment.[19] In fact, Paul argues later in the passage that God's *righteousness*, which is a complex term referring to God's faithful commitment to his covenant obligations, has been revealed in Christ—Israel's kingly representative—and his faithfulness to God (Rom 3:21–22).[20] We will have more to say about these topics in Chapter 37, but for now, it is clear that the Early Church believed and taught the faithfulness of the one true God.

These New Testament authors likely drew their understanding of this vital attribute from the portrayals of God in what we call the Old Testament scriptures, but it is also reasonable to conclude that Jesus was remembered as instructing his followers that God is faithful. In fact, several indicators in the teachings of Jesus suggest that belief in God as faithful to his people was a fundamental Christian teaching. For example, the Sermon on the Mount contains instructions detailing why the followers of Christ should not worry about food, drink, or clothing (Matt 6:25–32). Instead, Jesus encourages his disciples to seek the kingdom of God and his righteousness while assuring them that God's faithful provision will take care of their needs (Matt 6:33).[21] Furthermore, the gospel accounts record multiple instances where Jesus predicts that he will be handed

---

[19] Gaventa, *Romans*, 94–95
[20] Wright, "The Letter to the Romans," 397–406, 469–70.
[21] Keener, *The Gospel of Matthew*, 234–38.

over, killed, and vindicated from the grave (Matt 16:21; 17:22–23; Luke 9:22; 18:32–33; John 10:17–18). In these statements, Christ places his confidence in God's faithfulness to raise him from the dead—a fact to which all four gospel accounts attest. 1 Peter 2:23 recounts how Christ continued to entrust himself to God, the righteous judge who would vindicate Christ from the grave.[22] In other words, Jesus believed and taught his disciples that the true God is completely faithful in his character and being.

God is Just

The third moral attribute belonging to Yahweh is that he is *just*. The justice belonging to the only true God is closely tied to his role as the cosmic judge. Despite Yahweh revealing himself as compassionate, gracious, slow to anger, and abounding in covenant love and faithfulness (Exod 34:6), he will by no means leave the guilty unpunished (Exod 34:7). When Abraham was attempting to find righteous persons residing in Sodom and Gomorrah, he evoked the justice of God, "Far be it from You to do such a thing, to slay the righteous with the wicked, so that the righteous and the wicked are treated alike. Far be it from You! Shall not the Judge of all the earth deal justly?" (Gen 18:25). Since Yahweh serves as judge, lawgiver, and king, it naturally follows that he will bring salvation and deliverance to those who are in need (Isa 33:22). Even Ecclesiastes brings its book to a close by offering the persuasive reason to fear God and keep his commandments, "For God will bring every deed into judgment, with every secret thing, whether good or evil" (Ecc 12:13–14).[23] As we can see, the justice of God can be executed in the present or the future. Either way, God is shown to be just.

When we look at the various ways in which Yahweh serves as the cosmic judge of all creation, we may observe four defining features of this moral quality.[24] The first of these just characteristics is that God is an impartial judge. In other words, God justly renders judgment to all people fairly, without showing any favoritism. Moses told the Israelites that Yahweh "does not show partiality nor take a bribe" (Deut 10:17). Similarly, Jehoshaphat urged his judges to show care in what they do "for Yahweh our God will have no part in unrighteousness or partiality in the taking of a bribe" (2 Chron 19:7).[25] In the Book of Job, Elihu declares that the Almighty shows no partiality to princes, nor does he regard the rich above the poor (Job 34:19).[26] After the conversion of the Gentile Cornelius, Peter authoritatively declared the implications of God issuing forth salvation in this manner: "I most certainly understand that God does not show partiality, but in

---

[22] Elliott, *I Peter*, 531–32.
[23] Fox, *Ecclesiastes*, 85.
[24] Wright, "The Letter to the Romans," 399.
[25] Allen, "The First and Second Books of Chronicles," 555.
[26] Newsom, "The Book of Job," 577.

every nation anyone who fears Him and does what is right is acceptable to Him" (Acts 10:34–35). In the Book of Romans, where the topic of God's justice is thematic, Paul offers an extended exposition of the impartiality of the just judge:

> But because of your stubbornness and unrepentant heart you are storing up wrath for yourself in the day of wrath and revelation of the righteous judgment of God, who will render to each person according to his deeds: to those who by perseverance in doing good seek for glory and honor and immortality, eternal life; but to those who are selfishly ambitious and do not obey the truth, but obey unrighteousness, wrath and indignation. There will be tribulation and distress for every soul of man who does evil, of the Jew first and also of the Greek, but glory and honor and peace to everyone who does good, to the Jew first and also to the Greek. For there is no partiality with God. (Rom 2:5–11)

It appears abundantly clear that the moral character of God's justice meant that he would be impartial in his judgments, showing no favoritism with regard to race, wealth, or social status.

The second defining feature of the just judge is that he must uphold the law. The covenantal requirements for the people of God must be upheld by the righteous; otherwise, the moral quality of God's being just compels him to enter into judgment with the offender. For those who hate God and refuse to obey his commandments, Moses warns that the offender will be repaid with destruction (Deut 7:10).[27] Just as humanity disobeyed God in Eden, resulting in a curse and exile (Gen 3:16–24), so too was Israel warned that their disobedience to the commandments would result in a guilty verdict, curses, and exile (Deut 28:15, 63–64). The same portrayal of God as a just judge appears in the New Testament. The Apostle Paul is remembered as preaching that the true God has fixed a day in which he will judge the world in righteousness through the man Jesus (Acts 17:31). Paul's own words confirm this coming Day of Judgment, when even believers will give an account of themselves at God's judgment seat (Rom 14:10–12). First Peter depicts the Father as the one who impartially judges according to each person's work (1 Pet 1:17). Along the same lines, the Book of Revelation offers a glimpse into a judgment scene where the dead are raised to face judgment, each one being evaluated according to their works (Rev 20:13).

The justice of the righteous judge is evident in a third defining feature: he will defend and vindicate the helpless. A just judge must ensure that justice is served for the weak and the needy, as they often lack representation. When Yahweh describes his role as judge, he frequently pays attention to vulnerable groups as especially deserving of his just concern.[28] Consider these examples:

---

[27] Clements, "The Book of Deuteronomy," 350.
[28] Oswalt, "God," 282.

> "You shall not afflict any widow or orphan. If you afflict him at all, and if he does cry out to Me, I will surely hear his cry" (Exod 22:22–23)

> He executes justice for the orphan and the widow, and shows His love for the alien by giving him food and clothing. (Deut 10:18)

> O Yahweh, You have heard the desire of the humble; You will strengthen their heart, You will incline Your ear to vindicate the orphan and the oppressed, so that man who is of the earth will no longer cause terror. (Ps 10:17–18)

> Father of the fatherless and a judge for the widows, is God in His holy habitation. (Ps 68:5)

God's unrelenting commitment to the helpless extended to the human judges who decided between the people as God's judicial agents (Isa 10:1–2; Jer 5:28–29; Ezek 22:6–7; Ps 82:1–4; Zech 7:9–12). In essence, Yahweh's faithfulness to his role as judge and defender of the defenseless extended to his human representatives, who were tasked with judging on God's behalf.[29]

When we turn to the beliefs and practices of the Early Church, we can observe continuity with the Old Testament's portrayal of God as the just judge committed to the helpless. Jesus, who functions as the messianic agent of the only true God, was remembered as impressing upon his followers God's just concern for those who had no one to defend them (Mark 12:41–44; Luke 4:18–19; 6:40; 7:11–15), sometimes in the context of judgment (Matt 25:35–40).[30] The Book of Acts shows evidence of early Christians dividing the labor, empowering seven deacons to dutifully look after the widows (Acts 6:1–6). James gives attention to the Father's concern for the distressed widow and the orphan, while also encouraging the community to look after them (James 1:27). Similarly, 1 Timothy offers instructions for the care and concern for widows in the Christian community of Ephesus (1 Tim 5:3–5). In short, the Early Church demonstrates continuity with the Old Testament by portraying God the Father as showing concern for the just treatment of the helpless, and Jesus, along with the earliest Christians, acted as agents of God's just care.

The fourth and final function of the role of the judge that Yahweh carried out is that he must punish evil and wrongdoers. God shows compassion and grace towards those who repent and seek him with all their heart, but for those who refuse to relent, the judge must issue a "guilty" verdict and punish the wicked. "Vengeance is Mine, and retribution," says Yahweh (Deut 32:35).

As the Old Testament unfolds, the biblical authors began to sense that there is a day coming in which God will sit as judge in order to vindicate and reward the righteous

---

[29] Hayes, "Justice, Righteousness," 471.
[30] Culpepper, *Matthew*, 373–74; Nolland, *Matthew*, 1028–30.

but also punish and destroy the wicked. As the righteous judge, God gets angry with those who commit wickedness: "If one does not repent, God will whet His sword; He has bent and strung His bow" (Ps 7:11–12). His judicial purview extends beyond the nation of Israel to all creation: "But Yahweh sits enthroned forever; He has established His throne for judgment and He judges the world in righteousness; He executes judgment for the peoples with equity" (Ps 9:7–8). In other words, the necessity for the cosmic judge to punish evil is closely bound up with God's own righteousness.

The depiction of God who punishes the wicked as an extension of his role as the righteous judge appears frequently among the oracles of the Old Testament prophets. Take, for example, this sampling:

> For behold, Yahweh is about to come out from His place to punish the inhabitants of the earth for their iniquity (Isa 26:21)
>
> Let the nations be aroused and come up to the valley of Jehoshaphat, for there I will sit to judge all the surrounding nations. (Joel 3:12)
>
> And He will judge between many peoples and render decisions for mighty, distant nations. (Mic 4:3)
>
> A jealous and avenging God is Yahweh; Yahweh is avenging and wrathful. Yahweh takes vengeance on His adversaries, and He reserves wrath for His enemies. Yahweh is slow to anger and great in power, and Yahweh will by no means leave the guilty unpunished. (Nah 1:2–3)
>
> "Then I will draw near to you for judgment; and I will be a swift witness against the sorcerers and against the adulterers and against those who swear falsely, and against those who oppress the wage earner in his wages, the widow and the orphan, and those who turn aside the alien and do not fear Me," says Yahweh of hosts. (Mal 3:5)

When we examine the beliefs and teachings of the Early Church, it becomes clear that the true God continues to be characterized as the cosmic judge whose duty is to punish and defeat evil. The biblical data is complex, primarily because God has shared the prerogative of judgment with Jesus, an act that effectively empowers the son of God to function as God's agent of judgment (John 5:22, 27, 30; 8:16).[31] This results in Jesus sometimes describing God as the judge, while also describing himself as the newly empowered judge. Within Jesus' parables, we may observe the characterization of the Father as a king who wishes to settle accounts with his servants, forgiving the penitent and issuing punishment for the "wicked slave" (Matt 18:23–35). More to the point is the Parable of the Wicked Tenants (Matt 21:33–43; Mark 12:1–11; Luke 20:9–18), where God the Father owns a vineyard, rents it out to Israel, and enters into judgment with the tenants who act disobediently. In fact, the particular language of judgment that Jesus

---

[31] Thompson, *The God of the Gospel of John*, 230–31; Borgen, "God's Agent in the Fourth Gospel," 171.

employs in this parable is that of "destroying" the wicked (Mark 12:9), taking the kingdom away from the original recipients, and giving it to those who faithfully bear fruit (Matt 21:43). Similarly, God is characterized as a king who gave a wedding feast for his son (Matt 22:1–14). When the recipients killed the messengers whom the king sent to invite others to the wedding, the enraged king destroyed the murderers, set their city on fire (Matt 22:7), and even had an uninvited guest bound and thrown into the place where there is weeping and gnashing of teeth (Matt 22:13). God, as it seems, is intent on serving as a righteous judge who must punish sin and wickedness.

Jesus Christ, the highly empowered son of God who bears the prerogative of judgment from his Father, likewise offered parables in which Jesus served as the judge who punishes evil. The Parable of the Nobleman describes a man who enters into judgment with his servants after returning, having received a kingdom (Luke 19:11–27). While the master of the servants rewarded those who were faithful while he was away, he punished the disobedient, called him "worthless" (Luke 19:22), and had him slain in his presence (Luke 19:27). Jesus depicts himself as the coming son of man in his description of the Sheep and the Goats, who sits on his promised throne as king, shepherd, and judge (Matt 25:31–46).[32] While the righteous sheep enter into the kingdom of God at that time, the wicked goats are issued the verdict that labels them as "accursed ones" whose destiny lies with the Devil and his angels in the prepared fire (Matt 25:41). Their punishment will have its end that is eternal (Matt 25:46).[33] This recalls a saying of judgment from an earlier parable in Matthew, the Parable of the Tares in the Field, in which the son of man will have the wicked thrown into the furnace of fire at the end of the age (Matt 13:36–43). In all these examples, Jesus functions as the agent of God's judgment, punishing the disobedient and committing them to destruction.

Jesus' portrayal of God as the righteous judge who will deal with sin and evildoers was passed on to his followers, and we can examine how these early Christians thought of God in this key judicial role. The Apostle Paul spoke of a coming Day of Judgment, "the day of wrath and revelation of the righteous judgment of God, who will render to each person according to his deeds" (Rom 2:5–6). God, functioning as the impartial judge (Rom 2:11), will respond to the wicked with wrath and indignation, regardless of ethnicity or religious orientation. "On this day," Paul continues, "God will judge the secrets of man through Christ Jesus" (Rom 2:16). Later in Romans, Paul reminds his readers that "we will all stand before the judgment seat of God . . . each one of us will give an account of himself to God" (Rom 14:10–12). We can gather several key points of continuity between Paul's understanding of God's coming judgment and the

---

[32] Beasley-Murray, *Jesus and the Kingdom of God*, 307, observes that this passage is "neither a parable nor an allegory," noting that only the initial description of sheep and goats being separated by the shepherd is loosely parabolic. The entire passage is more appropriately characterized as an apocalyptic "representation of the Last Judgment."

[33] France, *Matthew*, 966–67.

teachings of Jesus. First, God will judge through his agent, Jesus Christ, thereby allowing Jesus to serve as one who is empowered with the prerogative of judgment.[34] Second, the impartial judge will summon all people to give an account, including Christians. Third, the timing of this Day of Judgment will occur on a single, set date in the future. Lastly, the sinfully wicked will be issued a guilty verdict, resulting in the righteous judge's wrathful indignation. These points can be observed in several other places in the New Testament (Heb 10:27; James 2:13; 1 Pet 4:17; Jude 1:14–15; Rev 20:11–15), but our survey thus far aptly demonstrates God as the cosmic judge who is committed to defeating and punishing evil.

The justice of God not only serves to punish evil and the wicked; it also serves to vindicate the righteous. The just judge must also restore the innocent when they are wronged, and another word for this restorative judgment is *vindication*. Imagine for a moment a scenario where an innocent person gets robbed by a thief, but it was all caught on camera. The innocent person brings the thief before a judge, and the evidence is examined impartially. When the judge finds in favor of the innocent person, it is not only the robber who is issued a verdict. The innocent person is restored to what was stolen, thereby vindicating the situation. It is the responsibility of the just judge not only to punish evil, as this scenario explains, but also to restore, deliver, and vindicate those who have been wronged.

While the authors of the biblical texts spare no expense in portraying God as the judge who will execute judgment upon the sinful, there is an equal emphasis placed upon characterizing God as the cosmic judge who vindicates his people when they are wronged by evil. The Psalms regularly depict the oppressed person calling out to Yahweh and praying for rescue and vindication from one's enemies (Ps 7:8–9; 26:1; 43:1–2; 54:1–4; 140:1–6).[35] God's just commitment to vindicate his people from their enemies is closely tied to his faithfulness to his promises made to the patriarchs. God's rescue of Israel from the nation of Egypt is directly linked to his role as the just judge and his quality of faithfulness (Exod 2:23–25; 3:7–8; 6:5; Deut 4:37–38; 1 Sam 10:18). The Book of Daniel displays several examples of the true God justly intervening to vindicate Daniel and his three friends when they were wrongly punished for doing what was right (Dan 1:9, 17; 3:24–28; 6:20–23), examples that served to motivate the readers of Daniel to place their trust in God's commitment to vindicating his faithful people from the wicked (Dan 7:17–18, 21–22, 25–26).[36] All of these examples culminate in Jesus Christ and his resurrection from the dead. Jesus was innocent and wrongly put to death, so it was the responsibility of the just judge to vindicate Jesus from the dead (Acts 2:23–24; 3:14–15).[37] In other words, the resurrection of Jesus was an act of the cosmic judge

---

[34] Richardson, *Theology of the New Testament*, 77.
[35] Oswalt, "God," 249–50.
[36] Seow, *Daniel*, 18; Goldingay, *Daniel*, 240–42; Pace, *Daniel*, 210–11.
[37] Schnabel, *Acts*, 142–43.

rescuing and delivering one of his people, and the Early Church anticipated a similar verdict on the Day of Judgment when the cosmic judge would raise the dead and grant immortality to all of his righteous people (1 Cor 6:14; 2 Cor 4:14; 13:4).

Conclusion

As we sum up this chapter, it is prudent to summarize our findings in order to better understand the key moral qualities of Yahweh, the only true God. First, we explored the *gracious* attribute of God, which serves to encompass his goodness, mercy, love, and forgiveness that he demonstrates towards his creation. Second, we closely looked at God's *faithfulness* in his commitments and dealings with his people. By recognizing God as faithful, we can rest assured that he is trustworthy, reliable, and a keeper of his covenant promises. Lastly, we examined the many ways in which God is *just*. In his role as the cosmic judge, God demonstrates his justice and judgment, both towards the righteous and towards the wicked. By defining God the Father as a gracious, faithful, and just God, we can gain a deeper understanding of him and discuss him more effectively in our evangelistic efforts.

Since we have already begun to see instances where the only true God works in and through Jesus Christ, who serves as the messianic agent of God's justice, we are now poised to explore another key feature of biblical theology. Yahweh is committed to saving, delivering, and redeeming his creation, and the way that he often works to accomplish these feats is by working through his creation when they function as his obedient agents. We will turn in the next chapter to this important relationship between God and his agents.

6
GOD'S AGENTS

The Jewish principle of agency, which establishes how a sender can send forth a representative agent on a mission, is a concept observed in Scripture, believed by the Early Church, and continues to be in practice in several Jewish circles in the modern era. Human beings, who are made in the image of God (Gen 1:27), frequently function as God's agents within the biblical narrative. Yahweh employs several other agents as well, including heavenly angelic messengers. Since the principle of agency was assumed in the culture of the biblical authors, those who encountered any of the commissioned representatives of Yahweh would talk to, treat, honor, and respect that agent as if he were Yahweh himself, without confusing the agent for the sender.

In this chapter, we will explore how Yahweh, the one true God, utilized qualified agents in his regular dealings with his creation.[1] First, we will discuss the arrangement between God and his representatives, while giving attention to the important roles of "sender" and "agent" as they are understood by the authors of the biblical texts. Second, we will examine how God regularly used heavenly angels as his messengers. Third, we will focus on the personified attributes that God sends forth as his agents, particularly his Spirit, word, and wisdom. Fourth, we will explore several different human agents of the only true God, including prophets, priests, and, most importantly, the anointed king of Israel. Finally, we will take stock of how Yahweh shares his name, titles, and prerogatives with these qualified human agents. By giving attention to the various ways God employs his agents as his empowered representatives, we can better understand the intentions and character of the sender—God himself.

The Sender and His Agent

Before examining the biblical examples of God sending forth an agent to fulfill a mission, we must first take the time to understand the social convention of agency within the Jewish world. The arrangement was made between a *sender* (sometimes called the "principal") and an *agent* (often referred to by the Hebrew term *shaliach*). While our current study will focus on God as the sender, it was also extremely common for human beings to function as senders. The relationship between sender and agent involves the

---

[1] Haight, *Jesus Symbol of God*, 91.

investment of the sender's authority, status, and prerogatives in the person of the agent, who, in turn, is sent on a mission.[2] The appointment of an agent could take place simply with a verbal agreement, and no formal writing or witnesses were required to verify this agentival arrangement.[3]

The recognized relationship between the sender and the agent can be summarized into six important tenets. The first tenet of the Jewish principle of agency is arguably the most important, namely, the agent fully represents the sender. This means that the commissioned agent was not merely a representative, but rather, they were the functional equivalent of the sender in terms of status, authority, and rights.[4] The second tenet recognizes that the sender is greater than the agent. The subordinate agent would, naturally, set aside any will or agenda in order to give room to the will of the sender.[5] Since the commissioned agent is the subordinate of the sender, it follows that he would fully obey the sender, thereby providing the third tenet. The sender possessed an inherent authority over the agent, and the agent's mission necessitated a faithful and obedient posture to the will of the sender.[6] Fourth, the agent functioned as the legal partner of the sender. An agent would bear the legal rights to act on behalf of the sender in judicial matters, including serving as a witness in a lawcourt setting, entering into a marriage contract, or taking possession of property.[7] The fifth tenet deals with the requirement of the agent to return to the sender when the mission has come to completion. If the sender entrusted the agent with a message to give to a third party or with a job to fulfill, it was assumed that the agent's commission would be incomplete until the moment that he or she delivered it to the sender.[8] The sixth and final tenet of the Jewish principle of agency is that a commissioned agent can recruit, authorize, and send forth his or her own agents. This would occur if the initial agent needed assistance with the mission or desired to extend the influence in a particular geographical region beyond the scope of what only a single agent could accomplish.[9] These six points can be observed in the ways that God sends forth an agent to accomplish his purposes within the biblical narrative. We will have the opportunity to more thoroughly examine these six tenets of the principle of agency in Chapter 24: Jesus as God's Agent.

---

[2] McGrath, *The Only True God*, 51, helpfully summarizes the data: "In ancient Judaism, God could empower his agent to wield his full power and authority, *precisely because* any figure so empowered always remained by definition subject and subordinate to the one empowering him, namely, God."
[3] Levinthal, "The Jewish Law of Agency," 138.
[4] Simmons, "The Rabbinical Law of Agency," 618. Dembitz, "Agency, Law of," 233; Bruce, *The Gospel and Epistles of John*, 100.
[5] Smith, *Wisdom Christology*, 92.
[6] Thompson, "John, Gospel of," 378.
[7] Borgen, "God's Agent in the Fourth Gospel," 169–71; Simmons, "The Rabbinical Law of Agency," 615; Dembitz, "Agency, Law of," 232–33.
[8] Borgen, "God's Agent in the Fourth Gospel," 172.
[9] Dembitz, "Agency, Law of," 232; Levinthal, "The Jewish Law of Agency," 136.

Angels as Agents of God

Having defined the roles in the sender-agent relationship as well as the six individual tenets of Jewish agency, we are now in a better place to begin exploring the biblical data. The first category of agents utilized by Yahweh is heavenly angels, who are frequently the object of the verb "to send" in Scripture (Gen 19:13–15; Dan 10:11; Acts 12:11). Although it is not clear with the English translation "angel," the Hebrew and Aramaic word (*malak*) means a messenger or envoy.[10] The same is true for the Greek word *angelos*, from which we get our English equivalent, angel. A messenger is, by definition, a designated agent, and it therefore follows that all heavenly angels function as authorized agents of Yahweh.[11] Once we understand that heavenly angels are God's representatives, we can start to make sense of passages where angels appear to humans and speak as if they were Yahweh himself. If we fail to consider that heavenly angels are representative messengers of Yahweh, then we may mistakenly collapse the agent and the sender by assuming that the messenger just is Yahweh himself.

If we examine how God's heavenly angels speak as authorized agents, we can begin to appreciate the Jewish principle of agency.[12] Note carefully the interaction between the angel of Yahweh and Hagar in this passage:

> Now the angel of Yahweh found her by a spring of water in the wilderness, by the spring on the way to Shur. He said, "Hagar, Sarai's maid, where have you come from and where are you going?" And she said, "I am fleeing from the presence of my mistress Sarai." Then the angel of Yahweh said to her, "Return to your mistress, and submit yourself to her authority." Moreover, the angel of Yahweh said to her, "I will greatly multiply your descendants so that they will be too many to count." The angel of Yahweh said to her further, "Behold, you are with child, and you will bear a son; and you shall call his name Ishmael, because Yahweh has given heed to your affliction. He will be a wild donkey of a man, his hand will be against everyone, and everyone's hand will be against him; and he will live to the east of all his brothers." Then she called the name of Yahweh who spoke to her, "You are a God who sees"; for she said, "Have I even remained alive here after seeing Him?" (Gen 16:7–13)

In this exchange, the author identifies the angel of Yahweh four times. This authorized agent speaks of Yahweh as someone other than himself (Gen 16:11), which we would expect when a sender commissions a messenger. However, the angel speaks as if he is uttering the very words of God, which we would also expect from a delegated agent of God.[13] In fact, after the conversation is over, the narrator informs us that Yahweh has spoken to Hagar, implying that the reader would conclude that Yahweh has spoken

---

[10] Davidson, "Angel," 148–49; Watson, "Angels," 248; Köhler et al., *Hebrew and Aramaic Lexicon*, 585–86.
[11] Watson, "Angels," 250; Routledge, *Old Testament Theology*, 119.
[12] Eichrodt, *Theology of the Old Testament*, 2:23.
[13] Sarna, *Genesis*, 383; Arnold, *Genesis*, 164.

through his angel, who fully represents him. The close association between God, the sender, and his heavenly angelic messenger is discernible when we recognize the Jewish principle of agency.

In another example, Moses encounters the angel of Yahweh in the burning bush. The narrator illustrates the dialogue between Moses and this angel as if Moses were talking directly to God:

> The angel of Yahweh appeared to him in a blazing fire from the midst of a bush; and he looked, and behold, the bush was burning with fire, yet the bush was not consumed. So Moses said, "I must turn aside now and see this marvelous sight, why the bush is not burned up." When Yahweh saw that he turned aside to look, God called to him from the midst of the bush and said, "Moses, Moses!" And he said, "Here I am." Then He said, "Do not come near here; remove your sandals from your feet, for the place on which you are standing is holy ground." He said also, "I am the God of your father, the God of Abraham, the God of Isaac, and the God of Jacob." Then Moses hid his face, for he was afraid to look at God. (Exod 3:2–6)

During this interaction, the angelic messenger simply appears in the bush. However, the rest of the exchange between Moses and the angel characterizes the angel in its capacity as an agent, to the point where the angel, in the midst of the bush, is referred to as "God."[14] Furthermore, the angel speaks for Yahweh in the first person, "I am the God of your father" (Exod 3:6). Moses hides his face for fear of looking at "God," despite the fact that it is clearly a representative angel in the bush. When the Early Church retold this story, the distinction between the angel who spoke to Moses and the Lord who spoke through this angel was maintained (Acts 7:30–31).[15] The most natural way to make sense of an angelic messenger of Yahweh speaking the very words of Yahweh himself, along with being addressed by Moses as "God," is to read the account in light of the context of the Jewish principle of agency. The angelic messenger in the bush fully represented Yahweh and spoke on his behalf.[16]

Later, during the Exodus wilderness experience, Yahweh informs the children of Israel that he will send them one of his angels to both guard and bring them into the prepared place (Exod 23:20). As an angelic agent of Yahweh, the Israelites are to obey his voice, which, naturally, conveys the words of God himself (Exod 23:21). Of noteworthy interest is the summons to not rebel against this angel of God, because God has shared his name with him: "since My name is in him." This passage reports how Yahweh invests his personal name into his angels—those heavenly agents who fully represent him.[17]

---

[14] Houtman, *Exodus*, 1:335–36.
[15] Keener, *Acts*, 2:1397.
[16] Davies, *Exodus 1–18*, 1:238–39; Propp, *Exodus 1–18*, 198; Meyers, *Exodus*, 52.
[17] Sarna, *Exodus*, 148; Hamilton, *Exodus*, 435; McGrath, *The Only True God*, 49.

God's heavenly messengers can thus be addressed as if they are God himself, without confusing the agent for God the sender.[18]

There are several other Old Testament passages where heavenly angels speak in their role as Yahweh's authorized agents, often by declaring the words of Yahweh himself in the first person (Gen 21:17–19; 31:11–13; 32:24–30; Exod 32:34–33:2; Num 20:16; Judg 2:1; Hos 12:3–4).[19] But for now, our sampling of passages should be sufficient to demonstrate that God employs heavenly angels to represent him as his delegated agents.

The authors of the New Testament continued to believe and depict heavenly angels as qualified agents of God who speak on God's behalf. An angel of the Lord, who revealed himself as Gabriel, appeared to Zacharias in Luke 1:11–20. The angel Gabriel acknowledges that he has been sent from God (Luke 1:19), which allows Gabriel to function as an authorized agent.[20] He distinguishes himself from the Lord (God) during his interaction with Zacharias, while also indicating that he was sent in response to the prayerful petition of Zacharias that was made to God (Luke 1:13). Moreover, Gabriel exercises the divine prerogative of judgment by making Zacharias mute in light of his failure to believe this authorized messenger (Luke 1:18–20). Luke, the author of this account, clearly wants his readers to regard Gabriel as a heavenly agent of the Lord God.

Towards the end of the Book of Acts is another instance where one of the angels of God functions in the role of an agent who fully represents his sender. While the Apostle Paul was on his way to Rome, his ship encountered a violent storm, causing the sailors to lose hope of reaching their destination safely. Paul announced to the crew that an angel belonging to the God he served had appeared to him (Acts 27:23). This angel shared with Paul a message from God, indicating that the ship's inhabitants would arrive safely. In light of the angel's message of hope, Paul states his confidence in the communication he received: "I believe God that it will turn out exactly as I have been told" (Acts 27:25). The stated object of Paul's belief is *God*, even though it was one of God's *angels* who spoke the message of hope to Paul. Unlike Zacharias, the Apostle Paul faithfully believed the angelic messenger who spoke the words of God as God's commissioned agent.[21]

The biblical record depicts several different categories of angels, all of whom represent God as his authorized messengers. The "cherub" (plural *cherubim*) is a winged angel whose first appearance in the Old Testament occurs when Yahweh drove humanity out of the Garden of Eden, placing the cherubim as his guardian agents of the path to the tree of life (Gen 3:24). Two massive cherubim, made from olivewood overlaid with

---

[18] Durham, *Exodus*, 335.
[19] Wright, "Angels," 329.
[20] Green, *Luke*, 78; Marshall, *Luke*, 60.
[21] Dunn, *Acts*, 339; Johnson, *Acts*, 449; Keener, *Acts*, 4:3630–31.

gold and having wings spanning approximately seven and a half feet in length, functioned as a covering in the Jerusalem temple over the ark of the covenant (1 Kgs 6:23–28; 8:6–7), which itself had its own two golden cherubim hammered to the mercy seat (Exod 25:18–22). The Israelites believed that God's presence sat enthroned above these two cherubim (2 Sam 6:2; 2 Kgs 19:15; 1 Chron 13:6). In fact, the prophet Ezekiel envisioned God's throne chariot riding upon the heads of the cherubim (Ezek 10:1–22), and other Old Testament authors confirm this angelic function (2 Sam 22:11; Ps 18:10). As angelic creatures that guard on Yahweh's behalf, uphold his throne, and sometimes move him from place to place, the cherubim are closely associated with the only true God.[22]

The "seraph" (plural *seraphim*) is a different class of heavenly angels, primarily distinguished by them having six wings (Isa 6:2). They participate in offering worship to Yahweh, and presumably their worship is intended to encourage participation from the people of God (Isa 6:3; Rev 4:8). One of the seraphs touches Isaiah on the mouth with a lump of burning coal, which results in the prophet having his iniquity taken away and his sins forgiven (Isa 6:6–7). Since the prerogative to forgive iniquity innately belongs to Yahweh (Isa 33:22–24), it naturally follows that his seraphs are here acting as Yahweh's agents, issuing forth forgiveness to the prophet Isaiah on God's behalf.[23] This should not be a surprise to those who situate the actions of God's representative seraphs in the context of the Jewish principle of agency. Other passages indicate that the seraphim resemble fiery serpents, rather than having a humanoid appearance (Num 21:6–9; Isa 14:29).[24] These rather unique serpentine creatures nevertheless function as angelic agents of Yahweh.

Among the heavenly messengers appear to be a higher class of angels that are referred to as archangels (literally "chief angel").[25] In some of the extra-biblical Jewish texts, there are seven named archangels, and this belief probably lies behind the greetings offered in the Book of Revelation, where "the seven spirits who are before His throne" contribute to the sending of the letter (Rev 1:4).[26] Within the New Testament, one named archangel is explicitly mentioned, Michael (Jude 1:9). The Old Testament refers to Michael the archangel as one of the chief princes, confirming the suggestion that he is one of several others who possess a rank of priority over the other heavenly angels (Dan 10:13).[27] The might and the authority of the "archangel" rank can be observed in Revelation 12:7–8 where Michael has his own group of heavenly angels belonging to him,

---

[22] Meyers, "Cherubim," 900.
[23] Roberts, *First Isaiah*, 99–100. Brueggemann, *Isaiah 1–39*, 59, observes how the seraphs serve as Yahweh's "functionaries" in this passage.
[24] Skelley-Chandler, "Seraph, Seraphs," 178; Dozeman, "The Book of Numbers," 163–64.
[25] Bauer et al., *Greek-English Lexicon*, 137.
[26] Boring, *Revelation*, 75; Aune, *Revelation 1–5*, 34–35; Koester, *Revelation*, 216.
[27] Collins, *Daniel*, 374–75; Newsom and Breed, *Daniel*, 332; Pace, *Daniel*, 315.

and together they go to war with the Dragon and his heavenly angels. The text highlights the superior strength of the archangel Michael and his army of angels. As one of the head (or leading) messengers, Michael represents the heavenly military interests of the true God.

Personified Attributes as Agents of God

As we transition from angels as agents of God to the topic of his personified attributes, we encounter several texts written in Hebrew poetry, which we need to keep in mind as we engage in the act of interpretation. God's Spirit, which is also referred to by the biblical authors as the Holy Spirit, functions as the presence and power of Yahweh that is extended throughout creation.[28] We will talk more about the Holy Spirit in Part 5, which is dedicated to Pneumatology. For now, we can briefly introduce one important way in which Yahweh uses his Spirit as an agent. To do so, we need to recognize the frequency of the biblical poets to personify, which means to give personality to an object or thing, the attributes of God. The Spirit, which ordinarily is depicted as just another way of talking about Yahweh himself in action, is personified as an agent in Psalm 104:30: "You send forth Your Spirit, they are created; and You renew the face of the ground." In this passage, the psalmist portrays Yahweh as commissioning his personified Spirit on a task to breathe life into the next generation of humanity.[29] Furthermore, the Spirit's mission includes bringing renewal to creation—the ground that was cursed in light of humanity's sin (Gen 3:17–19).[30] In other words, the Spirit of God functions as an agent of both creation and new creation.

The Early Church continued to view the personified Spirit as a sent agent of God. Using the particular personification of a "Helper" (sometimes translated as an "Advocate"), the Gospel of John mentions the Spirit being sent on a mission to empower Jesus' disciples.[31] Consider these texts:

> "But the Helper, the Holy Spirit, which the Father will send in My name, will teach you all things, and bring to your remembrance all that I said to you." (John 14:26)

> "When the Helper comes, whom I will send to you from the Father, the Spirit of truth that proceeds from the Father, it will testify about Me" (John 15:26)

The Apostle Paul similarly speaks of God *sending* the Spirit of the son of God in Galatians 4:6, which results in believers imitating Jesus' cry, "Abba!" Father!" This passage strongly hints that this commissioned Spirit enables believers to share in the risen

---

[28] Dunn, *Christology in the Making*, 133.
[29] Köhler et al., *Hebrew and Aramaic Lexicon*, 1515.
[30] Goldingay, *Psalms*, 2:194.
[31] Carter, *John*, 211; Lincoln, *John*, 411–12; Thompson, *John*, 320, 334.

Christ's character.[32] Since we have already observed that God sends forth his Spirit to bring about the renewal of creation (Ps 104:30), we can reasonably conclude that Paul regarded those believers who are the recipients of the sent Spirit as those who are newly created in Christ—a conviction confirmed later in Galatians 6:15.[33] Together, these passages demonstrate how the biblical authors characterized the personified Spirit of God, sent forth as an agent of God's life-giving purposes.

The Holy Spirit is not the only attribute of God that the authors of the biblical texts personified as a sent agent. The creative and powerful utterance of the Creator, his own word, is often the product of personification. Readers of the creation account in Genesis chapter one will recall the repeated illustration, "And God said," which demonstrates the Creator bringing order to his creation through the act of speaking.[34] The biblical poets picked up on this characterization and portrayed God as sending out his own word as an agent on missions to heal, deliver, and accomplish any number of God's purposes.[35] Take, for example, the following texts:

> He sent His word and healed them, and delivered them from their destructions. (Ps 107:20)
>
> He sends forth His command to the earth; His word runs very swiftly. (Ps 147:15)
>
> He sends forth His word and melts them; He causes His wind to blow and the waters to flow. (Ps 147:18)
>
> The Lord sends a word against Jacob, and it falls on Israel (Isa 9:8)

In fact, one of the clearest examples of Yahweh sending his personified speech out on a mission can be observed in Isaiah 55:11, where God defines precisely how his word acts as his commissioned agent: "So will My word be which goes forth from My mouth; it will not return to Me empty, without accomplishing what I desire, and without succeeding in the matter for which I sent it." This personified word, coming directly from the mouth of God, is the agent tasked with carrying out the will and purposes of God, the sender.[36] Ultimately, the sending of God's personified word runs parallel with the redemptive purposes realized with the sending of God's Spirit.

When it comes to the attribute of God's wisdom—his wise interactions with and instructions to creation—the authors of the biblical texts have not made "wisdom" the object of the verb "to send." However, there are several passages in which personified

---

[32] Dunn, *Galatians*, 219–22; Williams, *Galatians*, 112–13; Oakes, *Galatians*, 138.
[33] De Boer, *Galatians*, 402–3; Dunn, *Galatians*, 342–43.
[34] Arnold, *Genesis*, 39; Wenham, *Genesis 1–15*, 17–18; Westermann, *Genesis 1–11*, 110–11.
[35] Dunn, *Christology in the Making*, 217–18.
[36] Paul, *Isaiah 40–66*, 443–44; Goldingay and Payne, *Isaiah 40–55*, 2:378; Watts, *Isaiah 34–66*, 247–48

wisdom is on full display, particularly in the early chapters of the Book of Proverbs.[37] For example, the personified wisdom of God takes up the role of a prophetess in Proverbs 1:20–33. As we will soon see in this chapter, prophets were widely considered to be agents of Yahweh, so the portrayal of God's wisdom as a female prophet, speaking forth the words, rebukes, and promises of Yahweh, certainly qualifies as relevant material for our study of God's agents.[38] It is prudent for our study to cite this passage in its entirety in order that we may fully appreciate how personified wisdom functions as an agent of Yahweh:

> Wisdom shouts in the street, she lifts her voice in the square; at the head of the noisy streets she cries out; at the entrance of the gates in the city she utters her sayings: "How long, O naive ones, will you love being simple-minded? And scoffers delight themselves in scoffing and fools hate knowledge? Turn to my reproof, behold, I will pour out my spirit on you; I will make my words known to you. Because I called and you refused, I stretched out my hand and no one paid attention; and you neglected all my counsel and did not want my reproof; I will also laugh at your calamity; I will mock when your dread comes, when your dread comes like a storm and your calamity comes like a whirlwind, when distress and anguish come upon you. Then they will call on me, but I will not answer; they will seek me diligently, but they will not find me, because they hated knowledge and did not choose the fear of Yahweh. They would not accept my counsel, they spurned all my reproof. So, they shall eat of the fruit of their own way and be satiated with their own devices. For the waywardness of the naive will kill them, and the complacency of fools will destroy them. But he who listens to me shall live securely and will be at ease from the dread of evil." (Prov 1:20–33)

We can confidently draw several conclusions from this passage's illustration of God's wisdom as his personified agent. First, personified wisdom situates herself in public places—the streets, town square, and city gates—in hopes that she can relay Yahweh's message to the people. Second, this prophetic message primarily consists of condemnations and warnings of judgment that will fall upon those who refuse to heed her wise counsel. Third, as Yahweh's agent, personified wisdom speaks Yahweh's promises in the first person: "I will pour out my spirit on you; I will make my words known to you" (Prov 1:23). Fourth, although this wise prophetess has been sent into the public arena, she will quickly become inaccessible to those who refuse to repent. And finally, those who do, however, respond appropriately to her God-given message will experience a life of security and ease. This lengthy poetic passage presents a compelling display of personified wisdom, serving as the agent of God's prophetic oracles.[39]

There are several other lengthy passages that depict God's personified wisdom as the agent of his wise purposes (Prov 3:13–24; 8:1–36; 9:1–6), but our sample passage

---

[37] Smith, *Wisdom Christology*, 15–21.
[38] Meyers et al., *Women in Scripture*, 549.
[39] Yoder, *Proverbs*, 17–20; Fox, *Proverbs 1–9*, 96; Longman, *Proverbs*, 110–14.

is sufficient to observe the way in which Yahweh sends the attribute of his wisdom into the world.[40] There are other personified attributes of God that he sends as his agents, including his furious burning *anger* (Exod 15:7; Ps 78:49) and his *light* and *truth* (Ps 43:3).[41] As the God who redeems his people and his creation, he can even send forth his *redemption* as a personified agent, according to Psalm 111:9. These examples demonstrate the need to carefully interpret poetic texts that portray God as a sender and his attributes as distinct agents, which are commissioned forth to fulfill the Creator's purposes in the world.

Human Beings as Agents of God

Yahweh is not simply invested in redeeming and restoring his creation; he also invites qualified human beings to be the agents of his redemption and restoration. The most common example of human agents of Yahweh is the role of the *prophet*. Put simply, a prophet is someone who speaks on behalf of another.[42] The message of a prophet is called a prophecy, which shouldn't be confused with the term defining the act of speaking a prophecy, which is "to prophesy." When God sends human prophets, the prophet speaks with the full authority of God himself. Along the same lines, when the recipients of the prophet's message respond to the prophet, it is as if they are responding to God, the sender of the prophet.[43]

We should not underestimate the importance that Yahweh gives to his desire to summon human beings to serve as his highly authorized prophets. Sometimes these figures are directly identified by the biblical authors as prophets, while other times they are simply the object of God's sending. Consider the following passages that reveal just how often God utilizes human agents to communicate his words:

> God, furthermore, said to Moses, "Thus you shall say to the sons of Israel, 'Yahweh, the God of your fathers, the God of Abraham, the God of Isaac, and the God of Jacob, has sent me to you.'" (Exod 3:15)

> Then Yahweh sent Nathan to David. (2 Sam 12:1)

> Now it happened after many days that the word of Yahweh came to Elijah in the third year, saying, "Go, show yourself to Ahab" (1 Kgs 18:1)

> Then I heard the voice of the Lord, saying, "Whom shall I send, and who will go for Us?" Then I said, "Here am I. Send me!" (Isa 6:8)

---

[40] For a thorough treatment of Proverbs chs. 3, 8, and 9, see Smith, *Wisdom Christology*, 16–19.
[41] Goldingay, *Psalms*, 2:32, 504.
[42] Petersen, "Prophet, Prophecy," 622.
[43] Brueggemann, *Theology of the Old Testament*, 622–23.

> But Yahweh said to me, "Do not say, 'I am a youth,' because everywhere I send you, you shall go, and all that I command you, you shall speak." (Jer 1:7)

> "I am sending you to them who are stubborn and obstinate children, and you shall say to them, 'Thus says the Lord Yahweh.'" (Ezek 2:4)

Within these examples of God sending human figures to function as his prophetic spokesmen, we may observe several common characteristics defining these important agents. First, some of the prophets are what we might call literary prophets in light of the fact that their oracles were written down in biblical books devoted to them (e.g., the books of Isaiah, Jeremiah, Ezekiel, and Hosea). Other prophets, such as Moses, Nathan, Elijah, and Elisha, can be categorized as non-literary prophets, and these prophets are no less important to God's purposes of bringing forth his message to the intended recipients. What mattered was that the prophet acted as a faithful vessel to convey God's message to the audience, whether that be the children of Israel, the king, or even Gentiles.[44]

Second, the prophecy that the prophets declared was the very words of Yahweh, not the words of the prophet. When we read the messages that these prophetic agents spoke, they are often arranged in what we might call formulaic ways.[45] For example, the prophet Ezekiel is commanded by God to state, "Thus says the Lord Yahweh," and this formulaic way of introducing the message regularly appears in biblical prophetic literature (Exod 4:22; 1 Sam 2:27; Amos 1:3). There are variations of this declaration of God's prophetic oracles spoken through prophets, such as "Hear the word of Yahweh" (1 Kgs 22:19; Isa 1:10; Jer 2:4), "declares Yahweh" (Isa 14:22; Jer 1:8; Hos 2:13), and the reoccurring conclusion "says Yahweh" (Jer 49:2; Zeph 3:20; Hag 1:8). The prophets were the mouthpieces of the only true God, which helped solidify their role as obedient agents.[46]

Third, each of these prophetic figures discerned a very real and convincing calling upon their lives, and the biblical authors regularly illustrate God *sending* these prophets (using the verb "to send"). The Hebrew word for "agent" is *shaliach*, which is derived from the Hebrew verb "to send," *shalah*.[47] It is reasonable to conclude that the biblical authors, by impressing upon their readers that Yahweh personally sent each of these prophets to speak forth God's own words, were intentionally illustrating the prophets as agents.[48]

---

[44] Verhoef, "Prophecy," 1071; Brueggemann, *Theology of the Old Testament*, 628.
[45] Brueggemann, *Theology of the Old Testament*, 630.
[46] Eichrodt, *Theology of the Old Testament*, 1:323, refers to them as "the authorized purveyors of divine declarations."
[47] Collins, "שׁלח," 122–23.
[48] Hossfeld et al., "סָלַח," 51–53.

The Early Church continued to view human prophets as authoritative agents of the only true God. John the Baptist, according to John 1:6, was a man sent from God.[49] Jesus Christ, the promised messiah and king, nevertheless played the role of a prophet of God (Matt 13:57; 21:11; John 6:14). After the resurrection of Jesus, the body of Christ was genuinely served by the continued existence of prophetic figures (Acts 11:27; 13:1; 15:32). According to the Apostle Paul, God gifts and appoints some individuals to function as prophets in the churches (1 Cor 12:28–29; 14:29–32, 37). As such, we observe continuity between the way God speaks his prophetic words through human agents in the Old Testament and in the New Testament.

When it comes to the role of priests who worked in the Jerusalem temple, the relationship between the holy God and the people who offered sacrifices at the altar is not entirely clear. It is clear that the Levites function in an important role, mediating forgiveness between the people of Israel and Yahweh, the holy one.[50] What is less clear, upon an initial inspection, is whether the priests, who are members of Israel themselves and thereby need the forgiveness that Yahweh offers, represent Israel to Yahweh or whether they represent Yahweh to Israel. The weight of the biblical data suggests that the priests function as agents of Yahweh, since Yahweh has chosen them and provided the role through which they could mediate God's forgiveness to the children of Israel.[51] As authorized agents of God, the priests embodied and represented the purity and holiness of Yahweh himself to Israel.[52]

Several characteristics of the Levitical priests indicate their role as God's agents. First, the Book of Leviticus, in describing the various offerings and the details surrounding each individual sacrifice, repeatedly demonstrates that it is the priests themselves who make atonement for the people, resulting in their forgiveness (Lev 4:20; 5:10; 6:7; 19:22).[53] This suggests an awareness that the priests were serving as intermediaries between the God who offers forgiveness and the people who need that forgiveness. Second, when the Israelites made the golden calf at the base of Mt. Sinai, Moses, who was of the tribe of Levi, declared his intent to personally make atonement for the people: "You yourselves have committed a great sin; and now I am going up to Yahweh, perhaps I can make atonement for your sin" (Exod 32:30). When Moses brings the matter before God, he makes it clear that it is God who is providing the forgiveness (Exod 32:32). Moses, in effect, had spoken to the children of Israel aware of his roles as both a prophetic agent and a priestly agent of God.[54] Third, we may draw attention to

---

[49] McHugh, *John 1–4*, 22–24; Lincoln, *John*, 100.
[50] Duke, "Priests, Priesthood," 653.
[51] Simmons, "The Rabbinical Law of Agency," 619–20; Kaiser, "The Book of Leviticus," 1112.
[52] Brueggemann, *Theology of the Old Testament*, 665.
[53] Eichrodt, *Theology of the Old Testament*, 2:446; Kaiser, "The Book of Leviticus," 1035.
[54] Houtman, *Exodus*, 3:670–73.

what is commonly referred to as the Aaronic Blessing, found in the Book of Numbers. Note how Aaron, the High Priest, mediates God's blessing to the people:

> Then Yahweh spoke to Moses, saying, "Speak to Aaron and to his sons, saying, 'Thus you shall bless the sons of Israel. You shall say to them: Yahweh bless you, and keep you; Yahweh make His face shine on you, and be gracious to you; Yahweh lift up His countenance on you, and give you peace.' So they shall invoke My name on the sons of Israel, and I will bless them." (Num 6:22–27)

The High Priest Aaron shall bless the Israelites, and in doing so, Aaron declares that it is, in fact, Yahweh who brings forth the blessing while additionally promising to bless them further when they invoke him personally.[55] In other words, Aaron functions as a priestly agent of God's blessing.[56] Lastly, we can call attention to the words of the prophet Malachi as he discusses the role of the Levitical priests. Malachi conveys the importance of the priestly role by calling attention to how the priest is to serve as an agent of Yahweh—a *messenger*: "For the lips of a priest should preserve knowledge, and men should seek instruction from his mouth; for he is the messenger of Yahweh of hosts" (Mal 2:7). Just as we have observed with our study of heavenly angels, human messengers also function as authorized spokespersons for Yahweh, and in this instance, the authorized agent is the priest who preserves the knowledge and instruction from Yahweh.[57] These examples should be sufficient to conclude that those who served God as his priests understood themselves as agents of God's forgiveness, purity, and holiness.

One of the most important categories of qualified human beings through whom the only true God brings about his plans and purposes is the king. As the Creator, Yahweh naturally exercises his sovereign rule over creation, but as we have already observed in Chapter Five, human beings were created and given a mandate to subdue and rule over everything on the earth (Gen 1:27–28). Adam, whose name means *humanity* in Hebrew, functions as the human agent through whom God would exercise his just rule and reign over the good creation.[58] It is essential to acknowledge how the biblical authors portray Yahweh as a king in his own right.[59] All of the earth belongs to Yahweh, and Israel was to serve as Yahweh's kingdom of priests (Exod 19:5–6). When the men of Israel requested that Gideon and his descendants serve as their king, Gideon responded, "I will not rule over you, nor shall my son rule over you; Yahweh shall rule over you" (Judg 8:22–23). Yahweh presented himself at the commissioning of the prophet Isaiah as an enthroned king who was lofty, exalted, and wearing a massive robe (Isa 6:1). Isaiah goes on to prophesy that the righteous will see "the King in his beauty . . . Yahweh is our king"

---

[55] Westermann, *Elements of Old Testament Theology*, 78; Dozeman, "The Book of Numbers," 66.
[56] Olson, *Numbers*, 41; Duke, "Priests, Priesthood," 653.
[57] Hill, *Malachi*, 212–23.
[58] Gerstenberger, *Theologies in the Old Testament*, 183.
[59] Köhler, *Old Testament Theology*, 31; Brueggemann, *Theology of the Old Testament*, 600; Goldingay, *Old Testament Theology*, 2:59–63.

(Isa 33:17, 22). The prophets likewise characterize God's role as Israel's true king (Zeph 3:15), the king over all the earth (Zech 14:9). In fact, several of the psalms have been described as enthronement psalms in light of their celebratory worship offered to Yahweh as king:

> For God is the King of all the earth; sing praises with a skillful psalm. God reigns over the nations, God sits on His holy throne. (Ps 47:7–8)

> Yahweh reigns, He is clothed with majesty; Yahweh has clothed and girded Himself with strength; indeed, the world is firmly established, it will not be moved. Your throne is established from of old; You are from everlasting. (Ps 93:1–2)

> For Yahweh is a great God and a great King above all gods (Ps 95:3)

> Say among the nations, "Yahweh reigns; indeed, the world is firmly established, it will not be moved; He will judge the peoples with equity." (Ps 96:10)

> Yahweh reigns, let the earth rejoice (Ps 97:1)

> Shout joyfully before the King, Yahweh. (Ps 98:6)

> Yahweh reigns, let the peoples tremble; He is enthroned above the cherubim, let the earth shake! (Ps 99:1)

The Early Church continued to characterize the true God, whom they knew as the Father, as the king of all creation on account of his being the Creator (Matt 22:2; 1 Tim 1:17; 6:15; Rev 15:3).

Having recognized that the biblical authors regarded Yahweh as the ultimate and highest king, we can gain a deeper understanding of the significance attributed to Adam's kingly role in the opening chapters of Genesis.[60] Despite the fact that human beings were created on the sixth day, after the rest of creation was already brought into being, God placed these image-bearing humans over every other creature (Gen 1:28).[61] In effect, Yahweh the king is ruling through his human agent, King Adam. God even lets Adam name all of the animals under his rule, which is a further indication that God is sharing his rule and reign with his human representative (Gen 2:19–20).[62]

The themes of God as king and humanity as God's ruling agents meet again in Psalm 8. It may be prudent for us to examine the psalm in its entirety:

> O Yahweh, our Lord, how majestic is Your name in all the earth, You have displayed Your splendor above the heavens! From the mouth of infants and nursing babes, You have established strength because of Your adversaries, to make the enemy and the

---

[60] Wolff, *Anthropology of the Old Testament*, 226.
[61] Wenham, *Genesis 1–15*, 33.
[62] Fretheim, "The Book of Genesis," 352; Arnold, *Genesis*, 60; Wenham, *Genesis 1–15*, 68.

revengeful cease. When I consider Your heavens, the work of Your fingers, the moon and the stars, which You have ordained; what is man that You take thought of him, and the son of man that You care for him? Yet You have made him a little lower than God, and You crown him with glory and majesty! You make him to rule over the works of Your hands; You have put all things under his feet, all sheep and oxen, and also the beasts of the field, the birds of the heavens and the fish of the sea, whatever passes through the paths of the seas. O Yahweh, our Lord, how majestic is Your name in all the earth! (Ps 8:1–9)

This psalm praises Yahweh, the Creator, for the ways in which he uses human beings as the agents of his rule and reign. In the opening and concluding verses, Yahweh is praised with the title "our Lord," pointing to his position as the master, and Yahweh demonstrates his lordship by subduing his enemies. The psalmist asks how humanity, seemingly insignificant, can even compare with the most visually stimulating elements of God's creation: the heavens, the moon, and the stars (Ps 8:3–4).[63] Upon contemplating this question, a surprising answer is revealed. Humanity was created just a little lower than God, but God also empowered humanity to share in God's own prerogatives. First, human beings are crowned, an image that involves an elevation to the role of kingship. Yahweh is Lord of all creation, but he authorizes human beings to rule as his agents. Second, humans are crowned with God's own glory, meaning that they are endowed with God's dignity and value, likely stemming from their relationship with God as his image-bearers (Gen 1:27).[64] Third, God crowns humanity with another one of his attributes, his majesty, which is another way of speaking about honor and grandeur. "Majesty" is the noun related to the Hebrew adjective translated into "majestic" that defines Yahweh in the opening and closing verses of the psalm. Fourth, God made humanity to rule over God's works, the works of his hands.[65] Earlier in the psalm, these works included the more cosmic elements of creation, but in Psalm 8:7–8 they are defined as all other creatures. The totality of this rule that Yahweh shares with his human agents can be observed in the description of the creatures; they are in the heavens, on the earth, and in the sea (recalling Gen 1:28). Finally, Yahweh's role as the one who causes evildoers to cease is likewise invested in his human representatives. God places all things "under the feet" of human rulers—imagery associated with victory over chaotic enemies and possessing kingship over one's environment.[66] In short, Psalm 8 firmly establishes human beings as highly authorized agents of Yahweh's rule—an interpretation that can also be observed by the authors of the New Testament (1 Cor 15:27; Heb 2:6–8).[67]

---

[63] Craigie, *Psalms 1–50*, 108.
[64] Brueggemann, *The Message of the Psalms*, 36; deClaissé-Walford et al., *Psalms*, 124.
[65] McCann, "The Book of Psalms," 712; Craigie, *Psalms 1–50*, 108, articulates this point helpfully, "God's role for mankind is that of master within the created universe . . . Mankind's mastery is to extend over all created things."
[66] Stendebach, "רָגַל," 319–20; deClaissé-Walford et al., *Psalms*, 125.
[67] Craigie, *Psalms 1–50*, 110.

Once the nation of Israel had entered the promised land, it was only a matter of time before the initial vision from Genesis of a human agent through whom God would rule would be realized. After a failed attempt at being king by Saul the Benjamite, Yahweh selects David and enters into a covenant with him and with David's descendants (2 Sam 7:12–16; 1 Chron 17:11–14). Yahweh would be the father of these Davidic kings, and they in turn would be God's sons (2 Sam 7:14; 1 Chron 17:13), effectively creating a royal title "son of God" that referred to the anointed Israelite king.[68]

This special relationship between Yahweh and the Israelite kings who acted as agents of Yahweh's rule and reign can be observed in several passages, particularly in the Psalms.[69] Just as God authorized and empowered Adam to bear God's prerogatives (Psalm 8), God similarly invests his attributes in the kings who rule on God's behalf. For example, Psalm 45, which is described as "a Song of Love" due to its praise of the king's wedding (Ps 45:1), illustrates the human monarch in exalted terms.[70] The human king (perhaps Solomon or Hezekiah) is summoned to gird his sword on his thigh "in your splendor and your majesty" (Ps 45:3). Splendor and majesty are attributes innately belonging to Yahweh, according to Psalm 104:1, so the human king bears them in Psalm 45 as Yahweh's highly authorized kingly agent.[71] A similar empowerment is evident in the opening line of Psalm 72: "Give the king Your judgments, O God, and your righteousness to the king's son" (Ps 72:1). The Psalmist petitions God to invest his acts of justice and judgment in the human king, God's representative.[72] This theme reappears in Psalm 89, which begins by praising Yahweh for his strong arm and mighty right hand (Ps 89:13). Very quickly in the psalm, Yahweh announces that the Israelite king, identified as "David My servant," will be established with God's own hand: "My arm also will strengthen him" (Ps 89:20–21).[73] This is the very definition of God empowering a human Davidic king.[74] Additionally, the psalm describes two other personified attributes of Yahweh, his faithfulness and covenant love (Ps 89:14), that are shared with the human king in 89:24. Moreover, God's dominion and rulership over the sea (Ps 89:9), which he naturally exercises as king, is realized in and through his agent: "I shall also set his hand on the sea and his right hand on the rivers" (Ps 89:25). In effect, God's strong arm and mighty right hand are giving strength to his human ruler in order that he may then rule the swelling of the seas and still the rising waves.[75] The impression that the biblical authors leave us with

---

[68] Gerstenberger, *Theologies in the Old Testament*, 182; Birch, "The First and Second Books of Samuel," 1257.
[69] Kraus, *Theology of the Psalms*, 121–22.
[70] McCann, "The Book of Psalms," 860.
[71] McCann, "The Book of Psalms," 861; Gerstenberger, *Theologies in the Old Testament*, 183; deClaissé-Walford et al., *Psalms*, 419.
[72] Hossfeld and Zenger, *Psalms 2*, 211–13; Kraus, *Theology of the Psalms*, 119; McCann, "The Book of Psalms," 963; deClaissé-Walford et al., *Psalms*, 577.
[73] Kirk and Young, "I Will Set His Hand," 336.
[74] Kirk, *A Man Attested by God*, 103.
[75] Gerstenberger, *Theologies in the Old Testament*, 184; Hossfeld and Zenger, *Psalms 2*, 410; McCann, "The Book of Psalms," 1036.

is that Yahweh exercises his kingship through a highly authorized human regent, bringing to reality the original intention of King Adam.[76]

The evidence that the human Israelite king functioned as the royal agent of God can be seen outside of the Psalms. For example, the chronicler depicts Yahweh investing his rule in the position that King Solomon occupies, resulting in a depiction of the human king sitting upon the throne of Yahweh (1 Chron 29:23). This is a remarkable admission that illustrates Solomon exercising God's own rule from the Davidic throne that was located in Jerusalem.[77] Elsewhere, God's throne is firmly located in the heavens (Pss 11:4; 103:19; Isa 66:1), so the portrayal of Solomon sitting upon the throne of God indicates that the rule and reign of God are coming to pass through his qualified human agent.[78] The prophet Ezekiel, while prophesying about the coming shepherd-king, illustrates this royal figure as bearing the prerogatives of Yahweh himself. In Ezekiel 34:11–16, Yahweh describes his role as the shepherd who cares for his sheep, promising to feed them and lead them to rest. The impression the reader is left with is that Yahweh himself is the shepherd-king in the ultimate sense until the passage further unpacks how this vision will come to fruition through the promised Davidic king: "Then I will set over them one shepherd, My servant David, and he will feed them; he will feed them himself and be their shepherd. And I, Yahweh, will be their God, and My servant David will be prince among them. I am Yahweh, I have spoken" (Ezek 34:23–24). Ezekiel thus characterizes Yahweh as sharing his role as the shepherd with "David," the coming Davidic king, who will, in turn, exercise the shepherding prerogative of Yahweh.[79] A similar image appears in the oracles of the prophet Micah, who prophesies about a ruler from the tribe of Judah who will go forth from the city of Bethlehem (Mic 5:2). This promised kingly figure is then illustrated as not just a ruling king, but a shepherd-king empowered and authorized by none other than Yahweh himself: "He will arise and shepherd his flock in the strength of Yahweh, in the majesty of the name of Yahweh his God" (Mic 5:4). Micah envisions this promised ruler to bear Yahweh's strength—clearly an image of God enabling the power of his human agent.[80] Furthermore, the text indicates that this agent will possess the majestic name of Yahweh, *his God*, which reflects the full extent of the king's role as the agent representing Yahweh who sent him.[81] Finally, the post-exilic prophet Zechariah looks forward to the day when the house of David (which is another way to talk about the Davidic dynasty of kings) will be "like God" (Zech 12:8). For a human king to be compared to God himself is surely no insignificant feat, but it is

---

[76] Kraus, *Theology of the Psalms*, 122.
[77] Allen, "The First and Second Books of Chronicles," 469; Irons et al., *The Son of God*, 44; McGrath, *The Only True God*, 19.
[78] Barker, "The High Priest and the Worship of Jesus," 94–95.
[79] Kirk, *A Man Attested by God*, 107; Tuell, *Ezekiel*, 240; Odell, *Ezekiel*, 428.
[80] Hillers, *Micah*, 67. Becking, *Micah*, 186, argues, "He will be endowed with power by God."
[81] Kirk, *A Man Attested by God*, 108. Becking, *Micah*, 186, brilliantly observes, "The ruler is presented as fully embedded in and empowered by the Israelite divinity."

to be expected when that king is the agent of God himself.[82] Ultimately, several biblical authors portray the human Israelite king as a highly empowered and thoroughly authorized agent of Yahweh, the only true God.[83] We will have the opportunity to revisit this theme in Part 4: Christology, since Jesus Christ is the final Davidic king and the premier human agent of God.

God Highly Empowers and Authorizes His Agents

Before we bring this chapter to a close, we need to take stock of how the biblical authors and the Early Church depicted Yahweh sharing his most glorious title with his human agents. In several key passages, Yahweh invests the title "God" in the person of his representatives—a remarkable indicator of the Jewish principle of agency. Upon examining the evidence already reviewed, this practice should not come as a surprise. We have already observed that heavenly angelic messengers speak on Yahweh's behalf, convey God's messages in the first person, and are even addressed as Yahweh, their sender. We have also seen evidence of Yahweh investing his personal name in his agents, including angels and the Israelite king. Moreover, the attributes and prerogatives belonging to Yahweh are shared with his human agents, including his throne of kingship. It seems only natural for Yahweh, the sender, to invest his title "God" in his agents who represent him fully.[84]

The first category of human agents referred to by the biblical authors as "God" is the prophetic spokesman. In particular, Moses is referred to as "God" (Hebrew: *elohim*) in his capacity as God's authorized agent.[85] Yahweh informed Moses that his brother Aaron would speak on behalf of Moses to the people of Israel, with Aaron functioning as Moses' mouthpiece and Moses being "as God to him" (Exod 4:16). We should not overlook the significance of Yahweh telling Moses that he will be "as God" to Aaron.[86] The same feat can be seen in Exodus chapter seven, where the title "God" is even more closely associated with the prophet Moses: "And Yahweh said to Moses, 'See, I have made you God to Pharaoh'" (Exod 7:1). In other words, God called Moses "God" precisely

---

[82] Meyers and Meyers, *Zechariah 9–14*, 331–32; Kirk, *A Man Attested by God*, 109.
[83] Beasley-Murray, *Jesus and the Kingdom of God*, 21, offers a helpful summary: "Despite lofty attributes sometimes attributed to the king and the Messiah in the Old Testament, neither the king nor the Messiah was viewed in Israel as 'metaphysically' divine."
[84] Irons et al., *The Son of God*, 141.
[85] Köhler et al., *Hebrew and Aramaic Lexicon*, 53.
[86] Gerstenberger, *Theologies in the Old Testament*, 183; Meyers, *Exodus*, 62; Davies, *Exodus 1–18*: 1:336. Sarna, *Exodus*, 22, helpfully observes how Moses was "playing the role of God."

because Moses is God's authorized human agent, the one who speaks as the authorized representative of Yahweh himself.[87]

The second category of human agents in whom Yahweh invests his title "God" is the judge. As representatives of Yahweh's justice, order, and concern for the helpless, it is understandable why God would share his title with human judges who judge on his behalf.[88] Most Bibles footnote the reference to "God" in Exodus 21:6 as a human judge who bears "God" as a title.[89] In the legal instructions outlined over property disputes in Exodus 22:8–9, the owner of the house must appear before the *judges*, yet the Hebrew noun translated as "judges" is *elohim*, the noun for "God." As the passage continues, breaches of trust must result in both parties appearing before the judges, and these judges will condemn the guilty party (Exod 22:9). In both instances of the English translation "judges," we have the underlying Hebrew noun for God (*elohim*).[90]

The third category of Yahweh's human representatives, who are referred to as "God," is the Israelite king. As royal agents through whom God's kingship is brought to pass, it naturally follows that these human kings can bear the title "God." In Psalm 45, we have an important witness to the highly authorized king, whom the psalmist identifies as *elohim*: "Your throne, O God, is forever and ever. The scepter of uprightness is the scepter of your kingdom. You have loved righteousness and hated wickedness. Therefore God, your God, has anointed you with the oil of joy above your companions" (Ps 45:6–7). In this wedding psalm, the human king is addressed as "God" in his role as the true God's anointed representative (Ps 45:6).[91] However, the following verse (Ps 45:7) clarifies that this highly empowered human king has a God ("your God") above him, namely the one who anointed the king and exalted him above his companions.[92] This passage applies *elohim* to both the human king and the God he represents while carefully distinguishing the two and never confusing one for the other.[93]

We can observe the same feat in Isaiah 9:6, in which Yahweh invests several of his titles in the Davidic king. Isaiah declares, "For to us a child is born, to us a son is given," which points to someone who was born in the prophet's own lifetime (the Hebrew tenses of the verbs indicate actions that have already taken place). In what is

---

[87] Brueggemann, "The Book of Exodus," 738; Davies, *Exodus 1–18:* 1:461–62; Meyers, *Exodus*, 69; Sarna, *Exodus*, 36. Houtman, *Exodus*, 1:524, comments, "Moses always acts as YHWH's representative who carries out the commands that he is given by YHWH."
[88] Köhler et al., *Hebrew and Aramaic Lexicon*, 53; Eichrodt, *Theology of the Old Testament*, 1:306.
[89] Propp, *Exodus 19–40*, 193, helpfully observes, "judges are called 'Deity' because God inspires their judgments, inasmuch as they are his representatives and, so to speak, junior colleagues."
[90] Houtman, *Exodus*, 3:121.
[91] Köhler et al., *Hebrew and Aramaic Lexicon*, 53; Kraus, *Theology of the Psalms*, 109; Gerstenberger, *Theologies in the Old Testament*, 183; deClaissé-Walford et al., *Psalms*, 419–20; Ringgren, "אֱלֹהִים," 282; Xeravits, "Son of God," 1248.
[92] Mowinckel, *The Psalms in Israel's Worship*, 48.
[93] Collins and Collins, *King and Messiah as Son of God*, 14–15; McCann, "The Book of Psalms," 862.

almost certainly a reference to the young Hezekiah,[94] the reader observes four exalted titles formerly belonging to Yahweh: "Wonderful Counselor, Mighty God, Everlasting Father, Prince of Peace."[95] What matters for our current study is that this human child bears the title "Mighty God," an astonishingly lauded designation for Yahweh's royal agent.[96] When we combine the evidence of Israelite kings who were called "God" with the references to the prophets and judges who were also called "God," we can gain a better appreciation of the importance Yahweh places on his human representatives.[97]

Conclusion

To summarize, we began by carefully observing the relationship between the sender, God, and his representatives within the Jewish principle of agency. We also explored how God frequently used heavenly angels to function as his messengers. Furthermore, we took note of several of God's attributes that, when personified, were sent forth as agents of God's will and purposes. Then, we examined the human agents of God who represent his prophetic, priestly, and kingly ambitions. Finally, we drew attention to a rather significant way in which Yahweh empowered his agents by sharing his name, prerogatives, and title with them without allowing the agent to be confused with Yahweh himself. We will be sure to revisit many of these foundational biblical teachings when we examine how the Early Church came to understand the person of Jesus Christ within this Jewish context.

Why should it matter that the biblical authors and the Early Church alike portrayed the only true God as the Father alone? Most churches teach something different, so why should we take God's identity seriously? Does it have any relevance to how we live our lives in the twenty-first century, what the Christians in the first century believed and taught about God? Our next chapter will explore the practical applications of theology, the study of God.

---

[94] Goldingay, *Old Testament Theology*, 2:478–81; Blenkinsopp, *Isaiah 1–39*, 249; Roberts, *First Isaiah*, 147; Kirk, *A Man Attested by God*, 105.

[95] Mowinckel, *He That Cometh*, 175, observes that "The source of this divine equipment is not a supernatural conception or birth, but the fact that '*the spirit of Yahweh rests upon him*' . . . The gift of the spirit manifests itself in superhuman powers which are physical, intellectual, and moral."

[96] Xeravits, "Son of God," 1248. Brueggemann, *Isaiah 1–39*, 83, refers to this child as "the royal agent." Regarding the title *mighty God*, Brueggemann insists that it "should not be understood in a belatedly substantive, trinitarian category nor as a claim to divinity. Rather, the language means that the new king will be filled with all the powers (especially military) that are required."

[97] Brueggemann, *Isaiah 1–39*, 85, draws similar conclusions: "God is always recruiting human agents to enact the Great Reversal about which Yahweh has persistent 'zeal.'"

7
APPLYING THEOLOGY TODAY

The task in this chapter is to focus on the practical application of the theological truths held and taught by Jesus' first followers for disciples in the twenty-first century. I will attempt to answer the question, "So what? What impact does my understanding of first-century theology have on my daily life today?"

A simplified summary of the theology of the early followers of Jesus can be stated as follows: Yahweh is the Father and only true God; eternal life comes from knowing him and Jesus, his sent one, the Messiah and his son. We are to seek first the Father's kingdom and way of living. This is lived out by loving God and others. We learn to love God and others by following Christ and being yoked to him as our teacher. I will now add a portion of Peter's sermon on the day of Pentecost:

> "Men of Israel, listen to these words: Jesus the Nazarene, a man attested to you by God with miracles and wonders and signs which God performed through him in your midst, just as you yourselves know—this man, delivered over by the predetermined plan and foreknowledge of God, you nailed to a cross by the hands of godless men and put him to death. But God raised him up again, putting an end to the agony of death, since it was impossible for him to be held in its power. For David says concerning him, 'I saw the Lord always before me, for he is at my right hand so that I will not be shaken; therefore my heart was glad, and my tongue rejoiced; moreover my flesh will live in hope. For you will not abandon my soul to Hades, or let your Holy One experience corruption. You have made known to me the ways of life; you will make me full of gladness with your presence.' Fellow Israelites, I may say to you confidently of our ancestor David that he both died and was buried, and his tomb is with us to this day. Since he was a prophet, he knew that God had sworn with an oath to him that he would put one of his descendants on his throne. Foreseeing this, David spoke of the resurrection of the Messiah, saying, 'He was not abandoned to Hades, nor did his flesh experience corruption.' This Jesus God raised up, and of that all of us are witnesses. Being therefore exalted at the right hand of God, and having received from the Father the promise of the Holy Spirit, he has poured out this that you both see and hear. For David did not ascend into the heavens, but he himself says, 'The Lord said to my Lord, "Sit at my right hand, until I make your enemies your footstool."' Therefore let the entire house of Israel know with certainty that God has made him both Lord and Messiah, this Jesus whom you crucified." Now when they heard this, they were cut to the heart and said to Peter and to the other apostles, "Brothers, what should we do?" Peter said to them, "Repent, and be baptized every one of you in the name of Jesus Christ so that your sins may be forgiven; and you will receive the gift of the Holy Spirit. For the promise is for you, for your children, and

for all who are far away, everyone whom the Lord our God calls to him." And he testified with many other arguments and exhorted them, saying, "Save yourselves from this corrupt generation." So those who welcomed his message were baptized, and that day about three thousand persons were added (Acts 2:22–41).

Through faith, repentance, and baptism, we access the saving work of Jesus, the crucified Lord and Messiah, whom God raised from the dead. This is the simple faith in the one God and Jesus Christ. In order to live out our first-century faith in the one God and Jesus, his son, our savior, we must believe, follow, and do all things out of love.

As we seek to apply the first-century theology of the Early Church today, I recommend focusing on Matthew, chapters 5–7, also known as the Sermon on the Mount. This passage offers a clear and comprehensive understanding of what Jesus means when he invites us to follow him in living as God's children, seeking first God's kingdom (Matt 6:33) in this present evil age (Gal 1:4). Christ's instruction in this lengthy sermon outlines how God's faithful covenant people (those who followed Christ) were to live. Jesus does not undo God's covenant promises to Abraham and his descendants (Gen 12:1–3), but he brings them to fulfillment, perfection, and completion. From the beginning, Abraham was meant to be a blessing, not only to his descendants but to all the people on earth. Jesus fulfills the mission that God entrusted to Abraham's descendants, the children of Israel: "It is too small a thing for you to be my servant to restore the tribes of Jacob and to bring back those of Israel I have kept. I will also make you a light for the Gentiles, that my salvation may reach to the ends of the earth" (Isa 49:6).

Jesus' ministry was about including those who had been previously rejected, considered unclean, and lost. He demonstrates God's love and grace in that he came to save the whole world, a direct fulfillment of Genesis 12:3. As Jesus' disciples in the twenty-first century, we are to continue that ministry as we are born again through the Spirit of God (John 3:3, 5). Being "born again" is about understanding God's love and adopting his redemptive purposes for creation by aligning our hearts with the kingdom's values and demonstrating his love to the world. To be born again from the Spirit entails loving all, including sinners, not in the often-superficial way seen in religious contexts, but in the profound, unconditional, and sacrificial manner exemplified time and again by Jesus in the New Testament gospel accounts.

Jesus Christ's teaching is a call to authentic spiritual living, reminding us that the path to true spiritual enlightenment is not found in outward displays of piety or legalism. The king of God's kingdom spoke these words to religious Jews, not secular ones, encouraging them to be transformed not into another religious denomination but into a deeply personal, transformative journey of aligning their lives fully with the will of God. This journey demands continual self-examination, a willingness to grow, and an unwavering commitment to living the truths of the spiritual path.

Life in the age to come, also known as eternal life, is attained by knowing Yahweh as the only true God and Jesus as the Messiah sent by God (John 17:3). This means living a life of rejecting idols and anything deemed more valuable than the one true God. It means following and living out the life and teachings of Jesus as he shows us how to love Yahweh with our whole being, and how to truly love others and be a light to show them the way to God and his kingdom (Matt 5:14–16).

As we embody the teachings of Jesus and his closest disciples, which have been passed down since the first century, let us do so with grace and gratitude. We have been gifted by those who came before us, who received the truth of God's scriptures and patiently taught it to us, so that we could know and love God and follow Jesus towards the kingdom of God.

As I reflect back on life experiences, I have been on both sides of the "rush to judgment" often associated with discussing our faith with others who have come to different doctrinal conclusions. I was guilty of assuming I knew more (and better) about what others believed about God. These events so long ago taught me to be "quick to listen, slow to speak" (James 1:19). I also know the sting of being immediately judged as a heretic and labeled as a non-Christian based upon my theological understanding of God as a simple unity and not a Trinity of persons, a conviction that denies the historic creeds. It took me most of a year and a lot of theological writing to convince one man that I was a Christian, even though I was not a trinitarian.

I suggest that when we approach people (or they approach us), we do so without a bag full of judgments and with ears to listen and the patience to hear their perspective and not to be quick to judge and condemn them as unchristian because they have been taught a different, complicated, strongly contested understanding of God. Let us commit to showing them what it means to follow Jesus Christ and approach them with an example of love. Let us strive to speak the truth as we understand it from Scripture, but with humility, patience, and love (Eph 4:15). Let's refrain from adopting attitudes and words of judgment or condemnation. Those things aren't in our job description and are above our pay grade.

I think God prefers us to speak accurately about what his Scripture teaches, but also with humility. To my knowledge, there is no final, written theological exam on biblical doctrine that we have to pass to enter the kingdom. Our test is this: Do we know and love God and Jesus, our Messiah? Are we lovingly following Jesus, turning away from sin to follow our Father's teachings, and being loving lights to our neighbors?

As you continue to study the systematic theology of the Early Church, I invite you to make these your priorities.

PART TWO: ANTHROPOLOGY

8
HUMANITY AND THE IMAGE OF GOD

One of the key distinctives of humanity that we can see in the creation narrative of Genesis 1 is that human beings are made in God's image. No other creature is said to be created in the image of God, which highlights humanity in several crucially important ways.[1] Although the phrase "image of God" does not appear very often in the texts of Scripture, when its meaning is understood, it becomes abundantly clear that its theology is absolutely pervasive, underlying several key doctrines like *hamartiology, christology, ecclesiology*, and even *eschatology*. It is imperative, therefore, that we come to realize the meaning and purpose of the Creator making human beings in his image before we attempt to swim into the deeper waters of doctrinal exploration.

This chapter will begin our study of anthropology—the study of humanity—by examining what it means for human beings to be created in the image of God. First, we will aim to define the term *image of God* so that we may better understand God's intended purpose for humanity. Second, we will explore other passages in the Old Testament that describe human beings as God's image-bearers, noting that this designation persists after humanity becomes sinfully corrupt. Third, we will consider how the redemption that the Early Church found in Christ brings restoration to the image of God. Lastly, we will look at the various ways in which the authors of the New Testament portray Christ as the second Adam, in whom believers begin to experience the restoration of their image-bearing vocation. Once we come to understand the image-bearing responsibilities of humanity, we will be in a better position to study the topics of mortality, death, sleep, and resurrection.

Defining *Image of God*

To begin, it is prudent for us to take a good look at the first thing that the author of Genesis chapter one has to say about God's crowning accomplishment in creation: humanity.[2] On the sixth day of creation, we are told the following:

> Then God said, "Let Us make humanity in Our image, according to Our likeness; and let them rule over the fish of the sea and over the birds of the sky and over the cattle and

---

[1] Fretheim, "Image of God," 18.
[2] Sarna, *Understanding Genesis*, 14–16.

over all the earth and over every creeping thing that creeps on the earth." God created humanity in His own image, in the image of God He created him; male and female He created them. God blessed them; and God said to them, "Be fruitful and multiply, and fill the earth, and subdue it; and rule over the fish of the sea and over the birds of the sky and over every living thing that moves on the earth." (Gen 1:26–28)

Since human beings are created in God's image, it would serve us well to give due consideration to the "God" part of that term. It is reasonable to assume that the image-bearing vocation of human beings relates to the Creator God. Unfortunately, the initial passage begins with an interpretive problem that has divided readers for thousands of years, namely, the plural references to God in Genesis 1:26 ("Let *Us* make humanity in *Our* image, according to *Our* likeness"). Some have attempted to interpret this passage as if God were addressing His heavenly court of angels, the divine council. The problems with this interpretation are as follows: nowhere else in Scripture are angels described as also being made in the image of God, and angels are never illustrated as participating in acts of creation, as even the following verse clearly indicates ("*God created* humanity in His own image, in the image of God *He created* him; male and female *He created* them" [Gen 1:27]). Since it is only human beings who are described as having been made in the image of God, it is unlikely that God's reference to "our image" and "our likeness" includes the heavenly angels.[3]

A second, but far less likely, interpretation proposes that God is talking to Jesus. This suggestion is even more problematic than the "divine council of angels" suggestion. For one, Jesus was not yet in existence, having not yet been created (Matt 1:18, 20; Luke 1:35), so it would be impossible for God to be talking to Jesus. Furthermore, the Early Church remembered Jesus' teaching that only one person made humanity male and female, namely God (Matt 19:4–6).[4] Jesus never claimed, suggested, or hinted at having participated in the creation of human beings, so we can safely set that interpretation aside.

A third interpretive option, which does not require reading into the text of Scripture the presuppositions of "angels" or "Jesus," argues that the plural references in Gen 1:26 are examples of the plural of majesty. The God who spoke in the plural, while creating by himself, makes these representative human rulers while talking with the royal "we," a majestically plural declaration.[5] In other words, the plural references in Genesis 1:26 are plural in number but singular in meaning.[6] We already introduced the grammatical concept of the plural of majesty in Chapter Two when we discussed the Hebrew noun for God, *elohim*, which also happens to be the noun appearing in Genesis 1:26–27. It is no surprise that a plurally majestic designation for God (*elohim*) introduces plural

---

[3] Goldingay, *Old Testament Theology*, 2:518.
[4] Hagner, *Matthew 14–28*, 548; Davies and Allison, *Matthew*, 3:9; Nolland, *Matthew*, 770.
[5] See especially the examples in Smith, "The Plural of Majesty in the Hebrew Bible."
[6] Westermann, *Genesis 1–11*, 145; Goldingay, *Old Testament Theology*, 2:98; Speiser, *Genesis*, 7.

pronouns that highlight the honor and majesty due to the one true God.[7] We can find confirmation of this interpretation in the theology of the Early Church, which illustrated the subject of Genesis 1:26 as "the one who created" humanity according to his image (Col 3:10).[8] If Jesus and Paul taught that the God who made human beings according to his image was only one person, not multiple persons, then we can safely conclude that the plural references in Genesis 1:26 are majestically plural, not proper numerical plurals.[9]

As those who are created in the image and likeness *of God*, what can we discern about his role in this unique vocation given to humanity? When we consider the idea of human beings serving as the Creator's image-bearers in the context of the Ancient Near East, we encounter an essential cultural parallel: a king would set up statues of himself in a region he controlled, thereby reminding the local citizens that his rule and reign were present. This expression of the king's dominion, which was represented by the statue, which bore the image and likeness of the king, conveyed to the locals that the king was in charge, even though he was not physically present.[10] The early Christians, especially those living in cities outside Judea, were familiar with this concept, as images and busts of the Roman emperor were often erected throughout his empire, reminding citizens that Caesar had dominion over these territories, although he resided in Rome. When we combine these parallels with the unique role that God assigns to his image-bearers, we can observe that human beings were created to reflect God's rule over all creation as his viceregents.[11] We have already seen that Adam's initial role was to serve as the agent of God's rule and dominion over all creation, effectively making Adam a king in his own right (Chapter Six). The five-fold mandate given to these image-bearing humans is to be fruitful, multiply, fill the earth, subdue it, and rule over it (Gen 1:28). The kingly responsibilities, referenced with the commands to "subdue" and "rule," clarify the role of the image-bearers as functioning as representative agents of King Yahweh.[12] The other three mandates ("be fruitful, multiply, fill the earth") suggest that God is sharing his role as a creative being with those who bear his image.[13] In other words, human beings, by bearing children in the male-plus-female dynamic of the human relationship, reflect the creative tendencies of their Creator. The life-giving role of God is thus imaged in his human agents on earth. It is no wonder that it is only after God created and blessed humanity made in his image that creation is deemed "very good" (Gen 1:31).[14]

---

[7] Goldingay, *Genesis for Everyone: Part One*, 18.
[8] Dunn, *Colossians and Philemon*, 221–22; Barth and Blanke, *Colossians*, 413–14; Sumney, *Colossians*, 202–3.
[9] Arnold, *Genesis*, 44, suggests that the plural references refer to the self-deliberation of one person, not multiple persons.
[10] Brueggemann, *Genesis*, 32; Curtis, "Image of God (OT)," 390–91.
[11] Kaiser, *Toward an Old Testament Theology*, 76; Köhler, *Old Testament Theology*, 147; Walton, *Genesis*, Zondervan, 21.
[12] Walton, *The Lost World of Genesis One*, 68; Fretheim, "The Book of Genesis," 345; Arnold, *Genesis*, 45.
[13] Fretheim, "Image of God," 20.
[14] Brueggemann and Linafelt, *An Introduction to the Old Testament*, 56.

Image-Bearing Humans in the Biblical Story

Did Adam and Eve lose their vocation as God's image-bearers after they sinned, resulting in punishment by God and being exiled from the Garden of Eden? This is an interesting and important question. As we observed, being made in the image of God came with five mandates that we summarized into life-giving mandates and rulership mandates. Did Adam and Eve's disobedience negatively affect their ability to be fruitful, multiply, and fill the earth? We can confidently answer this question in the affirmative based on several comments from God. Prior to humanity's disobedience, the tree of life was accessible (Gen 2:9), and God explicitly said, "From any tree of the garden you may eat freely" (Gen 2:16). However, when Adam and Eve were exiled from the garden, their access to the tree of life was forbidden (Gen 3:22, 24).[15] Furthermore, the curse that God gave to Adam as a result of his sin included death, explicitly defined as returning to the dust of the ground: "By the sweat of your face you will eat bread, until you return to the ground, because from it you were taken; for you are dust, and to dust you shall return" (Gen 3:19).[16] As for the woman, her punishment includes a painful experience in the bearing of children: "I will greatly multiply your pain in childbirth, in pain you will bring forth children" (Gen 3:16).[17] It is only after the woman is handed this punishment that Adam names her "Eve," which in Hebrew means "life" due to her role as the mother of *the living*.[18] Based on these clues, we can safely conclude that the particular life-giving mandates associated with being made in the image of God were hindered by not having access to the tree of life, the experience of living that concludes with death and returning to the dust of the ground, and the increased difficulty in bearing children. Are human beings' life-giving capacities limited due to sin and disobedience? Yes, but they are not completely removed. The image of God, after humanity's disobedience, is tarnished but not forgotten.[19]

The same hindrance to fully exercising the mandates of being image-bearers can be observed in humanity's capacity to subdue and rule over God's creation. After failing to subdue the serpent, choosing instead to listen to it (and disobeying God in the process), the kingdom was removed from humanity's oversight. Adam and Eve were driven out from the Garden of Eden (Gen 3:23). Prior to being exiled from the garden, God planted it in Eden (Gen 2:8), and then he installed King Adam in the garden to work it and keep it (Gen 2:15). God even made Adam a helper—a woman suitable to assist in these royal tasks fit for human image-bearers (Gen 2:22–23).[20] By exiling Adam and Eve from the garden that they were entrusted initially with exercising dominion over, the functions of

---

[15] Beale, *A New Testament Biblical Theology*, 36.
[16] Wenham, *Genesis 1–15*, 83.
[17] Goldingay, *Old Testament Theology*, 1:142.
[18] Goldingay, *Old Testament Theology*, 1:143.
[19] Curtis, "Image of God (OT)," 390.
[20] Beale, *A New Testament Biblical Theology*, 30–35.

image-bearers to subdue and rule the earth are left unfulfilled. The Psalms never forgot humanity's true potential to rule over the works of God's hands (Ps 8:6), a dominion that would, in time, extend to the ends of the earth (Ps 72:8).[21] Again, we are left with the conclusion that the image of God has become tarnished in light of the sinful behavior of human beings.

The narrator of the Book of Genesis offers a glimmer of hope for humanity and their image-bearing vocation. In an often overlooked (but essential) type of biblical narrative, the genealogy traces Adam and Eve's ability to be fruitful and multiply (Gen 5:1–32).[22] At the head of this genealogical record is a deliberate reference back to humanity as the Creator's image-bearers:

> This is the book of the generations of Adam. In the day when God created man, He made him in the likeness of God. He created them male and female, and He blessed them and named them humanity in the day when they were created. When Adam had lived one hundred and thirty years, he became the father of a son in his own likeness, according to his image, and named him Seth (Gen 5:1–3).

This passage confirms that the image of God is not lost, despite its tarnished condition.[23] Adam bears a son "in his own likeness, according to his image" (Gen 5:3), which indicates that the image of God continues to exist, even among newly born human children.[24] The reader can, therefore, reasonably assume that every subsequent human being who is born is made in the image of God.[25]

The next explicit reference to humanity's image-bearing vocation occurs after Noah and his family exit the ark upon dry ground. After blessing Noah and his sons, God reminds the survivors of the flood of the fact that they were made in his image:

> "Whoever sheds man's blood, by man his blood shall be shed, for in the image of God He made man. As for you, be fruitful and multiply; populate the earth abundantly and multiply in it" (Gen 9:6–7)

While discussing humanity's role as his image-bearers, God emphasizes their sacred value and worth. Human beings should not shed the blood of one another, and the reason given for this prohibition is that they are made in God's image.[26] As representative agents of God who are called to share in his creative, life-giving acts in addition to serving as rulers on his behalf, the murder of an image-bearer is strictly forbidden.[27] The author of Genesis then deliberately recalls the context of the original mandates given to the image-

---

[21] Tate, *Psalms 51–100*, 224.
[22] Kaiser, *Toward an Old Testament Theology*, 79.
[23] Brueggemann, *Genesis*, 68.
[24] Beale, *A New Testament Biblical Theology*, 36.
[25] Wenham, *Genesis 1–15*, 126; Sarna, *Genesis*, 42.
[26] O'Connor, *Genesis 1–25A*, 147–48.
[27] Walton, *Genesis*, NIV, 343.

bearers (Gen 1:26–28) by recording how God summons Noah and his family to "be fruitful and multiply; populate the earth abundantly and multiply in it" (Gen 9:7).[28] By bringing to remembrance humanity's role as the Creator's image-bearers, the author of Genesis emphasizes to his readers that human beings still maintain this crucial vocation even after being expelled from the Garden of Eden, while also stressing the sanctified value that God places upon His most prized creatures.[29]

Outside of the Book of Genesis, the authors of the Old Testament do not use the phrase "image of God." However, the reader is placed in a state of expectation for a time when God will renew his creation, including human beings. The image of God, formerly blessed and deemed to be the crowning accomplishment of the Creator's very good creation, is marred and in dire need of redemption. To this end, the prophets envision a future time in which humanity will be restored to its full potential as image-bearers. Consider these promises that deliberately recall the mandates spelled out in Genesis 1:27–28:

> "Then I Myself will gather the remnant of My flock out of all the countries where I have driven them and bring them back to their pasture, and they will be fruitful and multiply." (Jer 23:3)

> "Thus says Yahweh, 'Behold, I will restore the fortunes of the tents of Jacob and have compassion on his dwelling places; and the city will be rebuilt on its ruin, and the palace will stand on its rightful place. From them will proceed thanksgiving and the voice of those who celebrate; and I will multiply them and they will not be diminished; I will also honor them and they will not be insignificant.'" (Jer 30:18–19)

> "I will multiply men on you, all the house of Israel, all of it; and the cities will be inhabited and the waste places will be rebuilt. I will multiply on you man and beast; and they will increase and be fruitful; and I will cause you to be inhabited as you were formerly and will treat you better than at the first. Thus you will know that I am Yahweh." (Ezek 36:10–11)

> "I will make a covenant of peace with them; it will be an everlasting covenant with them. And I will place them and multiply them, and will set My sanctuary in their midst forever." (Ezek 37:26)

In their visions of the coming restoration, the prophets Jeremiah and Ezekiel reiterate the mandates for God's image-bearers to be fruitful, multiply, and fill the earth.[30] This indicates that God's promises spoken through the prophets to restore his creation include an assurance that faithful human beings will also be restored in their capacity to function as Yahweh's image-bearers.[31] Although the phrase "image of God" is absent from these

---

[28] Arnold, *Genesis*, 109; Wenham, *Genesis 1–15*, 193–94.
[29] Goldingay, *Old Testament Theology*, 1:181.
[30] Craigie et al., *Jeremiah 1–25*, 327; Block, *Ezekiel 25–48*, 334
[31] Beale, *A New Testament Biblical Theology*, 51.

promises of restoration, the concept is clearly echoed in the use of the same Hebrew verbs found in Genesis 1:28 ("be fruitful" and "multiply"). The Early Church anticipated the fulfillment of these passages in the consummated kingdom of God, when Christ would return and usher in the regeneration (Matt 19:28).

Additionally, these visions of the coming restoration frequently include among their prophetic oracles the insistence that God will establish a second figure like Adam to function as the human agent through whom God will reign, subdue, and rule over his creation. Take, for example, these words that give hope and anticipation for a ruler in whom the kingly mandates of the image of God are to be restored:

> "Behold, the days are coming," declares Yahweh, "When I will raise up for David a righteous Branch; and he will reign as king and act wisely and do justice and righteousness in the land. In his days Judah will be saved, and Israel will dwell securely" (Jer 23:5–6)

> "My servant David will be king over them, and they will all have one shepherd; and they will walk in My ordinances and keep My statutes and observe them. They will live on the land that I gave to Jacob My servant, in which your fathers lived; and they will live on it, they, and their sons and their sons' sons, forever; and David My servant will be their prince forever." (Ezek 37:24–25)

We will elaborate on these texts more fully in Part 4 (Christology) and Part 8 (Eschatology), but for now, we can draw a few conclusions. First, Yahweh promises to establish a royal figure that is variously described as a "Branch" of David (signifying a member of the human king's family tree) or simply as "David" (a king who is typologically likened to David).[32] Both of these descriptions indicate a figure associated with the famous King David, with the prophet Jeremiah indicating that the figure will "reign as king," while Ezekiel outright says that this coming ruler "will be king over them . . . their prince forever."[33] Second, when these prophets envision the dominion and reign of this promised king, we see what can best be described as a human figure in whom the formerly tarnished image of God has been fully restored to its original purpose, resulting in an era in which God's justice is known throughout the subdued and ruled land. In other words, the prophets anticipate a coming age in which the image of God and *all of its functions will be fully renewed*. One thing is for sure: the anticipation of the time when God would restore his faithful into image-bearers was closely linked with the arrival of the promised Davidic Messiah. It is little wonder that we find evidence of renewal and restoration already present in the ministry of the Messiah, Jesus. (We will have the opportunity to explore this point in forthcoming chapters, namely Chapters 36 and 47.)

---

[32] Craigie et al., *Jeremiah 1–25*, 331; Tuell, *Ezekiel*, 256.
[33] Holladay, *Jeremiah I*, 617–18; Zimmerli, *Ezekiel 2*, 276.

The Restoration of the Image-Bearing Role in Christ

The New Testament authors gave the Early Church insight into how the image of God, tarnished by sin and disobedience, is in the process of being restored, particularly as it relates to the promised Davidic ruler, Jesus Christ. The Apostle Paul offers some clues about what the redeemed members of his churches should think about the meaning of the image of God. In 1 Corinthians 11, Paul draws on the theology of humanity as image-bearers from descriptions prior to the sinful acts of Adam and Eve: "For a man ought not to cover his head, since he is the image and glory of God, but woman is the glory of man" (1 Cor 11:7).[34] In arguing that Christian men are the image and glory of God, Paul reflects on the creation of Adam, who was made directly by God himself (Gen 1:27; 2:7) and was crowned with God's glory (Ps 8:5).[35] By drawing upon the creation account in Genesis chapter two, Paul understands Christian women as possessing the glory of man, largely due to Eve being taken from Adam's rib.[36] This is not to suggest that Paul thought that only Christian men were made in the image of God, for Paul later indicates that everyone, men and women alike, has borne the image of the earthy man Adam: "Just as we have borne the image of the man of dust, we shall also bear the image of the man of heaven" (1 Cor 15:49).[37] We will return to this important contrast between the image inherited from Adam and the counter-image of those who are in Christ. For now, we can conclude that Paul was influenced by the theology of humanity as God's male and female image-bearers, believing that only through Christ can the new, redeemed image be realized.

Within the Epistle of James, we find another reference to human beings made in the image of God. In a discussion of the tongue and how the Christian community should use it, James makes the following moral argument: "With it we bless the Lord and Father, and with it we curse men, who have been made in the likeness of God; from the same mouth come both blessing and cursing. My brethren, these things ought not to be this way" (James 3:9–10). Drawing upon the value and worth that humanity possesses (Gen 1:26–28), James criticizes those who bless the Father but curse his image-bearers.[38] Human beings reflect the Father, so it is morally inappropriate to curse someone made in the Father's image. Presumably, these early Christians are not cursing other Christians. Unbelievers are, in all likelihood, the target of this unloving speech, but James is convinced that even unbelievers are made in God's image, even if it is tarnished. To subdue and rule God's creation, believers must begin by controlling and managing their speech.

---

[34] Fitzmyer, *First Corinthians*, 414–15.
[35] Thiselton, *The First Epistle to the Corinthians*, 834–35.
[36] Bruce, *Paul*, 123; Ciampa and Rosner, *The First Letter to the Corinthians*, 524.
[37] Thiselton, *First Corinthians*, 1290; Nash, *1 Corinthians*, 422–23.
[38] Johnson, *The Letter of James*, 262; McKnight and Church, *Hebrews–James*, 373.

Jesus Christ as the Second Adam

The Early Church became quickly convinced that Jesus Christ was the second Adam, bringing fulfillment to all that Adam was created to do. Where Adam failed, Christ succeeded. This christological portrayal led believers to see in the redemptive work of Christ a restoration of the image of God so that those who are "in Christ" would experience a process of renewal. Paul seems to be the first early Christian author to systematize the doctrine of the restoration of the image of God for those who are in Christ. When Paul describes the process of transformation into the same "image" that is beheld in a mirror, he appears to be referring to the image of God that is experiencing the process of renewal (2 Cor 3:18).[39] This renewal is described by Paul as being conformed to the image of God's son (Rom 8:29),[40] which indicates a transformation from possessing a tarnished image of God that Adam inherited to an image of the full potential for humanity that is located in Christ (1 Cor 15:49).[41] The summons for Christians to live in light of their conversion experience, when they put off the old Adamic self and put on the new self that is defined by the man Jesus, continues to appear in the Pauline letters:

> Do not lie to one another, since you laid aside the old self (literally: "humanity") with its evil practices, and have put on the new self who is being renewed to a true knowledge according to the image of the One who created him (Col 3:9–10)

> in reference to your former manner of life, you lay aside the old self (literally: "humanity"), which is being corrupted in accordance with the lusts of deceit, and that you be renewed in the spirit of your mind, and put on the new self (literally: "humanity"), which in the likeness of God has been created in righteousness and holiness of the truth. (Eph 4:22–24)

These passages reiterate that the new humanity replaces the old humanity that was defined by Adam's sinfulness.[42] Within this new humanity is the image of God that is in the process of being renewed. The language of this renewal suggests that it is a progression that has not yet reached its point of completion. We can also note that the regeneration of Christian image-bearers affects their behavior, as they represent God to his creation. The Early Church, seeing itself as the people of God who have been redeemed in Christ, believed and behaved in light of the reality that they were in the process of being made into persons who will one day be set in charge of God's world, just as Adam was. We will elaborate on these points in greater detail in Part 4 (Christology), Part 7 (Ecclesiology), and Part 8 (Eschatology).

---

[39] Sampley, "The Second Letter to the Corinthians," 71.
[40] Dunn, *Romans 1–8*, 483.
[41] Dunn, *Theology of Paul*, 468.
[42] Ladd, *A Theology of the New Testament*, 493.

Conclusion

To sum up, we have thoroughly explored how human beings, God's crowning creation, were made to serve as his image-bearers, reflecting his creative, life-giving acts and his just rule over all creation. We first traced this theme through the opening chapters of Genesis and observed how humanity functioned as those made in God's image while they were in Eden and after they were exiled from that place of Paradise. Second, we took note of the prophetic promises within the Old Testament that gave hope to a renewal of God's image-bearers, particularly in the person of the coming Davidic king. Third, we examined how the theme of the image of God reappeared in the writings of the Early Church, revitalizing the hope of the tarnished vocation that finds forgiveness and redemption in the Creator's purposes. Finally, we noted how Paul's theology illustrated Christians as in an ongoing process of renewal in their image-bearing status, particularly in light of Jesus serving as the second Adam of God. Lastly, we drew attention to the various ways in which the authors of the New Testament associated Christ himself as the second Adam, the human being in whom believers begin to experience the restoration of their image-bearing vocation.

Having situated our introduction to anthropology, the study of humanity, in its image-bearing vocational context, we are now in a better position to examine one of the defining characteristics of human beings, their mortality. When Yahweh punished Adam and Eve for their disobedience, resulting in their exile from the Garden of Eden, the mortality of humanity became increasingly their defining feature of their existence. Human beings were mortal, and it is on this subject that we will now turn our attention.

9
THE MORTALITY OF HUMANITY

Benjamin Franklin, in his famous 1789 letter to Jean-Baptiste Le Roy, memorably wrote that "in this world nothing can be said to be certain, except death and taxes." This chapter will focus on the former certainty, the fact that all living creatures inevitably die. This trait is called "mortality," and it refers to the quality of being susceptible to death. The biblical authors long for the day in which those who have died will be resurrected from the dead unto new life. The reason why the promise of resurrection is such a persuasive truth in Christian evangelism is that people recognize the power of death that eventually overtakes every human person.

This chapter will discuss the mortality of humanity as it pertains to the overall subject of biblical anthropology. We will begin by looking at the composition of human beings, namely, dust from the ground that is animated by God's breath of life, resulting in a living soul. Second, we will explore a common designation that the biblical authors use to stress humanity in its mortal state of weakness: flesh. Lastly, we will look at how every human person is described as a soul, a soul that, unlike popular views of natural immortality, is mortal and not immortal. Once we set forth how the biblical authors and the Early Church understood the innate mortality of every human person, we will be in a better position to consider the destination of the dead, their condition, and whether or not the dead are conscious.

Humanity is *Dust* and the *Breath of Life*

Our first task is to sketch out the physical composition of God's image-bearers, at least in terms that the biblical authors convey to the readers of Scripture. When God creates humanity in his own image, as the creation account in Genesis chapter one states, there are no specific details on how exactly human beings were formed.[1] The account of creation depicted in Genesis chapter two, however, does offer the best summary of what the biblical authors think of the composition of humans, particularly in Genesis 2:7: "Then Yahweh God formed man of dust from the ground, and breathed into his nostrils the breath of life; and man became a living soul." The formation of Adam, as presented in this passage, offers a helpful foundation from which we can understand how the

---
[1] Sarna, *Genesis*, 17.

biblical authors perceived human composition.² The first thing this passage indicates is that humanity is formed from the dust of the ground. At the most basic level, human beings are dust, and our English translations are unable to convey the wordplay in Hebrew, where "man" (Hebrew: *adam*) is formed from the dust of the "ground" (Hebrew: *adamah*).³ The impression we are left with is that the biblical authors wanted the readers to mentally picture the ground's dust when they think of human beings, as the words are closely related and deliberately laid out to be seen. Put simply, humanity is formed from the very earth over which it is to have dominion.⁴

Dust, in and of itself, does not amount to much at all, so God animates the dust with the breath of life, which is the second key point in Genesis 2:7. In particular, God the Creator breathes his breath into the nostrils of Adam. This brings to mind the regular act of breathing in and out of the nose. That breath comes from God, and it gives life to the mundane dust. It is only upon receiving the breath *of life* that the human becomes a *living* being. Herein lies the conviction that mortals can only live because of their dependence upon the gift of God's life-giving breath.⁵

This brings us to our third point, which is the result of the dust that is animated by God's breath of life. Upon receiving the life-giving breath from God, Adam became a living soul. Some English translations render the noun for soul as a "being," but it is important for our study that we recognize this Hebrew word for soul, *nephesh*. When Adam became a living soul, he then existed precisely as a living soul. To say that he possessed a soul as if the soul were something separate from Adam himself would be to go beyond the text.⁶ Adam (and by extension, all subsequent human beings) just is a soul, the totality of the entire person.⁷ As such, the person (i.e., soul) is alive while being animated by the breath of life, while a person who is no longer breathing would be a dead person—a dead soul.⁸

The idea that human beings are likened to mere dust is a recurring theme presented in the biblical texts. The fate of Adam, along with every single human being who comes after him, is to eventually die and return to the dust from which he or she came:

> "By the sweat of your face you will eat bread, until you return to the ground, because from it you were taken; for you are dust, and to dust you shall return" (Gen 3:19).

---

² Köhler, *Old Testament Theology*, 135.
³ Towner, *Genesis*, 35; Wenham, *Genesis 1–15*, 59; Sarna, *Genesis*, 17.
⁴ Fretheim, "The Book of Genesis," 349–50.
⁵ Wenham, *Genesis 1–15*, 60.
⁶ Di Vito, "Anthropology," 173; Köhler, *Old Testament Theology*, 142; Wolff, *Anthropology of the Old Testament*, 21.
⁷ Green, "Soul," 359; Eichrodt, *Theology of the Old Testament*, 2:137.
⁸ Wolff, *Anthropology of the Old Testament*, 20; Eichrodt, *Theology of the Old Testament*, 2:135.

God's declaration to human beings is clear. Humanity is dust, and to dust humanity will return. The mortality of human beings is clearly observable as Adam comes full circle, originating in dust and turning back to dust when he dies.[9] In other words, Adam returns to the *adamah*. When we look at the testimony of Abraham, the faithful patriarch of the Jewish people, we can discern an awareness that even great men understood themselves to be merely dust from the ground: "Now behold, I have ventured to speak to the Lord, although I am but dust and ashes" (Gen 18:27).[10] Compared to the immortal and all-powerful Creator God, Abraham the mortal rightly recognized that he is simply dust and ashes. The psalmist repeats this point in Psalm 103:13–14, where Yahweh, the Father, is portrayed as knowing the frame of his children, being mindful that they are merely dust.[11] The biblical authors make no distinction between the composition of the righteous and the unrighteous, for "all come from dust" (Ecc 3:20).[12]

As we observed in Gen 2:7, humans are formed from the dust of the ground by God breathing into them the breath of life. As long as human beings possess this breath, they continue living. Breath is said to reside in the nostrils of humanity (Isa 2:22).[13] As long as the breath of life flows in and out of the nostrils, life remains (Job 27:3).[14] Since God has given his breath to his people, it is only right that they use it to sing *Hallelu-Yah* (Ps 150:6). Paul's preaching in Athens, according to the Book of Acts, included a sermon wherein he described the Creator God as the one who gives to all people life and breath and all things (Acts 17:25).

Sometimes, the *breath* of God is closely paralleled with God's *spirit*, indicating that the two nouns are set in apposition. Consider the evidence in these passages:

> But it is a spirit in man, and the breath of the Almighty gives them understanding (Job 32:8).

> The Spirit of God has made me, and the breath of the Almighty gives me life (Job 33:4).

> Thus says the God Yahweh, who created the heavens and stretched them out, who spread out the earth and its offspring, who gives breath to the people on it and spirit to those who walk in it (Isa 42:5)

The reason why God's "spirit" overlaps in meaning with his breath is that the Hebrew noun *ruach* is very flexible, meaning (depending on the context) spirit, breath, or wind.[15] As such, the biblical authors frequently portrayed human beings as animated by God's

---

[9] Vanzant, "Dust," 168.
[10] Westermann, *Genesis 12–36*, 292.
[11] Hossfeld and Zenger, *Psalms 3*, 35–6; deClaissé-Walford et al., *Psalms*, 766;
[12] Crenshaw, *Ecclesiastes*, 104; Krüger, *Qoheleth*, 93; Murphy, *Ecclesiastes*, 37.
[13] Tull, *Isaiah 1–39*, 91–92.
[14] Newsom, "The Book of Job," 523.
[15] Köhler et al., *Hebrew and Aramaic Lexicon*, 1197–201.

spirit in some texts, and in other passages, humanity is animated by God's *breath*. These are synonymous images, strongly suggesting to readers that they should not be treated as distinct forces from God that give life.[16]

Since human beings only become living souls upon receiving the breath from God, it is only natural that they die if God takes away that breath. During the flood, every living thing, including human beings, in whose nostrils was the breath of life, died (Gen 7:22).[17] Those who are destroyed with the edge of the sword are obviously depicted as no longer breathing (Josh 10:40; 11:11, 14). Just as God told Adam that he would return to dust when he died (Gen 3:19), the psalmist declares, "When his breath departs, he returns to the earth; on that very day his plans perish" (Ps 146:4).[18] Note carefully that the person is not what departs; what departs is the breath of God.[19] The person returns to the earth, reduced to nothing more than dust. The same imagery reappears in Ecclesiastes 12:7, which states: "The dust returns to the earth as it was, and the spirit will return to God who gave it." Since human beings are dust, to dust they will return, while the spirit-breath of God that animates humanity will return to God.[20] These texts clearly distinguish what we as readers should never confuse.

The Early Church similarly portrayed how a person without God's life-giving breath would obviously die.[21] On the cross, Jesus announced, "Father, into your hands I commit my spirit." The narrator then comments that Jesus breathed his last (Luke 23:46).[22] The deaths of Ananias (Acts 5:5) and his wife Sapphira (Acts 5:10) are both illustrated in terms of taking their last breath, indicating that the breath of life had expired.[23] James, while attempting to convince his readers that faith without works is dead, offers a familiar parallel: "The body without the spirit is dead" (James 2:26).[24] Within the Book of Revelation, the image of the Two Witnesses who are martyred for their faithful preaching of the gospel of the kingdom depicts their vindication from death in terms of "the breath of life from God" entering into their dead corpse (Rev 11:8–11).[25] Overall, the language employed by the Early Church described the breath or spirit of God animating living human beings owes its dependence to the anthropological portrayal set forth in the Old Testament. In other words, the authors of the New Testament taught in continuity with the portrayal of mortal humanity expressed by the Old Testament writers.

---

[16] Wolff, *Anthropology of the Old Testament*, 33.
[17] Wenham, *Genesis 1–15*, 183.
[18] Hossfeld and Zenger, *Psalms 3*, 613.
[19] deClaissé-Walford et al., *Psalms*, 997.
[20] Weeks, *Ecclesiastes*, 2:617–18; Seow, *Ecclesiastes*, 382; Fox, *Ecclesiastes*, 82.
[21] Hatch, *Daring to Differ*, 19.
[22] Ryken et al., "Mortality," 569.
[23] Fitzmyer, *Acts*, 323, 325.
[24] Johnson, *James*, 245.
[25] Thompson, *Revelation*, 127.

The Weakness of Humanity's *Flesh*

One of the most common ways in which the biblical authors illustrate human beings in their mortality, weakness, and susceptibility to decay is that they are *flesh*.[26] Again, if we take Adam as the starting point for understanding biblical anthropology, we find several helpful leads. The formation of the woman by taking one of Adam's ribs involved Yahweh, upon completion, closing up Adam's flesh (Gen 2:21). As such, the woman is said to be "bone of my bones and flesh of my flesh" (Gen 2:23). "All flesh" possesses the breath of life from God (Gen 6:17), making them living creatures, i.e., souls (Gen 9:15). By portraying humanity as "flesh," the writers of Scripture emphasize the weakness of human beings and their utter dependence on God for life.[27] The psalmist describes the absence of soundness in his flesh with the lack of health in his bones (Ps 38:3). In fact, several biblical authors devote their poetic words to illustrating the mortality of the flesh of humanity:

> Thus He remembered that they were but flesh, a wind that passes and does not return. (Ps 78:39)

> My knees are weak from fasting, and my flesh has grown lean, without fatness. (Ps 109:24)

> All flesh is grass, and all its loveliness is like the flower of the field. The grass withers, the flower fades, When the breath of Yahweh blows upon it; surely the people are grass. The grass withers, the flower fades, but the word of our God stands forever. (Isa 40:6–8)

> Thus says Yahweh, "Cursed is the man who trusts in mankind and makes flesh his strength, and whose heart turns away from Yahweh" (Jer 17:5)

> He has caused my flesh and my skin to waste away, He has broken my bones. (Lam 3:4)

In the above sampling of passages, the reader gains the clear impression that fleshly humanity is mortal, susceptible to weakness, and should not trust in its strength. The flesh is not portrayed as a part of the person, as if only part of a human being is weak and mortal. Instead, it is the entire person who suffers weakness, and the person as a whole will wither and fade away.[28]

In several instances, "flesh" is just another way of speaking about the person in their totality.[29] To this end, the biblical authors refer to all humanity in terms of "all flesh." When the psalmist praises Yahweh for giving food to all flesh, he is indicating that God has provided for all persons (Ps 136:25). The nation of Israel is differentiated from its oppressors, but together they are collectively described as "all flesh" who will recognize

---

[26] Kraus, *Theology of the Psalms*, 144.
[27] Biddle, "Flesh in the OT," 463.
[28] Wolff, *Anthropology of the Old Testament*, 30–31; Kraus, *Theology of the Psalms*, 144.
[29] Biddle, "Flesh in the OT," 463.

that Yahweh is the one who saves and redeems Israel (Isa 49:26). When Jeremiah recounts the word of Yahweh that states, "Behold, I am Yahweh, the God of all flesh," the clear implication is that Yahweh is the God of all humanity (Jer 32:27). Job sets the phrase "all flesh" and "humanity" in parallel lines, indicating that the two are coreferential terms: "All flesh would perish together, and man would return to the dust" (Job 34:15).[30]

It should be clear at this point that the authors of the biblical texts used the term "flesh" to illustrate vulnerable, weak, and mortal human persons. The Early Church similarly depicted humanity as flesh in its attempt to underscore the weakness and perishable nature of the human self. Notably, 1 Peter 1:23–25 discusses the salvific gospel message in terms of an imperishable seed that was preached to and believed by the early Christians. In making this argument, the author quotes Isaiah 40:6–8 in a manner that deliberately contrasts the mortality of *perishable* flesh, namely, all persons, with the seed message of the gospel that will lead to *imperishable* life.[31] When the Early Church wanted to portray Jesus before his resurrection to immortality, he was depicted "according to the flesh" (Rom 1:3; 2 Cor 5:16; Eph 2:14; Heb 5:7), referring to the genuine human condition, mortal and dependent upon God.[32] Jesus informs Peter upon his confession of Jesus as the Christ that "flesh and blood" did not reveal this truth to Peter, but rather the Father in heaven (Matt 16:17). Similarly, Paul describes "flesh and blood" as that which is perishable and, therefore, unable to inherit the kingdom of God apart from being clothed with immortality at the resurrection (1 Cor 15:50–53).[33] When the perishable flesh is granted an immortal body, then death is, understandably, swallowed up for good, just as Paul promised in 1 Corinthians 15:54–55.[34]

The New Testament authors continued to depict the mortal human person with the descriptor "flesh." For example, John the Baptist is remembered citing Isaiah, saying that "all flesh will see the salvation of God," using in the process "flesh" to illustrate all people (Luke 3:6).[35] When Jesus was praying to God, he acknowledged that God had given to Jesus' authority over all flesh, meaning all persons (John 17:2).[36] On the Day of Pentecost, Peter preached a sermon indicating that on the last days the Holy Spirit would be poured out on all flesh, namely all persons who receive salvation (Acts 2:17–21). Throughout the Book of Acts, it becomes abundantly clear that the "flesh" upon whom the Holy Spirit is poured out refers to human beings who respond appropriately to the preaching of the gospel of the kingdom and the name of Jesus Christ.[37] When Jesus speaks of God intervening to deliver the persecuted, he refers to human lives as flesh, "Unless

---

[30] Clines, *Job 21–37*, 774–75.
[31] Michaels, *1 Peter*, 77–78.
[32] Dunn, *Romans 1–8*, 13; Pfitzner, *Hebrews*, 92.
[33] Murphy-O'Connor, *1 Corinthians*, 174–75.
[34] Sampley, "The First Letter to the Corinthians," 989.
[35] Tannehill, *Luke*, 80.
[36] Lindars, *The Gospel of John*, 518.
[37] Peterson, *The Acts of the Apostles*, 140–41.

the Lord had shortened those days, no life would have been saved" (Mark 13:20). The English word translated "life" in this passage is the Greek word for "flesh" (*sarx*). In sum, the authors of both testaments refer to human persons as flesh—those who are weak, mortal, and in need of God's salvation.

A Human Person is a *Living Soul*

We observed that Genesis 2:7 describes the first human being as a "living soul." This portrayal, as Genesis 2:7 lays out for its readers, is the standard way in which humanity is illustrated, namely, that living beings *are souls*.[38] When the breath of life is no longer present, the human person dies, and the biblical authors repeatedly portray this death in terms of the soul dying. Any person (Hebrew: *nephesh*) who fails to humble himself is to be cut off from his people, according to Leviticus 23:29. Twice, we are reliably informed by the prophet Ezekiel that "the soul who sins will die" (Ezek 18:4, 20).[39] Since the noun *nephesh* is the typical way to refer to the living individual himself, we encounter several references by the biblical authors to a soul that lives (translated as "a life"), while several other passages state that the soul has died.[40] Consider the following examples where the underlying Hebrew for the deceased "person" is *nephesh* ("soul"):

> nor shall he approach any dead person (*nephesh*), nor defile himself even for his father or his mother (Lev 21:11)

> All the days of his separation to Yahweh he shall not go near to a dead person (*nephesh*). (Num 6:6)

> Anyone who touches a corpse (*nephesh*), the body of a man who has died, and does not purify himself, defiles the tabernacle of Yahweh (Num 19:13)

Since the soul is merely another term for the entire human person, we regularly see instances where individual people are referred to with the Hebrew noun *nephesh*.[41] When Sodom's king asked Abram to give to him the people, the English word "people" comes from the Hebrew *nephesh* (Gen 14:21). If an Israelite kidnaps one of his countrymen, the kidnapped person is described as a *nephesh* (Deut 24:7). The innocent poor persons can be more literally translated as "poor souls" (Jer 2:34). Similarly, "every person" is actually "every soul" in Jeremiah 43:6. These are not isolated examples, as several other references could be provided (e.g., Pss 3:2; 6:4–5; Prov 28:17; Ezek 17:17), but they are sufficient to

---

[38] Brueggemann, *Theology of the Old Testament*, 453; Di Vito, "Old Testament Anthropology," 226.
[39] Zimmerli, *Ezekiel 1*, 378-79, 385.
[40] Fredericks, "נֶפֶשׁ," 133; Eichrodt, *Theology of the Old Testament*, 2:137.
[41] Köhler, *Old Testament Theology*, 145; Wolff, *Anthropology of the Old Testament*, 21; Seebass, "Nephesh," 512.

demonstrate that human beings were regarded as souls, rather than being depicted as possessing souls inside their bodies.

When the person dies, it logically follows that the soul dies.[42] The biblical authors never describe the soul as immortal or possessing immortality.[43] On the contrary, only Yahweh himself possesses immortality as an innate attribute, as we observed in Chapter 4. The consistent testimony of the biblical authors is that the soul is mortal, ceasing to live and function at the moment of death.[44] The data illustrating the mortality of the person is substantial, particularly when we realize that the Hebrew word for soul (*nephesh*) lies behind these references to death and dying:

> but the person (*nephesh*) who eats of the flesh of the sacrifice of Yahweh's peace offerings while an uncleanness is on him, that person (*nephesh*) shall be cut off from his people. (Lev 7:20)

> But if there is a man who hates his neighbor and lies in wait for him and rises up against him and strikes him (*nephesh*) so that he dies (Deut 19:11)

> Now Joshua captured Makkedah on that day, and struck it and its king with the edge of the sword; he utterly destroyed it and every person (*nephesh*) who was in it. (Josh 10:28)

> Zebulun was a people who risked their lives (*nephesh*) to the death (Judg 5:18)

> And they said to the king, "Here is the head of Ish-bosheth, the son of Saul, your enemy, who sought your life (*nephesh*)." (2 Sam 4:8)

> Therefore I will divide him a portion with the many, and he shall divide the spoil with the strong, because he poured out his soul (*nephesh*) to death and was numbered with the transgressors; yet he bore the sin of many, and makes intercession for the transgressors. (Isa 53:12)

> "Therefore now, O Yahweh, please take my life (*nephesh*) from me, for death is better to me than life." (Jonah 4:3)

The authors of the New Testament continue this holistic approach, viewing the human person as a mortal soul.[45] Jesus Christ taught his followers on several occasions that they needed to be willing to give up their entire *lives* in order to be genuine disciples. The underlying Greek behind the word "life" is the word for "soul" (Greek: *psyche*).[46] "Whoever finds his life will lose it, and whoever loses his life for my sake will find it,"

---

[42] Wolff, *Anthropology of the Old Testament*, 22; Routledge, *Old Testament Theology*, 305.
[43] Di Vito, "Old Testament Anthropology," 218; Köhler, *Old Testament Theology*, 144–145; Hatch, *Daring to Differ*, 41; Brown, "Resurrection," 304.
[44] Wright, *The Resurrection of the Son of God*, 91.
[45] Green, "Soul," 359.
[46] Bauer et al., *Greek-English Lexicon*, 1098–100. Seebass, "Nephesh," 503, helpfully observes, "for the LXX translators *psyche* has more of an OT than a specifically Gk. meaning."

Jesus characteristically declared (Matt 10:39; 16:25; Mark 8:36; Luke 9:24; 17:33; John 12:25). In a moment of controversy on the Sabbath, Jesus asked his opponents if it was lawful to save or to destroy a soul on the day of rest, implying that the soul can be killed (Mark 3:4; Luke 6:9). Jesus even described his own death as a giving of his life (i.e., soul) as a ransom for many (Matt 20:28), and as the Good Shepherd who lays down his life-soul for the sheep (John 10:11, 15, 17).[47] This courageous example, no doubt, served to motivate Peter when he declared that he lay down his life for Jesus (John 13:37). In fact, Jesus taught that there is no greater love than for someone to lay down his soul for his friends (John 15:13).[48] It seems rather apparent that Jesus not only believed that the soul was mortal (including his own), but he also taught the mortality of the soul to his disciples. Naturally, the Early Church continued to portray human individuals as souls (e.g., Rom 11:3; Heb 10:39; James 5:20; 1 John 3:16; Rev 12:11), vulnerable to death and in desperate need of resurrection life.[49]

Conclusion

To summarize our findings, we set out to determine to what extent, if any, the biblical authors portray human beings as mortal. We observed that Adam was formed from the dust, animated by God's breath of life, and thus became a living soul, a living person. This portrayal of humanity was the standard for illustrating the composition of humanity, particularly as it related to the dust of the ground and the dependence on the breath of life that God offers. We also saw that one of the regular designations for human beings in their vulnerable state of weakness and mortality is "flesh." From there, we noted how the entire human person is frequently described as a soul, and this soul is always mortal, never immortal. The realization that the soul (i.e., the person) is prone to death was a belief embraced by the Early Church, drawing on the characterization present in the Hebrew Scriptures as well as the teachings of Jesus Christ. We can safely conclude at this juncture that the doctrine of the immortality of the soul is entirely absent from the Early Church's teaching, as expressed by the biblical authors.

We are now in a better position to ask the important questions concerning the destination of the dying. If human beings are mortal, what happens when they die? Where do they go? Does the destination of the dead depend on whether the person was righteous or unrighteous during their life? We will take up these important questions in our next chapter.

---

[47] Ryken et al., "Mortality," 569.
[48] Thompson, *John*, 225–26.
[49] Cullmann, *Immortality of the Soul or Resurrection*, 15–18; Schweizer, "ψυχη," 639. Scott, "Immortality," 432, observes that human beings "do not by nature possess immortality. Instead they are mortal, perishable, made susceptible to corruption because of sin."

10
THE DESTINATION OF THE DYING

The question of the afterlife is meaningful to many religious people. The confidence people have in their final moments can bring them and their families peace. For Christians, the trust and confidence that the God who raised Jesus from the dead will also raise us up on the last day functions as an extension of faith. In order for us to consider the topic of the resurrection of mortal humans who have succumbed to death, we must first determine the specifics concerning the location of the dead.

This chapter will thoroughly explore how the biblical authors illustrate the location of the deceased, which directly ties into what many describe as the intermediate state (the condition of the dead between death and resurrection). First, we will examine the biblical data concerning the deceased persons returning to the dust. Sometimes, this destination is called the "ground" or even the "pit," each suggesting a grave in which the dead are buried. Second, we will look at the common designations that the biblical authors use for the grave, which are *Sheol* (in Hebrew) and *Hades* (in Greek). We will also differentiate these key terms from other phrases that are confusingly included in discussions about the location of the dead. Lastly, we will give attention to the widespread acceptance among the biblical authors that the dead, prior to the future resurrection, are all in a single location. Once we have adequately surveyed how the authors of the biblical texts illustrate the location of those who have died, we will be in a better position to examine the condition of the deceased and ask whether they are conscious or unconscious.

The Dead Return to the Dust of the Ground

To begin our exploration, it is prudent to recall what Yahweh said to Adam when announcing his punishment because it directly relates to the topic at hand. God said, "By the sweat of your face you will eat bread, until you return to the ground, because from it you were taken; for you are dust, and to dust you shall return" (Gen 3:19). Adam, the archetypal human being, is dust, and he will return to dust.[1] There is no confusion over where Adam went when he died. He himself went to the dust from which he was created.[2] Nor is there any suggestion that Adam's body merely went to the dust while his soul went

---

[1] Wolff, *Anthropology of the Old Testament*, 115; Hendel, *Genesis 1–11*, 190.
[2] Ryken et al., "Mortality," 568.

into the presence of God. The biblical authors offer no such dualistic portrayal of humanity. At the end of Adam's life, he descended to the dust of the ground.

We may be tempted to think that Adam was alone in being characterized as being returned to dust, but the biblical data suggest otherwise. Several texts indicate that those who die are, like Adam, described as dust.[3] Consider the following passages:

> "Your hands fashioned and made me altogether, and would You destroy me? Remember now, that You have made me as clay; and would You turn me into dust again?" (Job 10:8–9)

> "He has cast me into the mire, and I have become like dust and ashes." (Job 30:19)

> "Look on everyone who is proud, and humble him, and tread down the wicked where they stand. Hide them in the dust together; bind them in the hidden place. (Job 40:12–13)

> "Who has aroused one from the east whom He calls in righteousness to his feet? He delivers up nations before him and subdues kings. He makes them like dust with his sword, as the wind-driven chaff with his bow." (Isa 41:2)

As we can observe, these biblical authors illustrate those who have died as being turned into dust with a remarkable similarity to the fate of Adam.[4] We should not overlook the specificity that these texts give to the person who dies: God turns "*me* into dust," "*I* have become like dust," "hide *them* in the dust," and "He makes *them* like dust." The pronouns clearly indicate that the individual dies and becomes the dust of the ground.

The biblical authors consistently portray the destination of the dying as lying down in the dust of the earth. Both Joshua and David openly speak about and accept their fate at the conclusion of their lives: "Now behold, today I am going the way of all the earth" (Josh 23:14); "I am going the way of all the earth" (1 Kgs 2:2).[5] Job openly acknowledges this position: "I will lie down in the dust; and you will seek me, but I will not be" (Job 7:21).[6] When the topic arises again, Job poetically sets his descent into the dust in parallel with a place called *Sheol*—a term that we will discuss shortly: "Will it go down with me to Sheol? Shall we together go down into the dust?" (Job 17:16).[7] It doesn't matter if someone dies full of strength or in bitterness, both lie down together in the dust, in the place where worms cover them (Job 21:26).[8] Elihu, one of Job's younger friends, carefully describes what happens when the flesh perishes, "man would return to the dust"

---

[3] Boadt, *Reading the Old Testament*, 250; Wright, *The Resurrection of the Son of God*, 122.
[4] Balentine, *Job*, 174, 457.
[5] Routledge, *Old Testament Theology*, 303; Wolff, *Anthropology of the Old Testament*, 99; Johnston, "Death and Afterlife," 215.
[6] Clines, *Job 1–20*, 195.
[7] Seow, *Job 1–21*, 758
[8] Balentine, *Job*, 332.

(Job 34:15).[9] The author of the Book of Job, therefore, leaves no doubt in the mind of the readers. The destination of the dead is a descent into the dust of the ground—into the earth.[10]

The Book of Psalms presents a similar portrayal of the destination of the dying to what we observed in the Book of Job. In Psalm 7, the author asks if he has committed any injustice, and if so, he declares, "Let the enemy pursue my soul and overtake it; and let him trample my life down to the ground and lay my glory in the dust" (Ps 7:5). We note here the repeated themes of the *soul* being defined in the parallelism as the *life* of the psalmist, while additionally locating the overtaken and trampled soul in the dust. Psalm 22 offers much of the same: "You lay me in the dust of death" (Ps 22:15).[11] We also have indications that the "pit" is a comparable term to the dust in Psalm 30:9, helping the reader further clarify the destination of those who die: "What profit is there in my blood, if I go down to the pit? Will the dust praise You? Will it declare Your faithfulness?" These rhetorical questions imply a negative answer. Those who descend to the dust will not praise God, nor will they speak of God's faithfulness, for they are dead. In another passage that pinpoints the dust of the earth as the location of the deceased, we can observe that the body and the soul are understood as different ways of speaking about the holistic individual, rather than two distinct parts: "For our soul has sunk down into the dust; our body cleaves to the earth" (Ps 44:25).[12] Just as God turned Adam back into dust, the psalmist states, "You turn man back into dust and say, 'Return, O children of men'" (Ps 90:3). Adam's fate is no different from our own, it would seem.[13] When God takes away the breath from humans, the psalmist offers a familiar conclusion: "They die and they return to their dust" (Ps 104:29). A comparable expression is located in Psalm 146:4, which illustrates that when the breath departs from mortal man, "he returns to the earth; on that very day his plans perish." The portrayal of humanity's mortality in the Psalms is consistent with the depiction of Adam set forth in the opening chapters of the Book of Genesis.[14]

In the survey thus far, there does not appear to be any indication that the fate of the righteous is any different from the fate of the unrighteous when determining where one goes at the moment of death. The writer of Ecclesiastes sums up the shared fate of all persons in language reminiscent of Adam's fate in Genesis 3:19: "All go to one place. All are from the dust, and to dust all return" (Ecc 3:20). In what is arguably the best summary verse for detailing the destination of the dying, whether the person is good or

---

[9] Clines, *Job 21–37*, 531.
[10] Köhler, *Old Testament Theology*, 154.
[11] McCann, "The Book of Psalms," 763.
[12] Di Vito, "Old Testament Anthropology," 226.
[13] Ryken et al., "Mortality," 568.
[14] McCann, "The Book of Psalms," 1099.

evil, Ecclesiastes 3:20 locates every single dead person as having returned to the dust.[15] This passage flies directly in the face of modern religious assumptions about where the dead go when they die. Some assume that the Bible places the righteous in heaven and the wicked in a fiery hell. The writer of Ecclesiastes plainly and clearly sums up the theology expressed in Genesis, Job, Psalms, and Isaiah by declaring that every single person, no matter the life they lived, goes to the same place: the dust.[16] This common description of the intermediate state is repeated in Ecclesiastes 12:7, which says, "The dust will return to the earth as it was, and the spirit returns to God who gave it." The writer carefully distinguishes the breath of life that returns to God from the person consisting of dust that returns to the earth.[17]

Sheol and *Hades*

We have already seen glimpses of the realm of the dead that the authors of the Old Testament call *Sheol*, as seen in Job 17:16. This Hebrew designation functions as a synonym for the grave—the abode to which all who have died descend.[18] Those who go down to Sheol, that is, into the earth, are said to have perished (Num 16:33). When Yahweh kills, he brings the deceased down to Sheol (1 Sam 2:6; Job 7:9; 14:13–14; Ezek 31:17). The author of Proverbs chapter nine makes clear to the readers that "the dead are there . . . in the depths of Sheol" (Prov 9:18).[19] Sometimes, the biblical poets go so far as personifying Sheol as possessing a mouth that swallows up those who have perished (Num 16:32–34; Ps 141:7; Prov 1:12; 30:15–16; Isa 5:14).[20] While someone may choose to work mightily in life, there is no activity whatsoever in Sheol, according to Ecclesiastes 9:10.[21] We will return later to the subject of the state of the dead in Chapter 11, but we can take note that the dead in Sheol are portrayed as being completely inactive.

Since the biblical authors show no reservation about placing dead souls in the dust of the earth, it is no surprise that we find depictions of souls descending to Sheol. Furthermore, the recognition that souls go to Sheol upon dying moves the various writers of the Psalms and Proverbs to petition Yahweh to rescue them from near death.[22] Consider the following evidence of souls being illustrated as going to Sheol:

---

[15] Wolff, *Anthropology of the Old Testament*, 115–16; Horne, *Proverbs–Ecclesiastes*, 435–36; Murphy, *Ecclesiastes*, 37.
[16] Seow, *Ecclesiastes*, 176.
[17] Weeks, *Ecclesiastes*, 1:546–48; Murphy, *Ecclesiastes*, 120; Fox, *Ecclesiastes*, 82.
[18] Johnston, "Sheol," 227; Wolff, *Anthropology of the Old Testament*, 103; Routledge, *Old Testament Theology*, 304.
[19] Perdue, *Proverbs*, 154.
[20] Levine, *Numbers 1–20*, 417, 428; Boadt, *Reading the Old Testament*, 250.
[21] Weeks, *Ecclesiastes*, 2:440.
[22] Goldingay, *Psalms*, 2:626.

> "For You will not abandon my soul to Sheol; nor will You allow Your holy one to undergo decay." (Ps 16:10)
>
> "O Yahweh, You have brought up my soul from Sheol; You have kept me alive, that I would not go down to the pit." (Ps 30:3)
>
> "But God will redeem my soul from the power of Sheol, for He will receive me." (Ps 49:15)
>
> "For Your covenant love toward me is great, and You have delivered my soul from the depths of Sheol." (Ps 86:13)
>
> "For my soul has had enough troubles, and my life has drawn near to Sheol. (Ps 88:3)
>
> "You shall strike him with the rod and rescue his soul from Sheol." (Prov 23:14)

Since the soul (*nephesh*) is another way of describing a person's life, it logically follows that a person whose life has ended would descend to Sheol.[23] As such, there are poetic passages that parallel Sheol and Abaddon, a rarely used term referring to the place of destruction (Job 26:6; Prov 15:11; 27:20).[24] Since all persons in Sheol have died, illustrating Abaddon as a place of destruction made appropriate sense to these biblical poets, particularly in light of its parallel with the grave in Psalm 88:11.

Observing that human beings are mortal and that when they die, they return to the dust of the ground, often referred to as Sheol, it is only natural that Sheol itself is to be portrayed as the de facto place of all who have succumbed to death.[25] As it so happens, this particular identification is repeatedly emphasized by the authors of the biblical texts. Note how Sheol—the realm of the dead—is set in parallel with the noun "death" in these texts:

> "The cords of Sheol surrounded me; the snares of death confronted me." (2 Sam 22:6; Ps 18:5)
>
> For in death there is no remembrance of you; in Sheol who will give you praise? (Ps 6:5)
>
> As sheep they are appointed for Sheol; Death shall be their shepherd (Ps 49:14)
>
> What man can live and not see death? Can he deliver his soul from the power of Sheol? (Ps 89:48)
>
> Her feet go down to death, Her steps take hold of Sheol. (Prov 5:5)

---

[23] Routledge, *Old Testament Theology*, 304.
[24] Grether, "Abaddon," 6; Newsom, "The Book of Job," 518.
[25] Köhler, *Old Testament Theology*, 154; Ryken et al., "Mortality," 568.

"For Sheol cannot thank You, Death cannot praise You; those who go down to the pit cannot hope for Your faithfulness." (Isa 38:18)

Shall I ransom them from the power of Sheol? Shall I redeem them from death? O Death, where are your thorns? O Sheol, where is your sting? Compassion will be hidden from My sight. (Hos 13:14)

"Furthermore, wine betrays the haughty man, so that he does not stay at home. He enlarges his appetite like Sheol, and he is like death, never satisfied. He also gathers to himself all nations and collects to himself all peoples. (Hab 2:5)

Several other references offer the same comparison between Sheol and death (e.g., Ps 116:3; Prov 7:27; Isa 28:15, 18), but the above sampling should be sufficient to demonstrate the point. The writers of the Old Testament agree that the dead descend to Sheol, the realm of all who have experienced death.

Another important term to consider when studying the location of the dying is the Greek noun *hades*. When the Jews who translated the Old Testament Scriptures into the Greek version known today as the Septuagint sought to translate the Hebrew term Sheol, they almost exclusively rendered it into its Greek equivalent, Hades. In other words, for the translators of the Old Testament Scriptures into Greek, Hades was understood as an equally acceptable term to describe the realm of the dead to which all descend upon death.[26] The New Testament authors elected to use the term Hades, rather than its Hebrew counterpart (Sheol), to portray the location of the dead, particularly because they were writing in Greek.[27] In Peter's Pentecost sermon in Acts chapter two, he twice cites Psalm 16:10 in the Greek version to demonstrate that Jesus Christ descended to Hades during the few days of his death. Compare the original passage and the way that Hades functions as the equivalent of Sheol:

"For You will not abandon my soul to Sheol; nor will You allow Your holy one to undergo decay." (Ps 16:10)

"For You will not abandon my soul to Hades; nor will You allow Your holy one to undergo decay." (Acts 2:27)

"he foresaw and spoke about the resurrection of the Christ, that he was not abandoned to Hades, nor did his flesh suffer decay." (Acts 2:31)

---

[26] Jeremias, "ᾅδης," 146–47.
[27] Bauckham, "Hades, Hell," 14, helpfully observes that *hades* is "sometimes, but misleadingly, translated 'hell' in English versions of the NT." Furthermore, Bauckham writes that those who are dead in *hades* are "hardly conscious."

According to Peter's use of Psalm 16:10, the deceased soul of Jesus, God's holy one, went to Hades.[28] God, of course, raised Jesus from the dead before the body began to decay in the grave.

We have further evidence that Hades functions as the location of those who have died, as described in the highly symbolic Book of Revelation. Four passages, in particular, deserve our attention. First, in Revelation 1:18, Jesus openly admits that he was dead, but now he is alive forevermore. Having conquered the grave, Jesus acknowledges that he is in possession of "the keys of death and Hades" (Rev 1:18).[29] Just as we observed a close connection between death and Sheol, we can now take note of the related terms "death" and "Hades," which are under the authority of the risen and highly exalted Jesus.[30] The two terms appear again in Revelation 6:8 as personified riders upon horses to whom authority is given to end lives: "I looked, and behold, an ashen horse; and he who sat on it had the name Death; and Hades was following with him. Authority was given to them over a fourth of the earth, to kill with sword and with famine and with pestilence and by the wild beasts of the earth" (Rev 6:8). Personified Death and Hades appear to be unstoppable forces of evil, bent on bringing many to their mortal demise, but the readers have had the truth unveiled to them that Jesus is now in possession of the keys that can unlock and release the dead by resurrection.[31] This is precisely what takes place in the final two references to the "Death and Hades" pair. In Revelation 20:13, which illustrates the fateful Day of Judgment, the dead are raised and immediately brought into their sentence: "And the sea gave up the dead which were in it, and death and Hades gave up the dead which were in them; and they were judged, every one of them according to their deeds." The vision squarely locates the dead persons before being raised to judgment under the control of personified Death and Hades.[32] At the conclusion of this judgment, these two chaotic forces are thrown into the *lake of fire*, which is conveniently explained as the second death (Rev 20:14).[33] It is clear from this passage that Death and Hades are distinguished from the lake of fire, and the former duo should therefore not be confused with the latter (about which we will talk more in Chapter 13).[34] In short, the authors of the New Testament remain consistent with the writers of the Old Testament in portraying Hades, the Greek translation of Sheol, as the place where all human beings go when they die.[35]

The hope of those who have died is to be raised from the dead by bodily resurrection. This is the consistent promise offered by the writers of the New Testament

---

[28] Barrett, *Acts 1–14*, 145–46, 148; Keener, *Acts*, 1:948–49.
[29] Cullmann, *Immortality of the Soul or Resurrection*, 25.
[30] Reddish, *Revelation*, 42.
[31] Beale, *The Book of Revelation*, 382–83; Ryken et al., "Mortality," 570.
[32] Aune, *Revelation 17–22*, 1103.
[33] Cullmann, *Immortality of the Soul or Resurrection*, 24; Reddish, *Revelation*, 390.
[34] Witherington, *Revelation*, 251.
[35] Johnston, "Sheol," 227.

(John 5:28–29; 1 Cor 15:51–54; 1 Thes 4:16), and even a few of the authors of the Old Testament were given glimpses of this resurrection hope. It logically follows, therefore, that if the dead are going to be raised from their graves, then the dead must all be located in those graves prior to coming to life. Put differently, if the promise of the resurrection of the dead is going to reanimate those who have died, then this presupposes that "the dead" are all *in one central location*, known to the biblical authors variously as Sheol, Hades, the grave, and the dust of the ground. This is an often-overlooked component of scriptural anthropology, but it is important to our exploration of the destination of the dying.

All the Dead Are in a Single Location

If we begin with the evidence offered by the authors of the Old Testament, we have some clues that indicate a shared awareness that, prior to the resurrection, the dead are collectively located in the dust of the ground. The prophet Isaiah contributes a few passages to our study. The first is Isaiah 26:19: "Your dead shall live; their bodies shall rise. You who dwell in the dust, awake and sing for joy! For your dew is a dew of light, and the earth will give birth to the dead." While there is some debate as to whether this passage refers to the metaphorical restoration of Israel as a nation or to the bodily resurrection of corpses, what remains clear in either case is that "the dead" are clearly portrayed as dwelling in the dust prior to coming forth to new life.[36] The next passage within the Book of Isaiah offers a similar portrayal: "Shake yourself from the dust and arise; be seated, O Jerusalem; loose the bonds from your neck, O captive daughter of Zion" (Isa 52:2). We can be more confident that this passage is employing the metaphor of rising from the dust to describe the return from the Babylonian exile, particularly in light of the references to the chains around the neck and the descriptor of "captive."[37] Nevertheless, the return from exile, which is metaphorically illustrated as a coming to new life, demonstrates the presupposition that "the dead" are located precisely in the dust.[38] Ezekiel picks up this theme of Israel's return from exile in his vision of the Valley of Dry Bones, which is recorded in Ezekiel 37:1–14, but for our purposes, we need only to examine verses 9–12:

> Then He said to me, "Prophesy to the breath, prophesy, son of man, and say to the breath, 'Thus says Adonai Yahweh, Come from the four winds, O breath, and breathe on these slain, that they come to life.'" So I prophesied as He commanded me, and the breath came into them, and they came to life and stood on their feet, an exceedingly great army. Then He said to me, "Son of man, these bones are the whole house of Israel;

---

[36] Nickelsburg, *Resurrection, Immortality, and Eternal Life*, 30–31; Blenkinsopp, *Isaiah 1–39*, 370–71; Goldingay, *Old Testament Theology*, 2:423.
[37] Oswalt, *The Book of Isaiah: Chapters 40–66*, 361.
[38] Goldingay & Payne, *Isaiah 40–55*, 2:257; Whybray, *Isaiah 40–66*, 165.

behold, they say, 'Our bones are dried up and our hope has perished. We are completely cut off.' Therefore prophesy and say to them, 'Thus says Adonai Yahweh, Behold, I will open your graves and cause you to come up out of your graves, My people; and I will bring you into the land of Israel.'" (Ezek 37:9–12)

This vision, which characterizes the captive nation of Israel as dried-up bones (Ezek 37:11), portrays Yahweh promising to return Israel to her own land.[39] In doing so, the nation's hope will be revived.[40] To illustrate Israel's return from captivity, God sends forth his breath of life to breathe upon the slain—the dry bones that are located in graves.[41] Like the passages in Isaiah, Ezekiel employs the metaphor of resurrection to offer hope for the revival of the entire nation of Israel from exile, placing the "dead" nation in the dusty grave prior to their time of restoration.[42]

When we arrive at the conclusion of the Book of Daniel, there can be no denying that the author is talking about bodily resurrection from the dead, not the metaphor of a nation returning from exile.[43] In particular, Daniel 12:2 offers an informative description of where the dead are, what they are doing there, what will happen to them, and a description of the resurrection life they will possess. The passage reads, "Many of those who sleep in the dust of the ground will awake, these to everlasting life, but the others to disgrace and everlasting contempt." The dead are portrayed as sleeping, the common biblical euphemism for death, about which we will discuss more fully in the next chapter. The location of the sleeping dead is clearly articulated—in the dust of the ground.[44] These will awaken in resurrection, with the righteous being gifted eternal life, while the unrighteous will be punished with shame and contempt. Both groups, those who are considered worthy of eternal life and those who receive contempt, are raised from the dust of the earth, where all the deceased go upon dying.[45] In sum, we can confidently conclude that the images of resurrection offered by the authors of the Old Testament presuppose that the dead are located in the dusty grave, which establishes continuity with the portrayals of the deceased descending into the dust of the ground.

When we examine how the writers of the New Testament depict the location of the dead prior to the promised resurrection, it becomes clear that the Early Church has been deeply impacted by these Old Testament images, especially those which are conveyed in Daniel 12:2.[46] When Jesus Christ taught about the resurrection, he explicitly

---

[39] Odell, *Ezekiel*, 450–55; Block, *Ezekiel 25–48*, 379–87.
[40] Johnston, "Afterlife," 3–4; Routledge, *Old Testament Theology*, 306.
[41] Darr, "The Book of Ezekiel," 1501;
[42] Wright, *The Resurrection of the Son of God*, 119–21; Goldingay, *Old Testament Theology*, 2:422–23.
[43] Smith-Christopher, "The Book of Daniel," 148.
[44] Nickelsburg, *Resurrection, Immortality, and Eternal Life*, 30; Russell, *Daniel*, 218; Hartman and Di Lella, *The Book of Daniel*, 307.
[45] Newsom and Breed, *Daniel*, 363; Wolff, *Anthropology of the Old Testament*, 110; Wright, *The Resurrection of the Son of God*, 109.
[46] Wright, *The Resurrection of the Son of God*, 130.

spelled out that the dead are located "in their tombs" prior to being raised up: "Do not marvel at this; for an hour is coming, in which all who are in the tombs will hear his voice, and will come forth; those who did the good deeds to a resurrection of life, those who committed the evil deeds to a resurrection of judgment" (John 5:28–29).[47] By drawing a comparison with the life of the prophet Jonah, Jesus declares that he will be buried in a very specific location—in the *heart of the earth*: "So will the Son of Man be three days and three nights in the heart of the earth" (Matt 12:40). This reference is all the more relevant because the prophet Jonah poetically situated himself in the belly of Sheol (Jonah 2:2), suggesting that Jesus also believed that Sheol was located in the heart of the earth.[48] The Jewish crowds acknowledged that Lazarus was raised from the dead (i.e., out of his tomb) by Jesus, according to John 12:17.[49]

Since the resurrection of Jesus Christ from the grave is the key moment of victory in the Early Church's experience, we can infer widespread recognition among the authors of the New Testament about the location of the deceased based on the several references to Jesus rising from the dead. Nearly every book in the New Testament attests to God raising Jesus from the dead, which indicates an acceptance that *Jesus was formerly among the group of dead people* during the few days in which he was lifeless. Consider carefully the wording of these passages, which describe in unison the realization that Jesus arose from among the deceased, "the dead":

> "Go quickly and tell His disciples that He has risen from the dead" (Matt 28:7)

> He gave them orders not to relate to anyone what they had seen, until the Son of Man rose from the dead. (Mark 9:9)

> and He said to them, "Thus it is written, that the Christ would suffer and rise again from the dead the third day" (Luke 24:46)

> This is now the third time that Jesus was manifested to the disciples, after He was raised from the dead. (John 21:14)

> "let it be known to all of you and to all the people of Israel, that by the name of Jesus Christ the Nazarene, whom you crucified, whom God raised from the dead" (Acts 4:10)

> But now Christ has been raised from the dead, the first fruits of those who are asleep. (1 Cor 15:20)

> Now the God of peace, who brought up from the dead the great Shepherd of the sheep through the blood of the eternal covenant, even Jesus our Lord (Heb 13:20)

---

[47] Keener, *The Gospel of John*, 1:655; Osborne, "Resurrection," 677; Barrett, *The Gospel According to St. John*, 171.
[48] Graybill et al., 195–96; Davies and Allison, *Matthew*, 2:355–56; Hagner, *Matthew 1–13*, 354.
[49] Michaels, *The Gospel of John*, 680.

> Blessed be the God and Father of our Lord Jesus Christ, who according to His great mercy has caused us to be born again to a living hope through the resurrection of Jesus Christ from the dead (1 Pet 1:3)
>
> and from Jesus Christ, the faithful witness, the firstborn of the dead, and the ruler of the kings of the earth. (Rev 1:5)

The testimony of the Early Church is consistent and clear—"the dead" are all located in a single location. Jesus died and was buried in the grave, thereby placing him among the dead. When God raised Jesus, he rose from among *the dead people*, having been dead himself during those few days. By looking at the place from which Jesus was raised, we can be confident in our observation that the Early Church believed and taught in continuity with the truths expressed in the Hebrew Bible: all human beings are mortal, the destination of every single deceased person is the grave, and Jesus himself was among the dead until God raised him to immortality.[50]

Conclusion

In conclusion, we have observed how the biblical authors illustrate the intermediate state, particularly the location to which the deceased go upon dying. We first noted the evidence indicating that the dead descend into the dust (or some other comparable term, such as the "ground" or the "pit"). This illustration grants continuity with the destiny of the dead and the fate given to humanity's archetype, Adam. From there, we explored the designations for the abode of the dead, namely Sheol in the Hebrew portions of the Bible and Hades in the Greek portions. In several cases, Sheol and Hades functioned as parallel designations for the grave and, by extension, for death itself. Finally, we observed an often-overlooked piece of data pertaining to the location of the dead, namely, a widespread recognition among the biblical authors in both testaments that the deceased are located in a single place as they await the promised resurrection. The biblical evidence offers a compelling portrayal of those who have died; they are buried in the grave, their souls are lifeless, and they can do nothing until new life is breathed into them.

Having firmly established that the deceased reside in Sheol (i.e., Hades), we can now turn our attention to exploring the nature of the intermediate state. Are the dead souls conscious, praising God, or perhaps looking upon their living family members? Or are they unconscious in light of the animating breath of life being removed from their person? What are we to make of the hints that we have already seen that the dead are sleeping? In our next chapter, we will examine the answers that the biblical authors provide to these crucially important questions.

---

[50] Osborne, "Resurrection," 673.

11
THE CONDITION OF THE DEAD

Almost every adult has visited or at least driven past a cemetery. It is not uncommon for older church buildings to have a cemetery on their property. You have probably attended a funeral that was held at the graveside, at a cemetery itself. However, very few people are aware of the origins of the English noun "cemetery." The word cemetery is ultimately derived from the Greek term *koimeterion*, which means "a sleeping place." Yes, the word cemetery originally referred to a place where the dead are buried and were understood to be sleeping.[1] It is no wonder that gravestones and burial monuments are often engraved with the acronym RIP, "rest in peace."

This chapter will thoroughly explore the nature and condition of those human beings who have died. First, we will take stock of the evidence laid out by the writers of the biblical texts, indicating that the dead are indeed unconscious, unable to perform any actions whatsoever. Then we will look at how the euphemism of sleeping and resting has come to describe the nature of the unconscious dead, both for the Old Testament authors and for the Early Church. Once we give heed to these two main purposes for this chapter, we will be in a better position to discuss the hope for those who have died, namely the resurrection of the dead unto new life, as demonstrated by Jesus himself.

The Dead are Unconscious and Inactive

We may begin our investigation into the activity, or lack thereof, of those who have died with an observation. Most of the evidence pertaining to this topic is located in the poetic books, specifically Job, Psalms, and Ecclesiastes. There are a few references in the books of Kings and Chronicles, as well as a reference in the prophet Isaiah, but for the most part, the evidence resides in the books of the Old Testament poets. Beginning in Job, we can discern the author's perspective on the state of the dead in Job's first speech of lamentation. In his painful questioning of why he didn't die at the moment of his birth, he poetically describes what that would be like:

> "For now I would have lain down and been quiet; I would have slept then, I would have been at rest, with kings and with counselors of the earth, who rebuilt ruins for themselves; or with princes who had gold, who were filling their houses with silver. Or like a

---
[1] Ryken et al., "Sleep," 799.

miscarriage which is discarded, I would not be, as infants that never saw light. There the wicked cease from raging, And there the weary are at rest." (Job 3:13–17)

We can derive several relevant points for our study from Job's lament. First, he describes death in terms of lying down, sleeping, and resting.[2] In this condition, Job portrays death as a quiet time—a time in which raging ceases.[3] Furthermore, he indicates that this fate has overtaken several different types of people. Mighty kings, counselors, and princes in possession of great riches are also asleep in death. This same fate is true for the unfortunate child who never saw the light of day and for the wicked as well. All people who have died, Job explains, are quietly sleeping, having ceased from their activities.[4]

In Job chapter ten, the protagonist wrestles with the perceived injustice of his situation. In doing so, he again vents to God, asking, "Why then have You brought me out of the womb? Would that I had died and no eye had seen me! I should have been as though I had not been, carried from womb to tomb" (Job 10:18–19). Job, in his obviously frustrated stance, prefers death to his present situation.[5] When he refers to death, Job characterizes what that experience would be like in terms of being unseen by others and as lifelessness ("as though I had not been"). Furthermore, death is full of darkness and deep shadow (Job 10:21–22). The portrayal of death as an inactive, dark nonexistence is a stark contrast to the experience of living life.[6]

A similar illustration of the unconsciousness of the dead can be observed in Job 14:20–21. In this illustration of death, Job describes his perception of how God interacts with mortal human beings: "After You prevail forever against him, and he passes; you change his countenance, and send him away. His sons come to honor, and he does not know it; they are brought low, and he perceives it not." Humanity passes away, and God sends him away to death's abode. Those who have died have absolutely no knowledge of their children, whether they are honored or brought low.[7] The dead have no perception of what takes place in the land of the living because the dead are not alive.[8] Job portrays the deceased as unconscious and unaware of anything that is going on.[9]

When we turn to the Psalms, we are in possession of several passages that speak to the subject of whether the dead are conscious or unconscious. In particular, several individual psalms petition Yahweh to deliver the speaker from peril that, left unchecked, would lead to certain death. In the midst of these calls for deliverance, the psalmist would routinely discuss the state of those who have died and offer helpful descriptions. For

---

[2] Seow, *Job 1–21*, 330; Balentine, *Job*, 90.
[3] Clines, *Job 1–20*, 91.
[4] Habel, *The Book of Job*, 110–11; Newsom, "The Book of Job," 369; Balentine, *Job*, 90.
[5] Balentine, *Job*, 176.
[6] Newsom, "The Book of Job," 415.
[7] Seow, *Job 1–21*, 680.
[8] Pope, *Job*, 105; Newsom, "The Book of Job," 443; Balentine, *Job*, 221.
[9] Clines, *Job 1–20*, 336.

example, Psalm 6 records a request made to Yahweh to rescue the author's mortal soul. The reason given is stated in Psalm 6:5: "For in death there is no remembrance of you; in Sheol who will give you praise?" Those who have tasted death and reside in Sheol possess absolutely no remembrance of God due to being unconscious.[10] Furthermore, the question regarding who will praise Yahweh in Sheol is purely rhetorical. No one can praise or glorify God in death, because the dead are without life.[11] A similar summons to Yahweh is located at the beginning of Psalm 28: "To You, O Yahweh, I call; My rock, do not be deaf to me, for if You are silent to me, I will become like those who go down to the pit" (Ps 28:1). The psalmist urges God to heed his call, and in doing so, he likens the deaf response and the silence to what it is like for those who die and descend to the pit. Here, we can glean how the author understood the intermediate state's location and whether the dead can communicate with God. The answer is no, for the realm of the dead is a realm of silence and inactivity.[12] The same understanding can be observed in Psalm 30, where the petitioner makes a supplication to God for help and healing. In the course of this request, the psalmist remarks in Psalm 30:9, "What profit is there in my blood, if I go down to the pit? Will the dust praise You? Will it declare Your faithfulness?" We can discern from this passage that the author believes that those who descend to the pit are likened to dust.[13] As dust, they are clearly incapable of offering praise to God or speaking of his faithfulness.[14] Again, these questions are rhetorical, possessing an obviously implied negative answer. The dead are unconscious in the grave, unable to talk.[15]

At times within the Psalms, the authors recall how God has previously defeated Israel's enemies. During these recollections, the state of the dead and the intermediate state are discussed, offering several insightful perspectives on the authors' beliefs about these topics. In longing for deliverance from the hand of his adversaries, the writer of Psalm 31 requests God to intervene decisively: "Let me not be put to shame, O Yahweh, for I call upon You; let the wicked be put to shame, let them be silent in Sheol" (Ps 31:17). The psalmist conveys his wishes that the wicked would suffer a shameful death and be brought low to the realm of the dead, Sheol. In Sheol, the author's enemies are entirely silent, unable to talk because they are dead.[16] A comparable passage in Psalm 76 celebrates God as a warrior who fights on behalf of his people. The psalm remembers a moment in Israel's past in which he triumphed over its enemies: "The stouthearted were plundered, they sank into sleep; and none of the warriors could use his hands. At Your rebuke, O God of Jacob, both rider and horse were cast into a dead sleep" (Ps 76:5–6). These strong

---

[10] Goldingay, *Psalms*, 1:138; Terrien, *Psalms*, 1:113.
[11] Rad, *Old Testament Theology*, 1:369; McCann, "The Book of Psalms," 704; Craigie, *Psalms 1–50*, 93, 96.
[12] Craigie, *Psalms 1–50*, 238.
[13] Wächer, "שחת," 597–98; Goldingay, *Psalms*, 1:431.
[14] Kraus, *Theology of the Psalms*, 165; Terrien, *Psalms*, 1:283; Craigie, *Psalms 1–50*, 255.
[15] Bauckham, "Life, Death, and the Afterlife," 80; Boadt, *Reading the Old Testament*, 250–51.
[16] Craigie, *Psalms 1–50*, 262.

adversaries, described as stouthearted and as warriors, were no match for the God of Jacob, whose rebuke sent the oppressors into "sleep." This is likely a reference to the sleep of death—a time of unconscious inactivity where the dead are unable to use their hands.[17]

There are further indicators that Sheol, the realm of the dead, is a place where the deceased cannot talk. For example, Psalm 94:17 describes the inactivity of those who die: "If Yahweh had not been my help, my soul would soon have dwelt in the abode of silence." Note how the soul of this righteous psalmist is that which dies. Furthermore, the place to which the soul goes at death is not characterized as a location where lively praising or conversing with others is possible. Instead, it is explicitly illustrated as *an abode of silence*, which is what the reader would naturally expect of a dead person in whom there is no life.[18] We may observe a comparable passage in Psalm 115, which contrasts the praise and worship offering by the living with the complete lack thereof by the deceased: "The dead do not praise Yahweh, nor do any who go down into silence" (Ps 115:17). The parallelism of this verse describes the dead people as those who go down, presumably to the dust of the earth. The dead, being unconscious, cannot offer praise to Yahweh, for they are silent.[19] There is no worship taking place in the grave where the dead descend at death. We may gather the same impression from Psalm 146:4, which describes rather clearly what takes place to humanity when the animating breath of life leaves at the moment of death: "When his breath departs, he returns to the earth; on that very day his plans perish." The text carefully distinguishes the breath of life and the person, which is indicated by the pronoun "he." When that which gives life to the soul leaves, the person returns to the dusty earth.[20] His thoughts and plans die along with him, since death is a place of inactive lifelessness.[21] In short, the Psalms offer a clear and recurring description of the intermediate state: the dead are unconscious, unable to talk, praise, move, or plan anything at all.

When we examine the testimony of the Book of Ecclesiastes, we are fortunate to have some of the most explicit expressions of activity that takes place in Sheol. In a passage that contrasts the knowledge held by those who are alive and those who have died, we can observe the limits of those who reside in the grave: "For the living know they will die; but the dead do not know anything, nor have they any longer a reward, for their memory is forgotten" (Ecc 9:5). Being lifeless, the dead are unable to think, understand, or recognize anything.[22] Even their own memories have been forgotten. This reality of the unconsciousness of death is further elaborated a few verses later: "Whatever

---

[17] Hossfeld and Zenger, *Psalms 2*, 267; Craigie, *Psalms 51–100*, 265.
[18] Goldingay, *Psalms*, 3:83; McCann, "The Book of Psalms," 1058.
[19] Terrien, *The Psalms*, 2:774; Goldingay, *Psalms*, 3:334.
[20] McCann, "The Book of Psalms," 1263.
[21] Goldingay, *Psalms*, 3:709; Terrien, *Psalms*, 2:910.
[22] Seow, *Ecclesiastes*, 305; Horne, *Proverbs–Ecclesiastes*, 500–1; Brown, *Ecclesiastes*, 93; Weeks, *Ecclesiastes*, 2:422.

your hand finds to do, do it with all your might; for there is no activity or planning or knowledge or wisdom in Sheol where you are going" (Ecc 9:10).[23] Again, the physical capacity of the living and the dead are distinguished. Since those in Sheol cannot perform any physical or mental processes, those who are alive should make the most of their opportunities.[24] Not only does Ecclesiastes 9:10 identify where the dead, including the reader, go when they die, but the passage also describes the sorts of activities that do not take place in Sheol.[25] The author of Ecclesiastes, it would appear, regards those who reside in Sheol as unconscious, lifeless, and unable to do anything.[26]

The few remaining references to the inactivity of those who have died come from the narrative portions of Scripture and from the prophet Isaiah. Speaking through the prophetess Huldah, God informs King Josiah about the details surrounding his death in 2 Kings 22:20: "Therefore, behold, I will gather you to your fathers, and you shall be gathered to your grave in peace, and your eyes shall not see all the disaster that I will bring upon this place." Josiah, a righteous and faithful Israelite king, will be gathered to his fathers, who are located in the grave.[27] When Josiah is brought to the grave at the moment of his death, he will be completely unable to see what God will do to Jerusalem. Josiah's lack of ability to use his eyes is due to the fact that he will be unconscious in the grave, devoid of life. This prophetic message to the king was deemed necessary enough by the Chronicler to preserve and restate it in 2 Chronicles 34:28, so there is little merit in quoting it here. Finally, we can turn to the Book of Isaiah, which records a song of praise sung by Hezekiah after God granted him an additional fifteen years of life. Within Hezekiah's song, he offers a helpful contrast of what little the dead are capable of and what the living are capable of: "For Sheol cannot thank You, death cannot praise You; those who go down to the pit cannot hope for Your faithfulness" (Isa 38:18).[28] The following verse declares that it is the living who give thanks to Yahweh, a praise in which Hezekiah is actively participating. Those who descend to the pit, which is aptly illustrated as Sheol and death, are unable to thank, praise, or place their hope in Yahweh. The dead who reside in Sheol are without life and, thus, are incapable of talking or singing.[29] Therefore, only those who are among the living are privileged with the opportunity to offer acts of praise to God (Isa 38:19).[30]

---

[23] Fox, *Ecclesiastes*, 64.
[24] Longman, *The Book of Ecclesiastes*, 231; Brown, *Ecclesiastes*, 95.
[25] Seow, *Ecclesiastes*, 306; Routledge, *Old Testament Theology*, 305.
[26] Crenshaw, *Ecclesiastes*, 163; Towner, "The Book of Ecclesiastes," 341; Horne, *Proverbs–Ecclesiastes*, 502.
[27] Seow, "The First and Second Books of Kings," 282.
[28] Wächer, "שחת," 597; Tucker, "The Book of Isaiah 1–39," 301; Roberts, *First Isaiah*, 485; Blenkinsopp, *Isaiah 1–39*, 485; Watts, *Isaiah 34–66*, 61.
[29] Routledge, *Old Testament Theology*, 305.
[30] Blenkinsopp, *Isaiah 1–39*, 485–86.

The Sleep of Death

Having thoroughly examined how the biblical authors portray the intermediate state as a period of unconscious lifelessness, we can pivot to examining the standard euphemism for death that persisted into the beliefs and teachings of the Early Church, namely the characterization of the deceased as *sleeping* or *resting* in their graves.[31] There is some variety in the ways the authors of the biblical texts portray the state of death. The deaths of Abraham, Ishmael, Isaac, Jacob, and Aaron are illustrated in terms of the deceased being *gathered to their people* (Gen 25:8, 17; 35:29; 49:29, 33; Num 20:24; Deut 32:50). For Moses and David, they were to *lie down with their fathers* (Deut 31:16; 2 Sam 7:12).[32] The prophet Daniel *entered into rest* at the end of his life, as stated in Daniel 12:13.[33] The psalmist offers the helpful illustration that is still used by many today: "Consider and answer me, O Yahweh my God; enlighten my eyes, or I will sleep the sleep of death" (Ps 13:3).[34] Whether the terminology is that of lying down, resting, or sleeping, the meaning is the same. The sleep of death is the unconscious designation for those who have died and are completely inactive, being without life or breath.[35]

When the author of Kings and the Chronicler recorded the histories of the various kings of Israel and Judah, the individual deaths of the rulers were described in terms of sleeping.[36] It did not matter if the king did good in the eyes of Yahweh or whether they did evil; their fate was the same. Death is likened to sleep for the biblical authors, regardless of the amount of favor one has gained with God. Consider these texts describing how the kings "slept" (i.e., died) and were buried with their ancestors:

> Then David slept with his fathers and was buried in the city of David. (1 Kgs 2:10)

> And Solomon slept with his fathers and was buried in the city of his father David (1 Kgs 11:43)

> The time that Jeroboam reigned was twenty-two years; and he slept with his fathers (1 Kgs 14:20)

> And Rehoboam slept with his fathers and was buried with his fathers in the city of David (1 Kgs 14:31)

> And Abijam slept with his fathers and they buried him in the city of David (1 Kgs 15:8)

---

[31] Beuken, "שָׁכַב," 664, offers the standard summary: "the notion of '(going to) sleep' also functioned as a metaphor for 'dying, being dead.'"
[32] Christensen, *Deuteronomy 21:10–34:12*, 772.
[33] Gowan, *Daniel*, 155.
[34] Craigie, *Psalms 1–50*, 142.
[35] Tromp, *Primitive Conceptions of Death*, 169–70.
[36] Johnston, "Death and Afterlife," 217.

And Asa slept with his fathers and was buried with his fathers in the city of David his father (1 Kgs 15:24)

And Baasha slept with his fathers and was buried in Tirzah (1 Kgs 16:6)

So Omri slept with his fathers and was buried in Samaria (1 Kgs 16:28)

So Ahab slept with his fathers (1 Kgs 22:40)

And Jehoshaphat slept with his fathers and was buried with his fathers in the city of his father David (1 Kgs 22:50)

So Joram slept with his fathers and was buried with his fathers in the city of David (2 Kgs 8:24)

And Jehu slept with his fathers, and they buried him in Samaria (2 Kgs 10:35)

And Jehoahaz slept with his fathers, and they buried him in Samaria (2 Kgs 13:9)

So Joash slept with his fathers (2 Kgs 13:13)

So Jehoash slept with his fathers and was buried in Samaria with the kings of Israel (2 Kgs 14:16)

And Jeroboam slept with his fathers, even with the kings of Israel (2 Kgs 14:29)

And Azariah slept with his fathers, and they buried him with his fathers in the city of David (2 Kgs 15:7)

And Menahem slept with his fathers (2 Kgs 15:22)

And Jotham slept with his fathers, and he was buried with his fathers in the city of David his father (2 Kgs 15:38)

So Ahaz slept with his fathers, and was buried with his fathers in the city of David (2 Kgs 16:20)

So Hezekiah slept with his fathers (2 Kgs 20:21)

And Manasseh slept with his fathers and was buried in the garden of his own house (2 Kgs 21:18)

So Jehoiakim slept with his fathers (2 Kgs 24:6)

As we can observe, the constant refrain of a king sleeping and being buried acts as individual obituaries for the author of the Book of Kings.[37] Their careers are over, and their lives have come to an end, giving room for the next king to begin his rule. The Chronicler continued to use the euphemism of sleep to illustrate the death of kings (e.g.,

---

[37] Hens-Piazza, *1–2 Kings*, 26; Sweeney, *I & II Kings*, 60; Beuken, "שָׁכַב," 666–67.

2 Chron 9:31; 12:16; 14:1; 16:13; 21:1). In each of these descriptions, the narrator is careful with the subject and the verb, indicating quite clearly that it is the individual king who died (i.e., slept). It was the individual king who was buried. There is no suggestion or hint of a dualistic portrayal of the king as if only the body slept while the soul continued to live elsewhere. Rather, the reader is left with the clear impression that the entire person died, slept, and was buried.

We have already taken notice of the portrayal of death as sleep in the scriptural books of poetry (e.g., Ps 76:5–6). Job discusses what it would be like if he died by likening the experience to lying down, sleeping, and being at rest (Job 3:13; 7:21).[38] In Job 14:12–14, the death of human beings is plainly depicted in terms of lying down and sleeping in Sheol.[39] Within the poetic oracles of the prophet Jeremiah, we find two further references to the sleep of death, the first referring to the fate of the inhabitants of Babylon: "'While they are inflamed I will prepare them a feast and make them drunk, that they may become merry, then sleep a perpetual sleep and not wake,' declares Yahweh" (Jer 51:39).[40] A similar fate awaits Babylon's princes, wise men, governors, prefects, and mighty men: "they shall sleep a perpetual sleep and not wake" (Jer 51:57). The immediate context of judgment from God strongly suggests that the act of sleeping in these texts refers to the state of death, rather than an ordinary overnight slumber.[41]

We have previously introduced Daniel 12:2 in Chapter 10, but the impact that passage had on the Early Church, including the beliefs of Jesus himself, renders it worthy of discussion here. The primary Old Testament verse that illustrates the hope of bodily resurrection from the grave portrays the intermediate state as a time of sleeping: "Many of those who sleep in the dust of the ground will awake, these to everlasting life, but the others to disgrace and everlasting contempt." Since the resurrection to eternal life is contrasted with sleeping, we can safely assume that "sleep" is functioning as a euphemism for death, describing those who are located in the dust of the ground. Moreover, the contrast in Daniel 12:2 between sleeping and "waking up" lays the groundwork for further speculation by the Early Church surrounding resurrection as an occasion in which the dead are awoken from their unconscious sleep.[42] We will return to this point in Chapter 12.

The early Christian authors of the New Testament wrote in Greek, but their conception of the soul at death was anything but Greek. Instead of adopting a belief in the immortality of the soul, the Early Church maintained consistency with the portrayal represented in the Old Testament scriptures of an intermediate state in which the dead

---

[38] Seow, *Job 1–21*, 357–58; Habel, *Job*, 166–67.
[39] Habel, *Job*, 241–42.
[40] McKane, *Jeremiah 26–52*, 1330.
[41] Lundbom, *Jeremiah 37–52*, 477; Keown et al., *Jeremiah 26–56*, 371–72.
[42] Goldingay, *Daniel*, 564; Oepke, "ἐγείρω," 334–37.

are unconscious, asleep, and awaiting resurrection.[43] Naturally, the teachings of Jesus had a profound impact on the theology and preaching of his earliest followers, so it makes sense to begin our exploration of the New Testament's understanding of the intermediate state with the beliefs of Jesus. In the Gospel of John, both Jesus and the narrator clarify the intent to wake Lazarus up from the dead. Note how the narrator frames the discussion between Jesus and his disciples in a manner that clarifies the reference to "sleep" as the sleep of death:

> after that he said to them, "Our friend Lazarus has fallen asleep; but I go, so that I may awaken him out of sleep." The disciples then said to him, "Lord, if he has fallen asleep, he will recover." Now Jesus had spoken of his death, but they thought that he was speaking of literal sleep. So Jesus then said to them plainly, "Lazarus is dead" (John 11:11–14)

In one of the stereotypical examples of the theme of misunderstanding that permeates the narrative of the Gospel of John, Jesus informs his followers that Lazarus, their friend, has fallen asleep. He also indicates his intent to go wake Lazarus up. The disciples express their misunderstanding of what Jesus said by interpreting his words literally, thinking that Lazarus is merely taking part in the nightly slumber. The narrator quickly signals to the reader the nature of the misunderstanding, clarifying that Jesus' intentions were to convey the reality of Lazarus' death and his desire to wake him up from the dead by resurrection. To this end, Jesus openly clarifies what he meant with his original phrase, "Our friend Lazarus has fallen asleep," by helpfully clearing up the confusion: "Lazarus is dead."[44] Not only did Jesus believe in the sleep of the dead, but he also taught this theology to his followers and then proved his intentions by raising Lazarus back to life (John 11:43–44).

The preaching of the Early Church, as recounted in the Book of Acts, expresses a continued belief in the sleep of the dead. After a lengthy speech condemning Jewish attitudes towards the Jerusalem temple and their rejection of God's agents, the members of the Sanhedrin stoned Stephen to death. The narrator describes Stephen's martyrdom with the euphemism of sleep: "he fell asleep" (Acts 7:60).[45] A similar use of the phrase occurs in Paul's first sermon in Acts. In an attempt to contrast David, who underwent decay in the grave, and Jesus, whom God raised from the dead, Paul illustrates David's death in terms of falling asleep (Acts 13:36). Having fallen asleep, David was laid among his fathers, and he experienced corruption—clearly indicating that the reference to sleep is illustrating the state of death.[46]

The Apostle Paul expressed the concept of death in terms of sleep in his letters to his Gentile churches. In 1 Thessalonians, one of Paul's earliest letters, he offers

---

[43] Finnegan, *Kingdom Journey*, 160–61.
[44] Harrington, *John*, 326; Coloe, *John 11–21*, 323; Brant, *John*, 173.
[45] Walton, *Acts 1–9:42*, 483–84; Keener, *Acts*, 2:1462–63.
[46] Keener, *Acts*, 2:2073.

encouragement to the Thessalonian church as it grieves the loss of some of the Christians in their community.[47] Some of the Christians in Thessalonica had unfortunately died, and Paul clearly describes the deceased as "those who are asleep" (1 Thes 4:13).[48] In order to bolster the church's hope, Paul reminds them that God has already raised Jesus, proving that death is not the end. In fact, God will do the very same to those who have fallen asleep in Christ (1 Thes 4:14).[49] There is no need to grieve hopelessly, for those who have fallen asleep are not in a disadvantageous position compared to those who are still alive (1 Thes 4:15).[50] At this point, Paul has illustrated death as "sleep" three successive times in this passage, and readers can be confident that Paul is talking about the sleep of death because in 1 Thessalonians 4:16, he describes those who have fallen asleep as "the dead" who will rise in resurrection: "For the Lord himself will descend from heaven with a shout, with the voice of an archangel and with the trumpet of God, and the dead in Christ will rise first."[51] Indeed, those Christians who have fallen asleep in death will rise before those who are alive at Jesus' coming (4:17), proving that the dead will not be overlooked.[52] The promise that Jesus will return to wake up those who sleep the sleep of death is meant to bring comfort and encouragement to those who are in mourning.[53] The contrast between those who are alive and those who are asleep (i.e., dead) reappears in 1 Thessalonians 5:10: "whether we are awake or asleep, we will live together with him."[54]

We may observe several other places in which the Apostle Paul characterizes the dead as those who sleep, particularly in 1 Corinthians. In giving practical answers to questions that the Corinthians raised to Paul, he comments on death in the context of whether a woman can remarry: "A wife is bound to her husband as long as he lives. But if her husband dies, she is free to be married to whom she wishes, only in the Lord" (1 Cor 7:39). The English versions typically describe the husband in this scenario as the one who "dies," but the Greek verb that lies behind it, *koimaomai*, is the regular verb that the New Testament authors use to refer to "sleeping" (and modern translations helpfully footnote this important insight).[55] The verb reappears in Paul's discussion of the Lord's Supper (1 Cor 11:17–34), which is also known as the communion meal. We will discuss the significance of this sacramental meal in Chapter 41, but for now, it will suffice to show that the Corinthians were celebrating this meal in a manner with which Paul strongly

---

[47] Green, *How to Read Prophecy*, 26; Ryken et al., "Mortality," 569.
[48] Malherbe, *The Letters to the Thessalonians*, 263; Wanamaker, *The Epistles to the Thessalonians*, 167; Smith, "The First Letter to the Thessalonians," 723–24.
[49] Smith, "The First Letter to the Thessalonians," 724; Weima, *1–2 Thessalonians*, 317–18; Kim and Bruce, *1 & 2 Thessalonians*, 383.
[50] Boring, *I & II Thessalonians*, 166; Weima, *1–2 Thessalonians*, 322; Bridges, *1 & 2 Thessalonians*, 123.
[51] Kim and Bruce, *1 & 2 Thessalonians*, 399; Boring, *I & II Thessalonians*, 155.
[52] Jewett, *The Thessalonian Correspondence*, 95; Marshall, *1 and 2 Thessalonians*, 127; Morris, *The First and Second Epistles to the Thessalonians*, 142.
[53] Malherbe, *The Letters to the Thessalonians*, 275.
[54] Morris, *The First and Second Epistles to the Thessalonians*, 162; Marshall, *1 and 2 Thessalonians*, 141; Wanamaker, *The Epistles to the Thessalonians*, 188–89.
[55] Barrett, *The First Epistle to the Corinthians*, 185–86.

disagreed, provoking some words of correction. In fact, one of the supporting arguments that Paul used to argue that the believers in Corinth were eating and drinking within this meal outside of the will of God was to recall the ways in which God has already enacted his judgment upon some of them: "For this reason many among you are weak and sick, and a number sleep" (1 Cor 11:30). In other words, a number of those who were inappropriately participating in the Lord's Supper are sleeping the sleep of death.[56]

The Apostle Paul employs the euphemism "sleep" several times to illustrate those who have died in 1 Corinthians 15, the chapter containing the most extended biblical exposition on the bodily resurrection of the dead. The chapter begins with Paul calling attention to the death, burial, resurrection, and post-resurrection appearances of Jesus. In his listing of those who were eyewitnesses to the resurrected Jesus, Paul notes that there was an instance where Jesus appears to over five hundred believers, most of whom are still alive, but some "have fallen asleep" (1 Cor 15:6). We can confidently interpret this reference to the few who fell asleep as those who have died because Paul is contrasting this group with those eyewitnesses who still remain alive.[57] A similar reference appears in 1 Corinthians 15:18, where Paul concludes that if Christ had not been hypothetically raised from the dead, then all who have already fallen asleep in Christ would have truly perished.[58] However, Paul positively argues that Christ has been raised from the dead, and in doing so, the apostle calls attention to this category ("the dead") from which Christ arose. Jesus is the first fruits of those who are asleep (1 Cor 15:20). This statement indicates that while Jesus was dead, he was obviously sleeping the sleep of death.[59] Now that Jesus has been raised to immortal life, Paul can logically conclude that Jesus is the first human being to be given immortality, and many who are still sleeping will also receive this reward.[60] This coming resurrection of the dead, of which Jesus has already partaken, will take place at his second coming (1 Cor 15:23), the time when the bodies of those who are in Christ will be changed from corruptible to incorruptible. This irreversible change will affect both those who are alive and those who are asleep, i.e., dead (1 Cor 15:51).[61] At this point, it should be overwhelmingly apparent that Paul firmly believed and taught the sleep of the dead to the believers in his churches, offering the hope of the return of Christ to awaken the dead out of sleep, just as God woke Jesus up from the dead.[62]

---

[56] Hays, *First Corinthians*, 201; Witherington, *Conflict & Community in Corinth*, 252.
[57] Garland, *1 Corinthians*, 689–90.
[58] Fitzmyer, *First Corinthians*, 564; Thiselton, *First Epistle to the Corinthians*, 1220.
[59] Garland, *1 Corinthians*, 706.
[60] Beale, *A New Testament Biblical Theology*, 261.
[61] Perkins, *First Corinthians*, 191. Horsley, *1 Corinthians*, 214, offers helpful insight here: "By saying that the *body* becomes clothed with imperishability and immortality Paul is intentionally addressing and blocking the idea that the soul becomes disembodied with it takes on immortality."
[62] Ryken et al., "Mortality," 569–70.

Conclusion

There are several other passages in which the authors of the New Testament demonstrate their commitment to the belief in the sleep of the dead (e.g., Matt 9:24; 27:52; Eph 5:14; 2 Pet 3:4; Rev 6:11; 14:13), but we have examined enough evidence to firmly draw the conclusion that the Early Church continued to embrace the doctrine of the mortality of human beings and the understanding that those who have died are resting in their graves. We can take this moment to reflect on our observations of the biblical data concerning the condition of the dead. We first examined the statements pertaining to the lack of activity taking place among those who have died. Being without life or breath, it makes sense for the biblical authors to illustrate the dead as unconscious and unable to see, talk, praise, or perform any activity otherwise requiring a living awareness. We also observed that the way in which the authors of the biblical texts characterized the unconscious dead was to talk of them sleeping, resting, or lying down with their fathers. The Early Church continued to believe and teach that the dead sleep until they are given new life via resurrection from the dead. Not only was this a teaching of Jesus himself, but we also saw substantial evidence that the Apostle Paul taught the sleep of the dead to his churches. It appears that the resurrection of Jesus from the sleep of death and the promise that believers would come to share in Jesus' resurrection offered several new opportunities for the authors of the New Testament to make good use of the illustration of the deceased resting in their graves.

Since a complete picture of those who are unconsciously sleeping in the dust of the earth includes the anticipation of resurrection from the dead, it is only natural that our next area of focus should be to look at how the hope for those who have died is found in the promise of being raised from their graves. This act of vindication from God, which the authors of the Old Testament only glimpsed, comes to full expression in the theology of the Early Church, particularly in light of the fact that God has already raised Jesus from the grave in a triumphal victory. Therefore, we must turn in our next chapter to the hope for mortal human beings—resurrection from the grave.

12
THE HOPE OF RESURRECTION

It is hard to overstate the sheer importance that the resurrection of Jesus has upon the beliefs, self-understanding, hope, and practices of the Early Church.[1] The effects of God raising Jesus from his state of death's sleep can be observed in all eight of the major doctrines that this volume sets out to cover. We have already seen how the only true God's moral attributes include being the just judge, and one of the most important ways that God promises to judge humanity is to vindicate the righteous from the dead while also raising the wicked to face judgment. In our study of hamartiology, we will see how the Early Church interpreted the death and resurrection of Jesus as the means by which sin and death were defeated. Along the same lines, the sacrifice of Jesus, the human Messiah, and his subsequent exaltation by God offer several important implications for christology. The mortal bodies animated by God's breath of life are set in contrast by the Apostle Paul with the immortal bodies animated by God's Spirit, about which we will have more to say in our study of pneumatology. The fullest sense of salvation and deliverance will be realized when the righteous inherit immortality and incorruption, a concept we will explore in our discussion of soteriology. Furthermore, ecclesiology uses "resurrection" as a metaphor for Christian conversion, describing those who are in Christ and members of his body. Finally, the study of last things, eschatology, will detail how God's final victory will involve raising the dead to either the life of the age to come or to judgment and condemnation. As we can see, the hope of resurrection has had a profound theological impact on all aspects of the Early Church's theology.

In order not to steal the thunder of the other doctrines and the ways in which the concept of resurrection overlaps with them, this chapter's focus will be on how the promise of being raised from the sleep of death is the hope for human beings in their mortal state. As such, the most recent chapters have laid the vital groundwork (no pun intended) for the hope of the resurrection of those in their graves. First, we will look at how the promise of resurrection on the last day was incorporated into the theology of the authors of the biblical texts. Second, we will consider how the resurrection of Jesus in the middle of history prompted the Early Church to reconsider its views of the two ages of God's history. Lastly, we will take note of how the New Testament authors connected the resurrection of Jesus and the future resurrection of the people of God in a manner that gave meaning to the critical event in the past while also instilling hope for the future.

---

[1] Kreitzer, "Resurrection," 805–806.

Once we focus on these three key facets of the resurrection hope for humanity, we will be in a better position to discuss what will happen to the unrighteous at the judgment in relation to anthropology.

The Promised Resurrection of the Dead on the Last Day

We have already pointed out that Daniel 12:2 served as the premier text within the Hebrew Bible that unambiguously offered the hope of bodily resurrection of the dead. Prior to Daniel 12:2, which is one of the latest texts of the Old Testament, there were a few clues and glimmers of optimism suggesting that Yahweh would one day raise the dead from their graves.[2] For example, the prayer of Hannah praises God in a manner that may suggest a belief in resurrection: "Yahweh kills and makes alive; He brings down to Sheol and raises up" (1 Sam 2:6). The parallelism in this passage connects the idea of God making the dead alive with raising them up from Sheol. The text does not elaborate on this thought, so we are left to speculate in hindsight about the Early Church's fuller understanding of the resurrection.[3] One such book that we know lent itself to such speculation by ancient readers is the Book of Job. For example, Job 14:14 asks the question, "If a man dies, will he live again?" While the Hebrew text clearly frames this as a question, the Greek translator rendered the Hebrew in a way that suggests an awareness of the hope of resurrection: "If a man dies, he *will* live again."[4] Another relevant passage, Job 19:25–26, expresses hope that God, the Redeemer, lives and will vindicate Job so that he, in his flesh, will at last behold God.[5] The Greek translator saw the Hebrew text and translated it with a view to the resurrection of the body: "he *will* raise up my flesh upon the earth."[6] The conclusion, recorded in Job 42:17, offers an obituary of the main protagonist: "And Job died, an old man and full of days." The Greek translator offers a postscript that can only be viewed in the Septuagint: "And Job died, an old man and full of days: and it is written that he *will rise again* with those whom the Lord raises up."[7] Additionally, we may note the question raised by the eighth-century prophet Hosea concerning the fate of the dead in Sheol, located in Hosea 13:14: "Shall I rescue them from the hand of Sheol? Shall I redeem them from death?" Again, the questions leave us speculating about God's intent, but the Greek translator turned these into unambiguously positive statements: "I *will* rescue them from the hand of Hades, and I *will* redeem them from death."

---

[2] Wright, *The Resurrection of the Son of God*, 148.
[3] Levenson, *Resurrection and the Restoration of Israel*, 173; Klein, *1 Samuel*, 17; McCarter, *1 Samuel*, 76.
[4] Cavallin, *Life After Death*, 105; Hartley, *The Book of Job*, 235–37.
[5] Ryken et al., "Mortality," 569. Longman, *Job*, 261, suggests that this passage originally pointed to Job's expectation that this meeting would take place before his death.
[6] Cavallin, *Life After Death*, 106.
[7] Cavallin, *Life After Death*, 106; Hartley, *The Book of Job*, 543.

Returning to Daniel 12:2 once again, we no longer have to speculate about what Hannah, Job, or Hosea meant for their Hebrew readers to understand by their words. Daniel 12:2, plainly and without ambiguity, sets the stage for a future bodily resurrection from the grave: "Many of those who sleep in the dust of the ground will awake, these to everlasting life, but the others to disgrace and everlasting contempt." Although we have already explored this passage as it pertains to the activity of the dead (they are sleeping) and the location of the dead (in the dust of the ground), we now have the opportunity to explore the promised destiny of the deceased. Those who sleep in the ground will awaken to resurrection, either to "everlasting life" (more on this phrase shortly) or to disgrace and contempt. The following passage, Daniel 12:3, describes the condition of those who attain the resurrection of life in terms of a glorious brightness: "Those who are wise shall shine like the brightness of the sky." The impression we are left with is that the righteous are not going to be raised to frail and fleshly mortality, bound by weakness, but rather to glory befitting royalty.[8] Indeed, they will be exalted "like the stars," as Daniel 12:3 concludes.[9] This should not be read as though the resurrected righteous will become stars in the sky or that they will be located in the stars of heaven. Instead, the thrust is that when God raises the dead, he will restore his faithful people to exalted positions of rulership, as the biblical authors have laid the groundwork for us to see by associating royalty with the imagery of stars and celestial glory (Num 24:17; Ps 8:3–6).[10] The resurrection bodies will be a substantial improvement on the old bodies made of the dust of the ground.

Returning to the phrase "everlasting life" in Daniel 12:2, we possess a nugget that the authors of the New Testament snatched up and utilized for several important reasons. For our purposes here, we will discuss two of them. First, the Hebrew text lying behind the English translation "everlasting life" more literally (and accurately) reads "the life of the age."[11] This suggests that resurrection life is characterized as life that belongs to a particular age or era of time. The Jewish people who discussed such things as the ages of God's history saw their current era as the present age, with another age, described as the "age to come," immediately following the conclusion of this present age.[12] This certainly appears to be the understanding of the author of Daniel, who concludes his work with the heavenly angelic messenger informing Daniel himself that he will be resurrected at the end of this present age: "But as for you, go your way to the end; then you will enter into rest and rise again for your allotted portion at the end of days" (Dan 12:13).[13] When we connect the language of Daniel 12:2–3 about the resurrection of the righteous unto glorious bodies consisting of the life of the age with the clue that the

---

[8] Wright, *The Resurrection of the Son of God*, 113.
[9] Pace, *Daniel*, 337; Levenson, *Resurrection and the Restoration of Israel*, 189–90.
[10] Dozeman, "The Book of Numbers," 191.
[11] Ramelli and Konstan, *Terms for Eternity*, 41, 47.
[12] Tomasino, "עוֹלָם," 350; Guhrt, "Time," 829; Hill, *Greek Words and Hebrew Meanings*, 186.
[13] Newsom and Breed, *Daniel*, 368; Goldingay, *Daniel*, 552.

righteous prophet Daniel will rise at the end of days (Dan 12:13), we can conclude that the promised resurrection of the dead is the event that brings the present age to its conclusion and ushers in the age to come.[14] Therefore, the resurrection life to which the righteous will be raised from their dusty graves is not merely the life of the age, but, as it came to be understood by the time of Jesus, the life of the age to come.[15] We will have more to say about the two ages later in this volume, but for now, it is crucially important to note that the event that divides the present age and the age to come is the resurrection of the dead.

The second reason why we need to discuss the phrase "everlasting life" at this point is its association with the resurrection of the body. Daniel 12:2 serves as the first biblical appearance of the phrase "life of the age" (rendered as "everlasting life" or "eternal life" in English translations). This life is characterized by the newfound life given to those who were dead, specifically by raising them from the dust of the ground. In effect, everlasting life is not just a generic way to describe life that does not come to an end, but rather, it indicates at its core the life that God's faithful people will come to possess when they are resurrected with bodies that can no longer die. Eternal life is, therefore, immortal life, incorruptible life, the life that one receives when the dead are raised to live in the glorious age to come.[16] This is why the future resurrection of the dead, foretold in the oracles of Daniel 12:2–3, is the solution to humanity's mortality.

The Early Church firmly embraced these two key truths: the two-age schema of God's history and the promised life of the age to come as resurrection life that is to have no end.[17] The teachings of Jesus Christ are filled with sayings, parables, and promises that reaffirm the coming resurrection of the dead as the event that begins the age to come. In the Parable of the Tares in the Field (Matt 13:24–30, 36–43), Jesus teaches that the end of the age will be a time of judgment in which the righteous and the wicked will be separated. Included in this parable is a loose allusion to Daniel 12:3 in Matthew 13:43: "Then the righteous will shine like the sun in the kingdom of their Father."[18] The end of the age will conclude, therefore, with the resurrection of the righteous unto a glorious condition, shining like the sun, a rather large star in its own right. When Peter asked about the sacrifice that he and the disciples had made by giving up everything, Jesus replied that they would receive many things in this age, but in the age to come, their reward would be eternal life (Mark 10:30; Luke 18:30). The life of the age to come is plainly given in that

---

[14] Preuss, "עוֹלָם," 542–43; Russell, *Daniel*, 228; Cavallin, *Life After Death*, 30.
[15] Guhrt, "Time," 832; Hill, *Greek Words and Hebrew Meanings*, 172; Sasse, "αἰών, αἰώνιος," 208. Anderson, *Contours of Old Testament Theology*, 318, provides a helpful summary: "People 'sleep' until the final consummation, when they will be 'awakened' to celebrate God's dominion with those who are alive."
[16] Bauckham, "Life, Death, and the Afterlife," 81; Levenson, *Resurrection and the Restoration of Israel*, 187; Collins, *Daniel*, 392.
[17] Hill, *Greek Words and Hebrew Meanings*, 181, 188–201.
[18] Hartman and Di Lella, *The Book of Daniel*, 309; Nickelsburg, *Resurrection, Immortality, and Eternal Life*, 300.

coming age, Jesus clearly taught.[19] When the Sadducees, a priestly and high-class Jewish sect, asked Jesus about the specifics of marriage as it pertained to the doctrine of the future resurrection of the dead, a doctrine for which they saw no evidence in the Torah of Moses, Jesus affirmed his belief that the resurrection coincided with the age to come:

> "The sons of this age marry and are given in marriage, but those who are considered worthy to attain to that age and the resurrection from the dead, neither marry nor are given in marriage; for they cannot even die anymore" (Luke 20:34–36).

As we can observe, Jesus distinguishes between two ages: "this age," in which we currently live, and "that age," when the resurrection of the dead takes place.[20] In that coming age, those who have attained the resurrection of the dead are unable to die, having inherited immortality in their new, glorious body. Furthermore, there are several passages in the Gospel of John where Jesus declares himself, as God's agent, to be the one who will raise the dead on the last day.[21] Consider these passages:

> "This is the will of Him who sent me, that of all that He has given me I lose nothing, but raise it up on the last day." (John 6:39)

> "For this is the will of my Father, that everyone who beholds the son and believes in him will have eternal life, and I myself will raise him up on the last day." (John 6:40)

> "No one can come to me unless the Father who sent me draws him; and I will raise him up on the last day." (John 6:44)

> "He who eats my flesh and drinks my blood has eternal life, and I will raise him up on the last day." (John 6:54)

> Martha said to him, "I know that he will rise again in the resurrection on the last day." Jesus said to her, "I am the resurrection and the life; he who believes in me will live even if he dies, and everyone who lives and believes in me will never die." (John 11:24–26)

The *last day* about which Jesus speaks appears to be the final day of the present age. On this day, Jesus will raise the dead and offer eternal life—the life of the age to come—to the righteous.[22] This event ushers in the coming age, the age to come. If there was ever any question regarding whether Jesus embraced the hope of resurrection that we find in Daniel 12:2, it was quickly settled by taking notice of Jesus practically quoting the passage and expressing not only his agreement but also his involvement in the coming resurrection of the righteous and the wicked. Compare what Jesus taught in John 5:28–29 with Daniel 12:2: "Do not marvel at this; for an hour is coming, in which all who are in the tombs will hear his voice, and will come forth; those who did the good

---

[19] Hill, *Greek Words and Hebrew Meanings*, 191–92.
[20] Johnson, *Luke*, 313; Green, *Luke*, 720.
[21] Osborne, "Resurrection," 677.
[22] Carson, *John*, 292; Brown, *John I–XII*, 270.

deeds to a resurrection of life, those who committed the evil deeds to a resurrection of judgment." For the righteous, the life of the age to come will be found in a resurrection from their tombs, while the unrighteous will suffer an unfavorable judgment. In short, Jesus believed and taught that the coming resurrection of the dead is to take place on the last day, bringing the present age to a close and initiating the age to come.[23]

The Early Church placed its hope in the promised eternal life as a reward that the righteous were to inherit on the last day. In fact, not only did the early Christians believe and teach that a resurrection body of never-ending life was part of the promised inheritance, but there are instances where Jesus reaffirmed this common Jewish belief when the issue arose in conversation.[24] Take, for example, this sampling of passages that express the Early Church's affirmation of eternal life in a resurrected body as something that has *yet to be inherited*:

> "And everyone who has left houses or brothers or sisters or father or mother or children or lands, for my name's sake, will receive a hundredfold and will inherit eternal life." (Matt 19:29)
>
> Then the King will say to those on his right, "Come, you who are blessed of my Father, inherit the kingdom prepared for you from the foundation of the world." . . . the righteous into eternal life. (Matt 25:34, 46)
>
> And a lawyer stood up and put him to the test, saying, "Teacher, what shall I do to inherit eternal life?" (Luke 10:25)
>
> A ruler questioned him, saying, "Good Teacher, what shall I do to inherit eternal life?" (Luke 18:18)
>
> Now I say this, brethren, that flesh and blood cannot inherit the kingdom of God; nor does the perishable inherit the imperishable. (1 Cor 15:50)

It is clear to see the impact that Daniel 12:2 had on the theology of the Early Church, which longed for the coming day when the dead would be raised to immortality, thus providing a tangible solution to the problem of human mortality.[25] Resurrection life in the age to come is to be inherited by the faithful people of God on the last day.

The In-Breaking of the Resurrection of Jesus in the Middle of History

Having established that the belief in the coming resurrection of those who sleep in their graves was one of the readily available answers to the problem of death—an option that

---

[23] Guhrt, "Time," 832.
[24] Hammer, "Inheritance (NT)," 415–16; Herrmann and Foerster, "κλῆρος," 781–85.
[25] Newsom and Breed, *Daniel*, 369–71.

Jesus and the Early Church embraced—we now need to factor in what is arguably the most critical event that has taken place in history. Jesus, the Jewish Messiah, died, was buried, and was raised from the dead by God. The resurrection of Jesus was not like those select few who also experienced resurrection (e.g., 2 Kgs 13:21; Acts 20:9–10), for Jesus was raised to immortality.[26] Jesus was resurrected to a never-ending life. Paul describes the resurrection that Jesus experienced as one that resulted in him never being able to die again (Rom 6:9).[27] The resurrected Jesus can hold the office of high priest forever precisely because he continues forever, always living to make intercession (Heb 7:24–25).[28] Similarly, Jesus introduces himself to John of Patmos as one who has inherited immortality in Rev 1:18: "I was dead, and behold, I am alive forevermore."[29] The significance of the resurrection of Jesus unto eternal life should not be missed; the early Christians were effectively confessing that the resurrection of the dead, which was to occur on the last day, had already begun with the raising of Christ in the middle of history. The hope of new resurrection life, which was to usher in the age to come, was broken into history when Jesus awoke from the grave on Easter Sunday.[30]

Although there are several other reasons for us to consider (which we will discuss later in this volume), this pivotal event, which belonged to the end of the age breaking into the middle of history, prompted the Early Church to reorient its understanding of the two-age schema of God's history. Instead of the simple, linear view of the present age coming to an end, followed by the age to come, the earliest believers quickly adopted a modified view that understood the age to come breaking into the present in light of Christ's ministry, death, resurrection, and the gift of the Spirit. The present age still functioned as history continued to move along, and the age to come was still anticipated as the climactic moment when the resurrection of the dead would be fully consummated.[31] However, there was also a profound awareness that the powers of the age to come were already being experienced by the people of God in Christ (Heb 6:5).[32] The coming age had been inaugurated (1 Cor 10:11), but its complete consummation was still in the future.[33] Instead of the basic two-age schema, the Early Church adopted a theology of the overlap of the ages, and the resurrection of Jesus to eternal life was a primary reason for this significant shift.[34]

Let's observe how the resurrection of Jesus in the middle of history shifted how the Early Church understood its view of the age to come and the general resurrection of

---

[26] Brown, "Resurrection," 305.
[27] Jewett, *Romans*, 407; Dunn, *Romans 1–8*, 322; Wright, "The Letter to the Romans," 540.
[28] Craddock, "The Letter to the Hebrews," 92–93.
[29] Ladd, *The Revelation of John*, 34; Smalley, *Revelation*, 56.
[30] See the helpful charts in Dunn, *Theology of Paul*, 464–65.
[31] Fee, *God's Empowering Presence*, 803.
[32] Koester, *Hebrews*, 314.
[33] Fee, *The First Epistle to the Corinthians*, 506–7. Hays, *First Corinthians*, 162.
[34] Hagner, "Gospel, Kingdom, and Resurrection," 118; Dunn, *Theology of Paul*, 200.

the dead that was to act as the transition between the two ages. We have already examined 1 Corinthians 15:20 in our discussion of the sleep of the dead in Chapter 11, but it is essential to examine the context of this passage to gain a deeper understanding of why Paul regarded the resurrected Jesus as the "first fruits of those who sleep."

> But now Christ has been raised from the dead, the first fruits of those who are asleep. For since by a human being came death, by a human being also came the resurrection of the dead. For as in Adam all die, so also in Christ all will be made alive. But each in his own order: Christ the first fruits, after that those who are Christ's at his coming. (1 Cor 15:20–23)

If we follow the logic of Paul's argument in the wider discussion of the truthfulness of the future resurrection of the body, we can appreciate how he and other early Christian authors regarded the raising of Christ in relation to the shift in the two-age schema of God's history.[35] It is clear that the general resurrection of the dead is still regarded as a future event. The dead are still asleep (1 Cor 15:20), and they will be made alive at the second coming of Christ (1 Cor 15:23). However, in the person of Jesus, the resurrection of the dead has already begun. He is regarded as the first fruits—an agricultural image referring to the first sheaf of an ongoing harvest.[36] The resurrection of the dead, which was to bring the present age to an end and initiate the glorious age to come, has now extended backward into history, creating an overlap of the ages. Paul is well aware that death continues, having already mentioned that some of the eyewitnesses of the resurrected Christ have since fallen asleep in death (1 Cor 15:6). The present age, in which human beings are weak, frail, and mortal, continues to persist. However, the harvest of the sleeping dead being woken up in resurrection has already begun, as the resurrection of Jesus unto immortal life has clearly demonstrated.[37] Paul understood himself and the members of the Early Church as living between two pivotal events—the resurrection of Jesus Christ in the past and the firm conviction that all the dead will be raised in the future, on the last day.[38] Once we accept that early Christians understood that they were living in the overlap of the two ages, particularly in light of God raising Jesus from the dead, we may begin to make sense of the resurrection theology of the Early Church.

Another passage worth considering is Ephesians 1:20–21, in which the two ages are illustrated in relation to the resurrection and exaltation of Jesus by God himself:

> He raised him from the dead and seated him at His right hand in the heavenly places, far above all rule and authority and power and dominion, and every name that is named, not only in this age but also in the one to come. (Eph 1:20–21)

---

[35] Green, *Salvation*, 131.
[36] Dunn, *Theology of Paul*, 240.
[37] Fee, *The First Epistle to the Corinthians*, 829–30.
[38] Fee, *God's Empowering Presence*, 805.

As we may plainly observe, the two ages are described as one (the age to come) following the other (this age). However, God has raised Jesus from the dead in the middle of this present age, and in doing so, Christ has been enthroned at God's right hand. This highly exalted status that God has bestowed upon the crucified and risen Jesus grants him kingship over every other ruler, authority, power, and dominion.[39] In other words, the resurrection of the Jewish Messiah in the past has signaled an inauguration of his reign already in this present age, while the age to come is still something in the future.[40] Again, it is clear to see that the resurrection of the dead, which was to be the decisive event that transitions this age into the age to come, has already begun in and with the man Jesus Christ, and the results of that resurrection can already be experienced for those who are in Christ.

The Resurrection of Jesus and the Promised Resurrection of the Dead

Even the language that the Early Church used to illustrate God raising Jesus from the sleep of death indicates an awareness and belief that Christ has, in some sense, shifted the future resurrection of the dead into the present age. When the authors of the New Testament describe the triumphal act of God raising Jesus, the phrase employed is that he was raised *from the dead*. However, when discussing the future resurrection of the dead on the last day, the New Testament writers typically talk about the resurrection *of the dead* (Matt 22:31; Acts 17:32; 23:6; 24:21; 1 Cor 15:13; Heb 6:2). The key difference is that Christ is raised from the group of dead persons, namely, those who will be raised as a group on the last day. Paul carefully differentiates these two events with his precise use of language in 1 Corinthians 15:12: "Now if Christ is preached as raised from the dead, how do some among you say that there is no resurrection of the dead?"[41] Note how Paul's awareness of the future resurrection of the dead (which, admittedly, he needed to remind his readers) is something of which Jesus has already partaken. The Early Church, following the teachings of Jesus himself (Matt 17:9; Mark 9:9–10; Luke 24:46), invariably described what happened to him as having been raised "from the dead," that is, Jesus rose out of the group of dead people (Acts 3:15; Rom 1:4; Col 1:18; 1 Thes 1:10; 1 Pet 1:3). In fact, before Jesus called Paul to be an apostle, the early Christians were already preaching that the resurrection had broken into the present: "they were teaching the people and proclaiming in Jesus the resurrection from the dead" (Acts 4:2).[42] As readers seeking to understand the beliefs and convictions of the Early Church, we would do well not to

---

[39] Hoehner, *Ephesians*, 281–82.
[40] Fowl, *Ephesians*, 62. Lincoln, *Ephesians*, 65, offers a helpful summary: "It is true that the writer's emphasis on Christ's exaltation to heaven and its benefits for the Church indicates clearly that he believes the age to come has already been inaugurated."
[41] Fitzmyer, *First Corinthians*, 562; Thiselton, *First Epistle to the Corinthians*, 1216–17.
[42] Wright, *The Resurrection of the Son of God*, 452; Keener, *Acts*, 2:1131–32.

quickly read over this subtle distinction between the future resurrection of the dead and what God accomplished by raising Jesus out from among the group of dead persons.

At this point, there can be no denying that there is an essential connection between the past resurrection of Christ and the future resurrection of those who sleep in their graves. The two events are closely related, with each giving meaning and purpose to the other. It was due to a firmly established belief in the resurrection of the dead on the last day that convinced the Early Church to shift its understanding of the two-age schema of God's history when Christ was raised in the middle of the present age. Moreover, the realization that God had the power to rescue Jesus from death inspired hope that God can and will do it again on the last day. We have already observed that Paul's message of comfort to the Thessalonians grieving over those who have died was to remind them that just as God raised Jesus from the dead, they would have confidence that the dead will also be raised at the return of Christ (1 Thes 4:13–16).[43] When we examine the theology of the Early Church as it attempts to affirm the truth of the future day in which the dead will be raised from their graves, the fact that God has already demonstrated bodily resurrection is possible through Christ functions as the key motivator of inspiring hope.[44] In other words, if God raised Jesus, then believers can be absolutely confident that the coming resurrection of the dead will come to pass, just as Paul argues in Rom 8:11: "If the Spirit of Him who raised Jesus from the dead dwells in you, He who raised Christ from the dead will give life to your mortal bodies also through His Spirit that dwells in you."[45] Take, for example, these passages that look back at the resurrection of Jesus and use that event to build confidence in the promise that the dead will be raised on the last day:

> Now God has not only raised the Lord, but will also raise us up through His power. (1 Cor 6:14)

> knowing that He who raised the Lord Jesus will raise us also with Jesus and will present us with you. (2 Cor 4:14)

> For our citizenship is in heaven, from which also we eagerly wait for a Savior, the Lord Jesus Christ; who will transform the body of our humble state into conformity with the body of his glory, by the exertion of the power that he has even to subject all things to Himself. (Phil 3:20–21)

> It is a trustworthy statement: For if we died with him, we will also live with him (2 Tim 2:11)

We can imagine that this argument was necessary to convince Gentile converts to the Early Church about the truthfulness of the coming day in which the dead in Christ will

---

[43] Dunn, *Theology of Paul*, 300.
[44] Brown, "Resurrection," 303.
[45] Fitzmyer, *Romans*, 491; Keck, *Romans*, 204–5; Dunn, *Romans 1–8*, 432, 445;

be given new, immortal bodies, particularly because the concept of bodily resurrection was largely unknown outside of Judaism and the early Christian movement. Paul was so convinced that the resurrection of Jesus proved that the dead will be raised on the last day that he could argue from a negative stance that if one was not true, then the other would be negated in 1 Corinthians 15:16–17: "For if the dead are not raised, not even Christ has been raised; and if Christ has not been raised, your faith is worthless; you are still in your sins." Both events—the resurrection of Jesus in the past and the resurrection of the dead on the last day—stand or fall together.[46] Fortunately for the Early Church, the testimony of eyewitnesses to the resurrected Jesus not only offered assurance of what was promised to come but also motivated the evangelistic preaching of the resurrection hope for humanity, whose mortal state was in desperate need of rescue.

Conclusion

In concluding this chapter dedicated to the hope of resurrection, let's review what we have observed. First, we took stock of the texts that laid the groundwork for the conviction that the dead will be raised from the sleep of death on the last day. Then, we introduced the two-age schema of God's history and saw how the future resurrection of the dead functioned as the climactic event that was believed to transition the present age into the age to come. Having grasped the basic two-age framework, we then took note of how the Early Church's theology of the resurrection of Jesus in the middle of history necessitated a shift in the understanding of the ages, resulting in a modified overlapping of the ages. Finally, we perceived a connection between the resurrection of Jesus that broke into the present and the coming day in which all the dead will be woken up from their graves. The Early Church took advantage of the belief that God had already raised Jesus from the dead and used it to inspire hope in the promise of the future resurrection of the body, which is to take place on the last day. Since God has already proven that he can give immortality to the man Jesus, God can and will do it again by sending Jesus to give life to those who have died. For humanity in its mortal and weakened state, the resurrection offers much-needed hope, peace, and comfort.

Having discussed the immortality that the righteous will inherit at the return of Jesus, we now need to address an often overlooked but equally important topic. The wicked, according to Daniel 12:2, will be raised to disgrace and everlasting contempt. As the just judge, God must punish evil, holding them accountable for their wicked acts. If the fate of righteous human beings is to inherit the life of the age to come, what is to become of the wicked? Our next chapter will provide biblical answers to these questions, as they relate to the broader topic of anthropology.

---

[46] Hays, *First Corinthians*, 261.

13
THE ANNIHILATION OF THE WICKED

The topic that concerns the fate awaiting the wicked has been deliberately set as one of the final chapters in our study of the doctrine of anthropology. This study builds on the observations of biblical material presented in the previous chapters. For one, we noted that human beings are mortal persons, that is, living souls. We also observed that immortality is not an innate characteristic of humanity; rather, it is a gift given at the resurrection of the body when Jesus returns. Furthermore, we have seen evidence that the resurrection of the dead applies not only to the righteous but also to the wicked. So, if the wicked are to face judgment on the last day, and if the wicked are mortal, what fate awaits them? Some have argued that the wicked will suffer torment for all eternity. Others think that the wicked will be given a second chance to repent on the Day of Judgment. Still, some believe that the wicked will eventually be delivered unto salvation by a God who is so universally loving that he cannot bring himself to punish the unrighteous. There is also a view that the wicked will be completely cut off, destroyed, and brought to an end. This latter view, often called *annihilationism* in theological circles, will be demonstrated to best account for the biblical data, including the mortality of humanity and the just judgment of God.[1]

Our study of the fate of those deemed unrighteous and wicked, from an anthropological perspective, will be conducted through four major arguments. First, we will examine what the authors of the Old Testament have to say about what God will do with the wicked after they face judgment. Presumably, the position that the writers of the Old Testament take on this matter will be adopted by Jesus and his followers; therefore, our second task will be to see how the Early Church's theology contributes to the question surrounding the fate of the wicked. Third, we will explore the language and meaning of *Gehenna*, the fiery location of destruction that is popularly referred to as "hell" that will be revealed on the Day of Judgment. Lastly, we will discuss some New Testament passages that have traditionally led readers to, at face value, draw the conclusion that the wicked will be punished forever. This will give us an opportunity to present a fuller picture of the New Testament's portrayal of the judgment of the wicked. After addressing these four primary points, we can take a step back and reflect on the practical realities that the doctrine of anthropology sets before those deeply concerned with adopting the beliefs and theology of the Early Church.

---

[1] Grogan, "Conditional Immortality," 249–50.

The Fate of Destruction and Annihilation

In what may come as a surprise to some, the authors of the Old Testament frequently spoke about the fate of the wicked after facing the judgment of the only true God. We find several examples in the Psalms that provide insight into the punishment that awaits those who act unrighteously. Psalm 1 explicitly refers to the time of judgment that the wicked will face. In doing so, it contrasts what they can expect with the firmly planted righteous people: "The wicked are not so, but they are like chaff that the wind drives away" (Ps 1:4).[2] Comparing the wicked at the judgment to chaff suggests that they will be annihilated and made to exist no longer. The conclusion of the psalm confirms this by stating plainly that the way of the wicked will perish (Ps 1:6).[3] The ninth psalm offers a similar portrayal of the destruction of the wicked, which is the conclusion of Yahweh sitting for judgment. When the judge issues his verdict, the wicked are said to be "destroyed," the judge has blotted out their name "forever and ever," the enemy has come to an "end" in ruin, and even the memory of them has "perished" (Ps 9:4–6).[4] Instead of desiring to punish the evildoer forever, Yahweh plans to "cut off the memory of them from the earth" (Ps 34:16), suggesting complete destruction in death (Ps 34:21).[5]

Psalm 37 offers the contrasting fates of the righteous and the wicked in stark detail. Note carefully the language of finality and destruction used to portray the fate of the wicked:

> For they will wither quickly like the grass and fade like the green herb. (Ps 37:2)

> For evildoers will be cut off, but those who wait for Yahweh, they will inherit the land. Yet a little while and the wicked man will be no more; and you will look carefully for his place and he will not be there. (Ps 37:9–10)

> But the wicked will perish; and the enemies of Yahweh will be like the glory of the pastures, they vanish—like smoke they vanish away. (Ps 37:20)

> For those blessed by Him will inherit the land, but those cursed by Him will be cut off. (Ps 37:22)

> For Yahweh loves justice and does not forsake His godly ones; they are preserved forever, but the descendants of the wicked will be cut off. (Ps 37:28)

> When the wicked are cut off, you will see it. (Ps 37:34)

> Then he passed away, and lo, he was no more; I sought for him, but he could not be found. (Ps 37:36)

---

[2] McCann, "The Book of Psalms," 685.
[3] Mabie, "Destruction," 99–100; deClaissé-Walford et al., *Psalms*, 63.
[4] Otzen, "אָבַד," 22; Craigie, *Psalms 1–50*, 118.
[5] deClaissé-Walford et al., *Psalms*, 329; Craigie, *Psalms 1–50*, 281.

There is no suggestion or hint that the destiny of the wicked involves a long period of suffering. They are not offered a second chance at the judgment, nor are they eventually redeemed and counted among the righteous. The language and imagery are clear: the wicked will be annihilated, they will be no more, they will not be found, they will fade away and vanish.[6] Attempts at even finding the wicked after God has punished them will result in being unable to locate them, having been destroyed completely.[7]

The Old Testament poets illustrate the judgment of the wicked with several metaphors that signify the fate of destruction, perishing, and annihilation. Those who do evil are compared to a potter's vessel—earthenware that will be dashed "in pieces" (Ps 2:9). Yahweh declares that those who forget him will be torn apart, with no one to deliver them (Ps 50:22).[8] The wicked will be "blotted out of the book of life" (Ps 69:28), indicating that their fate will not be among the living.[9] Like a lamp whose light has been snuffed out, "the evil man has no future" (Prov 24:20).[10] When God arises for judgment, the wicked will be likened unto thorns that are cut down and consumed in the fire (Isa 33:10–12). The prophet Malachi's illustration of the evildoer's fate as burnt stubble is thorough: "For behold, the day is coming, burning like an oven, when all the arrogant and all evildoers will be stubble. The day that is coming shall set them ablaze, says Yahweh of hosts, so that it will leave them neither root nor branch" (Mal 4:1). The wicked will indeed burn in the judgment, but the result will be their consumption, leaving nothing left but ash.[11] The prophet goes on to describe how the righteous will tread down the wicked, being "ashes under the soles of your feet on the day that I am preparing" (Mal 4:3). By characterizing the fate of the wicked as becoming ashes under the feet of the righteous, Malachi indicates that those who do evil will be annihilated completely.[12] The collective imagery employed by these Old Testament poets suggests that the total elimination of the wicked will be the verdict issued on the Day of Judgment.

There are a few passages that often get pointed to as proof that the wicked are not annihilated at the judgment but are instead under a sort of perpetual suffering and punishment. One such passage occurs at the conclusion of Isaiah chapter sixty-six. In the new heavens and the new earth, humanity "shall go out and look on the dead bodies of the men who have rebelled against me. For their worm shall not die, their fire shall not be quenched, and they shall be an abhorrence to all flesh" (Isa 66:24). What should we make of these corpses that are to possess worms that will not die? What about the unquenchable fire? Helpful answers begin to emerge once we recall that the biblical

---

[6] McCann, "The Book of Psalms," 829; Craigie, *Psalms 1–50*, 297. deClaissé-Walford et al., *Psalms*, 353, helpfully summarize the fate of the wicked: "the wicked will simply *not exist*."
[7] Mabie, "Destruction," 99–100.
[8] deClaissé-Walford et al., *Psalms*, 452; Craigie, *Psalms 1–50*, 367.
[9] Hossfeld and Zenger, *Psalms 2*, 183.
[10] Murphy, *Proverbs*, 182–83; Treier, *Proverbs–Ecclesiastes*, 78–79.
[11] Smith, *Micah–Malachi*, 339; Brown, *Obadiah through Malachi*, 204; Prestidge, *Life, Death and Destiny*, 77
[12] Schuller, "The Book of Malachi," 872; Hill, *Malachi*, 354.

authors never described the soul as immortal, and we place this passage within its broader context. First, these dead bodies are the result of Yahweh coming in fire to execute judgment, and the outcome of this fiery judgment is that there will be many who are slain (Isa 66:15–16).[13] The slain are then further defined as those who will "come to an end altogether" (Isa 66:17). By describing the judged evildoers as slain, having come to an end, and as dead bodies, the prophet seems to be indicating their annihilation. As for the worms that will not die, these worms are often associated with decaying corpses (Job 17:14; 24:19–20; Isa 14:11), not living bodies.[14] The fire that will not be quenched is in reference to the overwhelming and complete destruction of these wicked persons, resulting in slain corpses. The imagery presented in Isaiah 66:24 is not that of ongoing, conscious punishment but of wicked persons who, having been burnt up in God's judgment, have come to their end.[15]

The other passage that is often paired with Isaiah 66:24 is one that should be deeply familiar to us by now: Daniel 12:2.[16] As we have plainly seen several times already, those who sleep in the dust of the earth will awaken to bodily resurrection, some to the life of the age to come, but "others to disgrace and everlasting contempt." Recalling our findings from Chapter Twelve, we observed that the resurrection life the righteous inherit is characterized by the English adjective "everlasting," behind which lies the Hebrew phrase literally rendered as "life of the age." Since this new age in which the dead are raised follows the present age, many writers of the New Testament took to identifying the second age as "the age to come" (e.g., Matt 12:32; Mark 10:30; Luke 18:30; Heb 6:5). The same Hebrew noun that literally means "age" also appears in the description of the wicked who are raised; they are raised to disgrace and the *contempt of the age*. If the resurrection to life is described as the life of the age to come, then it naturally follows that this "contempt" is also being modified by "the age to come." The righteous will be exalted, but the wicked will be humbled in shame. The resurrection that awaits the wicked will result in an unfavorable judgment that renders them disgraceful and full of abhorrent contempt by all those who witness the results of God's destruction, but this is plainly not a description of unceasing, eternal punishment of the wicked.[17] That concept is plainly not on the mind of the prophet.

---

[13] Paul, *Isaiah 40–66*, 632. Blenkinsopp, *Isaiah 56–66*, 313, describes the destruction in these verses as "annihilating judgment."
[14] Lawlor, "Worm," 902; Bacchiocchi, *Immortality or Resurrection?* 198.
[15] Fudge, *The Fire That Consumes*, 112. Maiberger, "פֶּגֶר," 480, interprets the verse as "the final destruction of God's enemies." Goldingay, *Isaiah 56–66*, 524, offers an alternative reading: "In the hyperbole of the description, the idea will not be that worm and fire are forever consuming the same corpses but that corpses for consuming will always be added to the pile."
[16] Goldingay, *Daniel*, 548, argues that the wording of Dan 12:2 is dependent on Isa 66:24.
[17] Bacchiocchi, *Immortality or Resurrection?* 199.

The Early Church's Belief in the Annihilation of the Wicked

As we examine the Early Church's beliefs about the fate of the wicked that awaited them at the final judgment, several clear descriptors emerge that point to a view of annihilationism. The writers of the New Testament employed such words as "perish," "destruction," "end," "corruption," and "death" to illustrate the fate of the wicked, and all of these terms favor a theology in which those who commit evil will be destroyed entirely, rather than suffering forever, being given a second chance, or being universally redeemed.[18] Consider the following passages that describe the judgment of the wicked in terms of being destroyed or having perished:

> "Enter through the narrow gate; for the gate is wide and the way is broad that leads to destruction, and there are many who enter through it." (Matt 7:13)
>
> "What will the owner of the vineyard do? He will come and destroy the vine-growers, and will give the vineyard to others." (Mark 12:9)
>
> "Unless you repent, you will all likewise perish." (Luke 13:3, 5)
>
> "For God so loved the world, that he gave his only Son, that whoever believes in him should not perish but have eternal life." (John 3:16)
>
> in no way alarmed by your opponents—which is a sign of destruction for them, but of salvation for you, and that too, from God. (Phil 1:28)
>
> For many walk, of whom I often told you, and now tell you even weeping, that they are enemies of the cross of Christ, whose end is destruction (Phil 3:18–19)
>
> For the sun rises with a scorching wind and withers the grass; and its flower falls off and the beauty of its appearance is destroyed; so too the rich man in the midst of his pursuits will fade away. (James 1:11)
>
> But by the same word the heavens and earth that now exist are stored up for fire, being kept until the day of judgment and destruction of the ungodly. (2 Pet 3:7)
>
> Now I desire to remind you, though you know all things once for all, that the Lord, after saving a people out of the land of Egypt, subsequently destroyed those who did not believe. (Jude 1:5)
>
> The beast that you saw was, and is not, and is about to come up out of the abyss and go to destruction. (Rev 17:8)

What is thought-provoking to note in several of these passages is the nature of the two options presented to the readers of the New Testament. The followers of Jesus must choose between the narrow gate (that leads to life) and the wide gate leading to

---

[18] Hahn et al., "Destroy," 462–70.

destruction.[19] Those who believe in God's unique son have everlasting life, but those who choose not to will perish. Paul encourages the Philippians by saying that God will give them salvation while giving destruction to their opponents. This is the theology of the Early Church, which believed that those who truly followed Christ would find life while those who chose otherwise would be destroyed.

The early Christians employed several additional metaphors to describe the fate of the wicked, each signaling their complete annihilation and destruction. Those who do not bear good fruit are likened to trees that will be cut down, thrown into the fire, to be completely burnt up (Matt 3:10, 12; 7:19).[20] The wicked will be scattered "like dust" (Matt 21:44), burnt up "tares" (Matt 13:40), and dried up "branches" that are cast into the fire and burnt (John 15:6). Rather than being put in charge of the master's possessions, the evil slave will be "cut into pieces" (Matt 24:51).[21] Instead of reaping eternal life, those who "sow to the flesh" will reap "corruption," according to Galatians 6:8.[22] Like those who perished in the flood during the time of Noah and the ark, so too will the wicked be destroyed on the day that the Son of Man is revealed (Luke 17:27). As in the days of Lot when fire and brimstone rained down from heaven on Sodom, so too will the wicked be destroyed at the revealing of the Son of Man (Luke 17:28–29). This imagery points to the annihilation of the wicked and their complete ruin.

Destruction in *Gehenna*

Within the teachings of Jesus, we find mention of the location where the wicked will be annihilated on the Day of Judgment.[23] This location is known in Latin as *Gehenna* and in Greek as *geenna*, although it is typically rendered in modern English translations as *hell*. As we will recall, "hell" is something quite different from Hades, the Greek word for the grave and the equivalent of the Hebrew noun Sheol.[24] Hell, on the other hand, seems to be the fiery pit that sporadically appears in the teachings of the Early Church.

Several times in the teachings of Jesus, hell is illustrated clearly as the destination of all who have been judged as wicked on the Day of Judgment. Drawing on the familiar imagery associated with the Valley of Hinnom (e.g., 2 Kgs 23:10; Jer 7:31–32; 19:6), Christ used the threat of being tossed into *Gehenna* at the time of judgment as a motivator for his followers to live righteously and obediently:

---

[19] Nolland, *Matthew*, 333; Luz, *Matthew 1–7*, 372; Davies and Allison, *Matthew*, 1:697.
[20] Davies and Allison, *Matthew*, 1:319; Luz, *Matthew 1–7*, 139.
[21] Nolland, *Matthew*, 1000.
[22] Harder, "φθείρω κτλ," 104. Longenecker, *Galatians*, 281, concludes that "'destruction' is their final end."
[23] Jeremias, "γέεννα," 658, rightly observes, "In the NT there is no description of the torments of hell."
[24] Watson, "Gehenna," 927.

"and whoever says, 'You fool,' shall be guilty enough to go into the fiery hell." (Matt 5:22)

"If your right eye makes you stumble, tear it out and throw it from you; for it is better for you to lose one of the parts of your body, than for your whole body to be thrown into hell. If your right hand makes you stumble, cut it off and throw it from you; for it is better for you to lose one of the parts of your body, than for your whole body to go into hell. (Matt 5:29–30)

"You serpents, you brood of vipers, how will you escape the sentence of hell?" (Matt 23:33)

"If your foot causes you to stumble, cut it off; it is better for you to enter life lame, than, having your two feet, to be cast into hell" (Mark 9:45)

"But I will warn you whom to fear: fear the One who, after He has killed, has authority to cast into hell; yes, I tell you, fear Him!" (Luke 12:5)

We can be certain that this imagery of *Gehenna* collaborates with the Early Church's teaching that the wicked will be annihilated entirely, based on several strands of evidence. First, Jesus states in Matthew 10:28 that hell is the location where those who are thrown will be *destroyed* by God, suggesting complete destruction.[25] Second, similar images of this fiery judgment of the wicked regularly feature language of destruction. When the Messiah comes to judge, the unrighteous will be "burnt up" like chaff, completely consumed (Matt 3:12; Luke 3:17). At the end of the age, the sons of the evil one are rounded up and burnt up with fire (Matt 13:40). Jesus paralleled the day in which he will be revealed to bring judgment with the fire and brimstone that destroyed the wicked in Sodom (Luke 17:29–30). Third, the coming judgment is regularly illustrated in terms of a raging fire that completely burns the wicked. The Epistle to the Hebrews offers a dire warning to those believers to continue to sin: "For if we go on sinning willfully after receiving the knowledge of the truth, there no longer remains a sacrifice for sins, but a terrifying expectation of judgment and the fury of fire which will consume the adversaries" (Heb 10:26-27).[26] In other words, the fires of judgment have the capacity to consume, which reinforces the view of the annihilation of the wicked. Second Peter 3:7 describes the Day of Judgment as the time when fire will be employed in the "destruction of ungodly men." When we put all this evidence together, it suggests that the *Gehenna* of fire, also known as the fiery hell, is an illustration of the fate of the wicked, namely, those who will be permanently destroyed and annihilated at the end of the age.[27]

---

[25] Luz, *Matthew 8–20*, 101, draws a similar conclusion: "The punishment for the wicked consists in their complete destruction, body and soul." Watson, "Gehenna," 927, observes, "The NT does not describe the torment of Gehenna or portray Satan as the lord of Gehenna. These are later literary accouterments."
[26] Bruce, *Hebrews*, 258–59; Craddock, "The Letter to the Hebrews," 122–23.
[27] Although the Book of Revelation does not use the language of *Gehenna*, it portrays this place of fiery annihilation as the lake of fire (Rev 19:20, 20:10, 14, 15; 21:8). John of Patmos twice clarifies the meaning of the lake of fire imagery as "the second death" (Rev 20:14; 21:8).

Eternal Torment?

Although the Early Church provided several other texts that plainly speak of the complete destruction of the wicked (Rom 1:32; 1 Cor 3:17; 1 Thes 5:3; 2 Pet 2:12; Jude 1:7; Rev 11:18), a few isolated passages may give the impression that the punishment issued on the Day of Judgment consists of unceasing torment which is to endure for all eternity. It will be prudent for our current study to consider these passages and attempt to make sense of what the early Christian authors meant by them. The first passage to consider is Matthew 25:46, which is set in Jesus' discussion of the Day of Judgment that is to take place when he returns and sits on his glorious throne (Matt 25:31–34). The passage in question reads, "These will go away into eternal punishment, but the righteous into eternal life." It is sometimes argued that the wicked are illustrated here as suffering eternally, but that is not precisely what the passage is conveying. For one, this is speaking of a "punishment" (noun), not the act of ongoing "punishing" (verb).[28] Another point to consider is the meaning of the adjective "eternal," especially since it relates to both the punishment and the life into which the righteous enter. As we noted in our discussions of Daniel 12:2, the righteous are raised to everlasting life, which refers to the life *of the age to come*. The Greek adjective *aionios*, which translates into English as "everlasting" or "eternal," often refers to a perpetual period of time, but it also describes, as it does in Matthew 25:46, the concluding outcome of an event.[29] In the case of "everlasting punishment," the punishment issued forth by the judge on the Day of Judgment will have its conclusion that is everlasting. In other words, the fire into which the wicked will be thrown (Matt 25:41), which Matthew elsewhere has clearly indicated is to result in one's annihilation (Matt 3:12; 13:40),[30] will produce an outcome of complete destruction that is to last eternally, that is, throughout the age to come.[31]

A similar conclusion should be drawn from Paul's description of the return of Jesus to bring forth judgment upon those who reject the gospel:

> Jesus will be revealed from heaven with his mighty angels in flaming fire, dealing out retribution to those who do not know God and to those who do not obey the gospel of our Lord Jesus. These will pay the penalty of eternal destruction, away from the presence

---

[28] Bauer et al., *Greek-English Lexicon*, 555.
[29] Richardson, *Theology of the New Testament*, 74; Fudge, *The Fire That Consumes*, 195. France, *Matthew*, 966–67, is helpful here: "'Eternal punishment,' so understood, is punishment which relates to the age to come rather than punishment which continues forever."
[30] Nolland, *Matthew*, 1034.
[31] Ladd, *The Presence of the Future*, 150. Richardson, *Theology of the New Testament*, 74, observes, "The real issue concerns the character of the punishment as that of the order of the Age to Come as contrasted with any earthly penalties." Similarly, France, *Matthew*, 967, acknowledges that annihilationism "does more justice to Matthew's language in general ... 'eternal punishment' here will not be 'punishment which does on forever but 'punishment which has eternal consequences,' the loss of eternal life through being destroyed by fire."

of the Lord and from the glory of his power, when he comes to be glorified in his saints on that day (2 Thes 1:7–10).

The passage shares several similarities with the events leading up to Matthew 25:46, particularly the return of Jesus, the judgment of the wicked, the punishment of fire, and the destruction that is "eternal." Since the noun "destruction" refers to the means by which someone or something is destroyed,[32] it is unlikely that Paul intended that the act of destroying the wicked would take place eternally.[33] It is more likely that "eternal" illustrates the *completed results* of the destruction of the wicked; the conclusion of the destruction will last eternally, that is, throughout the age to come that Jesus will usher in at his return.[34]

There are two passages in the Book of Revelation that, at face value, suggest that the wicked will suffer the punishment of being tormented forever and ever (Rev 14:11; 20:10). However, Revelation illustrates its message with *symbols and images*, so interpreting these images at face value often overlooks the intended meanings being signaled to the readers.[35] Since the two texts are similar, it seems appropriate to address both of them at the same time:

> Then another angel, a third one, followed them, saying with a loud voice, "If anyone worships the beast and his image, and receives a mark on his forehead or on his hand, he also will drink of the wine of the wrath of God, which is mixed in full strength in the cup of His anger; and he will be tormented with fire and brimstone in the presence of the holy angels and in the presence of the Lamb. And the smoke of their torment goes up forever and ever; they have no rest day and night, those who worship the beast and his image, and whoever receives the mark of his name." (Rev 14:9–11)

> And the devil who deceived them was thrown into the lake of fire and brimstone, where the beast and the false prophet are also; and they will be tormented day and night forever and ever. (Rev 20:10)

These two passages speak of a punishment that involves, in some sense, being tormented. The imagery is powerful and far-reaching, referring to suffering that will take place "day and night," "forever and ever." On the surface, this appears to refer to the eternal conscious torment of the wicked, that is, until we observe the imagery that Revelation is borrowing from the prophet Isaiah. The Book of Revelation frequently draws from a pool of symbols and images, with the Old Testament serving as the primary source of

---

[32] Bauer et al., *Greek-English Lexicon*, 702.
[33] Best, *First and Second Epistles to the Thessalonians*, 263, argues persuasively that "The sense 'everlasting, of infinite duration' is to be rejected but the meaning 'characteristic of the age to come' may well be present."
[34] Bacchiocchi, *Immortality or Resurrection?* 231; Fudge, *The Fire That Consumes*, 246. Boring, *I & II Thessalonians*, 254, similarly concludes that "Unbelievers are not actively punished . . . The returning Lord is not portrayed as inflicting fiery torment on unbelievers. Though the judgment is severe, the fire is the theophanic and fiery presence of God, not the hellfire of punishment."
[35] Gorman, *Reading Revelation Responsibly*, 69.

inspiration for John of Patmos. In the case of Revelation 14:11 and 20:10, these images draw upon the prophetic judgment oracle against the nation of Edom, recorded in Isaiah 34:9–10:

> "Its streams will be turned into pitch, and its loose earth into brimstone, and its land will become burning pitch. It will not be quenched night or day; its smoke will go up forever. From generation to generation it will be desolate; none will pass through it forever and ever." (Isa 34:9–10)

The land of Edom, which suffered a devastating defeat in the fifth century BC, is characterized in Isaiah's prophetic imagery as burning day and night, with smoke perpetually rising.[36] The language employed by Isaiah is surely hyperbolic, intending to convey the complete defeat of the Edomites and their removal from their land, but the language of the ongoing burning and never-ending smoke should not be pressed beyond the bounds of its poetic exaggeration.[37] For one, the burning and smoke did, in fact, cease, as can be verified this very day. It is this imagery of the sure defeat of Edom, together with its overemphasis on continual burning and smoke that ascends forever, that Revelation draws upon in both Revelation 14:11 and 20:10.[38] In Revelation 14:11, the function of the borrowed imagery from Isaiah aimed to both dissuade the readers of Revelation from compromising with idolatrous worship practices and to encourage the faithful commitment to God and the Lamb.[39] The scene of judgment that occurs in Revelation 20:10 similarly ascribes the hyperbolic images of Edom's demise to the torment of the Devil, the beast, and the false prophet. If this fate, though exaggerated within the poetic license of Revelation's image-filled portrayals, awaits these evil figures, it would have significant implications for early Christian readers.[40] Those who have compromised their faith by allying with these guilty parties would be motivated to immediately break ties and commit themselves fully to the true God and the Lamb.[41] One final point that should not be overlooked is the way that John of Patmos defines for his readers the meaning of the lake of fire, describing it in Revelation 20:14 and 21:8 as "the second death." In other words, the lake of fire is a metaphor for dying a second time, not living under endless torment.[42] In short, if the imagery of Edom's demise cannot be taken literally, since the fire and smoke did come to an end, we would not expect the

---

[36] Watts, *Isaiah 34–66*, 10.
[37] Fudge, *The Fire that Consumes*, 298; Roberts, *First Isaiah*, 436.
[38] Bauckham, *The Climax of Prophecy*, 317–18.
[39] Smith, *Paradoxical Conquering*, 150; Koester, *Revelation*, 622. Blount, *Revelation*, 276, argues that "This language was not meant to be taken literally . . . His language is rhetorical, not literal."
[40] Bowles, "Does Revelation 14:11 Teach Eternal Torment?" 30.
[41] Blount, *Revelation*, 371–72; Paul, *Revelation*, 331.
[42] Carter, *What Does Revelation Reveal?* 115, remarks, "For those who have not lived accordingly, their fate is 'the lake of fire,' not an eternal torture chamber but a place of destruction (20:15)."

reapplication of that imagery to be intended to be read literally as unceasing, eternal torment.[43]

Conclusion

There is more to the topic of the annihilation of the wicked that we must set aside until we discuss eschatology, especially the Early Church's understanding of the second coming, the events surrounding the Day of Judgment, and the timing of the destruction. For now, we can conclude what the chapter set out to accomplish, which is to discern the fate of the wicked that is to be issued by the judge on the last day. First, we examined how the writers of the Old Testament anticipated that the wicked would be annihilated in judgment, that is, they would cease living. Second, we looked at the beliefs and theology of the Early Church, including the teachings of Jesus himself, and observed that there was continuity with the portrayal of the destruction of the wicked, which was extensively characterized by the authors of the Old Testament. In several passages, the plain and unambiguous meaning of the New Testament texts repeatedly depicts the wicked suffering *complete destruction*. We saw no evidence that the Early Church held out hope that the unrighteous would be offered a second chance at repentance on the Day of Judgment. Nor did we see any way to reconcile the admirable hope that God would universally redeem all humanity, including the wicked, with the constant illustrations of their complete and utter annihilation. Third, we looked closely at the language of hell (i.e., *Gehenna*) that illustrated the location where the wicked will be wholly annihilated when Christ returns to judge the living and the dead. Finally, we clarified some confusion with passages that appear to some readers as offering a contrary position to the dominant theology of annihilation of the wicked, as advocated by Jesus and the Early Church. Since the immortality of the soul is not a biblical teaching and immortality is conditioned upon a resurrection unto the life of the age to come, it is difficult to posit a theory that the wicked could physically endure unending torment. Will the wicked suffer on the day of fiery judgment? Yes. Will the suffering last forever, with no end in sight? No, it will come to an end, resulting in the destruction and complete annihilation of those who reject God and his son, Jesus Christ.

Having trekked through this long journey of humanity, its mortality, and the hope of resurrection unto new life, it is essential to take this opportunity to pause and reflect on how the topic of anthropology should motivate practical living and good, godly works. It is this necessary task that we will turn our attention to in our next chapter.

---

[43] Caird, *Revelation*, 186; Paul, *Revelation*, 250, 331; Smalley, *Revelation* , 368; 515.

14
APPLYING ANTHROPOLOGY TODAY

Our study of the image of God, its meaning, and its purpose naturally raises the question of who precisely this God is whom we are imaging in creation. To be a faithful image bearer, in other words, requires a correct understanding of the one in whose image we were made. This is precisely the language of Colossians 3:10, which describes how believers have clothed themselves with the new man that is being renewed in the true knowledge according to the image of the one who created him. Since one of the key functions of human image bearers is to direct worship back to the Creator, those who faithfully carry out this vocation will possess the knowledge of who God is, namely, the one person who created them. In fact, mirroring a misguided or mistaken understanding of the Creator to his creation results in a failure to serve as his image-bearer at the most fundamental level. The Early Church was unified on many issues. There was also some tolerance for differing opinions on a few select matters. The identity of God himself was not open for debate. All early Christians within the first century AD, based on all available evidence, understood the God of Jesus to be one single person, the Father alone. Getting this fact correct was profoundly important, as God's original mandate to human beings included the summons to be fruitful, multiply, and fill the earth (Gen 1:28). If human image bearers are multiplying and procreating, then they are producing more image-bearing human beings, those who are also purposed to reflect and mirror their Creator to the world. Since the tarnished image of God is being restored in Christ, it naturally follows that the mission of the Church would include discipling and teaching others to fulfill their image-bearing functions, including the need to know who the Creator God is. This God in whose image we are made is not Jesus, for Jesus is the second Adam in whom humanity is being restored so that we can carry out our image-bearing functions. The one who created us is just that, one person. The Creator is not two or three persons. He is only one person, the Father alone. Even sincere attempts at mirroring a God who is not revealed in Scripture are doomed to fail, no matter what the post-biblical creeds have to say on the matter. Therefore, let us, in our desire to live as faithful image-bearing human beings, strive to know our Creator better, including who he is and the nature of his will, which he intended to perform through us. As we pray, "May your will be done," let us be intentional about our desire to obediently serve as images reflecting the only true God's truths, standards, love, and forgiveness. As we aim to be the people God has called us to be, let us take care to share with others the correct knowledge and understanding of his identity.

Another application that we can take away from this section on Anthropology is drawn directly from Paul's exhortation presented in 1 Thessalonians 4:18. Although God has demonstrated that he can raise the dead unto eternal life, the loss of loved ones continues to bring sorrow, pain, sadness, and feelings of loss. In the big picture of God's redemptive plan for faithful humanity, death only lasts for a short period of unconscious sleep in the grave. One day, Christ will return, raise all who are in the tombs, and grant immortality to the righteous (John 5:28–29). Paul's encouragement to the church in Thessalonica, which had several within its community die due, at least in part, to persecution, was to comfort one another with the words of promise. These promising words included the truth that those who died are not in some disadvantageous position. In fact, the dead in Christ will rise first compared to those who are alive at the second coming. Those who lived lives honoring God, obeying his standards, and remaining faithful to him can be confident that they will be with Jesus precisely when he returns to earth (1 Thes 4:16–17). Resurrection from the grave is God's answer to death, and we are urged to comfort one another with this truth. However, some feel the need to offer a different narrative in order to encourage those grieving the death of a loved one. Those who are unaware of the power of resurrection and God's promise to send Jesus back to raise the dead from their graves and to put the enemy of death itself under his feet attempt, sincerely, to suggest a different form of comfort. In order to ease the pain of those grieving the deceased, some have taken the approach of confidently claiming, "They are in a better place," "they are in the arms of Jesus right now," "they are looking down on us from heaven." Although these attempts at offering words of healing and consolation are given in sincerity, they are not the words of comfort with which Paul desired his churches to share. Moreover, they are not the words of truth that Jesus taught the Early Church. Let us, therefore, embrace the victory that Christ achieved from the grave when God raised him unto immortality, sharing this hope of resurrection with others. Let us provide a message of hope, drawn from the teachings of Jesus and the encouragement of Paul, that when death is finally defeated at the second coming, there will be no more mourning, crying, or pain (Rev 21:4). The faithful will one day be with the Lord Jesus Christ, and Paul was clear that the process by which we are united to his presence is not by dying and going to heaven, but rather by Jesus descending from heaven, raising the dead, and granting immortality. It is a matter of timing and location. We do not go to heaven at the moment of our death in some form of disembodied existence. Instead, Jesus comes to us at the resurrection. This is why the Early Church longed and prayed for Jesus' return, as it would reunite believers with the righteous dead. It is very important that we seek to provide words of comfort to those who grieve the unfortunate loss of someone they know, but it is equally crucial that we offer the correct message of comfort—a message of hope and truth. By encouraging others with the promise of Christ's return to raise the dead, we can build up those who are momentarily weak and, in the process, serve as a Christlike example to them.

Our third application concerns the problem of evil and God's promise to put all enemies under the feet of Christ at his second coming. One of the things that the internet, smartphones, and social media have made Christians aware of is just how truly evil some human beings actually are. Heinous acts, deeds of terrorism, murders, assassinations, and death threats have become relatively common, whereas these were perceived to be extremely rare a few decades ago. In several countries of the world, it is illegal to be a Christian. Many followers of Christ have experienced persecution, some more than others. Believing the truths that Jesus taught about who God is, about the humanity of the Messiah, about what happens when you die, and about the second coming can cost a Christian his or her job. Being disfellowshipped and labeled as a heretic might not result in being physically injured, but it is certainly painful on an emotional level. There can be no question that sin has led to the formation of evil persons, and the faithful followers of Jesus Christ are often on the receiving end of evil and wicked acts. Our findings in Chapter 13 revealed that the wicked will have to answer for their ungodly behavior. The wicked will stand in judgment and face the consequences of their actions. It does not matter if those who committed evil have already died; God has proven that he can (and will) raise the dead. Evil doers will rise in the resurrection and be forced to stand in the presence of the judge. Judgment will be impartial, and all will be repaid according to their works. The assurance that God provides his faithful people that the wicked will one day be called to account to answer for their ungodly actions serves as a means of comfort. For one, followers of Christ can have confidence that their suffering is not going unnoticed by God and his Messiah, Jesus. Rescue and intervention in the present may or may not occur, but what is certain is that the Day of Judgment has been set by Yahweh himself. Furthermore, we can trust that, although the wicked often go unpunished in the present age, God will ensure that evil deeds will be called to account. In light of these promises, let us respond appropriately. Put off attempts at dwelling on those who are wicked. Trust that God is faithful to his promises, including his promises to vindicate the righteous and repay the wicked for their deeds. The return of Christ will usher in the new creation on a worldwide scale, and there is no room in God's new world for wickedness, evil, sin, and the ensuing death. The righteous will suffer no longer, the innocent will be murdered no more, and tragedies will be completely a thing of the past. This is good news. This is gospel-worthy news. Let us, therefore, build one another up with these promises, encouraging those who are undergoing persecution with God's assurance that the wicked will be completely and utterly annihilated on the Day of Judgment. God will take care of evil, and the resurrection of Jesus serves as a notice to all creation that change is coming. The humble will be exalted to inherit the kingdom of God, but the unrepentant will certainly be repaid for their evil deeds, resulting in their destruction into nonexistence.

PART THREE: HAMARTIOLOGY

15
HUMANITY'S SIN AND GOD'S SOLUTION

Hamartiology is the study of sin, and at the risk of alienating our readers, this doctrine is historically the least favorite among students of the Bible. There is often a gloomy and depressing feeling that accompanies the close study of sin and its effects on creation. Every book in the canon of Scripture acknowledges, in some way or another, the reality of sin. The Early Church, conscious of the victory over sin and death that Jesus Christ accomplished upon rising from the grave, celebrated its shared experience of freedom from the clutches of sin's dominion. Paul frames the Christian life in terms of having "peace with God through our Lord Jesus Christ . . . we exult in the hope of the glory of God" (Rom 5:1–2). The peace that God offers heals the broken bond between Creator and creature that is caused by sinful rebellion.

This chapter will cover the origin story of humanity's disobedience to God, as it is portrayed in the opening twelve chapters of Genesis. Although human beings are made in the image of God and set in charge of God's creation, they fail to continue along that path and suffer the consequences of their unfaithful, sinful choice. After examining the effects of humanity's rebellion, we will look at how Genesis chapters 4–11 repeatedly illustrate just how sinful human beings have become. This primeval history encompasses the exile of humanity from Paradise, culminating in the punishment of pride and dispersion in the Tower of Babel story. Then we will look closely at the way in which God prepares to deal with the curse of sinful humanity by calling a member of humanity, Abraham, to be the means through whom God's redemption will be made known. These themes will set the tone for the upcoming stories about the growth of Abraham's family, the establishment of the Mosaic covenant at Mount Sinai, and the new covenant that was ratified in the blood of the man Jesus Christ.

The Failing of God's Image-Bearing Humans

In the beginning, God created the heavens and the earth. This summary statement is unpacked by the events that follow (Gen 1:2–2:4), with each day during the seven-day illustration of creation being given the stamp of approval: "and God saw that it was good." After the formation of human beings and their installation as image-bearing rulers, the Creator's work is deemed to be very good (Gen 1:31). As we observed in Chapter 8, the role of the image-bearer consisted in sharing in the God-given prerogatives of creating life ("be fruitful, multiply, fill the earth") and rulership ("subdue it and rule"). These responsibilities are further clarified when God took the man and placed him in the Garden of Eden, "to cultivate it and keep it" (Gen 2:15).[1] Adam was tasked with working and tilling *Paradise* (which is derived from the Greek word for "garden")[2] in addition to "keeping" it—a verb that contains nuances of guarding. Adam had dominion over all of the animals, birds, and fish, and God even shared his prerogative of naming the various created things (Gen 1:5, 8, 10) with the image-bearing human king, who in turn named all the creatures under his oversight (Gen 2:19–20). Adam even gave her the name "Woman" after she was taken from his side. The picture we see in the opening two chapters of the Book of Genesis is that image-bearing humanity is set in charge of the Paradise of Eden and all that is in it. Human beings were to rule, cultivate, and guard God's good creation. As God's vicegerents, humanity was to reflect God's reign by listening to God, that is, by obeying what God says. By heeding the Creator's instructions to take care of the Paradise over which human beings had dominion, they would carry out their purpose as kings and queens.[3] Paradise served as a testing ground for God's special image-bearers to prove themselves faithful.

The well-known events that transpired in Genesis chapter three have led many to describe the outcomes as "the Fall of Man," with some interpreters going as far as to say we now live in a "fallen world." While these phrases may be theologically accurate, we can get to the heart of the matter when we frame the story in terms of humanity's disobedience, failure, and loss. The Greek verb "to sin" (*hamartano*), from which we derive the word for the study of sin, hamartiology, was used widely to describe incidents where the subject missed the mark, either intentionally or unintentionally.[4] Homer used the verb in *The Iliad* to illustrate a thrown spear missing the intended target.[5] Plato's writings indicate that this verb refers to making mistakes, even unintentional ones.[6] Similarly, Aristotle used the term to illustrate the errors of human ways, which are numerous (and often evil).[7]

In what ways, then, did Adam and Eve miss the mark, make a mistake, and err? The interaction with the serpent yields some important answers to this question. The narrator describes the serpent as one of the living creatures that Yahweh had made (Gen 3:1), meaning it was supposed to be included in the group of living creatures over which image-bearing humans were to exercise rule and dominion according to Genesis 1:28. Instead of ruling over the serpent and bringing it into order, God's

---

[1] Brown, *The Ethos of the Cosmos*, 140; Fretheim, "The Book of Genesis," 351. For an important discussion of the priestly role of Adam within Eden, see Beale and Kim, *God Dwells Among Us*, 6–15.
[2] Wallace, "Eden," 282.
[3] Merrill, "Image of God," 443.
[4] Montanari et al., *The Brill Dictionary of Ancient Greek*, 102–3.
[5] Homer, *The Iliad*, 5.287; 10.372; 16.336.
[6] Plato, *Republic*, 334c, 336e.
[7] Aristotle, *Nicomachean Ethics*, 2.6.

viceregents listened to the serpent, which resulted in chaos. By setting aside what the Creator had explicitly said about the forbidden tree, both Adam and Eve committed acts of disobedience, thereby failing to reflect God's just rule as his image-bearers. Instead of listening to and obeying the Creator, humanity chose to listen to the creature instead—the creature that was supposed to be under their authority and dominion.[8] In order to impress the significance of this point, it is crucial to look closely at God's command and the changes to the wording that took place in the dialogue between the serpent and Adam's wife. Yahweh's stipulations were as follows:

> "From any tree of the garden you may eat freely; but from the tree of the knowledge of good and evil you shall not eat, for in the day that you eat from it you will surely die." (Gen 2:16–17)

If we compare the statements of God to the exchange between the serpent and Eve, we can note three significant changes that further illustrate humanity's disobedience.[9] First, Eve tells the serpent simply that from the fruit of the trees of the garden "we may eat" (Gen 3:2), although God had said, "you may eat *freely*." Eve minimizes the goodness of God's privileges to his image-bearing rulers. Second, Eve states that "you will die" (Gen 3:3), which diminishes how God said that he would judge when he declared "you will *surely* die." Third, the woman alters the nature of God's prohibition, "God has said, 'You shall not eat from it *or touch it*'" (Gen 3:3), when, in fact, God clearly stated, "you shall not eat." It is unlikely that these three changes were accidental on the part of Eve or that they were mere paraphrases, as each of the alterations is significant. The woman failed in her mandate as faithful image-bearer, and her husband Adam, who was right there "with her" when she ate (Gen 3:6), is also guilty of setting aside his God-given vocation.

Returning to the question of how humanity missed the mark, made mistakes, and erred, the opening chapters of Genesis paint a picture that can be summarized into three answers. First, Adam and Eve failed to live up to their vocation as image-bearing rulers who were to subdue and have dominion over the serpent. Second, humanity disobeyed God's clear and direct command not to eat of the forbidden tree, choosing instead to listen to the crafty serpent. Lastly, the stipulations that the Creator gave to humanity were altered in meaningful ways that almost certainly contributed to the choice to act unfaithfully. Did Adam and Eve sin? Most certainly. They sinned by failing to serve in their role as image-bearing viceregents who were tasked with maintaining order over God's creation, by acting contrary to his commands, and by distorting those commands.

---

[8] Cotter, *Genesis*, 34, draws attention to the pun in Hebrew between humanity's nakedness (*"arummim"*) that is mentioned in Gen 2:25 and the description of the serpent as "crafty" (*"arum"*) in the following verse. By seeking the crafty words of the serpent, humanity came to the realization that they were naked (Gen 3:7).
[9] Beale, *A New Testament Biblical Theology*, 33.

The way that the author of Genesis presents Yahweh as punishing these acts of unfaithfulness offers clarity to the nature of their sinful effects. When we examine Genesis 3:14–19, we can observe that the serpent, the woman, the man, and the ground itself are cursed. Beginning with the serpent's punishment, God declares that it is cursed more than all the cattle and the beasts of the field and that this curse includes enmity placed between the serpent's offspring and the woman's offspring (Gen 3:14–15). Although the narrator of Genesis tells us very little about the serpent's identity, it is clear that Yahweh regards the serpent as morally responsible, cursing the serpent precisely because it deceived the woman (Gen 3:13–14).[10] The woman is cursed with increased anguish in childbirth (Gen 3:16),[11] which, importantly, does not take away her role as an image-bearer.[12] The woman is named "Eve" (which in Hebrew means "life"), and as the mother of all the living (Gen 3:20), Eve will continue to be fruitful, multiply, and fill the earth. Adam's punishment and what became of the ground are intertwined, for God told the man, "Cursed is the ground because of you" (Gen 3:17). Instead of producing the sort of lush vegetation present in the Paradise of Eden, the cursed ground will now yield thorns and thistles. Adam will continue to work the ground, in toil and with sweat on his face, and the conclusion of Adam's life is also connected to the ground, as we observed in Chapters 9 and 10. Adam's life will expire, and he will return to the dust, as we have observed in Genesis 3:19. Readers of Genesis throughout history can attest that these punishments persist, even to our present day. Snakes continue to attack human beings, the act of giving birth is still very difficult, human life is full of hard work and sweat, coming to an end with death, and the ground is often barren, and only after hard work does it produce food. The results of the unfaithful, sinful behavior of God's image-bearing humans had tremendous consequences.

The conclusion of the Garden of Eden episode in Genesis chapters 1–3 offers two further points that are often overlooked by readers. First, Genesis 3:21 states that Yahweh made garments of skin to clothe Adam and Eve. The Hebrew behind the noun "skin" is often used to describe animal skin, suggesting that God provided clothing for the original human beings from the hides of the animals. By wearing animal skins as clothing, Adam and Eve would be reminded constantly that their disobedience and punishment resulted from listening to the voice of one of the very animals over which they were originally tasked to rule and have dominion. The second point is that Adam and Eve were *exiled* from the Garden of Eden; that is, they were forcibly removed from the land over which they were set in charge as God's viceregents. When readers frame humanity's expulsion from Eden in terms of exile and compare the details with Israel's exile into Babylon in 587 BC, several convincing parallels emerge.[13] One, in particular, is

---

[10] Wenham, *Genesis 1–15*, 78–79.
[11] Walton, *Genesis*, NIV, 227.
[12] Sarna, *Genesis*, 27.
[13] Wenham, *Genesis 1–15*, 90.

that the Babylonian exile was illustrated with the metaphor of "death," especially within Ezekiel's vision of the Valley of Dry Bones (Ezek 37:1–14). We will recall that, in reference to the forbidden tree of the knowledge of good and evil, God said, "In the day that you eat of it you will surely die" (Gen 2:17). What actually took place on the day that humanity ate from the forbidden tree? They were exiled from the Garden of Eden. Exile, it appears, is what was intended by the punishment of death.

Fallen Creation in Genesis Chapters 4–11

If Genesis 1–3 introduced the sinful behavior of humanity due to disobedience and failure to live in accordance with their vocation as God's image-bearers, then Genesis 4–11 demonstrates the monumental effects of sin. Not only did unfaithful acts of sinfulness cause a break in the relationship between human beings and the God whose image they were created to reflect, but the relationships between family members also broke down considerably. The first two offspring of Adam and Eve, Cain and Abel, respectively, started off well as brothers, demonstrating an awareness of their role as image-bearers by regarding Yahweh as a being worthy of offering sacrifices (Gen 4:1–4). When God showed favor to Abel and his offering but expressed no favor to Cain and his offering, Cain became very angry. Yahweh expresses his continued longing for a relationship with humanity by telling the deeply angered (and reasonably hurt) Cain, "If you do well, will you not be accepted? And if you do not do well, sin is crouching at the door. Its desire is for you, but you must rule over it" (Gen 4:7). Yahweh's response indicates that there remains the possibility to do well, but if Cain gives into sin—which is personified as an animal ready to pounce—he will not be doing well.[14] Despite the image of God being tarnished by sin, humanity is not completely devoid of agency in making good decisions.[15]

We can only speculate why God chose Abel and his sacrifice, and why he rejected Cain and his offering. Our best clue within the immediate context comes from the fact that Abel offers to God the firstborn of his flock and the fat portions, perhaps suggesting that Abel had a clearer grasp of the task of being an image-bearer, one who is to reflect a good Creator. If Yahweh created all the animals and entrusted humanity with their care, then Abel could have regarded Yahweh as worthy of the best Abel could offer. Cain, who presumably learned about what was required of image-bearers from his parents (Cain was the firstborn, after all), for whatever reason, decided to present an offering that, by comparison with what Abel gave, we can only assume was not the first fruits and the best of the land's harvest. Whatever the case may be, Yahweh offers Cain a choice between doing well and giving in to temptation. Cain, consumed with his rage, killed his brother while they were out in the field (Gen 4:8). The image of God, once the crowning

---

[14] Walton, *Genesis*, NIV, 263–64.
[15] Sarna, *Genesis*, 33.

accomplishment of Yahweh's good creation, has sunk to the point where one image-bearer puts another image-bearer to death. Sin, which was meant to be mastered and put into order by Cain, was allowed to sow chaos, resulting in a further breakdown in humanity's relationship with one another and with its Creator.

Genesis chapter five presents a genealogy that demonstrates that Adam and Eve were indeed fruitful and multiplied, fulfilling their part in filling the earth. As we have already observed in Chapter 8, humanity's vocation as God's image-bearers was passed down from parents to children (Gen 5:1, 3).[16] This genealogy not only traces the descendants of Adam all the way down to Noah and his three sons, but it also documents the years of life of each generation. The narrator details how long each person lived, followed by the notice of their death ("and he died"). This refrain served as a bleak reminder to the reader of the ongoing effects of sin and the consequences of Adam's actions. The exception to this rule is the elusive figure of Enoch. While the description of Enoch ("Enoch walked with God; and he was not, for God took him") in Genesis 5:24 has resulted in an overwhelming amount of speculation, it is best not to build one's theology on the deviation from the standard. The Hebrew verb "to take" (*laqach*) is elsewhere used for the taking of another's life (1 Kgs 19:10; Ps 31:13; Prov 1:19; Jonah 4:3),[17] which perhaps explains the less-than-clear reference to Enoch's removal from life ("he was not").[18] What we can say with confidence is that the primary purpose and function of this genealogy is to move the narrative from Adam to Noah and his family, whose life and deeds will occupy the attention of the next four chapters of Genesis (chapters 6–9).

The flood account begins with an unusual twist involving the unauthorized application of the mandate to be fruitful, multiply, and fill the earth. The narrator informs us twice (Gen 6:2, 4) that procreation took place between the sons of God and the daughters of men. While at first glance this may appear to refer to human men and human women reproducing, the Hebrew phrase *b'ne ha'elohim* ("sons of God") consistently refers to heavenly angelic beings in the Old Testament (Job 1:6; 2:1; 38:7).[19] When we set these passages in their wider context, it immediately becomes clear that the act of heavenly angels taking for themselves human women for the purposes of reproduction was certainly outside of the will of the Creator.[20] For one, the creation account in Genesis chapter two depicts the formation of the woman precisely because, as Yahweh said, "It is not good for the man to be alone" (Gen 2:18). By giving the man a woman, the two

---

[16] Merrill, "Image of God," 444; Sarna, *Genesis*, 41.
[17] Sarna, *Genesis*, 43.
[18] The phrase "he was not" in Hebrew indicates that the subject has died in Job 7:8, 24; Pss 37:10; 39:13; 104:35; Jer 49:10; Ezek 28:19.
[19] Hendel, *Genesis 1–11*, 265; Walton, "Sons of God, Daughters of Men," 794–95; *Genesis*, NIV, 291; Rad, *Genesis*, 113–14; Caragounis, "בן," 676; Sarna, *Genesis*, 45; Westermann, *Genesis 1–11*, 371.
[20] Arnold, *Genesis*, 90.

could fulfill their task as image-bearers to be fruitful, multiply, and fill the earth. In other words, God's life-giving prerogative was shared with those who were made in his image, that is, human beings. The second reason why the mention of heavenly angels taking the daughters of men should be regarded as bad is the intentional echoes it has with earlier parts of the story. We are told in Genesis 6:2 that "the sons of God saw that the daughters of men were beautiful; and they took wives for themselves, whomever they chose." The Hebrew adjective translated as "beautiful" is *tov*, and this adjective appears in a remarkably similar passage, namely Genesis 3:6: "When the woman saw that the tree was good (Hebrew: *tov*) for food, and that it was a delight to the eyes, and that the tree was desirable to make one wise, she took from its fruit and ate."[21] Eve "saw" that which was forbidden, she regarded it as "good" (*tov*), and she "took" it in a manner that was clearly disobedient to God. Both passages combine the act of seeing, the description of the forbidden object as "good" (*tov*), and the wicked deed of taking what was off limits. The effects of sin and the subsequent rebellion from God's original purposes continue to sink to a new low within the narrative of Genesis.

In what is certainly in the running for the saddest passage written by the biblical authors, God illustrates the utterly sinful character of his image-bearers in Genesis 6:5, "Then Yahweh saw that the wickedness of man was great on the earth, and that every intent of the thoughts of his heart was only evil continually." Whether we interpret this statement as hyperbole or not, it is abundantly clear that humanity, now in its tenth generation after Adam, has descended to a place that requires God to bring them into judgment.[22] After expressing sorrow and grief for making human beings, Yahweh declares his intention to do just that—blot out humanity from the face of the land (Gen 6:6–7). Noah, however, finds favor with God and is summoned to construct an ark and gather into it his family, two of each animal, and enough food to keep the occupants fed. After responding in obedience to all that God commanded him, Noah and his family entered the boat and were thus protected from the ensuing flood's judgment upon every living thing. Starting over with this family of eight, Yahweh reiterated the mandate that was given to Adam, along with its blessing, "God blessed Noah and his sons and said to them, 'Be fruitful and multiply, and fill the earth'" (Gen 9:1, 7). Furthermore, the vocation of image-bearers is recommitted to the surviving humans, with a particular emphasis given to the sanctity of human life, whose blood is never to be shed (Gen 9:6).[23] Whether this reminder that those made in the image of God are not to go on murdering one another is a reflection on the sort of wicked behavior mentioned in Genesis 6:5 or whether it is a deliberate echo to the Cain and Able story, the effects are the same. Human beings who

---

[21] Hendel, *Genesis 1–11*, 267.
[22] Sarna, *Genesis*, 47; Walton, *Genesis*, NIV, 308.
[23] Goldingay, *Old Testament Theology*, 1:181.

reflect the good Creator possess inherent worth, value, and sanctity, despite the clearly tarnished condition of these image-bearers.[24]

Readers at this point in the narrative of Genesis may begin to adopt a hopeful outlook on humanity, but this optimism is quickly dashed. From the three sons of Noah (Shem, Ham, and Japheth), we are told, the whole earth was populated (Gen 9:19). We are also informed that Noah took up farming, planning a vineyard in the process (Gen 9:20). While these point to a cheerful expectation that, perhaps, Noah and his family are fulfilling the roles given to Adam, the narrative quickly shows just how easy it is for God's image-bearers to be overtaken by the very creation they were entrusted to oversee. The vineyard that Noah planted produced wine, and Noah allowed himself to partake of too much, becoming drunk in the process. After lying down naked in his tent, unconscious in his sleep from intoxication, readers are informed that something terrible happened to Noah. Ham, the youngest son, "saw the nakedness of his father" (Gen 9:22). While the details are not entirely clear, the narrative makes it apparent that this act was a serious violation, resulting in Noah issuing a curse on Ham's son, Canaan.[25] It is possible that seeing "the nakedness of his father" is to be interpreted literally, but the phrase elsewhere refers, plainly, to incest (Lev 18:6–19).[26] Whatever the case may be, Ham's sin was compounded when he told all about it to his brothers, bringing shame upon his father. Unfortunately, the hope that the newly blessed image-bearers had held turned into yet another curse and a further breakdown in the relationship between family members.[27]

The second genealogy, which spans the entirety of Genesis 10, details the various nations established by Noah's three sons. In fact, there appears to be a deliberate emphasis on the term "nations," as it appears six times in this chapter, but not once in the previous nine chapters. The creation of these various nations is a subtle reminder that Noah's descendants are indeed being fruitful, multiplying, and filling the earth, just as God had tasked them to do. At some point in the development of civilization, we get the Tower of Babel story in Genesis 11. There are aspects of this story that are open to speculation and others that are intentionally clear to see. For one, the narrator makes the point of informing the readers that the whole earth journeyed eastward (Gen 11:2), which may suggest that the people were in search of the Garden of Eden, which was located in the east (Gen 2:8; 3:24). Perhaps their inability to find Paradise motivated them to do the next best thing: to build "a tower whose top will reach into heaven" (Gen 11:4). We can be more confident with the expressly stated purpose of building this tower, which was "to make for ourselves a name." This name likely refers to a *reputation of high standing*, and when we combine this desire to make a name for themselves with the building of a tower that will reach into heaven, it becomes clear that the motivations behind these endeavors

---

[24] Merrill, "Image of God," 444; Sarna, *Genesis*, 62.
[25] Sarna, *Genesis*, 66.
[26] Kaiser, "The Book of Leviticus," 1125–26.
[27] Walton, *Genesis*, NIV, 352.

are prideful.[28] In the story that is to follow, God tells Abram, "I will bless you and make your name great" (Gen 12:2), and the proximity of these two stories, set by the narrator side by side, indicates a belief that Yahweh is the one who makes one's name great, not the individual.[29] There is nothing, it seems, inherently wrong with desiring a great reputation, but the narrative has shown example after example of humanity setting aside its vocation as God's image-bearers in order to fulfill sinful desires and temptations. The builders of the Tower of Babel, as Abraham will demonstrate by counterexample, have gone about acquiring a great name the wrong way.

The prideful pursuit of a name and a desire to break through the barrier between heaven and earth result in God confusing the language of the people (Gen 11:7). Instead of a united goal of building a tower into the heavens, Yahweh scatters them over the face of the whole earth (Gen 11:8–9), which conveniently sets humanity back on course to "fill the earth" as was initially tasked to his image-bearers. We may speculate whether the arrogant intention to make a name and produce a tower that crossed into the heavens was a violation not unlike the unlawful mixing of heavenly angels and the daughters of men in Genesis 6:2, 4. Whatever the case may be, we can be sure that the positive emphasis the narrator gives to God making a great name for Abram is intended to contrast with the vain efforts of the people attempting to make a name for themselves. God's image-bearers, originally the crowning accomplishment of the good creation, have sunk due to sin's effects and consequences. The former rulers of God's Paradise in Eden have been reduced to murderers, wicked, evildoers, drunkards, those who bring shame upon their parents, and lastly, prideful. If Genesis 1–2 was written to show humanity at its best, then Genesis 3–11 shows how sinful disobedience to God utterly undermines the potential of human beings. What hope can there be for humanity, cursed and sinful? Can anything, or anyone, break the spiral of perpetual ruin and unfaithful behavior?

God's Solution in Abraham

The answer to this dilemma, which the narrator has plainly indicated is a very real problem, comes at the beginning of Genesis chapter twelve. In what is clearly intended to transition from the repetitive episodes detailing the tumultuous effects of sin, Yahweh's choice to use Abram (whose name is later changed to Abraham) dominates not only the remainder of Genesis but also the rest of the Bible. Since the covenant struck with Abraham serves such a foundational role, it is worth exploring in detail here:

> Now Yahweh said to Abram, "Go forth from your country, and from your relatives and from your father's house, to the land which I will show you; and I will make you a great

---

[28] Sarna, *Genesis*, 83.
[29] Sarna, *Genesis*, 89; Walton, *Genesis*, NIV, 392.

nation, and I will bless you, and make your name great; and so you shall be a blessing; and I will bless those who bless you, and the one who curses you I will curse. And in you all the families of the earth will be blessed." (Gen 12:1–3)

We already introduced this passage in Chapter 5, drawing attention to the three tenets of the Abrahamic covenant (land, descendants, and blessing). Each of these promises serves to assist Yahweh in dealing with the sin of Adam, with the ultimate result being the redemption of the world.[30] By promising Abraham and his worldwide family the land, the function of God's image-bearers, being those tasked with the responsibility to subdue and rule over God's creation, can finally be realized on a global scale. In the land promise, God will again have his human viceregents possessing dominion, just as was initially intended with Adam. Unlike those who attempted to build a tower into the heavens in order to make a name for themselves, God will make Abraham's name great, as he will eventually take on the role of king of his own territory.

God's second promise to Abraham concerned the numerous descendants he would receive, enough to make Abraham a great nation. This assurance reincorporates the life-giving prerogatives that Yahweh shared with his image-bearing human beings, namely the mandates to be fruitful, multiply, and fill the earth. Abraham, who is seventy-five years old at this time (Gen 12:4), would view God's promise to make this old man into a great nation as nothing short of a miracle.

Finally, the blessing that will come to overtake all the families of the earth is of crucial importance for the subject of this chapter. A *blessing* is a well-known opposite of a *curse*, and the narrator of Genesis has just concluded several stories that bring into focus just how cursed human beings have become due to their sinful disobedience to their Creator.[31] We will recall that humanity's sin resulted in the punishment of the woman, the man, and the ground. "Cursed is the ground because of you," Yahweh told Adam, and this curse results in the death of humanity and their return to the dust. Abraham's blessing serves to undo the curse of Adam, thereby redeeming humankind and the world with which humanity is so closely linked.[32] In other words, God's promise to bless all the families of the earth in and through the man Abraham is not to suggest some generic, unspecified good thing. God plans to redeem his crowning accomplishment—his most favored creation—human beings, and to the surprise of many readers, God's purpose to redeem humanity involves faithful human beings acting as the means through whom sin's curse will be undone. This theme will continue to reappear in the Mosaic covenant and in the new covenant, as the unfolding narrative identifies the children of Abraham (the nation of Israel) and, ultimately, Israel's royal representative (Jesus Christ) as the agent of

---

[30] Wright, *New Testament*, 263, observes, "the narrative quietly insists that Abraham and his progeny inherit the role of Adam and Eve."
[31] Walton, *Genesis*, NIV, 229.
[32] Routledge, *Old Testament Theology*, 167.

this redemptive blessing of all humanity.[33] Once readers grasp the key fact that God has summoned Abraham to be the means through whom sin will be replaced with a creation-wide blessing, they can begin to focus on the Abrahamic family and the ways in which the biblical authors portray the family's journey along the path of their God-given purpose.

Conclusion

In conclusion, we have observed the introduction of sin, disobedience, and the breakdown in relationships between humanity and God, as well as the breakdown in humanity's relationships with one another. We saw that the ideal function of God's image-bearers became broken and tarnished in light of the events that transpired in Genesis 3. We also took notice of the deliberate effort of the narrator to detail, in episode after episode, just how broken and cursed humanity had become due to the influence of sin. Everything from murder, wicked intentions, and vain arrogance utterly demonstrated the sinfulness of God's image-bearers. Finally, we observed a clear turning point in the story when God summoned the man Abram and declared unto him the intention to not only restore the function of image-bearers as rulers of the land and producers of fruitful offspring but also to utilize Abram as the means through whom the curse of Adam would be replaced with a blessing. As such, our trek through the opening twelve chapters of Genesis ends on a note of hope, assuring the readers that God has not abandoned nor given up on human beings, his crowning accomplishment. The rest of the Old Testament will serve to tell the story of Abraham's children, the promised people through whom the worldwide blessing is to be realized, who come to grasp that they, too, are in need of redemption.

In far too many modern retellings of the biblical story of God's redemption, the history of Israel and the establishment of the Mosaic covenant at Mount Sinai get overlooked entirely. This unfortunate oversight fails to understand, as the Early Church came to see, that the law of Moses served a crucially important function in God's plan to undo the curse of Adam through Abraham and his faithful descendants. We cannot fully understand the significance of Jesus, the Jewish messianic king, until we grasp the people he was meant to represent. To this end, we need to examine the covenant God made with Moses, its purpose, and how it relates to our ongoing study of hamartiology. We will tackle these tasks in the next chapter.

---

[33] Wright, *New Testament*, 252, is helpful here: "Abraham's people are to be the means of undoing primeval sin and its consequences. This belief is a basic assumption throughout Jewish literature of our period."

16
THE MOSAIC COVENANT

Far too often, modern Christians describe the history of sin's relationship with humanity by beginning with the story of Adam and Eve eating the forbidden fruit and then jumping immediately to the death of Jesus. While it is true that the crucifixion, burial, and resurrection of Christ defeated sin and death, it would be a gross generalization to overlook how the covenant cut at Sinai between Yahweh and the newly redeemed children of Israel contributes to the conversation. The Apostle Paul plainly indicates his awareness of the Law's integral function between Adam's disobedience and Jesus' faithful act that resulted in redemption: "The Law came in so that the transgression would increase; but where sin increased, grace abounded all the more" (Rom 5:20). The pillars of the Law of Moses, including the sacrificial system, tabernacle, temple, and the priesthood, demonstrate that both God and the nation of Israel possessed a consciousness of sin, its effects, and the dangers it contained.

This chapter will discuss how the Mosaic covenant (also known as the Law of Moses) serves as an important contribution to our understanding of hamartiology. First, we will look closely at the inauguration of the covenant, particularly as it relates to Yahweh (the originator of the agreement) and the children of Israel (the recipients). Second, we will examine the priesthood, their roles, and the function of Israel's high priest as he relates to purifying the nation of their sin. Third, we will consider the meaning of the tabernacle and its successor, the Jerusalem temple, as the location where the children of Israel offered sacrifices and where the priesthood served their holy duties. Fourth, we will give careful attention to the promises of blessing and curses at the end of Deuteronomy, considering their relation to the sinfulness of unfaithful acts and the promise of covenant renewal. This brief survey of these otherwise complex biblical topics will help readers better understand how the Mosaic covenant attempted to address the overarching issue of humanity's sin, a topic about which the Israelites were acutely aware.

Defining *Covenant*

Before examining the specifics of how the Mosaic covenant relates to Israel's sinful behavior, it is necessary to define the covenant relationship. A covenant is an agreement or pact that is struck between two parties.¹ In the case of this covenant, the first party initiates and creates the covenant, while the second party accepts the terms of the covenant as the recipient. God, the initiator of the covenant, graciously offers benefits and promises to his people that they would be unable to acquire on their own. This demonstrates that the two parties in the Mosaic covenant relationship are not equals, since God is self-evidently greater than the children of Israel. The recipients of the covenant agreement, for their part, accept the gracious benefits and promises offered to them and respond to this unmerited act of love by responding with faithfulness to the terms set forth by the covenant's Creator. The nature of the relationship between God, the Creator of the Mosaic covenant, and the children of Israel, the party with whom God has entered into a covenant, can be observed in several key passages in Exodus:

> Moses went up to God, and Yahweh called to him from the mountain, saying, "Thus you shall say to the house of Jacob and tell the sons of Israel: 'You yourselves have seen what I did to the Egyptians, and how I bore you on eagles' wings, and brought you to Myself. Now then, if you will indeed obey My voice and keep My covenant, then you shall be My own possession among all the peoples, for all the earth is Mine; and you shall be to Me a kingdom of priests and a holy nation.' These are the words that you shall speak to the sons of Israel." So Moses came and called the elders of the people, and set before them all these words which Yahweh had commanded him. All the people answered together and said, "All that Yahweh has spoken we will do!" And Moses brought back the words of the people to Yahweh. (Exod 19:3–8)

In this passage, God reminds Israel of his redemptive acts of deliverance and salvation, something Israel was unable to accomplish on its own. Having established his role as the Creator of the covenant, God summons the other party to obey the terms of the covenantal agreement, promising further benefits if Israel holds up its end of the pact through obedience.² After hearing the Creator of the covenant's credentials as the one who redeemed them from Egypt, the people of Israel responded with their verbal commitment to faithfully obey all that God has said.³ The willingness of the Israelites to observe their covenantal obligations is motivated by reverence and love for Yahweh, rather than by any suggestion or hint of legalistic motivations.⁴

When the famous Ten Commandments are spoken to the children of Israel, Yahweh again begins by reminding the recipients of the covenantal agreement of his role

---

¹ Mendenhall and Herion, "Covenant," 1179; Williamson, "Covenant," 139; Hamilton, *Exodus*, 301.
² Brueggemann, "The Book of Exodus," 834–35; Goldingay, "Covenant, OT and NT," 770.
³ Williamson, "Covenant," 150–51. McConville, "בְּרִית," 749, rightly observes that "the emphasis falls on the responsibilities of the people to 'keep' the covenant."
⁴ Goldingay, *Old Testament Theology*, 1:380, helpfully reminds us that "Israel delights in God's statutes, longs for God's precepts, loves God's commands, and takes comfort in God's ordinances (Ps 119:16, 40, 48). There is no 'legalism' about Israel's attitude to God's commands."

as the mighty savior of Egyptian slavery.[5] As the one qualified to enter into a covenant relationship with his people, God can issue forth the specific terms of the agreement:

> "I am Yahweh your God, who brought you out of the land of Egypt, out of the house of slavery. You shall have no other gods before Me." (Exod 20:2–3)

After Moses received the instructions of the covenant agreement, which are known by their Hebrew term *torah*, Moses, the mediator of the covenant, brought these terms to the Israelites, who responded by reaffirming their verbal commitment to obey the commanded instructions faithfully:

> Then Moses came and recounted to the people all the words of Yahweh and all the ordinances; and all the people answered with one voice and said, "All the words which Yahweh has spoken we will do!" Moses wrote down all the words of Yahweh. Then he arose early in the morning, and built an altar at the foot of the mountain with twelve pillars for the twelve tribes of Israel. He sent young men of the sons of Israel, and they offered burnt offerings and sacrificed young bulls as peace offerings to Yahweh. Moses took half of the blood and put it in basins, and the other half of the blood he sprinkled on the altar. Then he took the book of the covenant and read it in the hearing of the people; and they said, "All that Yahweh has spoken we will do, and we will be obedient!" So Moses took the blood and sprinkled it on the people, and said, "Behold the blood of the covenant, which Yahweh has made with you in accordance with all these words." (Exod 24:3–8)

This passage highlights the significance of the sacrificial blood required to ratify the covenant agreement. After God detailed the terms of the covenant to the people of Israel through Moses, they agreed to them, leading to a public ceremony in which the blood of the sacrifice was sprinkled on the people.[6] In fact, the Hebrew verb that is behind the English translation "made" ("the blood of the covenant, which Yahweh has *made* with you") is more accurately translated as "cut," referring to the cutting of the animal whose blood was spilled to ratify the agreement.[7] In other words, covenants are sealed through the act of cutting, which concludes with the blood of a sacrifice spilling out for both parties to see.[8]

The Role of the Priesthood in the Mosaic Covenant

Before Yahweh issued forth the terms of the Mosaic covenant, he declared his intention to make the nation of Israel a kingdom of priests and a holy nation (Exod 19:5–6). Although the particular instructions within the Law of Moses identify a very select group

---

[5] Childs, *Exodus*, 401–2; Noth, *Exodus*, 161–62.
[6] Dozeman, *Exodus*, 565–66; Propp, *Exodus 19–40*, 295–96; Houtman *Exodus*, 3:290–91.
[7] Köhler et al., *Hebrew and Aramaic Lexicon*, 500–1.
[8] Brueggemann, "The Book of Exodus," 881; Meyers, *Exodus*, 206; Goldingay, *Old Testament Theology*, 1:370.

of Israelites as priests, this former statement should not be overlooked or downplayed. We recall that God's initial promise to Abraham was that he would make of him "a great nation" (Gen 12:2), with the result of blessing all of the families of the earth through Abraham himself (Gen 12:3).[9] If we connect the promise to make Abraham a great nation to Yahweh's declaration that Israel is to be a holy nation comprised of a kingdom of priests, then we can begin to see how Israel was to serve as the means through which God's curse-undoing blessing would extend to all the nations of the world. In other words, the children of Israel were to collectively be a priestly nation that, if they obeyed God, would serve as a conduit of blessings to the whole world.[10] It would seem that the role of the priest would be quite heavily involved in God's plan to deal with sin, thus bringing restoration to creation.

The priesthood within Israel, despite the corporate intention of the entire nation performing holiness, belonged to Aaron and his male children: "Then bring near to yourself Aaron your brother, and his sons with him, from among the sons of Israel, to minister as priest to Me" (Exod 28:1).[11] These priests were responsible for overseeing the sacrifices, maintaining the tabernacle (and later the temple), and regulating the rituals that God instructed Israel to observe. Within the Mosaic covenant, it was expected that the children of Israel would observe the commandments, but if a commandment was broken, there was a built-in way of dealing with sin within the covenant. By offering a variety of sacrifices, depending on the nature of the sin and the social status of the guilty party, atonement could be achieved. The priest would lay his hand on the head of the burnt offering, thereby making the animal acceptable for the act of forgiveness (Lev 1:4). The transgression of the sinner would be transferred to the animal through the priestly ritual, resulting in the animal's death. The awareness of the seriousness of sin was widely understood, even for unintentional sins, for which Leviticus 4:1–35 details the process by which these transgressions can be cleansed, again by ceremonially transferring the sin of the guilty party onto the animal through the hand of the officiant (Lev 4:4, 15, 24, 29, 33).[12] There were even provisions within the covenant to set apart the priests themselves for the work they were doing, which are spelled out in Leviticus 8:5-36.

The author of Leviticus appears to portray the holy work of the priests in a manner that resembles how God brought order out of chaos in the creation account within Genesis chapter one.[13] In the instructions contained in Leviticus 10:10, we read that the priests are obligated "to make a distinction between the holy and the profane, and between the unclean and the clean." The Hebrew verb translated "make a distinction" also appears in the opening chapter of Genesis, particularly when God separated the light

---

[9] Walton, *Genesis*, NIV, 393; Hamilton, *Exodus*, 304.
[10] Brown, *The Ethos of the Cosmos*, 72; Brueggemann, "The Book of Exodus," 835; Hamilton, *Exodus*, 304.
[11] Propp, *Exodus 19–40*, 430.
[12] Kaiser, "The Book of Leviticus," 1034; Hartley, *Leviticus*, 60, 62.
[13] Ko, *Leviticus*, 99; Gerstenberger, *Leviticus*, 125.

from the darkness (Gen 1:4), separated the waters below from the waters above the expanse (Gen 1:6–7), and even separated the day from the night (Gen 1:14, 18). Just as the Creator established order by making creational distinctions, the priestly duties served to recall the role of image-bearers in their acts of separating that which is ritually unclean from that which is ritually clean.[14] It is little wonder that so much attention was devoted to detailing the specific responsibilities of the priesthood, particularly as outlined in the Book of Leviticus.

A single high priest stood among the priests, functioning as the chief mediator between God and Israel within the bounds of the Mosaic covenant. Wearing custom garments (Exod 28:2–43), oversaw Israel's rituals and sacrificial offerings. In addition to ensuring that the priests were correctly performing their ceremonial duties as prescribed by God, the high priest played a significant role in the annual Day of Atonement (known in Hebrew as *Yom Kippur*). On this day, the high priest would enter the Holy of Holies within the tabernacle or temple in order to offer sacrifices, resulting in the atonement of the sins belonging to the entire nation of Israel, including himself (Lev 16:16–22). Prior to going into the Holy of Holies, where it was believed that the glory of God resided (Exod 40:34; 1 Kgs 8:11–12), the high priest would wash himself thoroughly: "He shall bathe his body with water in a holy place and put on his clothes, and come forth and offer his burnt offering and the burnt offering of the people and make atonement for himself and for the people" (Lev 16:24).[15] The role of the high priest, including his annual duties and the significance attached to the Day of Atonement, reflects a collective understanding of the seriousness of sin among the nation of Israel.[16]

Tabernacle and Temple

Before King Solomon commissioned the temple to be built in Jerusalem, Israel's priests served in a portable tabernacle that could be packed up as the people moved through the wilderness (Num 1:51).[17] This sanctuary, which was also known as the tent of meeting, housed the presence of God (Exod 25:8; 40:34). The primary purpose of the tabernacle was that it functioned as the site where the Israelite priests offered atoning sacrifices for the sins of the people. In the outer courtyard, in front of the door leading into the tabernacle, stood the altar of burnt offerings, where the majority of the sacrifices took place (Exod 40:6). Being the place where atoning sacrifices would be slaughtered on behalf of the transgressions of the people, this altar needed to remain holy, so it was anointed and consecrated (Exod 40:9–10; Lev 8:11). Integral to the holiness of the

---

[14] Duke, "Priests, Priesthood," 651.
[15] Milgrom, *Leviticus 1–16*, 1048–49.
[16] Hartley, "Atonement, Day of," 54–55.
[17] Goldingay, *Old Testament Theology*, 1:393–94.

tabernacle was the need to "keep the sons of Israel separated from their uncleanness," for those who profane the tabernacle with unclean defilement would be guilty of death (Lev 15:31).[18]

Once Israel entered the promised land, the capital city of Jerusalem became the location where the physical temple was built, thereby replacing the tabernacle. Although King David desired to build this house for Yahweh (2 Sam 7:5), Yahweh only permitted David's son Solomon to construct it (2 Sam 7:13).[19] According to the theology of Deuteronomy, this place was to be the location where Yahweh would establish his name to dwell (Deut 12:5; 11, 21; 14:23; 16:2, 6, 11).[20] Not only was the temple the location for the atonement of sin, but it also served as the place of worship, as expressed in many of the psalms (e.g., Pss 26:7–8; 42:4; 48:9–10; 84:4).[21] The presence of God, represented by the glorious cloud that descended upon the temple's completion according to 1 Kings 8:11, served to remind the children of Israel of Yahweh's direct involvement in the temple's daily sacrifices for the atonement of sin.[22] However, when the priests began failing in their role as mediators of God's forgiveness by committing sin (Jer 2:26; 6:13; Ezek 22:26; Mic 3:11), the cloud of glory abandoned the temple, leaving it nothing more than a vulnerable structure, open to attack: "Then the glory of Yahweh departed from the threshold of the temple and stood over the cherubim" (Ezek 10:18).[23] In other words, while the priests were properly performing their duties by overseeing the temple sacrifices that atoned for the people's sins, as mandated in the terms of the Mosaic covenant, there was order and peace. When, however, the temple and its priestly attendants failed to live in accordance with their covenantal roles relating to holding off sin, God removed his protection and allowed the Babylonians to destroy the temple in 587 BC. After returning from exile, the Jews began constructing a second temple, which they completed at the end of the sixth century BC. One might expect to witness the return of the cloud of glory to the temple at its dedication, just as it visibly descended into the Holy of Holies during the time of Solomon. But nothing of the sort took place, and, in fact, the post-exilic prophet Malachi looked forward to God returning to his temple, suggesting that the pivotal event had not yet taken place: "And the Lord, whom you seek, will suddenly come to His temple" (Mal 3:1).[24] The Early Church will have a definitive answer as to when, and in what capacity, Yahweh finally returned to his temple, but we will have to wait until Part Seven: Ecclesiology to unpack all the essential details.

---

[18] Kaiser, "The Book of Leviticus," 1106.
[19] Auld, *I & II Samuel*, 442; Gordon, *I & II Samuel*, 239; Anderson, *2 Samuel*, 119, 122.
[20] Clements, "The Book of Deuteronomy," 385.
[21] McCann, "The Book of Psalms," 782.
[22] Monson, "Solomon's Temple," 929, 934–35.
[23] Block, *Ezekiel 1–24*, 326–27; Zimmerli, *Ezekiel 1*, 255–56.
[24] Hill, *Malachi*, 289; Smith, *Micah–Malachi*, 329.

The Covenantal Blessings and Curses

As we have just observed, the temple, priesthood, and sacrifices were important components of the way in which the Mosaic covenant was to keep Israel's sins in check. When performing as intended, these interconnected mechanisms allowed for the transgressions of the children of Israel to be atoned for, and this process would inevitably continue on an ongoing basis. However, when Israel began to ignore their covenant obligations and turned instead to idolatrous practices, the ideal plan for the nation to be a holy kingdom of priests through whom the world would come to experience God's blessing became thwarted. In place of the blessings of God, the punishing curses were again issued, recalling again the scene from Genesis 3 where unfaithful humanity suffered the curses for their disobedience and failure to fulfill their role. Blessings and curses were a key element in the Adam and Eve story of Genesis chapters 1–3, and the same blessing and curses reappeared in God's covenant promises to Abraham, the chosen man through whom God would begin to deal with the sin of Adam: "I will bless those who bless you, and the one who curses you I will curse. And in you all the families of the earth will be blessed" (Gen 12:3). The blessings and curses resurface towards the end of Moses' exhortation to the children of Israel in Deuteronomy (chapters 27–28), and this theology serves to make sense of the ups and downs of Israel's journey to the promised land, the establishment of the monarchy, and the eventual defeat at the hand of the Babylonians that resulted in the exile of the people and the destruction of the temple.[25]

The list of blessings offered by Moses plainly instills the assurance that obedience to the instructions contained within the covenant will result in God exalting the Israelites in his favor.[26] The introduction to the lengthy list of promised blessings reaffirms the need for Israel to fulfill its part in the covenant agreement through faithfulness:

> "Now it shall be, if you diligently obey Yahweh your God, being careful to do all His commandments which I command you today, Yahweh your God will set you high above all the nations of the earth. All these blessings will come upon you and overtake you if you obey Yahweh your God" (Deut 28:1–2)

The passage continues with a lengthy list of blessings that God promised Israel for their faithful behavior. The people will be blessed in both the city and in the rural areas, an all-encompassing description, as described in Deuteronomy 28:3.[27] In particular, the promise includes a deliberate echo back to the initial blessing of Adam in Genesis 1:28: "Blessed shall be the offspring of your body and the produce of your ground and the offspring of your beasts, the increase of your herd and the young of your flock" (Deut 28:4). Although

---

[25] Miller, *Deuteronomy*, 198.
[26] Brueggemann, *Deuteronomy*, 255.
[27] Christensen, *Deuteronomy 21:10–34:12*, 672; Tigay, *Deuteronomy*, 258.

the list of blessings continues (Deut 28:5–14), the reader is left with the impression that the obedience of Israel would actually lead to the renewal of the vocation of Adam and the fulfillment of the promises made to Abraham.[28]

However, Moses also details the curses that will befall the children of Israel if they fail to fulfill their covenant obligations.[29] Beginning with Deuteronomy 28:15, we observe a list of punishments that will be issued as a response to unfaithful behavior: "But it shall come about, if you do not obey Yahweh your God, to observe to do all His commandments and His statutes with which I charge you today, that all these curses will come upon you and overtake you." The curses, which are clearly intended to be set in contrast to the aforementioned list of blessings,[30] include a curse over the people residing in the city and in the rural areas (Deut 28:16). Instead of a blessing that leads to fruitfulness and multiplication of one's offspring, disobedience will lead to a curse over the offspring of the body, the ground's produce, the herds, and the flocks (Deut 28:18). The list of curses, which is far lengthier than the list of blessings, was surely intended to dissuade sinful behavior.[31] The final curse concerns the exile of the people, which will remove them from their land, just as sinful acts exiled Adam and Eve from the Paradise of Eden.[32] Consider the following threat of punishment:

> "Yahweh will bring you and your king, whom you set over you, to a nation which neither you nor your fathers have known, and there you shall serve other gods, wood and stone . . . You shall have sons and daughters, but they will not be yours, for they will go into captivity" (Deut 28:36-41).

The punishment for sin, therefore, will resemble Adam's exile. Unfortunately, the conclusion of the narrative of the books of Kings details the exile of the children of Israel into a foreign land (2 Kgs 25:4–11), proving that Yahweh, in his role as the just judge, carried out the sentence of the curse about which Moses warned.[33]

In the Jewish canon of Scripture, the final book of the Hebrew Bible is what Christians call 2 Chronicles, which was originally a single book comprising both 1 and 2 Chronicles. This book concludes, marking the end of the Jewish canon, by recounting the Babylonian exile, the destruction of the temple, and the days of the land's desolation. Is the last word on Israel's history to be described in terms of a curse for sinful behavior? Fortunately, the Mosaic covenant contained within its stipulations an awareness that there would eventually need to be a renewal of the covenant with the people after they had

---

[28] Woods, *Deuteronomy*, 274.
[29] Brueggemann, *Deuteronomy*, 256.
[30] Woods, *Deuteronomy*, 276.
[31] Tigay, *Deuteronomy*, 261; Nelson, *Deuteronomy*, 327.
[32] Ryken et al., "Exile," 250.
[33] Brueggemann, *Deuteronomy*, 257.

experienced the curse of exile.[34] God, it would seem, prepared for the possibility that Israel would need to be restored after being thoroughly punished for its sinful rebellion against its Creator. The children of Israel were, after all, descendants of Adam. After the blessings and curses are committed to Israel by Moses, the hope of restoration and a new blessing is declared:

> "So it shall be when all of these things have come upon you, the blessing and the curse which I have set before you, and you call them to mind in all nations where Yahweh your God has banished you, and you return to Yahweh your God and obey Him with all your heart and soul according to all that I command you today, you and your sons, then Yahweh your God will restore you from captivity, and have compassion on you, and will gather you again from all the peoples where Yahweh your God has scattered you. If your outcasts are at the ends of the earth, from there Yahweh your God will gather you, and from there He will bring you back. Yahweh your God will bring you into the land which your fathers possessed, and you shall possess it; and He will prosper you and multiply you more than your fathers. Moreover Yahweh your God will circumcise your heart and the heart of your descendants, to love Yahweh your God with all your heart and with all your soul, so that you may live. (Deut 30:1–6)

The promise of covenant renewal after the period of curses involves, as we can observe, several key details. First, the people of God will be gathered out of their exile and into the promised land to possess it.[35] Second, God will ensure that his people will again prosper and multiply. Third, he will empower his people to obey the *Shema* (Deut 6:4–5), which summoned the listeners to love the one true God with all their heart and soul.[36] This empowerment will come in the form of a circumcised heart, a metaphor that suggests an inward commitment likened to the outward sign of physical circumcision.[37] Yahweh himself would perform the act of consecrating a heart, and presumably, its scope would include women and men. This new covenant would produce a renewed people with whom God would have a relationship.[38]

The Hebrew prophets also spoke of this promised time of covenant renewal, reaffirming Deuteronomy's commitment to the new heart that God himself would provide to those who returned to him, according to Deuteronomy 30:2.[39] The prophet Jeremiah demonstrates his commitment to continuing the hope that was spelled out in the Book of Deuteronomy:

> "Thus says Yahweh, God of Israel, 'Like these good figs, so I will regard as good the captives of Judah, whom I have sent out of this place into the land of the Chaldeans. For

---

[34] Christensen, *Deuteronomy 21:10–34:12*, 735.
[35] Nelson, *Deuteronomy*, 346, 348; Brueggemann, *Deuteronomy*, 266.
[36] Tigay, *Deuteronomy*, 284; Christensen, *Deuteronomy 21:10–34:12*, 738; Nelson, *Deuteronomy*, 348–49.
[37] Clements, "The Book of Deuteronomy," 513; Christensen, *Deuteronomy 21:10–34:12*, 739.
[38] McConville, "בְּרִית," 752.
[39] Christensen, *Deuteronomy 21:10–34:12*, 740.

> I will set My eyes on them for good, and I will bring them again to this land; and I will build them up and not overthrow them, and I will plant them and not pluck them up. I will give them a heart to know Me, for I am Yahweh; and they will be My people, and I will be their God, for they will return to Me with their whole heart.'" (Jer 24:5–7)

The trio of promises from Deuteronomy's covenant renewal—specifically, the land, prosperity, and a new heart—reappear here in Jeremiah's prophecy. The function of the new heart, which only God can provide, is to know Yahweh, allowing for a renewed covenant membership in which those in possession of this new heart will be the people of God who are truly capable of demonstrating a *Shema*-like commitment to faithfulness.[40] This insistence on receiving a new heart that would allow God's people to obey him (and presumably not commit sin) anticipates Jeremiah's fuller prophetic description of the new covenant:

> "Behold, days are coming," declares Yahweh, "when I will make a new covenant with the house of Israel and with the house of Judah, not like the covenant which I made with their fathers in the day I took them by the hand to bring them out of the land of Egypt, My covenant which they broke, although I was a husband to them," declares Yahweh. But this is the covenant which I will make with the house of Israel after those days," declares Yahweh, "I will put My law within them and on their heart I will write it; and I will be their God, and they shall be My people. They will not teach again, each man his neighbor and each man his brother, saying, 'Know Yahweh,' for they will all know Me, from the least of them to the greatest of them," declares Yahweh, "for I will forgive their iniquity, and their sin I will remember no more." (Jer 31:31–34)

Jeremiah's prophecy of covenant renewal plainly indicates that the Mosaic covenant was unquestionably broken due to Israel's sin.[41] Since the promise embedded in this new covenant is that God would inscribe his instructions upon the hearts of his people, we can again discern that this new heart is one that will possess the capacity to obey Yahweh faithfully.[42] Furthermore, this new covenant will be accompanied by the forgiveness of iniquity, which, in turn, will never be remembered again. The promised new heart that God will provide to his new covenant people will, therefore, replace a heart that has committed sinful iniquity.[43] The renewal of the covenant about which Jeremiah spoke would graciously address sin in a way that the Mosaic covenant was unable to accomplish.[44]

---

[40] Carroll, *Jeremiah*, 486; Thompson, *The Book of Jeremiah*, 508; Lundbom, *Jeremiah 21–36*, 232–33.
[41] Lundbom, *Jeremiah 21–36*, 466; Holladay, *Jeremiah 2*, 197.
[42] Allen, *Jeremiah*, 356; Holladay, *Jeremiah 2*, 198.
[43] Carroll, *Jeremiah*, 611; Allen, *Jeremiah*, 357.
[44] Thompson, *The Book of Jeremiah*, 581; Lundbom, *Jeremiah 21–36*, 470; Carroll, *Jeremiah*, 614.

The priestly prophet Ezekiel, who, like Jeremiah, lived through the horrific events of the Babylonian exile, spoke the prophetic word of Yahweh concerning the new heart:

> Therefore say, "Thus says the Lord Yahweh, 'I will gather you from the peoples and assemble you out of the countries among which you have been scattered, and I will give you the land of Israel.' When they come there, they will remove all its detestable things and all its abominations from it. And I will give them one heart, and put a new spirit within them. And I will take the heart of stone out of their flesh and give them a heart of flesh, that they may walk in My statutes and keep My ordinances and do them. Then they will be My people, and I shall be their God." (Ezek 11:17–20)

The theme of Yahweh gathering his people from exile and placing them into the land is familiar, as is the promise of the new heart that enables faithful living. What is new is the promise of God giving his spirit, presumably his Holy Spirit, with the covenant-renewing new heart.[45] This reorganization of the people of God will then be recognized by both a new heart and the coming of the Spirit in a new, dramatic way. The pairing of the new heart and the new spirit appears in a later prophetic oracle uttered by Ezekiel:

> "For I will take you from the nations, gather you from all the lands and bring you into your own land. Then I will sprinkle clean water on you, and you will be clean; I will cleanse you from all your filthiness and from all your idols. Moreover, I will give you a new heart and put a new spirit within you; and I will remove the heart of stone from your flesh and give you a heart of flesh. I will put My Spirit within you and cause you to walk in My statutes, and you will be careful to observe My ordinances. You will live in the land that I gave to your forefathers; so you will be My people, and I will be your God. Moreover, I will save you from all your uncleanness; and I will call for the grain and multiply it, and I will not bring a famine on you. I will multiply the fruit of the tree and the produce of the field, so that you will not receive again the disgrace of famine among the nations. (Ezek 36:24–30)

In addition to the recurring promises of God bringing his people into their own land and the reaffirmation of Adam's mandate to be fruitful and multiply in that land, the renewed covenant members will be cleansed with the imagery of clean water, and they will be delivered from all their uncleanness and impurity.[46] This again points to a definitive removal of sin, the sin that brought about the covenant curses in the first place. Yahweh will accomplish this great feat by granting his people a *new heart* and a *new spirit*, which is outright identified as the Spirit of God.[47] Importantly, the renewal of the covenant will bring renewal and restoration to God's people, marking them out by providing a heart to

---

[45] Odell, *Ezekiel*, 124; Tuell, *Ezekiel*, 60; Joyce, *Ezekiel*, 115.
[46] Allen, *Ezekiel 20–48*, 179; Greenberg, *Ezekiel 21–37*, 734; Odell, *Ezekiel*, 442.
[47] Tuell, *Ezekiel*, 247; Joyce, *Ezekiel*, 204.

obey and the Spirit to assist in fulfilling the obligations of this new covenantal agreement.[48]

Conclusion

As we summarize our exploration of the covenant that God made with the children of Israel through the mediator Moses, it is essential to consider the specific ways in which this covenantal agreement addressed the ongoing issue of sin and the curses that resulted from humanity's disobedience in the Garden of Eden. First, we examined the formation of the covenantal agreement between Yahweh and the children of Israel, noting carefully that Moses, the mediator, ratified the covenant with a sacrifice. The covenant provided many God-given benefits and promises offered to the Israelites, who were to respond to this act of unmerited grace by being faithful to the terms of the covenant, namely, the Law of Moses. Second, we noted God's desire that the entire nation would be a kingdom of priests, thereby functioning as a holy nation in fulfillment of the promise to make of Abraham a great nation through which blessings would flow. The role was concentrated on the office of the Levitical priests and their leader, the high priest, who each worked to mediate God's atonement through the overseeing of ritual animal sacrifices. The high priest, in particular, was central to the annual Day of Atonement, which served as a means of atonement for the sins of the entire nation. Third, we noticed that the location of these sacrifices to atone for acts of sinful disobedience took place in sacred places, first in the traveling tabernacle in the wilderness, and later in the Jerusalem temple. Finally, we saw how the promised blessings and curses at the end of Deuteronomy reiterated God's desire to extend his favor towards his people who responded in obedience, while also warning of the curses that would befall those who acted unfaithfully to the Law of Moses. The final curse, being exile, would not be the last word, for God promised in the Law and the Prophets of a renewed covenant, a new covenant, in which a new heart to obey would be provided, along with the gift of God's Spirit. It is within the parameters of this new covenant that Yahweh would definitively deal with sin and its curse over creation.

How did the Early Church understand sin in light of the new covenant that Jesus ratified in his death? How did the disobedience of Adam and its resulting curse find a salvific answer within the parameters of the new covenant? In what ways did God provide the early Christians the promised new heart and new Spirit that would accompany the covenant's renewal, and how do these two gifts help the faithful people of God overcome sinful temptations? Our next chapter will seek to provide answers to these important questions, thereby offering clarity on how God has dealt with sin and the curse through the death of his son, Jesus Christ.

---

[48] Allen, *Ezekiel 20–48*, 179–80; Greenberg, *Ezekiel 21–37*, 735–37; Joyce, *Ezekiel*, 206.

17
THE NEW COVENANT

Many readers of the New Testament are unaware that the word "testament" means covenant. This helpfully delineates a clear line between the Old Testament (i.e., Mosaic covenant) and the New Testament (i.e., new covenant). The Early Church understood the death of Jesus as the sacrifice that simultaneously dealt with sin and ratified the terms of the new covenant agreement between God and his people. Therefore, it is prudent for our ongoing study of Hamartiology to examine the relevance of the new covenant, especially as it pertains to the death of Jesus.

While there is a great deal that early Christians had to say about the blood of Christ and the defeat of sin, this chapter will concentrate its focus on the interrelationship between the new covenant and the defeat of sin (and its curse). First, we will complement our examination of the formation of the old covenant, mediated by Moses, with a close investigation of the new covenant and its mediator. Second, we must draw attention to the way that Jesus himself defined the new covenant and spoke about the ways in which it would usher in the forgiveness of sins. Third, we must also give weight to the Apostle Paul's teachings on the new covenant, especially where Paul points to the defeat of the curse at the death of Christ on the cross. Fourth, we will observe how the author of the Epistle to the Hebrews elaborates on the fulfillment of Jeremiah's prophecies concerning a new covenant in light of the salvific work of Jesus. And finally, we will look more broadly at the universal acceptance of the Early Church of the cleansing of sin that the death of Jesus accomplished. Once we give due attention to the interrelatedness of the new covenant and the problem of sin, we will be in a better position to focus on the universal effects of sin upon all creation.

Christ's Role as Mediator of the New Covenant

In our last chapter, we noted how the Mosaic covenant was formed between Yahweh and his people. God set forth the terms of the covenant, communicated them through the mediator Moses, and the agreement was ratified with a sacrifice involving blood. The Early Church remembered Jesus confirming the terms of the new covenant at a meal that Jesus shared with his closest disciples on the night before his death.[1] After taking a cup

---

[1] Stein, "Last Supper," 448.

and giving thanks, Jesus announced the symbolic value of the shared drink: "This is My blood of the covenant, which is poured out for many" (Mark 14:24; Luke 22:20). Matthew's version of this saying explicitly clarifies the purpose of the poured-out blood as being "for the forgiveness of sins" (Matt 26:28). In doing so, Matthew makes it clear that Jesus is referring to the new covenant about which Jeremiah prophesied, wherein iniquities would be forgiven, and sins would no longer be remembered (Jer 31:34).[2] In fact, Matthew's stylistic arrangement of his gospel account has displayed the person of Jesus as the new Moses, pointing to an intentional effort to depict Jesus as the mediator of the new covenant. For example, Matthew's gospel is divided into five blocks of teaching, perhaps in an effort to intentionally mirror the five books of Moses (Genesis through Deuteronomy).[3] Each of Matthew's blocks of teaching concludes with a refrain that is remarkably similar to the statements in Exodus 24:3–4, where "all the words of Yahweh" served as the terms of the covenant:

> When Jesus had finished these words, the crowds were amazed at His teaching (Matt 7:28)
>
> When Jesus had finished giving instructions to His twelve disciples, He departed from there to teach and preach in their cities. (Matt 11:1)
>
> When Jesus had finished these parables, He departed from there. (Matt 13:53)
>
> When Jesus had finished these words, He departed from Galilee (Matt 19:1)
>
> When Jesus had finished all these words, He said to His disciples, "You know that after two days the Passover is coming, and the Son of Man is to be handed over for crucifixion." (Matt 26:1–2)

After Jesus "finished" the final block of teaching, he announced the coming Passover and connected his death with that event. His mention of his blood that would ratify the covenant (Matt 26:28) appears to be a deliberate echo of Moses' declaration, "Behold the blood of the covenant, which Yahweh has made with you in accordance with all these words." (Exod 24:8).[4] Further parallels between Jesus and Moses include the attempt by Herod to kill all the male infants (Matt 2:16), which resembles Pharaoh's effort to put to death all newborn Hebrew sons (Exod 1:16), and Jesus' ascension to the mountain to deliver the Sermon on the Mount (Matthew 5–7) is surely intended to correspond to Moses going up on Mount Sinai to deliver the terms of the old covenant.[5]

In their own ways, each of the four New Testament gospel writers portrays Jesus as authoritatively teaching God's instructions and concluding this depiction with an

---

[2] Knowles, *Jeremiah in Matthew's Gospel*, 207–9; Allen, *Jeremiah*, 357; Boring, "The Gospel of Matthew," 472.
[3] Davies and Allison, *Matthew*, 1:59, 61, 72. See the discussion in Allison, *The New Moses*, 192–94, 293–98.
[4] Knowles, *Jeremiah in Matthew's Gospel*, 208, 212; Davies and Allison, *Matthew*, 3:473.
[5] Broyles, "Moses," 562. For a full treatment of Jesus as the new Moses, see Allison, *The New Moses*, 137–262.

account of Jesus' sacrificial death. The most common title that the crowds and disciples attribute to Jesus is "Teacher," indicating an acknowledgment that he possessed influence in his capacity as one who provided instruction to his disciples from God.[6] Furthermore, those who witnessed Jesus teach and perform miracles would frequently comment on his teaching that possessed authority (e.g., Matt 7:29; 9:8; Mark 1:27; 11:28; Luke 4:32; 7:8; John 5:27; 10:18).

Unlike Moses, who mediated Yahweh's covenant with the Israelites, Jesus mediated the new covenant to anyone who responded with repentance and faith at the announcement of the dawning kingdom of God (Matt 4:17; Mark 1:14–15, Luke 4:43), regardless of whether they were from among the people of Israel. Jesus' commitment to making the gospel of the kingdom the object of the faith of his followers demonstrated that the gospel was elevated in importance above the individual commands of Moses. This can be observed fairly easily in the ministry of Jesus. For example, the necessity to preach and respond appropriately to the gospel of the kingdom of God overshadowed the commitment one had to honor their parents, which is one of the Ten Commandments (Exod 20:12; Deut 5:16).[7] Consider the following evidence:

> He saw two other brothers, James the son of Zebedee, and John his brother, in the boat with Zebedee their father, mending their nets; and He called them. Immediately they left the boat and their father, and followed Him. (Matt 4:21–22)

> "For whoever does the will of God, he is My brother and sister and mother." (Mark 3:33–35)

> And He said to another, "Follow Me." But he said, "Lord, permit me first to go and bury my father." But He said to him, "Allow the dead to bury their own dead; but as for you, go and proclaim everywhere the kingdom of God." (Luke 9:59–60)

Jesus explicitly contrasted the Law and the Prophets with the proclamation of the message of the kingdom, which began with the preaching of John the Baptist: "The Law and the Prophets were proclaimed until John; since that time the gospel of the kingdom of God has been preached, and everyone is forcing his way into it" (Luke 16:16). In other words, the breaking in of the kingdom of God, which John and Jesus preached and was demonstrated with miraculous deeds of restoration, indicated that something new was taking place—something that was not just a continuation of the Mosaic covenant.[8]

---

[6] Riesner, "Teacher," 807.
[7] Davies and Allison, *Matthew*, 1:402; France, *Mark*, 178–80; Bovon, *Luke 2*, 13–14. Boring, *Mark*, 110, aptly captures the seriousness of Jesus' mission: "The appearance of Jesus as a representative of God's kingdom calls for a radical decision, and nothing can have a higher priority, not even family."
[8] Ladd, *Crucial Questions About the Kingdom*, 93; Culpepper, "The Gospel of Luke," 312–13; Bovon, *Luke 2*, 465; Green, *Luke*, 603.

The Forgiveness of Sins Made Possible in the New Covenant

At the end of Jesus' ministry, on the night before he was crucified, Jesus shared a meal with his followers, those who had responded appropriately to the preaching of the kingdom. During the meal, he took some bread, broke it, and shared it with the disciples, announcing that it symbolized his body (Luke 22:19). Jesus then took the cup and shared it with his disciples, declaring that it represented the blood that would ratify the covenant: "This cup which is poured out for you is the new covenant in My blood" (Luke 22:20). Essentially, Jesus indicated to his followers that the new covenant teachings were being confirmed with blood and that he himself would be the sacrifice that brought the covenant into full effect.[9] Instead of the blood of young bulls used by Moses to ratify the old covenant (Exod 24:5–8), the blood of Israel's representative, the Messiah, would bring the new covenant to completion.[10] Just as blood sealed the Law of Moses to the children of Israel, the teachings of Christ were sealed with his own blood, which was shed at the cross. According to Jesus in Matthew 26:28, the new covenant achieved the long-awaited forgiveness of sins that the old covenant prophets foresaw (Jer 31:34).[11]

The renewal of the covenant, as we have observed, was to accompany the giving of a new heart in order to obey Yahweh fully.[12] It should come as no surprise that Jesus frequently taught about the heart, its condition, and how those who participate in his ministry of the kingdom of God, which is breaking into the present, can come to possess a new heart. While someone may not commit the sinful act, to perform the wicked deed in one's heart nevertheless makes one guilty, according to Jesus (Matt 5:28). Evil and blasphemous words were regarded by Jesus as a reflection of an evil heart, out of which the mouth speaks (Matt 12:34; 15:18–19). In fact, Jesus would often rebuke those who were contemplating evil in their hearts (Matt 9:4; Mark 2:8). Humanity suffered from a hardness of heart (Mark 3:5; 6:52; 8:17), but the restoration that the kingdom of God would bring renewal to the heart, and the faithful members of the new covenant would benefit from this promised new heart.[13]

Those who accepted the gospel of the kingdom of God with faith and repentance began to experience a change in their heart. The large crowds who heard Jesus preach the gospel followed him, resulting in Jesus teaching the Sermon on the Mount, wherein Jesus declares that a pure heart is within their grasp (Matt 5:8).[14] Quoting Isaiah, Jesus taught that those who respond with understanding and repentance at the announcement of the kingdom of God that has drawn near would be healed from their

---

[9] Bovon, *Luke 3*, 159–60.
[10] Fitzmyer, *Luke X–XXIV*, 1391, 1402; Johnson, *Luke*, 342; Green, *Luke*, 763.
[11] Witherington, *Matthew*, 484–85; Nolland, *Matthew*, 1078–81.
[12] Schuele, "Heart," 765.
[13] Wright, *Jesus and the Victory of God*, 282–87.
[14] Nolland, *Matthew*, 205, draws attention to the promise in Matt 5:8 ("for they will see God") and recognizes the themes of possessing the land in God's presence and the restoration.

dull heart (Matt 13:15). Indeed, having the gospel of the kingdom in one's believing heart was so crucial that Jesus warned his followers that the evil one—the Devil—will attempt to snatch away the saving gospel from their hearts (Matt 13:19, Luke 8:12). However, the ideal member of the new covenant is one who listens to the message of the kingdom "with an honest and good heart" (Luke 8:15), holds it fast, and perseveres to bear fruit. In other words, the gospel of the kingdom, which promises a coming restoration of all creation, begins in the present with the transformation of the hearer's heart, resulting in fruit as evidence of the new creation that has already begun. Further proof that the renewal of the heart was at the core of Jesus' kingdom ministry can be observed in the necessity of new covenant members to forgive others from the heart (Matt 18:35), which is the conclusion to a parable that concerned the kingdom of God (Matt 18:23). In short, the emphasis Jesus gives to the condition of the heart and how to find restoration further demonstrates his awareness that he was inaugurating the new covenant throughout his ministry.

Paul's Theology of the New Covenant

After the resurrection of Jesus, the Apostle Paul offered several theological reflections on the new covenant ushered in by Jesus' death and resurrection.[15] In doing so, Paul discusses the defeat of sin and how Jesus took upon himself the curse in his death. In an attempt to remind the Galatians of their current position within the new covenant community, Paul recounts how God told Abraham that through him all the nations (i.e., Gentiles) would be blessed (Gal 3:8). Those who are defined by faith are already experiencing the blessing of Abraham, who was himself a believer, while those who derive their identity from the works of the Law are under a curse, according to Galatians 3:10.[16] In order to justify this characterization, Paul quotes Deuteronomy 27:26 ("Cursed is everyone who does not abide by all the things written in the book of the Law, to perform them") which, as we have seen in the previous chapter, describes the punishing curses that are to come upon those who are disobedient.[17] From Paul's perspective, the time of the curses outlined in Deuteronomy 28–29 is still in effect for those Jews under the old covenant. Christ, in his capacity as the messianic king who represents his people, embodied the curse as he died on the cross, redeeming those who are of faith from the curse (Gal 3:13).[18] In doing so, the new covenant blessings, which were to accompany those who returned to God with all their heart according to Deuteronomy 30:1–6, are now available (Gal 3:14), and they are not limited to the members of the Mosaic covenant.

---

[15] Campbell, "Covenant and New Covenant," 180–81.
[16] Wright, *Paul and the Faithfulness of God*, 864; De Boer, *Galatians*, 198; Dunn, *Galatians*, 171.
[17] Dunn, *Galatians*, 170; Oakes, *Galatians*, 109.
[18] Oakes, *Galatians*, 112–13; De Boer, *Galatians*, 210. Thielman, *The Law and the New Testament*, 17, contends that "the Messiah himself has absorbed the law's curse."

Membership in the new covenant, as Paul insists, is based upon faithfulness, which allows Jews and Gentiles to enter the covenant community on equal footing.[19] By ratifying the new covenant in his blood on the cross, Jesus bears in his role as the Jewish Messiah the curses of the Mosaic covenant, thereby making the blessings of Abraham available.[20]

Paul demonstrates his awareness of and agreement with the consummation of the new covenant at the death of Jesus, as we can observe in the discussion of the Lord's Supper in 1 Corinthians 11. In a tradition that Paul acknowledges that he received from Jesus, he recounts how Jesus at the Last Supper with his disciples, and in doing so, he describes the symbolism of the bread and the cup in terms of the new covenant that was to be ratified with his blood: "In the same way He took the cup also after supper, saying, 'This cup is the new covenant in My blood; do this, as often as you drink it, in remembrance of Me'" (1 Cor 11:25).[21] Not only does Paul corroborate the pivotal event depicted in Matthew, Mark, and Luke, but he also instructs his readers to recall these words of Jesus as they participate in the regular communion meals together.[22] As such, Paul contributed significantly to the Early Church's widespread acceptance of Jesus' death as the moment when the promised new covenant was ratified.

By the time Paul writes 2 Corinthians, he is able to speak about the new covenant as a concept with which his readers are well acquainted. In describing his apostleship and his traveling companions, Paul mentions how God has equipped them as ministers of the new covenant: "Our adequacy is from God, who also made us adequate as servants of a new covenant, not of the letter but of the Spirit" (2 Cor 3:5–6). Paul here observes that this new covenant is defined by the Spirit of God, which recalls Ezekiel's prophecies concerning the new Spirit that God would give to his people at the renewal of the covenant (Ezek 11:17–20; 36:24–30).[23] In fact, Paul contrasts the new covenant ministry in which he and his readers are active participants with the reading of the old covenant that the children of Israel experience (2 Cor 3:13–14).[24]

In Paul's letter to the Romans, he offers several comments that help bring further clarity to his understanding of the new covenant agreement between God and his people. For those who have received the circumcision of the heart, which is brought about by the Spirit, they bear the label "Jew who is one inwardly" (Rom 2:29). These two new covenant indicators recall Deuteronomy's illustration of the reorganization of God's

---

[19] Dunn, *Galatians*, 179–80.
[20] Wright, *Paul and the Faithfulness of God*, 867.
[21] Fee, *First Epistle to the Corinthians*, 605–7; Horsley, *1 Corinthians*, 160–61.
[22] Conzelmann, *1 Corinthians*, 201–2.
[23] Sampley, "The Second Letter to the Corinthians," 64; Fee, *God's Empowering Presence*, 806; Wright, *Paul and the Faithfulness of God*, 981.
[24] Wright, *Paul and the Faithfulness of God*, 677. Dunn, *Theology of Paul*, 148–49, offers clarity here: "the old covenant has been surpassed and replaced by something better . . . [Israel] simply have not realized the epochal shift brought about by Christ."

people after all the curses have occurred (Deut 30:6) in addition to Ezekiel's aforementioned prophecies concerning the new Spirit.[25] The new heart and the new Spirit promised in these oracles of the covenant's renewal by the prophet Ezekiel almost certainly impacted Paul's description of God's love for his people in Romans 5:5: "The love of God has been poured out within our hearts through the Holy Spirit that has been given to us."[26] Similarly, Paul contrasts the believer's experience prior to entering the new covenant with their current experience wherein they have become obedient from the heart to the form of teaching to which they were entrusted (Rom 6:17). This further indicates that believers have received the promised new heart that is circumcised, allowing them to perform the faithful behavior God desired.[27] It also indicates that this obedience consists of the doctrine (which is another way to translate the Greek noun rendered as "teaching" here) that God requires of his new covenant people. This newly organized family of God, consisting of believing Jews and Gentiles (Rom 1:16), functions as the redeemed family promised to Abraham, about whom Paul attributes the fulfillment of Jeremiah's prophecy of the new covenant (Jer 31:34) in Romans 11:27: "And this is my covenant with them, when I take away their sins."[28] Paul is deeply convinced that the Early Church is the new covenant people of God, bearing new hearts, possessing the Holy Spirit, and living faithfully to Jesus Christ.

The New Covenant in the Epistle to the Hebrews

Jeremiah's prophecy of the new covenant is given more attention in the Epistle to the Hebrews than in any other book in the New Testament.[29] The author of the Epistle to the Hebrews contrasts the Law of Moses with the new covenant, which is explicitly illustrated as the "better covenant" (Heb 7:18–22).[30] Jesus Christ serves as the mediator of the new covenant, which the author of Hebrews defines with a full citation of Jeremiah 31:31–34. In fact, Hebrews repeatedly applies the title "mediator" of the new and better covenant to the person of Jesus, indicating its importance and permanence (Heb 8:6; 9:15; 12:24). After offering the full quote of Jeremiah's prophecy, the author issues a contrast between the new covenant and the Mosaic covenant (about which Jeremiah described as being near its end): "In speaking of a new covenant, he makes the first one obsolete. And what is becoming obsolete and growing old is ready to vanish away" (Heb 8:13).[31] One of the reasons the new covenant is described in such glowing

---

[25] Wright, "The Letter to the Romans," 449.
[26] Fee, *God's Empowering Presence*, 812–13. Dunn, *Romans 1–8*, 253, detects here an allusion to Jer 31:31–34 in Paul's language of the heart and the Holy Spirit.
[27] Dunn, *Romans 1–8*, 353.
[28] Wright, *Paul and the Faithfulness of God*, 1248.
[29] Koester, *Hebrews*, 112–14.
[30] deSilva, *Perseverance in Gratitude*, 272–73; Attridge, *Hebrews*, 204–9; Bruce, *Hebrews*, 151.
[31] Attridge, *Hebrews*, 228–29.

terms is that Jesus has been raised to immortality, and in his role as the high priest, he can serve forever without needing to be replaced by subsequent priests. The death of Jesus brings redemption for the transgressions committed under the first covenant, the Mosaic covenant (Heb 9:15).[32] Since Jeremiah's prophecy promised that the new covenant would bring an end to God remembering sins and lawless deeds, there is no longer a required offering to atone for sinful acts (Heb 10:17–18).[33] The death of Christ on the cross functioned as the once-and-for-all offering: "we have been sanctified through the offering of the body of Jesus Christ once for all" (Heb 10:10).[34] Since Christ has been sacrificed for the forgiveness of sins, the Early Church did not practice the offering of animal sacrifices in the temple in Jerusalem. The terms of the new covenant made no such requirement of its members.

The Epistle to the Hebrews, in its attempt to persuade members of the new covenant to live faithfully, emphasizes the teachings of Jesus as the means to living loyally within this new agreement between God and his people. During a contrast between Moses' household and the household over which God placed Christ, the author of Hebrews identifies his readers as members of this second house, on the condition of their faithful commitment within that relationship: "but Christ is faithful over God's house as a son. And we are his house if indeed we hold fast our confidence and our boasting in our hope" (Heb 3:6).[35] This pledge of believers to "hold fast" is further defined in terms of obedience to the crucified and risen Jesus: "And having been made perfect, he became to all those who obey him the source of eternal salvation" (Heb 5:9).[36] In other words, obedience to the teachings of Jesus is the requirement for receiving unending salvation within God's new covenant. This salvation is illustrated in terms of the gospel that Jesus first spoke—the gospel of the kingdom of God—which was received and confirmed by the readers of Hebrews (Heb 2:3). Moreover, Jesus demonstrated himself to be one who was faithful to God, which makes Jesus an example worthy to follow and imitate: "consider Jesus, the Apostle and High Priest of our confession; he was faithful to Him who created Him" (Heb 3:1–2).[37] Indeed, the readers are summoned to run with endurance as they are fixing their eyes on Jesus, the "founder and perfecter of our faith" (Heb 12:1–2).[38] It is precisely because Jesus *endured* the cross (Heb 12:2) that his followers should run with *endurance*. In sum, obedience to the teachings of Jesus Christ and a commitment to imitate his example together serve as the terms of the new covenant that God has made with his renewed people.

---

[32] Craddock, "The Letter to the Hebrews," 109; Lane, *Hebrews 9–13*, 242; Johnson, *Hebrews*, 239.
[33] Bruce, *Hebrews*, 242.
[34] Lane, *Hebrews 9–13*, 266; Koester, *Hebrews*, 439–40.
[35] Ellingworth, *Hebrews*, 195.
[36] Craddock, "The Letter to the Hebrews," 63; Johnson, *Hebrews*, 148–49; deSilva, *Perseverance in Gratitude*, 194.
[37] Johnson, *Hebrews*, 107, helpfully observes, "Like Moses, Jesus is, as a human being, created by God, the source of all reality."
[38] deSilva, *Perseverance in Gratitude*, 432.

The Death of Jesus in the Theology of the Early Church

The Early Church universally accepted the death of Jesus and the shedding of his blood as the means by which God offers the forgiveness of sins. Peter's sermon on the Day of Pentecost proclaimed that by God raising Jesus from the dead, the agony of death was put to an end, being powerless to hold Jesus in the grave (Acts 2:24). In his second sermon in Acts, Peter summons his Jewish hearers to repentance and to heed the sayings of Jesus, effectively indicating that Jesus' teachings are the standard of behavior for the people of God (Acts 3:19, 22–23).[39]

The Epistle of James insists that faith without works is dead (James 2:17), and the good works that James has in mind include several of the teachings of Jesus.[40] For example, James' illustration of the implanted saving word (James 1:21) parallels Jesus' Parable of the Sower, which likens the word of the kingdom to a seed that saves those who receive it (Matt 13:19; Luke 8:12). The promise that the kingdom belongs to those who are poor in this world (James 2:5) almost certainly has been impacted by Jesus' memorable beatitude, "Blessed are the poor, for theirs is the kingdom of God" (Luke 6:20). Furthermore, the command in James 5:12 to not swear, but instead let your "Yes" be yes and your "No" be no, clearly have been impacted by Jesus' preaching in Matthew 5:34–37.

The Epistles of Peter also indicate the theology of the new covenant. Christians are illustrated as those who obey Jesus and are sprinkled with his blood (1 Pet 1:2), and salvation is promised to those who persist in their faith (1 Pet 1:9). The process by which one receives the purification of sins is closely associated with the true knowledge of Jesus Christ, according to 2 Peter 1:8–9.

We may observe further evidence of the close association between the salvific death of Jesus and the new covenant in the First Epistle of John and in the Book of Revelation. The "propitiation" of sin, that is, the atoning sacrifice, is none other than the person of Jesus Christ (1 John 2:1–2). The epistle then calls attention to the teachings and commandments of Christ himself, while also setting him up as the moral example that his followers are to maintain (1 John 2:3–6).[41] Finally, the Book of Revelation regularly portrays Jesus as the sacrificial Passover lamb, and with twenty-eight total occurrences, "the Lamb" is the most common way in which the book describes him. Christ is the one who "released us from our sins by his blood" (Rev 1:5),[42] and the plan for him to be slain preexisted in God's purposes (Rev 13:8). The blood of Christ is the metaphorical

---

[39] Walton, *Acts 1–9:42*, 278, offers helpful insight: "it is membership in Israel that is at stake here, true Israelites are those who pay attention to Jesus, the prophet like Moses, and correspondingly, those who reject Jesus are no longer true members of the people of God."
[40] Davids, *James*, 47–50.
[41] Painter, *1, 2, and 3 John*, 167–70; Parsenios, *First, Second, and Third John*, 68–9; Smalley, *1, 2, 3 John*, 52.
[42] Mounce, *Revelation*, 49; Roloff, *Revelation*, 26.

ingredient that believers use to wash their robes (Rev 7:14).[43] Without question, the sacrificial death of Jesus served as the widely accepted means by which one receives forgiveness within the new covenant, while obedience to Jesus served as the standard for remaining in good standing within that relationship.

Conclusion

To sum up, this chapter set out to examine the relationship between the new covenant and the defeat of sin. We first took note of how Jesus Christ serves in his role as the mediator of this new covenant relationship between God and his people, just as Moses functioned as the mediator of the Mosaic covenant. As a mediator, the words, teachings, and example of Jesus Christ serve as the binding terms for those within the new covenant, just as the Law of Moses functioned as the terms of the Mosaic covenant. Second, we observed how Jesus defined the new covenant as the means by which his followers were to be forgiven of their sins, drawing upon the prophecy in Jeremiah 31:31–34 in the process. Third, we examined several ways in which Paul the Apostle depicted his communities as members of the new covenant, drawing upon Deuteronomy, Jeremiah, and Ezekiel in the process to illustrate the body of Christ as possessing a new heart and the Spirit of God. Fourth, we saw how the Epistle to the Hebrews drew extensively upon the theology of the new covenant from Jeremiah in order to frame the Christian life in terms of the death of Jesus and a committed faithfulness to him. Lastly, we surveyed how the rest of the New Testament authors understood the shed blood of Jesus as the means by which the people of God find forgiveness while also summoning them to obey Christ and his teachings as members of the new covenant. What remains clear is that the Early Church believed and taught that they were now within the new covenant relationship that God had cut with his people, sealing it with the blood of the man Jesus Christ and summoning members of the Church to observe all that Christ commanded faithfully.

With the hindsight that Christ dealt with sin and the curse in his death on the cross, the Early Church reflected on the nature of sin and its powerful grasp on humanity. Although it was clear that believers had been set free from the law of sin and death (Rom 8:2), there is still more that we can explore about the impact that humanity's disobedience and rebellion have had on God's creation. Our next chapter will give close attention to the seriousness of sin, its impact on God's world, and how the figure of Adam fits into the spread of sin among humanity. By drawing attention to the effects of sin, we may come to appreciate Christ's faithful life, which ultimately resulted in his death on the cross.

---

[43] Fee, *Revelation*, 114–15.

18
THE UNIVERSAL EFFECTS OF SIN

Having examined the disobedience of humanity and the various provisions for dealing with sin, both within the Mosaic covenant and the new covenant, it should be clear at this point that the concept of sin is a matter of serious importance for the biblical writers. Sinful disobedience creates a barrier between human beings and the fellowship they might otherwise experience with their heavenly Father, their Creator. Although Adam's sinful actions resulted in conflict among fellow human beings, sin is primarily seen as an offense against Yahweh himself. The writers of the New Testament celebrate the shared conviction that sin has been completely and utterly defeated for those who are in Christ. In light of sin's defeat, the faithful have nothing to fear, either in this age or in the age to come. "There is no condemnation for those who are in Christ Jesus," Paul triumphantly declares in Romans 8:1.

This chapter will closely examine how the Early Church understood and explained the devastating effects of sin, not only on humanity but also on God's good creation.[1] We will begin by looking backward from the starting point of the solution of sin to the original human couple's sinful behavior, Adam and Eve. In doing so, we will assess how the Early Church perceived sin's universal contamination in relation to the person of Adam. Second, we will observe the problem of the universality of sin, affecting both Jews and Gentiles. The Jews, as we know, were in possession of the Law of Moses, which leads us to our third topic of discussion: the role of the Law within God's larger plan to deal with sin once and for all. Fourth, we will consider the deadly effects of sin and Paul's understanding of Adam's role in this death that all human beings will inevitably experience. After discussing how sin relates to death, the natural place to turn is to the crucifixion of Jesus Christ, who is repeatedly illustrated as dying for our sins. The death of Jesus will, therefore, be our fifth point. Finally, we will give careful attention to how the early Christians viewed their relationship with sin and Adam, especially in light of Christ's sacrificial death and victorious resurrection. Since the Early Church saw itself between two pivotal events in history—the cross in the past and the consummation of the kingdom of God at the future return of Christ—those believers began to self-identify in ways that accepted the implications of these two crucial moments in history. What the early Christians believed about sin, in other words, made a demonstrable impact on how they viewed themselves and their place in the only true God's salvation history.

---

[1] Morris, "Sin, Guilt," 877–81.

The Results of Adam's Deception and Disobedience

The Apostle Paul discusses the figure of Adam and the results of his sinful disobedience more than any other New Testament author. Rather than speaking of the *fall* of Adam, Paul portrays the events of Genesis chapter three in terms of original humanity being *deceived*. Take, for example, 2 Corinthians 11:3: "But I am afraid that as the serpent deceived Eve by his cunning, your thoughts will be led astray from a sincere and pure devotion to Christ."[2] It is clear from Paul's statement, "Through one man sin entered into the world" (Rom 5:12), that sin was not part of the original creation. It resulted from human disobedience.[3] Creation itself, which Adam was tasked to rule over and steward, was subjected by God to futility (Rom 8:20), again indicating that sin was nowhere present in the beginning.[4] Paul is convinced that sin (and the death that followed) was brought into the world by Adam, and human beings have been practicing sin ever since. It is easy to get the impression that every human being has committed sinful acts based on the wording of Romans 3:23 ("All have sinned and fall short of the glory of God"), but upon closer inspection, the tense of the Greek verb "to sin" indicates a single completed action in the past (literally, "all sinned"). This particular wording has led interpreters to see a deliberate connection between Adam's original sin and the sinful behavior in which all humanity finds itself entangled, and this suggestion finds confirmation in Romans 5:12: "Therefore, just as through one man sin entered into the world, and death through sin, and so death spread to all men, because all sinned."[5] What we can discern about Paul's theology of sin's origins is that creation was originally flawless. After sin and death came into the world, things were very different.

The Universal Problem of Sin

According to the purpose statement of Romans, the gospel message is the power of God unto salvation to everyone who believes, that is, for Jews and for Gentiles alike (Rom 1:16). If the gospel is what brings salvation to Jews and Gentiles, then it stands to reason that both groups are in need of salvation. This is a conclusion that Paul often draws in his assessment of the universal reach of sin, not least of which is the fact that all human beings descend from Adam. "Both Jews and Greeks are all under sin," Paul concludes in Romans 3:9.[6] During the time of Christ, the standard Jewish understanding of Gentile behavior was that their race was idolatrous, ignorant of their Creator and his ways, and outside of the bounds of the promises made to the patriarchs. The average Jew

---

[2] Furnish, *II Corinthians*, 487–88; Collins, *Second Corinthians*, 214–15; Keener, "Man and Woman," 591.
[3] Fitzmyer, *Romans*, 411; Dunn, *Romans 1–8*, 272, 289; Wright, "The Letter to the Romans," 526.
[4] Wright, "The Letter to the Romans," 596; Longenecker, *Romans*, 722–23; Dunn, *Romans 1–8*, 470, 488.
[5] Wright, "The Letter to the Romans," 470; Fitzmyer, *Romans*, 417.
[6] Moo, *Romans*, 201.

would have regarded the average Gentile as sinful, but God had given the Jewish people his laws through Moses. Does possession of the Law of Moses by the Jews vindicate them from the charge of being sinful?[7] Not if the Jews were unfaithful with the oracles with which God had entrusted them:

> Then what advantage has the Jew? Or what is the value of circumcision? Much, in every way. For in the first place the Jews were entrusted with the oracles of God. What if some were unfaithful? Will their faithlessness nullify the faithfulness of God? (Rom 3:1–3)

Paul includes himself in the denunciation of Israel's lack of faithfulness ("our unrighteousness") in Romans 3:5, eventually coming to the conclusion that the entire human race—Jews and Gentiles alike—is under sin (Rom 3:9). To justify this guilty label, Paul draws upon several passages from the Hebrew Scriptures that have already pointed out God's condemnation of Israel's disobedience (Rom 3:10–18). Clearly, sin has affected all humanity.

The Law of Moses in the Purposes of God

When Paul examines the role of the Law of Moses from his vantage point as a Christian, he draws some notable inferences about its function in the broader purposes of God. In our previous chapter, we drew attention to the role of Deuteronomy's curses as it pertains to those who identify with the works of the Law, particularly in Galatians 3:10: "For all who rely on works of the Law are under a curse." Furthermore, Paul adds in Romans 3:20 that he would not have known about sin if not for the Law ("for through the Law comes the knowledge of sin"). He is very careful not to equate the Mosaic Law with sin itself: "I would not have come to know sin except through the Law" (Rom 7:7).[8] In other words, the Law clearly indicates the difference between right and wrong. The sacrificial system and the priesthood, which were so fundamental to Judaism, might give one the impression that the Mosaic Law possessed a built-in answer to sin; however, the curses that Yahweh promised to those who disobeyed were poured out, as evidenced by the Babylonian exile and the events surrounding that national tragedy.

In the midst of Paul's argument, where he contrasts the first man, Adam, with the man Jesus Christ, the apostle provides an important detail about the function of the Mosaic Law in relation to these two contrasting figures. "The Law," Paul carefully argues, "came in so that the transgression would increase; but where sin increased, grace abounded all the more" (Rom 5:20). This densely packed statement offers several key truths concerning Paul's understanding of the relationship between the Law and sin. First, he personifies the Law as slipping in alongside Adam's single transgression. The active

---

[7] Dunn, *Romans 1–8*, 131, 139.
[8] Dunn, *Romans 1–8*, 400.

voice of the verb suggests an intentionality of purpose, and, paired with the purpose-defining conjunction "so that," we learn that this purpose was to increase the transgression that Adam committed. In other words, the Law was not aimed at preventing sin, but rather it served an unrecognized purpose during the period of the Old Testament; it actually *concentrated sin and increased it* within the covenant people.[9] This helps explain how those who rely on the works of the Law are under a curse (Gal 3:10). By increasing Adam's transgression and binding it to Israel, it could be taken upon Israel's royal representative, the Messiah, and defeated once and for all on the cross.[10]

The Sin of Adam and the Death of Humanity

Before we look closely at how the role of the Jewish Messiah could embody the sinful destiny of all the children of Israel in his death, we need to consider the connection that the Early Church observed between the sinful acts of humanity and death itself. The key figure is again Adam, whose name, as we have already seen, means *humanity*. The recognition that the rest of humanity shares Adam's fate is clear from Romans 5:12: "Therefore, just as sin came into the world through one man, and death through sin, and so death spread to all men because all sinned." Even though sin was not explicitly reckoned from Adam until Moses, death nevertheless reigned supreme during that period, even though not everyone's sins were like Adam's transgression (Rom 5:13–14). Since the punishment for sin is death (Rom 6:23), Paul can also say that death reigned and that sin reigned in death (Rom 5:21).[11] This reign of death becomes, for the apostle, a metaphor for the condition of an unconverted person, one who is outside of Christ.[12] Note how the imagery of death is used throughout Pauline theology to illustrate the unsaved person's existence:

> "I was once alive apart from the Law; but when the commandment came, sin became alive and I died; and this commandment, which was to result in life, proved to result in death for me; for sin, taking an opportunity through the commandment, deceived me and through it killed me." (Rom 7:9–11)

> "And you were dead in your trespasses and sins" (Eph 2:1)

> "even when we were dead in our transgressions, made us alive together with Christ" (Eph 2:5)

---

[9] Wright, "The Letter to the Romans," 530, describes the implications of Paul's argument: "The Torah, so far from delivering its possessors from the entail of Adam's sins, actually appears to exacerbate it for them."
[10] Wright, *The Climax of the Covenant*, 37–40.
[11] Dunn, *Romans 1–8*, 287, 299.
[12] Bultmann "θάνατος κτλ," 20; Scott, "Life and Death," 554.

"When you were dead in your transgressions and the uncircumcision of your flesh, He made you alive together with him, having forgiven us all our transgressions (Col 2:13)

"For you have died and your life is hidden with Christ in God." (Col 3:3)

Paul's own experience of the commandment deceiving him and killing him (Rom 7:11) appears to be a deliberate echo of the story in Genesis 3, where humanity was deceived, resulting in the death of exile.[13] As such, Paul interprets the experience of a Jew in terms of the transgression of Adam, whose influence upon all humanity has already been explored. In no uncertain terms, Paul's theology portrays the unconverted as darkened in their understanding and excluded from the life of God (Eph 4:18), implying that they are living under the dominion of death.[14] While living under death's rule and reign, the unconverted are "slaves to sin" (Rom 6:17, 20). Since the Law bound and increased Adam's transgression to Israel, Paul can describe those who have yet to believe the gospel with similar *slave* imagery: sold into bondage to sin (Rom 7:14) and a prisoner to the law of sin (Rom 7:23).[15] Those who are in Christ can rest upon the hope of a future in which creation will be set free from its slavery to corruption, according to Romans 8:21.

The Cross as the Solution to Humanity's Sin

Returning to the death of Jesus Christ, the anointed king of Israel, we can now begin to appreciate how the universal problem of sin that brought death into the world is dealt with on the cross. The Early Church had a strong awareness and conviction that the death of Jesus was, in some manner, associated with sin. In what was no doubt familiar jargon from the earliest period of Christianity, "Christ died for our sins" was received by Paul and shared with his churches, according to 1 Corinthians 15:3.[16] Jesus appears to have taken a voluntary role in going to his own death, as Galatians 1:4 indicates that he "gave himself for our sins."[17] In the Epistle to the Romans, Paul remarks that Christ "was delivered over because of our transgressions" (Rom 4:25) and that the death that Christ died, "he died to sin once for all" (Rom 6:10). Since all humanity has borne the sin of Adam, Christ died for the ungodly (Rom 5:6). Paul even includes himself in this group of sinful people, "while we were sinners, Christ died for us" (Rom 5:8; 1 Thes 5:10). As a single human individual, King Jesus was able to embody the sins of all persons, "one died for all" (2 Cor 5:14). Indeed, Paul stressed the redemptive death of the human Messiah: "by the grace of the one man Jesus Christ" God's gracious gift abounded to the many

---

[13] Fitzmyer, *Romans*, 468; Dunn, *Romans 1–8*, 384–85, 402.
[14] Lincoln, *Ephesians*, 278.
[15] Wright, "The Letter to the Romans," 566, 570–71.
[16] Garland, *1 Corinthians*, 683.
[17] Longenecker, *Galatians*, 7–8

(Rom 5:15).[18] Paul was even able to interpret the death of Jesus as an individual, despite Paul's awareness that he is one among many, "the Son of God who loved me and gave himself up for me" (Gal 2:20). Paul makes absolutely certain the fact that Christ was formerly not sinful, even though he embodied humanity's sin onto his own person, "He made him who knew no sin to be sin on our behalf" (2 Cor 5:21). This passage in particular observes that the Father was not absent and uninvolved in the process.[19] In fact, God actively and deliberately made Jesus the offering for sin, "For what the Law could not do, weak as it was through the flesh, God did: sending His own son in the likeness of sinful flesh as an offering for sin, he condemned sin in the flesh" (Rom 8:3).[20] Since Jesus, serving as Israel's kingly representative, embodied Israel's sin on the cross, redemption and the forgiveness of sins are now located in Christ (Col 1:14).

Since Adam's transgression was passed along to all humanity, human beings find themselves in solidarity with Adam. Paul describes this experience in terms of "the old self" (literally, "the old human being").[21] Consider how Paul's theology frames the human experience apart from being in Christ in terms of this *old man Adam*:

> knowing this, that our old self was crucified with him, in order that our body of sin might be done away with, so that we would no longer be slaves to sin (Rom 6:6)

> to put off your old self, which belongs to your former manner of life and is corrupt through deceitful desires, and that you be renewed in the spirit of your mind, and put on the new self, which in the likeness of God has been created in righteousness and holiness of the truth. (Eph 4:23–24)

> Do not lie to one another, since you laid aside the old self with its evil practices, and have put on the new self who is being renewed to a true knowledge according to the image of the One who created him (Col 3:9–10)

As we can see, the Early Church regarded the sinful effects of Adam's transgression to come to an end with the conversion of the believer.[22] Upon repenting, accepting the gospel of the kingdom, and being baptized in water, the new Christian transitions out of solidarity with Adam (the old human being) and moves into a brand-new solidarity, frequently described as being "in Christ" (the new human being). This is made possible by the believer identifying with the death and resurrection of Jesus. When someone converts to Christ, their sin is laid upon Christ, the one whose death deals with the sins of his people. By identifying with Jesus' resurrection, the new convert begins a new life

---

[18] Dunn, *Romans 1–8*, 293; Longenecker, *Romans*, 595.
[19] Dunn, *Theology of Paul*, 217–22.
[20] Wright, "The Letter to the Romans," 578, helpfully remarks, "What matters is that it was genuine humanity, not a sham . . . a true human being, bearing the true likeness."
[21] Kreitzer, "Adam and Christ," 9.
[22] Wright, *Paul and the Faithfulness of God*, 893, is in agreement: "the 'old human' refers back to Adam, the head of a humanity characterized by sin and death."

that is no longer under the lordship of sin and death but is instead under the lordship of Jesus, their new king.[23] We will elaborate on these topics in Part Six (Soteriology) and Part Seven (Ecclesiology), but for now, we can safely say that the Early Church portrayed the unconverted person as living under the rule of sin and death, and only by turning to Christ can someone be rescued and redeemed from these personified evil forces.

Living in the Overlap of the Two Ages

Despite Paul's insistence that sin is no longer the master of believers (Rom 6:11–14), Christians still live in this present age. The complete redemption of a believer will not take place until they receive their immortal resurrection bodies when Christ returns, at which point death will be defeated entirely (1 Cor 15:50–54).[24] Although Christians are already God's new creation in the present, according to 2 Corinthians 5:17, the believer nevertheless still has a responsibility to choose daily not to return to living under sin's enslavement. Paul offers up prayer in hopes that his readers "do no wrong," and that they may instead choose to "do what is right" (2 Cor 13:7).[25] Since the old Adamic self has died, Paul can logically urge believers to "consider the members of your earthly body as dead to immorality, impurity, passion, evil desire, and greed" (Col 3:5). In other words, believers need to think correctly about the implications of their new life in Christ that has replaced their former deadness, particularly by reckoning sinful desires as themselves dead.[26] Although evil still persists in this present age, the Early Church was committed to no longer fighting evil with evil (Rom 12:17; 1 Thes 5:15). Instead of being conquered by evil, believers should conquer evil with good (Rom 12:21). Operating out of a base of love, Christians strove to not take into account wrongs suffered or evil committed against them (1 Cor 13:5). By obeying the sound words of Jesus Christ (1 Tim 6:3), the Early Church continued to under his reign and rule in anticipation of the final victory over death that will occur at the resurrection of the dead.[27]

Conclusion

In conclusion, we set forth in this chapter to observe how early Christians made sense of sin and its effects on human beings and upon God's world. We first took note of how the Early Church understood Adam and Eve's disobedient behavior, the events

---

[23] Jewett, *Romans*, 405–6.
[24] Fitzmyer, *1 Corinthians*, 606. Scott, J. Julius Jr. "Immortality," 432.
[25] Thrall, *2 Corinthians 8–13*, 895; Matera, *II Corinthians*, 309; Roetzel, *2 Corinthians*, 120–21.
[26] Dunn, *Colossians and Philemon*, 212–16; Lincoln, "The Letter to the Colossians," 642–43; Gupta, *Colossians*, 131–32.
[27] Knight, *Pastoral Epistles*, 249–50; Dunn, "The First and Second Letters to Timothy," 827; Bassler, *1 Timothy, 2 Timothy, Titus*, 109.

surrounding their sinful decision, and the catastrophic aftermath that came to be linked with the person of Adam. We also discerned an awareness among Paul, in particular, that all humanity—Jews and Gentiles alike—was deeply sinful, having been affected by Adam's fateful choice in Eden. Third, we saw that the Mosaic Law played a vital role in the wider purposes of God's plan to deal with Adam's sin, namely by concentrating Adam's transgression into the children of Israel until Israel's messianic representative, Jesus Christ, could embody their sin and curses in his death on the cross. Recognizing a significant connection between sin and death led to our fourth observation, which highlighted the mortal consequences of those who commit sin. One of the most central tenets of the Early Church was that Jesus, the king of God's kingdom, not only died but also died for sinners. This was our fifth point of examination. Lastly, we explored how those who had converted to Christ understood their relationship with sin, especially in light of the realization that their former solidarity with the old man Adam had been broken, being replaced with an awareness that they were now in Christ, the new man. So, although Christians began to describe their experience in terms of a new life rather than using language associated with death, these believers still looked forward to a time in which their redemption would be completed at the return of Christ, resulting in the possession of immortal bodies.

While our study of sin has thus far intentionally been focused on human beings, the ideal readers of the Bible, humanity was by no means the only part of God's creation that consciously acts in rebellion towards its Creator. The writers of the Old Testament and the Early Church also talked about the elusive figure of Satan, in addition to several demonic beings and disobedient heavenly angels that do not act in accordance with the purposes of God. To fairly assess the universality of the sinful effects of rebellious creation, we cannot limit our scope to human beings alone. As such, our next chapter will attempt to make sense of these other non-human beings, thereby providing a fuller picture of not only God's creation that is in rebellion against his ways but also how God will deal with these forces on the Day of Judgment.

19
CREATION IN REBELLION

The subject of non-human rebellious entities, namely Satan, demons, and fallen angels, might appear to be fairly straightforward. The biblical authors, both in the Old Testament and the New Testament, presuppose that their readers know about the existence of these beings. As such, they are never formally introduced to the uninitiated reader by the writers of the biblical text, leaving interested persons having to piece together clues about the origins, activities, and meaning behind these members of rebellious creation. A plethora of extra-biblical Jewish texts also discuss and presuppose belief in the figure of Satan, various demons, and disobedient heavenly angels, but for the purposes of this volume, we are narrowing our scope to the biblical texts and what the Early Church believed about such malevolent figures.[1]

Our exploration of the non-human created beings that are in sinful rebellion against Yahweh will proceed with four phases. First, we will look at the figure that the biblical authors variously described as Satan, the Devil, and the tempter. We will carefully examine the Old Testament evidence before considering what Jesus taught and what his earliest followers believed about this figure. Second, we will explore the subject of demons and the various ways in which the biblical authors, in both the Old and New Testaments, depict them. In doing so, we will give particular attention to the exorcisms that Jesus and Paul performed against these unclean spirits. Third, we will address the subject of heavenly angels who have chosen to no longer align with God but instead elect to act contrary to his purposes. Lastly, we will give heed to the various depictions of the Day of Judgment, the time in which all rebellious creation will be called to account and suffer punishment for their evil and sinful deeds.

Defining *the Satan*

As we begin with our exploration of the figure called Satan, it is important that we first define our terms. The Hebrew noun *satan* simply means an adversary or opponent, and the corresponding verb (coincidentally also pronounced "*satan*") means "to oppose."[2] When the authors of the Old Testament employed the noun *satan* to refer to a generic

---

[1] Smith, "An Inquiry into the Identity," 43–74.
[2] Baloian, "שטן," 1231; Hamilton, "Satan," 985.

adversary, whether human or angelic, the Hebrew definite article ("the") would be omitted. Examples of this casual use of *satan* without the article ("an adversary") include David (1 Sam 29:4), the sons of Zeruiah (2 Sam 19:22), unnamed opponents or wicked people (1 Kgs 5:4; 1 Chron 21:1; Ps 109:6), Hadad the Edomite (1 Kgs 11:14), Rezon, son of Eliada (1 Kgs 11:23), and even the angel of Yahweh (Num 22:22, 32). What appears clear based on this survey is that the noun *satan* (without the Hebrew definite article) always refers to conscious beings, usually humans, who act adversarially towards someone else.[3] When the Hebrew Bible was translated into the Greek Septuagint, the omission of the definite article in these instances was consistently maintained.

However, when the Old Testament writers use the definite article ("the") with *satan* (*ha'satan*), the figure in question is much more specific. No longer were the authors describing a generic accuser or adversary (a *satan*), for the definite article drew attention to a specific figure—the *satan*, the accuser. Consider the account in the narrative portions of the Book of Job:

> Now there was a day when the sons of God came to present themselves before Yahweh, and Satan also came among them. Yahweh said to Satan, "From where do you come?" Then Satan answered Yahweh and said, "From roaming about on the earth and walking around on it." Yahweh said to Satan, "Have you considered My servant Job? For there is no one like him on the earth, a blameless and upright man, fearing God and turning away from evil." Then Satan answered Yahweh, "Does Job fear God for nothing? Have You not made a hedge about him and his house and all that he has, on every side? You have blessed the work of his hands, and his possessions have increased in the land. But put forth Your hand now and touch all that he has; he will surely curse You to Your face." Then Yahweh said to Satan, "Behold, all that he has is in your power, only do not put forth your hand on him." So Satan departed from the presence of Yahweh. (Job 1:6–12)

In this passage, we observe a meeting of God and his angels, the sons of God. Just as the sons of God are illustrated as coming into the presence of Yahweh, so too is the figure described in Hebrew as "the Satan." In Job 1:6 and 2:1, the Satan "came among" the angelic sons of God, and this phrase in Hebrew (*b'tavek*) regularly indicates membership of the group in question.[4] This vital detail demonstrates that this figure, whom the author identifies as "the Satan," is also an angelic son of God.[5] At this meeting of Yahweh and the heavenly angels, Satan discusses his activity of roaming the earth, and when Yahweh informs him of the blameless man Job, the Accuser serves as a prosecuting attorney. By auditing Job's virtue, Satan argues that Job would spurn God if God's protection were

---

[3] Wray and Mobley, *The Birth of Satan*, 52.
[4] Clines, *Job 1–20*, 19; Newsom, "The Book of Job," 347; Wharton, *Job*, 16; Longman, *Job*, 82. Other examples include Gen 23:10; 40:20; 2 Kgs 4:13.
[5] Baloian, "שטן," 1231; De La Torre and Hernandez, *Quest*, 62; Wray and Mobley, *The Birth of Satan*, 59–60; Kelly, *Satan*, 22; Hamilton, "Satan," 986.

lifted. After God grants him permission to test Job, this angelic adversary departs from the presence of God. In the following chapter of Job, we observe the extent of Satan's power: "So Satan went out from the presence of Yahweh and struck Job with loathsome sores from the sole of his foot to the crown of his head" (Job 2:7). Satan possessed the ability to assault Job with a body full of painful sores.[6] It should also be pointed out that this adversarial figure is not depicted as God's equal in any way; rather, *ha'satan* needed permission to test Job, demonstrating that Yahweh was the supreme being even among his angelic council.[7] This adversary, it would appear, is quite different from the other generic opponents, for "the Satan" is illustrated by the author of Job as an angelic son of God, one who harms God's people and possesses the capacity to strike them with harmful bodily sicknesses malevolently.

A similar portrayal of the Adversary (*ha'satan*) occurs in one of the visions given to the prophet Zechariah, where Satan again serves as a prosecuting attorney, this time acting in opposition to the high priest Joshua:

> Then he showed me the high priest Joshua standing before the angel of Yahweh, and Satan standing at his right hand to accuse him. And Yahweh said to Satan, "Yahweh rebuke you, O Satan! Yahweh who has chosen Jerusalem rebuke you! Is not this man a brand plucked from the fire?" (Zech 3:1–2)

Satan is portrayed as a figure standing counter to Joshua, ready to act as his accuser. In other words, *ha'satan* (the noun) stands ready to accuse, that is, to *satan* (the verb). Before Satan is able to get a word in, Yahweh thoroughly rebukes Satan. God does to the accuser what the accuser desires to do to God's chosen priest. Zechariah's brief description of "the Satan" contains several remarkable parallels to the opening two chapters of the Book of Job. Both passages plainly portray, in prose, an accusatory figure bent on finding fault in human individuals.[8] He appears in the presence of heavenly angels—almost certainly the divine council—and Yahweh speaks to him.[9] In short, the authors of the Old Testament carefully distinguish between ordinary accusers and the accuser who is portrayed as a heavenly angel intent on actively opposing the people of God.

In the instances where the Hebrew text employs the definite article for the accuser (*ha'satan*), the Jewish translators of the Septuagint carried over that article in the Greek, rendering "the Satan" into "the *diabolos*" (Job 1:6, 7, 9, 12; 2:1, 2, 3, 4, 6, 7, 8; Zech 3:1, 2).[10] The Greek noun *diabolos* also carries with it the meaning of one who accuses, but its primary definition is that of a slanderer. Just as the authors of the Old

---

[6] Estes, *Handbook on the Wisdom Books*, 33; Longman, *Job*, 88; Wray and Mobley, *The Birth of Satan*, 63.
[7] Hamilton, "Satan," 987.
[8] Smith, *Micah–Malachi*, 199; Brown, *Obadiah through Malachi*, 147.
[9] Goldingay and Scalise, *Minor Prophets II*, 219; De La Torre and Hernandez, *Quest*, 62; Wray and Mobley, *The Birth of Satan*, 64–65; Nogalski, *Micah–Malachi*, 847.
[10] Kelly, *Satan*, 31.

Testament maintained the distinction, the Early Church preserved distinct meanings behind *diabolos* (without the definite article) and *o diabolos*, referring to the Devil. References to ordinary slanderers with the noun *diabolos* include gossiping women (1 Tim 3:11; Tit 2:3) and generic slanderers in the last days (2 Tim 3:3).[11] However, when the New Testament authors do employ the definite article ("the Devil"), we again encounter a very specific figure that bears a remarkable resemblance to the accuser from the Old Testament.

Take, for example, the account of Jesus' post-baptism temptation in the wilderness, which is mentioned briefly in Mark 1:12–13 but given a fuller telling in Matthew 4:1–11 and Luke 4:1–13. We can discern several clues about this figure, whom Matthew variously describes as *the Devil* (Matt 4:1, 5, 8, 11), *the tempter* (Matt 4:3), and *Satan* (Matt 4:10). First, the Devil is the subject of the active verb "to approach" as he comes up to Jesus (Matt 4:3), and the narrator uses the same verb to illustrate the angels approaching Jesus after the temptation (Matt 4:11).[12] Second, Jesus and Satan have real conversations with each other about the nature of the temptations that are taking place. Third, Satan possesses the ability to supernaturally take Jesus out of the wilderness and into the holy city to stand on the highest point of the temple (Matt 4:5; Luke 4:9). Fourth, another of the temptations involves the Devil showing Jesus all of the kingdoms of the world, about which Luke recounts, "I will give you all this domain and its glory; for it has been handed over to me, and I give it to whomever I wish. Therefore if you worship before me, it shall all be yours" (Luke 4:6–7). Since Jesus does not dispute Satan's claim and chooses only to refuse to offer worship, we can confidently discern that Satan has indeed been handed all the kingdoms of the world, presumably by God.[13] We can safely conclude that Jesus' ministry began with a thorough temptation by the Devil, a powerful figure bearing considerable authority and a pointed motive to dissuade Jesus from acting in his role as the messianic son of God.[14]

Within the ministry of Jesus, he demonstrates the reign of God in the present by performing exorcisms, thus freeing the possessed from demonic activity.[15] While these periodic demonstrations of Jesus' authority as the messianic king and inaugurator of the kingdom were awe-inspiring to the crowds, the Pharisees, who were unconvinced of the legitimacy of Jesus' God-given ministry, attributed the empowerment resulting in the casting out of demons to the ruler of the demons: "But the Pharisees were saying, 'He casts out the demons by the ruler of the demons'" (Matt 9:34; Mark 3:22; Luke 11:15).[16]

---

[11] Rad and Foerster, "διαβάλλω, διάβολος," 81.
[12] Hagner, *Matthew 1–13*, 64, 69.
[13] Nolland, *Luke 1–9:20*, 182; Wray and Mobley, *The Birth of Satan*, 119.
[14] Twelftree, "Temptation of Jesus," 821. Hagner, *Matthew 1–13*, 63, remarks, "There is no reason . . . why we may not have here a historical tradition that Jesus himself mediated to his disciples, perhaps as a means of encouragement in the face of the testing they were to confront."
[15] Twelftree, *Jesus the Exorcist*, 218.
[16] Pagels, *The Origin of Satan*, 20.

Later in the narrative of Jesus' life, this criticism reappears, and Jesus offers a clarifying response that explicitly identifies this ruler of the demons as "the Satan":

> But when the Pharisees heard this, they said, "This man casts out demons only by Beelzebul the ruler of the demons." And knowing their thoughts Jesus said to them, "Any kingdom divided against itself is laid waste; and any city or house divided against itself will not stand. If Satan casts out Satan, he is divided against himself; how then will his kingdom stand? If I by Beelzebul cast out demons, by whom do your sons cast them out? For this reason they will be your judges. But if I cast out demons by the Spirit of God, then the kingdom of God has come upon you. Or how can anyone enter the strong man's house and carry off his property, unless he first binds the strong man? And then he will plunder his house." (Matt 12:24–29)

The Pharisees, unable to accept that Jesus was performing the exorcisms through the empowerment of God's Spirit, attributed the power to a figure called Beelzebul, which in Hebrew means "master of the house" (*ba'al* and *zebul*).[17] Jesus, in disagreeing with the logic behind the accusation that the Pharisees made, questions why Satan would cast out Satan, which would result in Satan dividing his own kingdom.[18] In doing so, Jesus identifies Satan as the ruler of the demons, which confirms the claim that Satan (i.e., Beelzebul) is associated with demonic activity.[19] The exchange between the Pharisees and Jesus demonstrates a shared belief between both parties of Satan as a powerful figure who exercised lordship over demonic unclean spirits.

In the Parable of the Tares—a title that puts the focus on the opponents of Jesus' ministry—we are able to discern some further clues about what the Early Church believed about the Devil.[20] When Jesus offers his explanation to the parable, he emphasizes the opposition he faces from the enemy: "The field is the world; and as for the good seed, these are the sons of the kingdom; and the tares are the sons of the evil one; and the enemy who sowed them is the devil, and the harvest is the end of the age; and the reapers are angels" (Matt 13:38–39). Within this parable, Jesus essentially divides all humanity into one of two mutually exclusive groups: one is either a son of the kingdom or a son of the evil one.[21] Jesus further defines this evil one as "the enemy" and, more explicitly, *the Devil*. According to Jesus, the Devil is actively influencing people in the world in a manner that directly opposes the preaching of the gospel of the kingdom, which would transform its listeners into the sons of the kingdom.[22] While several of Jesus' Jewish contemporaries would have regarded the Roman Emperor Tiberius as the enemy, or

---

[17] Twelftree, "Beelzebul," 418; Wahlen, *Jesus and the Impurity of Spirits*, 125–26; Hagner, *Matthew 1–13*, 282.
[18] Twelftree, *Jesus the Exorcist*, 106.
[19] Wray and Mobley, *The Birth of Satan*, 121; Rad and Foerster, "διαβάλλω, διάβολος," 80.
[20] Boring, "The Gospel of Matthew," 310.
[21] Ladd, *A Theology of the New Testament*, 51; Pagels, *The Origin of Satan*, 83.
[22] France, *Matthew*, 535, offers an apt summary: "To depict Satan as a spiteful enemy trying to spoil the good work of the landowner and ruin his harvest expresses graphically his status in biblical literature: he is a spoiler, not a constructive authority in his own right."

perhaps Herod Antipas, or maybe even the corrupt priests running the temple in Jerusalem, Jesus identifies the true enemy who is actively fighting against the dawning of the kingdom of God as the Devil.

When the Apostle Paul took the opportunity to discuss the topic of the opponents of the Corinthian community, he provided a glimpse into the Early Church's understanding of the malevolent figure known as the Devil. Consider how Paul illustrates the schemes of the pseudo-apostles:

> "For such men are false apostles, deceitful workers, disguising themselves as apostles of Christ. No wonder, for even Satan disguises himself as an angel of light. Therefore it is not surprising if his servants also disguise themselves as servants of righteousness, whose end will be according to their deeds." (2 Cor 11:13–15)

If we assume for a moment that Paul is consistently using the verb "to disguise" in these three verses, we may discern a helpful pattern.[23] The false apostles disguise themselves as true apostles, apostles of Christ. The act of disguising hides the subject (in this case, the apostles) from the reality of their moral standing. So, when Paul applies the same verb to "the Satan" (*o satanas*), who, by taking the disguise as an angel of light, logically implies that he is hiding the fact that he is actually an *angel of darkness*. This is one of the few places in the New Testament where we receive confirmation of the Devil's identity as a fallen heavenly angel. Moreover, Paul employs the intensive use of the third-person masculine Greek pronoun in his description of Satan in this passage ("Satan disguises *himself*"), leaving no question about the personality of this deceptive angelic figure.[24] Satan even has unrighteous servants who follow him, disguising themselves as servants of righteousness. The resulting picture offered by Paul to the Corinthians is that Satan is an angel of darkness who is powerful enough to masquerade as a good angel to deceive others and capable of influencing his servants to imitate that deceptive plot.

The figure of Satan is linked with the man of lawlessness—someone whose arrival on the scene of history will preclude the second coming of Christ—according to the Apostle Paul. In 2 Thessalonians, Paul dedicates the primary purpose of the letter to bringing clarity to the local church regarding the Day of the Lord and what must occur before it arrives. Within Paul's argument, he notes how this man of lawlessness will be empowered by the Devil to perform astonishing feats: "The one whose coming is in accord with the activity of Satan, with all power and signs and false wonders and with all the deception for those who perish" (2 Thes 2:9–10). The Devil is portrayed here as energizing and empowering this lawless man to perform supernatural works that an ordinary human person would be unable to do on their own.[25] The legitimacy of these

---

[23] Barnett, *Second Corinthians*, 523–24
[24] Harris, *The Second Epistle to the Corinthians*, 773.
[25] Kim and Bruce, *1 & 2 Thessalonians*, 606; Weima, *1–2 Thessalonians*, 538; Wanamaker, *The Epistles to the Thessalonians*, 259.

mighty works will cause, according to Paul, several to be misled, which further emphasizes Satan's active role in this empowerment.[26] In short, the figure of Satan is presented by Paul as possessing the compelling ability to grant power, miracles, and wonders to human individuals who oppose Christ.

Just as the Devil departed from Jesus at the conclusion of the temptation narratives (Matt 4:11; Luke 4:13), the Epistle of James encourages early Christian believers to resist the Devil, which will result in him running away from them: "Resist the devil, and he will flee from you" (James 4:7).[27] The Greek preposition translated as "from" (*apo*) employed by James denotes that this act of the Devil outwardly departing will move him away from the resisting Christian, rather than suggesting that this is an internal struggle. The external tempter will retreat away from the resisting believer, just as Satan retreated from Jesus when he resisted the temptations.

The Epistle of First John contains a few noteworthy references to the Devil that are important for our study. Beginning with 1 John 3:8, the author portrays the Devil as an ancient figure that is characterized by his sinful behavior: "Whoever makes a practice of sinning is of the devil, for the devil has been sinning from the beginning" (1 John 3:8).[28] Anyone who continues in a lifestyle of sinning is deriving their identity from the Devil, who himself is associated with wicked behavior. Since the sinner and the Devil are active subjects of the verb "to sin," we can conclude that both are morally responsible for their actions.[29] Although the author here illustrates the Devil as having sinned "from the beginning," he does not clarify further on the nature of that timing until 1 John 3:12, where Cain is illustrated as the one "who was from the evil one and murdered his brother."[30]

Another passage of note is 1 John 5:19, which attributes the evil influence found in the world to a single figure. The passage reads: "We know that we are from God, and the whole world lies in the power of the evil one." By ascribing tremendous power and authority to a single evil individual, the author clearly delineates the contrast between the world (i.e., creation in need of redemption) and the early Christians who belong to God.[31] As such, the evil one stands in opposition to God and his people. The "evil one" is almost certainly to be identified with the figure of the Devil,[32] namely, he who was already mentioned in 1 John 3:8, not to mention the teachings of Jesus that have already branded

---

[26] Witherington, *1 and 2 Thessalonians*, 223–24.
[27] Martin, *James*, 153. Davids, *James*, 166, illustrates this as the "flight of the devil."
[28] Houlden, *The Johannine Epistles*, 95; Lieu, *I, II, & III John*, 133–35; Rad and Foerster, "διαβάλλω, διάβολος," 80–81.
[29] Brown, *The Epistles of John*, 430; Thompson, *1–3 John*, 95–6.
[30] von Wahlde, *The Gospels and Letters of John*, 3:119; Painter, *1, 2, and 3 John*, 229; Brown, *The Epistles of John*, 441.
[31] Lieu, *I, II, & III John*, 231; Strecker, *The Johannine Letters*, 99–101; von Wahlde, *The Gospels and Letters of John*, 3:214.
[32] Strecker, *The Johannine Letters*, 209; Painter, *1, 2, and 3 John*, 324.

the evil one as "the enemy" and "the Devil" in Matthew 13:38–39.[33] This powerful evil being is not some internal struggle with sin or an ordinary human adversary. Instead, he has within his sphere of influence all who are not currently members of the Early Church.[34]

One of the primary functions of revelatory literature, such as the Book of Revelation, is to reveal to readers what is actually taking place from God's heavenly perspective. For example, the faithful within the church at Smyrna are warned that some in their community are about to be imprisoned. While the local Smyrnaean civic authorities will be the ones who drag those Christians off to jail, Revelation pulls away the veil and shows who is really behind this persecution: "Behold, the devil is about to cast some of you into prison, so that you will be tested, and you will have tribulation for ten days" (Rev 2:10). The Devil is revealed to be the real enemy behind the persecution of the church in Smyrna, as he is illustrated as possessing the power, influence, and capacity to incarcerate.[35] Those who are thrown in prison will be tested, and they must prove themselves faithful against the Devil's temptations. There is no question about the identity of the Devil for Revelation's readers, as the book, on multiple occasions, outright illustrates him with several titles and behaviors we have come to observe over the course of our study: "And the great dragon was thrown down, that ancient serpent, who is called the devil and Satan, the deceiver of the whole world—he was thrown down to the earth, and his angels were thrown down with him" (Rev 12:9). The same unveiling of the identity of the dragon occurs in Revelation 20:2: "And he seized the dragon, that ancient serpent, who is the devil and Satan."[36] Not only is the satanic dragon illustrated as the deceiver, but the Book of Revelation also recalls the serpent from Genesis 3 and makes the explicit connection between that serpent of old and the Devil in a manner that was left unsaid by the author of Genesis.[37] Furthermore, the Devil has several heavenly angels at his disposal, which we can only assume are fallen angels. The Book of Revelation, true to its name, unveils and reveals several truths, and in the case of our study, it makes plainly clear Satan's aliases, activities, and angelic subordinates.

Although there are several other texts we could explore (John 8:44; Rom 16:20; Eph 6:11–12; Jude 1:9), we have surveyed enough data to draw some conclusions about what Jesus taught and the Early Church believed about the evil figure of the Devil. This conscious, external tempter appears to be, by all available biblical data, a wicked heavenly angel intent on adversarially prosecuting the people of God. He possesses a tremendous

---

[33] Bauer et al., *Greek-English Lexicon*, 851, defines *o poneros* as "the evil one = the devil."
[34] Brown, *The Epistles of John*, 623, draws attention to "the article before *poneros* and the clear reference to 'the Evil One' in the preceding verse" (i.e., 1 John 5:18).
[35] Rowland, "The Book of Revelation," 577; Beale, *Revelation*, 242; Reddish, *Revelation*, 57
[36] We will have the opportunity to explore these passages more fully in Chapter 49: The Millennial Reign.
[37] Thompson, *Revelation*, 135; Boring, *Revelation*, 165–66; Schüssler Fiorenza, *Revelation*, 81; De La Torre and Hernandez, *Quest*, 75.

amount of influence and power, and he holds sway over many people who are not saved. Not to be confused with normal adversaries or slanderers, this enemy is repeatedly identified as *the Satan*, *the Devil*, and *the evil one*. Christians are summoned to follow the example of Jesus and resist the Devil, and in doing so refuse to give in to his temptations and deceptions. The Devil, in other words, is a very real angelic figure with whom the Early Church needed to contend.

Defining *Demons* and *Unclean Spirits*

When we turn our attention to examine what the biblical authors had to say about demons and unclean spirits (the two terms are often interchangeable), they are presented in Scripture so casually that it appears that their existence was simply taken for granted. No biblical author introduces demons or discusses their origins or appearance. Matters are further complicated by the fact that the biblical authors employ multiple Hebrew words to describe these demonic creatures. As far as the authors of the biblical texts are concerned, demons and unclean spirits are simply present, and their activities are contrary to the will of God that he has for his covenant people.

Take, for example, Deuteronomy 32:17, in which we find the Hebrew noun *shed* (plural: *shedim*) used to portray demonic creatures: "They sacrificed to demons that were not God, to gods they had never known, to new gods that had come recently, whom your fathers had never dreaded."[38] These demons were the object of sacrifice by some of the unfaithful Israelites, and the parallelism of this passage suggests that the demons were regarded as false gods.[39] As such, these demons are looked upon unfavorably by the author of Deuteronomy, particularly because they were associated with illicit worship practices.[40] Another passage that links demons with false gods is Psalm 106:37–38. Note, again, the parallelism within the poetry: "They sacrificed their sons and their daughters to the demons; they poured out innocent blood, the blood of their sons and daughters, whom they sacrificed to the idols of Canaan, and the land was polluted with blood." These demons, the *shedim*, are idols to whom the children of Israel offered their own children as sacrifices.[41] These abhorrent practices of the nations are strongly denounced by the psalmist.

The second type of demon presented by the authors of the Old Testament is the goat demon, coming from the Hebrew noun *sair* (plural: *sairim*).[42] These demons appear in four passages, and they, like the *shedim* we already examined, were the objects

---

[38] Köhler et al., *Hebrew and Aramaic Lexicon*, 1417.
[39] Kuemmerlin-McLean and Reese, "Demons," 139.
[40] Clements, "The Book of Deuteronomy," 528.
[41] Hossfeld and Zenger, *Psalms 3*, 92.
[42] Köhler et al., *Hebrew and Aramaic Lexicon*, 1341.

of unlawful worship practices.[43] Moses informed the sons of Israel of this unauthorized sacrifice: "They shall no longer sacrifice their sacrifices to the goat demons with which they play the harlot. This shall be a permanent statute to them throughout their generations" (Lev 17:7). By offering sacrifices to these goat demons, some of the disobedient among Israel were being unfaithful to the covenant agreement and were thus rightly labeled as playing the "harlot" by Moses.[44] The second occurrence of the goat demons appears in 2 Chronicles, where the chronicler is spelling out the sins of Jeroboam.[45] This terrible king, we are told, "appointed his own priests for the high places, and for the goat demons, and for the calves that he had made" (2 Chron 11:15). Jeroboam went so far as to establish a priesthood dedicated to paying honor to these goat demons, who again find themselves as the object of illicit devotion. When the prophet Isaiah prophesied about the downfall of the glorious nation of Babylon, he foretold that its land would be uninhabited by people. However, several unclean creatures will make their dwellings in the wake of Babylon's desolation: "But wild animals will lie down there, and its houses will be full of howling creatures; there ostriches will live, and there goat-demons will dance" (Isa 13:21).[46] The prophet thus illustrates these demons as frolicking among other non-kosher beings. The once beautiful kingdom of Babylon will become a den for celebrating goat demons, demonstrating the utter destruction that the judgment of Yahweh will bring upon that realm. Later in Isaiah, the destruction of Edom is prophesied, and readers encounter a similar picture of a wholly ruined land that will come to be inhabited by a variety of unclean creatures, including the goat demons: "Wildcats shall meet with hyenas, goat-demons shall call to each other; there too Lilith shall repose, and find a place to rest" (Isa 34:14). Set in parallel with the gathering of the wildcats and hyenas, the goat demon (*sair*) shall meet with another of its kind. Paired with these goat demons is a female night monster called "Lilith," which many scholars identify as a demon in her own right. It is difficult to say much more about her since this is the only scriptural passage in which she is mentioned, but her pairing with the goat demons suggests that she is yet another unclean demonic creature.

Several of the texts we have already surveyed (Deut 32:17; Ps 106:37; Isa 13:21; 34:14) were interpreted by the Jewish translators of the Septuagint with the Greek word *daimonion*, which means "demon."[47] This Greek word is the regular designation that the Early Church used to denote the demonic creatures. Although the sense in which demons functioned as false objects of worship and sacrifice was retained by early Christians, there emerged a new way in which these creatures opposed God. We begin to see several instances where demons come to inhabit human individuals, resulting in what the New

---

[43] Van Pelt and Kaiser, "שָׂעִיר," 1260; Kuemmerlin-McLean and Reese, "Demons," 139.
[44] Milgrom, *Leviticus 17–22*, 1462.
[45] Allen, "The First and Second Books of Chronicles," 521.
[46] Van Pelt and Kaiser, "שָׂעִיר," 1260.
[47] Foerster, "δαίμων κτλ," 11–12.

Testament authors describe as demon possession (without any suggestion that the host serves in the capacity of an owner).[48] During the ministry of Jesus, which was characterized by the announcement of the kingdom of God and its ensuing reign breaking into this age, Jesus would often cast out demons from the body of the possessed person. As such, there is frequently a close association between the preaching of the gospel of the kingdom of God and Jesus' exorcising demonic, unclean spirits. For example, Matthew offers a summary statement about how Jesus was proclaiming the good news of the kingdom (Matt 4:23), and he immediately follows up this sentence by observing that many who heard of the fame of this kingdom preacher "brought to him all who were ill, those suffering with various diseases and pains, demoniacs, epileptics, paralytics; and he healed them" (Matt 4:24). These "demoniacs" are human beings in whom demons have taken up residence and imprisoned.[49] Matthew is careful to distinguish these demoniacs from those who were ill and those who suffered from disease and pain, and in doing so, Matthew here did not identify those experiencing demon possession as being sick, mentally, or otherwise.[50]

In another story of Jesus encountering demon-possessed people, we observe some helpful clues about the potential effects of demonic inhabitation and the cognitive abilities of the demons themselves. Consider this account of Jesus traveling into Gentile territory:

> And when he came to the other side, to the country of the Gadarenes, two demon-possessed men met him, coming out of the tombs, so fierce that no one could pass that way. And behold, they cried out, "What have you to do with us, O Son of God? Have you come here to torment us before the time?" Now a herd of many pigs was feeding at some distance from them. And the demons begged him, saying, "If you cast us out, send us away into the herd of pigs." And he said to them, "Go." So they came out and went into the pigs, and behold, the whole herd rushed down the steep bank into the sea and drowned in the waters. (Matt 8:28–32)

The story indicates that the demons who inhabited the two men empowered them mightily to the point where they would withstand anyone who attempted to walk on that road. Of incredible note is the fact that, without Jesus saying a word, the demon-possessed men immediately knew Jesus' messianic identity ("O Son of God") and recognized that Jesus' arrival indicated a time of radical reversal. Furthermore, they are also aware of the coming Day of Judgment and Jesus Christ's key role on that day as the appointed judge.[51] Since the country of the Gadarenes is not a prominent Jewish settlement and the locals were swine-herders, we can reasonably assume that Matthew is deliberately portraying these men as Gentiles, who normally would be completely

---

[48] Kuemmerlin-McLean and Reese, "Demons," 140.
[49] Nolland, *Matthew*, 184.
[50] Keener, *Matthew*, 155–56.
[51] Wahlen, *Jesus and the Impurity of Spirits*, 122–23; Twelftree, *Jesus the Exorcist*, 83.

ignorant of Jewish expectations of the coming Messiah and the Day of Judgment.[52] Not only do these demon-possessed men possess this supernatural knowledge, which they clearly received from the empowering demons who inhabit them, but the demons themselves speak to Jesus ("If you cast *us* out, send *us* away").[53] Moreover, while the whole herd rushed down into the sea, the Greek text makes it clear that they (i.e., the demons) drowned in the water.[54] Matthew presents the demons as conscious, malevolent beings that have the capacity to impart strength and theological knowledge to ordinary human beings.[55]

The Gospel of Mark presents a similar story in a much more concise manner. According to Mark 1:34, Jesus both exercised demons from their human hosts, and he demonstrated his authority over the demons by not allowing them to reveal Jesus' true messianic identity: "And he healed many who were ill with various diseases, and cast out many demons; and he was not permitting the demons to speak, because they knew who he was." Mark, like Matthew, is careful to distinguish the demon-possessed from those suffering from diseases, presumably not to give the reader the impression that demons are just another form of ailing sickness. We again encounter evidence that the demons have access to supernatural knowledge of the messianic identity of Jesus, something the disciples are unaware of at this point in the narrative.[56] Despite the demons' ability to communicate verbally with Jesus and their unique theological insights, Jesus nevertheless demonstrates that, as the anointed Messiah, he is empowered to exercise his rule and dominion over the demons.[57]

When Luke illustrates a similar story in which the demons have the opportunity, albeit briefly, to verbally reveal who Jesus is, the evangelist offers a few additional clues that are helpful for our study. Luke 4:40–41 describes the scene in question: "Now when the sun was setting, all those who had any who were sick with various diseases brought them to him, and he laid his hands on every one of them and healed them. And demons also came out of many, crying, 'You are the Son of God!' But he rebuked them and would not allow them to speak, because they knew that he was the Christ." While it is not apparent in the English translation, Luke's Greek makes a careful distinction in this passage between the many people whom Jesus healed and the demons, to whom the grammar attributes *the act of coming out* of the many, the verb *crying*, and *the object* of not being allowed to speak. In other words, Luke clearly and unmistakably distinguishes the

---

[52] Hagner, *Matthew 1–13*, 227.
[53] Davies and Allison, *Matthew*, 2:81.
[54] Gundry, *Matthew*, 160.
[55] Hagner, *Matthew 1–13*, 229, offers an apt summary: "The demons with their supernatural knowledge know immediately who stands before them."
[56] Kelly, *Satan*, 82; Perkins, "The Gospel of Mark," 543; Guelich, *Mark 1–8:26*, 66–67.
[57] France, *Mark*, 110.

demons, who consciously speak and know Jesus' identity as the Christ, and the possessed persons.[58] Jesus rebuked the demons, not the demon-possessed people.[59]

Moving from the teachings of Jesus to the theology of the Apostle Paul, we encounter some familiar overlap from the portrayals of demons by the authors of the Old Testament. In Corinth, Paul attempted to settle a dispute concerning whether it was acceptable within the bounds of the new covenant to consume food that came from sacrifices to pagan gods. Some of the Corinthians, assuming that the idols weren't even real in the first place, regarded the eating of this meat as an innocent practice.[60] Paul disagrees that the practice is of no consequence, and in doing so, he alludes to a passage we surveyed above (Deut 32:17) in his response that is found in 1 Corinthians: "No, I imply that what pagans sacrifice they offer to demons and not to God. I do not want you to be participants with demons. You cannot drink the cup of the Lord and the cup of demons. You cannot partake of the table of the Lord and the table of demons" (1 Cor 10:20–21).[61] So, despite the fact that idols appear to be harmless and inanimate, Paul regarded them as something more, as demons.[62] Furthermore, it was important to Paul that his communities not commune, either intentionally or unintentionally, with these demons by partaking of the meat sacrificed to these idols. The threat was so serious that Paul insists that a Christian, who partakes of the Lord's Supper and communes with the risen Jesus in that meal, cannot also eat at the table with demons.[63] Influenced by Deuteronomy 32:17, Paul took a firm stance on this issue, thereby protecting the sanctity of the early Christian sacramental meal.

Within the Epistle of James, we may discern some further evidence that demons are conscious, evil creatures with the capacity to understand important theological truths. In the discussion about the importance of good works in order to supplement a believer's faith, James offers a supporting argument that happens to mention demons: "You believe that God is one; you do well. Even the demons believe—and shudder" (James 2:19). As James compliments a foundational tenet of the early Christian faith—the oneness of God—he observes that even demons admit to this truth. In other words, the demonic creatures have the conscious ability to recognize the Creator, know that he is only one person, and understand the implications of where they stand in opposition to the one God, which results in fearful trembling.[64] James shows an awareness that even the demons possess the capability to recognize the only true God mentally, but their works, being malevolent, will certainly not save them on the Day of Judgment.[65] To convince his

---

[58] Marshall, *Luke*, 196–97.
[59] Nolland, *Luke 1–9:20*, 214; Green, *Luke*, 226.
[60] Garland, *1 Corinthians*, 479–80.
[61] Fitzmyer, *First Corinthians*, 393.
[62] Paige, "Demons and Exorcism," 210.
[63] Thiselton, *First Corinthians*, 776.
[64] Davids, *James*, 125–26
[65] McKnight and Church, *Hebrews and James*, 361.

readers that they need to produce good works to accompany their faith, James cites the demons as a counterexample of creatures that possess intelligence but lack good deeds to support it. The argument of James presupposes that the demons are real, intelligent beings, albeit evil in their behavior.[66]

While there are undoubtedly other passages we could explore to demonstrate further what the Early Church believed about demons (e.g., Luke 8:29; 11:14–26; Eph 6:12; Rev 9:20; 16:14; 18:2), we have surveyed enough clear passages in order to draw some firm conclusions. First, these demonic entities are unquestionably conscious creatures, often linked with inciting idolatrous worship and sacrifice. Second, demons frequently possessed human persons (and on occasion, pigs), and in doing so, the demons oppress their victims in a variety of ways. Third, demons have the ability to listen, talk, beg, and even show fear. In other words, these creatures demonstrate their cognitive functions. Fourth, demons often possess knowledge of theological truths that ordinary human beings do not possess. These include the oneness of God, the messianic identity of Jesus, Jesus' role as the judge, and the coming Day of Judgment. Fifth, the writers of the New Testament are extremely careful to distinguish the demonized human beings and the conscious demonic entities within them, often noting the difference when the demons speak and when the demon-possessed persons speak so as not to confuse the two. Lastly, the demons function as an extension of Satan, the ruler of the demons, and his realm of influence. When Jesus casts out demons, he exercises the rule and reign of God while simultaneously tearing down the Devil's dominion. Although the Early Church does not explain the origins of demons, it universally acknowledges that these sinful beings are in opposition to the kingdom of God that Christ inaugurated and that they will be finally defeated on the coming Day of Judgment.

Fallen Heavenly Angels

Having now examined the two most significant examples of non-human creatures rebelling against the Creator, we can turn to the fallen heavenly angels. In a sense, we have already seen clear evidence that the biblical authors believed some of the heavenly hosts of angelic messengers chose to rebel against God rather than work with him. We have observed, for example, that the sons of God, which in Hebrew is a phrase that always refers to heavenly angels, took for themselves human women and bore offspring (Gen 6:2–4). Furthermore, we saw evidence that the figure of Satan was one of these angelic sons of God in Job 1:6 and 2:1. As we have already seen, the Devil is an enemy that strongly works against the interests of Yahweh. Moreover, the Apostle Paul demonstrates his acceptance that Satan is an angel of darkness by informing the

---

[66] Sleeper, *James*, 81, offers a common-sense reading: "This is the first mention of demonic powers in James. We can assume that his readers would have taken their existence for granted."

Corinthians that he disguises himself as an angel of light (2 Cor 11:14). If Satan is a rebellious heavenly angel, might there be others who have sided with his rebellion?

Luckily for us, the biblical authors and the Early Church have provided readers with several clear passages that illustrate these rebellious angels. The Book of Daniel, the premier example of apocalyptic (i.e., revelatory) literature in the Old Testament, reveals several details about heavenly conflicts that have corresponding ramifications on earth between rival kingdoms. In Daniel chapter ten, the narrator tells of how the protagonist, the Jewish exile Daniel, received a visionary message involving great conflict (Dan 10:1). The contents of this vision compelled Daniel to go into mourning for a period of three weeks, at the end of which a messenger, dressed in linen, arrives and stands before Daniel. This messenger announces that he has been sent "in response to your words" (Dan 10:12). However, the messenger then acknowledges that he was withstood during that period of three weeks: "But the prince of the kingdom of Persia was withstanding me for twenty-one days; then behold, Michael, one of the chief princes, came to help me, for I had been left there with the kings of Persia" (Dan 10:13). From this passage, we may discern several vital truths. First, Michael, whom we know to be an archangel (Jude 1:9), is described as "one of the chief princes," which strongly suggests that the noun *prince* refers to a heavenly angelic being.[67] If this is the case, then the prince who was opposing Daniel's visitor, the prince of the kingdom of Persia, would likewise be understood to be a heavenly angel.[68] The second point of relevance in this passage is that the angelic prince of Persia, physically opposing Michael the archangel, is displaying himself as a rebellious heavenly angel.[69] Third, this rebellious angel represents, in some capacity, the kingdom of Persia.[70] By extension, we can look at how other angelic princes are associated with kingdoms within the Book of Daniel in order to bring further clarity to this point:

> "I shall now return to fight against the prince of Persia; so I am going forth, and behold, the prince of Greece is about to come. However, I will tell you what is inscribed in the writing of truth. Yet there is no one who stands firmly with me against these forces except Michael, your prince." (Dan 10:20–21)

Not only is there a rebellious angel representing the kingdom of Persia, but we are informed that Greece has its own heavenly angel, which presumably will act against the interests of Israel, whose angel is none other than the archangel Michael.[71] In short, the

---

[67] Rowland, *The Open Heaven*, 89, observes, "It is clear from the context (Michael is referred to as one of the chief princes in the same verse), that the prince here is no human king but the angelic representative of the Persian kingdom."
[68] Eichrodt, *Theology of the Old Testament*, 2:199; Collins, *Daniel*, 374; Hammer, *Daniel*, 103; Towner, *Daniel*, 153.
[69] Smith-Christopher, "The Book of Daniel," 137. Collins, *The Apocalyptic Imagination*, 136–37, draws similar conclusions: "There is an ongoing battle between Michael, 'one of the chief princes,' and the princes of Persia and Greece."
[70] Pace, *Daniel*, 314–15.
[71] Newsom and Breed, *Daniel*, 335; Collins, *Daniel*, 376.

apocalyptic Book of Daniel reveals to its readers that conflicts on earth between opposing nations bear resemblance to conflicts in heaven against good angels and evil angels.

Having already mentioned the angelic sons of God from Genesis chapter six, it is interesting to observe how the Early Church fixated on their sinful behavior and discussed it in several passages. Within these New Testament texts, we receive confirmation that the beings referred to as "sons of God" in Genesis 6:2–4 are indeed heavenly angels. Beginning with the Epistle of Jude, we observe a lengthy argument that attempts to dissuade unfaithful behavior. In the midst of this exhortation, Jude refers to angels who, after abandoning their proper dwelling, indulged in strange flesh: "And the angels who did not stay within their own position of authority, but left their proper dwelling, he has kept in eternal chains under gloomy darkness until the judgment of the great day—just as Sodom and Gomorrah and the surrounding cities, which likewise indulged in sexual immorality and pursued unnatural desire" (Jude 1:6–7). These angels are clearly heavenly angels and not human messengers because they are still alive, being imprisoned in chains, which is not something that could be true of human beings due to their life expectancy.[72] Jude tells us that these angels, like those in Sodom and Gomorrah, indulged in sexual immorality, which is precisely what the angels in Genesis 6:2–4 committed by taking for themselves the daughters of men and producing unnatural offspring.[73] Jude, therefore, recalls the account in Genesis six, identifies the sons of God and "angels," details their sinful acts, and indicates that they await the Day of Judgment.[74]

Second Peter, a letter that demonstrates an awareness of the contents of the Epistle of Jude, also discusses these fallen angels from heaven.[75] While arguing that God has judged evildoers in the past and that he will do it again on the Day of Judgment, 2 Peter 2:4 points to the events described in Genesis 6:2–4: "For if God did not spare angels when they sinned, but cast them into hell and committed them to chains of gloomy darkness to be kept until the judgment."[76] It should be noted that the phrase "cast them into hell" in this passage is more accurately rendered as "cast them into Tartarus,"[77] and should therefore not be confused with the location in which the wicked will be annihilated on the Day of Judgment (see Chapters 13 and 48). What we can say with certainty is that these angels committed sin and were subsequently bound with chains of darkness, where they remain imprisoned until the coming Day of Judgment.[78] Once again, these angels must be heavenly angels, not human messengers, because they currently reside in the

---

[72] De La Torre and Hernandez, *Quest*, 77; Neyrey, *2 Peter, Jude*, 61.
[73] Bauckham, *Jude, 2 Peter*, 50–52.
[74] Donelson, *I & II Peter and Jude*, 116–17, 179; Noll, "Angels, Heavenly Beings, Angel Christology," 46; Watson, "The Letter of Jude," 488–89; Mbuvi, *Jude and 2 Peter*, 38.
[75] Noll, "Angels, Heavenly Beings, Angel Christology," 46.
[76] Watson, "The Second Letter of Peter," 347.
[77] Bauer et al., *Greek-English Lexicon*, 991.
[78] Davidson, "Angel," 155; Mbuvi, *Jude and 2 Peter*, 108.

location of Tartarus, the prison of darkness.[79] One further suggestion that 2 Peter 2:4 refers to the account of the angels who sinned in Genesis 6:2–4 comes from the recognition that the passage continues with three other instances where God issued judgment, namely Noah's flood, the destruction of Sodom and Gomorrah, and the rescue of Lot from unprincipled men (2 Pet 2:5–7). Since the author orders these accounts chronologically and places the story of the sinful angels before Noah's flood, we can reasonably conclude that the author is identifying these fallen heavenly angels as the sons of God presented in Genesis 6:2–4.[80]

Working backwards from the contents of Second Peter, we can shine some much-needed light on a remarkably similar passage in First Peter. After the resurrection of Jesus, 1 Peter 3:19–20 indicates that the risen one preached to those who now reside in prison, namely those disobedient angels during the time of Noah: "He went and made proclamation to the spirits now in prison, who once were disobedient, when the patience of God kept waiting in the days of Noah." These imprisoned "spirits" refer to heavenly angels (see 1 Kgs 22:19–23; Heb 1:13–14; Rev 1:4), and the timing of the event during Noah's lifetime points again to the events of Genesis 6, where the sons of God cohabited with human women.[81] The appearance of this story in 1 Peter and its reappearance in 2 Peter suggest that the recipients were well aware of the story and that the identification of the sons of God in Genesis 6:2–4 as fallen heavenly angels was an established tradition in the Early Church.

Several other texts indicate that the Devil is accompanied by a host of fallen angels. When Jesus discussed the Day of Judgment that is to take place when he returns, he describes the fate of the wicked as headed to the eternal fire that God has prepared for Satan and his angels: "Then he will also say to those on his left, 'Depart from me, accursed ones, into the eternal fire which has been prepared for the devil and his angels'" (Matt 25:41). Since this place of judgment is for those who are wicked, it naturally follows that the angels of Satan for whom the fire is prepared are themselves evil.[82] Furthermore, we can observe that the fate of these fallen angels, along with Satan himself, is described in terms of a punishment that will conclude with eternal results (Matt 25:46). The pairing of the Devil and his fallen angels appears again in Revelation 12:7–8, which clearly identifies these angels as the heavenly messengers: "And there was war in heaven, Michael and his angels waging war with the dragon. The dragon and his angels waged war, and they were not strong enough, and there was no longer a place found for them in heaven."

---

[79] The Greek translators of Job 41:32 rendered "the deep" as "the Tartarus of the abyss." This suggests an underwater location of Tartarus, which is quite different from the description of *Gehenna* (hell) or even the dusty grave of Sheol.
[80] Neyrey, *2 Peter, Jude*, 198. Callan (Watson and Callan, *First and Second Peter*, 180) offers the following summary: "The author of 2 Peter likewise seems to presume that Gen. 6:1–4 narrates the sin of angels."
[81] Elliott, *1 Peter*, 656; Achtemeier, *1 Peter*, 255–56; Boring, *1 Peter*, 140; Donelson, *I & II and Jude*, 112.
[82] Davies and Allison, *Matthew*, 3:431.

The dragon, which is unambiguously identified as the Devil and Satan in Revelation 12:9, fights alongside his army of fallen angels against the archangel Michael and his angels.[83] This heavenly battle between good angels and wicked angels bears a remarkable resemblance to the confrontations observed in Daniel 10.[84] Just as Daniel portrayed the skirmishes in heaven between good and evil angels as having an impact on the events that take place on earth, so too does Revelation reveal the clash between Michael's angels and Satan's angels, which has parallels to the persecution that faithful people of God experience.[85] Michael's angelic army is able to best Satan's evil angels in combat, resulting in their expulsion from heaven: "he was thrown down to the earth, and his angels were thrown down with him" (Rev 12:8–9). The eviction of the Devil's angels from heaven confirms that these are fallen heavenly angels and not sinful human messengers.[86]

The Day of Judgment and the Fate of Rebellious Creation

How will the Creator judge these rebellious creatures? In what way will God deal with those beings who persist in their sinful and defiant ways? We have already seen clear evidence that these wicked non-human creatures will have to stand before the judge on the Day of Judgment (Matt 25:41, 46; 2 Pet 2:4; Jude 1:6). The demons expressed awareness that they will be punished on this coming day (Matt 8:29). Paul the Apostle assumes that the exalted positions of rulership promised to faithful believers wherein they will judge the angels is common knowledge among his readers: "Do you not know that we will judge angels?" (1 Cor 6:3).[87] The Book of Revelation assures its readers that the Devil will indeed be punished on the Day of Judgment, particularly in light of his deceptive practices: "And the devil who deceived them was thrown into the lake of fire and brimstone, where the beast and the false prophet are also; and they will be tormented day and night forever and ever" (Rev 20:10). The reference to the unending torment is almost certainly intended to be hyperbolic, since the passage goes on to define the imagery of the lake of fire as "the second death" in Revelation 20:14. In other words, the end of these rebellious creatures would be death, that is, their annihilation. In any case, the Early Church was confident that the entire world would be judged on the date set by God (Acts 17:30–31), and this judgment would include all creation, both human and non-human. Those who have rebelled against God will be called to account and forced to answer for their insubordinate behavior. The wicked will be cut off completely, including sinful angels, and the righteous will inherit the earth (Ps 37:9; Matt 5:5; Rev 5:10).

---

[83] Davidson, "Angel," 154; Moloney, *The Apocalypse of John*, 180.
[84] Beale, *Revelation* , 650–52.
[85] Paul, *Revelation*, 219; Blount, *Revelation*, 234.
[86] Koester, *Revelation*, 549, notes, "Revelation simply assumes that the devil has angelic allies."
[87] De La Torre and Hernandez, *Quest*, 75.

Conclusion

In conclusion, we have observed several essential facts about non-human creatures who have sinfully rebelled against their Creator. First, we looked at the figure of Satan, the fallen angel who accuses the righteous people of God. The Early Church regarded this angel as the Devil, the evil one, the tempter, and the serpent of old. Satan possesses incredible influence and authority, having the capacity to deceive susceptible human beings and even empower his evil agents. Second, we examined the malicious beings known as demons and unclean spirits. These conscious, intelligent beings are associated with illicit sacrifices and worship, and the early Christians acknowledged that demons often inhabit the bodies of unsuspecting human beings. Jesus was remembered as casting out these unclean spirits as an expression of the reign of God breaking into history. Third, we saw evidence that the Old Testament authors were aware that not all heavenly angels were siding with Yahweh, for some had chosen to rebel and act wickedly. The Early Church continued to hold to this understanding, noting that Satan has his own fallen angels at his disposal, while other angels who sinned during the time of Noah were being imprisoned until the Day of Judgment. Finally, we observed that this coming Day of Judgment will be the time in which all evildoers will be judged and suffer the punishment of destruction. By destroying those who continually sin against him, God will again bring order to chaos, allowing for the righteous to live in a kingdom without sin or death, just as God originally intended.

The Early Church understood the death of Jesus on the cross as an act that atoned for the sins of God's people. Additionally, members of the new covenant need to reject disobedient and sinful behavior actively, choosing instead to live in accordance with the teachings of Jesus. The next chapter will offer some much-needed pastoral reflections on the modern Christian and the daily choice to obey Christ, rather than obey sinful impulses.

20
APPLYING HAMARTIOLOGY TODAY

It is far too easy to underappreciate the covenant promises that Yahweh made to Abraham, especially the assurance that all the families of the earth will be blessed (Gen 12:3). For many readers of this volume, the promises that Yahweh made to Abraham are foundational. For first-time readers of the Bible (or even the Book of Genesis, for that matter), the plan to undo the curse laid upon humanity by summoning a faithful member of humanity is not only new but also a surprising twist to the narrative. Particularly when we have encountered instance after instance of the negative effects of sin upon creation that are laid out for the reader to see in Genesis chapters 4-11, the prospect that God is assuredly going to rescue the crowning accomplishment of his creation—human beings—in and through faithful humanity, is a rather welcome turn of events. The way in which God plans to utilize humanity to be the means of blessing the world eventually culminates in Christ, the human Messiah, who will rule the world when he returns to earth. The narrative shift in Genesis 12:3 deliberately reorients our way of reading the rest of the Bible. It encourages us to keep a close eye on Abraham's descendants and the various ways in which Yahweh uses them to bless others, help others, rescue others, and so on. Even when several members of Abraham's family show themselves to be unfaithful and disobedient, God continues to work with those who are loyal to his larger plan. Although there are several examples we can point to from Israel's history, no one is more important to this plan than the man Jesus Christ. Not only did Jesus announce the saving gospel of the kingdom of God, but he also lived faithfully to God, culminating in his redemptive death on the cross. What resulted from Christ's faithful ministry was that the blessing of Abraham was extended to the nations (Gal 3:14). How does the body of Christ fit into this big picture? Having already benefited from the forgiveness of sins and the experience of becoming God's new creation people by receiving the Holy Spirit, Christians must continue to be the people through whom God is extending his redemptive blessing to the world. By virtue of our union with Christ, we are Abraham's children (Gal 3:29), which means we can actively participate in the ministry of reconciliation. Let us, therefore, make the deliberate and committed choice to preach the message of the kingdom of God when the opportunity arises. Let us pray, "May your will be done" (Matt 6:10), so that God can use us to bring about his redemptive reign by our actions done in obedience. Let us find ways to participate in God's purpose of bringing healing to the nations, forgiveness to sinners, and saving truths believed by the Early Church to those with ears to hear. In other words, let us demonstrate that we genuinely are Abraham's family by our words and deeds, not merely by our personal beliefs.

Our second practical application, drawn from our study of Hamartiology, focuses on the new covenant, particularly on the human side of the pact struck with God. For Christians, God has already done so much for us. He continues to provide for us in the present, and he has many great things in store when his son returns to consummate the kingdom upon the earth. God has forgiven us and adopted us into his family. He presently guides us and empowers us with his Holy Spirit. Moreover, he assures us that we will see him face-to-face in the kingdom of God, having bestowed upon us immortality and an everlasting inheritance in his renewed world. In other words, there are so many reasons to be appreciative, grateful, and thankful. The natural human tendency is to show gratitude towards those who do nice things for them. When someone offers to buy us dinner, we say, "Thank you." We teach our children to express gratitude verbally when they receive gifts. In fact, it is widely considered to be rude not to acknowledge when someone does something nice for you. Now, when it comes to the new covenant, we can observe all that God has done, is doing, and will do for us. We can attempt to reciprocate with thanksgiving and good works, but nothing we do will ever pay God back for all that he has done for us. Even with perfect obedience, we would never arrive at a place where we could say to our Creator, "Now we are even." So, if we cannot repay God, no matter how appreciative we are for what he has done, is doing, and will do for us, how should we respond to his goodness? What is the proper answer when we desire to express our gratitude to Yahweh? The answer lies in the new covenant, the agreement between Yahweh and all who respond to the gospel of the kingdom with faith. Our faithful response, which is also described as our righteous acts, consists of obeying the terms of the covenant agreement set forth by the mediator. Since this mediator is Jesus Christ, we are to keep his teachings and commands. We are to be faithful to his words. We respond to God's gracious and unmerited act of favor—to his loving action of sending his son— by observing all that his son commanded (Matt 28:20). Christ himself even taught his followers that "If you love me, you will keep my commandments . . . you are my friends if you do what I command you" (John 14:15; 15:14). The Greek text of these two passages reveals emphatic stress upon the pronouns governing Jesus' commands ("*my* commandments . . . what *I* command"). Even the conclusion of the Sermon on the Mount summons Jesus' audience to listen to his teachings and obey them, comparing these faithful followers to a wise builder who will weather the storms with endurance (Matt 7:24–25). On the other side of the coin are those who listen to Christ's teachings but refuse to observe them. They are compared to a fool whose fall will be great (Matt 7:26–27). Let us, therefore, show our appreciation, gratitude, and reverence towards the God who has entered into a covenant with us through the death of Jesus by committing ourselves to Jesus' words. Let us be faithful to our part of the covenant agreement by reading the commands of Christ, committing them to memory, and living them out in our daily lives. By doing so, we will prove to be kingdom citizens, the rulers in training for our eternal role that we will inherit at Christ's return.

Our third and final application point emphasizes the need for holiness and repentance, especially in light of the sinful condition from which we have been liberated. Several texts illustrate the momentous contrast between one's life prior to conversion and after converting to become a Christ follower. Take, for example, Ephesians 2, which describes how believers were formerly "dead in your trespasses and sins . . . we too all formerly lived in the lusts of our flesh" (Eph 2:1, 3). The scene appears pretty grim, but the illustration after experiencing one's new life in Christ and his or her union with him is much more positive: "God . . . made us alive together with Christ . . . and raised us up with him, and seated us with him in heavenly places in Christ Jesus" (Eph 2:4–6). The resulting appeal in light of this transformation from deadness to sharing in Christ's victory is that believers serve as God's workmanship, having been created in Christ Jesus to perform good works (Eph 2:10). How does one go from a life of deadness, characterized by fleshly lusts, to walking in newness of life through the working of good deeds? The answer lies in holy living and repentance. Holiness refers to the quality of a life set apart for the service of God and Jesus Christ. Rather than trying to protect one's holy state by retreating from the world, God's holy people are engaged in mission, serving as God's redemptive presence in a world in need of his rule and reign. Instead of hiding one's lamp under a basket, Christians are summoned to be the light of the world (Matt 5:14–15). Your character, in other words, is marked by a holy calling to carry out the will of God and the mission of Jesus in the very same world out of which you have been redeemed. Another factor that is closely tied to a believer's holiness is the subject of repentance, the reorientation of one's mind towards honoring one's Creator. Naturally, when you change the way you think, your behavior will also change. Holiness, therefore, is a result of genuine repentance. Although repentance is a core element of Christian conversion, it also occurs in the life of Christians, encouraging them to confess their mistakes in their pursuit of performing good works in holiness (1 John 1:9). As we consider our findings from this section on Hamartiology, let us commit to living holy lives, eager to perform good works. Let us also take the time to reflect on our repentance from deadness, recognizing the tremendous shift in thinking and behavior that results from such a dramatic turn. If we discern that we are not currently living as the light to the world, as the workmanship that God created us to be, then we need to consider repenting. Becoming a follower of Jesus is not merely a matter of learning the truths within this book; it demands and necessitates a genuine change in priorities, resulting in good works and holy living. Human beings were made for a purpose. Humanity was created in Christ Jesus in order to perform good works, to be the people through whom God's just rule, grace, love, and truth are made known. Let us truly be the repentant and holy people of God, carrying out good deeds so that his will may be done on earth as it is in heaven.

PART FOUR: CHRISTOLOGY

21
THE MESSIANIC EXPECTATIONS FROM THE OLD TESTAMENT

Christology, which is the study of the person of Christ, is at the heart of the early Christian movement. Matthew's Gospel opens by explicitly illustrating Jesus as the son of David and the son of Abraham (Matt 1:1), indicating the sheer importance of these titles. At the death of Jesus, Mark tells of how one of the most unlikely persons to identify Jesus' messianic status, a Roman centurion, correctly confessed, "Truly this man was the Son of God" (Mark 15:39). The Gospel of John famously sets its purpose statement to encourage its readers to believe the simple truth that Jesus is the Christ, the son of God (John 20:31). The Early Church was eager to make disciples, and a crucial part of that process was teaching the converts the true identity of the man Jesus Christ.

This chapter will closely examine how the authors of the Old Testament laid the groundwork for the roles, qualifications, and lineage belonging to the coming Messiah. Not just anyone could claim to be the promised Jewish king of God's kingdom, for there were several expectations set forth by these Old Testament writers that make the office of Messiah unique. First, we will examine closely how Yahweh makes promises to the famous patriarch Abraham concerning his descendants, out of whom the Jewish Messiah will eventually be born. Second, we will look at one of Abraham's great-grandsons, Judah, and the promises made concerning the royal figures who will descend from his line. Third, we will observe how the covenant God made with King David, one of Judah's royal descendants, heightened the anticipation for a messianic figure to come forth from David's family tree. Since the christological understanding of the person of Jesus was essential to the preaching, theology, and hope of the Early Church, it is prudent that we begin our study by carefully listening to the expectations that the writers of the Old Testament set forth for their readers. In doing so, we have a much better chance of avoiding much of the modern confusion over who Jesus is, the nature of his humanity, his origins, and his relationship to Yahweh, the only true God.

Christ, the Son of Abraham

We have already encountered the Abrahamic covenant in our discussions of theology and hamartiology, and these crucial promises are incredibly relevant to our current study of christology (as Matt 1:1 has already indicated for us). The passage is worth quoting again in full:

> Now Yahweh said to Abram, "Go forth from your country, and from your relatives and from your father's house, to the land which I will show you; and I will make you a great nation, and I will bless you, and make your name great; and so you shall be a blessing; and I will bless those who bless you, and the one who curses you I will curse. And in you all the families of the earth will be blessed." (Gen 12:1–3)

Abraham—known at this point in the narrative of Genesis as simply Abram—is to function as the most important patriarch of the people of God. Not only is God reenergizing humanity's image-bearing mandate to be fruitful and multiply in the person of Abraham by promising to make him a great nation, but the curse-ending blessing will come forth from him as well. This sets the bar high for the children of Abraham and what the reader can expect of their potential. In fact, the story of the Old Testament, especially the narrative sections, closely follows the descendants of the great patriarch Abraham, watching and waiting to see how God's promises will come to fruition in and through this chosen man.[1]

Luckily for us, the narrative of Genesis continues to portray God appearing to Abraham, and in these appearances, the promises continued to be supplemented and further defined. One such appearance occurs in a vision (Gen 15:1), where Yahweh assures Abram that his reward "will be very great." Abram, recalling that the earlier promises involved a large number of descendants—enough to constitute an entire nation—would come from him, explains that he is still childless.[2] The word of Yahweh came to Abram with an answer, giving clarity to the promise of offspring and resulting in Abram committing his full trust in Yahweh:

> "Your very own son shall be your heir." And he brought him outside and said, "Look toward heaven, and number the stars, if you are able to number them." Then he said to him, "So shall your offspring be." And he believed Yahweh, and he counted it to him as righteousness. (Gen 15:4–6)

When Genesis chapter seventeen recounts the terms of the covenant agreement, we observe a new element within Yahweh's promises to Abram, which is the declaration that kings will descend from him:

> "Behold, my covenant is with you, and you shall be the father of a multitude of nations. No longer shall your name be called Abram, but your name shall be Abraham, for I have made you the father of a multitude of nations. I will make you exceedingly fruitful, and I will make you into nations, and kings shall come from you." (Gen 17:4–6)

---

[1] Wenham, *Genesis 1–15*, 278; Hamilton, *Genesis 1–17*, 375–76.
[2] Fretheim, "The Book of Genesis," 445.

In God's attempt at renewing the human race through the faithfulness of Abraham and his family, we begin to see how the role of an image-bearing ruler will be restored. The offspring of Abraham will consist of royalty—kings who will presumably attempt to live up to the standards that originally belonged to King Adam, who was to exercise dominion over God's creation.[3] Yahweh's promise to make Abraham's descendants a group of kings will receive even further precision when Jacob blesses his sons, particularly his son Judah. In any case, the reader of Genesis is now beginning to be filled with anticipation that God will actually do what he promised to bring about in and through Abraham—bless the families of the earth in a manner that undoes the curse of Adam and results in the restoration of human beings as God's image-bearers to positions of kingship.

Christ, the Descendant of Judah

As the narrative of Genesis continues, the Abrahamic promises are reiterated to his son Isaac (Gen 26:3–5) and to his grandson Jacob (Gen 32:13).[4] The particular oath to provide Abraham with an abundance of descendants begins to take shape with the birth of twelve sons to Jacob. These sons will eventually become large Israelite clans in their own right, but in the final days of Jacob's life, they are simply twelve individuals. Right before he dies, the patriarch Jacob summons his sons in order that he may offer to each of them a personal blessing, and it is in the promises made to Judah that we observe several important details concerning the coming Messiah:

> "Judah, your brothers shall praise you; your hand shall be on the neck of your enemies; your father's sons shall bow down before you. Judah is a lion's cub; from the prey, my son, you have gone up. He stooped down; he crouched as a lion and as a lioness; who dares rouse him? The scepter shall not depart from Judah, nor the ruler's staff from between his feet, until tribute comes to him; and to him shall be the obedience of the peoples." (Gen. 49:8–10)

Jacob here promises Judah that his clan will receive praise, victory over its enemies, and even worship. Judah is even likened unto a ferocious lion, which is certainly an image of a warrior. The most important part of this blessing is found in the promises of royalty that are intertwined with Judah's offspring.[5] Images of a scepter—a ruler's staff—confirm the kingly overtones of these descendants. Not only will a line of kings come forth from Judah's clan, but the people will give obedience to it. The translator of this passage into the Septuagint rendered the terms "scepter" and "ruler's staff" in Greek as a single ruler, a prince. This suggests that the promises made to Judah's offspring were being read in

---

[3] Rose, "Messiah," 567; Sarna, *Genesis*, 124.
[4] Wenham, *Genesis 16–50*, 189, 291.
[5] Arnold, *Genesis*, 381–82.

some circles as referring to one particular ruler.[6] What we can say for certain is that the patriarch Jacob blesses his son, Judah, promising that Judah's descendants will serve as kings to whom the people will give their obedience.[7]

In Numbers 24:17, we encounter Balaam's oracle, which offers a further promise of a coming royal figure. The prophetic oracle declares that "a star shall come out of Jacob, and a scepter shall rise out of Israel; it shall crush the forehead of Moab and break down all the sons of Sheth." The imagery of the scepter again points to a coming king—a ruler who will be a descendant of the nation of Israel.[8] This single monarch is also described as a warrior in his own right, one who defeats Israel's enemies.[9] By illustrating this promised warrior-king as a "human being," the Greek translator of this passage into the Septuagint made abundantly clear what was already obvious. The mighty monarch who is to descend from Israel will himself be a member of the human race.

Christ, the Son of David

Once the nation of Israel entered the promised land and asked Yahweh for a king, they were granted the Benjamite Saul, who turned out to be an unfaithful ruler. King Saul's successor, David, would be from the line of Judah, not Benjamin. In one of the most influential texts on Jewish messianic expectation, God enters into a covenant with David, promising the human king that his house (dynasty), throne, and kingdom would endure forever. Yahweh conveyed the covenant to David through the prophet Nathan with these critical words:

> "When your days are complete and you lie down with your fathers, I will raise up your descendant after you, who will come forth from you, and I will establish his kingdom. He shall build a house for My name, and I will establish the throne of his kingdom forever. I will be a father to him and he will be a son to Me; when he commits iniquity, I will correct him with the rod of men and the strokes of the sons of men, but My covenant love shall not depart from him, as I took it away from Saul, whom I removed from before you. Your house and your kingdom shall endure before Me forever; your throne shall be established forever." (2 Sam 7:12–16)

The promise of a line of kings that is to descend from Abraham and Judah is brought into complete focus in the Davidic covenant. God declares that after King David dies and goes to sleep with his ancestors, one of David's sons will be installed as the new ruler. In particular, this king will "come forth from" David, meaning he will be a lineal,

---

[6] Irons et al., *The Son of God*, 129.
[7] Sarna, *Genesis*, 336; Fretheim, "The Book of Genesis," 665.
[8] Levine, *Numbers 21–36*, 200–2; Irons, et al., *The Son of God*, 129–30.
[9] Dozeman, "The Book of Numbers," 191; Rose, "Messiah," 567.

biological son of David.¹⁰ Yahweh makes it clear in this covenantal agreement that he will establish this human king's kingdom, and in doing so, Yahweh talks about his relationship with this paramount ruler. Yahweh declares that he will be the father of this king and that the king will be the son of God. This is a crucially important title, indicating that the son of David is also the *son of God*—a designation for the Israelite king through whom God's rule and reign will be made known.¹¹ The reference to the "house" that this descendant of David will build—a house that will endure forever—probably carried with it the dual meanings of the house of God (i.e., a temple) as well as a dynasty. Either way, Yahweh assures David that this house, the throne upon which the covenanted line of kings will sit, and their kingdom will endure forever. It is difficult to overemphasize the impact that the covenant God made with David had on the theology of the Early Church.¹²

When the chronicler—the author of what we call the books of First and Second Chronicles—reworked the materials from the Davidic covenant for Jewish readers living after the exile and a subsequent return to the land, he provided several helpful clues pertaining to how the particular elements of Yahweh's agreement with David were being understood in his time. In the version of the Davidic covenant in 1 Chronicles 17:11–14, we find confirmation that David's royal offspring "who will come forth from you" (2 Sam 7:12) is "one of your descendants after you, who will be of your sons" (1 Chron 17:11).¹³ The reference to Yahweh correcting the disobedience of the Davidic son of God is removed in the version of the chronicler, who points to an awareness that there has been a narrowing of focus upon a faithful coming king. Furthermore, the promise of the house that is to last forever is clarified by referring to a temple in which God will settle this human king (1 Chron 17:14).¹⁴ Finally, the emphasis on the enduring and everlasting reign of this kingly son of God suggested to many that once he began to rule in his kingdom, it would never come to an end. Each of these promises contributed to a momentum of hope, expectation, and longing for the time when the Father would definitively install the son of David upon David's covenanted throne, so that he might rule the kingdom forever.¹⁵

The characterization of the promised royal figure, who was to descend from King David's line, continued to appear in the oracles of the Old Testament prophets.¹⁶

---

[10] Auld, *I & II Samuel*, 419. Cartledge, *1 & 2 Samuel*, 452, observes, "Yahweh promised to bestow his blessing upon an offspring of David . . . so that the throne would pass from father to son and a strong dynasty would be born in Israel."
[11] Klein, *1 Chronicles*, 380; Birch, "The Book of 2 Samuel," 1257.
[12] Campbell, *2 Samuel*, 72; Firth, "Messiah," 539.
[13] Japhet, *I & II Chronicles*, 333.
[14] Knoppers, *I Chronicles 10–29*, 672.
[15] Braun, *1 Chronicles*, 200; Mowinckel, *He That Cometh*, 157.
[16] Mowinckel, *He That Cometh*, 160, observes that "the ideal future king, the 'Messiah,' was always thought of in the Old Testament as a scion of David, 'a shoot from the stump of Jesse,' descended from the ancient Bethlehemite line."

Isaiah, for example, tells of how this highly anticipated kingly figure will be empowered by the Spirit of God in order to rule and judge well:

> There shall come forth a shoot from the stump of Jesse, and a branch from his roots shall bear fruit. And the Spirit of Yahweh shall rest upon him, the Spirit of wisdom and understanding, the Spirit of counsel and might, the Spirit of knowledge and the fear of Yahweh. And his delight shall be in the fear of Yahweh. He shall not judge by what his eyes see, or decide disputes by what his ears hear, but with righteousness he shall judge the poor, and decide with equity for the meek of the earth; and he shall strike the earth with the rod of his mouth, and with the breath of his lips he shall kill the wicked. Righteousness shall be the belt of his waist, and faithfulness the belt of his loins. (Isa 11:1–5)

Isaiah illustrates this ideal king as a *shoot* from the stump of Jesse, the father of King David. This shoot is further defined as a *branch*, a metaphor from the family tree that other prophets will reuse after Isaiah. There is no question that this coming king will be a lineal descendant of David's line.[17] Nor is there any confusion regarding how he will perform his kingly duties, as he will be highly empowered with the Holy Spirit.[18] The relationship between this Davidic king and Yahweh is characterized in terms of the king possessing the fear of Yahweh, a reverent posture in which the king will delight (Isa 11:2–3). Of important note is the Spirit's empowerment of this anointed king in a manner that grants him *God's own knowledge*, thereby allowing the human being to possess insight and awareness of matters that God reveals to him.[19] Additionally, the king will judge the poor and meek fairly while issuing punishments to the wicked. All in all, this ideal Davidic king, upon whom the Spirit of God rests, will be empowered to rule and judge faithfully.[20]

The prophet Jeremiah also uses the *branch* metaphor to describe the promised messianic figure. In Jeremiah 23:5, we again encounter the anticipation for an ideal king through whom Yahweh's justice and righteousness will be realized: "'Behold, the days are coming,' declares Yahweh, 'when I will raise up for David a righteous Branch, and he shall reign as king and deal wisely, and shall execute justice and righteousness in the land'" (Jer 23:5). Much of the same descriptions we have come to expect with this promised messianic figure are present here. Jeremiah prophesied about a coming member of David's lineage, one of David's descendants, described here as a righteous *Branch*.[21] In fulfillment of the covenant Yahweh made with David, this promised king will exercise his royal duties wisely and with righteousness. Yahweh will "raise up" the Davidic king,

---

[17] Blenkinsop, *Isaiah 1–39*, 263; Firth, "Messiah," 540–41.
[18] Mowinckel, *He That Cometh*, 162, 174, is helpful here: "The future king is thought of as endowed with superhuman *divine powers and qualities* in at least as great measure as the idealized historical king."
[19] Roberts, *First Isaiah*, 179.
[20] Brueggemann, *Isaiah 1–39*, 99–100.
[21] McKane, *Jeremiah 1–25*, 561; Thompson, *Jeremiah*, 489.

recalling the language in the covenant wherein God would "raise up" a descendant after David (2 Sam 7:12). Furthermore, we see that the coming king will perform deeds of judgment by executing justice in the land. The resulting impression left upon the reader is that Yahweh will take an active role in placing this human descendant from David's family tree in the role of the faithful king, who is to act as both ruler and judge.[22]

Ezekiel, a prophetic contemporary of Jeremiah, likewise foretold a time when God would fulfill the promises he swore in the Davidic covenant. In the midst of several assurances that creation will be restored, Yahweh declares his intent to install a ruler from David's lineage: "Then I will set over them one shepherd, My servant David, and he will feed them; he will feed them himself and be their shepherd. And I, Yahweh, will be their God, and My servant David will be prince among them; I, Yahweh, have spoken" (Ezek 34:23–24). Within this prophecy, God calls the promised messianic shepherd-ruler to come, "David," which clearly intends to recall the former figure of King David, who was remembered as a shepherd. What is made clear is that Yahweh himself will be the God of the redeemed people and that this promised Davidic ruler will be the people's prince.[23] The readers of Ezekiel's oracles rightly distinguished the two figures: Yahweh (their God) and the human Davidic prince.[24] These promises reappear in a later prophecy, in which we can observe the same distinction between Yahweh and the promised messianic king who is likened to David:

> "My servant David will be king over them, and they will all have one shepherd; and they will walk in My ordinances and keep My statutes and observe them. They will live on the land that I gave to Jacob, My servant, in which your fathers lived; and they will live on it, they, and their sons and their sons' sons, forever; and David, My servant, will be their prince forever" (Ezek 37:24-25).

Once again, we observe Yahweh assuring his people that he will bring forth a Davidic shepherd who will rule as king forever.[25]

The prophet Micah offers a similar hopeful outlook for a coming king. Micah's prophecy illustrates this coming ruler as one whom Yahweh highly empowers, offering several important details about just how powerful this promised messianic figure would be:

> "But you, O Bethlehem Ephrathah, who are too little to be among the clans of Judah, from you shall come forth for me one who is to be ruler in Israel, whose coming forth is from of old, from ancient days. Therefore he shall give them up until the time when she who is in labor has given birth; then the rest of his brothers shall return to the people of Israel. And he shall stand and shepherd his flock in the strength of Yahweh, in the majesty

---

[22] Lundbom, *Jeremiah 21–36*, 172; Firth, "Messiah," 541–42.
[23] Allen, *Ezekiel 20–48*, 163; Firth, "Messiah," 543
[24] Block, *Ezekiel 25–48*, 297, refers to this Davidic king as the "Human Agent of Peace."
[25] Tuell, *Ezekiel*, 256; Allen, *Ezekiel 20–48*, 193–94; Block, *Ezekiel 25–48*, 418.

of the name of Yahweh his God. And they shall dwell secure, for now he shall be great to the ends of the earth." (Mic 5:2–4)

Micah, writing nearly three hundred years after the installation of the Davidic covenant, offers several connections between David and the prophesied coming ruler. First, Micah recalls David's hometown of Bethlehem (1 Sam 16:4). Second, reference is made to the clans of Judah—the son of Jacob from whom a line of kings would descend (Gen 49:8–10). Third, Micah indicates that there will be a ruler who comes forth from Bethlehem, which is what the reader would expect from the king that God promised he would raise up from David's own lineage (2 Sam 7:12). Fourth, Micah refers back to the Davidic covenant from hundreds of years in the past as the time of old—from ancient days—that readers could trace this promised Davidic ruler.[26] Fifth, the anticipated leader will perform the functions of a shepherd-king (another nod to his ancestor David), and the people are likened to his "flock." What is really fascinating about this coming messianic king is that Yahweh will greatly empower him, sharing Yahweh's own strength with this human son of David. In other words, this promised king will be able to perform works of power because God has given him strength.[27] Moreover, Micah clearly states that this ruler will serve as shepherd "in the majesty of the name of Yahweh his God," indicating that Yahweh is not only sharing his strength with this human king but also Yahweh's own name.[28] By bearing the name of Yahweh, this descendant of David will be Yahweh's human agent, fully representing Yahweh in every way. Micah is careful to leave no room for confusion concerning the relationship between this highly anticipated ruler and Yahweh by plainly indicating that Yahweh is "his God," the God of the promised king. Needless to say, this promised Davidic ruler will be no mere man; instead, he will be highly empowered by Yahweh to the point where he rules and shepherds the people as Yahweh's human agent.[29]

The metaphor of the *branch* used by Isaiah and Jeremiah to illustrate the promised king descending from David's lineage reappears twice in the oracles of the prophet Zechariah. The anticipated ruler is first mentioned by the angel of Yahweh when he admonishes High Priest Joshua in Zechariah 3:8: "Hear now, O Joshua the high priest, you and your friends who sit before you, for they are men who are a sign: behold, I will bring my servant the Branch." God, speaking through a representative heavenly angel, informs Joshua that the *Branch* is indeed coming. Yahweh makes plain the relationship that will take place between him and the coming king, for the Branch is "my servant."[30] Despite the "branch" imagery recalling the promises of an ideal messianic son of David,

---

[26] Simundson, "The Book of Micah," 571; Mowinckel, *He That Cometh*, 185; Firth, "Messiah," 542.
[27] Mowinckel, *He That Cometh*, 175–76; Ben Zvi, *Micah*, 126–27.
[28] Ben Zvi, *Micah*, 127.
[29] Hillers, *Micah*, 67, offers the following helpful summary of the passage: "The rule is by human agency, for the king is separate from God and under him, but through the king flow divine power and majesty."
[30] Meyers and Meyers, *Haggai, Zechariah 1–8*, 202; Smith, *Micah–Malachi*, 201.

this king will nevertheless be subordinate to Yahweh.[31] The second passage reaffirms several key details of this coming messianic figure that we have already observed: "Thus says Yahweh of hosts, 'Behold, the man whose name is the Branch: for he shall branch out from his place, and he shall build the temple of Yahweh'" (Zech 6:12). In this prophecy, Yahweh clearly identifies this messianic *Branch* as a man, a human being, which is what everyone expected of a descendant of King David.[32] We also see confirmation of the role of temple-builder that was given to this promised Davidic king in 2 Samuel 7:13. In other words, the *Branch* will possess complete authority over the house of God, having the capacity to build up, reshape, and edify the place where God dwells.[33] Zechariah is again careful to distinguish between Yahweh of hosts and the anticipated Branch of David, who is to be a member of the human race.[34]

When we examine the Book of Psalms, we encounter several idealized illustrations of the anointed king of Israel, the Messiah, that formed the heart of messianic expectation. Beginning in Psalm 2, we begin to recognize how God will bring order to the world, including its rebellious inhabitants, through the installation of an anointed king. Psalm 2:2 describes the conflict of the nations that oppose Yahweh and his anointed one. "Anointed" is a translation from the Hebrew noun *mashiach*, from which we get the English word "Messiah." Yahweh declares his intention to establish his anointed ruler in Jerusalem: "But as for Me, I have installed my king upon Zion, my holy mountain" (Ps 2:6).[35] The process of installing, that is, coronating the anointed king in order that he may perform his royal duties, is further defined as identifying him with the title Son of God: "Yahweh said to me, 'You are my Son; today I have begotten you'" (Ps 2:7).[36] By using the metaphor of "begetting" to illustrate the installation of the anointed king to his position of rulership, God becomes the father of this king, and the king takes on the title "son of God."[37] This recalls the language of the Davidic covenant where Yahweh would be the father of this son of David, and the king would, in turn, be the son of Yahweh (2 Sam 7:14). This ideal king is to extend his rule and reign from Zion to eventually encompass "the very ends of the earth" as an inheritance from Yahweh (Ps 2:8). Moreover, this anointed king, who is again described to as Yahweh's "son" in Psalm 2:12, is to be the rightful recipient of worship in the form of offering a kiss to a human king, which was a traditional way of paying homage to human superiors in Israel's history (Gen 27:26; 50:1; 1 Sam 10:1; 2 Sam 15:5). In sum, Psalm 2 offers a comprehensive

---

[31] Ollenburger, "The Book of Zechariah," 766.
[32] Mowinckel, *He That Cometh*, 161, similarly argues, "When Zechariah uses the term ['Branch'] as a title of the ideal king, he is also thinking of legitimate descent from David's line."
[33] Petersen, *Haggai and Zechariah 1–8*, 276; Ollenburger, "The Book of Zechariah," 788.
[34] Meyers and Meyers, *Haggai, Zechariah 1–8*, 355.
[35] deClaissé-Walford et al., *Psalms*, 68, point out that God's agency is expressed in this verse.
[36] Craigie, *Psalms 1–50*, 67, insists, "It is important to stress, nevertheless, that the Davidic king, as son of God, was a *human being*, not a divine being."
[37] McCann, "The Book of Psalms," 689, aptly describes this king as a "new agent of God's rule."

description of the ideal messianic ruler, who is called Yahweh's anointed, king, and son of God.

Promises of the coming Davidic king continue to emerge throughout the Psalms. For example, Psalm 18:50 characterizes the expected messianic figure with the parallel descriptors of *king, anointed one,* and *David's offspring*: "Great salvation he brings to his king, and shows steadfast love to his anointed, to David and his offspring forever." This portrayal reinforces the qualification of the coming anointed king as a biological descendant of David, the seed of David.[38] Psalm 89 continues to underscore the reality that God has not abandoned his covenant with David despite the suspension of the kingship due to the Babylonian exile. Psalm 89:3–4 offers words of comfort: "I have made a covenant with my chosen one; I have sworn to David my servant: I will establish your offspring forever, and build your throne for all generations."[39] The promise to establish the descendants of King David so that they may rule on David's throne forever is reassured to the readers (Ps 89:29, 36).[40] The promise that the coming messianic king will be a lineal descendant of King David shows up again in Psalm 132:11: "Yahweh swore to David a sure oath from which he will not turn back: 'One of the sons of your body I will set on your throne.'"[41] The impression left upon the reader of the Psalms is that the idealized anointed king to come will indeed be a son of David.

Conclusion

While there are undoubtedly other passages we could survey that would each reinforce the facts we have already observed (e.g., Ps 45:6–7; Isa 9:6–7; Jer 30:8–9; 33:15–17; Hos 3:5; Amos 9:11; Zech 12:8), we have gathered enough evidence at this point in order to paint a clear picture of the sort of anticipated messianic figure that the authors of the Old Testament outline for their readers. We first observed that this promised figure was to be realized in conjunction with the covenant promises that Yahweh made with Abraham. In particular, God assured Abraham on multiple occasions that his offspring would be instrumental in blessing the world, and this promise included the expectation of a group of kings being among Abraham's seed. Second, we carefully noted how the messianic anticipation came into sharp focus with the guarantee that Judah, one of

---

[38] deClaissé-Walford et al., *Psalms*, 68; Longman, "Messiah," 468, describes the Davidic king in this passage as "the human monarch."
[39] McCann, "The Book of Psalms," 1034. Goldingay, *Psalms*, 2:669, draws similar conclusions: "it is important that Yhwh's commitment to David explicitly referred to establishing his offspring and building up his throne generation after generation, not just in David's own day."
[40] Hossfeld and Zenger, *Psalms 2*, 411.
[41] deClaissé-Walford et al., *Psalms*, 936; Hossfeld and Zenger, *Psalms 3*, 464, emphasize how the promised descendant is illustrated as the "'fruit of your body' . . . reflects the idea that the seed that has come from the abdomen of the man develops into a fruit into the abdomen of the mother."

Abraham's great-grandsons, would have among his descendants a line of scepter-wielding human rulers worthy of being the object of worship. As the narrative of the Old Testament continues, it becomes clear that the anticipation of the promised king, who would descend from the line of Judah and his great-grandfather Abraham, is pinpointed in the family tree of the famous King David. Therefore, our third key insight is the way in which the covenant assurances Yahweh made with David, a descendant of Judah, would produce a human regent who would rule from the covenanted throne in Jerusalem forever. The impact of the Davidic covenant was observed throughout the Hebrew prophets, who likened the promised king from David's line to a "Branch," an authentic member of David's family tree. The prophets also foretold that Yahweh himself would empower this coming descendant of David with his Holy Spirit, with his strength, and even by sharing his own name with this human king. The Psalms complemented these hopes of the long-awaited Messiah with ideal pictures of his reign, his relationship with his God (Yahweh), his royal title "Son of God," and the reassurance that he would come forth from David's family tree. The authors of the Old Testament leave their readers with a clear picture of a promised anointed king in fulfillment of the promises God made to Abraham, Judah, and David. This anointed ruler would be a genuine member of the human race, a man who would count Abraham, Judah, and David as his legitimate ancestors.[42] In other words, the promised Jewish messianic king would not be a heavenly angel or, confusingly, the God of Israel himself. As we will soon see, the New Testament opens with confirmation of all of these insights that the authors of the Old Testament have made apparent to their readers.

How do the New Testament writers illustrate Jesus' birth? Do they trace Jesus back to David, Judah, and even to the famous patriarch Abraham? Why do two writers of the gospel accounts devote so much attention to these genealogies? What roles do God's angels from heaven play in announcing the birth and identity of the newborn Jesus? Did the Early Church, in its portrayals of the birth of Jesus, confirm the expectations of a coming human being, or do they contradict them? To answer these crucial christological questions, we must now turn our attention to the descriptions of the promised Messiah's birth within the pages of the New Testament.

---

[42] Mowinckel, *He That Cometh*, 159, offers a similar conclusion: "It is in keeping with the character of the future restoration of the Davidic kingdom that its king is not a divine being from above but *a mortal man of David's line*."

22

THE BIRTH OF JESUS

It is common for churches to devote time in December to celebrating the season of Advent. These observances are often accompanied by the singing of hymns on the topic of Christ's birth, lighting candles, elaborate Christmas plays, and sermons focusing on the New Testament birth narratives. It is even popular for Christians to decorate their front yards with various arrangements of the nativity scenes portrayed by Matthew and Luke. While Jesus was probably not born exactly on December 25, the practice of devoting time to reflect on his birth (and all the events that surrounded it historically) is a worthy pursuit. The New Testament authors had much to say about the birth of the promised Jewish Messiah, and the details reinforce the genuine humanity of this long-expected figure.

This chapter will examine what the Early Church believed and taught about Jesus Christ's birth and his relationship with the key ancestors Abraham, Judah, and David. First, we will give attention to the genealogies and birth narratives presented in our earliest gospel accounts, and in the process, we will look closely at the language the biblical authors use to explain Jesus' coming into existence. Second, we will look at the Gospel of John, which does not possess a birth narrative but nevertheless offers insights into the birth of Jesus. Third, we will examine the preaching in the Book of Acts in order to discern the connection between King David and his offspring, Jesus Christ. Fourth, we will survey the letters of the Early Church to take stock of all they have to report about Christ and his descent from the famous patriarchs of the Old Testament. Finally, we will look into the Book of Revelation, which provides helpful imagery to illustrate Jesus' birth and his relationship to his ancestor, King David. As we gather evidence from the New Testament documents, we will consider whether there is continuity or discontinuity with the Jewish messianic expectations observed in the previous chapter.

The Birth of Jesus in the Synoptic Gospels

The opening line of the Gospel of Matthew indicates the book's intention to portray Jesus as the direct fulfillment of the Old Testament's long-anticipated Messiah: "The book of the genealogy of Jesus Christ, the son of David, the son of Abraham" (Matt 1:1).[1] This

---

[1] Keener, *The Gospel of Matthew*, 73

introduction confirms Jesus as the lineal human descendant of King David and the famous patriarch, Abraham.[2] Using the standard formula for genealogies in the Old Testament ("A begat B, B begat C, etc."), Matthew traces Jesus' origins all the way back to the forefather Abraham:

> Abraham was the father of Isaac, Isaac the father of Jacob, and Jacob the father of Judah and his brothers. Judah was the father of Perez and Zerah by Tamar, Perez was the father of Hezron, and Hezron the father of Ram. Ram was the father of Amminadab, Amminadab the father of Nahshon, and Nahshon the father of Salmon. Salmon was the father of Boaz by Rahab, Boaz was the father of Obed by Ruth, and Obed the father of Jesse. Jesse was the father of David the king. David was the father of Solomon by Bathsheba who had been the wife of Uriah. (Matt 1:2–6)

This passage continues until the birth of Jesus, and in the process, Matthew uses the Greek verb "to become the parent of another" (*gennao*) over forty times to illustrate the act of a father bringing his child into existence, also known as the act of *begetting*.[3] Occasionally, Matthew's genealogy provides even more detail, stating that the child came out of (Greek: *ek*) his respective mother (Matt 1:3, 5 [twice], 6, 16). Both of these points coalesce when it comes to the birth of Jesus in Matt 1:16: "Jacob the father of Joseph the husband of Mary, of whom Jesus was born, who is called Christ." In this passage, Jesus is said to have come out of (Greek: *ek*) Mary, in addition to being described as having been born (literally: "begotten"). Matthew is careful not to suggest that Joseph, Mary's husband, was the father of Jesus. The text has taken care to reserve that role for God the Father. Matthew, however, has made it entirely clear that Jesus was begotten, that is, brought into existence, by the Holy Spirit through Mary, his mother.

After the genealogy concludes, the birth narrative begins by drawing attention to the *genesis* of Jesus: "Now the birth of Jesus Christ took place in this way" (Matt 1:18). The word for "birth" in this passage is the Greek noun *genesis*, which naturally points to the origin and beginning of Jesus' life.[4] How did Jesus begin to exist? Matthew tells us. Joseph, upon realizing that Mary is pregnant, encounters an angel of the Lord in a dream (Matt 1:19). The angel informs him, "Joseph, son of David, do not be afraid to take Mary as your wife, for the child who has been conceived in her is from the Holy Spirit" (Matt 1:20). Again, Matthew employs the verb *gennao* to describe the act of bringing the child into existence, which is somewhat obscured by the English translation "conceived."[5]

---

[2] Davies and Allison, *Matthew*, 1:155, helpfully point out that the word translated as "genealogy" in Matt 1:1 "probably includes not only the idea of 'birth' or 'origin' but in addition extends beyond that to the thought of 'creation.' Hence the best translation is transliteration: 'genesis'."
[3] Nolland, *Matthew*, 72.
[4] Smith, "Virginal Conception or Begetting?" 46; Carter, *Matthew*, 109; Nolland, *Matthew*, 92; Brown, *Birth*, 124.
[5] Bauer et al., *Greek-English Lexicon*, 193; Brown, *Birth*, 130.

Through the creative power of God's Holy Spirit, Jesus was brought into existence in the womb of Mary.[6] According to Matthew, this is how the *genesis* of Jesus took place.

There is absolutely no hint or suggestion that Jesus was already alive, in heaven, or elsewhere, and descended into Mary in order to become human.[7] The genealogy and birth narrative of Matthew simply do not offer that perspective. Like every other child, Jesus began to live in the womb of his mother, but unlike every other child, the Holy Spirit of God created Jesus. This is why Jesus can call God his father, not because God had intercourse with Mary—Matthew says nothing of the sort—but rather because the Father begat Jesus by means of his creative Spirit.[8] The result is a fully human figure who did not consciously preexist his birth, not for a single moment. Matthew's portrayal of Jesus' birth fulfills the expectation that the human Messiah would descend from the lines of Abraham and David.

Unfortunately, the Gospel of Mark, which is almost certainly the earliest of the four New Testament gospel accounts, does not possess an infancy narrative or a genealogy of Jesus. However, Mark does portray Jesus as the son of Mary and as the brother of four named brothers (James, Joses, Judas, Simon) and an unspecified number of sisters (Mark 6:3). This description is the conclusion of those in his hometown synagogue who knew Jesus from his youth. Their impression of him is that he is a man with siblings and a mother, the woman who bore him.[9] Furthermore, Mark portrays Jesus as the son of David on multiple occasions, indicating an awareness that Jesus descended from the famous king's ancestry:

> And when he heard that it was Jesus of Nazareth, he began to cry out and say, "Jesus, Son of David, have mercy on me!" And many rebuked him, telling him to be silent. But he cried out all the more, "Son of David, have mercy on me!" (Mark 10:47–48)

> And those who went before and those who followed were shouting, "Hosanna! Blessed is he who comes in the name of the Lord! Blessed is the coming kingdom of our father David!" (Mark 11:9–10)

In sum, while the Gospel of Mark does not explicitly mention the birth of Christ, it nevertheless depicts Jesus as the human son of Mary, the brother of multiple siblings, and the royal offspring of King David.[10]

---

[6] Davies and Allison, *Matthew*, 1:200, 208; Horn, "Holy Spirit," 278; Kleinknecht et al., "πνεῦμα κτλ," 402
[7] Dunn, *Christology in the Making*, 50; Kuschel, *Born Before All Time?* 319. Brown, *Birth*, 141, fiercely defends this interpretation: "there is no suggestion of an incarnation whereby a figure who was previously with God takes on flesh."
[8] Davies and Allison, *Matthew*, 1:220.
[9] Marcus, *Mark 1–8*, 375; Guelich, *Mark 1–8:26*, 310.
[10] Irons et al., *The Son of God*, 135; Haight, *Jesus Symbol of God*, 162.

When we turn to Luke's Gospel, we are greeted with an extensive birth narrative and a genealogy that traces Jesus' lineage all the way back to the first human being, Adam himself. Beginning with the announcement of Jesus' birth, Luke tells the story from Mary's perspective rather than Joseph's. God sends the angel Gabriel to announce to Mary that she will bear a son whose name is to be Jesus. Gabriel's declaration and Mary's response are worth looking at in full:

> "And behold, you will conceive in your womb and bear a son, and you shall call his name Jesus. He will be great and will be called the Son of the Most High. And the Lord God will give to him the throne of his father David, and he will reign over the house of Jacob forever, and of his kingdom there will be no end." And Mary said to the angel, "How will this be, since I am a virgin?" And the angel answered her, "The Holy Spirit will come upon you, and the power of the Most High will overshadow you; therefore the child to be born will be called holy—the Son of God." (Luke 1:31–35)

Gabriel makes several predictions about this soon-to-be-born child: Jesus will be great and *will be* called the Son of the Most High.[11] The angel also reaffirms the covenant promises made to David, and in the process, he states that David is the ancestor of this promised child.[12] These descriptions are consistent with the messianic expectations we gathered from the Old Testament authors, but they would be strange if Jesus were already in existence, alongside the Father in heaven, prior to being born. The Early Church did not share that understanding of Jesus, and Luke is quite explicit that the child's miraculous birth is due to the creative act of God's Holy Spirit (Luke 1:35).[13] The Spirit of God, which is further defined in the parallelism as God's power, overshadows Mary, resulting in the begetting of this son. Luke is also quite careful to draw a crucially important link between the creative work of the Holy Spirit bringing Jesus into existence (Greek: *gennao*) and his description as the Son of God.[14] In a few verses, the angel Gabriel reveals to Mary that, without the help of Joseph, she will conceive the long-awaited Jewish Messiah, who *will be* the Son of God, and at the moment of his coming into existence, he will *then be* that promised Son of God.[15] Furthermore, we find confirmation that Jesus will be the human descendant of David, a key feature that we already observed in Matthew and Mark.

---

[11] Kuschel, *Born Before All Time?* 321, states the obvious: "nor was he Son of God 'from eternity'; he was Son of God from his birth."
[12] Johnson, *The Gospel of Luke*, 37.
[13] Fitzmyer, *Luke I–IX*, 193, 350–51; Kleinknecht et al., "πνεῦμα κτλ," 402.
[14] Kuschel, *Born Before All Time?* 320; Brown, *Birth*, 291. Dunn, *Christology in the Making*, 51, states that "it is sufficiently clear that is it a begetting, a becoming which is in view, the coming into existence of one who will be called, and will in fact be the Son of God, not the transition of a pre-existent being to become the soul of a human baby or the metamorphosis of a divine being into a human foetus."
[15] Fitzmyer, *Luke I–IX*, 351; Haight, *Jesus Symbol of God*, 162; Kirk, *A Man Attested by God*, 390. Brown, *Birth*, 31, observes the similarity in Jesus' coming into existence in Matthew and Luke: "I shall stress that Matthew and Luke show no knowledge of pre-existence; seemingly for them the conception was the becoming (begetting) of God's Son."

Luke's christological understanding of Jesus' coming into existence at his conception is reaffirmed by his lengthy genealogy (Luke 3:23–38), a record that traces Jesus' ancestry farther back than simply the key figures of the likes of David, Judah, and Abraham. Luke argues that Jesus comes from a long line of human beings that began with Adam himself. What is interesting is that Adam is illustrated as being the son of God at the genealogy's conclusion (Luke 3:38).[16] This description of the first human being is relevant in light of Luke's placement of the genealogy, which occurs directly after the baptism of Jesus when he is publicly declared to be the Son of God:[17]

> Now when all the people were baptized, and when Jesus also had been baptized and was praying, the heavens were opened, and the Holy Spirit descended on him in bodily form, like a dove; and a voice came from heaven, "You are my beloved Son; with you I am well pleased." (Luke 3:21–22)

By placing the genealogy that ends with Adam, the son of God, immediately after Jesus' public coronation ceremony in which God himself announces that Jesus is the newly anointed son of God, Luke draws an essential connection between King Jesus and Adam, who was created to rule God's creation (Gen 1:28).[18] Where Adam failed as God's viceregent, Jesus, the second Adam, will succeed. In sum, Luke's genealogy not only portrays Jesus as a genuine human figure who descends from a long line of key figures in Israel's history, but he also functions as the royal son of God in a manner that likens him to King Adam.[19]

The Birth of Jesus in the Gospel of John

When we turn our attention to the Gospel of John, we do not have the benefit of either a genealogy or a birth narrative. John's Gospel begins with a lengthy prologue (John 1:1–18) that we will examine in full detail in Chapter 25: Wisdom Christology and Logos Christology. As far as indicators of Jesus' birth go, we have several references to Jesus' family, particularly his mother. Despite the lack of a genealogy and a birth narrative, readers are presented with the fact that Mary is Jesus' human mother (John 2:1–5, 12; 19:26–27). The Jews demonstrate their awareness that Jesus was raised by Joseph and Mary (John 6:42). By portraying Jesus as having a human mother, we can reasonably deduce that Jesus is a human son of Mary. The fact that Jesus was born a human is

---

[16] Dunn, *Christology in the Making*, 112; Kirk, *A Man Attested by God*, 221, 334.
[17] Johnson, *The Gospel of Luke*, 70.
[18] Kirk, *A Man Attested by God*, 223.
[19] Fitzmyer, *Luke I–IX*, 504. Bovon, *Luke 1*, 137, offers an apt summary: "Jesus is the Son of God through God's creative work with Adam, through his promise to David."

confirmed with references to his siblings (John 2:12; 7:3–5, 10).[20] The Gospel of John also portrays Jesus as the promised descendant of David:

> Others said, "This is the Christ." But some said, "Is the Christ to come from Galilee? Has not the Scripture said that the Christ comes from the offspring of David, and comes from Bethlehem, the village where David was?" So there was a division among the people over him. (John 7:41–43)

While the crowds enter into a disagreement about Jesus' precise place of birth, there is no disagreement that the promised Christ is to be a descendant of King David. That the Gospel of John depicts Jesus as the Christ, the son of God, is clear from its purpose statement in John 20:31.[21] We do have a helpful exchange between Jesus and Pontius Pilate towards the end of his ministry, where Jesus speaks about his birth:

> Then Pilate said to him, "So you are a king?" Jesus answered, "You say that I am a king. For this purpose I was born and for this purpose I have come into the world—to bear witness to the truth. Everyone who is of the truth listens to my voice." (John 18:37)

Jesus' admission to being born to be the Jewish king is accompanied by a reference to coming "into the world," which was a common idiom still in use today that illustrates a person's birth.[22] When Jesus gives an illustration of a woman giving birth, he describes the newborn child as being born "into the world" in John 16:21. When we put all these pieces together, we are left with a picture of the person of Jesus who has a human mother and siblings, who descends from the ancestry of David in order to be the promised Christ, and who admits to being born for this royal purpose.

The Birth of Jesus in the Book of Acts

The Book of Acts, being the second of Luke's volumes, continues the story of the formative years of the early Christian movement. Within this account, we are fortunate to have a few more passages that express Luke's theology of Christ's birth and his origins. The first occurs in Peter's Pentecost sermon, which is full of scriptural references from the Old Testament that, Peter argues, anticipate the coming Messiah. One of those passages is Psalm 132:11, which Peter draws upon in order to demonstrate that Jesus is the offspring of King David: "Being therefore a prophet, and knowing that God had sworn with an oath to him that he would set one of his descendants on his throne"

---

[20] Keener, *The Gospel of John*, 1:518, 704–5.
[21] Lincoln, *John*, 506, observes that "the narrative attempts to make clear what is involved in claiming that Jesus is the sort of Messiah who is the Son of God."
[22] Sasse, "κοσμέω κτλ," 888–89; Barrett, *The Gospel According to St. John*, 160, 493; Irons et al., *Son of God*, 138–39.

(Acts 2:30).[23] As a descendant of David, Jesus would, obviously, be a human being. We also find evidence of another passage, Deuteronomy 18:15, being applied to Jesus on two occasions: in Peter's second speech (Acts 3:22) and in Stephen's speech (Acts 7:37).[24] This passage from Deuteronomy, which we will examine more fully in the next chapter, is not, strictly speaking, a prediction of the coming Messiah but rather anticipates a prophetic figure who is to be a member of the people of Israel. By applying the role of the promised prophet from Deuteronomy 18 to Jesus, the early Christians were, among other things, identifying him as an Israelite counted among their brothers:

> "Moses said, 'The Lord God will raise up for you a prophet like me from your brothers. You shall listen to him in whatever he tells you.'" (Acts 3:22)

> "This is the Moses who said to the Israelites, 'God will raise up for you a prophet like me from your brothers.'" (Acts 7:37)

By portraying Jesus as one of the Israelite brethren, Luke locates the origins of this anticipated prophetic figure in human ancestry. Even the preaching of the Apostle Paul traces Jesus to his ancestor, King David: "From the descendants of this man, according to promise, God has brought to Israel a Savior, Jesus" (Acts 13:23).[25] To sum up, the portrayal of Jesus within the Book of Acts that plainly illustrates him as a member of the people of Israel and as a royal descendant of David stands in continuity with the accounts of his birth presented in the Gospel of Luke.[26]

The Birth of Jesus in the New Testament Epistles

The Apostle Paul provides our study with several references to Jesus' birth and his place in the lineage that goes back to the figures of Abraham and David. The opening lines of the Letter to the Romans offer several relevant clues as to what Paul believed about the origins of Jesus, particularly his relationship to David as foretold by the prophets of the Old Testament:

> Paul, a servant of Christ Jesus, called to be an apostle, set apart for the gospel of God, which he promised beforehand through his prophets in the holy Scriptures, concerning his Son, who was descended from David according to the flesh and was declared to be the Son of God in power according to the Spirit of holiness by his resurrection from the dead, Jesus Christ our Lord. (Rom 1:1–4)

---

[23] Watson, *Acts 1–9:42*, 196; Fitzmyer, *Acts*, 258; Barrett, *Acts 1–14*, 148.
[24] Fitzmyer, *Acts*, 289; Pervo, *Acts*, 188.
[25] Barrett, *Acts 1–14*, 636.
[26] Irons et al., *The Son of God*, 135–36.

In his definition of "the gospel of God," Paul mentions "his Son" (i.e., God's son), and then he carefully traces the origins of the son of God to the lineage of King David.[27] The English translation does not quite capture the specificity that Paul offers when he illustrates Jesus in Greek as he who was "born out of the seed of David."[28] This description reaffirms the promises of the Davidic covenant, where David's offspring would be given the title "Son of God" (2 Sam 7:12–14).[29] Paul also indicates that this Jesus is in fulfillment of the holy Scriptures, by which he means the Old Testament. The long-anticipated Jewish Messiah, Jesus Christ, is indeed the offspring of David, just as the prophets declared he would be. The Davidic descent of Jesus appears later in Romans when Paul reaffirms his belief that the Messiah is the offspring of Jesse, David's father, with a quote from Isaiah 11:10 in Romans 15:12: "And again Isaiah says, 'The shoot of Jesse will come, even he who arises to rule the Gentiles; in him will the Gentiles hope.'"[30] By illustrating Jesus as the royal son of David at the beginning and conclusion of Romans, Paul demonstrates his commitment to the theology of the human Messiah as the climactic fulfillment of God's promises within the Davidic covenant, which provides the famous king with an heir from his own offspring.

When we turn to Paul's Epistle to the Galatians, we find several key passages that overlap with the evidence observed in Romans. For example, Paul's argument in Galatians chapter three hinges on Jesus being a descendant of Abraham. In particular, the line of reasoning in Galatians 3:16 draws upon the collective noun "offspring" in order to show Christ to be the sole representative of the family God promised to Abraham: "Now the promises were made to Abraham and to his offspring; it does not say, 'And to offsprings,' as of many; but it says, 'And to your offspring,' that is, to one person, who is Christ." Jesus, functioning in the role of the Jewish anointed king who represents his people, is illustrated as a legitimate member of Abraham's family.[31] Although Paul does not explicitly mention the virgin birth, he does mention the climactic action of the birth of the son of God: "But when the fullness of the time came, God sent forth His Son, born of a woman, born under the Law" (Gal 4:4).[32] With a clear distinction between God and God's son, Paul illustrates the birth of Jesus with the familiar phrase "born of a woman," indicating the common act of a mother giving birth to a human child.[33] Consider the following parallels:

> "Man who is born of a woman is few of days and full of trouble." (Job 14:1)

---

[27] Dunn, *Romans 1–8*, 23. Fitzmyer, *Romans*, 233, similarly acknowledges that "God is Jesus' father."
[28] Gaventa, *Romans*, 28, rightly observes, "That Jesus is from David's lineage already establishes that he is a biological descendant of David."
[29] Fitzmyer, *Romans*, 234–35.
[30] Dunn, *Romans 9–16*, 850; Gaventa, *Romans*, 409; Fitzmyer, *Romans*, 707–8.
[31] Wright, *Galatians*, 223–27; Dunn, *Galatians*, 183–85.
[32] deSilva, *Galatians*, 355, argues, "The Son 'came into being from a woman,' thus sharing our humanity."
[33] Betz, *Galatian*, 206; Martyn, *Galatians*, 390, 407.

> "What is man, that he can be pure? Or he who is born of a woman, that he can be righteous?" (Job 15:14)
>
> "How then can man be in the right before God? How can he who is born of woman be pure?" (Job 25:4)
>
> "Truly, I say to you, among those born of women there has arisen no one greater than John the Baptist. Yet the one who is least in the kingdom of heaven is greater than he." (Matt 11:11)

By illustrating Jesus' birth in the same way Jesus described the common birth that every human being experiences, Paul expresses his belief that Jesus was a fully human product of his mother's womb.[34] The following description, "born under the Law," indicates that Jesus was born a Jew, a member of the people of Israel. The Epistle to the Galatians, in short, confirms the truths that Jesus is a lineal descendant of the patriarch Abraham and that he was born of a woman as a genuine Jewish person.[35]

The Pauline insistence on Jesus' authentic Davidic descent as a key feature in the gospel message is evident in the Second Epistle to Timothy. Not unlike the inclusion of Jesus as the son of David into the saving gospel message that we observed in Romans 1:1–4, 2 Timothy 2:8 stresses the same christology: "Remember Jesus Christ, risen from the dead, descendant of David, according to my gospel." While portraying Jesus Christ as the descendant of David surely evoked the promises of the Davidic covenant and the kingdom of God, of no less importance is the origin that Jesus owed to David as his royal ancestor.[36] These key features, 2 Timothy 2:8 reminds us, were part of Paul's gospel message, not miscellaneous speculation.

The Epistle to the Hebrews has much to contribute to the subject of christology. Regarding the topic of the birth and origins of Christ, we need to look no further than a fact that the author remarks is plainly obvious and uncontested: "For it is evident that our Lord was descended from Judah" (Heb 7:14).[37] The Greek verb translated "was descended" (*anatello*) appears in the perfect tense, which indicates not only that Christ descended from the tribe of Judah but also that he presently endures in that state. By drawing attention to Jesus' ancestor Judah, the author of Hebrews portrays Jesus as a

---

[34] Dunn, *Galatians*, 215, similarly concludes that the phrase "'born of woman' was a typical Jewish circumlocution for the human person."
[35] Oakes, *Galatians*, 137, comments, "Paul is emphasizing the idea of the Son of God being a real human."
[36] Collins, *I & II Timothy and Titus*, 223; Knight, *The Pastoral Epistles*, 397; Johnson, *The First and Second Letters to Timothy*, 374. Dibelius and Conzelmann, *Pastoral Epistles*, 108, state the obvious conclusion to Jesus descending from David: "It implies no preexistence."
[37] Attridge, *Hebrews*, 201; Johnson, *Hebrews*, 187; Craddock, "The Letter to the Hebrews," 89. We could add Heb 3:2, which probably speaks of God as the one who created Christ. On this point, see Johnson, *Hebrews*, 54.

human being who qualifies for all the promises God made to Judah's royal offspring in Genesis 49:8–10.[38]

The Birth of Jesus in the Book of Revelation

To the surprise of many, the Book of Revelation uses prophetic imagery to illustrate Jesus' birth and link him to his key ancestors, Judah and King David. The first time the book portrays Jesus with animal symbolism is in Revelation 5:5, which combines two key Old Testament messianic prophecies: "Weep no more; behold, the Lion of the tribe of Judah, the Shoot of David, has conquered, so that he can open the scroll and its seven seals." The first key image with which Jesus is associated is that he is the Lion of the tribe of Judah, a portrayal that deliberately recalls the lion related to the royal line of kings who were to descend from Judah (Gen 49:8–10).[39] The second image, the Shoot of David, is also saturated with royal overtones. It recalls several of the prophetic promises pertaining to David and his family tree, as well as the messianic shoot (e.g., Isa 11:1, 10). In other words, both of these image-filled depictions of the person Jesus display him as a lineal human descendant who traces his origins back to Judah and David.[40] The following noteworthy passage pertaining to our present study appears in Revelation twelve:

> A great sign appeared in heaven: a woman clothed with the sun, and the moon under her feet, and on her head a crown of twelve stars; and she was with child; and she cried out, being in labor and in pain to give birth. Then another sign appeared in heaven: and behold, a great red dragon having seven heads and ten horns, and on his heads were seven diadems. And his tail swept away a third of the stars of heaven and threw them to the earth. And the dragon stood before the woman who was about to give birth, so that when she gave birth he might devour her child. And she gave birth to a son, a male child, who is to shepherd all the nations with a rod of iron; and her child was caught up to God and to His throne. (Rev 12:1–5)

While there is much we could say about this passage, its function in the narrative of Revelation, and its dependence on a contemporary story at the time of the composition of the Book of Revelation, for the purposes of studying Jesus' birth, we shall limit our attention to that topic.[41] The vision depicts a woman, who probably represents the people of God, giving birth to a child who is undoubtedly Jesus Christ.[42] Although the child-to-be-born is under the threat of attack by the great red dragon, God rescues the child and

---

[38] Koester, *Hebrews*, 354–55.
[39] Blount, *Revelation*, 105; Koester, *Revelation*, 375.
[40] Smith, *Paradoxical Conquering*, 60. Aune, *Revelation 1–5*, 351, helpfully comments, "The emphases on the tribe of Judah and on the Davidic descent together underline one of the crucial qualifications of the Jewish royal Messiah: he must be a descendant of the royal house of David."
[41] For more details, see Paul, *Revelation*, 214; Carter, *What Does Revelation Reveal?* 86–87; Koester, *Revelation*, 547.
[42] Koester, *Revelation*, 546, argues, "It is best to take this scene as a portrayal of Jesus' birth."

exalts him to God and his throne. It would appear that the image-filled vision moves rather quickly from the birth of Jesus to his post-death exaltation to heaven.[43] But the reference to the child's birth is unmistakable, and there is no indication that the child was already in heaven alongside God before his birth. As the Book of Revelation comes to a close, Jesus offers an autobiographical reminder to the churches: "I, Jesus, have sent my angel to testify to you about these things for the churches. I am the shoot and the descendant of David, the bright morning star" (Rev 22:16).[44] For the second time in Revelation, Jesus is defined as the royal offspring, the shoot of King David's family tree, making Jesus a human being in whom the covenantal promises God made to David find their fulfillment.[45] In sum, the Book of Revelation portrays through its series of signs, symbols, and Jewish images the person of Jesus Christ as having been born from a long line that can be traced back to the famous King David and even as far back as the patriarch Judah. As such, Jesus is the long-anticipated Jewish Messiah, the human king who is to rule God's kingdom.

Conclusion

In conclusion, we have observed that the Early Church had much to say about the birth of Jesus, the period in time during which he was brought into existence in the womb of Mary. We also saw several passages in which the messianic promises offered by the writers of the Old Testament, namely, the assurances that one who would descend from the lineage of Abraham, Judah, and David, were explicitly confirmed by the New Testament authors. Matthew begins his gospel account with a genealogy that traces Jesus' human lineage through these three key figures, demonstrating that he is indeed the long-awaited Jewish Messiah. The birth narratives also describe how Jesus was begotten in his mother's womb through the help of the creative power of the Holy Spirit. Despite not having an infancy narrative, the Gospel of Mark nevertheless portrays Jesus as Mary's son and the brother of Mary's children while also highlighting Jesus' legitimacy as the offspring of King David. Luke, like the Gospel of Matthew, provides a helpful birth narrative in addition to a genealogy, both of which depict Jesus as a legitimate human being who descended from a long line of famous figures in Israel's history. The Gospel of John, like Mark, emphasizes Jesus' familial relationship with his mother and his brothers while also confirming him as the son of David. The Book of Acts presents much of the same christology expressed in the Gospel of Luke, portraying Jesus as the royal offspring of David and a member of the people of Israel. The writings of the Apostle Paul conveyed his acceptance that Jesus was born, was the legitimate descendant of Abraham and King David, and that he was an authentic Jewish person. The author of the Epistle to the

---

[43] Smalley, *Revelation*, 319–20
[44] Smalley, *Revelation*, 577.
[45] Charles, *Revelation*, 2:219; Blount, *Revelation*, 411.

Hebrews noted the self-evident truth that Jesus was a real human descendant of Judah. Finally, we looked into the image–rich Book of Revelation to take note of its illustration of Jesus as a powerful and mighty lion figure descending from Judah, in addition to being a royal offspring of David. Furthermore, Revelation also briefly mentions Jesus' birth in one of its visions, with no suggestion that he was alive in heaven before being born. To put the beliefs and teachings of the Early Church, as they are presented in the New Testament, plainly, we can conclude that the early followers of Jesus were convinced that Jesus was a genuine member of the human race who was begotten by God's Spirit in the womb of Mary, and was the heir of the promises made to the offspring of Abraham, Judah, and David. Since Jesus was the human descendant of all these key Old Testament figures, it follows that Jesus did not consciously preexist his birth in any way. It is obvious and rather self-evident that a son cannot exist before his ancestors.

As the Jewish Messiah, what sort of roles did Jesus carry out during his earthly ministry? We have already seen some evidence of the centrality of the title "Son of God" associated with the promised king from David's line, but how did the writers of the New Testament gospel accounts illustrate Jesus in this way? What about Jesus' favorite self-designation, the "Son of Man"? What data can we gather that would explain why he values this title so highly? There is also evidence that Jesus was aware of his fate to be a suffering figure. Why is this role vital to his self-understanding, and what meaning did the Old Testament offer to this discussion? We will address these key questions in our next chapter.

23
JESUS' MESSIANIC ROLES

The Early Church understood Christ as bearing in his person several functions that contribute to his messianic identity and mission. For the early Christians, Jesus of Nazareth was not some mere man, just an average guy. On the contrary, Jesus was to his earliest followers their redeeming savior, their instructive teacher, their lord to whom they owed their obedience, their anointed king whose rule they were under, their forerunner who modeled how to be faithful to God, their mediating high priest, and the coming judge of the living and the dead. There can be no denying that the person of Jesus served in many roles that made an impact upon the Early Church, and that impact is still experienced today by those who commit to following him.

This chapter will concentrate on three of the most significant messianic roles that Jesus Christ performed. The first christological role is the *son of God*, a role that was clearly central to Jesus' ministry, his death, and his highly anticipated second coming to occupy the throne of David and rule as king over God's kingdom. The second messianic role that we will explore is Jesus' favorite self-designation, the *son of man*. This designation, which certainly finds its origins in the vision contained in Daniel chapter seven, functioned in several important ways during Jesus' ministry and in building expectations for his second coming. Lastly, we will observe how Jesus appears to have voluntarily taken upon himself the role of the *suffering servant* described in the prophetic oracles of Isaiah. Not only did Jesus speak of himself in terms of a servant who is to be killed, but the Apostle Paul illustrates Jesus as Isaiah's suffering servant in an attempt to make sense of his self-sacrificial humility and the example it serves for Paul's churches. By drawing attention to Christ as the son of God, son of man, and the suffering servant, we hope to better appreciate the christology believed and taught by the Early Church.

Christ as *Son of God*

One of the most impactful titles that early Christians applied to Jesus is that he is the son of God. This title bore many of the hopes and expectations that we have already observed in the Old Testament writers, particularly those who anticipated a royal figure from the line of descendants coming forth from King David.[1] As a reminder, let's look at how the promised messianic king would be the son of God:

> "I will be a father to him and he will be a son to Me" (2 Sam 7:14)
>
> "I will be his father and he shall be My son" (1 Chron 17:13)
>
> "You are my son; today I have begotten you." (Ps 2:7)
>
> "He shall cry to me, 'You are my Father, my God, and the Rock of my salvation!' I will make him firstborn, the highest of the kings of the earth." (Ps 89:26–27)

This concept that the promised royal offspring of David would bear this special relationship with the Father, Yahweh himself, was maintained by the early Christians. Being the messianic son of God meant, obviously, that he wouldn't be Yahweh but would instead be the human king that Yahweh would anoint to serve as the king of the promised kingdom of God.[2] In other words, when the early Church placed their trust in Jesus as the son of God, they were confessing that Jesus was the long-anticipated Jewish Messiah who was the promised descendant and heir of King David.

Several New Testament authors demonstrate their awareness and acceptance that Jesus' title "son of God" referred to the promised Jewish Messiah, the Christ. The evidence for this crucial fact is overwhelming. Consider the following sample:

> Simon Peter replied, "You are the Christ, the Son of the living God." (Matt 16:16)
>
> And the high priest said to him, "I adjure you by the living God, tell us if you are the Christ, the Son of God." Jesus said to him, "You have said so." (Matt 26:63–64)
>
> The beginning of the gospel of Jesus Christ, the Son of God. (Mark 1:1)
>
> And demons also came out of many, crying, "You are the Son of God!" But he rebuked them and would not allow them to speak, because they knew that he was the Christ. (Luke 4:41)
>
> Nathanael answered him, "Rabbi, you are the Son of God! You are the King of Israel!" (John 1:49)
>
> but these have been written so that you may believe that Jesus is the Christ, the Son of God; and that believing you may have life in his name. (John 20:31)
>
> For the Son of God, Jesus Christ, whom we proclaimed among you, Silvanus and Timothy and I, was not "Yes and No"; but in him it is always "Yes." (2 Cor 1:19)

---

[1] Xeravits, "Son of God," 1248.
[2] Dunn, *New Testament Theology*, 60, observes, "In the NT writings, therefore, the way is well prepared for what became the principal language to express the relation between God, as Father, and Jesus, as Son."

> until we all attain to the unity of the faith, and of the knowledge of the Son of God, to a mature man, to the measure of the stature which belongs to the fullness of Christ. (Eph 4:13)

So vital is this designation for the person of Jesus that all four authors of the New Testament gospel accounts begin their biographies by describing how John the Baptist baptizes Jesus in what serves as a public anointing ceremony. Stated differently, the writers of the New Testament gospels each mark the beginning of Jesus' ministry with a public coronation of Jesus as the royal son of God:

> In those days Jesus came from Nazareth in Galilee and was baptized by John in the Jordan. Immediately coming up out of the water, he saw the heavens opening, and the Spirit like a dove descending upon him; and a voice came out of the heavens: "You are my beloved Son, in you I am well-pleased." (Mark 1:9–11)

Both Matthew (Matt 3:17) and Luke (Luke 3:22) agree with Mark's portrayal that it is God himself who announces authoritatively that Jesus is the messianic son of God, now anointed to begin his earthly ministry.[3] In the Gospel of John, it is John the Baptist who authoritatively claims to have witnessed the Spirit resting on Jesus during John's activity of baptizing in water (John 1:31–33). Having witnessed Jesus' anointing by the Spirit, John the Baptist announces Jesus as the promised royal Messiah: "I myself have seen, and have testified that this is the Son of God" (John 1:34).[4] By each stressing Jesus as the long-awaited son of God, the four New Testament gospels emphasize to their readers the importance of this title for making sense of the rest of his ministry.

Along with the royal and Davidic overtones that the title "son of God" carried with respect to the person of Jesus, it also conveyed a key nuance involving the nation of Israel. Just as the royal meaning of "son of God" began in the Old Testament, so too does the connection between *Israel* and *son of God* find its roots in the same Hebrew scriptures.[5] In particular, there are several passages where the nation of Israelites is corporately identified as God's "son." Consider the following passages:

> Then you shall say to Pharaoh, "Thus says Yahweh, 'Israel is my son, my firstborn.' So I said to you, 'Let my son go that he may serve me; but you have refused to let him go.'" (Exod 4:22–23)

> Yahweh your God who goes before you will himself fight on your behalf, just as he did for you in Egypt before your eyes, and in the wilderness where you saw how Yahweh your God carried you, just as a man carries his son, in all the way which you have walked until you came to this place. (Deut 1:30–31)

---

[3] Dunn, *Jesus Remembered*, 371–74.
[4] Brown, *John I–XII*, 66; Schnackenburg, *John*, 1:304; Beasley-Murray, *John*, 25–26.
[5] Donaldson, "Son of God," 336; Xeravits, "Son of God," 1248.

> Thus you are to know in your heart that Yahweh your God was disciplining you just as a man disciplines his son. (Deut 8:5)
>
> When Israel was a child, I loved him, and out of Egypt I called my son. (Hos 11:1)

Israel, as a nation, was regarded by Yahweh as "son of God," and in turn, Yahweh was depicted as the Father.[6] While it is also true that individual descendants of Israel are described as "sons of God" (that is, God's children) in passages like Deuteronomy 14:1; Jeremiah 3:19; and Hosea 1:10, these individuals made up the larger nation of Israel—God's son because of the covenant, creating a relationship involving protection, love, and discipline.[7]

The authors of the Old Testament portrayed an interesting relationship between the nation of Israel and its Davidic king, particularly in the way that the single ruler served as the representative of the people.[8] This is not a surprising move in Jewish theology of the king, since he bore the title "son of God" as the leader of the nation, which was also regarded as "son of God." Consider how a single fighter, young David, represented the entire nation of Israel in his fight against the Philistines and their representative, Goliath (1 Sam 17:8–10, 50). This theology of the king representing his people is apparent when David's unwarranted census resulted in the punishment of all of his people for his sinful decision (2 Sam 24:10–17). After the death of Solomon, the kingdom of Israel was divided when the northern tribe no longer wanted to be represented by the Davidic monarchy: "When all Israel saw that the king did not listen to them, the people answered the king, saying, 'What portion do we have in David? We have no inheritance in the son of Jesse; to your tents, O Israel! Now look after your own house, David!' So Israel departed to their tents" (1 Kgs 12:16; 2 Chron 10:16).[9] The phrases "in David" and "in the son of Jesse" indicate that the people saw themselves as either in solidarity with the Davidic king, their representative, or outside of this solidarity. The ten northern tribes chose the latter. We have already seen evidence in Chapter 21 that the promised Jewish Messiah from the line of David will serve as a shepherd-king over the flock, God's people, in Ezekiel 34:23; 37:24; Micah 5:4. Readers need to look no further than the writings of the Apostle Paul to see how the Jewish theology of the king representing his people came to be foundational for illustrating how Jesus represents the new covenant people of God with "in Christ" language.

The Early Church, in addition to wholeheartedly believing that Jesus was the Christ, the son of God, also portrayed Jesus as Israel's representative. Take, for example, Matthew's use of typology to depict the newborn king who embodies the nation of Israel,

---

[6] Caragounis, "בֵּן," 676; Durham, *Exodus*, 56; Tijay, *Deuteronomy*, 18; Dearman, *Hosea*, 278–80.
[7] Dearman, *Hosea*, 104.
[8] See especially Wright, *Climax of the Covenant*, 46–47; *Paul and the Faithfulness of God*, 825–29.
[9] A similar event occurred during the life of David in 2 Samuel 20:1, which foreshadows what took place in 1 Kings 12:16.

using a quote from Hosea 11:1: "And he rose and took the child and his mother by night and departed to Egypt and remained there until the death of Herod. This was to fulfill what the Lord had spoken by the prophet, 'Out of Egypt I called my son'" (Matt 2:14–15). Matthew has, in effect, taken a passage about the son of God (i.e., Israel) being called out of Egypt during the story of the exodus and applied it in a new way to a single individual, to Jesus.[10] As such, Jesus acts as the royal son of God, representing his people, Israel.[11]

We can observe a second example of Christ's title *son of God* functioning as a representative of the people within the temptation narratives contained in Matthew and Luke, who both portray the Devil tempting Jesus in the wilderness (Matt 4:1; Luke 4:2). Jesus' trial that occurred over a period of forty days and nights (Matt 4:2) surely was meant to recall the period of forty years in which the Israelites were tested (Deut 8:2).[12] Both periods of testing took place in the wilderness, but with different outcomes. Israel succumbed to idolatry by worshipping the golden calf, but Jesus refused to bow down and worship the Devil. Rather than grumbling about the lack of food and water, as Israel displayed, Jesus relied on God's provision. Instead of the episodes of frequent disobedience demonstrated by Israel, Jesus remained faithful and obedient during his trial.[13] Noteworthy is the repeated element in Jesus' temptation by the Devil, which concerned whether Jesus truly was the Son of God (Matt 4:3, 6; Luke 4:3, 9). By succeeding in his trial, Jesus confirms that he rightfully bears this title.[14] The obvious ways in which Matthew and Luke parallel Israel's experience in the wilderness with Jesus' temptation suggest that the title "son of God" functioned in a representative capacity, with Jesus succeeding where the nation of Israel failed.

The third example of Christ serving as the sole representative of his people is arguably the most important. As the royal son of God, Jesus was able to die on the cross on behalf of God's people. All four writers of the New Testament gospels acknowledge their awareness that Jesus' death represented the fate of sinners. Matthew records Jesus teaching his followers that his death is "poured out for many for the forgiveness of sins" (Matt 26:28). Hecklers who looked upon Jesus as he hung on the cross echo the temptations that Jesus experienced in the wilderness by deliberately calling into question whether he really was the Messiah, the son of God: "If you are the Son of God, come

---

[10] Gundry, *Matthew*, 33–34.
[11] Davies and Allison, *Matthew*, 1:263–64, astutely observe, "For Matthew, 'Son of God' must have to do in part with Jesus as the personification or embodiment of true, obedient Israel."
[12] Clements, "The Book of Deuteronomy," 355.
[13] Carter, *Matthew*, 172, is instructive here: "Future audiences, shaped by the creeds that emerged from the fourth- and fifth-century debates, understand this term as indicating Jesus' divinity, but the authorial audience brings different and diverse understandings to the text . . . Rather than referring to a divine nature, the audience understands the term to indicate special relationships with God marked by loyalty to God's will."
[14] Bauer, "Son of God," 273–74.

down from the cross" (Matt 27:40).[15] Here we again have the title "son of God" serving to identify the individual Jesus as he actively suffers on behalf of others. Even the inscriptions on the cross, which the Roman soldiers mockingly placed above Jesus, signified him as Israel's representative, the King of the Jews (Matt 27:37; Mark 15:26; Luke 23:38). The apostle Paul regards Jesus' faithfulness unto death as affecting Paul in a deep and personal way: "I have been crucified with Christ. It is no longer I who live, but Christ who lives in me. And the life I now live in the flesh I live by the faithfulness of the Son of God, who loved me and gave himself for me" (Gal 2:20).[16] The Early Church was convinced that Christ, King Jesus, was able to atone for the sins of all humanity because he was the Jewish Messiah, the son of God, the only human being whose role uniquely qualified him to represent his people on the cross.

Christ as *Son of Man*

The title *son of God* was not the only role that the Early Church attributed to the person of Christ. In fact, all four New Testament gospel writers remembered Jesus referring to himself with what seems to be his favorite self-designation: the *son of man*.[17] The frequency with which each evangelist employs this title for Jesus demonstrates its importance to Jesus' self-understanding, his mission, and his humanity. Matthew uses the title thirty times, Mark has fourteen occurrences, Luke has twenty-five, and John uses it thirteen times. Nearly all of these instances of the title *son of man* in the four gospel accounts are on the lips of Jesus rather than the crowds, opponents, or narrators. What could account for Jesus' obsession with the designation *son of man*?

Like the christological title *son of God*, the designation *son of man* owes its meaning to its origins in the Old Testament. Although it is certainly true that an ordinary human being, a mortal, is often described as a son of man by the writers of the Old Testament (Num 23:19; Ps 8:4; Ezek 2:1, 3, 6, 8), Jesus' distinctive use of the title was drawn directly from Daniel chapter seven.[18] Before examining how Jesus applied this title to himself, we must first determine its meaning in the Book of Daniel.

The seventh chapter of Daniel records a vision that Daniel received in a dream (Dan 7:1–14), as well as the interpretation of that vision that one of the heavenly angels authoritatively provided (Dan 7:15–28). The vision consisted of four successive beasts that emerged from the chaotic sea, which indicated that they were malevolent and evil in their orientation.[19] These animals (a lion, a bear, a leopard, and a monstrous beast) would

---

[15] Senior, *The Passion of Jesus in Matthew*, 96, 132; Luz *Matthew 21–28*, 538.
[16] Wright, *Galatians*, 156–58; de Boer, *Galatians*, 162.
[17] Dunn, *Jesus Remembered*, 724–25.
[18] Collins, "Son of Man," 344.
[19] Seow, *Daniel*, 101–2; Kirk, *A Man Attested by God*, 141.

have been familiar to the readers of Daniel as representing the kingdoms of Babylon, Media, Persia, and Greece, respectively.[20] While these four beasts are mentioned in Daniel's dream, the bulk of the attention is given to the fourth beast. This terrible beast possessed ten horns and another little horn, which receives an even more concentrated focus within the vision and its interpretation. This little horn is portrayed as a man of violence, characterized as making war with the saints and overpowering them (Dan 7:21, 25), subduing three other kings (Dan 7:24), speaking against the Most High God, and altering various aspects of the Law of Moses. Furthermore, the saints will, unfortunately, be given into the powerful hand of this little horn and suffer a period of harsh persecution (Dan 7:25). However, the vision concludes on a positive note with the vindication of this suffering group of God's people when judgment is passed (Dan 7:26). This vindication includes receiving possession of the kingdom (Dan 7:18, 22, 27).

Where does the figure of the *son of man* fit into this vision? The answer is found in Daniel 7:13–14, which is the initial description of vindication from the deeds of the boastful little horn. This passage states:

> I saw in the night visions, and behold, with the clouds of heaven there came one like a son of man, and he came to the Ancient of Days and was presented before him. And to him was given dominion and glory and a kingdom, that all peoples, nations, and languages should serve him; his dominion is an everlasting dominion, which shall not pass away, and his kingdom is one that shall not be destroyed. (Dan 7:13–14)

Within Daniel's retelling of his vision, he sees a single human individual, one like a son of man. This "son of man" figure is clearly distinguished from the Ancient of Days—an obvious reference to the true God. What is fascinating is that the Ancient of Days gives this "son of man" figure dominion, glory, and a kingdom. This is a remarkable act of *empowering a single human being on the part of God*. God effectively shares his own dominion, his own glory, and his own kingdom with this human being.[21] The result is that this son of man will possess an everlasting kingdom in addition to honor from all nations.[22]

Now that the "one like a son of man" has been introduced in the vision, how does the interpreting angel make sense of this figure for Daniel (and for the readers of Daniel chapter seven)? When Daniel approaches the angel and requests an interpretation of his visionary dream, something very important takes place. The interpretation explains the vision's portrayal of the one like a son of man who receives dominion and kingship from God as a group of people—the suffering people of God—who are eventually

---

[20] Goldingay, *Daniel*, 374; Pace, *Daniel*, 231; Newsom and Breed, *Daniel*, 221–25; Collins, *Daniel*, 312.
[21] Nickelsburg, *Resurrection, Immortality, and Eternal Life*, 283.
[22] Towner, *Daniel*, 104, views the *son of man* as thoroughly human: "he is a figure for a fifth human monarchy."

vindicated and given possession of God's dominion and kingdom.[23] Stated differently, the vision portrays a single individual (the son of man), and the vision is authoritatively interpreted to reveal that this human person actually represents an entire group of people who suffer persecution but find deliverance when judgment is passed in their favor.[24] This means that Daniel's vision of the son of man portrays him as a representative figure for the suffering people of God.[25]

To summarize, Daniel chapter seven offers a multi-faceted depiction of a unique human individual, the one like a son of man. First, the son of man is highly empowered by the Ancient of Days, who shares his own prerogatives with this qualified human being. Second, the son of man is portrayed as coming on the clouds of heaven. Third, the son of man functions as the representative of the saints—the people of God—particularly as they suffer. This facet is combined with the assurance that the Ancient of Days will vindicate his persecuted people after a period of intense suffering. With this in mind, we can now turn to the writings of the New Testament in order to see how the Early Church understood Jesus' claim to be the son of man.

When we look at the gospel accounts in the New Testament, particularly Matthew, Mark, and Luke, it becomes clear that Jesus was impacted by Daniel's portrayal of the unique "son of man" figure, and this impact resulted in Jesus embodying the role, functions, and destiny of the son of man. There are several examples of Jesus claiming to be the highly authorized and empowered son of man. When Jesus declares to the paralytic that his sins are forgiven, the scribes regard this act by Jesus to be blasphemous (Matt 9:1–3). Jesus responds with a claim to be the son of man who bears the authority from God to offer the forgiveness of sins legitimately: "'But that you may know that the Son of Man has authority on earth to forgive sins'—he then said to the paralytic—'Rise, pick up your bed and go home'" (Matt 9:6; Mark 2:10; Luke 5:24).[26] In other words, Jesus is not committing blasphemy because God has shared the prerogative of *forgiving sins* with Jesus, the son of man.[27]

Another example occurs on the Sabbath when Jesus allows his disciples to pick heads of grain on this day of rest (Mark 2:23). The Pharisees, who held to a much stricter interpretation of the commandment to do no work on the Sabbath, repeatedly asked Jesus why he was allowing his disciples to act unlawfully (Mark 2:24). Jesus responds to this

---

[23] Wright, *Jesus and the Victory of God*, 524, is helpful here: "There is nothing particularly modest or understated about the vindication of the 'son of man' in Daniel 7:14, 18 and 27 . . . He is the true representative of YHWH's people, and will be vindicated as such."
[24] Nickelsburg, *Resurrection, Immortality, and Eternal Life*, 283; Gowan, *Daniel*, 108; Pace, *Daniel*, 245; Goldingay, *Daniel*, 367; Kirk, *A Man Attested by God*, 143.
[25] Dunn, *Jesus Remembered*, 752, arrives at the same conclusion: "The tradition was of Jesus using Daniel's vision of the manlike representation of the saints of the Most High to express his own hopes for vindication."
[26] Irons et al., *The Son of God*, 140; Carter, *Mark*, 47; Kirk, *A Man Attested by God*, 273–85; McIntosh, *One God, Three Persons*, 102.
[27] Collins, *Mark*, 186, similarly concludes that Christ can "forgive sins as God's representative."

criticism by reminding his critics with a claim to be the son of man who possesses authority over the Sabbath: "The Sabbath was made for man, not man for the Sabbath. So the Son of Man is lord even of the Sabbath" (Mark 2:27–28). Essentially, Jesus recalls how God instituted the seventh day *after* the original image-bearing humans had already been created and granted authority over God's creation. In light of this, Jesus draws upon his role as the highly authorized son of man from Daniel 7:13–14 that he possesses the God-given authority and lordship to allow aid to be given to his disciples who suffer from hunger, the disciples whom he represents.[28]

A third example is located in one of Jesus' many statements about his second coming. Jesus promised to return as the son of man who bears the Father's own glory: "For the Son of Man is going to come with his angels in the glory of his Father, and then he will repay each person according to what he has done" (Matt 16:27; Mark 8:38; Luke 9:26). By this point in the narrative, the reader has already associated Jesus' claim to be the son of man with the figure illustrated in the vision of Daniel chapter seven, so Jesus' claim to come in the Father's glory owes its dependence on the portrayal of the Ancient of Days sharing his glory with the one like a son of man (Dan 7:14).[29] As such, Jesus makes a claim to bear in his person the glory of the Ancient of Days, whom Jesus plainly defines as "his Father."[30]

Having now seen evidence that Jesus saw himself as embodying the role of the coming son of man, whom Daniel depicts as coming on the clouds of heaven, we can examine other ways in which Jesus emphasizes this aspect of his favorite self-designation. Fortunately, the writers of the New Testament gospels provide readers with several indicators that Jesus spoke about his second coming in terms of him embodying the role of the son of man. The son of man will come in his kingdom, according to Matthew 16:28. When the son of man comes, he will sit on his promised throne and begin the process of judgment (Matt 19:28; 25:31–34). Matthew uses a Greek word (*parousia*) for the visible arrival and coming of the son of man, at which time he will be physically present (Matt 24:27, 37, 39).[31] We will discuss the importance of the Early Church's use of the "coming" (*parousia*) in Chapter 48. At this point, we can draw attention to how Jesus linked the coming of the son of man on the clouds of heaven with the end of the age (Matt 24:3, 27–30).[32] The followers of Jesus were encouraged to be ready and faithful, for the son of man was coming at an unexpected hour (Luke 12:40; 18:8). The beginning

---

[28] Carter, *Mark*, 59; Collins, *Mark*, 204–5; Marshall, "Son of Man," 776.
[29] Carter, *Mark*, 235.
[30] Kirk, *A Man Attested by God*, 312; Collins, *Mark*, 412.
[31] Marshall, "Son of Man," 777.
[32] Ladd, *The Presence of the Future*, 117; Beasley-Murray, *Jesus and the Kingdom of God*, 314.

of the Book of Acts explicitly connects Jesus' second coming with the cloud imagery from Daniel 7:13.[33] Note the familiar image of the cloud:

> And when he had said these things, as they were looking on, he was lifted up, and a cloud took him out of their sight. And while they were gazing into heaven as he went, behold, two men stood by them in white robes, and said, "Men of Galilee, why do you stand looking into heaven? This Jesus, who was taken up from you into heaven, will come in the same way as you saw him go into heaven." (Acts 1:9–11)

Just as Jesus ascended into heaven with a cloud after his resurrection, so too will he return on the cloud from heaven (Luke 21:27).[34] In short, by taking upon himself the role and destiny of the son of man, Jesus promised the early Christians that his return to sit on his throne, enact judgment, and consummate the kingdom of God would be visibly seen in terms of coming on the clouds of heaven.

In the Gospels of Matthew, Mark, and Luke, most of Jesus' sayings about the son of man concern his fate as one who suffers persecution, rejection, and even death. Recalling the key point from Daniel's vision, the one like a son of man was interpreted to serve as a representative figure for the suffering people of God, and it appears that Jesus believed that he was to bear this destiny, even unto the cross.[35] Consider just a sample of passages that demonstrate Jesus describing himself in terms of the rejected and suffering son of man:

> Foxes have holes, and birds of the air have nests, but the Son of Man has nowhere to lay his head. (Matt 8:20)

> But I tell you that Elijah has already come, and they did not recognize him, but did to him whatever they pleased. So also the Son of Man will certainly suffer at their hands. (Matt 17:12)

> You know that after two days the Passover is coming, and the Son of Man will be delivered up to be crucified. (Matt 26:2)

> And he began to teach them that the Son of Man must suffer many things and be rejected by the elders and the chief priests and the scribes and be killed, and after three days rise again. (Mark 8:31)

> he was teaching his disciples, saying to them, "The Son of Man is going to be delivered into the hands of men, and they will kill him. And when he is killed, after three days he will rise." (Mark 9:31)

---

[33] Keener, *Acts*, 1:727, 731–32.
[34] Nolland, *Luke 18:35–24:53*, 1006.
[35] Marshall, "Son of Man," 778.

> Blessed are you when people hate you and when they exclude you and revile you and spurn your name as evil, on account of the Son of Man! (Luke 6:22)

> Jesus said to him, "Judas, would you betray the Son of Man with a kiss?" (Luke 22:48)

It seems rather apparent that Jesus willingly accepted his fate as the son of man who was to act as *the representative* of the persecuted people of God.[36] By recognizing this crucial aspect of the multifaceted role of Daniel's son of man, we can begin to make sense of the predictions of his death that Jesus makes. When Jesus attempted to explain and clarify to his disciples his destiny to be handed over, rejected, and killed, he frequently offered these predictions in terms of what would befall the Son of Man. It is the son of man who would suffer (Matt 17:12; Mark 8:31) and be killed by the torturous act of crucifixion (Matt 17:22; 20:18–19; 26:2). The rejection of the son of man would include the act of being betrayed (Matt 26:24, 45; Mark 14:21). As the son of man, Jesus would give his life as a ransom for many (Matt 20:28; Mark 10:45), demonstrating his acceptance of his role as the representative of many others. However, Jesus also believed, just as the vision in Daniel chapter seven reassured its readers, that the suffering people of God would indeed be vindicated, and he, as the people's representative, would experience God's vindication by being raised from the dead (Matt 20:18–19; Mark 9:9; Luke 9:22).[37] In fact, the only way to make sense of Jesus' claim that "it is written of the Son of Man that he should suffer many things and be treated with contempt" (Mark 9:12) is to identify Jesus with the son of man from Daniel 7:13, which is the only passage in the Old Testament scriptures speaking of the ill-treated people of God as being represented by a single human figure.[38]

All of these features of Daniel's vision of the one like a son of man converge at Jesus' trial, where he utters what is arguably the most climactic claim to be the son of man in the New Testament. The passage is worth reading in full:

> Now the chief priests and the whole Council were seeking testimony against Jesus to put him to death, but they found none. For many bore false witness against him, but their testimony did not agree. And some stood up and bore false witness against him, saying, "We heard him say, 'I will destroy this temple that is made with hands, and in three days I will build another, not made with hands.'" Yet even about this their testimony did not agree. And the high priest stood up in the midst and asked Jesus, "Have you no answer to make? What is it that these men testify against you?" But he remained silent and made no answer. Again the high priest asked him, "Are you the Christ, the Son of the Blessed?" And Jesus said, "I am, and you will see the Son of Man seated at the right hand of Power, and coming with the clouds of heaven." And the high priest tore his garments and said,

---

[36] Perkins, "The Gospel of Mark," 551.
[37] See especially Kirk, *A Man Attested by God*, 334–39.
[38] See also Matt 26:24; Mark 14:21; Luke 18:31; 22:22, which all portray the suffering of the son of man as having been written about formerly in the scriptures (i.e., Daniel 7).

"What further witnesses do we need? You have heard his blasphemy. What is your decision?" And they all condemned him as deserving death. (Mark 14:55–64)

There is much we could draw from this important passage. At the heart of the exchange is Jesus' acceptance of the claim to be the Christ, the Jewish Messiah.[39] However, Jesus follows up his claim to be the Christ with a direct quote from Daniel 7:13 ("the Son of Man . . . coming with the clouds of heaven") combined with an allusion to Psalm 110:1, in which Yahweh summons a second figure to sit at his right hand. Not only does Jesus claim to be the son of man from Daniel 7:13, but he also announces that, despite his current circumstances of arrest, his captors will see and experience Jesus' vindication by Yahweh as he is highly exalted to sit at Yahweh's right hand.[40] However, Jesus is currently surrounded by the members of the Sanhedrin and the chief priests, including the high priest himself. If Jesus foresees his vindication from his persecuted situation, which will soon end in his death, in terms of the role of the son of man from Daniel 7, then we can begin to understand why his claim was regarded as blasphemous. In Daniel's vision, the people of God suffer at the hands of four terrifying animals that symbolize pagan nations. If Jesus prophetically interpreted his trial in terms of the role of Daniel's son of man, then it reasonably follows that he not only saw himself as embodying the fate of the persecuted saints, but he also saw the Jews surrounding him in this unfair trial as embodying the pagan beasts from Daniel's vision.[41] Once Caiaphas read between the lines of Jesus' confession to be the soon-to-be-vindicated son of man, he regarded the implicit illustration of his priestly role as an unclean pagan animal to be utterly blasphemous. The high priest's sentencing of Jesus to death, ironically, reinforced Jesus' claim to be the representative of the persecuted people of God.

The Gospel of John also portrays Jesus as the son of man. This gospel account continues to draw on the vision in Daniel chapter seven by illustrating Jesus as being highly empowered and authorized by the Father, he who gave Jesus "authority to execute judgment, because he is the Son of Man" (John 5:27).[42] Jesus makes this point again in John 6:27, where he describes himself as the son of man upon whom "the Father, God, has set his seal."[43] Daniel's portrayal of the son of man, the representative of the suffering people who receive glory from God, has also influenced several passages. According to John 3:14, the son of man will be "lifted up," which is a double entendre, meaning that

---

[39] Boring, *Mark*, 413, clarifies Jesus' messianic intentions: "The revelatory *ego eimi* . . . is not a claim to be YHWH or an enunciation of the sacred name of God."
[40] Collins, *Mark*, 705.
[41] Wright, *Matthew*, 2:168. See also his *Jesus and the Victory of God*, 525–25: "[Caiaphas'] court has become part of the evil force which is opposing the true Israel, and which will be overthrown when YHWH vindicates his people. Caiaphas, the High Priest, has become the new Antiochus Epiphanes, the great tyrant oppressing YHWH's people. The Sanhedrin was playing the Fourth Beast to Jesus' Son of Man."
[42] Smith, *Wisdom Christology*, 137.
[43] Witherington, *John's Wisdom*, 155, observes, "This verse uses agency language—the Son of man is the one upon whom God has set his seal of approval and authorization, to act on the Father's behalf."

he will be exalted and that he will be hoisted up onto the cross to suffer. When Jesus speaks about his anticipated time of suffering on the cross, he links this pivotal event with the son of man receiving glory: "The hour has come for the Son of Man to be glorified" (John 12:23); "Now is the Son of Man glorified, and God is glorified in him; if God is glorified in him, God will also glorify him in himself, and will glorify him immediately" (John 13:31–32). The Gospel of John, however, does add an important new dimension to the role of the son of man that Jesus embodies, and this is the role of the authoritative revealer of the Father in heaven, as we can see in passages like John 1:51; 3:13; 8:28. Thus, while maintaining its dependence on the vision in Daniel chapter seven, the Gospel of John displays Jesus as the multi-faceted son of man while adding to this title the role of the revealer of the Father.[44]

Christ as *Suffering Servant*

So far, we have noticed that the Early Church believed and taught that Jesus served as humanity's representative in the roles of the *son of God* and the *son of man*. The third role that we will explore in this chapter—the *suffering servant*—also carries with it the function of one who voluntarily suffers in place of others. We have already seen the paradoxical dynamic of Jesus' ministry where he both functions as the messianic king of God's kingdom and as the rejected and crucified son of man. How can it be that those very same enemies must first conquer the one who is to conquer God's enemies? Jesus believed that the real enemies were sin and death, not the Romans, the Caesars, the corrupt priesthood, the Herodian family, or any other sinful group of people. When Jesus announced that "the Son of Man came not to be served but to serve, and to give his life as a ransom for many" (Mark 10:45), he deliberately drew attention to his deeply felt conviction that he must embody the role of a *servant* who must *give up his life* on behalf of others.[45] These two pieces—servant and one who dies for others—are combined in the portrayal of the suffering servant that appears in the Book of Isaiah.

The middle portion of the Book of Isaiah (chapters 40–55) contains several references to a figure whom Yahweh calls "my servant." It is also from these chapters that Jesus took his cue to embody the role and function of Yahweh's servant. There are four significant passages in this section of Isaiah, often described by specialists as "songs" due to their poetic structure, continuity of theme, and affinity with the biblical psalms.[46] We only need to explore a sampling of these sections in Isaiah to become familiar with their content and message:

---

[44] Smith, *Wisdom Christology*, 134–37.
[45] Boring, *Mark*, 303.
[46] Collins, "Servant of the Lord," 193–94; Goldingay, "Servant of Yahweh," 704.

> Behold my servant, whom I uphold, my chosen, in whom my soul delights; I have put my Spirit upon him; he will bring forth justice to the nations. He will not cry aloud or lift up his voice, or make it heard in the street; a bruised reed he will not break, and a faintly burning wick he will not quench; he will faithfully bring forth justice. (Isa 42:1–3)
>
> I am Yahweh; I have called you in righteousness; I will take you by the hand and keep you; I will give you as a covenant for the people, a light for the nations, to open the eyes that are blind, to bring out the prisoners from the dungeon, from the prison those who sit in darkness. (Isa 42:6–7)
>
> "It is too light a thing that you should be my servant to raise up the tribes of Jacob and to bring back the preserved of Israel; I will make you as a light for the nations, that my salvation may reach to the end of the earth." Thus says Yahweh, the Redeemer of Israel and his Holy One, to one deeply despised, abhorred by the nation, the servant of rulers: "Kings shall see and arise; princes, and they shall prostrate themselves; because of Yahweh, who is faithful, the Holy One of Israel, who has chosen you." (Isa 49:6–7)
>
> I gave my back to those who strike, and my cheeks to those who pull out the beard; I hid not my face from disgrace and spitting. But the Lord Yahweh helps me; therefore I have not been disgraced; therefore I have set my face like a flint, and I know that I shall not be put to shame. He who vindicates me is near. Who will contend with me? Let us stand up together. Who is my adversary? Let him come near to me. Behold, the Lord Yahweh helps me; who will declare me guilty? Behold, all of them will wear out like a garment; the moth will eat them up. Who among you fears Yahweh and obeys the voice of his servant? Let him who walks in darkness and has no light trust in the name of Yahweh and rely on his God. (Isa 50:6–10)

These examples from the first three servant songs in Isaiah 42, 49, and 50 portray a figure through whom Yahweh will accomplish his salvific and redemptive purposes. God will empower his servant with his Spirit to extend God's justice on a worldwide scale, extending from the servant to the Gentile nations.[47] This mission will be restorative in nature, particularly through the imagery of bringing light to darkness, opening blind eyes, and rescuing those who are imprisoned. Not only will the servant help Yahweh bring his salvation to the ends of the earth, but it will also restore the people of Israel to freedom and wholeness.[48] Unfortunately, the servant of Yahweh will not be universally accepted in his mission, as he will suffer rejection. Despite this shameful treatment, the servant will be faithful to Yahweh, carrying out his commissioning.[49] In doing so, the servant places his confidence and trust in Yahweh's provision, protection, and promise of vindication.

The themes of the servant who, in the midst of suffering and rejection, faithfully brings Yahweh's salvation to the ends of the earth while also believing that Yahweh will help and rescue him in times of distress coalesce in the fourth servant song that is located

---

[47] Oswalt, *Isaiah 40–66*, 110.
[48] Paul, *Isaiah 40–66*, 190.
[49] Goldingay and Payne, *Isaiah 40–55*, 2:210–11.

in Isaiah 52:13–53:12. While this fourth song is the lengthiest, making it difficult to cover in detail, we can observe several key points of interest with only a selection of quotations:

> See, my servant shall prosper; he shall be exalted and lifted up, and shall be very high. (Isa 52:13)

> He was despised and rejected by others; a man of suffering and acquainted with infirmity; surely he has borne our infirmities and carried our diseases; yet we accounted him stricken, struck down by God, and afflicted. But he was wounded for our transgressions, crushed for our iniquities; upon him was the punishment that made us whole, and by his bruises we are healed ... Yahweh has laid on him the iniquity of us all. He was oppressed, and he was afflicted, yet he did not open his mouth; like a lamb that is led to the slaughter, and like a sheep that before its shearers is silent, so he did not open his mouth ... For he was cut off from the land of the living, stricken for the transgression of my people. They made his grave with the wicked and his tomb with the rich, although he had done no violence, and there was no deceit in his mouth. (Isa 53:3–9)

> The righteous one, my servant, shall make many righteous, and he shall bear their iniquities ... he poured out himself to death, and was numbered with the transgressors; yet he bore the sin of many, and made intercession for the transgressors. (Isa 53:11–12)

The description of the servant of Yahweh begins with a promise to highly exalt and lift up this noteworthy figure. The exaltation of the servant, however, comes after a mission of suffering and rejection.[50] The servant is clearly identified as a human being who bears the iniquities and transgressions of others.[51] Isaiah's servant songs make it clear that Yahweh is distinguished from this suffering human servant, for it is God who strikes down the servant, God lays the iniquity of the people on the servant, and presumably, it is God who exalts this servant after his death. Indeed, it is the death of this suffering servant, being cut off from the land of the living, that is the conclusion of his role as the one bearing the people's iniquities, and after pouring himself out to death, he is buried in a grave. Throughout the servant's mission, his demeanor is portrayed as one of silent acceptance of his fate, choosing not to respond with violent acts or deceitful speech.

Who is this servant that the Book of Isaiah portrays in the servant songs of chapters 42, 49, 50, and 52–53? While it is easy to see how the person of Jesus Christ embodies this role as the suffering servant, Isaiah appears to originally depict the servant quite explicitly as Israel in some capacity: "But you Israel, my servant" (Isa 41:8), "You are my servant, O Israel" (Isa 44:21).[52] However, the Book of Isaiah also portrays God using his servant in various redemptive ways towards Israel, particularly with the servant

---

[50] Blenkinsopp, *Isaiah 40–55*, 349, offers an apt summary: "the Servant, once humiliated and abused, will be exalted; once counted among criminals, will be in the company of the great and powerful."
[51] Paul, *Isaiah 40–66*, 401–3; Oswalt, *Isaiah 40–66*, 382–83. Goldingay and Payne, *Isaiah 40–55*, 2:291–92, remark, "he suffered in a way which marked him more than any other human being."
[52] See also Isa 44:1–2; 45:4; 48:20; 49:3; Collins, "Servant of the Lord," 194. Goldingay, "Servant of Yahweh," 706, similarly draws attention to the emphasis in Isaiah to the *role* of the servant, rather than to a *person*.

gathering Israel (Isa 49:5), restoring Israel (Isa 49:6), bearing "our" transgressions and "our" iniquities (Isa 53:5). The iniquity of "us all" has fallen on this servant (Isa 53:6). It would appear that the servant of Isaiah is a faithful group of the members of the nation of Israel who serve as Yahweh's means of redeeming wayward Israel.[53] One could rightly detect echoes of the Abrahamic covenant, which promised to bless the entire world through Abraham's faithful family members (Gen 12:3).

The Early Church portrayed Jesus Christ as embodying the role of the suffering servant of Isaiah, as described in his own mission.[54] In other words, Jesus believed, spoke about, and acted in a manner that demonstrated that he saw himself as exemplifying the role of Isaiah's suffering servant, carrying out the part belonging to faithful Israel in his own person.[55] This can be observed in several texts of the New Testament gospel accounts. One such example appears in Matthew 12:14–21, where Jesus, despite the conspiring attempt by the Pharisees to destroy him, amasses a following to whom he offers healing. Matthew, after noting how Jesus warned these followers not to talk about who he was, openly notes how these actions are to fulfill Isaiah 42:1–3, the first servant song in Isaiah.[56] In another example, Jesus clarified his role as one who "came not to be served but to serve and to give his life as a ransom for many" (Matt 20:28; Mark 10:45).[57] By casting out demons from those who were possessed and offering healing to the ill, Jesus fulfilled that which Isaiah said in the fourth servant song: "He himself took our infirmities and carried away our diseases" (Matt 8:16–17).[58] The narrator in the Gospel of John attributes the lack of belief of the crowds to the signs Jesus performed as a fulfillment of a line of Isaiah's fourth servant song (John 12:37–38).

In Matthew, Mark, and Luke, Christ repeatedly makes bold predictions about the suffering that will come his way. After Peter confesses Jesus to be the Christ (Mark 8:29), Jesus plainly declares that he "must suffer many things and be rejected by the elders and the chief priests and the scribes, and be killed, and after three days rise again" (Mark 8:31–32). Similar predictions of Jesus' rejection and suffering continue in the narrative (Mark 9:31; 10:33–34), each indicating that Jesus not only accepted his role as Isaiah's suffering servant but also attempted to inform his disciples of his decision. Luke records Jesus' prediction that Jesus will be spat upon in accordance with "all things which are written through the prophets" (Luke 18:31–32), which appears to include the

---

[53] Collins, "Servant of the Lord," 194; Goldingay, "Servant of Yahweh," 706.
[54] Goldingay, "Servant of Yahweh," 706, states, "Christians know that Jesus is the supreme embodiment of the servant vision."
[55] Wright, *Jesus and the Victory of God*, 603, frames it as such: "It is therefore highly probable that, in addition to several other passages which informed his vocation, Jesus regarded Isaiah 53, in its whole literary and historical context, as determinative."
[56] Davies and Allison, *Matthew*, 2:322–29.
[57] Dunn, *Jesus Remembered*, 813–14.
[58] Davies and Allison, *Matthew*, 2:36–38.

third servant song (Isa 50:6).[59] Matthew and Mark similarly recount how this spitting occurred in their descriptions of the humiliation and crucifixion of Jesus (Matt 26:67; 27:30; Mark 15:19).

We have evidence outside of the New Testament gospels that indicates an acceptance among the Early Church of Jesus taking upon himself the role of Isaiah's suffering servant. Philip, one of the seven initial deacons of the Early Church, informed a traveling eunuch from Ethiopia that the passage he was reading (Isa 53:7–8) found its fulfillment in Jesus (Acts 8:26–35). When the Apostle Paul wanted to set Jesus as an example to the Philippians as one who gave up his privileges in order to serve others (Phil 2:5–11), Paul drew heavily on Isaiah's fourth servant song. In particular, Paul portrays the human messianic king as emptying himself by taking the form of a servant (Phil 2:7), a direct echo of Isaiah's suffering servant.[60] By embodying the role of Isaiah's suffering servant, Jesus demonstrated his humble self-emptying "to the point of death" (Phil 2:8). Paul here has quite clearly drawn upon Isaiah 53:12 ("he poured out himself to death").[61] Moreover, Paul's train of thought shifts from Christ's death to his resurrection and exaltation: "For this reason, God highly exalted him" (Phil 2:9), which recounts the opening line of the fourth servant song, "See, my servant shall prosper; he shall be exalted and lifted up, and shall be very high" (Isa 52:13).[62] As such, Paul not only believed that Jesus voluntarily emptied himself of his messianic prerogatives in order to carry out the role of Isaiah's suffering servant, but he also summons his Philippian readers to imitate Jesus' humility in their daily lives: "Have this attitude in yourselves, which was also in Christ Jesus" (Phil 2:5).[63] First Peter similarly urges its readers to follow in the footsteps of Jesus by calling to mind how he acted in fulfillment of the role of Isaiah's servant,[64] quoting explicitly Isaiah 53:9:

> For to this you have been called, because Christ also suffered for you, leaving you an example, so that you should follow in his steps. "He committed no sin, and no deceit was found in his mouth." When he was abused, he did not return abuse; when he suffered, he did not threaten; but he entrusted himself to the one who judges justly. He himself bore our sins in his body on the cross, so that, free from sins, we might live for righteousness; by his wounds you have been healed. For you were going astray like sheep, but now you have returned to the shepherd and guardian of your souls. (1 Pet 2:21–25)

It should be apparent by this point that the Early Church not only believed that Jesus took upon himself the role of the suffering servant spoken about in the Book of Isaiah but also that Jesus' example was a model that should be imitated and obeyed in the lives

---

[59] Nolland, *Luke 9:21–18:34*, 895–96.
[60] Wright, *Paul and the Faithfulness of God*, 683; Reumann, *Philippians*, 349.
[61] Bockmuehl, *Philippians*, 139.
[62] Oswalt, *Isaiah 40–66*, 379.
[63] Smith, "Taking Philippians 2:6-11 Out of the Vacuum," 28–29.
[64] Bartlett, "The First Letter of Peter," 281–84.

of Jesus' followers. We should not, however, miss the key christological point about Jesus' role as Isaiah's suffering servant, namely that Jesus saw himself as the one person who could appropriately embody the mission formerly given to faithful Israel. Put differently, by accepting the mission of the suffering servant, Jesus embodied the mandate given to faithful Israel as the one faithful representative of Israel. Moreover, when we combine the representative function of the suffering servant with the similar representative roles of the royal *son of God* and the *son of man*, we can gain a deeper appreciation for Jesus as a genuine human figure who stands and acts on behalf of his people. As the Early Church illustrated Jesus as the son of God, the son of man, and the suffering servant, it emphasized his authentic humanity as a member of the human race who acted as the royal king, as the one who suffered, and as the one who bore Israel's destiny to be the means through which God would bless the world by dealing with sin once and for all.

Conclusion

This chapter focused on three important christological titles that the authors of the New Testament attributed to Jesus. First, we explored Jesus as the son of God, the royal Jewish messiah who was not only anointed to be king of God's kingdom but also acted as the king who represented his people, even to the point of dying for them on a cross bearing the title "King of the Jews." Second, we examined the one like a son of man from the Book of Daniel, a character highly authorized by God and who represented God's righteous people who suffered at the hands of evil. Finally, we looked closely at the servant figure in the four servant songs of Isaiah, each of which contributed to a God-given mission to faithful Israel to be the means through which God would deal with sin, gather the lost, and ultimately bring salvation to the nations. Jesus willingly shouldered the role of the suffering servant as Israel's representative, taking transgressions on himself and pouring out his life unto death, resulting in Yahweh raising him from the dead and exalting him to heaven. These three key christological roles display Christ as a human being—the royal son whom Yahweh anointed, the son of man whom Yahweh empowered with his own prerogatives, and the suffering servant upon whom Yahweh laid the people's iniquities. As such, the Early Church was firmly convinced that Jesus Christ was distinguished from Yahweh, never to be confused with one another.

While remaining fully human, Christ possessed a special relationship with the Father, the only true God. As *son of God*, Jesus rules on God's behalf; as *son of man*, Jesus exercises God's prerogatives; and as *suffering servant*, Jesus is the means through which God deals with humanity's sin. To say that Jesus acts as the highly authorized and highly empowered agent of Yahweh is to accurately capture the sense in which the Early Church understood the unique role of the human Messiah. In our next chapter, we will dig deeper into Jesus' role as God's agent, the son who fully represents the only true God.

24
JESUS AS GOD'S AGENT

In Chapter 7, we introduced the concept of agency as it relates to Yahweh's regular practice of commissioning and sending forth his authorized representatives. In that chapter, we observed how the only true God utilizes several different agents, including heavenly angels, his personified attributes, and even qualified human beings such as prophets, priests, and the Israelite king. It should be no surprise, since the Early Church depicted Jesus as a prophetic figure, as the new high priest, and as the messianic king, that he also functioned in the role of God's agent. In particular, Jesus served as the most qualified agent that Yahweh could conceivably empower, since the Jewish principle of agency regarded a father's own son to be the most trusted representative of the father's interests (Mark 12:6).[1] Readers of the New Testament who fail to grasp the relationship between God as the sender and Jesus Christ as the sent agent will be unlikely to make sense of the nuance the Early Church attributed to Jesus' mission and exalted status. It is crucial, therefore, that we thoroughly explore what it means for Jesus to act as the agent of Yahweh.

This chapter will demonstrate how the New Testament portrayal of Christ's relationship with God is built upon the custom of the Jewish principle of agency. First, we will explore how the son of God fully represents his sender, the Father. Second, we will demonstrate that the God who commissioned Jesus as his agent is unquestionably greater than Jesus. Third, we will observe how Jesus, conscious of his role as the highly empowered human agent of God, chose to faithfully obey the mandate for which he was sent. Fourth, we will take note of how God authorized Jesus to function as his legal partner, particularly in the ways in which Jesus bears the judicial functions and prerogatives of God. Fifth, we will see how Jesus' ascension to heaven after his resurrection is crucial in completing the mission for which he was sent. Finally, we will investigate how Jesus, the premier agent of God, recruited the members of the Early Church to serve as his agents, thus demonstrating how an agent can appoint more agents. By the end of this chapter, we will possess a thorough understanding of how the human Jesus fully represented Yahweh, without confusing the agent who was sent with the God who sent him.

---

[1] Harvey, "Christ as Agent," 241; Carter, *Mark*, 328. Collins, *Mark*, 547, similarly remarks, "Jesus is God's last agent."

Jesus Fully Represented God as God's Agent

Our first task is to thoroughly explore the early Christian portrayal of the son of God, the human agent who fully represented Yahweh. One need not look any further than the frequently repeated "sending" indicators, which define the sender as God and God's agent as Jesus:

> He had still one other, a beloved son. Finally he sent him to them, saying, "They will respect my son." (Mark 12:6; Matt 21:37; Luke 20:13)

> "For God did not send his Son into the world to condemn the world, but in order that the world might be saved through him." (John 3:17)

> "He who does not honor the Son does not honor the Father who sent him" (John 5:23)

> "He who believes in me does not believe in me, but in Him who sent me." (John 12:44)

> "Whoever sees me sees the One who sent me." (John 12:45)

> "Whoever receives me receives Him who sent me." (John 13:20)

> "This is eternal life, that they may know You, the only true God, and Jesus Christ whom You have sent." (John 17:3)

As the one whom God has sent, Jesus acts as God the Father's agent. The passages above indicate a particular emphasis in the Gospel of John that stresses the roles of Jesus as the Father's agent and the Father as the one who authorizes Jesus for his mission.[2] In fact, the illustration of Jesus as the one whom God has sent occurs over forty times in the Gospel of John, making this christological point a recurring theme throughout the text.[3] Furthermore, Jesus is called an *apostle* in both John 13:16 and Hebrews 3:1, further solidifying his role as the only true God's agent.

The Gospel of John and the Book of Acts explicitly portray Jesus as a highly authorized prophetic agent of Yahweh, drawing upon the characterization in Deuteronomy 18:15–19 and applying it to Jesus. In this passage, Yahweh informs Moses that there will come a time when another prophet will arise, in whom Yahweh will place his words to speak in his name:

> Yahweh your God will raise up for you a prophet like me from among you, from your countrymen, you shall listen to him . . . "I will raise up a prophet from among their countrymen like you, and I will put My words in his mouth, and he shall speak to them all that I command him. It shall come about that whoever will not listen to My words which he shall speak in My name, I Myself will require it of him." (Deut 18:15, 18–19)

---

[2] Smith, *Wisdom Christology*, 89–93.
[3] Charlesworth, "Lady Wisdom and Johannine Christology," 107.

This promised prophet is characterized by several noteworthy traits that should not be overlooked. First, Yahweh is establishing this prophet and setting him on the scene of history. The two figures are clearly distinguished in this passage, and they are never confused. Second, the prophet is from the stock of Israel, being from among Moses' countrymen.[4] This is a genuine human figure, not a heavenly angelic figure or a divine being. Third, Yahweh puts his own words into the mouth of this prophet, resulting in a human spokesperson whose speech is the very speech of Yahweh.[5] Fourth, Yahweh declares that this human prophet speaks in Yahweh's name, that is, bearing Yahweh's authority.[6] Finally, refusing to obey what the prophet says is tantamount to refusing Yahweh, since the prophet is Yahweh's prophetic agent. There can be no doubt that the promised prophet like Moses from Deuteronomy 18:15–19 is a highly authorized human figure.[7]

As mentioned, the Gospel of John insists that Jesus is the promised prophet from Deuteronomy 18:15–19. The Samaritan woman and the blind man speak of Jesus in prophetic terms (John 4:19; 9:17), and the crowds openly declare him to be *the prophet* (John 6:14; 7:40). Throughout the narrative, Jesus openly admits that his words and teachings do not belong to him, for they belong to the Father who sent him as his agent:

> For He whom God has sent speaks the words of God (John 3:34)

> So Jesus answered them and said, "My teaching is not mine, but His who sent me. If anyone is willing to do His will, he will know of the teaching, whether it is of God or whether I speak from myself. He who speaks from himself seeks his own glory; but he who is seeking the glory of the One who sent Him, he is true, and there is no unrighteousness in him." (John 7:16–18)

> So Jesus said, "When you lift up the Son of Man, then you will know that I am he, and I do nothing on my own initiative, but I speak these things as the Father taught me." (John 8:28)

> "I speak the things which I have seen with the Father" (John 8:38)

Just as the prophet speaks forth God's words as one who bears God's authority, Jesus acknowledges that he speaks and acts in his Father's name:

> "I have come in my Father's name, and you do not receive me; if another comes in his own name, you will receive him." (John 5:43)

---

[4] Clements, "The Book of Deuteronomy," 429. Brueggemann, *Deuteronomy*, 194, contends that this promised prophet "must be a member of Israel."
[5] Nelson, *Deuteronomy*, 235, captures well the sense of the text: "Yahweh commands the prophet, so what this prophet speaks is unequivocally Yahweh's word in its entirety."
[6] Tigay, *Deuteronomy*, 177, observes, "This declaration establishes the prophet as the highest authority in the land."
[7] Anderson, "The Having-Sent-Me Father," 34.

> So they took branches of palm trees and went out to meet him, shouting, "Hosanna! Blessed is the one who comes in the name of the Lord—the King of Israel!" (John 12:13)

The Gospel of John even warns those who choose to ignore Jesus' God-given words of the consequences of their unfaithful actions, just as Yahweh said it would happen in Deuteronomy 18:19:

> He who believes in him is not judged; he who does not believe has been judged already, because he has not believed in the name of the unique Son of God. (John 3:18)

> He who rejects me and does not receive my sayings, has one who judges him; the word I spoke is what will judge him at the last day. (John 12:48)

In the preaching of Peter and Stephen, presented in the Book of Acts, Jesus is outright identified as the promised prophet. This conclusion can be observed with two direct quotations from Deuteronomy 18:15:

> Moses said, "The Lord God will raise up for you a prophet like me from your brethren; to him you shall give heed to everything he says to you. And it will be that every soul that does not heed that prophet shall be utterly destroyed from among the people" (Acts 3:22–23)

> This is the Moses who said to the sons of Israel, "God will raise up for you a prophet like me from your brethren." (Acts 7:37)

It should be clear at this point that Jesus, the human Messiah, functioned as the authorized and empowered agent of God, speaking forth the very words of Yahweh. This is exactly what one would expect from an agent within the Jewish culture, where the principle of agency was simply a given concept. As we will recall, the promised Davidic ruler would operate in the strength and the majesty of the name of Yahweh, according to Micah 5:4. Furthermore, this promised king would be "like God" (Zech 12:8). Moreover, the one like a son of man from Daniel 7:13–14 is quite explicitly given God's own dominion, glory, and kingship. The New Testament authors do not shy away from displaying Jesus as one who bears the prerogatives of God; that is, God has shared his unique roles with his son in a manner consistent with the investment of an agent with the status of the sender.[8] The first example of God authorizing Jesus with his prerogatives is the ability to forgive sins. Consider this account where the narrator makes it abundantly clear that God has given this authority to Jesus, a human being:

> And just then some people were carrying a paralyzed man lying on a bed. When Jesus saw their faith, he said to the paralytic, "Take heart, son; your sins are forgiven." Then some of the scribes said to themselves, "This man is blaspheming." But Jesus, perceiving their thoughts, said, "Why do you think evil in your hearts? For which is easier, to say, 'Your sins are forgiven,' or to say, 'Stand up and walk'? But so that you may know that

---

[8] Bauckham, *Jesus and the God of Israel*, 138.

the Son of Man has authority on earth to forgive sins"—he then said to the paralytic—"Stand up, take your bed and go to your home." And he stood up and went to his home. When the crowds saw it, they were filled with awe, and they glorified God, who had given such authority to human beings. (Matt 9:2–8)

In this passage, Jesus acknowledges that he possesses the authority to forgive sins, and in doing so, he refers to himself as the son of man. We will recall that Daniel 7:13–14 portrays the one like a son of man as being empowered by God's prerogatives, so it is no surprise that even the crowds who witnessed the healing miracle acknowledged that God has shared his authority with Jesus, a member of the human race.[9] By forgiving sins, Jesus was not claiming to be God; rather, he was claiming to be God's agent.[10]

The second example of God authorizing Jesus Christ occurs in John 5, where Jesus heals a man who was unable to walk. Since this took place on the Sabbath, Jesus' actions caused a stir among those who did not accept him to be the Messiah, God's anointed son. Among the many things Jesus said in his defense is a recognition that he is able to bestow life on the man's lame legs because God has empowered Jesus to do so:

> "For just as the Father raises the dead and gives them life, even so the Son also gives life to whom he wishes ... Truly, truly, I say to you, an hour is coming and now is, when the dead will hear the voice of the Son of God, and those who hear will live. For just as the Father has life in Himself, even so He gave to the Son also to have life in himself" (John 5:21, 25–26)

God the Father, the Creator and sustainer of life itself, has shared the life-giving prerogative with Jesus.[11] This allows Jesus to perform healings, raise the dead, and offer salvific life through his gospel.

The third example comes from the same context as Jesus' lengthy response to the criticisms that arose from healing the lame man on the Sabbath in John chapter five. In particular, Jesus states that God has shared his role as the judge with Jesus:

> "For not even the Father judges anyone, but He has given all judgment to the Son, so that all will honor the Son even as they honor the Father. He who does not honor the Son does not honor the Father who sent him. Truly, truly, I say to you, he who hears my word, and believes Him who sent me, has eternal life, and does not come into judgment, but has passed out of death into life ... and He gave him authority to execute judgment, because he is the Son of Man." (John 5:22–24, 27)

---

[9] Davies and Allison, *Matthew*, 2:93; Nolland, *Matthew*, 382.
[10] Kirk, *A Man Attested by God*, 282, 306
[11] Lincoln, "I am the Resurrection," 128. Borgen, *Bread from Heaven*, 162, argues, "The life of the Father as the sender is transferred to the agent, the Son."

As God's messianic agent, Jesus represents God by performing the role of judge.[12] In doing so, Jesus functions in a way that fully represents the Father who sent him as his agent.[13] To show disrespect to God's agent is akin to disrespecting God himself. Furthermore, Jesus is given the authority to judge because he is the highly empowered son of man portrayed in Daniel 7:13–14.

The fourth way in which God authorizes Jesus can be observed at the conclusion of the Gospel of Matthew. After Jesus died, was buried, and raised to immortality by God, he appeared to his disciples and boldly declared his new exalted status: "All authority in heaven and on earth has been given to me" (Matt 28:18). This is a substantial announcement that should not be overlooked. After God raised Jesus from the dead, God shared with Jesus all authority in creation itself, in both heaven and on earth. We have already seen that God has given authority on earth to Jesus during Jesus' earthly ministry (Matt 9:6; Mark 2:10; Luke 5:24). Now, after the resurrection, the level of empowerment is much greater, including all authority in heaven. This makes the resurrected Jesus the fully empowered agent of the one true God, displaying the human Messiah as possessing all the rights and privileges formerly belonging to God alone.[14]

One final way in which God establishes Jesus as his representative agent is by sharing his titles and even his own name with the son of God. While this level of empowering an agent might seem extreme to modern readers, it was the normal consequence of the Jewish principle of agency, wherein the agent fully represented his sender. When Jesus announced, "I have come in my Father's name" (John 5:43), he openly identified himself as the Father's authorized agent.[15] Again, when Jesus declares to his disciples, "Whoever has seen me has seen the Father" (John 14:9), he is plainly stating his role as the Father's agent.[16] The Jewish crowds attest that Christ, by virtue of his messianic role as the son of David, serves as the agent of God: "The crowds that went ahead of him and that followed were shouting, 'Hosanna to the Son of David! Blessed is the one who comes in the name of the Lord'" (Matt 21:9).[17] The Apostle Paul remarks how God raised Jesus to an exalted status, and in doing so, God shared his name with his son: "Therefore God also highly exalted him and gave him the name that is above every name" (Phil 2:9).[18] A similar expression can be located in the opening of the Epistle to the Hebrews, where the author argues for Jesus' superiority over the heavenly angels because the highly exalted Jesus is the heir a better name: "having become as much better

---

[12] Lincoln, "I am the Resurrection," 128.
[13] Anderson, "The Having-Sent-Me Father," 42; Fuller, "Incarnation," 61; Thompson, "John, Gospel of," 377.
[14] Kirk, *A Man Attested by God*, 332; Luz, *Matthew 21–28*, 623–24.
[15] Meyer, "The Father," 265. Keener, *John*, 1:660, offers a refreshingly honest take: "to come in the Father's name meant to come as his representative."
[16] Thompson, *John*, 309, states, "Jesus has identified himself as the Son, the representative of God who speaks the words and does the life-giving works of the Father."
[17] Hagner, *Matthew 14–28*, 596.
[18] Hurtado, *One God, One Lord*, 97; Kirk, *A Man Attested by God*, 108; McGrath, *Only True God*, 49–50.

than the angels, as he has inherited a more excellent name than they" (Heb 1:4).[19] Sharing God's name with Christ is certainly included in the expression that God appointed the son the "heir of all things" (Heb 1:2).

When we consider the many ways in which Jesus functions as the agent of the only true God, by speaking the words of God, exercising God's prerogatives, bearing God's authority, and carrying in himself God's personal name, it is no surprise that Jesus is called "God" on a few occasions.[20] To be sure, by God sharing his title with Christ, this is not, in effect, collapsing God and Jesus into a single being. Rather, it is displaying Jesus as one who is fully authorized and empowered by the only true God, acting as God's duly appointed agent. Not surprisingly, the passages that apply the title "God" to Jesus both occur after the resurrection and in the context of Jesus being described as having a God above him (i.e., the Father). Take, for example, Thomas answering Jesus by confessing "My Lord and my God" (John 20:28) just a few verses after Jesus plainly acknowledged that *he has a God*, the Father alone (John 20:17).[21] Similarly, Hebrews 1:8–9 calls Jesus "God" while at the same time making it very clear that Jesus still has a God ranked above him:

> But of the Son he says, "Your throne, O God, is forever and ever, the scepter of uprightness is the scepter of your kingdom. You have loved righteousness and hated wickedness; therefore God, your God, has anointed you with the oil of gladness above your companions." (Heb 1:8–9)

This passage, which calls Christ "God" and recognizes that the one who anointed Jesus is "your God," is quoting directly from Psalm 45:6–7. We observed in Chapter Six that Yahweh was frequently illustrated as empowering the human Israelite king as his royal agent. Psalm 45 is one such passage that calls the human king, who rules on behalf of the true God as God's agent, "God."[22] It is precisely with this understanding of a human agent bearing the title of God that the author of Hebrews carries over in his citation of Psalm 45:6–7 in Hebrews 1:8–9. The resurrected and exalted Jesus, who has been appointed the heir of all things (Heb 1:2) and the bearer of God's personal name (Heb 1:4), is given the title "God" in his capacity as God's human agent. The author of Hebrews makes it clear to his readers that Jesus, God's agent, has a God above him in Hebrews 1:9 ("your God, has anointed you"). This christology is consistent with the human Messiah who currently possesses all authority in heaven and on earth (Matt 28:18).

---

[19] Johnson, *Hebrews*, 74.
[20] Irons et al., *The Son of God*, 140–41.
[21] Carter, *John and Empire*, 196; Nemes, *Trinity & Incarnation*, 197–98. Thompson, *God of the Gospel of John*, 234–35, helpfully states that "The Father has authorized the Son precisely to exercise divine activities and prerogatives . . . Thomas's confession cannot mean that the risen Jesus is the only God. That epithet has already been used by Jesus himself in a context that clearly distinguishes the Father and the Son (17:3)."
[22] Johnson, *Hebrews*, 80, acknowledges: "The king who is the subject of the psalm is thoroughly human . . . Yet, because of his enthronement, this human king can be designated as God."

God is Greater than His Agent, Jesus

Although God invested his prerogatives, roles, authority, name, and titles in his agent, the human Jesus, there was never any question in the beliefs of the Early Church regarding who was in charge. The Jewish principle of agency holds that the sender always outranks the commissioned agent, and the New Testament authors are abundantly clear in acknowledging the subordination of Christ to God. In the culture of the Ancient Near East, it was never questioned that a father outranked his children, as every father was older than and begat his sons. Although Jesus, in his role as the agent of God, fully represented the Father, he nevertheless taught his disciples that *the Father was greater than his son*: "The Father is greater than I" (John 14:28).[23] Even after the resurrection, the Apostle Paul clearly explains the hierarchy of creation in terms of its relation to the one true God: "all things belong to you, and you belong to Christ; and Christ belongs to God" (1 Cor 3:22–23).[24] Later in 1 Corinthians, Paul again illustrates Christ's subordinate status to God in terms of headship: "But I want you to understand that Christ is the head of every man, and the husband is the head of his wife, and God is the head of Christ" (1 Cor 11:3).[25] When Paul describes the return of Christ to bring all creation into subjection under God's rule, Paul makes it clear that this includes Jesus: "When all things are subjected to him, then the Son himself will also be subjected to the one who put all things in subjection under him, so that God may be all in all" (1 Cor 15:28).[26] Based on these clear, straightforward passages, we can deduce that Jesus understood his role as God's agent to be subordinate to God during his ministry, and this subordination continued to remain after Jesus' post-resurrection exaltation, and it will remain even after the second coming.

Jesus Christ Fully Obeyed God

When an agent was commissioned for a set task by his sender, the agent would be expected to faithfully obey the sender, and the relationship between Jesus and God is similarly illustrated by the authors of the biblical texts.[27] The mission of Jesus is to obey the will of the Father: "My food is to do the will of him who sent me and to accomplish

---

[23] Barrett, "The Father Is Greater than I," 28; Brown, *John XII–XXI*, 655. Anderson, "The Having-Sent-Me Father," 41, observes that Jesus "can do nothing without the Father, and the Father is greater than he."

[24] Fitzmyer, *First Corinthians*, 208–9. Conzelmann, *1 Corinthians*, 81, offers a reading of clarity: "Christological subordinationism emerges in the reference back to God."

[25] Fitzmyer, *First Corinthians*, 409, writes, "As God is preeminent over Christ, so Christ is preeminent over every man, and man is preeminent over woman."

[26] Hays, *First Corinthians*, 266, provides an apt summary: "It is impossible to avoid the impression that Paul is operating with what would later come to be called a subordinationist christology. The doctrine of the Trinity was not yet formulated in Paul's day."

[27] Ladd, *A Theology of the New Testament*, 251; Robinson, "Christology Today," 68, illustrates Christ's obedient posture in terms of an "*absolutely intimate dependence*" upon God as his Father.

his work" (John 4:34).[28] Jesus' mission was to preach the gospel of the kingdom of God: "I must preach the good news of the kingdom of God to the other towns as well; for I was sent for this purpose" (Luke 4:43). As the highly authorized prophet, Jesus acknowledged that he obediently spoke what God told him to say: "the Father who sent me has himself given me a commandment about what to say and what to speak" (John 12:49).[29] Jesus' mission even included performing the Father's deeds, about which Jesus stated, "I have shown you many good works from the Father" (John 10:32).

Unfortunately, not everyone believed that Jesus was the promised Jewish Messiah, regarding him instead as a messianic pretender who claimed God's prerogatives illegitimately. When Jesus was accused of rebelliously "making himself" into someone or something (John 5:18), he immediately clarified the misunderstanding by calling attention to his role as the obedient agent of God.[30] "The son can do nothing of himself," Jesus declares in John 5:19, "unless it is something he sees the Father doing, for what the Father does, the son does in like manner."[31] We may observe a similar misunderstanding in John 10:30–36, where Jesus again responds to his confused opponents by drawing attention to his role as the sanctified *agent of the Father*. "Do you say of him whom the Father consecrated and sent into the world, 'You are blaspheming,' because I said, 'I am the Son of God'"? (John 10:36).[32] This is precisely what we would expect of one who is not only an agent but also a son—the premier agent of his God and Father.

Christ is the Legal and Judicial Representative of God

According to the Jewish principle of agency, the agent may perform judicial and legal functions belonging to the sender, and the Early Church illustrated Jesus as taking over the role of the cosmic judge from God the Father. We have already observed that Jesus claimed that the Father authorized Jesus to bear the prerogative of enacting judgment (John 5:22–24, 27), and this gets unpacked in several noteworthy ways.[33] Consider how the following passages point to Jesus serving as the agent of God as it pertains to judicial matters:

> "Yet even if I do judge, my judgment is true, for it is not I alone who judge, but I and the Father who sent me." (John 8:16)

---

[28] Borgen, *Bread from Heaven*, 155.
[29] Carter, *John: Storyteller, Interpreter, Evangelist*, 60, rightly observes that Jesus' role as agent is *"dependent on and derivative of* God."
[30] Gaston, "Does the Gospel of John Have a High Christology?" 133.
[31] Anderson, "The Having-Sent-Me Father," 41; Robinson, "Christology Today," 68.
[32] Robinson, *Twelve More New Testament Studies*, 175.
[33] Thompson, *God of the Gospel of John*, 230–31.

> "And He ordered us to preach to the people, and solemnly to testify that this is the one who has been appointed by God as Judge of the living and the dead." (Acts 10:42)

> "Therefore having overlooked the times of ignorance, God is now declaring to men that all people everywhere should repent, because He has fixed a day in which He will judge the world in righteousness through a man whom He has appointed, having furnished proof to all men by raising him from the dead." (Acts 17:30–31)

> on the day when, according to my gospel, God will judge the secrets of men through Christ Jesus. (Rom 2:16)

> For after all it is only just for God to repay with affliction those who afflict you, and to give relief to you who are afflicted and to us as well when the Lord Jesus will be revealed from heaven with His mighty angels in flaming fire, dealing out retribution to those who do not know God and to those who do not obey the gospel of our Lord Jesus. (2 Thes 1:6–8)

Based on these verses, it is plainly apparent that the New Testament authors were convinced that Jesus was going to judge the world on God's behalf.[34] Once we grasp this key role of Jesus as God's agent, we can begin to make sense of several of his sayings that, without the context of Jewish agency, would remain obscure. For example, when asked about the authority Jesus possesses to explain his actions in the temple, he responds by saying, "Destroy this temple, and in three days I will raise it up" (John 2:18–19). This response leads to some confusion among those with whom Jesus is speaking, but the narrator helpfully clarifies the misunderstanding with a straightforward conclusion: "He was speaking of the temple of his body" (John 2:21). The question remains how it is possible for Jesus, being dead, to raise himself back to life personally. The answer comes later in the narrative of the Gospel of John, where Jesus acknowledges that he possesses the authority to take up his life precisely because God has given it to him: "I have authority to lay it down, and I have authority to take it up again. This commandment I received from my Father." (John 10:18). As God's legal agent, Jesus takes possession of what rightfully belongs to the Father: "No one can come to me unless the Father who sent me draws him" (John 6:44). Later, Jesus describes his loyal followers "my sheep," those whom the Father has given over to Jesus' care and protection: "I give them eternal life, and they will never perish. No one will snatch them out of my hand. What my Father has given me is greater than all else, and no one can snatch it out of the Father's hand" (John 10:28–29).[35] As the agent of God, Jesus and the Father share a oneness of purpose, both working to achieve the same goal (John 10:30).[36] As we can observe, the early Church embraced the understanding of Christ's role as agent of the only true God.

---

[34] Fitzmyer, *First Corinthians*, 466.
[35] Loader, "The Central Structure of Johannine Christology," 202.
[36] Smith, *Wisdom Christology*, 96–98; Carter, *John: Storyteller, Interpreter, Evangelist*, 60.

The Ascension and the Completion of the Agent's Mission

When an agent finished his mission, it was customary to return to the sender.[37] For Jesus, this involved his post-resurrection ascension to God's right hand, which would bring his earthly ministry to a conclusion. Jesus was aware of the need to ascend to God once he completed his mission as God's highly empowered agent: "Jesus, knowing that the Father had given all things into his hands, and that he had come from God and was going to God" (John 13:3).[38] After his resurrection, Jesus tells Mary Magdalene that he still needs to ascend to his God and Father: "Do not cling to me, for I have not yet ascended to the Father; but go to my brothers and say to them, 'I am ascending to my Father and your Father, to my God and your God'" (John 20:17). The author of Hebrews repeatedly observes how Jesus ascended to heaven after dealing with sin: "After making purification for sins, he sat down at the right hand of the Majesty on high" (Heb 1:3; 10:12; 12:2). It seems apparent that Jesus' ascent into heaven after his earthly mission was brought to completion resulted in connecting the agent with his sender.

Christ, as God's Agent, Commissioned Further Agents

Finally, we may observe several indicators that point to the fact that Jesus, the agent of God, sent forth his own agents. In other words, the only true God's *apostle* sends forth his own *apostles*. In our earliest Gospel accounts, Jesus sends out the twelve apostles to act as his agents (Matt 10:7; Mark 6:7; Luke 9:1–2). Their message, "The kingdom of heaven is at hand" (Matt 10:7; Mark 6:12; Luke 9:2), was the message Jesus also spoke (Matt 4:17; Mark 1:15; Luke 4:43). Even their deeds of healing, raising the dead, cleansing, and casting out demons (Matt 10:8) reflect that activity of their sender, Jesus. The Gospel of Luke records an additional sending where Jesus commissions seventy agents (Luke 10:1–3) to perform healing and to announce the kingdom of God: "heal those in it who are sick, and say to them, 'The kingdom of God has come near to you'" (Luke 10:9). The chain of command is plain to see in Jesus' instruction about those who accept the preaching of his agents: "Whoever receives you receives me, and whoever receives me receives him who sent me" (Matt 10:40; Luke 10:16; John 13:20).[39] In other words, those who accept the preaching of the agent (the apostles) of an agent (Christ) are, in reality, accepting the one who sent Christ, namely God.[40] Jesus openly acknowledges in his

---

[37] Smith, *Wisdom Christology*, 92; "The Jewish Principle of Agency," 10–11.
[38] Borgen, "God's Agent in the Fourth Gospel," 172.
[39] See similar statements in Mark 9:37; Luke 9:48.
[40] Luz, *Matthew 8–20*, 120, captures the sense of agency well in commenting on Matt 10:40: "In them Jesus himself confronts the people, and in Jesus God confronts them . . . In the background are the Jewish emissary law (an emissary represents with full authority the one who commissioned him)."

lengthy prayer to God how he has commissioned forth his own agents: "As you sent me into the world, so I have sent them into the world" (John 17:18).

At the conclusion of Jesus' ministry, he sends his disciples out to be his agents, tasked with proclaiming the gospel of the kingdom of God and the resurrection. Christ's commissioning of his agents is described in several texts (Matt 28:19–20; Luke 24:46–48; John 20:21; Acts 1:8). The Gospel of John notably records how Jesus equipped his agents with the Holy Spirit at the moment of their commissioning: "'Peace be with you; as the Father has sent me, I also send you.' And when he had said this, he breathed on them and said to them, 'Receive the Holy Spirit'" (John 20:21–22).[41] In this way, the disciples, acting as Jesus' highly empowered agents, are given the same Holy Spirit that God gave to Jesus at the beginning of his ministry (Matt 3:16; Mark 1:10; Luke 3:22; John 1:32). In short, Jesus, the Spirit-empowered, kingdom-preaching, miracle-working apostle of the only true God sent out his own agents—those who would also be empowered with the Spirit, proclaim the same kingdom message, perform the same miracles, and be identified as his apostles.[42]

Conclusion

This chapter has demonstrated the many ways that Jesus functioned as the authorized and empowered agent of the only true God, the Father. We first examined how Jesus served in the capacity of an agent that fully represented God, which included bearing God's prerogatives, roles, and even the title "God" in two passages. Second, we saw how the relationship between God, the sender, and Jesus, the agent, is and continues to be illustrated in terms of a superior and one who is subordinate to his sender rather than being coequal with each other. Third, we noticed that Jesus faithfully carried out the will of the Father as an obedient agent. Fourth, we explored how Christ, bearing the legal and judicial responsibilities of his sender, performed these duties in his role as God's agent. Fifth, we saw how the post-resurrection ascension to heaven allowed Jesus, the agent, the necessary opportunity to report back to his sender. Finally, we demonstrated that Jesus appointed his own agents—his disciples—to continue his ministry. The Early Church agreed that Jesus functioned as the highly empowered agent of God in a manner that fit appropriately into the expectations set forth in the Jewish principle of agency.

What are we to make of the Early Church's tendency to portray Jesus as the embodiment of the wisdom and word of God? Did the Early Church think of Jesus as having preexisted his birth? These questions will be discussed in our next chapter.

---

[41] Keener, *John*, 2:1204.
[42] McIlhone, "Jesus as God's Agent," 311.

25
WISDOM CHRISTOLOGY AND LOGOS CHRISTOLOGY

When we set Jesus in his Jewish context, we begin to observe several fascinating ways in which the Early Church drew upon earlier traditions in order to uniquely illustrate Jesus. Drawing upon books like Proverbs, early Christians not only portrayed Jesus as embodying the wisdom of God, but they also recounted times when Jesus spoke of himself in terms of God's wisdom. The opening eighteen verses of the Gospel of John, often called the *prologue*, build upon this characterization by depicting Jesus as the word that became flesh (John 1:14) and, in doing so, draws upon several Old Testament portrayals of God's creative and powerful speech. What is the significance of these christological representations, which are commonly referred to as "Wisdom Christology" and "Logos Christology"? Furthermore, since the writers of the Old Testament speak about Yahweh using his wisdom and his word in order to perform acts of creation, what does this say about whether Christ preexisted his birth?

This chapter sets out to explore these questions in order to make sense of the Early Church's repeated attempts at illustrating Jesus as the embodiment of God's wisdom and God's word. Our first task will be to offer a comprehensive examination of the Wisdom Christology in the New Testament, noting its origins and its significance. Second, we will examine how Wisdom Christology was eventually combined with Logos Christology in the opening prologue of the Gospel of John. These christological portrayals raise important questions about the subject of preexistence, so our third task will be to explain how early Christians understood the preexistence of Jesus, particularly as it pertains to God's foreknowledge and his personified wisdom and word. Once we possess a clear understanding of the Christology that the Early Church believed and taught, we will be able to fully appreciate the importance of Jesus as the genuinely human Messiah, descendant of David, and descendant of Abraham.

New Testament Wisdom Christology

Beginning with the Early Church's Wisdom Christology, we can observe several instances where the authors of the gospel accounts display Jesus in ways that represent or even embody God's wisdom.[1] For example, Matthew chapter eleven notes how the imprisoned

---

[1] Dunn, *Christology in the Making*, 163–212; Smith, *Wisdom Christology*, 3–10; "New Testament Portrayals of Wisdom Christology," 5–17.

John the Baptist heard about the "deeds of Christ" (Matt 11:2), and the passage continues with Jesus lamenting the reception that both he and John have received from their audiences. In doing so, he speaks of his own deeds as those belonging to a female figure, Wisdom:

> "For John came neither eating nor drinking, and they say, 'He has a demon!' The Son of Man came eating and drinking, and they say, 'Behold, a gluttonous man and a drunkard, a friend of tax collectors and sinners!' Yet wisdom is vindicated by her deeds." (Matt 11:18–19)

Matthew has carefully framed this episode with John inquiring about the deeds of Christ, and Christ describing his deeds in terms of the *deeds of Wisdom*. This suggests that Jesus understood himself as embodying the wise works of the wisdom of God, which Jesus personifies as a female figure by using the feminine pronoun ("her deeds").[2] Luke's version of the same story suggests that both John the Baptist and Jesus are disciples of this personified wisdom figure—her children: "Yet wisdom is vindicated by all her children" (Luke 7:35).[3] Another relevant passage is found in Matthew 12:42 (and its parallel in Luke 11:31) where Jesus, hinting at himself, speaks of something greater than Solomon's wisdom: "The Queen of the South will rise up with this generation at the judgment and will condemn it, because she came from the ends of the earth to hear the wisdom of Solomon; and behold, something greater than Solomon is here." What is greater than the wisdom taught by King Solomon? Naturally, the wisdom taught by King Jesus, the promised Messiah.[4] In another parallel passage between Matthew and Luke, Jesus recounts how the wisdom of God promises to send prophets who will, unfortunately, suffer rejection and death: "Therefore also the Wisdom of God said, 'I will send them prophets . . . some of whom they will kill'" (Luke 11:49). However, in Matthew's version of the same story, it is Jesus himself who speaks: "I am sending you prophets . . . some of whom you will kill" (Matt 23:34).[5] In effect, Matthew is saying that Jesus, by speaking on behalf of this Wisdom figure, is the embodiment of the Wisdom of God.[6] Moreover, Jesus describes himself as the one to whom the Father has handed all things, particularly the knowledge and insight that Jesus is now able to reveal:

> "I thank you, Father, Lord of heaven and earth, that you have hidden these things from the wise and understanding and revealed them to little children . . . All things have been handed over to me by my Father, and no one knows the Son except the Father, and no one knows the Father except the Son and anyone to whom the Son chooses to reveal him." (Matt 11:25–27; Luke 10:21–22)

---

[2] Wainwright, *Shall We Look for Another?* 68–79; Davies and Allison, *Matthew*, 2:264.
[3] Reid, "Wisdom's Children," 46.
[4] Nolland, *Matthew*, 513.
[5] Suggs, *Wisdom, Christology, and Law*, 13–15; Wilson, "Works of Wisdom," 1–20.
[6] Boring, "The Gospel of Matthew," 356; Keener, *Matthew*, 555; Juce, "Wisdom in Matthew," 135–36.

This saying of Jesus draws upon Jewish traditions describing the wisdom of God, such as the wisdom poem in Job chapter twenty-eight:

> "But where can wisdom be found? And where is the place of understanding? Man does not know its value, nor is it found in the land of the living . . . Where then does wisdom come from? And where is the place of understanding? Thus it is hidden from the eyes of all living and concealed from the birds of the sky. Abaddon and Death say, 'With our ears we have heard a report of it.' God understands its way, and He knows its place. For He looks to the ends of the earth and sees everything under the heavens . . . Then He saw it and declared it; He established it and also searched it out. And to man He said, 'Behold, the fear of the Lord, that is wisdom'" (Job 28:12–13, 20–24, 27–28)

Job poetically recounts how God's wisdom is "hidden from the eyes of all living" and that only the Creator God knows where wisdom is to be found. The poem concludes by encouraging the readers to demonstrate the fear of the Lord, for this is how the hidden and elusive wisdom of God can be found. Jesus, who understood himself as the climactic embodiment of God's wisdom, is the one who reveals God's hidden wisdom to the disciples (Matt 11:25–27).[7]

There are indicators that the writers of the New Testament gospel accounts regarded Jesus as one filled with the wisdom of God. One example comes from a time when Jesus was in his hometown preaching in the local synagogue. His teaching amazed those present, leading them to comment on the wisdom he had received, according to Mark 6:2: "Where did this man get these things? What is the wisdom given to him? How are such mighty works done by his hands?" There was no question that Jesus possessed wisdom; the question regarded what manner of wisdom it was, which implicitly calls into question the source of Jesus' wisdom.[8] Another example appears in Luke's gospel account as he describes how the young Jesus grew up and increased in God's wisdom: "And the child grew and became strong, filled with wisdom" (Luke 2:40). Luke repeats this description at the conclusion of the story of Jesus as a twelve-year-old: "Jesus kept increasing in wisdom and stature, and in favor with God and men" (Luke 2:52). There can be no doubt that Jesus continued to grow and be filled with God's wisdom.

The Gospel of John has the most substantial Wisdom Christology of the four New Testament gospel accounts. Although it can be shown that its opening prologue (John 1:1–18) is indebted to former Jewish portrayals of God's wisdom—a feature we will explore later in this chapter—the wider narrative of the Gospel of John consists of several descriptions of Christ that illustrate him as the embodiment of the wisdom of God. Observe how Jesus' response to the less-than-receptive crowds ("You will seek me, and you will not find me") in John 7:34 appears to quote one of the sayings made by the figure of personified wisdom in Proverbs 1:28: "They will seek me diligently, but they will

---

[7] Deutsch, *Lady Wisdom, Jesus, and the Sages*, 64; *Hidden Wisdom and the Easy Yoke*, 21–112.
[8] Smith, "New Testament Portrayals of Wisdom Christology," 11–12.

not find me."[9] At the wedding at Cana, the mother of Jesus immediately knew whom to go to in order to address the crisis of the wine that ran out, pointing the attendants to Jesus (John 2:3–10). No doubt this is due to an awareness that Jesus embodies the wisdom of God, the personified figure from Proverbs that mixes her own wine and offers it unto others (Prov 9:1–5).[10] Similarly, personified wisdom's invitation to drink her wine is accompanied by a summons to "eat of my bread" in Proverbs 9:5, which is probably the basis for Jesus' claims to be the bread of life (John 6:35).[11] Not only does Jesus identify himself with the imagery of bread, but he also invites his listeners to partake of this bread, promising life to those who eat (John 6:51). This guarantee draws upon personified wisdom's promise that those who share in her meal will live (Prov 9:5–6).[12] Several other titles applied to Jesus in the Gospel of John owe their dependence upon characterizations of God's wisdom in Proverbs. Among these include the saying "I am the door of the sheep" (John 10:7), which recalls personified wisdom offering a blessing to those who listen to her voice as she waits beside her doors (Prov 8:34).[13] As the Good Shepherd who leads the sheep that "listen to my voice" (John 10:11, 16), Jesus embodies the invitation offered by personified wisdom who summons her audience to listen to her (Prov 1:33).[14] One of the most famous expressions of Jesus, "I am the way, the truth, and the life" (John 14:6) draws upon three characteristics of God's wisdom from Proverbs. All of the wisdom's ways are pleasant ways (Prov 3:17); out of wisdom's mouth comes truth (Prov 8:7), and the figure of wisdom repeatedly promises the reward of life (Prov 1:33; 3:16; 8:35; 9:11).[15] There can be no question that one of the main themes in the Gospel of John is to illustrate the person of Jesus as the embodiment of God's personified wisdom, especially the figure of wisdom presented in Proverbs.

The realization that Jesus Christ embodied the wisdom of God can be observed in other New Testament authors,[16] but none more noteworthy than Paul. The Apostle Paul plainly identifies Christ as God's wisdom in several passages. Consider the following verses:

> but to those who are the called, both Jews and Greeks, Christ the power of God and the wisdom of God. (1 Cor 1:24)

> But by his doing you are in Christ Jesus, who became to us wisdom from God, and righteousness and sanctification, and redemption (1 Cor 1:30)

---

[9] Culpepper, *The Gospel and Letters of John*, 167–68.
[10] Smith, *Wisdom Christology*, 192–93; Brown, *John I–XII*, 106–7; McHugh, *John 1–4*, 196.
[11] Brown, *John I–XII*, 273; Thompson, *John*, 151; Witherington, *John's Wisdom*, 149–50; Lincoln, *John*, 229.
[12] Ringe, *Wisdom's Friends*, 61; Witherington, *Jesus the Sage*, 375; Koester, *Symbolism*, 101.
[13] O'Boyle, *Wisdom Christology*, 166–67; Witherington, *Jesus the Sage*, 375; Ringe, *Wisdom's Friends*, 61.
[14] Dunn, "Let John Be John," 331; Smith, *Wisdom Christology*, 149–50;
[15] O'Boyle, *Wisdom Christology*, 171–72; Ringe, *Wisdom's Friends*, 60–61.
[16] For a comprehensive summary, see Smith, "New Testament Portrayals of Wisdom Christology," 5–11.

> But we impart a secret and hidden wisdom of God, which God decreed before the ages for our glory. None of the rulers of this age understood this, for if they had, they would not have crucified the Lord of glory. (1 Cor 2:7–8)
>
> Christ, in whom are hidden all the treasures of wisdom and knowledge. (Col 2:2–3)

In one of Paul's most christologically-rich hymns, located in Colossians 1:15–20, the apostle applies nine of the traits of God's personified wisdom to the person of Jesus.[17] The purpose of such a vibrant and powerful presentation is to encourage Paul's readers to view Jesus as *the climactic embodiment of wisdom*.[18] Those who seek after God's wisdom, just as the Old Testament encourages (Job 28:28; Prov 3:13; 4:5), need to look no further than the man Jesus Christ. These wisdom-inspired descriptions in the hymn include the portrayal of Christ as "the firstborn of all creation" (Col 1:15), which draws heavily on the image of personified wisdom in Proverbs, who poetically says, "Yahweh created me at the beginning of his work, the first of his acts of long ago" (Prov 8:22).[19] Paul's deep theology of Jesus only gets deeper in Colossians 1:16: "For in him all things in heaven and on earth were created." Attentive readers of Paul's hymn and its Wisdom Christology would have readily recalled earlier descriptions of God creating all things with his wisdom, such as we find in Psalm 104:24: "O Yahweh, how manifold are your works! In wisdom have you made them all." The same theology depicting God creating in and with his wisdom appears, unsurprisingly, in Proverbs: "Yahweh by wisdom founded the earth; by understanding he established the heavens; by his knowledge the deeps broke open" (Prov 3:19–20). More parallels of the same idea occur in Jeremiah 10:12; 51:15, demonstrating the pervasiveness of the concept that Yahweh creates with his wisdom.[20] Paul's hymn concludes by emphasizing the peace that was made through the blood of Christ (Col 1:20), which recalls how all of the paths of personified wisdom come to be described as peace (Prov 3:17).

How should we attempt to make sense of Paul's hymnic presentation of Christ in Colossians 1:15–20? It seems unlikely that Paul intended his audience to read Jesus back into those Old Testament portrayals of God's personified wisdom, especially in light of Paul's clear statements regarding Jesus' birth (Rom 1:3; Gal 4:4). It is far more likely

---

[17] Hurtado, *One God, One Lord*, 41, states that Paul in Col 1:15–20 seems "to have drawn upon the language used by Jews to describe Wisdom . . . in articulating the significance of the exalted Jesus." Caird, *Paul's Letters from Prison*, 177, offers similar remarks: "there can be little doubt that the personified Wisdom is somewhere in the background of this passage." Dunn, *Colossians and Philemon*, 86, notes that Col 1:15–20 "can be quite properly classified as an early Christian hymn in which Christ is praised in language used commonly in Hellenistic Judaism in reference to divine wisdom."

[18] Dunn, *Colossians and Philemon*, 89, makes a crucially important observation worth our attention: "The effect is the same: not to predicate the actual (pre)existence of . . . Christ prior to an in creation itself, but to affirm that . . . Christ . . . be understood as the climactic manifestations of the preexistent divine wisdom, by which the world was created."

[19] Arnold, *Colossians*, 352–53; Dunn, *Colossians and Philemon*, 90; Barth and Blanke, *Colossians*, 197.

[20] Smith, "New Testament Portrayals of Wisdom Christology," 9.

that Paul is using typology in order to see the person of Jesus in the present as a type of God's personified wisdom that was depicted in the Old Testament, long before Jesus was even born.[21] This interpretation is strengthened by Paul's own admission that he was using *types* (1 Cor 10:6) and speaking *typologically* (1 Cor 10:11) when applying to Christ the image of "the rock that followed" the Israelites in the wilderness (1 Cor 10:4) that earlier Jewish sources applied to the wisdom of God.[22] In other words, Paul is *not saying* that Jesus is God's firstborn wisdom and the wise agent through whom God created all things; rather, the wisdom of God that was so highly valued and sought after is *now definitely and climactically found in the human being, Jesus Christ*. The resurrected and exalted Jesus is the antitype—the corresponding reality—of the personified wisdom of God, the prototype.

What was it about the Old Testament portrayal of God's wisdom that led the Early Church to begin thinking of the person of Christ in terms of wisdom? The answer to this question primarily lies in the theology of the Book of Proverbs. Since it has become apparent in our survey thus far that portrayals of God's wisdom from Proverbs have deeply impacted the Early Church's christology, it would be beneficial to take this opportunity to look closely into what made Proverbs so important. The book begins by encouraging its readers to "know wisdom and instruction" (Prov 1:2), and these wise instructions from God are clarified in the passage's parallelism as "sayings of understanding," "instruction in wise behavior," "prudence," and "knowledge and discretion" (Prov 1:2–4). The author, taking the role of a father figure, summons his sons to listen carefully to his instruction, which is further clarified to be "teaching" (Prov 1:8). The opening lines of the Book of Proverbs, therefore, portray God's wisdom as the wise instructions and knowledge that are relayed to a prudent student, resulting in the practice of wise behavior. It is no surprise that the earliest readers of Proverbs interpreted God's wise instruction in terms of the various commandments in the Law of Moses.

After the opening passage introduces God's wisdom, its next appearance in Proverbs 1:21–31 occurs with a fresh personification as wisdom speaks in the first person and takes on the role of a prophetess. In other words, the wise instructions and teachings of God have undergone a literary shift, now appearing as personified wisdom, or as many have taken to addressing her, Lady Wisdom. This personification of God's wisdom—his wise instructions to his creation—should not be confused with a different category, that of a conscious female person. By taking wisdom, the wise instruction of God, and personifying it, the writer of Proverbs chapter one is giving God's wisdom a fictional personality by employing highly metaphorical language within the bounds of Hebrew

---

[21] Kuschel, *Born Before All Time?* 280–85.
[22] Perriman, *In the Form of a God*, 51–54; Fitzmyer, *First Corinthians*, 385. Hays, *First Corinthians*, 161, helpfully observes that "it is not difficult to see how Paul might have hit upon the notion of identifying the rock metaphorically with Christ, since the transference of the attributes of divine Wisdom to Christ was already a common interpretive practice in early Christianity."

poetry.²³ To state the matter differently, the personified figure of Lady Wisdom is not to be confused with a conscious female person; rather, she is to be viewed as the personification of God's wise interactions with and his instruction to his creation.

The opening nine chapters of Proverbs provide several key passages in which the author illustrates the wisdom of God as a personified female figure.²⁴ The first passage in which Lady Wisdom appears is Proverbs 1:21–31, where she functions as a prophetess who summons the naïve to listen to her words. In Proverbs 3:13–18, the wisdom of God is personified as a tree of life that is to be grasped and held close. Proverbs chapter eight has the lengthiest personification of wisdom, highlighted by Lady Wisdom taking the roles of a teacher who offers her students wise instruction (Prov 8:1–21) and a child who delights in all that Yahweh created (Prov 8:22–36). Finally, Proverbs 9:1–6 depicts personified wisdom as the owner of a house that she built, which serves as the place into which her listeners are invited to partake of her bread and wine. By personifying God's wise instruction, the author aims to utilize this female figure to encourage the original readers of Proverbs (all of whom would likely have been young men) to seek and embrace the wisdom of God.

This literary strategy reaches its climax in Proverbs 31:10–31, a passage that fully details the excellent wife, a woman whom the ideal male readers of Proverbs would do well to pursue. The lengthy passage, which illustrates the many traits of this excellent wife, has been deliberately shaped by the earlier descriptions of God's personified wisdom from the opening nine chapters of Proverbs. In other words, the excellent wife is the embodiment of Lady Wisdom—*wisdom made flesh*.²⁵ Consider the intentional ways in which the woman in Proverbs 31:10–31 embodies the roles, traits, and characteristics formerly applied to the personified wisdom of God in Proverbs chapters 1–9:

> At the entrance of the gates in the city she utters her sayings (Prov 1:21); Her husband is known in the gates (Prov 31:23)
>
> She is more precious than jewels (Prov 3:15); She is far more precious than jewels. (Prov 31:10)
>
> My fruit is better than gold (Prov 8:19); with the fruit of her hands she plants a vineyard. (Prov 31:16)
>
> Wisdom has built her house (Prov 9:1); and gives food to her household (Prov 31:15)
>
> She has sent out her maidens (Prov 9:3); and portions for her maidens. (Prov 31:15)

---

²³ Treier, *Proverbs–Ecclesiastes*, 18.
²⁴ For a detailed treatment, see Smith, *Wisdom Christology*, 15–19.
²⁵ Perdue, *Proverbs*, 280, describes the woman in Prov 31:10–31 as "the incarnation of wisdom in female form." See also Yoder, *Proverbs*, 299; McKinlay, *Gendering Wisdom the Host*, 127; Longman, *Proverbs*, 542.

"Come, eat of my food" (Prov 9:5); She brings her food from afar. (Prov 31:14)

These are just a sample of a total of eleven characteristics describing God's personified wisdom that the author purposefully used to illustrate the wife of Proverbs 31:10–31.[26] It would appear that this closing section of the Book of Proverbs was put together to offer practical applications for the potentially overlooked female readers, allowing them tangible ways to apply God's wisdom. The main point of the multifaceted description of the excellent wife is that she (and any female reader who imitates her) embodies the preexistent wisdom of God.

The Early Church looked back at passages like Proverbs 31:10–31, recognized how human beings could function as the embodiment of the wisdom of God, and used the same Jewish theology to apply passages about wisdom to Christ.[27] In doing so, the Early Church no doubt followed the lead of Jesus, who openly taught that he was the climactic revelation of God's wisdom, the one in whom those who seek wisdom may find it. In order to make sense of the Wisdom Christology present in the New Testament, one must begin with the Jewish portrayals of God's wisdom, primarily those in Job, Psalms, and especially Proverbs.

How Logos Christology Developed out of Wisdom Christology

While the Early Church embraced Wisdom Christology from its inception, a similar christological portrayal that depicted Jesus in terms of God's creative and powerful word only began to appear at the end of the first century AD. Since the Greek noun for "word" is *logos*, many have come to describe this christology as *Logos Christology*.[28] The most notable passage that illustrates Christ as the embodiment of the word that was in the beginning with God is the opening prologue of the Gospel of John:

> In the beginning was the Word, and the Word was with God, and the Word was God. He was in the beginning with God. All things came into being through him, and without him not one thing came into being. What has come into being in him was life, and the life was the light of all people. The light shines in the darkness, and the darkness did not overcome it . . . And the Word became flesh and lived among us, and we have seen his glory, the glory as of a father's only son, full of grace and truth. (John 1:1–5, 14)

---

[26] For a complete list, see Smith, *Wisdom Christology*, 19–20.
[27] Several other Jewish texts between Proverbs and the New Testament similarly portrayed human beings as the embodiment (incarnation) of God's personified wisdom. See the details in Smith, *Wisdom Christology*, 22–39.
[28] Brown, *John I–XII*, 523, draws attention to the foundation of Jewish wisdom texts from which *Logos Christology* emerged: "In the OT presentation of Wisdom, there are good parallels for almost every detail of the Prologue's description of the Word."

The prologue, often called a hymn due to its poetic structure, speaks about God's word, its prehistory, its role as the instrument in God's acts of creation, its relation to life and light, its interaction with creation, the rejection it suffered, and, most importantly, the way that it became embodied in the man Jesus Christ. Although there is much that can be said about the intricate details of this influential passage, we can offer a few secure observations that are relatively non-controversial and widely acknowledged.[29]

The first point is that the author of the prologue is directing his readers to the opening chapter of Genesis with several key pointers. By starting the opening verse of the prologue ("In the beginning") with a direct quote from Genesis 1:1 (*"In the beginning God created the heavens and the earth"*), we can be confident that the argument that will unfold concerns the way in which God formed creation in the initial chapter of the Old Testament.[30] Other parallels support this interpretation, including the portrayal of God creating through the act of speaking, as well as the themes of life, light, and darkness. These recognizable elements of the creation account in Genesis chapter one point the reader of the prologue to that story, its themes, and its Creator.

Within the account of creation in Genesis chapter one, readers repeatedly observe God forming each part of creation by speaking that creation into existence. When light was needed, "God said, 'Let there be light'" (Gen 1:3). When an expanse was required, God spoke, and it was so (Gen 1:6–7). When the waters needed to be gathered into a single place, the Creator again used his powerful utterance to make it so (Gen 1:9). When vegetation was brought forth, it happened according to God's spoken word (Gen 1:11). In fact, the phrase "And God said" acts as a deliberate and constant refrain in this section, emphasizing the fact that the Creator made all things by speaking, that is, by using his word. Not one thing was created apart from God speaking. This includes the sun, moon, and stars (Gen 1:14–16), the creatures in the water and the birds in the sky (Gen 1:20), the animals on the ground (Gen 1:24), and even image-bearing human beings (Gen 1:26–27). It is no doubt a fair summary of this creation account to observe that everything that was made came to be by God's creative and powerful speech.[31] This is what took place, as the author of Genesis chapter one remarks, "In the beginning."[32]

The contributors to the collection of Psalms often praised Yahweh for his glorious and beautiful creation. One author, in particular, drew upon the theology expressed in Genesis chapter one in order to depict Yahweh creating with his word. Consider the language and the parallelism occurring in Psalm 33:6: "By the word of Yahweh the heavens were made, and by the breath of his mouth all their host." The

---

[29] Smith, *Wisdom Christology*, 49–80.
[30] Gaston, *Dynamic Monarchianism*, 14; Beasley-Murray, *John*, 10; Brown, *John I–XII*, 4; ; McHugh, *John 1–4*, 6; Haenchen, *John 1*, 109; von Wahlde, *The Gospel and Letters of John*, 2:2.
[31] Brueggemann, *Theology of the Old Testament*, 148, 163.
[32] Boyarin, *Border Lines*, 96; Gaston, "High Christology," 131.

psalmist portrays God creating the heavens with his word, demonstrating the influence of the Genesis chapter one creation account. Furthermore, the parallelism in the second line of Psalm 33:6 further describes Yahweh's creative speech as the breath of his mouth. In other words, the psalmist is describing the spoken utterance that comes from God's mouth.[33] This creative word is not alive or conscious; rather, it is God's own powerful speech, representing the intentions of the maker in a declaration.

The spoken utterance of God was not only active in the formative days of creation. In fact, Yahweh continued to use his creative words to interact with his world and those who lived within it.[34] Consider the following passages that illustrate just how the Old Testament authors understood the ongoing activity of Yahweh's powerful word, particularly by personifying the word as an agent that Yahweh sends on a mission:

> He sent His word and healed them, and delivered them from their destructions. (Ps 107:20)
>
> He sends forth His command to the earth; His word runs very swiftly. (Ps 147:15)
>
> He sends forth His word and melts them; He causes His wind to blow and the waters to flow. (Ps 147:18)
>
> The Lord has sent a word against Jacob, and it will fall on Israel (Isa 9:8)
>
> So will My word be which goes forth from My mouth; it will not return to Me empty, without accomplishing what I desire, and without succeeding in the matter for which I sent it. (Isa 55:11)

These biblical poets, in a similar fashion to the portrayal of personified wisdom in Proverbs chapters 1–9, give personality to one of God's key attributes: his powerful and creative speech. God's personified word acts as an agent that is sent by God to meaningfully interact with creation, such as offering healing, bringing deliverance, melting ice, and even rebuking Israel. The personification of God's creative word even goes so far as to give it legs with which it runs swiftly. Moreover, the personified word is an obedient agent that accomplishes the mission for which it was sent, which, in turn, carries out God's desire. It is essential to remember that the personification of God's word, such as personified wisdom, should not be misconstrued as a conscious person, as if the word were a second person alongside Yahweh in heaven.[35] What we find in Psalms, Proverbs, and the prophets like Isaiah is Hebrew poetry, and poetic depictions of personified attributes like the wisdom of God and the word of God need to be interpreted precisely as poetry.

---

[33] Craigie, *Psalms 1–50*, 272–73; McCann, "The Psalms," 810.
[34] Dunn, *Christology in the Making*, 217–19.
[35] Robinson, *The Priority of John*, 380–81; Collins and Collins, *King and Messiah*, 176.

Returning to the Prologue of the Gospel of John, we can now read through its portrayal of Logos Christology as well-informed interpreters. In fact, John 1:1–5 offers the very same portrayal of God's personified word that we observed in the Old Testament. The word that was in the beginning (John 1:1–2) is a blatant and obvious echo of the opening chapter of Genesis. The word is portrayed as having been "with God" (John 1:1), indicating a distinction familiar to the Hebrew poets, who thoroughly personified Yahweh's creative and powerful speech to function as an agent. It naturally follows that an agent is positioned alongside the sender prior to being commissioned for its appointed task, so there is no surprise that the personified word was with God.[36] The final phrase in John 1:1 (and the Word was God) does not collapse the clear distinction that the verse articulated immediately prior to where the personified word was with God. Instead, the phrase "the Word was God" is a well-known grammatical construction in Greek that, in this occurrence, displays "God" as an adjective that describes the word.[37] God's personified word, stated differently, was fully expressive of God, representing God in a manner that speech naturally reflects the character.[38] This is very similar to the poetry in Isaiah 55:11, where the word acts as God's personified agent that accomplishes what God desires. John 1:2 repeats what was already stated in John 1:1, namely that this personified word was in the beginning with Yahweh.

When the Prologue portrays the act of creation, it is illustrated in continuity with the depictions that we observed throughout Genesis chapter one and Psalm 33:6, precisely with God as the Creator who made all things through his creative and powerful word (John 1:3).[39] The masculine pronoun "him" demonstrates that the Prologue is certainly personifying the word as a masculine agent, due to the Greek noun *logos* being grammatically masculine. Just as Genesis chapter one shows how God's powerful utterance ("and God said") made light and all living things, so too does the Prologue attribute these results to the creative workings of the personified word, in whom was life that gave light to humanity (John 1:4). With a crucially important shift in verbal tense, John 1:5 moves to describe the present, noting how the light that the personified word made is currently shining in the darkness, with the unfortunate result that the darkness is unable to overcome that light. In this verse, *darkness* serves not merely to denote the absence of illumination but also to represent those people who live in darkness, and as such, they are incapable of conquering the light produced by God's word. This suggests that the light is stronger than the darkness, and it additionally draws upon the activity of God's word that interacts with humanity, sometimes with healing and deliverance (Ps 107:20), but other times with rebuke (Isa 9:8). It is clear that the Logos Christology in the opening verses of the Prologue is deeply indebted to the depictions of God's creative

---

[36] Smith, *Wisdom Christology*, 57–58.
[37] For similar examples of this Greek construction, see 1 John 1:5 ("God is light"), where the noun *light* functions adjectively, as well as 1 John 4:8 ("God is love"), where the noun *love* acts as an adjective describing God.
[38] Zerwick and Grosvenor, *Grammatical Analysis*, 285; Wallace, *Greek Grammar*, 269; Novakovic, *John 1–10*, 2–3.
[39] Bernard, *The Gospel According to St. John*, 1:3

and powerful speech—often personified as an agent of God's activity—within the Old Testament scriptures.

When the Prologue arrives at John 1:14, where "the Word became flesh and lived among us," we have a powerful statement of God's personified word becoming embodied in the human being, Jesus Christ.[40] This theology, which posits that one of God's personified attributes becomes flesh, owes its meaning and dependence primarily to Old Testament portrayals of God's wisdom. In particular, the poetic depiction within Proverbs 31:10–31 of the excellent wife who serves as the embodiment of personified wisdom functions as the clearest parallel to John 1:14, where the personified word becomes embodied in the man Jesus Christ.[41] As such, the person of Jesus within the Gospel of John bears in his person the same creative and powerful words of God, resulting in several instances where Jesus openly admits that he is not speaking his own words but those belonging to the Father. For example, take into consideration these cases:

> For he whom God has sent speaks the words of God (John 3:34)

> "My teaching is not mine, but His who sent me (John 7:16)

> "For I did not speak on my own initiative, but the Father Himself who sent me has given me a commandment as to what to say and what to speak. I know that His commandment is eternal life; therefore the things I speak, I speak just as the Father has told me." (John 12:49–50)

There can be no doubt that the human Jesus speaks the words of God, and this is made so because he is the embodiment of the personified speech that was in the beginning with God. This is not to say that Jesus personally was in the beginning with God. The Prologue has been very clear that it was *the word*, not Christ, that was with God in the beginning. Furthermore, John 1:14 indicates that it was the word that became flesh, not the preexisting son of God who became flesh. The Early Church, which regarded the Old Testament scriptures as deeply important, read the Prologue of the Gospel of John in light of the earlier Jewish depictions of God's word, which was active in creation and often personified as God's agent, but God's word was never portrayed in the Hebrew Bible as a conscious person alongside Yahweh.

---

[40] Dunn, *Christology in the Making*, 243, famously wrote, "the revolutionary significance of v.14 may well be that it marks *not only the transition in the thought of the poem from pre-existence to incarnation, but also the transition from impersonal personification to actual person.*"

[41] The Early Church noticed several parallels between God's word and God's wisdom, and these parallels had a significant bearing on the original meaning of the Prologue of the Gospel of John. For example, wisdom was in the beginning (Prov 8:22–23), wisdom was with God (Prov 8:27, 30), wisdom was the means through which Yahweh created all things (Ps 104:24; Prov 3:19–20; Jer 10:12; 51:15), she offers life (Prov 3:18; 8:35), and she provides light in the midst of darkness (Prov 2:10–13; 4:18). For a thorough account of the parallels between wisdom and word, see Smith, *Wisdom Christology*, chs. 2–3.

The Preexistence of Jesus

If the Early Church believed and taught that the human Messiah, Jesus Christ, was the embodiment of God's wisdom and God's word, in what sense can we speak of Jesus' preexistence? Stated differently, what is the correct way to make sense of the early Christian belief about the wisdom of God and the word of God that became flesh in the person of Jesus? This is an important question that deserves thoughtful consideration and a nuanced answer that takes into account all the available facts, including the birth of Jesus and the nature of personification as it relates to wisdom and the word.

First, we should allow the authors of the New Testament to have their say on the matter of defining in what sense Jesus possessed a preexistence. Beginning with the clear texts, we can observe the preaching of Peter in the opening sermon in Acts:

> "Men of Israel, listen to these words: Jesus the Nazarene, a man attested to you by God with miracles and wonders and signs which God performed through him in your midst, just as you yourselves know—this man, delivered over by the predetermined plan and foreknowledge of God, you nailed to a cross by the hands of godless men and put him to death." (Acts 2:22–23)

Peter, the de facto leader of the twelve apostles, proclaimed, under the influence of the Holy Spirit, that the human Jesus was a key part of God's *predetermined plan*. Peter further clarified this plan as God's *foreknowledge*.[42] In other words, Jesus was in God's plans and purposes, preexisting in the mind of God. This is not *literal preexistence*, as if the son of God were consciously alive before his birth. This, instead, is what we might refer to as *notional preexistence*—preexisting in the plans and purposes of God.[43]

Another passage is located in the opening chapter of First Peter, which discusses God's foreknowledge that he possessed prior to the creation of the world. Note carefully the wording here:

> knowing that you were not redeemed with perishable things like silver or gold from your futile way of life inherited from your forefathers, but with precious blood, as of a lamb unblemished and spotless, the blood of Christ. For he was foreknown before the foundation of the world, but has appeared in these last times for the sake of you (1 Pet 1:18–20)

---

[42] Keener, *Acts*, 1:925–27, 938–39; Pervo, *Acts*, 81; Barrett, *Acts 1–14*, 142–43; Fitzmyer, *Acts*, 255; Walton, *Acts 1–9:42*, 192. Irons et al., *The Son of God*, 166, is worth repeating: "If Jesus only preexists in God's mind and plan, then his physical existence chronologically begins at the moment of his begetting in the womb of Mary."

[43] Biblical scholars openly acknowledge the distinction between literal and notional preexistence. See Irons et al., *The Son of God*, 165–66; Craddock, *The Pre-existence of Christ*, 80; Hurtado, "Pre-Existence," 744; Hamerton-Kelly, *Pre-Existence*, 11, 21; Capes, "Preexistence," 956; Dunn, *Theology of Paul*, 273; Richardson, *Theology of the New Testament*, 155; Harnack, *History of Dogma*, 1:318; Smith, *Wisdom Christology*, 82–83.

Prior to the foundation of the world, that is, the world's creation, Jesus, the spotless lamb, was already in God's foreknowledge. That is to say, Jesus preexisted notionally in God's plans and purposes, and these plans existed before the founding of the world.[44] It is also important to draw attention to Peter's insistence that it is in these last times that Jesus showed up on the scene of history. In other words, Jesus did preexist, but only in the foreknowledge of God, and his first appearance was in these last days, not during the period of the Old Testament. It is also interesting to note that the Greek verb used here in 1 Peter 1:20 to describe God "foreknowing" (*proginosko*) has its related noun "foreknowledge" (*prognosis*) appearing earlier in 1 Peter 1:2, which describes how the recipients of First Peter were chosen "according to the foreknowledge of God the Father."[45] This indicates that obedient Christians were also in the preexistent foreknowledge of God, just like Jesus Christ. Since it is highly unlikely that the Early Church viewed itself as a group of persons possessing a literal preexistence, it follows that 1 Peter 1:20 is best viewed in terms of notional preexistence.

The Book of Revelation contains yet another reference to Jesus possessing a notional preexistence. Revelation's image-filled visions describe the book of life, and in Revelation 13:8, this book belongs to the Lamb (one of the primary images describing the person of Jesus). According to this verse, the Lamb was slain "from the foundation of the world." Since it would be nonsensical to interpret this image literally as if Jesus was actually slaughtered at the creation of the world, it seems like the more likely interpretation is to understand this reference as taking place in the purposes and plans of God.[46] This fits well with an earlier description in Revelation of the one seated upon the throne, who is described as the Creator. In Revelation 4:11, the enthroned Creator God is praised, in part due to his purpose in which all created things existed prior to being made: "for You created all things, and because of Your will they existed, and were created." Because of God's will, that is, his desire within his purposes, all that has been created already existed within those plans and foreknowledge prior to being brought into existence.[47] It follows that the Lamb also was in God's will prior to being created and suffering the death described in Revelation 13:8. In short, the most likely way that John of Patmos intended his readers to understand the reference to the Lamb who was slain from the foundation of the world is to attribute the act to God's plans and purposes, resulting in the Lamb of God again being attributed a notional preexistence.

---

[44] Elliott, *I Peter*, 376–77; Donelson, *I & II Peter and Jude*, 48; Watson and Callan, *First and Second Peter*, 36. Boring, *1 Peter*, 85, states, "God is the one who foreknew/destined Christ before the foundation of the world."
[45] Bartlett, "The First Letter of Peter," 259.
[46] Osborne, *Revelation*, 503; Reddish, *Revelation*, 255; Charles, *Revelation of St. John*, 1:354–55; Paul, *Revelation*, 233; Boxall, *Revelation*, 191; Harrington, *Revelation*, 139; Rowland, "The Book of Revelation," 657;
[47] Mulholland, "Revelation," 463–64; Mounce, *Revelation*, 127; Charles, *Revelation of St. John*, 1:134.

Conclusion

Let's take this opportunity to gather all of the data we have observed thus far, since the topic of preexistence is complex and nuanced. The early Christians portrayed Jesus with a Wisdom Christology by attributing to Jesus the roles, attributes, characteristics, and functions formerly belonging to God's personified wisdom. As such, Jesus was portrayed as embodying God's wisdom in all its fullness. Within this christological model, Jesus can be accurately described as preexisting as personified wisdom; however, since a personification is not a conscious person, this preexistence is not literal. The Early Church also attributed to Jesus a Logos Christology that built on the efforts of its earlier Wisdom Christology, and in the process, these believers depicted Jesus as the flesh that the word became. Like Wisdom Christology, the Logos Christology of the early Christians applied to Jesus the characteristics, roles, and functions formerly belonging to God's personified word, allowing Jesus to carry out those roles and authoritatively speak the life-giving oracles of God during his ministry. Since the personified word that was with God in the beginning was also not a conscious person, but rather the creative and powerful utterance of God, this would not imply that Jesus literally preexisted as this word. These observations can be confirmed by our extensive findings from Chapter 3, where we noted that Yahweh created the heavens and the earth all alone, by himself. We also observed in Chapter 21 that the writers of the Old Testament looked forward to the birth of the Messiah—a figure who did not exist during that period of history. Furthermore, the birth of Jesus in Chapter 22 demonstrates that Jesus was brought into existence at the moment of his conception, proving that he did not exist consciously prior to that time. When we add to all this evidence the plain, straightforward testimony of the Early Church, indicating that Jesus was in the plans, purposes, and foreknowledge of God, we can firmly conclude that the biblical authors did not believe in the literal preexistence of Jesus Christ. Instead, Christ possessed a notional preexistence within God's will, desire, and plans. The resulting picture is an authentic member of the human race, in whom the roles of God's wisdom, the life-giving words, and the purposes of the one true God find their fulfillment.

Of course, this highly empowered and highly authorized human Messiah, Jesus Christ, suffered, died, was buried, and was raised unto eternal life on the third day. After his resurrection, Jesus was highly exalted to heaven and enthroned at God's right hand. It goes to show that the Early Church had much to say about the importance and lasting impact of Jesus' death, his subsequent resurrection, and his post-resurrection exaltation to sit at the right hand of Yahweh himself. In our next chapter, we will examine how these key facts about the person of Jesus contributed to shaping the Early Church's christology.

26

THE DEATH, RESURRECTION, AND EXALTATION OF JESUS

Several key figures within the early Christian movement were martyred for their commitment to the God of Israel. John the Baptist was brutally beheaded for his commitment to summoning people to repent in light of the dawning kingdom of God. Stephen was one of the first followers of Christ to be killed for his faith, having died from being stoned shortly after Jesus' resurrection. The Apostle James, the son of Zebedee and brother of John, sadly met his end at the point of the sword of Herod Agrippa I. Although the details are scarce, early Christian tradition places the deaths of both Peter and Paul during the reign of the Emperor Nero in the mid-60s. These brave and courageous believers died for their faith, but unlike Jesus Christ, none of them were raised from the dead, highly exalted, or ascended to heaven to sit alongside God. Christ, on the other hand, did rise from the grave on the third day, demonstrated his resurrection to several eyewitnesses, was taken up to heaven, and enthroned at God's right hand. What was it about Jesus that distinguished him from all the other martyrs within the Early Church?

This chapter will explore the christological significance of the death, resurrection, and highly exalted ascension of Jesus. The Early Church spoke often and at length about each of these three pivotal events relating to the person of Jesus, allowing us a wealth of data to read through and appreciate. First, we will look closely at the crucifixion of Jesus on the cross and ask how it relates to the question of who Jesus is. Second, we will examine the resurrection of Jesus, that is, the way in which God granted immortality to his human son. Third, we will investigate the christological significance that the Early Church attributed to Jesus' exaltation to heaven, particularly in the way that it evoked the frequent use and citation of Psalm 110:1. During our exploration of these three noteworthy topics, we will keep a close eye on how they relate to the subject of Christology, especially as they concern Jesus as a genuine member of the human race.

The Death of Jesus and Christology

Beginning with Jesus' death, all the New Testament authors unambiguously agree that the promised Messiah, the anointed king of God's kingdom, died.[1] The fact that Jesus died

---

[1] Ryken et al., "Mortality," 569, remark: "That Jesus was mortal was a consequence of his humanity."

was never called into question by the biblical authors. Nor do we find any suggestion that Jesus only partially died, or that he died in some sense, but that he continued to live in some other sense. What we instead observe is a consistent use of clear and straightforward language indicating that Jesus hung on a cross, died of suffocation that regularly accompanied Roman crucifixion, and was buried. Even secular historians acknowledge the historicity of the person of Jesus, who died by this common first-century Roman form of capital punishment.

Our earliest gospel, the Gospel of Mark, offers several details about the death of Jesus that are christologically relevant. Jesus, who primarily spoke Aramaic, had his final words remembered and preserved by Mark, who recalls how Jesus cited Psalm 22:1 in Aramaic: "And at the ninth hour Jesus cried with a loud voice, 'Eloi, Eloi, lema sabachthani?' which means, 'My God, my God, why have you forsaken me?'" (Mark 15:34). Psalm 22, a psalm of David, initially lamented the abandonment of God experienced by the author, who, after pleading for rescue and deliverance, praises Yahweh for his intervention to save him from his predicament. We may reasonably presume, since Jesus frequently spoke boldly about his belief that God would raise him from the dead (Mark 8:31; 9:9, 31; 10:34), that Jesus recited the opening line of the twenty-second psalm in full confidence that he too would be vindicated by God after this period of suffering.[2] By drawing on the experience of David and applying it to himself, Jesus expressed his belief that he was to be viewed as another David, *a new David*, not only by his followers but also by God himself. Since David was the human Israelite king, readers of Mark would likely view Jesus as a human being who was also destined to rule the kingdom of Israel. As such, Jesus' citation of Psalm 22:1 points to him being a human being, just as David was, while also acknowledging that Jesus has a God above him, one who is able to rescue and deliver Jesus from death.[3]

Mark's narration continues and confirms these points by portraying the death of Jesus in terms of him breathing his last, a clear indication of someone taking his dying breath (Mark 15:37). Moreover, the centurion, whom Mark recounts was "standing right in front" of Jesus and observing how Jesus died, declared, "Truly this man was the Son of God" (Mark 15:39). This christological confession, coming from the unlikely source of a Gentile member of the Roman military, directly acknowledges Jesus as a human being, while also carrying out Mark's christological theme of portraying the messianic son of God as a figure who must suffer and die.[4] The fact that Jesus had indeed died was

---

[2] Brown, *The Death of the Messiah*, 2:1050–51.
[3] Kirk, *A Man Attested by God*, 513, observes how Mark's use of Psalm 22 for Jesus portrays him as "the righteous human king who has faithfully represented God's reign to the earth. However, they are fully consonant with Mark's idealized human Christology, in which the distinction between Jesus and God as characters in the story is never breached."
[4] Rhoads et al, *Mark as Story*, 112, remark, "The only triumph Mark depicts in Jesus' death is his human faithfulness to God."

confirmed by the centurion to Pilate (Mark 15:44–45) and by Joseph, who personally took Jesus' body down from the cross, wrapped *him*, and placed *him* in a tomb (Mark 15:46). According to Mark's christology, the human son of God suffered and died on the cross, and, in the process, Jesus distinguished himself from his God, whom he addressed as "My God" in fulfillment of Scripture.

The Gospel of Matthew, drawing upon Mark's story and using it for Matthew's own audience, similarly portrays the death of Jesus. Once again, Jesus is depicted as being crucified for his messianic claims, claims for which he is repeatedly mocked. These claims included the royal title "son of God" (Matt 27:40, 43) and its equivalent, "King of the Jews" (Matt 27:37) and "King of Israel" (Matt 27:42).[5] Matthew includes Jesus' citation of Psalm 22:1, this time putting the words into Hebrew: "My God, my God, why have you forsaken me?" (Matt 27:46). Jesus' final actions involved crying out with a loud voice before breathing his last, which clearly points to his death (Matt 27:50). After being removed from the cross and placed in a tomb by Joseph, Jesus' corpse was verified by two further witnesses: "Mary Magdalene and the other Mary were there, sitting opposite the tomb" (Matt 27:61). Matthew notes how Pilate provided a guard to watch over the tomb that was secured by some of the Pharisees and chief priests, having the express aim of preventing anyone from removing Jesus (Matt 27:62–66). Without a doubt, Matthew portrays Jesus as one who suffered and died on the cross, and his burial was witnessed by several within hours of taking his last breath.

The Gospel of Luke also draws on Mark's narrative as a source, adding its own distinctive emphases. Luke, like Matthew and Mark, plainly describes Jesus breathing his last (Luke 23:46). The centurion, having witnessed Jesus' last breath, praised God and declared, "Certainly this man was innocent" (Luke 23:47).[6] As one of the closest eyewitnesses to Jesus' death on the cross, this soldier's testimony, which plainly distinguishes the God to whom he praised and the human being who just innocently suffered, offers a helpful glimpse into Luke's theology. Several crowds observed Jesus' death, including his acquaintances and several Galilean female followers (Luke 23:48–49). Joseph is again credited with requesting the body from Pilate, taking it down from the cross, and wrapping it. Then, Luke carefully notes that Joseph placed *him* in the tomb, making clear that Jesus, albeit dead, was precisely who was being buried (Luke 23:53). In sum, Luke's depiction of the death of Jesus presents the human Messiah dying on a cross, seen by many observers, and eventually buried in a tomb that very day.

The Gospel of John presents its own retelling of Jesus' death, without explicitly drawing upon the three earlier gospel accounts. John tells how Caiaphas, the high priest, predicted that the man Jesus would die on behalf of all the people: "You know nothing

---

[5] Carter, *Matthew*, 173; Brown, *The Death of the Messiah*, 2:1152.
[6] Brown, *The Death of the Messiah*, 2:1160–67.

at all, nor do you take into account that it is expedient for you that one man die for the people, and that the whole nation not perish" (John 11:49–50). What is interesting about this declaration is that Caiaphas was actually arguing that the leadership in Jerusalem should get rid of Jesus in order to save the nation from perishing at the hands of the Romans, but Caiaphas was unaware, as the narrator informs the reader, that he was actually speaking under the prophetic inspiration of God, which announced that a human being, Jesus Christ, would die for the nation (John 11:51).[7] This ironic prophetic declaration by the high priest, which John takes up and presents truthfully to his readers, is repeated for emphasis later in the narrative: "Caiaphas was the one who had advised the Jews that it was expedient for one man to die on behalf of the people" (John 18:14). The Gospel of John, therefore, not only illustrates Jesus as a crucified human being but also as the human being who atones for the people in his death. In other words, a human being died for the sins of the nation.[8]

The theme of irony continues among those who condemned Jesus to death, with Pontius Pilate proclaiming to the mob, "Behold the man!" in John 19:5. Shortly after, he declares to the same mob that this human being is the King of the Jews: "Behold your King" (John 19:14). The crucifixion of this human king is layered with details that confirm Jesus' full humanity. Jesus announces, while hanging on the cross, that he is thirsty (John 19:28). After taking a drink, he gives up his spirit and dies, a fate that was confirmed by the nearby soldiers who took notice that Jesus "was already dead" (John 19:33). One of these soldiers thrust a spear into the deceased Jesus' side, which resulted in blood and water spilling out, giving further confirmation that the one whose body hung on the cross was indeed a human person (John 19:34).[9] Joseph is again remembered as taking Jesus' body, preparing it for burial, and laying it in a new tomb. With the help of Nicodemus, Joseph placed Jesus in the nearby tomb (John 19:42), assuring the reader that *Jesus himself* was buried when he died, not just his body. The resulting portrayal in the Gospel of John, like the three earlier gospel accounts, is of a genuinely human person, Jesus the Jewish king, who completely dies on the cross for the sake of others.

The theology of the Apostle Paul also indicates an awareness in the Early Church that Jesus, a genuine member of the human race, gave himself up for our sins. In Paul's Letter to the Romans, the death of Christ is contrasted with the transgression of the first human being, Adam (Rom 5:12–21). While Paul details how the transgression of one man, Adam, resulted in sin and death being brought into the world, Paul also juxtaposes Adam with another man, namely Jesus Christ. For example, Adam is illustrated as "a type of him who was to come" (Rom 5:14). Jesus, the antitype of the human being Adam, is also described by Paul as a human being: "the one man, Jesus Christ"

---

[7] Coloe, *John 11–21*, 329.
[8] *John: Storyteller, Interpreter, Evangelist*, 113.
[9] Brown, *The Death of the Messiah*, 2:1177, is helpful here: "This strong attestation of the death of Jesus in John was not for apologetics (to prove that Jesus rose *from the dead*) but for christology."

(Rom 5:15).[10] The disobedience of Adam to God had terrible results, but this was countered by the obedience of man Jesus Christ to God (Rom 5:19), obedience that Paul elsewhere depicts as a disposition that led to Christ's death on a cross (Phil 2:8). This theology of the death of the human Jesus resurfaces in the confessional statement in 1 Timothy 2:5–6: "For there is one God, and one mediator also between God and men, the man Christ Jesus, who gave himself as a ransom for all." It is through the death of a member of the human race that the redemptive ransoming of sinners back to God is accomplished.[11]

The Resurrection of Jesus and Christology

All four gospel accounts are in agreement that God raised Jesus from the dead on the first day of the week, leaving behind an empty tomb. Mark's account of the resurrection concludes with a messenger announcing to the three women that Jesus has risen and that he would meet the disciples in Galilee, a declaration that produced trembling and astonishment (Mark 16:8). Matthew fills in some of the gaps in Mark's story by recounting two resurrection appearances, one to the women who witnessed the empty tomb (Matt 28:9) and the other to the eleven disciples (Matt 28:17). Luke also builds upon Mark's account by retelling an encounter between two men on the Road to Emmaus and the resurrected Jesus, although they initially did not recognize him (Luke 24:13–31). Later, Jesus appeared to the eleven apostles, seeking to convince them by showing his hands and feet. Although at first glance, the disciples thought that they were seeing a spirit (Luke 24:37), Jesus reassured them of the truth of the bodily resurrection by drawing attention to his raised condition: "Touch me and see, for a spirit does not have flesh and bones as you see that I have" (Luke 24:39). These helpful words of the resurrected Jesus indicate that he was raised from the dead in a condition that *remained thoroughly human*, albeit an immortalized human.[12] The Gospel of John observes how the risen Jesus appeared to Mary Magdalene (John 20:14), who is promptly commissioned to tell the other disciples that she witnessed the truth of the resurrection (John 20:17–18). Later that day, Jesus appears in the midst of his disciples, exposes his hands and feet to them, and shares with them the Holy Spirit (John 20:19–23). Furthermore, Jesus appeared to eyewitnesses on two separate occasions, once to the group of disciples that included Thomas (John 20:26) and again on the shore of the Sea of Tiberias, where he shared a meal with those present, according to John 21:15. The testimony of the gospel accounts

---

[10] Dunn, *Romans 1–8*, 280.
[11] Towner, *The Letters to Timothy and Titus*, 183, argues, "What Jesus did to execute God's universal will to save he did as a human being, in complete solidarity with the human condition."
[12] Nolland, Luke 18:35–24:53, 1213–14; Culpepper, "The Gospel of Luke," 485.

reinforces the christology of the human Jesus, both before and after God raised him from the dead.

The Book of Acts summarizes the spread of the gospel message, beginning in Jerusalem, and in the process, it frequently discusses the resurrection of Jesus. Three examples will suffice to give an adequate sampling of what the Early Church believed about the christology surrounding the risen Jesus. The first passage comes from Peter's Pentecost sermon, which, under the inspiration of the Spirit, declares Jesus to be a human being:

> "Men of Israel, listen to these words: Jesus the Nazarene, a man attested to you by God with miracles and wonders and signs which God performed through him in your midst, just as you yourselves know—this man, delivered over by the predetermined plan and foreknowledge of God, you nailed to a cross by the hands of godless men and put him to death. But God raised him up again, putting an end to the agony of death, since it was impossible for him to be held in its power." (Acts 2:22–24)

Luke recounts how the Apostle Peter defines the person of Jesus in thoroughly human terms—as a man attested to by deeds that God performed through Jesus. Not only does Peter illustrate Jesus as a genuine human being, but he also distinguishes him from the God who empowered Jesus to do these miraculous powers, wonders, and signs.[13] This human Jesus was crucified, but God raised him to immortality, a condition that God granted to Jesus by freeing him from death and its power.

The second relevant passage in the Book of Acts also comes from Peter's testimony. Preaching to Cornelius and those present with him, the Apostle Peter recounts how God raised Jesus on the third day and granted that Jesus be made visible to several witnesses (Acts 10:40–41). Peter was one of those witnesses, and he convincingly demonstrates that this resurrection appearance was not a hallucination, declaring that he and his fellow disciples "ate and drank with him after he arose from the dead" (Acts 10:41).[14] By recalling his experience and the experience of others sharing a meal with the risen Jesus, he expresses confidence in the enduring humanity of Jesus, who consumed food after being immortalized from the grave.

The third passage is drawn from Luke's retelling of Paul's preaching to the Athenians at Mars Hill. In this sermon, the Apostle Paul summons his Gentile audience to repent in light of the resurrection of Jesus Christ, the human being whom God has appointed to return and judge the world. Note carefully Luke's summary of Paul's sermon:

---

[13] Pervo, *Acts*, 80–81.
[14] Dunn, *Jesus Remembered*, 859–60.

"While God has overlooked the times of human ignorance, now he commands all people everywhere to repent, because he has fixed a day on which he will have the world judged in righteousness by a man whom he has appointed, and of this he has given assurance to all by raising him from the dead." (Acts 17:30–31)

According to Paul, Jesus is the human being whom God raised from the dead, and since he will return on a set date in the future to judge the world as a human being, we can confidently conclude that Jesus remained human after his resurrection. Furthermore, Paul illustrates Jesus as the human being whom God empowers to share in God's prerogative as the cosmic judge, making the human Jesus an agent of God.[15] The simplest reading of the christology in the Book of Acts leaves its readers with a clear impression that when God raised Jesus from the dead, Jesus continued to endure as a genuine human person.

The rest of the New Testament affirms the resurrected state of Jesus Christ in terms of an immortalized state, indicating a shared awareness that God has bestowed eternal life on one who formerly was mortal, which is the self-evident condition of human beings. Paul's opening lines in the Epistle to the Romans are relevant here, as they illustrate Jesus as the son of God, both before and after his resurrection:

Paul, a servant of Christ Jesus, called to be an apostle, set apart for the gospel of God, which he promised beforehand through his prophets in the holy Scriptures, concerning his Son, who was descended from David according to the flesh and was declared to be the Son of God in power according to the Spirit of holiness by his resurrection from the dead (Rom 1:1–4)

Observe carefully how Paul depicts Jesus as "his son" (i.e., the son of God) by virtue of being a descendant of David. However, Paul also portrays Jesus as the son of God with power due precisely to his resurrection. While Jesus was the human descendant of King David prior to his death, he retains this title after rising from the dead, albeit in an exalted, more powerful position. We will have more to say about Jesus' exalted status shortly. For now, we can look deeper into Romans, where Paul plainly indicates that God raised Jesus to immortality: "We know that Christ, being raised from the dead, will never die again; death no longer has dominion over him" (Rom 6:9). Within 1 Corinthians chapter fifteen, which is the Bible's most extended exposition on the topic of resurrection, Paul carefully contrasts the regular human body with the glorious body given at the resurrection. In doing so, he illustrates our present body as "perishable" and the resurrected body as "imperishable" (1 Cor 15:42, 53).[16] It follows that Christ, whose resurrection from the dead is the first fruits of those who have fallen asleep (1 Cor 15:24), was also raised to immortality, that is, to having an imperishable body. The Epistle to the Hebrews observes how the resurrected Jesus as perpetually serve as a priest "through the power of an

---

[15] Dunn, *Beginning from Jerusalem*, 689–90.
[16] Scott, "Immortality," 432.

indestructible life" (Heb 7:16).[17] In light of being raised to immortality, Jesus "holds his priesthood permanently, because he continues forever" (Heb 7:24).[18] Even Jesus himself spoke about his never-ending life that he received after dying and being raised from the dead: "I was dead, and behold, I am alive forevermore" (Rev 1:18). In short, the Early Church believed and taught that Christ's post-resurrection life was an indestructible, never-ending immortality that God gave to him.

The Christology of Jesus' Exaltation

It is now appropriate to examine how God exalted Jesus after raising him from the dead. It became clear to the Early Church that Jesus was resurrected to a promoted position, specifically to a place of enthronement at God's right hand in the heavens. The key text that inspired this belief is Psalm 110:1, which is the most quoted, alluded to, and echoed Old Testament passage within the pages of the New Testament. This opening verse from Psalm 110 reads, "Yahweh says to my lord, 'Sit at my right hand until I make your enemies your footstool.'" This psalm, which bears the title "Psalm of David," depicts Yahweh speaking to another figure who is referred to as "my lord." Presumably, this is David's lord, that is, one whom David would regard as ranked higher than he is, but distinct from Yahweh himself. In fact, the Hebrew term that lies behind "my lord" is *adoni*, which appears 195 times in the Old Testament, always refers to a high-ranking figure, but never refers to Yahweh himself. Naturally, the Early Church saw the Jewish Messiah, Jesus, as the intended referent to this exalted figure whom Yahweh summons to sit at his right hand. Since Yahweh is the heavenly Father who is enthroned in heaven, a summons to sit at his right hand would be an invitation to ascend into heaven. This is precisely what the Early Church described of Jesus, who ascended into heaven and sat down at the right hand of God. Consider the following testimony:

> This Jesus God raised up, and of that we all are witnesses. Being therefore exalted at the right hand of God (Acts 2:32–33)
>
> He is the one whom God exalted to His right hand as a Prince and a Savior (Acts 5:31)
>
> Christ Jesus is the one who died—more than that, who was raised—who is at the right hand of God, who indeed is interceding for us. (Rom 8:34)
>
> He raised him from the dead and seated him at his right hand in the heavenly places (Eph 1:20)

---

[17] Koester, *Hebrews*, 355, admits that "Christ truly died, but did not remain subject to death. He received indestructible life through his exaltation to God's right hand."
[18] Shogren, "Mortality and Immortality," 776, points out, "Jesus is not only human, but he also lives forever."

After making purification for sins, he sat down at the right hand of the Majesty on high (Heb 1:3)

But when Christ had offered for all time a single sacrifice for sins, he sat down at the right hand of God (Heb 10:12)

who has gone into heaven and is at the right hand of God, with angels, authorities, and powers having been subjected to him. (1 Pet 3:22)

Several other passages speak of Jesus at the right hand of God in heaven (Acts 7:55–56; Col 3:1; Heb 1:13; 8:1; 12:2), and even Jesus himself anticipated his post-resurrection ascension to God's right hand (Matt 22:44; 26:64). However, we have observed enough to firmly establish the impact that Psalm 110:1 had on the Early Church's understanding of the significance of Jesus' ascension.

Since Psalm 110:1, which identifies two figures as Yahweh and one whom the psalmist refers to as "my lord," was understood by early Christians as referring to the Father and to Jesus, we can begin to make sense of the title of lordship often attributed to Jesus after rising from the dead. It became a common and widespread practice for the authors of the New Testament to describe the resurrected Jesus as "our lord," "the Lord Jesus Christ," or simply as "lord." This should not be confused with the Father's personal name, Yahweh, who is clearly distinguished from the second figure in Psalm 110:1. When the Early Church called Jesus "lord" in light of his post-resurrection exaltation to Yahweh's right hand, this was indeed an application of an exalted title to Jesus.[19] Observe how the title "our lord" was so readily applied to Jesus after this resurrection:

Barnabas and Paul, men who have risked their lives for the sake of our Lord Jesus Christ (Acts 15:25–26)

who was declared the Son of God with power by the resurrection from the dead, according to the Spirit of holiness, Jesus Christ our Lord (Rom 1:4)

awaiting eagerly the revelation of our Lord Jesus Christ (1 Cor 1:7)

Blessed be the God and Father of our Lord Jesus Christ (2 Cor 1:3)

the God of our Lord Jesus Christ, the Father of glory, may give you a spirit of wisdom and of revelation in the knowledge of him (Eph 1:17)

For it is evident that our Lord was descended from Judah (Heb 7:14)

Blessed be the God and Father of our Lord Jesus Christ (1 Pet 1:3)

---

[19] Dunn, *Beginning from Jerusalem*, 219, similarly argues that Psalm 110:1 "envisages two Lords—the Lord God, and another exalted to God's right hand and described as 'my Lord'. It would be entirely understandable if the first Christians allowed this text to determine the language they used for Jesus, and if their initial use of 'Lord' in reference to Jesus made somewhat indiscriminate use of other appropriate 'Lord' texts."

to the only God, our Savior, through Jesus Christ our Lord, be glory, majesty, dominion, and authority, before all time and now and forever. Amen. (Jude 1:25)

It has become rather apparent in our study that Jesus' ascension to sit at Yahweh's right hand involved a considerable promotion in rank, or as Paul articulated it, "God has highly exalted him" (Phil 2:9).[20] In the second half of the Colossian hymn, there are several indicators of Jesus' exalted status. As an expression of Paul's Wisdom Christology, the resurrected Christ is the head of the body, being he who has attained first place among God's creation (Col 1:18). Since God has empowered Jesus with all authority in heaven and on earth (Matt 28:18), this highly exalted human being now possesses the capacity to "hold all things together" (Col 1:17), or as the Epistle to the Hebrews puts it, he "upholds all things by the word of his power" (Heb 1:3).[21] Drawing upon Psalm 8 and its portrayal of Yahweh putting all things under the feet of human beings, the ascended Christ is the first to come to realize this empowerment. For example, Ephesians 1:22 emphatically states that God "put all things under his feet and gave him as head over all things to the church." Hebrews offers a similar depiction, while observing that the full extent of this rule is not yet fully realized: "For in subjecting all things to him, He left nothing that is not subject to him. But now, we do not yet see all things subject to him," according to Hebrews 2:8.[22] Indeed, one of the key truths that the Book of Revelation reveals to its Christian readers is that Jesus is already functioning as "the ruler of the kings of the earth" (Rev 1:5).[23] Although the Early Church eagerly anticipated the second coming of Christ to sit upon the throne of David in Jerusalem, there was nevertheless an acceptance that he was already reigning as a consequence of his post-resurrection exaltation to heaven to sit enthroned at God's right hand.

One of the key roles Jesus was presented with after being raised from the dead is that of the high priesthood. Paul briefly comments on this without much elaboration in Romans 8:34: "Christ Jesus is he who died, yes, rather who was raised, who is at the right hand of God, who also intercedes for us." It is, however, in the Epistle to the Hebrews where the role of high priest is fleshed out in greater detail. As one who was made like his human brother and sisters, Jesus could serve God in the capacity of high priest, both mercifully and faithfully (Heb 2:17).[24] As one who has overcome sin, temptation, and death, Jesus the High Priest can sympathize with other human beings (Heb 4:15). Although all of those who previously held the position of high priest came

---

[20] Osiek, *Philippians, Philemon*, 64.
[21] Dunn, *Colossians and Philemon*, 94; Ellingworth, *Hebrews*, 100; Koester, *Hebrews*, 181.
[22] Koester, *Hebrews*, 221–22.
[23] Reddish, *Revelation*, 34–35, is helpful here: "Faced with persecution and discrimination, John's audience may have felt discouraged and fearful, believing that the powers of oppression and tyranny were in control. John states otherwise, however, reminding them that Jesus Christ is the one who is "the ruler of the kings of the earth."
[24] Ellingworth, *Hebrews*, 185, notably states, "It is therefore impossible to force 'Son' and 'high priest' respectively into the categories later defined as the human and divine natures of Christ."

from the line of Levi, Jesus, who descended from the line of Judah (Heb 7:14), has become high priest according to the order of Melchizedek, based on another verse from Psalm 110.[25] In particular, the exalted lord that sits alongside Yahweh in heaven (Ps 110:1) is also designated as a priest forever, not according to the Tribe of Levi, but according to a much older figure: "You are a priest forever after the order of Melchizedek" (Ps 110:4).[26] The author of Hebrews picks up on this passage, observes how the resurrected Jesus now possesses "indestructible life" (Heb 7:16), which qualifies Jesus to serve in the role as high priest forever, with no need of anyone to replace him since he will never die (Heb 7:24, 28).[27] As one who offered himself once and for all, there is no longer the need for the offering of animal sacrifices (Heb 7:27). In short, High Priest Jesus serves a crucially important role as one who can now, having been raised to immortality and exalted to heaven, forever intercede on behalf of those who follow him.

Conclusion

As we bring this chapter to its conclusion, it is prudent that we summarize our findings as they pertain to the christology illustrated by Christ's death, resurrection, and exalted status. We first observed that the New Testament authors were in agreement that the human Jesus died on the cross for our sins. The Early Church was quite explicit that a member of the human race was able to die and atone for sin. Second, we saw that when God raised Jesus from the dead, God immortalized the human Jesus, and he remains a human being to this day, never to die again. Furthermore, we saw several strands of evidence pertaining to the highly exalted status that Jesus was given at his post-resurrection ascension into heaven, including his enthronement at the right hand of Yahweh himself, the superior title "lord," universal authority over all creation, and the role of the high priesthood forever. It is utterly amazing what the Creator God was able to do with a member of the human race: the man Jesus Christ.

Reflecting on Christ as a genuine human being offers several points of practical application, particularly in the way in which Jesus' faithful obedience and trust in God set an example that the Early Church was keen on following. Our next chapter will explore this and other ways in which the christology of the Early Church coincides with discipleship and practical Christian living.

---

[25] Goldingay, *Psalms*, 3:296–97.
[26] Lane, *Hebrews 1–8*, 184.
[27] Ellingworth, *Hebrews*, 397.

27
APPLYING CHRISTOLOGY TODAY

One common question that gets asked among those who discuss Christology with one another is whether it even matters *what you believe about Jesus*. Some people blindly follow the creeds invented in the fourth and fifth centuries, even when those creedal statements directly contradict the clear teachings of the Old and New Testaments. Others (almost blindly) follow what their pastor tells them without reading the Bible for themselves to see if the doctrines they are hearing match the teachings of Jesus. The unfortunate result of these all-too-common scenarios is that different christological portrayals of Jesus are believed by those who claim to be his followers. Two of our findings in this section on Christology bear considerably on how we practically follow his example. The first truth is that Jesus Christ, the Son of God, *was a genuine human being*. He was a real man, the son of Abraham, Judah, and David. Many others identified him as a human being, and even Christ himself admitted to being a man in John 8:40. The second truth is equally important: the human Jesus *obeyed God by placing his trust and faith in him*, remaining faithful to Yahweh throughout his ministry. The Epistle to the Hebrews helpfully informs us that Christ "learned obedience from the things which he suffered" (Heb 5:8). Although Jesus is primarily remembered for teaching in the Lord's Prayer to pray, "May Your will be done" (Matt 6:10), Jesus himself made this petition to God in Gethsemane: "My Father, if this cannot pass away unless I drink it, may Your will be done" (Matt 26:42). On several occasions, we can observe Christ openly speaking about his willingness to obey God, e.g., "My food is to do the will of Him who sent me and to accomplish His work" (John 4:34). What is impressive is that Christ's obedient and faithful posture towards his God and Father was accomplished while being fully human—as a real member of the human race. The correlation for Christ's followers is clear to see: if Jesus, as a genuine man, possessed the capacity to obey God, then we, too, as human beings, can do the same. In other words, if the Spirit empowered Jesus with the ability to reject sin and do the will of God, then we, too, by the power of the same Holy Spirit, can live faithfully towards God. In light of the truth that Jesus was an actual member of the human race, his example for Christians to follow is unquestionably attainable. We can live like Christ and be pleasing to God (Eph 5:2). We can walk as he walked (1 John 2:6). We can have his mindset among ourselves (Phil 2:5). Let us, therefore, set our eyes on Jesus, the faithful human Messiah, and follow his example by obeying God. Let us study how he lived in obedience to Yahweh by reading the four gospel accounts, praying that God would empower us to enact his will on earth as it is in heaven. Only then can we begin to appreciate how Christology and practical living were intended to go hand-in-hand.

Our second practical application drawn from our study of Christology concerns how we should relate to the risen Jesus, having concluded that he is the son of God, not the creator God. What sort of devotion is appropriate to give to God's highly exalted human Messiah? Does worshipping Jesus as the Messiah offend or cause God to be jealous? What about prayer and petitions? Can we pray to Jesus? Can he even hear us when we pray? These are essential questions to many, as they seek to give honor to God and to Jesus Christ. Beginning with the question of worship, we can already observe in the Old Testament that it was appropriate to give homage to both Yahweh and to the human king of Israel: "all the assembly blessed Yahweh, the God of their fathers, and bowed their heads and paid homage to Yahweh and the king" (1 Chron 29:20). Jesus, the Messiah and highly exalted son of God, is worthy of all creation bowing the knee (Phil 2:10), an act of worship that ultimately gives glory to the God who raised Jesus (Phil 2:11). Among the many hymns in the Book of Revelation, we can observe worship directed towards God because he is the Creator: "Worthy are You, our Lord and our God, to receive glory and honor and power, for You created all things" (Rev 4:11). The Lamb of God is also worthy of worship, but for a different reason. He is worthy because he died as a redemptive sacrifice for humanity: "Worthy are you to take the scroll and to open its seals, for you were slain, and by your blood you ransomed people for God from every tribe and language and people and nation" (Rev 5:9). So, God and the human Jesus are the objects of prostration, but for two different reasons. Both are legitimate forms of worship in which the Early Church engaged. Regarding the issue of prayer, Christ taught that the normative requests are made to the Father (Matt 6:9). However, Jesus also taught his followers that "If you ask me anything in my name, I will do it" (John 14:14). In fact, we find prayer language and requests directed towards the risen Jesus within the New Testament (Acts 7:59; 1 Cor 16:22; 2 Cor 12:8). The early Christians understood the resurrected and highly exalted Jesus—who had been granted all authority in heaven and on earth by God (Matt 28:18; Phil 2:9)—as possessing the God-given capacity to hear prayers. As such, believers could address Jesus in prayer, although the standard prayers were addressed to God in the name of Jesus (John 15:16; Rom 1:8; Eph 5:20; Col 3:17). What should stand out in the Early Church's practices of offering worship and prayer is the complete absence of the Holy Spirit being the object of these religious acts. No biblical author worshipped the Holy Spirit, and along the same lines, there is no evidence of anyone in Scripture praying directly to the Holy Spirit. The focus, after the resurrection, was solely on Yahweh and the highly exalted human Messiah. Let us, therefore, seek to honor the human Messiah by offering worship appropriate to his role as the Christ, the son of God, whose death redeemed us. Let us not refrain from honoring Jesus for what God has accomplished through him. Furthermore, let us embrace the practices of the Early Church, which offered up thanks to God in the name of our lord Jesus Christ. By following these early Christian practices, we can confidently honor God and his human son appropriately, without fear or concern that we might be ignoring one in favor of the other.

Our third practical application drawn from our study of Christology pertains to the subject of atonement and the value of the person of Jesus. The biblical authors were quite explicit that it was the death of a perfect human being, Christ Jesus, that ransomed and atoned for the sins of humanity. Yes, a member of the human race was sufficient in the eyes of God to cover the transgressions of sinners by the shedding of blood. The death of Jesus and his atoning for sins bear considerable weight when it comes to defining who he is. At the moment of Jesus' death on the cross, Mark's gospel account records the words of a Gentile centurion, who identified the crucified one as a human being: "Truly this man was the Son of God" (Mark 15:39). On multiple occasions, the Gospel of John portrays Jesus as the one man that should die for the people (John 11:50–52; 18:14). The same christological understanding of atonement appears in the theology of Paul, who repeatedly illustrates Jesus as the "one man" whose obedience to the point of death resulted in justification of life and righteousness (Rom 5:12–19). Furthermore, we observe in the creedal statement of 1 Timothy 2:4–6 that God wants all human beings to come to the knowledge of truth, which includes the understanding that "the human being Messiah Jesus" gave himself as a ransom for all. Never in Scripture is there any passage, explicit or implicit, that suggests that Jesus had to be God in order to die for the sins of the world. No New Testament author thought that God died for their sins. Even the idea that God could die on the cross is incoherent, for God possesses the innate attribute of immortality, as we demonstrated in Chapter 4. Furthermore, God couldn't have been the one who died on the cross and was buried in a tomb, for the Early Church was unanimous that it was God who raised the crucified Jesus from the grave. In other words, God, the Creator and giver of life, gave resurrection life to someone else, that is, to Jesus Christ, the human Messiah. A famous post-biblical attempt at addressing this issue appears in later Chalcedonian developments following the Council of Chalcedon in the fifth century, which affirmed the divine person of Christ, while later theologians (e.g., in the sixth century) interpreted the assumed human nature as lacking independent personhood. In this post-biblical christological reconstruction, the divine person, being innately immortal, did not die, but rather suffered and died in his impersonal human nature on the cross for the sins of the world. This attempt at maintaining that Jesus is God while also affirming the death of a human is an unconvincing reading of the New Testament, which never portrays Christ as an impersonal human nature. Jesus is a real man, a human being, a genuine member of the human race. He isn't a God-man; he is *God's man*. Let us, therefore, align ourselves with the will of God, which desires that all human beings come to the knowledge of the truth, a truth that includes the simple fact that Jesus is the human mediator between the one God and humanity (1 Tim 2:4–5). This human mediator, not some impersonal human nature, was the one who gave himself as a ransom (1 Tim 2:6). These are simple truths that God wants his people to embrace and share with others. Let us proclaim the realities expressed by the Early Church, not by incoherent creeds developed hundreds of years after the New Testament was written.

PART FIVE: PNEUMATOLOGY

28
HOLY SPIRIT AS GOD'S POWER AND PRESENCE

The Holy Spirit is a complex topic in Scripture. The biblical authors employ a variety of complementary designations to illustrate the Spirit of God, including the Spirit of the Lord, the Spirit, the Spirit of Yahweh, the Spirit of Truth, the Helper, the Spirit of Wisdom, the Eternal Spirit, and, of course, the Holy Spirit. These different titles for the same Spirit of God make it difficult for a modern reader of the biblical texts to grasp the concept and form a definition of the Spirit. Furthermore, matters can become complicated when readers notice that there is often no discernible difference between Yahweh's activity and the Spirit's activity, leading to the conclusion that the Spirit is simply the outworking and action of God himself.

This chapter will begin exploring the primary meanings and purposes of God's Holy Spirit, as conveyed by the authors of the biblical texts. First, we will consider how the Spirit functions as the Creator God's power, the dynamic workings of God observable in creation and among God's people. Second, we will consider how the biblical authors intentionally portrayed the Holy Spirit as the extended presence of God. Finally, we will examine the personification of God's power and presence and the Spirit of God, which is illustrated in personal terms. Although there is much more to say about the Holy Spirit, this introduction outlines the Spirit's basic and most essential roles and functions.

The Holy Spirit as God's *Power*

One of the most common ways that Yahweh uses his Spirit is to empower human individuals to perform their God-given tasks. Beginning with the Old Testament, there was a widespread acceptance that the Holy Spirit equipped and strengthened key figures.[1] The Book of Judges characteristically illustrates its leaders as bearers of God's Spirit:

> The Spirit of Yahweh was upon him, and he judged Israel. He went out to war, and Yahweh gave Cushan-rishathaim king of Mesopotamia into his hand. And his hand prevailed over Cushan-rishathaim. (Judg 3:10)

---

[1] Matthews, "Holy Spirit," 262–63; Levison, "Holy Spirit," 861; Webb, *Judges*, 160–61; Van Pelt et al., "רוּחַ," 1076; Sasson, *Judges 13–21*, 702–3, 715, 731.

> But the Spirit of Yahweh clothed Gideon, and he sounded the trumpet, and the Abiezrites were called out to follow him. (Judg 6:34)
>
> Now the Spirit of Yahweh came upon Jephthah . . . So Jephthah crossed over to the sons of Ammon to fight against them; and Yahweh gave them into his hand. (Judg 11:29–32)
>
> The Spirit of Yahweh came upon him mightily, so that he tore him as one tears a young goat though he had nothing in his hand (Judg 14:6)
>
> And the Spirit of Yahweh rushed upon him, and he went down to Ashkelon and struck down thirty men of the town (Judg 14:19)
>
> And the Spirit of Yahweh came upon him mightily (Judg 15:14)

During the times of the monarchy, the Spirit of Yahweh was vital in energizing the various kings to lead effectively and charismatically, in addition to fighting their battles.[2] The first king, Saul the Benjamite, received the empowerment of the Spirit, enabling him to prophecy among the prophets (1 Sam 10:10) and to lead Israel successfully in battle against the Ammonites (1 Sam 11:6, 11). When Samuel anointed the young David to be the next king, we are told that "the Spirit of Yahweh rushed upon David from that day forward" (1 Sam 16:13). It is no wonder that the next chapter reports that David was able to best Goliath in battle, for the Holy Spirit had certainly given power and strength to the youth. The Spirit similarly empowered King Azariah (2 Chron 15:1) and the Persian king Cyrus (2 Chron. 36:22). The prophet Isaiah predicted that the Spirit of Yahweh would give power to the promised messianic king, the shoot of Jesse. Consider the many ways in which the Holy Spirit would empower this anointed human ruler:

> Then a shoot will spring from the stem of Jesse, and a branch from his roots will bear fruit. The Spirit of Yahweh will rest on Him, the spirit of wisdom and understanding, the spirit of counsel and strength, the spirit of knowledge and the fear of Yahweh. And he will delight in the fear of Yahweh, and he will not judge by what his eyes see, nor make a decision by what his ears hear; but with righteousness he will judge the poor, and decide with fairness for the afflicted of the earth; and he will strike the earth with the rod of his mouth, and with the breath of his lips he will slay the wicked. Also righteousness will be the belt about his loins, and faithfulness the belt about his waist. (Isa 11:1–5)

The Early Church saw in this passage several promises that were fulfilled in Jesus Christ, the king whose ministry publicly began at his baptism. This event served as the defining moment when God empowered Jesus with God's Spirit.[3]

In addition to judges and kings, the authors of the Old Testament frequently depict the Holy Spirit energizing the ministries of various prophetic figures. The Book of Numbers portrays Moses as one who bears the Spirit, to such an extent that Yahweh took

---

[2] Eichrodt, *Theology of the Old Testament*, 2:50–51; Kleinknecht et al., "πνεῦμα κτλ," 362–63.
[3] Tengström and Fabry, "רוּחַ," 390–91, 394; Van Pelt et al., "רוּחַ," 1076.

"some of the Spirit that is on you and put it on" the elders (Num 11:17, 25–26). Balaam the Gentile received the Spirit of Israel's God, which allowed him to deliver oracles and see visions (Num 24:2-4). Yahweh himself describes Joshua, the successor of Moses, as "a man in whom is the Spirit," in Numbers 27:18. The Spirit also came upon the Levite Jahaziel (2 Chron 20:14), which empowered him to speak to King Jehoshaphat and the people of Judah and Jerusalem. The priest Zechariah was clothed with the Holy Spirit, giving him the words and boldness to speak against King Joash's idolatry (2 Chron 24:20). Not surprisingly, the more well-known prophetic figures, such as Isaiah, Ezekiel, Daniel, and Micah, were remembered as prophesying under the inspiration of God's empowering Spirit.[4] The prophet Micah provides an illustrative example of the Holy Spirit being outright defined as God's power: "But as for me, I am filled with power, with the Spirit of Yahweh" (Mic 3:8). Since it was widely accepted that God's Spirit empowered these prophetic figures, it was forbidden for the Israelites to do them any harm (1 Chron 16:22; Ps 105:15).

The powerful Spirit of God is also evident in Yahweh's acts as the Creator.[5] In the creation account in Genesis chapter one, we can observe the Spirit of God hovering over the chaotic waters right before God's creative and powerful word brings forth light (Gen 1:2–3). This portrayal of the Spirit hovering employs a rare Hebrew verb that elsewhere describes an eagle hovering over its young in the nest (Deut 32:11), suggesting that the Spirit in Genesis 1 is brooding and fostering creation itself.[6] Although we will return to the concept of personification shortly, Yahweh tasks his powerful Spirit on a mission to create life and to renew creation: "You send forth Your Spirit, they are created; and You renew the face of the ground" (Ps 104:30).[7] Elihu outright acknowledges that "the Spirit of God has made me, and the breath of the Almighty gives me life" in Job 33:4. Moreover, Yahweh's powerful Spirit can reconstitute the fallen people of God from their deadness of exile, according to Ezekiel's vision of the Valley of Dry Bones:

> "Then you will know that I am Yahweh, when I have opened your graves and caused you to come up out of your graves, My people. I will put My Spirit within you and you will come to life, and I will place you on your own land. Then you will know that I, Yahweh, have spoken and done it" (Ezek 37:13-14)

The same Holy Spirit that was instrumental in the acts of creation continues to be active in the workings of the Creator God in the present.

---

[4] Isa 61:1; Ezek 2:2; Dan 4:8; Mic 3:8.
[5] Dunn, *New Testament Theology*, 48. Kleinknecht et al., "πνεῦμα κτλ," 366, offer the definition, "the personal, creative power of God."
[6] Köhler et al., *Hebrew and Aramaic Lexicon*, 1219–20; Tengström and Fabry, "רוּחַ," 384.
[7] Kleinknecht et al., "πνεῦμα κτλ," 363. Van Pelt et al., "רוּחַ," 1075, draw attention to the Spirit's role as "the agent of creation."

The Early Church experienced the impact of God's empowering Spirit.[8] One needs to look no further than Christ, who was anointed with the Holy Spirit at his baptism, empowering him to perform mighty deeds and miracles. We often find statements indicating how Jesus "was filled with the power of the Spirit" (Luke 4:14). Jesus openly taught that the Holy Spirit empowered him to perform exorcisms: "But if I cast out demons by the Spirit of God, then the kingdom of God has come upon you" (Matt 12:28). Peter's sermon in the Book of Acts described how "God anointed Jesus of Nazareth with the Holy Spirit and with power" in Acts 10:38.[9] Even the angel Gabriel attributes the begetting of Jesus in the womb of Mary to the creative act of the Spirit: "The Holy Spirit will come upon you, and the power of the Most High will overshadow you" (Luke 1:35). The parallelism of this passage demonstrates, quite clearly, how God's Spirit is further identified as his power to create.[10]

During his ministry, Jesus taught his disciples that, in their mission work to share the gospel of the kingdom, they would suffer persecution. When this took place, the Spirit would empower the disciples with words to speak to their persecutors: "for it is not you who speak, but the Spirit of your Father speaking through you" (Matt 10:20). Jesus makes clear in this passage that the powerful Holy Spirit is the Father's own Spirit, an extension of God the Father himself. Right before ascending to the right hand of God in heaven, Jesus announced to his followers that they "receive power when the Holy Spirit has come upon you" (Acts 1:8). This powerful Spirit from God would equip them to be faithful witnesses of Jesus and his gospel of the kingdom.

The idea that the Holy Spirit is God's power in action regularly featured in the Apostle Paul's letters.[11] Consider how the theology of Paul closely links God's power and God's Spirit:

> Now may the God of hope fill you with all joy and peace in believing, so that you will abound in hope by the power of the Holy Spirit. (Rom 15:13)
>
> For I will not presume to speak of anything except what Christ has accomplished through me, resulting in the obedience of the Gentiles by word and deed, in the power of signs and wonders, in the power of the Spirit (Rom 15:18–19)

---

[8] Dunn, "Spirit," 693, provides a helpful summary: "But by far the most frequent use of *pneuma* in the NT (more than 250 times) is as a reference to the Spirit of God, the Holy Spirit, that power which is immediately of God as to source and nature."
[9] Dunn, *Jesus Remembered*, 373.
[10] Dunn, "Spirit," 697.
[11] Kleinknecht et al., "πνεῦμα κτλ," 433, acknowledge, "it would be a mistake to think that Paul finds in 'the third person of the Trinity' the original meaning of πνεῦμα."

> my message and my preaching were not in persuasive words of wisdom, but in demonstration of the Spirit and of power, so that your faith would not rest on the wisdom of men, but on the power of God. (1 Cor 2:4–5)

> He would grant you, according to the riches of His glory, to be strengthened with power through His Spirit (Eph 3:16)

> for our gospel did not come to you in word only, but also in power and in the Holy Spirit (1 Thes 1:5)

These examples expressed by early Christians can be multiplied (e.g., Gal 3:5; 2 Tim 1:7; Heb 2:4). However, we have observed sufficient evidence to conclude that the Early Church embraced the truth that the Spirit of God effectively empowers God's people in mighty ways.

The Holy Spirit as God's *Presence*

The biblical authors express an awareness that the Holy Spirit often functioned as the extended presence of the one true God. The purpose of such an illustration would affirm the nearness of God to his people, reminding them of his imminent involvement. For example, the rhetorical question appearing in some of the Psalms attributed to David identifies God's Spirit and his presence:

> Do not cast me away from Your presence and do not take Your Holy Spirit from me. (Ps 51:11)

> Where can I go from Your Spirit? Or where can I flee from Your presence? (Ps 139:7)

These passages illuminate our initial exploration of the meaning and purpose of the Holy Spirit. On the one hand, we can observe that the Spirit belongs to the one true God. It is defined as *your* Spirit, which further elaborates on the concept of being in your presence through parallelism of these verses.[12] On the other hand, it is clear that when the psalmist and his implied readers experience the Holy Spirit, they are in the very presence of God.[13] We can go even further by pointing out that the Hebrew phrase behind the English translation "your presence" is, quite literally, "from your face." In other words, those who experience and possess the Holy Spirit are before the face of the one God, since the Spirit

---

[12] Goldingay, *Psalms*, 2:134; 3:631, who declares, "it is impossible to escape from Yhwh, and specifically to escape from Yhwh's spirit or face."
[13] Dunn, *New Testament Theology*, 48.

is God's presence.[14] Those who experience the Spirit of God naturally regard the Father as close, personal, and involved in the lives of his children.[15]

Several other texts clarify that the biblical authors regarded the Spirit of God as his presence. In the midst of several promises of the restoration of the people of God, Yahweh commits to pouring out his Spirit in a manner that will bring his face out of hiding: "And I will not hide my face anymore from them, when I pour out my Spirit upon the house of Israel" (Ezek 39:29). In effect, Israel will be able to experience God's presence when he gives them his Spirit. Along the same lines, God spoke through the prophet Haggai to reassure his audience that "I am with you" (Hag 2:4). In the following verse, Haggai clarifies how it is that God is with his people: "My Spirit is abiding in your midst" (Hag 2:5). With the Holy Spirit present among the people, Yahweh's presence is felt and experienced.[16] Paul conveys much of the same to his Christian communities, particularly as he argues that God's freedom can be experienced where the Spirit is present: "Now the Lord is the Spirit, and where the Spirit of the Lord is, there is freedom," in 2 Corinthians 3:17. Paul here identifies the Lord God as the Spirit itself, while also noting how the presence of the Spirit of God results in liberty for the new covenant people of God.[17]

The First Epistle of John illustrates precisely how God abides in those who believe and love one another: "And by this we know that he abides in us, by the Spirit that he has given us" (1 John 3:24). This passage makes it clear that God himself abides in his people with his Spirit—another indicator that the Spirit is just another way of speaking about the presence of the one true God. When the Father gives his Spirit to his faithful children, he extends his abiding presence in a very personal and perceptible manner. This theme reemerges later in the epistle:

> No one has seen God at any time; if we love one another, God abides in us, and His love is perfected in us. By this we know that we abide in Him and He in us, because He has given us of His Spirit. (1 John 4:12–13)

While early Christians affirmed that they had never seen Yahweh, they experienced his abiding presence through his own Spirit. When the Early Church expressed God's love towards one another, they recognized that he was in their midst, particularly through the gift of his Holy Spirit.

---

[14] Van Pelt et al., "רוּחַ," 1075, acknowledge how the Spirit of God often "functions as the alter ego of Yahweh."
[15] Brueggemann, *Theology of the Old Testament*, 292, brilliantly states, "the witness of the Old Testament does not move in the direction of what became in the Christian formulation the third person of the Trinity."
[16] Meyers and Meyers, *Haggai, Zechariah 1–8*, 52, state that the Holy Spirit "can also refer to God's presence or a manifestation thereof... In this instance it stands for Yahweh's potent presence."
[17] Sampley, "The Second Letter to the Corinthians," 71; Dunn, *Theology of Paul*, 422; Thrall, *2 Corinthians 1–7*, 271–74.

We will thoroughly examine the early Christian understanding of the body of Christ as the new temple in Chapter 40. Still, for now, we can observe Paul's insistence that God's presence was extended into the midst of the new covenant community. In other words, the Early Church functioned as a temple dwelling for the one true God, and God made his dwelling among his people by giving his Spirit to them. The Holy Spirit legitimized the Early Church's belief and conviction that God's presence was among them as a new temple community. For example, Paul illustrates the body of Christ as a temple because God dwells and walks among them: "What agreement has the temple of God with idols? For we are the temple of the living God; as God said, 'I will make my dwelling among them and walk among them, and I will be their God, and they shall be my people'" (2 Cor 6:16).[18] How is it exactly that God is present among his people? By giving the Holy Spirit—the presence of the one true God—to dwell among them: "Do you not know that you are God's temple and that God's Spirit dwells in you?" (1 Cor 3:16). The insistence that the Spirit of God functions as his real and personal presence within the temple community of believers appears often: "Or do you not know that your body is a temple of the Holy Spirit within you" (1 Cor 6:19); "you also are being built together into a dwelling of God in the Spirit" (Eph 2:22). In short, the belief that the new covenant community functioned as the new house in which God personally dwells through the Holy Spirit demonstrates that the Spirit was recognized as God's presence.

The *Personification* of the Holy Spirit

In reviewing what we have already discovered, the Spirit of Yahweh is his power, both in acts of creation and in equipping his people to perform mighty deeds. The Spirit is also Yahweh's presence, a common way in which the biblical authors illustrate God personally dwelling among his faithful people. As such, we have seen that the Holy Spirit is personal—the presence of a loving and active heavenly Father who is in a deep covenant commitment with his children. At times, the Holy Spirit appears to undergo personification, attributing emotions, actions, and a personality to the Spirit of the Father. We will recall from Chapter 25 that the biblical authors personified God's wisdom and God's word; therefore, the act of the Holy Spirit undergoing personification should not come as a surprise. By recognizing the frequent instances where the biblical authors personified the Holy Spirit, we are never left with the impression that the Spirit is something (or someone) distinct from God himself. Just as we observed with the personification of God's wisdom and word, giving personality to a key attribute of

---

[18] Fee, *God's Empowering Presence*, 337–38, admits, "Thus, by God's Spirit the church becomes 'the temple of the living God,' by his Spirit, God 'dwells among them,' and by his Spirit, God 'has become a father for you.'"

Yahweh does not mean that the attribute is a fully-fledged person, distinct from Yahweh himself.[19]

Take, for example, how the psalmist personifies the Holy Spirit—the power and presence of Yahweh—as an agent that Yahweh can send forth on a mission in Psalm 104:30: "You send forth Your Spirit, they are created; and You renew the face of the ground."[20] God commissions his Spirit as a personified agent to enact his powerful creation, and the psalmist makes it clear that God himself is credited with the deeds ("*you* renew").[21] Similarly, the Book of Isaiah details how Yahweh has sent both the prophet and his Spirit: "And now Adonai Yahweh has sent me, and His Spirit" (Isa 48:16).[22] This passage sheds light on how the human prophet, an agent in his own right, is sent forth on a mission along with God's Spirit, which is depicted as a personified agent alongside the prophet.[23] In the New Testament, the Holy Spirit continues to undergo personification as a commissioned agent, and this personification is illustrated through the depiction of God's Spirit as a "Helper." Observe how the Spirit is personified as a sent agent and as a helper:

> "But the Helper, the Holy Spirit, that the Father will send in my name, he will teach you" (John 14:26)

> "But when the Helper comes, whom I will send to you from the Father, the Spirit of truth, which proceeds from the Father, he will bear witness about me." (John 15:26)

The personification of the Spirit appears to be taking place in these passages. The Holy Spirit, which is grammatically neuter in Greek, undergoes personification as a masculine "Helper." In personification, the personified Spirit is referred to with masculine pronouns. These masculine indicators are nothing more than the act of personifying God's Spirit—his power and presence—as a helpful agent that assists, teaches, and bears witness among the Christian community.[24] There are other examples of early Christians believing that the Spirit has been sent as a personified agent (e.g., John 16:7; Gal 4:6; 1 Pet 1:12), and in each case, the Spirit carries out God's purpose. Notably, when we

---

[19] Richardson, *Theology of the New Testament*, 104–5, stresses that "the Spirit of God has no existence apart from God any more than the spirit of Elijah can exist apart from Elijah. God's Spirit is God acting." He continues (120), "The Spirit of God, is, of course, personal; it is God's [power] in action. But the Holy Spirit is not a person existing independently of God; it is a way of speaking of God's personality in history."
[20] Tengström and Fabry, "רוּחַ," 387.
[21] Dunn, *Did the First Christians Worship Jesus?* 73.
[22] Goldingay and Payne, *Isaiah 40–55*, 2:143–4.
[23] Paul, *Isaiah 40–66*, 316, helpfully points out that "This is one of the very few verses where the prophet speaks in the first person."
[24] Moloney, *John*, 434, shows respectable restraint by acknowledging that John 15:26 "is not to be read in light of fourth-century trinitarian debates." Wallace, *Greek Grammar*, 331–32, similarly draws attention to the "erroneous" claim often made that the Holy Spirit can be argued to be a masculine person. The far demonstrative pronoun (*ekeinos*) is governed by the masculine "Helper," not the neuter Spirit of truth.

compare the examples of God *sending* his Spirit to the passages illustrating God *giving* his Spirit, the similarities suggest that sending and giving are functionally the same.

The personified Holy Spirit also leads God's faithful people in obedient living. The psalmist humbly requests of God that he would instruct him to obey his will, particularly by providing God's Spirit to lead him: "Teach me to do Your will, for You are my God; let Your good Spirit lead me on level ground" (Ps 143:10). The Spirit of God undergoes personification, resulting in the Spirit bearing the function as a leader and guide.[25] The psalmist is clear on two points: God is one person (as the second-person singular pronouns illustrate) and the Spirit belongs to God. The Early Church possessed a heightened awareness of the Spirit's role in leading the faithful community of the new covenant. Paul was adamant that those who followed the leading of the Holy Spirit are members of the renewed people of God—his children: "For all who are led by the Spirit of God are children of God" (Rom 8:14). Similarly, the role of the personified Spirit leading the Early Church required that its members follow accordingly: "But I say, walk by the Spirit, and you will not carry out the desire of the flesh . . . But if you are led by the Spirit, you are not under the Law" (Gal 5:16, 18). The portrayal of the Holy Spirit's personification as a leader and a sent agent is remarkably similar to depictions of God's light and truth in Psalm 43:3, both of which are personified to perform the functions of leading and carrying out the mission for which God sent them.

We may observe several other ways the biblical authors personify the Spirit of Yahweh. The personification of the Holy Spirit allows for it to be depicted as being grieved (Isa 63:10; Eph 4:30), talking (Acts 8:29; 1 Tim 4:1; Rev 2:7), teaching (Luke 12:12; John 14:26), helping (John 15:26; Rom 8:26–27), writing on our hearts (2 Cor 3:3), and inviting readers to respond faithfully (Rev 22:17).[26] Furthermore, lying to the Spirit (Acts 5:3) was understood as lying to the God himself (Acts 5:4), since the personified Spirit present in the early Christian community displayed the very presence of God.[27] Along the same lines, insulting or outraging the personified Spirit of grace (Heb 10:29) was an affront to the one God: "For we know Him who said, 'Vengeance is Mine, I will repay'" (Heb 10:30). In short, the Holy Spirit often underwent personification, both in the Old and New Testaments, but the biblical authors never took this personification a step further to suggest that the Spirit was a conscious, separate person alongside the Father himself.[28] The Early Church's theology of the Holy Spirit personified can be traced

---

[25] Hossfeld and Zenger, *Psalms 3*, 575–76; Dunn, *Did the First Christians Worship Jesus?* 73.
[26] The portrayal of the Holy Spirit speaking to the churches is repeated in Rev 2:11, 17, 29; 3:6, 13, 22.
[27] Tuggy, *What is the Trinity?* 46. Walton, *Acts 1–9:42*, 359, arrives at the same conclusion: "Luke presents the presence of the Spirit in the community (cf. 4:31) as the very presence of YHWH himself."
[28] Richardson, *Theology of the New Testament*, 103, rightly points out that the concept of the personhood or personality of the Holy Spirit is "unknown to the biblical writers."

to the teachings of Jesus, who clearly taught his followers that the Spirit was "the Spirit of your Father," according to Matthew 10:20.

Conclusion

To summarize our findings, this chapter has introduced the Holy Spirit's most fundamental and basic meanings and purposes. We first noticed that the biblical authors frequently illustrated the Holy Spirit as the power of God. As such, the Spirit powerfully equipped God's people to serve him in the past and present faithfully. The Spirit was also instrumental in forming and creating all things, further cementing its portrayal as the power of God. Second, we observed how the authors of the biblical texts portrayed God's Spirit as his presence, regularly extending it to be present in the midst of his people. In this investigation, we examined several texts that convey the reality that God himself was truly among his people when his Holy Spirit was in their midst, an experience that highlights the definition of the Spirit as the very real presence of God. Finally, we saw the common tendency of both the authors of the Old Testament and the early Christians to personify the Holy Spirit, that is, to poetically give the presence and power of the Father a personality and emotions. The portrayal of the Holy Spirit's personification parallels God's personified wisdom and word, and we even observed similarities between the poetic personification of similar attributes, such as the light and the truth of God. Although it was commonplace to personify God's Spirit—his power and presence—this personification was never misunderstood by the Early Church as if the Spirit was a separate divine person alongside the Father, alive and conscious. That view of the Spirit took several hundred years to develop, but it was not believed and taught by the Early Church.

Having displayed the Holy Spirit as God's power and presence, often personified, we can now focus on exploring how the biblical authors related to the Spirit. If the Holy Spirit is just another way of talking about God's power and God's presence, is the Spirit worthy of worship? Is the Spirit the object of prayer, animal sacrifices, or songs? Do any of the 150 psalms dedicate their praise to God's Spirit? What about the many hymns recorded in the Book of Revelation? Do they sing to the Spirit? Our next chapter will offer clear answers to these questions as we continue to seek understanding of what the Early Church believed and taught on matters of Pneumatology.

29
HOW THE SPIRIT RELATES TO THE FATHER AND THE SON

The early Christians produced what we might call creedal statements that reflected their beliefs and experiences in light of coming to faith in Christ. One such creedal statement is in 1 Timothy 2:5, which states, "For there is one God, and one mediator also between God and men, the man Christ Jesus." This creed summoned the Early Church to embrace the truth that the one God has made Jesus, the human Messiah, the mediator between God and humanity. The passage emphasized the key role of God and the human Jesus, particularly in their relationship with human beings. What is missing is any mention of the Holy Spirit. God's Spirit, his presence and power, was surely important in the lives of the early Christians. However, the Early Church appears to have prioritized the one true God and the risen Jesus. How did the Holy Spirit relate to God the Father in the beliefs and practices of the biblical authors?

This chapter will explore how biblical authors understood and perceived the Spirit, God's presence and power, particularly in the context of devotion traditionally offered to God himself. We will begin by examining the various ways human beings participated in worship, including acts of prostration, prayer, and offering animal sacrifices. Second, we will investigate how the experience of the Holy Spirit relates to acts of singing and praise, specifically psalms, songs, and hymns. Third, we will consider prophetic throne room visions to locate the Spirit in God's heavenly court, both in the Old and New Testaments. Fourth, we will inquire whether God or Jesus Christ ever talks to, dialogues with, or communicates with the Spirit. Finally, we will look into how the Spirit's role overlaps with that of the resurrected and highly exalted Jesus. This chapter's investigation will surely shed much-needed light on what the Early Church believed and taught about the Holy Spirit.

Is the Holy Spirit the Object of Worship, Prayer, or Sacrifice?

First, we can examine how the people of God in both the Old and New Testaments offered acts of worship to God. It is pretty self-evident that the Father, the only true God, was the object of worship. When Moses informed Pharaoh that Israel is God's son, his firstborn, and that Pharaoh must "Let My son go that he may serve Me" (Exod 4:22–23), Yahweh portrays himself as the Father. Psalm 2:11 invites the readers to "Worship Yahweh with reverence and rejoice with trembling." Even Jesus taught that true worshipers would worship the Father in spirit and in truth (John 4:23). In addition to worshiping God, the anointed human king was considered worthy of receiving worship. First Chronicles 29:20 records how Yahweh and King David are objects of worship: "all the assembly blessed Yahweh, the God of their fathers, and bowed their heads and paid homage to Yahweh and the king."[1] Returning to Psalm 2, the readers, in addition to giving worship to Yahweh (Ps 2:11), the kingly son of God is to receive homage in the form of a kiss (Ps 2:12).[2] After Jesus walked on water, his disciples worshiped him as the son of God, not as God: "You are certainly God's son" (Matt 14:33). When it comes to the Holy Spirit, however, there is no evidence that anyone directed their worship to it. None of the famous patriarchs worshiped the Spirit, nor did the Israelites after them. Similarly, the Early Church never offered worship to the Spirit of God. God never summons his people to prostrate themselves before his Spirit, and Jesus never commanded his disciples to make the Spirit their object of worship.[3] Early Christians worshiped the Father and Jesus, the human Messiah, but they never worshiped the Holy Spirit.[4]

When we examine the practice of offering prayer, is there any evidence that the people of God made petitions to the Spirit? Yahweh, the Father, is obviously the most common recipient of prayer (Isa 63:16–17), a practice that Jesus inherited and taught to his disciples: "Pray then in this way: 'Our Father'" (Matt 6:9). After his resurrection and exaltation to heaven, even Jesus could be the object of prayerful petitions (Acts 7:59–60; 1 Cor 16:22; 2 Cor 12:8–9). More specifically, the early Christians would pray to the Father in Jesus' name (John 14:13; 15:16; 16:23). The Holy Spirit, however, is never the object of prayers or petitions. There is no evidence that anyone, in either testament, entreated, made pleas, appeals, or any other requests to the Spirit.[5] While early Christians would often pray to God the Father in the name of Jesus, there is absolutely no evidence in the Bible of prayer offered to the Father, son, and Holy Spirit collectively.[6]

It was extremely common to offer animal sacrifices to God as an act of worship and reverence. Cain and Abel instinctively brought offerings before Yahweh (Gen 4:3–4), a practice that was a routine part of the tabernacle and temple functions under the old covenant. After the once-and-for-all sacrifice of Jesus on the cross, the animal sacrifices ceased, but the concept of living a sacrificial life to God continued to

---

[1] Irons et al., *The Son of God*, 179; McGrath, *The Only True God*, 50; Dunn, *Did the First Christians Worship Jesus?* 8.
[2] Other examples of this verb "to kiss" being used of worship given to human beings include Isaac (Gen 27:26); Jacob (Gen 33:4); Moses (Exod 4:27), Jethro (Exod 18:7); and David (1 Sam 10:1).
[3] Dunn, *Did the First Christians Worship Jesus?* 74, helpfully admits, "Neither in the language of worship nor in the practice of worship do we find it thought to be appropriate that the Spirit should be seen as the one worshipped or to be worshipped."
[4] Tuggy, *What is the Trinity?* 45; Aune, "Worship, Early Christian," 974. Hurtado, "Worship, NT Christian," 916, argues extensively that the objects of worship within the New Testament are "Jesus as well as God (the Father)."
[5] McIntosh, *One God, Three Persons*, 105.
[6] Aune, "Worship, Early Christian," 980–81.

endure. For example, Paul appealed to his readers to "present your bodies as a living sacrifice, holy and acceptable to God" in Romans 12:1. Additionally, the author of Hebrews directs the "sacrifice of praise" to the one true God (Heb 13:15). It appears that the biblical authors reserved the offering of sacrifices, whether real or spiritual, to God alone. Christ is never the object of sacrificial offerings, and neither is the Holy Spirit.[7] Sacrifices were reserved for the Father alone.

Is the Holy Spirit the Object of Psalms, Songs, or Hymns?

When we turn to examine how the people of God offered praise to him, the results are strikingly similar. Nearly all of the psalms are sung to Yahweh, who is clearly identified as the Father in light of the references to the intended readers as his "children."[8] Psalm 45:1 indicates that wedding psalms can be addressed to human kings.[9] However, not one of the 150 psalms is directly sung to the Spirit of Yahweh.

In addition to psalms, we can look at the practice of singing songs outside of the Psalter. When the biblical authors record the songs of their subjects, they are always directed towards Yahweh, the God of Israel, in the Old Testament (e.g., Exod 15:1, 21; Deut 32:3; Judg 5:2–3). Within the New Testament, songs are traditionally addressed to God, such as the Magnificat (Luke 1:46–55), the Benedictus (Luke 1:68–79), and the Gloria (Luke 2:14). Early Christians sang songs *about Jesus*, such as we find in Colossians 1:15–20, but this is not, strictly speaking, sung *to Jesus*. The Holy Spirit, once again, was never considered worthy of being the object of singing.

One key feature of the Book of Revelation is its use of early Christian hymns, which are interwoven throughout the narrative. These hymns encouraged the readers of Revelation to not only imitate the acts of worship prescribed in the lyrics but also to refrain from offering worship to those whom John of Patmos deemed unworthy and illicit. Naturally, the one seated upon the throne, the Almighty, is the object of many hymns (e.g., Rev 4:8–11; 7:12; 19:1–7). We even find Christ, illustrated as a Lamb, as the object of hymnic singing (Rev 5:9–12). On occasion, hymns are sung to both God and the Lamb (Rev 5:13; 7:10).[10] However, there is no indication that Revelation directs any manner of singing of hymns to the Holy Spirit. The Spirit's exclusion is all the more striking in light of Revelation's insistence that only correct forms of worship should be

---

[7] Dunn, *Did the First Christians Worship Jesus?* 56, observes, "in earliest Christianity, *Christ was never understood as the one to whom sacrifice was offered*, even when the imagery of sacrifice was used symbolically for Christian service."
[8] Pss 2:7; 34:11; 82:6; 89:26–27; 103:13.
[9] Mowinckel, *The Psalms in Israel's Worship*, 73–74.
[10] Blount, *Revelation*, 95–96.

practiced by the early Christians. Directing hymns to the Spirit never occurs, not even once.

The Holy Spirit in the Throne Room Visions of God

On rare occasions, the biblical prophets catch a visionary glimpse of what the only true God is doing in the heavenly realm. These throne room visions typically portray the Father anthropomorphically, usually seated on a throne. We can examine these glimpses into God's throne room in order to locate the Holy Spirit. In 1 Kings, the prophet Micaiah declares what he observed:

> "Therefore, hear the word of Yahweh. I saw Yahweh sitting on His throne, and all the host of heaven standing by Him on His right and on His left. Yahweh said, 'Who will entice Ahab to go up and fall at Ramoth-gilead?' And one said this while another said that. Then a spirit came forward and stood before Yahweh and said, 'I will entice him.' Yahweh said to him, 'How?' And he said, 'I will go out and be a deceiving spirit in the mouth of all his prophets.' Then He said, 'You are to entice him and also prevail. Go and do so.' (1 Kgs 22:19–22)

In this Old Testament vision of heaven, the prophet describes the throne room of God and details those present. The occupants include an enthroned Yahweh and the angelic host of heaven flanking him on both sides. Jesus is not present in this heavenly vision because he has not yet been created. The Holy Spirit is also not present.[11] The Father is envisioned as seated upon his throne, but there is no anthropomorphic portrayal of the Holy Spirit. There is only one throne, and only one person sits upon it.[12] It should be said that when Yahweh sends a spirit that volunteers for the mission, this is not a reference to the Holy Spirit. As the context strongly suggests, this spirit belongs to one of the heavenly hosts of angels.[13]

A familiar scene reemerges in the prophet Isaiah's retelling of his own commissioning. In Isaiah 6:1–8, the prophet has a vision of Yahweh seated upon the throne. Angels surround him, seraphs to be exact. When a mission is discussed and the question is raised, "Whom shall I send, and who will go for Us?" (Isa 6:8), Isaiah volunteers for the job. Once again, the throne room vision portrays a single person on the throne—Yahweh himself. Several seraphs accompany Yahweh. No preexistent son of God is present in Yahweh's throne room, nor do we catch any glimpse of the Holy Spirit. The vision of God shows only one person, Yahweh alone.[14] Ezekiel's vision of

---

[11] Kleinknecht et al., "πνεῦμα κτλ," 387, admit the same concerning the Spirit, which "is never present in the heavenly assembly before the throne of God."
[12] Barlow, "The Throne Room Problem," 4.
[13] Heavenly angels are referred to as "spirits" in Heb 1:13–14.
[14] Brueggemann, *Isaiah 1–39*, 59.

God repeats these common features (Ezek 1:4–22). This portrayal shows four living creatures, each bearing four wings. Ezekiel's description of God, which is heavily qualified ("something like") in order not to give the impression that the prophet laid eyes on his enthroned Creator: "there was something resembling a throne, like lapis lazuli in appearance; and on that which resembled a throne, high up, was a figure," according to Ezekiel 1:26. Yahweh is upon his throne, surrounded by flying angelic creatures. Christ is absent, since he wasn't in existence yet, and the Holy Spirit is nowhere to be found.

The consistent absence of the Holy Spirit in the throne room visions continues into the New Testament. As we observed in Chapter 26, the resurrected Jesus was highly exalted to Yahweh's right hand, a fact that the Early Church frequently affirmed by drawing upon the language of Psalm 110:1. Naturally, the throne room visions that take place after Jesus' exaltation feature Christ in heaven alongside God.[15] This feature was absent in the Old Testament heavenly visions. We can consider several throne room visions in our search for the Holy Spirit:

> But being full of the Holy Spirit, he gazed intently into heaven and saw the glory of God, and Jesus standing at the right hand of God; and he said, "Behold, I see the heavens opened up and the Son of Man standing at the right hand of God." (Acts 7:55–56)

> After these things I looked, and behold, a door standing open in heaven, and the first voice which I had heard, like the sound of a trumpet speaking with me, said, "Come up here, and I will show you what must take place after these things." Immediately I was in the Spirit; and behold, a throne was standing in heaven, and One sitting on the throne. And He who was sitting was like a jasper stone and a sardius in appearance; and there was a rainbow around the throne, like an emerald in appearance. (Rev 4:1–3)

> And I saw between the throne (with the four living creatures) and the elders a Lamb standing, as if slain, having seven horns and seven eyes, which are the seven Spirits of God, sent out into all the earth. And he came and took the book out of the right hand of Him who sat on the throne. (Rev 5:6–7)

These revelations of what the heavenly throne room looks like, even with all of their imagery and symbolism, never portray the Holy Spirit as a figure present alongside God. Moreover, the Spirit does not have its own throne. As Stephen declared, Christ is seated at the right hand of God, but the Spirit of God is neither seen nor enthroned in any throne room vision.[16] The consistent testimony of the heavenly visions throughout Scripture indicates an awareness among the biblical authors that the Holy Spirit was not a conscious, separate person alongside God the Father. Rather, the Spirit was God's personal presence and power.

---

[15] Barlow, "The Throne Room Problem," 8.
[16] McIntosh, *One God, Three Persons*, 105, presents the observation of Dale Tuggy: "While God has a throne, which he now shares with the exalted Jesus, this spirit is nowhere portrayed as enthroned."

Communicating with the Holy Spirit

Another way to distinguish God, the Messiah, and God's Spirit is to examine their communication closely. The biblical authors record hundreds of instances in which people speak to, pray, and cry out to God the Father. Similarly, in the ministry of Jesus, people had regular conversations with Jesus, asking him questions and engaging with his teachings. However, when we carefully search for occasions where people talked to the Holy Spirit, we again come up empty. Neither in the Old Testament nor the New Testament do we find the people of God speaking, conversing with, or otherwise communicating with God's Spirit. This is one of many reasons why the Holy Spirit does not have a personal name, such as the Father (Yahweh) and the son of God (Jesus) possess.[17]

The Holy Spirit and the Highly Exalted Jesus

Despite the universal reservation of the biblical authors and the Early Church to portray the Holy Spirit as a distinct, conscious person alongside the Father in heaven, there was an awareness that the Spirit that powerfully raised Jesus from the dead unto immortality came to be very closely associated with Christ. In fact, several passages give the impression that the highly exalted Jesus has now taken the role of the giver of the Holy Spirit, no doubt due to his position as the agent who represents the only true God. This is most apparent in the theology of Paul, such as we can observe in Galatians 4:6, where "the Spirit of His Son" enables believers to intimately cry "Abba! Father!" In other words, the Holy Spirit is characterized in a similar manner to Jesus, who prayed the same prayer during his earthly ministry (Mark 14:36).[18] The Spirit, therefore, transforms the children of God into conformity with the character of the son of God himself.[19]

The resurrection has provided Jesus with an incorruptible body (1 Cor 15:42), belonging to the new creation. In this capacity, Christ, whom Paul regards as a resurrected human being (1 Cor 15:45, 47), serves as the source of resurrection life for those who are in Christ: "The last Adam became a life-giving spirit" (1 Cor 15:45).[20] Just as Paul understands Adam as the source of perishable humanity, Christ, the second Adam, by virtue of having been raised to receive an immortal body energized by the Holy Spirit, functions as the spiritual human locus of resurrection life to be given at his second

---

[17] McIntosh, *One God, Three Persons*, 105.
[18] Hays, "The Letter to the Galatians," 285.
[19] Oakes, *Galatians*, 138; Dunn, *Theology of Paul*, 263. de Boer, *Galatians*, helpfully points out, "the act of addressing God as "Abba" and/or as "Father" is not an action thought up by human beings themselves, but a human action wrought by God. It is the mark of God's beneficially invasive presence and activity."
[20] Dunn, *Theology of Paul*, 242, remarks, "The last Adam stands for eschatological humankind, the life of the new creation, from resurrection onwards."

coming.²¹ To be clear, Paul's portrayal of the resurrected Jesus in terms of the life-giving Spirit is not to suggest that Jesus is no longer a genuine human being.²² Paul's theology is quite clear that the risen and highly empowered Messiah is an immortalized member of the human race (Rom 5:15–19; 1 Cor 15:21, 47; 1 Tim 2:5; see also Acts 17:31).

In Romans chapter eight, Paul appears to illustrate the concepts of the Spirit of God, the Spirit of Christ, and Christ's indwelling presence as interchangeable realities for faithful believers. Consider the passage in question:

> However, you are not in the flesh but in the Spirit, if indeed the Spirit of God dwells in you. But if anyone does not have the Spirit of Christ, he does not belong to him. If Christ is in you, though the body is dead because of sin, yet the spirit is alive because of righteousness. If the Spirit of Him who raised Jesus from the dead dwells in you, He who raised Christ from the dead will give life to your mortal bodies also through His Spirit that dwells in you. (Rom 8:9–11)

Paul portrays the Spirit of God residing in the midst of the community, only to swap an interchangeable term, "the Spirit of Christ," in the following verse. This phrase likely refers to the Spirit that the risen and exalted Christ now gives, a Spirit that possesses the capacity to give life, both at conversion and at the resurrection of the dead. Paul then speaks of Christ dwelling in the presence of the community, no doubt due to the extension of his presence that the Spirit of Christ provides. One final interchangeable term, "the Spirit of Him who raised Jesus," refers to the only true God as the one who not only raised Jesus but also is the source of life for his faithful children.²³ This theology could only be produced in light of Christ's post-resurrection exaltation and empowerment to share in God's authority (Matt 28:18; Phil 2:9). A remarkably similar passage appears in Ephesians 3:16–17, where the Father's Spirit grants power to the believing community of faith "so that Christ may dwell in your hearts." In other words, the Early Church would experience the Spirit of God that the risen Christ sends as if it were Christ himself.²⁴

There are several other noteworthy examples of Jesus and the Spirit overlapping in their roles. Believers who are in Christ are illustrated as being joined to his body by the Holy Spirit: "anyone united to the Lord becomes one spirit with him" (1 Cor 6:17).²⁵ The

---

²¹ Dunn, *Christology in the Making*, 145–46, clarifies that the Spirit "is the medium of union between the exalted Christ and the Christian . . . for Paul *no distinction can be detected in the believer's experience between exalted Christ and the Spirit of God*."
²² Wright, "The Letter to the Romans," 419, insists that Paul's christology believes that the resurrected Christ is still a genuine human being: "'Jesus' for Paul regularly refers to the human being, Jesus of Nazareth, now risen and exalted by still the same human Jesus."
²³ Dunn, *Baptism in the Holy Spirit*, 148, states that "Christ was experienced through the Spirit . . . These three phrases describe precisely the same fact and experience."
²⁴ Lincoln, *Ephesians*, 206, agrees: "Believers do not experience Christ except as Spirit and do not experience the Spirit except as Christ. The implication, as far as this prayer is concerned, is that greater experience of the Spirit's power will mean the character of Christ increasingly becomes the hallmark of believers' lives."
²⁵ Dunn, *Theology of Paul*, 264, helpfully remarks, "The Spirit is the medium of Christ's union with his own."

"Spirit of Jesus Christ" provided the Apostle Paul with provision, according to Philippians 1:19.[26] Similarly, the missionary work within the Book of Acts shows an awareness that the Spirit of Jesus, which appears to be an interchangeable way of portraying the Holy Spirit, restricted some evangelistic activity (Acts 16:6–7).[27] Within the First Epistle of Peter, we find mention of the Spirit that inspired the oracles of the prophets, presumably the Old Testament prophets, being illustrated as "the Spirit of Christ within them" (1 Pet 1:10–11). Once again, we encounter the Early Christian understanding that the Holy Spirit, which believers receive in light of Christ's post-resurrection exaltation and empowerment, is the same Spirit that gave awareness to the former prophets of the promised Jewish Messiah.[28] Finally, the revelatory words of Jesus Christ, sent to the seven Asian churches, are repeatedly depicted within the Book of Revelation as the Spirit speaking to the churches. Each of the letters to the seven churches (Revelation 2–3) begins with an instruction describing Jesus himself and his exhortation to the specific congregation. However, each letter concludes with the refrain "He who has an ear, let him hear what the Spirit says to the churches." The resurrected Christ, highly empowered with the Holy Spirit by God, exercises his mediating rule and reign by making the Spirit accessible to the members of the new covenant.[29]

Conclusion

To sum up, we have observed several reasons to conclude that the Holy Spirit, the presence and power of Yahweh, was not understood to be a distinct person alongside Yahweh. We first examined how the people of God interacted with him through various forms of worship, including offering prayers and sacrifices. The Holy Spirit was never illustrated as the object of worship, prayer, or sacrifice. Second, we looked carefully at the common acts of praise, including the collection of Psalms, individual songs, and the hymns presented in the Book of Revelation. We could not find evidence that people sang psalms, songs, or hymns to the Holy Spirit. Third, we investigated the prophetic throne room visions in both testaments, looking for any depiction of the Spirit. Yet again, we came up empty-handed, for the Spirit of God is never anthropomorphized like the Father, nor does the Spirit possess its own throne. Even though the resurrected and ascended

---

[26] Hawthorne, *Philippians*, 41; Osiek, *Philippians, Philemon*, 41–42
[27] Fitzmyer, *Acts of the Apostles*, 578, observes, "This is the only time in the Lucan writings that the Spirit is described as that of Jesus; it stands in parallelism with the 'Holy Spirit' (v.6)."
[28] Dunn, *Christology in the Making*, 160, usefully states, "Peter may simply mean that the Spirit which forecast the sufferings of Christ thus proved itself to be the Spirit of Christ. That is to say, just as the character of the Christ-event provided a definition of the Spirit which enabled the first-century believer to distinguish what power and inspiration was to be recognized as of the Spirit, so the character of the Christ-event enabled the first-century believer to recognize what OT prophecies pointed to Christ, were inspired by the Spirit that inspired Christ."
[29] Beale, *Revelation*, 234, concurs: "The formular also shows that Christ's words are none other than the words of the Spirit and that Christ dwells among the Churches through the Spirit."

Jesus has a throne unto himself, the Spirit does not. Fourth, we considered whether God's people ever spoke to the Spirit in the way they talk to Yahweh and the Messiah. No verse in Scripture indicates that people spoke to the Holy Spirit. However, there was a widespread acknowledgment among the Early Church that the risen Jesus had taken over God's role as the giver of the Holy Spirit, to the point that those who experienced the Spirit would often regard it as if it were Christ himself. Taken together, this evidence strongly suggests that the Early Church believed and taught that God's Spirit was not a conscious person, but rather served as God's power and personal presence, now made available in and through the last Adam, Jesus.

After finishing this chapter, readers might wonder about the tangible and meaningful purposes that the Holy Spirit served in the new covenant, especially after spending all of this effort to demonstrate what the Spirit is not. Fortunately for us, the New Testament authors have several crucial things to say about the functions of the Holy Spirit within the body of Christ. We will explore the Spirit's role among God's renewed people in the next chapter.

30
THE SPIRIT'S ROLE IN THE NEW COVENANT

The authors of the Old Testament acknowledge that, on occasion, Yahweh empowered a select few individuals with his Spirit. These unique empowerments occurred so infrequently under the Mosaic covenant that the biblical authors emphasized the occasions for their readers. Yahweh fills Bezalel with the Holy Spirit to equip him to perform important works of craftsmanship in the tabernacle (Exod 31:2–5). The narrator of the Book of Numbers presupposes that God has shared his Spirit with Moses in order to empower him to lead and bear "the burden of the people" (Num 11:17). Joshua, Moses' successor, has also received the Holy Spirit, providing him with wisdom to lead (Deut 34:9). However, most of the people of God under the old covenant were not as fortunate as these examples. The vast majority did not receive God's Spirit. In the new covenant, however, things changed. Every single person in the body of Christ, that is, each member of the new covenant, possesses the Holy Spirit.

This chapter explores how the Holy Spirit functions within the community of the renewed people of God, that is, those who are members of the new covenant. We will begin by observing how the Spirit served as the defining badge of individual members of the worldwide family of God that was promised to Abraham. Second, we will examine how the Spirit served for the Early Church as a present installment: a down payment of the incorruptible body to be awarded to the faithful at the resurrection of the dead. Third, we will consider some of the many ways the Holy Spirit gifts and empowers the body of Christ for mission, evangelism, and service. Finally, we will look into the Spirit's role in granting Christians direct access to God, allowing his children to commune and fellowship with him in meaningful ways. This survey will help us appreciate how the Early Church viewed the Spirit as relevant and active in their daily lives and their self-understanding as the people of the only true God.

The Holy Spirit Identifies the Family of God

Let us first consider how one's possession of the Holy Spirit demonstrates membership in the new covenant people of God. In other words, Yahweh demonstrated that he has accepted people into his renewed family by gifting them his Spirit, definitively marking them out as his children.[1] Within the Book of Acts, we can observe how the early Christians slowly came to this realization. At the preaching of the gospel by Peter, we are told that "the Holy Spirit fell upon all those who were listening to the message . . . on the Gentiles" (Acts 10:44–45). After Peter and several witnesses observed demonstrable proofs of the conversion of these Gentiles, "he ordered them to be baptized in the name of Jesus Christ" (Acts 10:48). From the perspective of Peter and the early Christians, the God of Israel had brought these Gentiles into the new covenant by gifting them his Spirit.[2] When questions arose later as to whether Gentiles in the Church needed to be physically circumcised and observe the Law of Moses, Peter responded by arguing from his experience preaching the gospel that when God gave the Gentiles the Spirit, there was no longer a difference between Jews and Gentiles:

> "Brethren, you know that in the early days God made a choice among you, that by my mouth the Gentiles would hear the word of the gospel and believe. And God, who knows the heart, testified to them by giving them the Holy Spirit, just as He also did to us; and He made no distinction between us and them, cleansing their hearts by faith. (Acts 15:7–9)

By acknowledging that God has poured out his Spirit upon Gentile believers, the Jewish Christians agreed that the Gentiles were now part of the same family.

Paul the Apostle makes the same argument in his Epistle to the Galatians. After Paul departed the believers in Galatia, others came in and attempted to convince Paul's converts that they needed to observe the works of the Law of Moses. When Paul learned of this, he wrote to the Galatians, reminding them that God had given them the Holy Spirit, marking them as members of the new covenant, after they had believed the gospel.[3] Paul asks the Galatians, "Having begun by the Spirit, are you now being perfected by the flesh?" (Gal 3:3). His argument suggests that his converts began their Christian experience by receiving the Holy Spirit, the demonstrable indicator that God had accepted them.[4] Therefore, they should not seek to be perfected along fleshly and ethnically Jewish boundary-marking works. Furthermore, Paul argues that God has sent his Spirit, which transforms people into sons of God and heirs: "Because you are sons, God has sent forth the Spirit of His Son into our hearts, crying, 'Abba! Father!' Therefore you are no longer a slave, but a son; and if a son, then an heir through God" (Gal 4:6–7). In other words, the Spirit identifies believers in the Early Church as children of God.[5]

---

[1] Beale, *A New Testament Biblical Theology*, 577.
[2] Keener, *Acts*, 2:1809. Dunn, *Beginning from Jerusalem*, 400, observes that "What happened to Cornelius and his companions was manifestly no different from what happened to the first disciples on the day of Pentecost."
[3] Wright, *Paul and the Faithfulness of God*, 971–72.
[4] Levison, "Holy Spirit," 873.
[5] Dunn, "Galatians," 181.

The insistence that possession of the Spirit marks out people as genuine members of the renewed family of God permeates Paul's theology, and this truth is evident in letters other than Galatians. Those being led by the Spirit are God's children, having been adopted into the renewed family of God: "For all who are led by the Spirit of God are sons of God. For you did not receive the spirit of slavery to fall back into fear, but you have received the Spirit of adoption as sons, by which we cry, 'Abba! Father!'" (Rom 8:14–15). Furthermore, the Spirit itself bears witness that we are sons and daughters of God, having been marked out with that very Spirit (Rom 8:16).[6] We will have the opportunity to unpack and explain in detail the important meaning of justification in Chapter 37. Still, for now, we can preemptively state that Paul's converts were justified, that is, declared to be members of the new covenant "by the Spirit of our God" (1 Cor 6:11). Paul later in 1 Corinthians makes it clear that every single person in the body of Christ, regardless of race and socio-economic class, possesses the same Holy Spirit: "For in one Spirit we were all baptized into one body—Jews or Greeks, slaves or free—and all were made to drink of one Spirit" (1 Cor 12:13).[7] The theology of Paul matches the experience of Peter; anyone who receives the Holy Spirit from God has been made a child of God, a member of the family of Abraham, and a member of the new covenant.

The Holy Spirit and the Promised Resurrection Body

Although the Early Church was convinced that every believer receives the Spirit at the moment of conversion, the Spirit was believed to be a down payment of the resurrection body that Jesus would bestow upon the faithful at his second coming. Stated differently, possession of the Spirit indicated that the process of salvation had indeed begun. Still, it will not reach its full potential until the believer receives the glorified body that is immortal, incorruptible, and energized by the same Spirit of God.[8] This crucially important function of the Holy Spirit regularly appears in the writings and theology of Paul:

> We know that the whole creation has been groaning in labor pains until now; and not only the creation, but we ourselves, who have the first fruits of the Spirit, groan inwardly while we wait for adoption, the redemption of our bodies. (Rom 8:22–23)

> Now He who establishes us with you in Christ and anointed us is God, who also sealed us and gave us the Spirit in our hearts as a pledge. (2 Cor 1:21–22)

---

[6] Wright, *Into the Heart of Romans*, 105.
[7] Fee, *God's Empowering Presence*, 181. Dunn, *Theology of Paul*, 421, notes "it was their reception of the Spirit which constituted each one of them members of the body of Christ."
[8] Beale, *A New Testament Biblical Theology*, 579, helpfully declares, "The Spirit is the 'down payment' for the future consummation of resurrection life."

> we do not want to be unclothed but to be clothed, so that what is mortal will be swallowed up by life. Now He who prepared us for this very purpose is God, who gave us the Spirit as a pledge. (2 Cor 5:4–5)
>
> In him you also, when you had heard the word of truth, the gospel of your salvation, and had believed in him, were marked with the seal of the promised Holy Spirit; this is the pledge of our inheritance (Eph 1:13–14)
>
> And do not grieve the Holy Spirit of God, with which you were marked with a seal for the day of redemption. (Eph 4:30)

As Paul's theology makes clear, receiving the Spirit indicates that the work of redemption has begun.[9] Still, the full measure of redemption occurs at the resurrection, when the mortal body is swallowed up by life. In other words, possessing the Spirit anticipates the promised inheritance of resurrection life.[10]

Paul can draw these conclusions because he defines our present bodies that we possess in our mortality as a physical body, which is *energized by our living soul*. The Spirit energizes the incorruptible resurrection body, which Jesus already possesses and is promised to the faithful. This is most clearly articulated in 1 Corinthians 15:42–44, where Paul contrasts the present body with the immortal body of the resurrection:

> So it is with the resurrection of the dead. What is sown is perishable, what is raised is imperishable. It is sown in dishonor, it is raised in glory. It is sown in weakness, it is raised in power. It is sown a physical body, it is raised a spiritual body. If there is a physical body, there is also a spiritual body. (1 Cor 15:42–44)

We can gain further insight into these two bodies by examining 1 Corinthians 15:44, where the phrase "physical body" could be more accurately translated as a "soulish body" (using the Greek adjective for "soul").[11] Paul unpacks this in the following verse (1 Cor 15:45), where he cites Genesis 2:7 to recall that the first human being, Adam, became a living soul. The resurrection body of glory is illustrated as a "spiritual body," meaning it is a body defined and empowered by the Holy Spirit.[12] The spiritual body is not an inanimate, ghostly vapor. It is a real, corporeal, and tangible body, the renewal of God's good creation.[13] As such, Paul connects the hope of the incorruptible body, energized by the Holy Spirit, with the present installment of the Holy Spirit that each

---

[9] Fee, *God's Empowering Presence*, 806–8.
[10] Levison, "Holy Spirit," 875; Beale, *A New Testament Biblical Theology*, 580;
[11] See especially Wright, *Resurrection of the Son of God*, 348–56.
[12] Green, *Salvation*, 134. Dunn, *Theology of Paul*, 60, provides remarkable clarity: "The soulish body takes after Adam, of the earth, made of dust; the spiritual body will be patterned after Christ's resurrection body."
[13] Wright, *Resurrection of the Son of God*, 354, insists that Paul is describing "a body animated by, enlivened by, the Spirit of the true God."

believer possesses. The redemption that has already occurred at conversion (Col 1:14) anticipates the future redemption of the body (Rom 8:23).

The Gifts and Empowerment of the Holy Spirit

The Early Church effectively utilized the Holy Spirit's empowerment in the mission field, in sharing the gospel of the kingdom, and by serving one another. Before ascending to heaven, Jesus informed his followers that they would receive the Holy Spirit, which would equip them to be his witnesses: "But you will receive power when the Holy Spirit has come upon you; and you will be my witnesses in Jerusalem, in all Judea and Samaria, and to the ends of the earth" (Acts 1:8). The power of the Spirit energized and empowered the early Christians to preach the gospel with boldness, effectively continuing the spread of the gospel that Jesus began. The Spirit fell upon the Church definitively on the Day of Pentecost (Acts 2:1–4), and Peter, under the inspiration of this Spirit, proclaimed that the last days have arrived, just as the prophet Joel predicted: "But this is what was uttered through the prophet Joel: 'And in the last days it shall be, God declares, that I will pour out my Spirit on all flesh'" (Acts 2:16–17).[14] The Book of Acts testifies to the Holy Spirit's enablement of the early Christians in their proclamation of the gospel message. For example, the Spirit motivated Philip to evangelize the Ethiopian eunuch (Acts 8:29), called Barnabas and Paul for a missionary trip (Acts 13:2), emboldened Paul to rebuke Elymas when he opposed the preaching of the gospel (Acts 13:9), and equipped overseers to serve in the Church (Acts 20:28). In other words, the power of the Holy Spirit was vital for the success of the Early Church's missionary work.[15]

Another way the Spirit of God equipped early Christians was by giving them the courage and confidence to speak the gospel of the kingdom, even in dangerous circumstances. Jesus made it clear to his disciples that their evangelistic efforts would land them before governors and kings, at which time they were not to worry about how or what they should say in their defense, "for it is not you who speak, but the Spirit of your Father speaking through you." (Matt 10:18–20). In fact, Jesus declared that "the Holy Spirit will teach you in that very hour what you ought to say" (Luke 12:12). This is precisely what we observe in the Book of Acts where, for example, Peter, "filled with the Holy Spirit, said to" the rulers in Jerusalem the gospel truths about Christ (Acts 4:8). The rulers responded by recognizing the boldness that the Spirit-empowered Peter possessed: "Now when they saw the boldness of Peter and John and realized that they were uneducated and ordinary men, they were amazed and recognized them as companions of Jesus" (Acts 4:13). Similarly, the early Christians, who were already in possession of the Spirit, could be filled with the same Spirit "and continued to speak the word of God with

---

[14] Dunn, *Jesus and the Spirit*, 163.
[15] Ladd, *A Theology of the New Testament*, 345–46.

boldness" (Acts 4:31). The Early Church could even pray in the Spirit that others be given boldness to announce the gospel message, such as we see in Ephesians 6:

> With all prayer and petition pray at all times in the Spirit, and with this in view, be on the alert with all perseverance and petition for all the saints, and pray on my behalf, that utterance may be given to me in the opening of my mouth, to make known with boldness the mystery of the gospel (Eph 6:18–19)

In fact, the conclusion of the Book of Acts indicates that Paul preached the kingdom of God and taught about Christ "with all boldness and without hindrance" (Acts 28:31).

In addition to preaching the gospel of the kingdom and its restorative reign, many evangelists were empowered by the Holy Spirit to perform signs and wonders, thus enacting the kingdom's restoration already in the present. The accompanying of the gospel of the kingdom with restorative miracles was already on display in the ministry of Jesus (Matt 4:23; 9:35), who performed such deeds due to the power of the Spirit that God gave to him: "God anointed Jesus of Nazareth with the Holy Spirit and with power; how he went about doing good and healing all who were oppressed by the devil" (Acts 10:38).[16] At the pouring out of the Spirit on the Early Church on the Day of Pentecost, Peter's citation of Joel included the empowerment to perform *wonders* and *signs* (Acts 2:19; quoting Joel 2:30). Throughout the Book of Acts, his pairing of Spirit-enabled wonders and signs thematically accompanied the preaching of the gospel message (e.g., Acts 2:43; 4:30; 5:12; 6:8).[17] Similarly, when Paul evangelized the city of Thessalonica, his gospel "came to you not only in word, but also in power and in the Holy Spirit and with full conviction" (1 Thes 1:5).[18] The same can be seen in the way Paul spoke with the believers in Corinth; his message was "in demonstration of the Spirit and of power" (1 Cor 2:4). The experience of the Early Church included an awareness that God had gifted them his Holy Spirit to not only speak the gospel with boldness but also to perform miraculous works of power that verified the kingdom of God had broken into the present.

Naturally, the Early Church had numerous needs, as it consisted of a diverse group of believers living in various parts of the world. When the true God equipped the body of Christ with the Holy Spirit, he empowered believers to meet the needs and address the issues that arose. Although the reign and rule of God had broken into the present through the ministry of Jesus, his announcement of the kingdom, his resurrection, and the sending of the Spirit, the present evil age nevertheless continued. As such, believers possessing the powers of the age to come (Heb 6:5) had to contend with the difficulties presented in the overlap of the ages. The gifts of the Spirit offered the

---

[16] Dunn, *Jesus and the Spirit*, 70–76; Keener, *Acts*, 2:1802–4.
[17] See also Acts 7:36; 14:3; 15:12; Rom 15:19; 2 Cor 12:12; Heb 2:4.
[18] Fee, *God's Empowering Presence*, 44–45.

members of the new covenant the power of God to enact his will on earth as it is in heaven.

We could say several things about how the Holy Spirit gifted and equipped the body of Christ, so it is best to summarize the key features. First and foremost, love was to be the motivating factor in using one's Spirit-enabled gifting towards others in the Church and outsiders.[19] When Paul lists the fruit of the Spirit in Galatians 5:22–23, love sits prominently at the head of the list for good reason. When Paul summons his converts to "pursue the greater gifts" (1 Cor 12:31), followed by the claim that "the greatest of these is love" (1 Cor 13:13), it becomes apparent that Christ's selfless sacrifice served as the nonnegotiable standard for members of his body.[20] Similarly, the discussion of spiritual gifts in First Peter prioritizes love for one another "above all" (1 Pet 4:8).

Second, the purpose of the gifts is to build one another up, that is, to edify. Prophecy—the act of speaking God's words to exhort others—naturally has more edification potential than speaking in languages (also known as "tongues"), which only edifies the speaker (1 Cor 14:4).[21] Spiritual gifts should be exercised for the edification of one another (1 Cor 14:26), not for selfish reasons or to divide the body into factions. By prioritizing the building up of one another, the Early Church demonstrated that the reign of God has indeed broken into the present, resulting in love, peace, and service towards one another.

Third, God has personally provided different gifts to a diverse group of believers to foster unity in the single body of Christ. Paul stresses diversity of early Christians, but not at the expense of the unity of the body: "For just as we have many members in one body and all the members do not have the same function, so we, who are many, are one body in Christ, and individually members one of another" (Rom 12:4–5). Although the same Spirit energizes the spiritual gifts, God's will is accomplished among the different members of the body (1 Cor 12:11, 18). In other words, God is the one who wills and brings to pass the gifts of the Spirit, rather than the gifted individual.

Fourth, the early Christians found encouragement to take their personal giftings of the Spirit to serve their God-given potential. Paul strove to motivate his converts along these lines: "Since we have gifts that differ according to the grace given to us, each of us is to exercise them accordingly" (Rom 12:6).[22] First Peter echoes these encouraging remarks: "As each one has received a special gift, employ it in serving one another" in 1 Peter 4:10. Whether one has the gift of teaching, healing, prophecy, speaking in

---

[19] Dunn, *Theology of Paul*, 596.
[20] Fee, *First Epistle to the Corinthians*, 690–91, 721. Hays, *First Corinthians*, 221, argues that "love must govern the exercise of all gifts of the Spirit."
[21] Thiselton, *The First Epistle to the Corinthians*, 1084; Hays, *First Corinthians*, 235–26; Fitzmyer, *First Corinthians*, 509–10.
[22] Gaventa, *Romans*, 342; Wright, "The Letter to the Romans," 710–11.

languages, leadership, evangelism, showing mercy, or serving, one should use that spiritual gift to the glory of God. Regardless of the specific gifts one has received, the Early Church was encouraged to "do your work heartily" (Col 3:23) and to love Yahweh with *all of one's heart, soul, mind, and strength* (Mark 12:30).

Communion with God through the Holy Spirit

The Holy Spirit additionally gives members of the new covenant access to the true God, the Father. We can observe this already in the teachings of Jesus, who described the Father as the God who desired his worshipers to engage him in the Spirit: "But the hour is coming, and is now here, when the true worshipers will worship the Father in spirit and truth, for the Father seeks such as these to worship him" (John 4:23). In fact, Jesus drives the point home by insisting that those who worship God "must worship in spirit and truth" (John 4:24). In Ephesians 2:18, this point is clearly echoed: "we both have access in one Spirit to the Father."[23] Since the Father is the only true God, making him the most deserving of worship, it is to be expected that he is the goal of the act of praise. The Spirit makes this possible by transitioning strangers and aliens into the household of God, that is, into the Father's renewed family (Eph 2:19). Paul is even able to contrast the efforts of those pushing circumcision on his converts with we "who worship in the Spirit of God and glory in Christ Jesus" (Phil 3:3). We have already observed that the gift of the Spirit encourages those in the body of Christ to offer worship to "Abba! Father!" (Gal 4:6; Rom 8:16), which directly imitates how Jesus called out to God in Mark 14:36.

The Spirit also assists in prayer to God, serving an intercessory role in times of weakness. Paul illustrates the function of the Spirit interceding for the people of God in times of prayer in his Epistle to the Romans:

> Likewise the Spirit helps us in our weakness; for we do not know how to pray as we ought, but that very Spirit intercedes with sighs too deep for words. And God, who searches the heart, knows what is the mind of the Spirit, because the Spirit intercedes for the saints according to the will of God. (Rom 8:26-27)

Although believers hope for the redemption of the body—the time when the Spirit's transformation of the individual will be complete—the Spirit already offers support to the believer in the present. The Early Church *longed and groaned* for the resurrection of the body (Rom 8:23). As such, the Spirit intercedes in conveying those *inexpressible longings and groanings* to God the Father in prayer (Rom 8:26).[24] Elsewhere, Paul can speak of the common experience believers have in terms of fellowship that the Holy Spirit provides,

---

[23] Lincoln, *Ephesians*, 149–50; Best, *Ephesians*, 273–76; Ladd, *A Theology of the New Testament*, 484.
[24] Dunn, *Romans 1–8*, 476–79.

that is, a participation in the Spirit (2 Cor 13:14; Phil 2:1).[25] This fellowship was experienced among the diverse group of believers who viewed themselves as children of the only true God, the Father (Eph 2:18). Similarly, Jude can describe his readers as "praying in the Holy Spirit" (Jude 1:20)[26] when they direct their petitions "to the only God our Savior, through Jesus Christ our Lord" (Jude 1:25). This gift of the Spirit allows the renewed family of believers access to the true God.

Conclusion

To summarize, we examined several key ways in which the Early Church experienced the Spirit of God in its communities of faith. We began by noting how the Spirit marked out and identified members of the new covenant, both Jewish and Gentile believers in Jesus. Second, we observed how the overlap of the ages and the inauguration of the kingdom of God situated the Holy Spirit as the present installment of a much fuller gift to come when the dead will be raised from their graves. In this manner, the present possession of the Spirit indicated that the new creation had already broken into the present in the lives of God's people. Still, it directed the hope of those believers to the future when the mortal bodies would be clothed with immortality through the gift of eternal life. Third, we looked at various ways in which the Holy Spirit empowered members of the Early Church. In particular, we observed an emphasis on self-sacrificial love as the foremost gift, the intentional use of spiritual gifts to edify the body of Christ, the diversity of gifts given to believers, and the encouragement to use those gifts to the best of one's God-given ability. Finally, we examined the Spirit's role in granting access to the Father. Whether it be through worship or prayer, the Early Church, despite its diversity, was able to interact with God personally and intimately through God's Spirit. It is hard to deny that the early Christians experienced the Holy Spirit on a daily basis, as it was integral in the lives of the renewed family of God.

Having already noted the emphasis among the authors of the New Testament on the Holy Spirit producing love among members of the Early Church, we can now turn our attention to exploring how the Spirit leads God's children to live faithfully. Possession of the gift of the Spirit was to produce good fruit, godly living, and a way of life that is pleasing to God. In our next chapter, we will focus on the critical role of the Holy Spirit, ensuring that we are well-informed about what the Early Church believed and taught regarding the Spirit's influence on the kind of behavior appropriate for the new covenant agreement between the Father and his people.

---

[25] Dunn, *Theology of Paul*, 561–62.
[26] Watson, "The Letter of Jude," 497.

31
WALKING BY THE SPIRIT

For the early Christians, living with the Holy Spirit was an everyday experience. The involvement of the Spirit of God in the lives of God's people was so common that Paul could presuppose its regularity in his attempts to encourage his converts to walk by the Spirit's guidance: "If we live by the Spirit, let us also walk by the Spirit" (Gal 5:25). In other words, the very same Spirit that gifted, equipped, and empowered the Early Church should also help direct righteous behavior. This extremely practical function of the Holy Spirit, which was foretold by the prophets of the Old Testament, helped set early Christians apart morally and ethically from those outside of the Church, the unredeemed.

This chapter will investigate three important ways in which the biblical authors portrayed the Holy Spirit as leading God's people, particularly in the new covenant. We will begin by looking at the role that the Spirit was to play in the prophetic predictions of Ezekiel and Joel as they give rise to the hope of the renewal of the people of God and his covenant. Second, we will examine how Paul illustrates the Holy Spirit as leading God's people in the righteous behavior that is appropriate for members of the new covenant. Finally, we will observe how those who live by the Spirit find themselves fulfilling the requirements of the Law of Moses by walking according to love and holiness. This study will provide us with a deeper understanding of how God intended his people to walk in accordance with the leading of his Spirit, producing the faithful obedience that God always desires among his children.

The Promised Renewal of the People of God by His Spirit

In Chapter 16, we studied the Mosaic covenant, how Israel broke it through disobedience, and the promises of God's renewal, restoration, and forgiveness. These promises were spoken by the prophets, and within these prophetic oracles that offered comfort and hope, we find mention of Yahweh giving his Spirit to his people. The function of this Spirit within these prophetic promises of restoration was to equip and empower God's people to live faithfully.[1] Consider these promises from the prophet Ezekiel:

---

[1] Beale, *A New Testament Biblical Theology*, 560–62.

> "And I will give them one heart, and put a new spirit within them. And I will take the heart of stone out of their flesh and give them a heart of flesh, that they may walk in My statutes and keep My ordinances and do them. Then they will be My people, and I shall be their God." (Ezek 11:19–20)

> "Moreover, I will give you a new heart and put a new spirit within you; and I will remove the heart of stone from your flesh and give you a heart of flesh. I will put My Spirit within you and cause you to walk in My statutes, and you will be careful to observe My ordinances." (Ezek 36:26–27)

The promise is given in Ezekiel eleven and reaffirmed in chapter thirty-six. When Yahweh decides to renew his people, he will give them a heart that is neither hard nor unresponsive to his ways.[2] Instead, his people will receive a new heart and a new Spirit. This Holy Spirit will empower the new heart to love Yahweh with all one's heart, which echoes back to the Shema of Deuteronomy 6:4–5. The renewal of God's people will involve the gift of the Holy Spirit in order to enable them to obey God fully, from the heart.[3]

A similar prophetic oracle foretelling the gift of the Holy Spirit appears in the prophet Joel. After describing a vision of the restoration of God's people, including assurances that the land, the beasts of the field, and the children of Zion will experience an era of abundance and blessing (Joel 2:21–27), the prophet details how God will give his Holy Spirit freely to all of his people:

> "And it shall come to pass afterward, that I will pour out my Spirit on all flesh; your sons and your daughters shall prophesy, your old men shall dream dreams, and your young men shall see visions. Even on the male and female servants in those days I will pour out my Spirit." (Joel 2:28–29)

The gift of the Holy Spirit will accompany an era of blessing and renewal, which will serve to characterize the Spirit as a contributor to those promises of restoration. What is interesting to note is that Joel emphasizes that, unlike Israel's past (when the Spirit was only given to key figures like kings and prophets), Yahweh will empower men and women alike. Both sons and daughters will be able to speak forth the words of God, regardless of whether they are free or servants. Furthermore, age would not be a factor, because the Spirit will empower the old and the young alike. Joel envisions a time of new creation that will be accompanied by God giving his Spirit freely and without distinction, empowering his children to know the will of God.

When we turn our attention to the New Testament and examine how the Early Church interpreted the promises of the restored heart and the gift of the Spirit, we are fortunate again to find help in the theology of the Apostle Paul. In the second chapter of the Epistle to the Romans, Paul teases out a thought that will require several further

---

[2] Goldingay, *Biblical Theology*, 416.
[3] Horn, "Holy Spirit," 275.

chapters in his argument to unpack, namely that the renewed people of God—the body of Christ—has experienced the new heart and the new Spirit: "But a Jew is one inwardly, and circumcision is a matter of the heart, by the Spirit, not by the letter" (Rom 2:29). We can detect the clear allusions to Ezekiel 11:19–20 and 36:26–27, which both anticipate the time when Yahweh would renew his people by giving them a heart of flesh and the Holy Spirit.[4] It is also likely that Paul included in his thinking the promise of the renewal of the covenant in Deuteronomy 30:6, which speaks of a *circumcised heart* which would allow the people to love God fully and experience life: "Moreover Yahweh your God will circumcise your heart and the heart of your descendants, to love Yahweh your God with all your heart and with all your soul, so that you may live."[5] Quite clearly, Paul concluded that these promises were fulfilled by the Early Church. A close parallel to Paul's theology in Romans 2:29 appears in 2 Corinthians 3:3, where Paul speaks to the believers in Corinth: "And you show that you are a letter from Christ delivered by us, written not with ink but with the Spirit of the living God, not on tablets of stone but on tablets of human hearts." We again see the pairing of the new heart and the new Spirit, foretold by the prophet Ezekiel.

How does the Holy Spirit enable the people of the new covenant to live faithfully and righteously? Stated differently, how does the gift of the Spirit circumcise the hearts of all who possess it, males and females, so that they may love Yahweh with all their heart? The Early Church recognized that the Spirit had started a process of renewal among God's people, and that this renewal anticipates the regeneration of all creation at the second coming of Christ. We read in the Epistle to Titus that the Holy Spirit has already started the process of salvation and new creation: "He saved us, not on the basis of deeds which we have done in righteousness, but according to His mercy, by the washing of regeneration and renewing by the Holy Spirit (Titus 3:5). What is remarkable in this passage is an awareness that the regeneration and the renewal—promises that belong in the kingdom of God that has yet to be fully consummated—have broken into the present among the early Christians.[6]

The Leading of the Holy Spirit in the New Covenant

Although the new creation began at the moment of conversion, when the Spirit produces regeneration and renewal among the believers, the role of the Spirit continues to be vital. Recalling our findings from Chapter 30, Paul anticipates that his converts will follow the

---

[4] Fitzmyer, *Romans*, 323.
[5] Wright, "The Letter to the Romans," 449. Dunn, *Romans 1–8*, 127, provides an apt summary: "The circumcision God looks for is the circumcision of the heart, which the prophets called for . . . something which could be fully accomplished only by the Spirit of God."
[6] Dunn, *Baptism in the Holy Spirit*, 166.

Spirit as it leads them, proving that these converts really are members of God's renewed family: "For all who are led by the Spirit of God are sons of God" (Rom 8:14). This theology also appears in Galatians, where Paul taught that God has sent the Spirit (Gal 4:6), and Christians should follow the leading of the Spirit (Gal 5:18). Since Christians possess the Spirit, they are able to obey God from the heart. The Old Testament recounts how the children of Israel were led through the wilderness by a cloud and a pillar of fire. Deuteronomy, for example, describes how God led his children, explaining that the period in the wilderness was when God was disciplining his children:

> "You shall remember all the way which Yahweh your God has led you in the wilderness these forty years, that He might humble you, testing you, to know what was in your heart, whether you would keep His commandments or not . . . Thus you are to know in your heart that Yahweh your God was disciplining you just as a man disciplines his son." (Deut 8:2, 5)

Paul portrays the Spirit in the lives of the early Christians as similarly leading God's people, and those who faithfully and obediently follow the Spirit's leading are the children of God.[7]

As children of God in whom the new creation has already begun, the early Christians were to live in accordance with this new identity. The former life before conversation is often illustrated as the *flesh*, a life defined by frail mortality that is headed towards death. Now that believers possess the Spirit, they are children of God who are to live in a manner that is appropriate for those headed towards the fullness of the new creation, which is to come at the return of Jesus. How did the Early Church live as new creation people who followed the leading of the Spirit? Paul answers this by directing his readers to walk in light of their new identity in Christ, rather than according to their former solidarity with flesh: "walk by the Spirit, and you will not gratify the desires of the flesh" (Gal 5:16). The regeneration and renewal that has already begun should produce fruit, demonstrating the ongoing effects of the Spirit's empowerment and moral formation of those in the renewed family of God.[8] This righteous fruit, which characterizes those who are truly headed towards entrance into the kingdom of God, includes "love, joy, peace, patience, kindness, goodness, faithfulness, gentleness, self-control (Gal 5:22–23). This is not an exhaustive list, as Ephesians 5:8–9 lists goodness, righteousness, and truth as the fruit produced by those who walk as children of light. Paul hopes that his converts remain sincere and blameless until the day that Christ returns (Phil 1:10), which is only made possible by being "filled with the fruit of righteousness"

---

[7] The link between God *leading* and the identity of the *children of God* also appears in Isa 63:14–16; Jer 3:14, 19; 31:9.
[8] Hays, "The Letter to the Galatians," 328, calls attention to Paul's emphasis "on the peaceful and community-building character of the Spirit's work."

(Phil 1:11). A life consisting of Spirit-filled fruit was the standard that Paul expected of his readers, not the exception to the rule.

To follow the leading of the Holy Spirit, one must willingly and obediently choose to walk according to this new creation way of life—a life that anticipates the full redemption of all creation in the kingdom of God. However, believers felt a tension due to the inevitable fact that the overlap of the ages has left Christians in mortal bodies for the time being, despite the process of regeneration and redemption having already begun. Paul was well aware of this struggle, and he encouraged those who are in Christ to view in light of Christ's own crucifixion: "Now those who belong to Christ Jesus have crucified the flesh with its passions and desires" (Gal 5:24). In other words, those who are in Christ have followed Christ's lead by putting to death the passions and desires of the *flesh*—the former manner of life that believers lived prior to conversion.[9] In fact, the Holy Spirit empowers believers to crucify the flesh: "For if you live according to the flesh you will die, but if by the Spirit you put to death the deeds of the body, you will live" (Rom 8:13) Paul offers two choices here: either cut off completely the sinful fleshly deeds, with the help of the Holy Spirit's power, or continue living according to the flesh, which will result in death. Walking by the Spirit, as we can see, was absolutely necessary and essential in the daily lives of the Early Church.

Paul desired that his readers bear fruit that is in keeping with the Spirit's leading. He encourages those who already possess the Spirit to continue following the Spirit faithfully: "If we live by the Spirit, let us also walk by the Spirit" (Gal 5:25). There are several practical ways that walking by the Spirit can produce fruit for those who are in Christ. For example, if someone in the community of faith is caught in a trespass, those who are spiritual, that is, those who are walking by the Spirit, should show the fruit of *gentleness* in restoring the weaker person (Gal 6:1). Walking by the Spirit certainly included being receptive to the Spirit's prompting to speak the gospel to someone, as evidenced in several places in the Book of Acts.[10] The Spirit should also orient the *hope* of Christians forward to the return of Jesus, producing in them an eagerness of anticipation (Rom 15:13; Gal 5:5). Additionally, the Spirit produces the fruit of *love*, and this love can be expressed in praying for one another (Rom 15:30). Even if believers suffer persecution, the Spirit produces *joy* (1 Thes 1:6). We also find evidence that the Spirit motivated some within the Early Church to *prophesy*, that is, to speak the words of God in ways that exhorted and edified others in the body (1 Thes 5:19–20). Additionally, the Holy Spirit empowers believers with the power to exercise *self-discipline* in their lives (2 Tim 1:7). By producing these Spirit-enabled fruits, early Christians demonstrated that the new creation had indeed begun in their conversion, and this work of regeneration continued in their

---

[9] Longenecker, *Galatians*, 264.
[10] E.g., Acts 8:29 (Philip), 10:19; 11:12 (Peter), 13:2 (Barnabas and Paul).

daily lives as they looked forward to the return of Christ to consummate creation's renewal.

How Those Who Walk by the Spirit Fulfill the Law of Moses

Thus far, we have examined the promises of covenant renewal that involved God giving his people a new heart and his Spirit, noting how the Early Church experienced the fulfillment of these promises in their conversion to Christ. Furthermore, we observed how early Christians actively followed the leading of the Holy Spirit, producing fruit in accordance with the new creation that had already begun in their lives. When we examine Paul's theology closely, it becomes apparent that he is adamant that those who walk by the Holy Spirit's leading have fulfilled the obligations of the Law of Moses. As such, the early Christians who walked by the Spirit were living the sort of lives that God had expected from his people all along, and this obedience was now attainable through the circumcised heart and the empowerment of his Spirit. While we will have to wait until Chapter 42 for a fuller treatment of the Early Church's understanding of the Law of Moses, we can focus here on how the early Christians who walked by the Spirit understood their relationship to the Mosaic covenant.

We may begin by examining how those who live by the Holy Spirit fulfill the righteous requirements of the Law of Moses. Consider carefully how Paul illustrates how those who walk by the Spirit bring fulfillment to the obligations of Torah:

> For what the Law could not do, weak as it was through the flesh, God did: sending His own son in the likeness of sinful flesh as an offering for sin, he condemned sin in the flesh in order that the righteous requirement of the law might be fulfilled in us, who walk not according to the flesh but according to the Spirit. (Rom 8:3–4)

The Law of Moses was powerless to do what it was supposed to, which was to give life (Rom 7:9–10). This weakness was not the fault of the Law of Moses, as if it were bad, broken, or in any way evil. On the contrary, Paul is quite clear that "the Law is holy, and the commandment is holy and righteous and good," according to Romans 7:12.[11] The weakness was located in the flesh, that is, the unredeemed human condition in solidarity with Adam.[12] God, however, was able to offer the life that the Torah promised by commissioning Christ to take upon sinful humanity on the cross as a sacrifice. The death of Jesus made it possible for those who walk according to the Spirit to produce the life that the Law wanted to offer. In the process of living according to the Spirit, believers no

---

[11] Longenecker, *Romans*, 642; Fitzmyer, *Romans*, 469; Dunn, *Romans 1–8*, 385–86, 402.
[12] Wright, "The Letter to the Romans," 566, provides helpful clarity: "In order to exonerate Torah, Paul now analyzes further the 'I' that is caught up in sin and hence in death. To do this, he contrasts the true nature of Torah with the nature of the human being (and the Jew precisely as a person 'in Adam')."

longer walk according to the flesh—the unredeemed human condition—and in doing so, they produce the life that Deuteronomy 30:6 promised to those who love God with the heart offered in the renewed covenant. Those who live by the Spirit accomplish what the Law of Moses was unable to do.

Similarly, Paul can say that those who produce the Spirit-enabled fruit of love are living in fulfillment of the obligations of Torah.[13] Note how those who produce the fruit of love and exercise it towards their neighbor have fulfilled the Law:

> Owe no one anything, except to love one another; for the one who loves another has fulfilled the law. The commandments, "You shall not commit adultery; You shall not murder; You shall not steal; You shall not covet"; and any other commandment, are summed up in this word, "Love your neighbor as yourself." Love does no wrong to a neighbor; therefore, love is the fulfilling of the law. (Rom 13:8–10)

> For the whole law is fulfilled in one word: "You shall love your neighbor as yourself." (Gal 5:14)

Since love is the foremost fruit of the Spirit (Gal 5:22), Paul can argue here that the one who loves their neighbor is walking by the Spirit. In any case, it is clear that those who, by the Spirit, produce the fruit of love, are fulfilling the demands of the Law of Moses.

Paul taught his converts, both Jewish and Gentile believers in Jesus, that walking by the Spirit has effectively replaced the need to observe the Mosaic covenant. Quite explicitly, Paul argues that those who obediently follow the leading of the Holy Spirit are not under the obligation of the Law of Moses: "But if you are led by the Spirit, you are not under the Law" (Gal 5:18). For the Early Church, the Law of Moses was the old covenant, and since the Spirit had been given to those in the new covenant, the old covenant was no longer the binding agreement between God and his children. Paul makes this clear in Romans 7:6: "But now we have been released from the Law, having died to that by which we were bound, so that we serve in newness of the Spirit and not in oldness of the letter." Having *died with Christ* in the waters of baptism during conversion (Rom 6:4), the early Christians began walking according to the Spirit's leading, not according to the Mosaic commandments from which they were released. For those who were formerly bound in the Mosaic covenant, converting to Christ and receiving the Spirit initiated them into the new covenant. Naturally, the abundant life and the fruit that the Holy Spirit produces among those who follow its lead removes any obligation to carry

---

[13] Räisänen, *Paul & the Law*, 63, observes, "Whoever accepts the Torah, must fulfill it *in its totality;* as for Christians, the same law *in its totality* is fulfilled in the love command." Wright, "The Letter to the Romans," 725, argues that "Those who are justified by faith 'apart from the works of the Torah' (3:28) are now, perfectly logically, instructed to live as the people through whom what Torah by itself could not do is accomplished (8:3–8; 10:1–11). People who love their neighbors thus 'fulfill Torah,' both in the immediate sense that they will never do any of the things Torah forbids, and in the wider sense that through them God's way of life will be seen to advantage."

out the Mosaic Law. After listing out the fruit of the Spirit (Gal 5:22–23) and contrasting those new creation behaviors with the deeds of the flesh (Gal 5:19–21), Paul contends that those who produce this spiritual fruit live in a way that *makes the Law redundant*: "against such things there is no law" (Gal 5:23).[14] By drawing significant attention to the Spirit's role as the fulfillment of the renewal of God's people that the Law and the Prophets promised, the Early Church honored the gift of the Spirit without speaking poorly of the Law of Moses.

Conclusion

To sum up, this chapter has explored three significant ways that the authors of Scripture illustrated the Spirit of God leading and guiding the early Christians. We first investigated Ezekiel's and Joel's prophetic oracles of the renewal of God's people, particularly calling attention to the promises of the new heart and the new Spirit that God would provide during the coming restoration. The Early Church experienced this promised restoration by receiving the Spirit at their conversion to Christ, thus entering the new covenant. Second, we saw how the Holy Spirit served as a guide that led the early Christians to live righteously and produce fruit in accordance with their identity as new creation people. Finally, we surveyed Paul's theology that unflinchingly argued that those who walk by the Spirit have fulfilled the demands of Torah. By loving God from a circumcised heart and loving one's neighbor, a member of the new covenant, in possession of the Holy Spirit, is not under obligation to the Mosaic Law and its covenantal stipulations. Those who walk by the Spirit inevitably produce the life that the Law wanted to offer, but was unable to produce due to sinful humanity, not to any fault of its own. Paul repeatedly encouraged his readers to live by the Spirit's leading, thus proving to be authentic children of God— the renewed family of God in Christ. Living by the Holy Spirit was synonymous with the common Christian experience within the Early Church.

Having observed how the Early Church understood the experience of the Holy Spirit in very practical ways, readers may be asking how to live faithfully in step with the Spirit's leading in the twenty-first century. Does God still equip and empower his people with spiritual gifts? Is the Spirit still active in the body of Christ today? We will wrestle with these crucial questions in the next chapter.

---

[14] Williams, *Galatians*, 151, suggests that "Paul is actually claiming that the character produced by the Spirit fulfills the Law."

32
APPLYING PNEUMATOLOGY TODAY

Our first practical application that is drawn from our larger study of Pneumatology might appear to be the most obvious takeaway, but it is also one of the most important. It deals with the fruit of the Spirit presented in Galatians 5:22–23, emphasizing that these behaviors are ideals to which those who are being led by the Spirit are to aspire. Since those who possess the Holy Spirit are members of God's new creation already (Gal 6:15), we may view these nine behaviors as defining one who is a kingdom citizen, one destined to share in the rule and reign of Christ, which will be consummated on a worldwide scale at his return. The intersection between Pneumatology, ethics, and Eschatology makes passages like Galatians 5:22–23 extremely important. It is no surprise that Paul begins his list of characteristics defining Spirit-enabled believers with love. *Love* is the benevolent affection that God desires of his people (Deut 6:5), an act that expresses goodwill towards one's neighbor. *Joy* is the next fruit, and it conveys the gladness of one deeply moved by what God has done, is currently doing, and promises to do in the future. When we look at *peace*, we find the disposition of inner tranquility from being reconciled to God, resulting in a peacemaking orientation towards others. Since there will be peace on the earth when Christ returns to put all his enemies under his feet, possessing peace in the present anticipates what will one day become a creation-wide reality. *Patience* is the next spiritual fruit, and it refers to the ability to endure difficult people and circumstances. Patience is absolutely essential for those who are committed to remaining obedient to Christ in this present evil age, where those who are opposed to the Christian agenda seek to harass and persecute. Moving on to *kindness*, we have the quality of one who is graceful and helpful, often in the face of harsh behavior. *Goodness* is similar to kindness, although it reflects one who is ethically upright, seeking to virtuously benefit others with what God defines as good. The following fruit, *faithfulness*, is the unwavering commitment to God, his son, and their teachings. Faithfulness overlaps with being loyal and obedient, and it is often used in illustrations of marriage (to a spouse or covenantally to God). *Gentleness* is the disposition of mildness and humility. It refers not to someone who is weak and frail, for those who possess a strong conviction must channel it without being harsh or rude. Finally, we have *self-control*, which describes the mastery a person exercises over their impulses and desires. This includes control over one's speech, eating, drinking, anger, and sexual urges. Let us prayerfully embody these characteristics, seek to strengthen them in our own lives and among those in our communities of faith. Moreover, if we are performing deeds contrary to the Fruit of the Spirit, let us engage in sincere repentance, striving for the genuine change of mind that leads to godly behavior worthy of a citizen of the kingdom of God—a "new creation" person.

The second practical application drawn from our exploration into Pneumatology seeks to motivate good works from one's identity as a Spirit-led follower of Christ. One of the most notable changes between the accessibility of the Holy Spirit in the old covenant and the new covenant is that it is no longer reserved for prophets or kings. Instead, the Spirit of God has been poured out on all who believe in the gospel of the kingdom, transforming strangers into God's renewed family. The Early Church observed people from every tribe and nation receiving the Spirit, being gathered into the body of Christ. Today, those who claim Christ as their Messiah appear to be more divided than ever, despite the Early Church's ideal of a shared identity. But the function of the Holy Spirit does not stop at identification; it is also our down payment on the promised glory. The Spirit serves as the pledge of our inheritance (Eph 1:13–14), a taste of the resurrection body that swallows mortality in immortal life (2 Cor 5:4–5). We groan together with the rest of creation as the Spirit stirs within us, longing for bodies raised imperishable—sown in weakness, raised in power. Too often, believers dwell on the discomfort, pain, and difficulties of this life, longing for the life of the age to come, and in the process, many completely overlook how God's gift of the Spirit serves as a bridge from this life to the next. Your Spirit-sealed life anticipates the fullness of renewal, but the process has already begun. We have already tasted the powers of the coming age (Heb 6:5). The new birth, the renewal of the mind, the identification as God's new creation, and the transformative fruit developed by the Spirit's leading prove, without question, that God "who began a good work in you will perfect it until the day of Christ Jesus" (Phil 1:6). This empowerment by the Spirit—the very same Spirit that empowered Jesus in his ministry—propels us in mission. Jesus promised power for witness (Acts 1:8), and Pentecost marked the beginning of the Spirit's outpouring with bold proclamation and signs that confirmed the truth of the promised kingdom. The Spirit gave utterance, emboldened those proclaiming the gospel message, and nudged the faithful in the direction of those willing to listen to the Early Church's truths. In light of these vital ways that God's Spirit interacts with his faithful people, let us live out our identity as the Spirit-possessing family of God by pursuing unity and a oneness of mission. God's family should not be divided, and as agents of restoration, we can work toward healing, peacemaking, and forgiveness in the present age among our brothers and sisters. If we groan amid our mortal bodies of flesh and weakness, longing for resurrection bodies energized by the Spirit, then we collectively, as a community of faith, should orient our focus toward the future. While it is certainly true that we are individuals who often differ from one another, we are members of Christ's body, God's new family, and kingdom citizens. In other words, our identity within the new covenant is a group identity, not a solo mission. We should strive, with the fruit of patience, goodness, and love, to work together. Finally, let us deeply consider how the gift of the Holy Spirit can equip us for mission. Pray that God may fill us, empower us, and give us the bold words to speak forth his message of the kingdom of God, so that many others might know God's salvation, grace, and forgiveness.

The third application relating to our study of Pneumatology concerns how the Spirit relates to new covenant worship practices. It is fairly well documented that the Early Church worshipped, sang songs, and directed acts of cultic devotion to God and to the risen Messiah, Jesus. The Holy Spirit, however, is notably excluded from these practices as their direct object. No one is commanded to pay homage or sing to the Spirit anywhere in Scripture. Even prayer language was reserved for the true God and for the risen Jesus alone. The common Greek verbs used by the authors of the New Testament (*proskeneo* and *latreuo*) never once have the Spirit as their direct object. The book within the New Testament that contains the largest number of hymns is the Book of Revelation, and upon examining each of its hymns and the explicitly intended objects of the hymnic singing, God is most commonly the person to whom they are directed. Occasionally, the Lamb is the object of Revelation's hymns, but the Holy Spirit is never once sung to within this worship-filled book. Does this mean that the Spirit is not involved at all in Christian acts of paying homage? The answer appears to be that the Holy Spirit has been incorporated into worship, *without being the object of songs, hymns, and prayers*. Within the ministry of Jesus, he taught that true worshippers will worship the Father in the Spirit and in truth: "those who worship Him must worship in spirit and truth" (John 4:23–24). As we can observe, paying homage to God in the Spirit is closely related to worshipping "in truth" (not in doubt, unbelief, or misunderstandings). A similar illustration of Spirit-filled worship appears in Ephesians, which describes believers being filled with the Holy Spirit as they participate in several forms of worship and thanksgiving that are directed explicitly to God the Father in the name of our Lord Jesus Christ: "be filled with the Spirit, speaking to one another in psalms and hymns and spiritual songs, singing and making melody with your heart to the Lord; always giving thanks for all things in the name of our Lord Jesus Christ to God, even the Father" (Eph 5:18–20). In fact, the community of believers is exhorted to pray at all times in the Spirit (Eph 6:18; Jude 1:20), which refers to the Spirit's enabling empowerment and guidance, granting Christians full access to God. It should be apparent that the Holy Spirit was deeply integrated into acts of early Christian worship and prayer, without being the object of those acts. As we too seek to worship the true God in Spirit and in truth, let us honor God's desire by directing our songs, hymns, and prayers in accordance with approved practices—and in doing so, engaging in these devotional acts in the power of God's Holy Spirit. Let us draw on the joy that the Spirit produces in praising God and his Messiah with gladness and enthusiasm. Let us also exhibit the spiritual fruit of self-control in directing our praise to the only true God and to Jesus Christ, not to other objects of unauthorized worship. In doing so, we too can be the true worshippers that the Father seeks.

PART SIX: SOTERIOLOGY

33

THE GOSPEL OF THE KINGDOM OF GOD

One of the defining characteristics of Jesus that all four of the New Testament gospel writers present is that he was a preacher of the message of salvation. In fact, the reason the Early Church described the books of Matthew, Mark, Luke, and John as *gospels* was largely due to their interest in retelling all that Jesus said in his role as an evangelist, which resulted in his crucifixion and vindication. For example, Mark begins his biography of Jesus with the opening line, "The beginning of the gospel of Jesus Christ, the Son of God" (Mark 1:1). Mark then introduces Jesus' ministry by depicting him as a herald of the good news, the gospel of God (Mark 1:14). In other words, the four gospel accounts of Jesus' life and deeds contained summaries of Jesus preaching the gospel message, to the point that the literary genre of "gospel" owes its meaning to the main subject, Jesus, the evangelist of the gospel. It should come as no surprise that the four authors of the New Testament gospels were deeply concerned that their readers listen carefully to what Christ preached and take note of how his hearers largely rejected that evangelistic preaching.

This chapter will examine the contents of the saving gospel message, which Jesus described as the gospel of the kingdom of God. We will begin by looking carefully at the preachers of the gospel within the ministry of Jesus, and in the process, pay special attention to the contents of their message of salvation. Then we will look at the announcement of the gospel in the rest of the New Testament in order to see how the key events of the death and resurrection of Jesus affected the contents of the gospel of the kingdom. Finally, we will take stock of how the Early Church employed a variety of terms to describe the gospel message. The findings from this chapter will be significant in laying the foundation for our ongoing study of salvation, soteriology.

The Kingdom of God as the Contents of the Saving Gospel Message

When we consider the announcement of the kingdom of God, we find that John the Baptist, not Jesus, was the first to preach this message of salvation. The beginning of the Baptist's ministry is illustrated in terms of him preaching the kingdom: "In those days John the Baptist appeared in the wilderness of Judea, proclaiming, 'Repent, for the kingdom of heaven has come near'" (Matt 3:1–2). When John spoke about the kingdom, its nearness was intended to provoke a change of behavior. This change is called *repentance*, and John emphasized the need for this life-reorientation as he preached the kingdom: "Who warned you to flee from the wrath to come? Bear fruit worthy of repentance" (Matt 3:7–8; Luke 3:7–8). God's reign and rule have drawn near, and this meant that judgment was close at hand. Those who accepted John's announcement of the kingdom of God demonstrated their belief by being baptized in the Jordan River, repenting of their sins, and producing fruit. Luke summarizes the ministry of the Baptist in terms of preaching the good news: "So with many other exhortations he preached the gospel to the people" (Luke 3:18).

One of those who accepted John's preaching of the kingdom and submitted to his summons to be baptized was none other than Jesus. In fact, we see that Jesus preaches the very same message that John preached after he was imprisoned: "From that time Jesus began to proclaim, 'Repent, for the kingdom of heaven has come near'" (Matt 4:17).[1] The Gospel of Mark, importantly, situates Jesus' preaching of the gospel of the kingdom as the purpose statement of his entire work:

> Now, after John had been taken into custody, Jesus came into Galilee, preaching the gospel of God, and saying, "The time is fulfilled, and the kingdom of God is at hand; repent and believe in the gospel." (Mark 1:14–15)

These verses contain four key elements that we should not overlook.[2] First, Jesus declared that the climactic time had come to fulfillment. This is a seismic shift, as the overlap of the ages has begun with the reign and rule of God breaking into the present. By announcing that the time is fulfilled, Jesus is employing some of the strongest possible language to draw attention to the significance of his proclamation.[3] Second, the kingdom of God has drawn near. The tense of the verb "to draw near" is the perfect tense, indicating that something has happened and that its effects remain in the present. In terms of the nearness of the kingdom of God, Jesus is stating exactly what John said before him: the promised redemptive reign of God is close at hand, and it remains within reach in the present.[4] Comparing the preaching of the *kingdom of heaven* and the *kingdom of God* results in concluding that the two terms mean the same thing; for it is the God of heaven who sets up a kingdom (Dan 2:44).[5] Third, the appropriate response to this good news is to repent—to change one's thinking in light of the dawning kingdom of God. Again, the summons to repentance echoes the preaching of John the Baptist. Lastly, Jesus commands his listeners to believe in the gospel of the kingdom.[6] By placing one's trust in the gospel that Jesus preached, the believer is inevitably committing to Jesus himself, the

---

[1] Ladd, *The Presence of the Future*, 110.
[2] Beasley-Murray, *Jesus and the Kingdom of God*, 72. Dunn, *Jesus Remembered*, 408, asks, "What was it that had drawn near? God's kingdom, the exercise of God's kingship, the manifestation of God's sovereignty."
[3] Boring, "Gospel, Message," 631.
[4] Chilton, *Pure Kingdom*, 60–61.
[5] Dodd, *The Parables of the Kingdom*, 21; Ladd, *Crucial Questions About the Kingdom*, 122.
[6] Perkins, "The Gospel of Mark," 536.

one who both announces the kingdom of God and demonstrates exactly how this kingdom has broken into the present. In other words, to believe in the gospel of the kingdom that Christ preached is to, in effect, believe in Christ, the king of the kingdom.

The preaching of the gospel of the kingdom is a staple feature of Jesus' ministry.[7] Several summary statements describe Christ proclaiming the kingdom, and these summary statements often portray Jesus as habitually preaching his gospel. Consider the following passages:

> Jesus was going throughout all Galilee, teaching in their synagogues and proclaiming the gospel of the kingdom, and healing every kind of disease and every kind of sickness among the people. (Matt 4:23)
>
> Jesus was going through all the cities and villages, teaching in their synagogues and proclaiming the gospel of the kingdom, and healing every kind of disease and every kind of sickness. (Matt 9:35)
>
> "I must proclaim the good news of the kingdom of God to the other cities also; for I was sent for this purpose." (Luke 4:43)
>
> Soon afterwards he went on through cities and villages, proclaiming and bringing the good news of the kingdom of God. (Luke 8:1)
>
> When the crowds found out about it, they followed him; and he welcomed them, and spoke to them about the kingdom of God, and healed those who needed to be cured. (Luke 9:11)
>
> "Truly, truly, I say to you, unless one is born again he cannot see the kingdom of God." (John 3:3)
>
> "Truly, truly, I say to you, unless one is born of water and the Spirit, he cannot enter into the kingdom of God." (John 3:5)

The preaching of the gospel (or good news) is described with its content, and the content of the gospel that Jesus preached is repeatedly illustrated as the kingdom of God.[8] Proclaiming the gospel of the kingdom was the defining activity of Christ's ministry. Furthermore, we see evidence that the announcement of the kingdom—God's restorative reign—was regularly accompanied by what might be best described as "kingdom miracles." These restorative acts of healing offered convincing proofs that the kingdom of God had indeed broken into the present and that God's rule was nearby. As such, Jesus was remembered as not only announcing the restorative reign of God, but also as

---

[7] Ladd, *Crucial Questions About the Kingdom*, 64. Dunn, *Jesus Remembered*, 383, observes, "The centrality of the kingdom of God (*basileia tou theou*) in Jesus' preaching is one of the least disputable, or disputed, facts about Jesus."
[8] Finnegan, *Kingdom Journey*, 14.

demonstrating the truth of the promised restoration breaking into the present with healings.

Jesus did not preach the kingdom of God by himself. He recruited help in the form of disciples, those who had already placed their faith in the gospel of the kingdom. We find several passages indicating that Jesus commissioned his followers to assist in the proclamation of the gospel of the kingdom, further underscoring the importance of the message within the ministry of Jesus:

> "As you go, proclaim the good news, 'The kingdom of heaven has come near.'" (Matt 10:7)

> "This gospel of the kingdom shall be preached in the whole world as a testimony to all the nations, and then the end will come." (Matt 24:14)

> Then Jesus called the twelve together and gave them power and authority over all demons and to cure diseases, and he sent them out to proclaim the kingdom of God and to heal. (Luke 9:1-2)

> But He said to him, "Allow the dead to bury their own dead; but as for you, go and proclaim everywhere the kingdom of God." (Luke 9:60)

> "Heal the sick in it and say to them, 'The kingdom of God has come near to you.'" (Luke 10:9)

The urgency behind getting the message about the kingdom out is apparent in Jesus' attempts to recruit the disciples to share in the evangelistic mission. Matthew is careful to inform his readers that the message of the disciples ("The kingdom of heaven has come near") is the same script used by John the Baptist and Jesus alike (Matt 3:2; 4:17). Readers get the impression that Jesus valued the gospel so highly, especially when he prioritized the announcement of the kingdom over the commandment to honor one's parents in Luke 9:60.[9] The in-breaking of the kingdom of God was undoubtedly worthy of a reorientation of one's thinking, requiring the believer to prioritize the kingdom above everything else (Matt 6:33).

Before examining the preaching of the gospel after Jesus' death and resurrection, we need to consider how Jesus commanded his followers to continue preaching the kingdom after he ascended into heaven. What we find is Jesus instructing the disciples in the Great Commission to continue teaching all that Jesus taught, which would naturally include the gospel of the kingdom of God. For example, Matthew concludes with Jesus exhorting his followers to go, make disciples, baptize them, and teach them to observe all that Jesus commanded them (Matt 28:19-20). The Gospel of John portrays Jesus' post-resurrection commissioning differently: "Peace be with you; as the Father has sent me, I

---

[9] Ladd, *The Gospel of the Kingdom*, 98.

also send you" (John 20:21). The beginning of the Book of Acts details Christ's final words to his followers: "you will be my witnesses in Jerusalem and in all Judea and Samaria, and to the end of the earth" (Acts 1:8). It is reasonable to interpret Jesus' parting words before ascending to God's right hand as an exhortation to the early Christians to continue preaching the same message Jesus preached, the gospel of the kingdom of God.

The Preaching of the Gospel of the Kingdom after Christ's Resurrection

When we examine the evangelistic testimony of the Early Church for the thirty years after Jesus' resurrection, we find confirmation that the disciples continued to preach the kingdom as the contents of the saving good news.[10] However, the events of the cross, burial, and resurrection of Christ were added to the gospel of the kingdom without undermining the original message that Jesus preached. We can observe this message in several passages. For example, Acts 8:12 records the successful preaching of Philip that resulted in several in Samaria submitting to water baptism: "But when they believed Philip preaching the good news about the kingdom of God and the name of Jesus Christ, they were being baptized, men and women alike." The gospel is still defined as the gospel of the kingdom of God, while *the name of Jesus Christ* refers to everything Jesus stands for (including his death, burial, and resurrection). Philip's message consisted of both the kingdom and Jesus, not just Jesus. We find the same emphasis in the preaching of Paul. Having arrived in Rome, Paul's message to the local Jews was also about God's kingdom and Christ: "When they had set a day for Paul, they came to him at his lodging in large numbers; and he was explaining to them by solemnly testifying about the kingdom of God and trying to persuade them concerning Jesus, from both the Law of Moses and from the Prophets, from morning until evening" (Acts 28:23). The gospel Paul preached was, predictably, about the kingdom of God, while also arguing that Jesus is the fulfillment of the promises in the Law and the Prophets. The Book of Acts comes to a close by describing how Paul boldly preached the gospel of the kingdom and Jesus to the Gentiles for two full years:

> "Therefore let it be known to you that this salvation of God has been sent to the Gentiles; they will also listen." And he stayed two full years in his own rented quarters and was welcoming all who came to him, preaching the kingdom of God and teaching concerning the Lord Jesus Christ with all openness, unhindered. (Acts 28:28–31)

Once again, we see that the gospel spoken was about the kingdom and about Jesus Christ. Although the key elements of Christ's death, burial, and resurrection were a vital part of the gospel, *the message continued to be, first and foremost, the gospel of the kingdom.*[11]

---

[10] Ladd, *The Gospel of the Kingdom*, 115–16.
[11] Beasley-Murray, *Jesus and the Kingdom of God*, 75; Finnegan, *Kingdom Journey*, 14.

The Book of Acts places considerable emphasis on the preaching of the gospel message by Jesus' witnesses, the early Christians. Not only does the Book of Acts conclude with the unhindered preaching of the kingdom (Acts 28:31), but it also begins with Jesus speaking about the things concerning the kingdom of God for a period of forty days after his resurrection (Acts 1:3).[12] The themes of the kingdom and its king, Jesus Christ, serve as bookends for the Book of Acts, suggesting that the evangelism taking place within the narrative also reflects the announcement of the kingdom. We have already drawn attention to the book's purpose statement in Acts 1:8, where the risen Jesus commissions the disciples to be his witnesses from Jerusalem to Judea and Samaria, and to the ends of the earth. We have also observed that the Early Church preached the gospel of the kingdom and Jesus Christ to the Jews (Acts 28:23), to the Samaritans (Acts 8:12), and to the Gentiles (Acts 28:31). Moreover, the early Christians continued to proclaim the kingdom, including the encouragement that one must enter the kingdom amidst persecution (Acts 14:22), speaking about the kingdom in the synagogues (Acts 19:8), and preaching the kingdom to the elders in Ephesus (Acts 20:25). Without question, the Early Church's gospel message of salvation was rooted in the kingdom of God and sustained by Christ's death and resurrection. The Book of Acts demonstrates the continuity between Jesus' own preaching of the kingdom prior to his ascension and Paul's missionary efforts that brought the kingdom message to Rome.

The letters of Paul show further indication that the kingdom of God continued to be at the very heart of the gospel message. When Paul offers an autobiographical account of his conversion from a Pharisee to a Christian in the Epistle to the Galatians, he offers some details about how the churches in Judea perceived his evangelism. Those churches were hearing that, "He who once persecuted us is now preaching the faith he once tried to destroy" (Gal 1:23). Paul, in other words, was proclaiming the very same Christian faith that he formerly persecuted, meaning that Paul's gospel was the same gospel as those who were before him—the earliest Christians. When Paul describes the gospel that he preaches, he emphasizes Jesus as the son of David, which makes Jesus the *heir of David's dynasty, throne, and kingdom*:

> Paul, a bond-servant of Christ Jesus, called as an apostle, set apart for the gospel of God, which He promised beforehand through His prophets in the holy Scriptures, concerning His Son, who was born of a descendant of David according to the flesh, who was declared the Son of God with power by the resurrection from the dead (Rom 1:1–4)

The same emphasis on Christ as the descendant of David, which makes him the fulfillment of the Davidic covenant and heir of David's kingdom, appears again in 2 Timothy 2:8: "Remember Jesus Christ, risen from the dead, descendant of David,

---

[12] Dunn, *Beginning from Jerusalem*, 1008, astutely observes, "The chief features of Paul's message—'proclaiming the kingdom of God and teaching what related to the Lord Jesus Christ'—match the initial emphasis of Acts (1:3) and continue to imply complete continuity with the preaching of Jesus."

according to my gospel." The need to bring to remembrance the connection between the promised son of David and the everlasting kingdom that rightfully belonged to him was vitally important for the Early Church, especially when they preached to Gentiles who did not have the typical background in Jewish messianic expectation that the average Jew would possess from basic instruction in the synagogue. The same holds true for the important title of "Christ," which would be all too familiar to Jewish audiences, but that title was simply not in the vocabulary of Gentiles. This would require the early Christian evangelists to teach and explain these key concepts that are vital to the gospel of the kingdom. Gentiles who were introduced to the faith would be instructed in the importance of Jesus as the *son of David* and his roles as the *Christ*, the king of the kingdom of God. We can imagine Paul spending several hours explaining the person of Jesus and his role as the anointed king of the true God's kingdom to his audience in the Roman colony of Philippi, as he states, "Christ is proclaimed; and in this I rejoice" (Phil 1:18). Paul portrays himself as an evangelist of the gospel of the kingdom of God in continuity with the ministry of Jesus.

Even the Book of Revelation portrays the faithful proclamation of the gospel as preaching what Jesus proclaimed: his gospel of the kingdom of God.[13] This illustration is achieved in many ways. For example, Revelation often speaks of "the testimony of Jesus Christ," which probably refers to Jesus' own spoken testimony, the witness he gave as a preacher of the gospel. We find helpful confirmation of this interpretation by comparing the Greek word for "testimony" or "witness" (*martyria*) with the Greek word for a "martyr" (*martys*). A martyr, of course, is someone who dies because of testimony he or she offered, and the Book of Revelation is noteworthy for the fact that it is the first piece of Christian literature that defines those who suffered and died because of what they preached as "martyrs." The most noteworthy martyr that the Book of Revelation highlights is none other than Jesus Christ, whom John of Patmos illustrates in the greetings as "Jesus Christ, the faithful witness" (literally, "the faithful martyr" [Rev 1:5]). Similarly, Revelation 3:14 begins the letter to Laodicea as coming from Jesus, "the faithful and true witness" (literally, "martyr"). We know that this noun conveys one who has died for their spoken testimony because every single other instance of the noun appearing in the Book of Revelation depicts faithful Christians who were killed for their faith (Rev 2:13; 11:3, 7; 17:6). As such, the references to *the testimony of Jesus* almost certainly refer to the message Jesus testified that led to his death as a martyr:

> John, who testified to the word of God and to the testimony of Jesus Christ (Rev 1:1–2)
>
> I, John, your brother and fellow partaker in the tribulation and kingdom and perseverance which are in Jesus, was on the island called Patmos because of the word of God and the testimony of Jesus. (Rev 1:9)

---

[13] Smith, *Paradoxical Conquering*, 194–235.

> And I saw the souls of those who had been beheaded because of their testimony of Jesus and because of the word of God (Rev 20:4)

In other occurrences, Jesus' testimony, his gospel of the kingdom of God, is the faithful message that leads to early Christians suffering martyrdom. For example, the vision of the slaughtered martyrs describes that they died "because of the word of God and because of the testimony which they had maintained" (Rev 6:9). What we can observe in each of these passages is a close link between Jesus' testimony and the word of God. The phrase "word of God" was a typical early Christian shorthand reference for the gospel message. The close proximity, therefore, between Jesus' testimony and the word of God in Revelation suggests that the two phrases are interconnected; the word of God is the testimony of Jesus. All of these images highlight Jesus as a faithful preacher of the gospel of the kingdom, as well as an example of what Christian evangelists should sound like when they proclaim the gospel, even if they must also suffer as martyrs.

Early Christian Terminology for the Gospel of the Kingdom

The description of the gospel that Jesus preached as *the word of God* bears a resemblance to similar descriptors employed by the authors of the New Testament. In fact, several terms and phrases function as synonyms of the gospel of the kingdom of God. The most common example of this gospel terminology is the *word*, which has slight variations such as *the word of God*, *the word of the Lord*, and *the word of Christ*. Take, for instance, Mark's version of the Parable of the Sower, which portrays the seed message of the gospel as the *word*: "The sower sows the word" (Mark 4:14). Matthew clarifies what would have been obvious: "When anyone hears the word of the kingdom" (Matt 13:19), while Luke opts for, "the seed is the word of God" (Luke 8:11). Another clear indicator that the *word* is a shorthand for the gospel of the kingdom occurs in Luke 4:43–5:1, where Jesus announces his purpose of preaching the kingdom, while the narrator summarizes Jesus' proclamation as *the word of God*. The same connection occurs in the Book of Acts, where those scattered by persecution "went about preaching the word" (Acts 8:4), which is later unpacked as "the good news of the kingdom of God and the name of Jesus Christ" in Acts 8:12. Two verses later, this message of the kingdom is abbreviated as "the word of God" (Acts 8:14). Similarly, the evangelistic effort to speak boldly on the topic of the kingdom of God is aptly summarized as "the word of the Lord" (Acts 19:8–10). Paul carefully traces faith back to the gospel that Jesus preached, the *word of Christ*: "So faith comes from what is heard, and what is heard comes through the word of Christ" (Rom 10:17). Overall, the New Testament authors use the terms *word*, *word of God*, *word of the Lord*, and *word of Christ* as synonyms for the gospel of the kingdom over sixty times.[14]

---

[14] Boring, "Gospel, Message," 630.

It may also be helpful to distinguish these synonyms ("word" and its equivalents) with the designation that the writers of the New Testament employed to refer to the sacred texts of Scripture. When referencing scriptural books or texts, these authors use the term "Scripture," which is also sometimes rendered as the "writings." For example, Jesus would sometimes ask the question, "Have you never read the Scriptures" (Matt 21:42; Mark 12:10) or speak of some event in fulfillment of the Scriptures (Luke 4:21; John 13:18). The preaching of the word of God, however, was not a generic exposition of the texts of Scripture. When almost the entire city "assembled to hear the word of the Lord" (Acts 13:44), they were gathering to listen to the gospel of the kingdom being preached. Within the New Testament, portrayals of *preaching the word* involved proclaiming the saving gospel of the kingdom of God.

Conclusion

This chapter has examined the evangelistic testimony of the Early Church. We observed that the saving gospel message had a title, the gospel of the kingdom. John the Baptist prepared the way by summoning people to repentance and baptism in light of the kingdom drawing near. Jesus preached the same gospel, heralding it in all towns and villages. Those who repented and placed their faith in Jesus' gospel of the kingdom became disciples, and Jesus trained these followers to go forth and preach the very same message. After Jesus' death, resurrection, and ascension, the Early Church faithfully continued to proclaim the gospel of the kingdom, incorporating into this message the truths of the cross and Christ's victory over death. We also observed Paul speaking the gospel of the kingdom, which required further teaching to Gentiles who had no context or background with Judaism's expectations of the kingdom covenanted to the son of David. Furthermore, we noted how the imagery within the Book of Revelation illustrates the faithful preaching of Jesus' own testimony. Finally, we drew attention to many of the synonymous terms used by early Christians as shorthand language for the gospel of the kingdom of God, such as "word" and "word of God." Hearing and believing in the gospel of the kingdom was a crucial and nonnegotiable step in becoming a follower of Jesus.

A question may have arisen during the study of this chapter regarding the faith that Jesus called his audience to place in his saving message about the kingdom of God. What did it mean to have faith (or to believe) in Jesus and his gospel? Is faith a single action in the life of a Christian, or is it an ongoing commitment? In our next chapter, we will thoroughly explore faith and belief in order to offer some much-needed answers.

34
FAITH AND BELIEVING

When anyone translates a concept from its original language into a target language, there is almost always something lost in translation. This is inevitably the case when bringing the language of the New Testament, Greek, into English. Many are unaware that the noun *faith* (i.e., *belief*) and its verbal equivalent, *believing*, offer only a small sample of what the original Greek words can convey. Unfortunately, there is no single English word that contains all of the meanings that these crucial Greek words meant during the time of Jesus and the inception of the early Christian movement.[1] Since Jesus summoned his audiences to believe and place their faith in his gospel of the kingdom of God, we would do well to fully understand what the Greek word that lies behind "faith" meant in the context of the Early Church.

This chapter will discuss the three major meanings of the Greek noun for "faith" (*pistis*), which also apply to the Greek verb for "believing" (*pisteuo*). The first definition that we will explore is that of "trust," the dependence and reliance upon someone or a promise. The second definition of *pistis* and *pisteuo* is "loyalty," the faithful commitment that one person shows another. Lastly, the third definition, "obedience," is arguably the most important for English speakers, since the words *faith* and *believing* do not carry within them the nuance of one obeying the person in whom they place their faith. Throughout this chapter, we will examine how the preaching of the gospel among the Early Church summoned its hearers to respond with trust, loyalty, and obedience. Once we grasp these three crucially important meanings of the Greek noun and verb in question, we can better appreciate the measure of commitment that early Christians made to the initial proclamation of the kingdom and Jesus' death on the cross.

Faith as *Trust*

Beginning by looking at faith and believing as *trust*,[2] we find the Early Church following in the footsteps of the famous patriarch Abraham. This key figure was remembered as a pivotal man of trust, drawing primarily on the illustration in Genesis 15:6: "Then he believed in Yahweh; and He reckoned it to him as righteousness." Abraham's response

---

[1] Bauer et al., *Greek-English Lexicon*, 816–20.
[2] Bultmann and Weiser, "πιστεύω κτλ," 206–7. Michel, "Faith," 594, observes that "In classical Gk. literature *pistis* means the trust that a man may place in men or the gods."

to the promises of God, including a worldwide family that would descend from him as numerous as the stars of heaven, involved trusting in the certainty of God to carry out all that he said he would do. In this manner, Abraham *trusted* in Yahweh, and this confident belief in God and his promises was credited to Abraham as righteousness (i.e., covenant membership).[3]

It did not escape the notice of Paul the Apostle that Yahweh credited Abraham with righteousness in Genesis chapter fifteen, two chapters before Abraham was physically circumcised. This observation was crucial in Paul's argument that circumcision (or any other works of the Law of Moses) cannot define a person's righteous covenant status with God. Those who exhibit a trusting faith like Abraham become his children:

> so that he might be the father of all who believe without being circumcised, that righteousness might be credited to them, and the father of circumcision to those who not only are of the circumcision, but who also follow in the steps of the faith of our father Abraham which he had while uncircumcised. For the promise to Abraham or to his descendants that he would be heir of the world was not through the Law, but through the righteousness of faith. (Rom 4:11–13)

As we can see, Abraham functions as a father figure for all who believe if they "follow in the steps of faith of our father Abraham." In other words, the *trust* that Abraham had in God's promises should be imitated by his children. Paul also reaffirms one of the most important promises contained within the Abrahamic Covenant, namely, the land promise, which is expressed in Romans 4:13 as the inheritance of the entire world.[4] This significant pledge allowed early Christians who exhibited what might be called "Abrahamic faith," who confidently *trusted* in God's intentions, to embrace their roles as heirs of the world. *Trusting* God to carry out the promises he made to Abraham was a crucial aspect of faith and believing for the Early Church.

We can find several instances of Jesus praising people's *trust* in his ability to perform miracles, which verified that the kingdom of God was breaking into history through Jesus' ministry. Jesus marveled at the centurion who *trusted* in Jesus' God-given authority to heal by simply saying that it would be done: "Truly I say to you, I have not found such great faith with anyone in Israel" (Matt 8:10). When the four friends brought the paralytic to Jesus, he observes the *trust* they had in his ability to bring restoration into the present situation: "Seeing their faith, Jesus said to the paralytic, 'Take courage, son; your sins are forgiven'" (Matt 9:2). Similarly, the hemorrhaging woman put her *trust* in Jesus into action when she merely wanted to touch his garment, resulting in Jesus encouraging her confidence that he would make her well: "Daughter, take courage; your faith has made you well," according to Matthew 9:22. In fact, there are several instances

---

[3] Wright, "The Letter to the Romans," 491.
[4] Ryken et al., "Inheritance," 421; Wright, "The Letter to the Romans," 495.

in which Jesus speaks positively of someone's faith or belief, when the context makes it clear that he is primarily acknowledging one's *trust*. Look closely at these examples where faith equates to one expressing their *trust* in someone or something:

> When he entered the house, the blind men came up to him, and Jesus said to them, "Do you believe that I am able to do this?" They said to him, "Yes, Lord." Then he touched their eyes, saying, "It shall be done to you according to your faith." (Matt 9:28–29)

> "Because of the littleness of your faith; for truly I say to you, if you have faith the size of a mustard seed, you will say to this mountain, 'Move from here to there,' and it will move; and nothing will be impossible to you. (Matt 17:20)

> "Truly I say to you, if you have faith and do not doubt, you will not only do what was done to the fig tree, but even if you say to this mountain, 'Be taken up and cast into the sea,' it will happen. And all things you ask in prayer, believing, you will receive." (Matt 21:21–22)

> "And if he sins against you seven times a day, and returns to you seven times, saying, 'I repent,' forgive him." The apostles said to the Lord, "Increase our faith!" (Luke 17:4–5)

> Martha said to him, "I know that he will rise again in the resurrection on the last day." Jesus said to her, "I am the resurrection and the life; he who believes in me will live even if he dies" (John 11:24-25)

Several other passages in Jesus' life and teachings equally convey that "faith" refers to *trusting* in Jesus and his promises, but for now, we have adequately demonstrated the point.

The rest of the New Testament authors contribute to the understanding that *trust* is one of the three meanings of faith and believing. We have already seen evidence that Paul has drawn quite heavily on Abraham's example of showing faith in God and his promises. In his efforts to lay out his argument to get to the point where he can point to the faith of Abraham, Paul asserts that human beings are declared to be righteous covenant members by their initial act of *trust*, that is, their faith: "For we maintain that a man is justified by faith apart from works of the Law" (Rom 3:28).[5] The same resolute *trust* must be placed in the truth that God raised Jesus from the dead: "if you confess with your mouth Jesus as Lord, and believe in your heart that God raised him from the dead, you will be saved" (Rom 10:9). The resurrection of Christ, which presupposes the truth that all will be raised from the dead when Jesus returns, was so foundational for the Early Church that Paul could hypothesize that if Christ was not woken up from the grave, then a believer's *trust* would be futile and empty: "if Christ has not been raised, your faith is worthless; you are still in your sins" (1 Cor 15:17). Moreover, Paul can rejoice over the firmness of one *trusting* in Christ, which is the first step in following Christ: "For even

---

[5] Wright, *Paul and the Faithfulness of God*, 847, arrives at a similar conclusion: "one is reckoned to be within the justified people, those whom this God has declared 'righteous', 'forgiven', 'member of the covenant', on the basis of *pistis* and that alone."

though I am absent in body, nevertheless I am with you in spirit, rejoicing to see your good discipline and the stability of your faith in Christ. Therefore as you have received Christ Jesus the Lord, so walk in him" (Col 2:5–6).

There are even some passages in Paul that probably point to Christ as the subject of *trusting* in God.[6] One such instance appears in Galatians 2:20, where the Greek text speaks of the *faith of the Son of God*, that is, Jesus' own faithful trust in God. Paul elaborates on the *trust* that Jesus exhibited: "the Son of God who loved me and gave himself for me" (Gal 2:20). Since the end of this verse details the deeds of Christ where he served as the subject, it is almost certainly true that Christ is also the subject of the faithful *trust* earlier in the verse. A similar passage occurs in Romans 3:22, where Paul describes how God's own righteousness has been revealed through *Jesus Christ's faith*. Does this refer to a believer's faith in Jesus, or does it mean Jesus' own faithful trust in God? Although the phrase in Greek is ambiguous, the verse immediately continues by illustrating how God's righteousness is "for all those who believe; for there is no distinction." Since it would be redundant for Paul to begin by describing Christians having "faith in Jesus Christ" and then to immediately speak about all who believe, it seems more probable that the phrase "Jesus Christ's faith" refers to Jesus' *trust* in God that demonstrated God's righteousness for all who believe. These obscure passages, in all likelihood, show that Paul was aware that the ministry of Jesus was characterized by Jesus' enduring *trust and reliance on God*, resulting in Christ becoming obedient to the point of death on the cross (Phil 2:8).

Faith as *Loyalty*

Having observed several places in the New Testament where faith and believing refer to one's *trust*, we can turn to look at the second meaning of these words: *loyalty*.[7] One can understand how expressing trust in God and Christ would naturally generate an enduring commitment of faithfulness. When the early Christians placed their faith in the gospel of the kingdom, they were committing themselves to a life of *loyalty* to Jesus, the king of that kingdom. In other words, expressing belief and faith was not a one-time decision with no discernible change afterwards. One's trust would naturally lead to a firm *loyalty* between the believer and the object of their trust. It is crucially important to recognize how the Early Church expressed *loyalty* in their acts of faith and belief because, while *loyalty* is not contained within the definitions of the modern English words "faith" and "believing," *loyalty* was undoubtedly one of the key meanings of the Greek words (*pistis* and *pisteuo*).

---

[6] The full list of these disputed passages where Jesus is arguably the subject of faithful trust in God, rather than the object, is Rom 3:22, 26; Gal 2:16, 20; 3:22; Eph 3:12; Phil 3:9; Rev 14:12.
[7] Bultmann and Weiser, "πιστεύω κτλ," 208. See the helpful discussion in Wright, *Jesus and the Victory of God*, 250–51.

Several texts express the Early Church's understanding of its faithful *loyalty* to both God and Christ. In Matthew's Gospel, Christ rebukes the hypocritical scribes and Pharisees because they have neglected the weightier matters of the Law: "justice and mercy and faithfulness" (Matt 23:23). The third item in this list, faithfulness, is another word for the *loyalty* that the true God expects from all of his people. In Luke 16:10–12, we find the Greek adjective related to faith and believing, and this adjective (*pistos*) is almost always translated into English as "faithful." Naturally, "faithful" and "*loyal*" are synonyms, so this passage is worth consideration:

> "Whoever is faithful in a very little is faithful also in much; and whoever is dishonest in a very little is dishonest also in much. If then you have not been faithful with the dishonest wealth, who will entrust to you the true riches? And if you have not been faithful with what belongs to another, who will give you what is your own? (Luke 16:10–12)

In this contrasting teaching about the faithful and the dishonest, Jesus is clearly encouraging loyalty. Those who have been *loyal* to God, who entrusted them with his own wealth, will be rewarded with true wealth of their own. By offering this saying, Jesus was encouraging his audience, especially the Pharisees, to consider how they had already been entrusted with much from God and to respond appropriately. Otherwise, they will be labeled as dishonest stewards.

When Paul and Barnabas were edifying and encouraging the churches with the hope of the kingdom of God, they charged their converts to demonstrate their steadfast *loyalty* to the gospel, even in the midst of persecution. The rallying call exhorted the disciples "to continue in the faith, and saying, 'Through many tribulations we must enter the kingdom of God'" (Acts 14:22). By reminding the converts that the consummated kingdom is still in the future, they would be motivated to remain *loyal* and committed to entering what lies ahead.

The opening and conclusion of Paul's Epistle to the Romans place a crucial emphasis on living faithfully and *loyally* by obeying God and Jesus. At the beginning of the letter, Paul lays out his gospel, and in doing so, he describes how the risen Jesus has commissioned him to bring the Gentiles into a relationship that is defined by obedience and *loyalty*: "through whom we have received grace and apostleship to bring about *the obedience of faith* among all the Gentiles for his name's sake, among whom you also are the called of Jesus Christ" (Rom 1:5–6). The key phrase here, "the obedience of faith," makes abundantly clear that the purpose of one's faith and belief is to lead to an obedient relationship of *loyalty*, not just an initial decision at the time of conversion.[8] When Paul brings the epistle to a close, his final words call attention to the obedient *loyalty* that early

---

[8] Wright, "The Letter to the Romans," 420. Gaventa, *Romans*, 31, offers a helpful summary: "'The obedience that comes from faith,' then, is behavior that reflects the realm of faith—not in an abstract sense of believing as opposed to doing, but faith, reliance, and trust in the gospel of Jesus Christ, from which conduct springs."

Christians possessed to the only true God: "the obedience of faith—to the only wise God, through Jesus Christ, to whom be the glory forever! Amen" (Rom 16:26–27). Since the Epistle to the Romans begins by emphasizing this *loyal* covenant relationship between believers and the Father and concludes by stressing the very same *loyal* covenant relationship, we can confidently conclude that the heart of Romans itself is deeply interested in producing this faithful posture among its readers.[9]

The beginning of Romans chapter three is one visible expression of the loyalty that God expects among his covenant people. Paul begins by asking about what advantage there is to being Jewish, to which he affirms their privileged position as indeed valuable: "Great in every respect. First of all, that they were entrusted with the oracles of God" (Rom 3:1–2). Paul acknowledges that Yahweh shared his oracles, namely, his commandments, with Israel. Importantly, the language of "entrusting" makes it clear that God expected Israel to share these oracles with others, and in doing so, serve as the light of the world. Paul then raises the question about Israel's lack of *loyalty* in their covenant agreement with God, asking if Israel's *disloyalty* will make it impossible for God to be *loyal* to his end of the covenant agreement: "What if some were unfaithful? Will their faithlessness nullify the faithfulness of God?" (Rom 3:3). This passage demonstrates the *loyalty* nuance of God's faithfulness to his covenant promises.[10]

In several other places in the theology of Paul, we can find the concept of *loyalty* expressed in the English words "faith" and "believing." In the list of the fruit of the Spirit, we can clearly see *loyalty* (i.e., faithfulness) as evidence that the new creation has already begun among the renewed people of God: "But the fruit of the Spirit is love, joy, peace, patience, kindness, goodness, faithfulness, gentleness, self-control" (Gal 5:22–23). A similar list of fruitful behaviors appears in 1 Timothy 6:11, where *loyalty* ("faith") appears in the collection of other well-known fruits, such as love and gentleness. Paul helpfully defines for the Corinthians a steward as one who *loyally* carries out the mission they have been entrusted: "Moreover, it is required of stewards that they be found trustworthy" (1 Cor 4:2). The gospel of the kingdom summons all who believe in it to remain *loyal* and to continue to be faithful: "if indeed you continue in the faith firmly established and steadfast, and not moved away from the hope of the gospel that you have heard" (Col 1:23). Christ, the one with whom the early Christians have died in baptism, can be counted on to be absolutely *loyal* to his followers, even if they show *disloyalty*: "If we are faithless, he remains faithful, for he cannot deny himself" (2 Tim 2:13).

We can even find instances in the rest of the New Testament of a believer's faith commitment being expressed in terms of *loyalty*. The Epistle of James, for example, encourages a celebratory response to undergoing trials because the testing of one's *loyalty*

---

[9] Dunn, *Romans 1–8*, 17–18, 24.
[10] Wright, "The Letter to the Romans," 452–54; Dunn, *Romans 1–8*, 131–32

to God results in endurance: "Consider it all joy, my brethren, when you encounter various trials, knowing that the testing of your faith produces endurance" (James 1:2–3). Along the same lines, First Peter calls for great joy among its readers when their *loyalty* is tested with fire: "the proof of your faith, being more precious than gold which is perishable, even though tested by fire, may be found to result in praise and glory and honor at the revelation of Jesus Christ" (1 Pet 1:7). Furthermore, a believer's response to facing the advances of the Devil should be resistance and remaining steadfast in their *loyalty*: "Resist him, firm in your faith" (1 Pet 5:9). Finally, in the Book of Revelation, readers are urged to remain *loyal* in the midst of persecution, choosing to endure even if they have to suffer martyrdom. Consider Jesus' exhortation to the Church in Smyrna:

> Do not fear what you are about to suffer. Behold, the devil is about to cast some of you into prison, so that you will be tested, and you will have tribulation for ten days. Be faithful until death, and I will give you the crown of life. (Rev 2:10)

Testing and tribulation should not cause a believer to forgo loyalty and compromise faith. Instead, one must remain faithful, following in the example of Jesus, who died and was raised to new life because of his *loyalty* to God (Rev 2:8). Those believers who live faithfully for Christ as his witnesses may endure suffering, and this persecution of early Christians often included imprisonment and being put to death.[11] Instead of responding with violence or abandoning the faith, the readers of Revelation are exhorted to endure and remain *loyal*: "If anyone is to be taken captive, to captivity he goes; if anyone is to be slain with the sword, with the sword must he be slain. Here is a call for the endurance and faith of the saints" (Rev 13:10). This passage defines "endurance" as a nonviolent faithfulness, that is, remaining *loyal* as God's holy people. Quite clearly, the New Testament authors sought to encourage loyalty among believers, rather than simply making an empty confession of faith.

Faith as *Obedience*

Having examined how the early Christians perceived "faith" and "believing" in terms of both trust and loyalty, we can turn our attention to the third meaning, *obedience*.[12] Although obedience is closely associated with loyalty, the former emphasizes the active and willing behavior of doing the works that God expects in the new covenant agreement. It is important to recognize the nuance of obedience within the Greek terms *pistis* and *pisteuo*, particularly because the English terms "faith" and "believing" do not bring out the sense of obeying the one in whom one believes. Within the Early Church, when someone committed to believing in Jesus and his gospel of the kingdom, it went without saying

---

[11] Smith, *Paradoxical Conquering*, 79, 112; Reddish, *Revelation*, 57; Koester, *Revelation*, 280–82.
[12] Bultmann and Weiser, "πιστεύω κτλ," 205–6. Michel, "Faith," 594, summarizes the verb's usage in Greek literature: "With reference to people, *pisteuō* means to obey."

that the believer was obliged to obey the terms of that gospel message. One could not have faith without a commitment to obedience.

Within the Gospel of John, the verb "to believe" is heavily concentrated, appearing ninety-eight times. This high frequency is greater than all of the verb's occurrences in Matthew, Mark, Luke, and the Book of Acts combined.[13] In several of these instances within the Gospel of John, we can observe the sense that one's ongoing belief is exhibited in obedience to Jesus, the son of God. Take, for example, John 3:36, where the narrator portrays the ongoing act of believing in Christ as the opposite of disobeying him: "He who believes in the Son has eternal life; but he who does not obey the Son will not see life, but the wrath of God abides on him." If refusing to obey Jesus is the reverse of "believing," then believing clearly means *obeying*. The present participle "believing" illustrates an ongoing act, a continuing disposition of active obedience. Therefore, whoever is actively obeying the Son of God possesses eternal life, while those who are disobeying him bear God's wrath and will not experience life in the age to come.

Seeing how the ongoing, participial use of the verb "to believe" in the Gospel of John suggests *obedience*, we may tentatively hypothesize that the same construction in other passages might also carry the nuance of an ongoing posture of *obeying* Christ. The same construction occurs earlier in the chapter, such as in John 3:15 ("whoever believed in him may have eternal life") and 3:16 ("whoever believes in him should not perish but have eternal life"). The parallel themes in these verses with what we observed in John 3:36 suggest that the ongoing act of believing illustrates one who is actively *obeying* Jesus. We can be more confident in our interpretation when we look at how John 5:24 describes those who are listening to Jesus' gospel (that is, obeying it) and believing the God who commissioned Jesus: "Truly, truly, I say to you, he who hears my word, and believes Him who sent me, has eternal life, and does not come into judgment, but has passed out of death into life." We find confirmation that these acts of listening and believing involve true *obedience* just a few verses later, where Jesus declares that the resurrection unto new life will be given to those who perform good works: "those who did the good deeds to a resurrection of life, those who committed the evil deeds to a resurrection of judgment" (John 5:29). In any case, we can be confident that the figure of Jesus presented in the Gospel of John expected those who believed in him to *obey* his gospel message and to produce good works.

Within the Book of Acts, we find *obedience* and faith closely associated. In a description of the growing success of the gospel message, we find that both the quantity of the disciples was increasing, as well as the quality of their faithful *obedience*: "The word of God kept on spreading; and the number of the disciples continued to increase greatly in Jerusalem, and a great many of the priests were becoming obedient to the faith"

---

[13] The occurrences of the verb *pisteuo* are numbered as follows: Matthew (11), Mark (14), Luke (9), Acts (37).

(Acts 6:7). Since the faith was considered by the Early Church as something to be *obeyed*, it was obviously not regarded as a single event of belief at the moment of conversion.

When Paul describes the second coming of Christ in Second Thessalonians, he describes the judgment that will be poured out on the unfaithful and disobedient. In this illustration, Paul helpfully contrasts those who have truly believed with those who were disobedient to the gospel of the kingdom. Note carefully the difference:

> when the Lord Jesus will be revealed from heaven with his mighty angels in flaming fire, dealing out retribution to those who do not know God and to those who do not obey the gospel of our Lord Jesus. These will pay the penalty of eternal destruction, away from the presence of the Lord and from the glory of his power, when he comes to be glorified in his saints on that day, and to be marveled at among all who have believed—for our testimony to you was believed. (2 Thes 1:7–10)

On one hand, Paul portrays the destruction of the wicked here, and in doing so, he characterizes this group as those who do not know God and those who do not obey Jesus' gospel. On the other hand, those who will be glorified when Jesus returns are those "who have believed," including those who believed Paul's testimony. If belief is the opposite of disobedience, then belief must include *obedience*, particularly obedience to Jesus' gospel of the kingdom of God.

In the Epistle to the Hebrews, an entire chapter is devoted to describing what we might call the Hall of Fame of people of faith. The eleventh chapter of Hebrews describes eighteen named persons who exhibited faith, as well as several other unnamed persons. As the author describes each of these heroes of faith with the recurring introduction "By faith," it becomes clear that the author understands faith to be an obedient posture that involves good works. Several examples from this chapter bear out the practical nature of faith. Abel showed his faith by offering a better sacrifice than Cain (Heb 11:4), Noah demonstrated his faith by building an ark to rescue his family (Heb 11:7), and Abraham gave evidence of his faith: "By faith Abraham obeyed when he was called" (Heb 11:8).[14] We may observe further evidence that faith requires obedience in the description of Rahab: "By faith Rahab the harlot did not perish along with those who were disobedient, after she had welcomed the spies in peace" (Heb 11:31). By contrasting her faith with the disobedient, readers come away with the clear impression that her faith demonstrated *obedience*. The passage continues into Hebrews chapter twelve with the climactic hero of faith, Jesus Christ, the author and perfector of faith. Naturally, Jesus had faith in God, and he demonstrated his faithful obedience when he "endured the cross, despising the shame," according to Hebrews 12:2.[15] Since the author of Hebrews has earlier illustrated Jesus as one who "learned obedience from the things

---

[14] deSilva, *Perseverance in Gratitude*, 393.
[15] Johnson, *Hebrews*, 317, observes that the race set before the readers in Heb 12:2 "is a matter of moral and religious transformation in which the 'faithful' Jesus (3:1) and believers are intimately linked."

which he suffered" (Heb 5:8), we can reasonably conclude that he perfected faith specifically by *obeying* God.

One cannot study the correlation between faith and obedient works without examining the lengthy treatment of the subject in the Epistle of James. In James 2:14–26, the author thoroughly argues that true faith demands *obedient* works. He begins in 2:14 by asking whether faith without works can bring salvation, and the Greek construction of the question requires a negative answer ("no, faith without works will not save").[16] By drawing on the examples of our father Abraham and Rahab, both of whom were justified by their obedient works (James 2:21, 25), the argument is presented that faith without works is dead and empty. In fact, the only verse in Scripture that talks about "faith alone" appears in this section, where the author concludes that "a man is justified by works and not by faith alone" (James 2:24). Genuine faith must be expressed with good works performed in *obedience* to God and to Christ.

Conclusion

This chapter has examined the three primary meanings of the Greek terms *pistis* and *pisteuo*, which are translated into English as "faith" and "believing." The first definition of this noun and verb is *trust*, the steadfast and unwavering reliance on God and his promises. We also observed that faith and believing often refer to *loyalty*, which is faithful commitment and devotion within the new covenant agreement. Finally, we saw how *obedience* was the product of true faith and ongoing acts of believing, leading to a willingness to hear and do the will of God and Christ. Rather than portraying believers as making a single decision at their conversion, the authors of the New Testament illustrate the early Christians making lifelong commitments of faithfulness.

In the ancient world, each religious group had its own initiation ritual that all converts had to undergo. We have already glimpsed several elements of the Early Church's conversion process, including repentance, belief in the gospel of the kingdom of God, baptism in water, and receiving the Holy Spirit. What else took place at the moment of conversion? What did repentance look like for early Christians? And what did the life of a believer within the new covenant look like? We will have the opportunity to explore these important questions in our next chapter.

---

[16] Johnson, *James*, 237–38.

35
WHAT CONVERSION LOOKED LIKE

In the first-century Greco-Roman empire, a pagan could worship several different gods and goddesses, unconcerned about any fear of jealousy or rivalry among these deities. Pagans could honor Caesar as son of God and savior, as was common during the early period of Christianity. They could also worship Jupiter, the chief Roman god, along with Apollo, Artemis, and even Asclepius, the god of healing. Pagans could participate in the rituals present at any of the temples dedicated to these deities, take part in any festivals that honored the gods, and even offer prayers for their guidance. When a pagan converted to Christianity, however, everything changed. Being introduced to the Father, the Creator of heaven and earth, would not be adding another god to one's already existing pantheon of deities, like one might do when they make a new friend. On the contrary, when a pagan converted to Christ, all other gods and goddesses were abandoned and replaced by the God of Jesus.[1] For the Early Church, conversion was a complete life overhaul and reorientation of priorities. Paul was not exaggerating when he described early Christian converts as a "new creation" (2 Cor 5:17; Gal 6:15).

This chapter will outline the events that took place for converts of the Early Church. First, we will look at the summons for the potential convert to repent, that is, to change their thinking and behavior in solidarity with Christ. Second, the convert would respond to the gospel of the kingdom with understanding, acceptance, and belief. Third, believers would participate in the ritual act of being baptized in water by someone who has already been initiated into the early Christian movement. Fourth, the convert would receive the gift of the Holy Spirit, thereby marking them as a member of God's renewed family. Finally, believers would commit to a life of faithfulness and obedience to Jesus' teachings as they continued in the faith. These five key steps defined the salvific conversion process of early Christianity, and they are helpful for those interested in rediscovering ancient Christian practices and views of salvation as an experience in the present. Each of these topics is more fully explored in different chapters, but the aim of this chapter is to examine how they all fit together for each person entering the body of Christ.

---

[1] Dunn, *Beginning from Jerusalem*, 574, observes, "Paul was in effect requiring of Gentiles responsive to his message that they affirm the Jewish credo (Deut. 6.4—'The Lord our God is one Lord') and the first two of the ten commandments (Exod. 20.3–5; Deut 5.7–9). This Jewish understanding of God and belief about God was a fundamental stratum of Paul's gospel which continued to run through his theology."

Repentance

Beginning with the topic of repentance, it is important to define the concept as it was presented in the early Christian movement. For Jews, the idea of repenting was familiar, since it was frequently mentioned in the preaching of the Hebrew prophets. The Hebrew verb "to repent" (*shuv*) referred to the act of turning, usually turning away from behavior that was forbidden in the covenant relationship between God and Israel. For example, the prophet Jeremiah spoke the word of Yahweh to the disobedient: "Return, faithless Israel" (Jer 3:12), "Return, O faithless sons" (Jer 3:14). The prophetic summons to repent was seen as returning to a forgiving God, thereby performing a complete transformation of behavior. Both the Greek noun "repentance" (*metanoia*) and the related verb "to repent" (*metanoeo*) clearly conveyed a change of mind. To repent was to completely reorient one's thinking. This was no mere addition of spiritual knowledge to the convert. Rather, it was an incredible change in priorities, lifestyle, behavior, and motivation.[2]

The summons to repentance was often paired with the proclamation of the gospel of the kingdom of God in the preaching of the Early Church. In fact, these two elements of the early Christian message were crucially interrelated. When John the Baptist announced the gospel, he exhorted his audiences to repent, for the kingdom has come near (Matt 3:2), indicating that the dawning of the reign and rule of God was *the motivation* for repentance. In other words, the nearness of the kingdom of God, properly understood, was to persuade the listener to change their mind.[3] The urgent need to repent, because the kingdom of God was breaking into the present, was also preached by Jesus (Matt 4:17; Mark 1:15). We have already observed in Chapter 33 that Christ's preaching of the kingdom in Mark 1:15 included the call to repent in light of the climactic time arriving and the kingdom having drawn near. Indeed, *repentance* was a regular part of the preaching of Jesus:

> Then he began to denounce the cities in which most of his miracles were done, because they did not repent. (Matt 11:20)

> "The men of Nineveh will rise up at the judgment with this generation and condemn it, for they repented at the preaching of Jonah, and behold, something greater than Jonah is here." (Matt 12:41)

> "I have not come to call the righteous but sinners to repentance." (Luke 5:32)

---

[2] Dunn, *Jesus Remembered*, 500, provides the following definition of the summons to repent: "a call to 'convert', that is, for individuals to radically alter the manner and direction of their whole life, in its basic motivations, attitudes and objectives, for a society to radically reform its communal goals and values."
[3] Boring, "Gospel, Message," 632; France, *Matthew*, 104.

"Woe to you, Chorazin! Woe to you, Bethsaida! For if the mighty works done in you had been done in Tyre and Sidon, they would have repented long ago, sitting in sackcloth and ashes. (Luke 10:13)

"unless you repent, you will all likewise perish." (Luke 13:3, 5)

The in-breaking of God's reign and rule, which was taking place in and through the ministry of Jesus, motivated this habitual summons to repentance.[4] When the disciples asked Jesus to explain the Parable of the Sower, he groups his followers together as insiders who have "been given the mystery of the kingdom of God, but those who are outside get everything in parables" (Mark 4:11). As Jesus unpacks the experience of the outsiders, he cites Isaiah 6:9–10 and explains that those who see and hear, but neither perceive nor understand, are unable to return and be forgiven (Mark 4:12). In effect, Jesus is requiring belief and comprehension of his gospel of the kingdom as a prerequisite for repenting.[5]

Those who refused this invitation to repentance would find that the nearness of the kingdom included a nearness of judgment. John the Baptist illustrated the closeness of God's judgment in terms of an axe that is already laid at the root of the trees (Luke 3:9). Those who responded appropriately by demonstrating true repentance were no longer identified as outsiders, as tax collectors and sinners. In fact, Jesus responded to criticism he received for dining with repentant sinners (Luke 15:2) by telling parables detailing how there was abundant celebration in heaven over even one converted sinner (Luke 15:7, 10).[6] No doubt, the earliest disciples of Jesus learned the importance of repentance and the necessity of incorporating it into their own preaching of the gospel, in light of the thorough example set by Jesus.

In the version of the Great Commission presented in the Gospel of Luke, the disciples are commanded to proclaim "repentance for forgiveness of sins . . . to all nations" (Luke 24:47). Indeed, this emphasis on summoning potential converts to repent is precisely what we encounter in the evangelistic message of the Early Church.[7] On the Day of Pentecost, Peter summoned those present to "Repent and each of you be baptized" (Acts 2:38). A similar exhortation to repent and turn to God occurs in Peter's sermon at the temple: "Repent therefore, and turn to God so that your sins may be wiped out" (Acts 3:19). Within the Book of Acts, the call to repent is a regular feature in the preaching of the gospel:

"God exalted him at His right hand as Leader and Savior, to give repentance to Israel and forgiveness of sins." (Acts 5:31)

---

[4] Ladd, *The Gospel of the Kingdom*, 97–101; Luz, *Matthew 1–7*, 135.
[5] Marcus, *The Mystery of the Kingdom of God*, 90–96; Wright, *Jesus and the Victory of God*, 236–38; Collins, *Mark*, 249.
[6] Nolland, *Luke 9:21–18:34*, 772–74, 776; Green, *Luke*, 575–76.
[7] Keener, *Acts*, 1:972–74.

And they praised God, saying, "Then God has given even to the Gentiles the repentance that leads to life." (Acts 11:18)

"Therefore having overlooked the times of ignorance, God is now declaring to men that all people everywhere should repent, because He has fixed a day in which He will judge the world in righteousness through a man whom He has appointed, having furnished proof to all men by raising him from the dead." (Acts 17:30–31)

"I testified to both Jews and Greeks about repentance toward God and faith toward our Lord Jesus." (Acts 20:21)

"I did not prove disobedient to the heavenly vision, but kept declaring both to those of Damascus first, and also at Jerusalem and then throughout all the region of Judea, and even to the Gentiles, that they should repent and turn to God, performing deeds appropriate to repentance." (Acts 26:19-20)

Although we can confidently assume that the earliest readers of the New Testament documents were already repentant initiates of the Early Church, we can still observe evidence that repentance was the standard act of those coming to the faith. Paul reminds the Romans that God's gracious kindness leads people to repentance (Rom 2:4), but those who are stubborn and unrepentant are storing up wrath to be poured out in the Day of Judgment (Rom 2:5).[8] The Epistle to the Hebrews reinforces our findings that repentance was a fundamental and foundational part of a believer's conversion: "let us press on to maturity, not laying again a foundation of repentance from dead works" (Heb 6:1). When Second Peter responds to concerns about the delay of Christ's return, it draws attention to God's desire "for all to come to repentance" (2 Pet 3:9).

At times, however, some in the Early Church began to waver in their faithfulness to Christ, which prompted rebuke and a call to repentance. Paul wrote to the Corinthians of his fear that some who had formerly sinned "have not repented of the impurity, sexual immorality, and sensuality that they have practiced" (2 Cor 12:21). Jesus summons several churches unto repentance in the Book of Revelation.[9] For example, the Christian community in Ephesus was threatened to lose their church if they failed to demonstrate genuine works of repentance, according to Revelation 2:5. Some within the Church of Pergamum, due to compromising in ways that were unfaithful to the new covenant commitment, were summoned by Jesus to repent (Rev 2:14–16). Jesus similarly demanded repentance from the early Christian communities of faith in Thyatira (Rev 2:21–22), Sardis (Rev 3:3), and Laodicea (Rev 3:19). This evidence indicates that the people of God were not just called upon to reorient their thinking in repentance at the time of their conversion. The summons to repentance could reemerge if a believer faltered in their obedient commitment to the terms of the new covenant.

---

[8] Dunn, *Romans 1–8*, 81–84; Gaventa, *Romans*, 77–79.
[9] Smith, *Paradoxical Conquering*, 73–74, 86, 91, 97, 108–9.

Believing the Gospel of the Kingdom of God

We have already drawn attention to the pairing that regularly occurred with the call to repentance and placing one's faith in the gospel of the kingdom. The summary statement in the Gospel of Mark records the first two commands of Jesus: "Now, after John had been taken into custody, Jesus came into Galilee, preaching the gospel of God, and saying, 'The time is fulfilled, and the kingdom of God is at hand; repent and believe in the gospel'" (Mark 1:14–15). This outline of Jesus' habitual announcement of the saving gospel message urged his audiences to repent and believe. Within the life of Jesus, those who responded appropriately to his summons to repent and believe in the gospel of the kingdom showed their faith by *following* Jesus.[10] For example, after Matthew mentions how Jesus would customarily preach the kingdom and perform restorative miracles, he illustrates how many responded to his preaching: "Large crowds followed him" (Matt 4:25). Jesus often praised the faith of those who responded appropriately to his evangelistic mission (Matt 9:22, 29; 15:28; Mark 10:52; Luke 7:50). All three of the Synoptic gospel accounts headline their large collection of Jesus' parables with the Parable of the Sower, where Jesus portrays the one soil that bears fruit appropriate for reception of the gospel of the kingdom as the person who "hears the word and understands it" (Matt 13:23; Mark 4:20; Luke 8:15). One must fully accept the kingdom of God in order to have entrance into it, making belief in Jesus' gospel mandatory for salvation: "Truly I say to you, whoever does not receive the kingdom of God like a child will not enter it at all" (Luke 18:17).[11] The purpose statement of the Gospel of John explicitly draws attention to its function, which is to lead people to place their faith in Jesus as the Christ, the son of God: "these have been written so that you may believe that Jesus is the Christ, the Son of God; and that believing you may have life in his name" (John 20:31). We can reasonably conclude that all four Gospel accounts aim to convince their readers to believe in Jesus' saving gospel message.

In our previous chapter, we drew attention to the early Christian understanding of faith and believing as *trust, loyalty,* and *obedience*. When someone produces repentance as a result of hearing the gospel preached, that reorientation of their thinking would generate the full effect of faith, including trust in God and his kingdom promises, a loyal and faithful relationship, and obedience to the teachings of Jesus. The importance of believing the gospel of the kingdom, that is, wholeheartedly trusting and committing to its truth claims, cannot be overemphasized during the conversion process.

As expected, the summaries of the evangelistic efforts presented in the Book of Acts provide several instances of early Christian converts coming to believe in the

---

[10] Wright, *Jesus and the Victory of God*, 258–64; Dunn, *Jesus Remembered*, 500–3.
[11] Nolland, *Luke 9:21–18:34*, 882–83.

gospel. Having faith and believing in the gospel is portrayed as the normative response for those being initiated into the Early Church:

> But many of those who had heard the word believed, and the number of the men came to about five thousand. (Acts 4:4)

> And all the more believers in the Lord, multitudes of men and women, were constantly added to their number (Acts 5:14)

> But when they believed Philip preaching the good news about the kingdom of God and the name of Jesus Christ, they were being baptized, men and women alike. (Acts 8:12)

> And the hand of the Lord was with them, and a large number who believed turned to the Lord. (Acts 11:21)

> When the Gentiles heard this, they began rejoicing and glorifying the word of the Lord; and as many as had been appointed to eternal life believed. (Acts 13:48)

> They said, "Believe in the Lord Jesus, and you will be saved, you and your household." And they spoke the word of the Lord to him together with all who were in his house. (Acts 16:31-32)

> they received the word with great eagerness, examining the Scriptures daily to see whether these things were so. Therefore many of them believed, along with a number of prominent Greek women and men. (Acts 17:11-12)

As we can observe, the ideal response to hearing the gospel of the kingdom is to believe, that is, to place one's faith in the message and the truths expounded within it.

The theology of Paul the Apostle is one of the clearest indicators of the function that faith in the gospel had in the process of early Christian conversion. Paul demonstrates the importance of belief in several key passages. Consider, for example, the purpose statement of his Epistle to the Romans: "For I am not ashamed of the gospel, for it is the power of God for salvation to everyone who believes, to the Jew first and also to the Greek" (Rom 1:16). The salvation that God offers to all who believe in this gospel message motivates Paul's boldness to preach it.[12] Paul can also portray belief in the gospel as *receiving* and *standing* in it: "Now I make known to you, brethren, the gospel which I preached to you, which also you received, in which also you stand" (1 Cor 15:1). Believers were expected to partner with Paul in "striving together for the faith of the gospel" (Phil 1:27). Converts were exposed to the Christian hope when they listened to and placed their faith in the gospel (Col 1:5). Ephesians even recounts how members of the Early Church became believers after hearing the gospel preached: "when you had heard the word of truth, the gospel of your salvation, and had believed in him" (Eph 1:13). Paul

---

[12] Gaventa, *Romans*, 45–46.

demonstrates that believing in the saving gospel message was a standard part of initiation into the Early Church.

Baptism in Water

One of the most visible ways early Christian converts expressed their public solidarity with Christ was by being immersed in water after repenting and believing in the gospel of the kingdom. It was not uncommon for the evangelist who proclaimed the gospel to also perform the baptismal ritual upon the new believer, although this was not a requirement. Although we will offer a thorough treatment of the meaning and purpose of water baptism in Chapter 41, we can sketch out a summarized picture of how this ritualistic practice functioned for converts into the Early Church.

Beginning with the ministry of John the Baptist, we can already see the foundation of this initiation ritual, which accompanies repentance and the proclamation of the gospel of the kingdom of God. All three elements are present, as we can observe:

> Now in those days John the Baptist came, preaching in the wilderness of Judea, saying, "Repent, for the kingdom of heaven is at hand." . . . Then Jerusalem was going out to him, and all Judea and all the district around the Jordan; and they were being baptized by him in the Jordan River, as they confessed their sins (Matt 3:1–6)

Although Jesus needed no repentance, he indeed accepted John's preaching of the kingdom, choosing to preach the same message verbatim (Matt 4:17). Jesus demonstrated his agreement with John's proclamation of the kingdom of God's nearness by submitting to baptism in water (Matt 3:13–17). The Gospel of John indicates that Jesus immersed people in water, following the lead of John the Baptist (John 3:26).[13] Eventually, Jesus instructed his disciples to baptize new converts on his behalf (John 4:1–2). After dying and rising, Christ commissioned his followers to continue his evangelistic mission by making disciples, baptizing the new converts into water, and instructing them to observe all that Jesus taught (Matt 28:19–20). The practices of the Early Church demonstrate that Jesus' disciples continued to summon their audiences to repentance and belief in the gospel of the kingdom, followed by the immersion of those converts into the waters of baptism.

Luke's summaries of early Christian practices over the initial thirty years offer a helpful insight into the practice of water baptism. Peter pointedly commanded those who expressed approval with his gospel to "Repent, and each of you be baptized in the name of Jesus Christ for the forgiveness of your sins" (Acts 2:38). Luke explicitly indicates that *baptism was a required step* to be counted as a member of the new covenant community:

---

[13] von Wahlde, *The Gospels and Letters of John*, 2:157, 161; Moloney, *John*, 109; Beasley-Murray, *John*, 52.

"So then, those who had received his word were baptized; and that day there were added about three thousand souls" (Acts 2:41). Philip's preaching of the gospel of the kingdom and the name of Jesus Christ was believed, resulting in both men and women being immersed in water (Acts 8:12). After preaching to the Ethiopian eunuch, Philip baptized him immediately upon arriving at a suitable body of water (Acts 8:36–39). The same sense of urgency to baptize the new convert in water also occurs in the conversion of the repentant persecutor, Saul of Tarsus: "And immediately there fell from his eyes something like scales, and he regained his sight, and he got up and was baptized" (Acts 9:18). After the Holy Spirit was given to Cornelius and several other Gentiles with him, Peter "ordered them to be baptized" (Acts 10:48), an act that was eventually met with approval by the Jewish believers in Jerusalem (Acts 11:18). This trend continued among the Early Church's preaching to Gentiles, including the entire household of Lydia (Acts 16:14–15) and the Philippian jailor's family (Acts 16:33). Many Corinthians, including the synagogue leader Crispus and his household, "believed and were baptized" by Paul (Acts 18:8). Baptism, like repentance and faith in the gospel of the kingdom, was a standard initiation rite for early Christian converts as they publicly expressed their new solidarity with Jesus.

When we examine how the rest of the New Testament authors describe baptism in water, we find further confirmation that this initiation ritual was administered to all converts. In Romans 6, Paul presupposes that his readers have all partaken in water baptism. In typical Pauline fashion of rhetorically reminding his audience of the fundamentals of the faith, he recalls the experience of descending into the water as an act of solidarity to Christ's death: "Or do you not know that all of us who have been baptized into Christ Jesus have been baptized into his death?" (Rom 6:3). The wording of Paul's argument here presupposes that he and his readers have already participated in the baptismal act of immersion in water, being dipped down and raised up in imitation to the death and resurrection of Jesus.[14] The reality of the convert's experience in baptism can thus be spoken of as having already taken place: "we have been buried with Him through baptism into death . . . our old self was crucified with him" (Rom 6:4, 6). Similarly, Paul recalls how his Corinthian converts have already been washed in the waters of baptism: "Such were some of you; but you were washed" (1 Cor 6:11).[15] Paul takes it for granted that the Galatians have already been immersed in water, putting on Christ as a result: "For all of you who were baptized into Christ have clothed yourselves with Christ" (Gal 3:27).[16] Other statements show comparable evidence of the widespread practice of baptism:

> having been buried with him in baptism (Col 2:12)

---

[14] Dunn, *Baptism in the Holy Spirit*, 140.
[15] The only other instance of this verb "to wash" in the New Testament appears in Acts 22:16, which is in the context of water baptism.
[16] Dunn, *Baptism in the Holy Spirit*, 109, states, "Gal. 3.27 does describe the rite of water-baptism as a 'putting on Christ or state that in baptism we put on Christ.'"

> one Lord, one faith, one baptism (Eph 4:5)
>
> He saved us, not on the basis of deeds which we have done in righteousness, but according to His mercy, by the washing of regeneration and renewing by the Holy Spirit (Tit 3:5).
>
> baptism now saves you (1 Pet 3:21)

In the discussion of the elementary and foundational teachings of the Early Church, the author of the Epistle to the Hebrews lists "instruction about baptisms" after repentance and faith (Heb 6:1–2). This mention of baptisms in the plural is probably what the author means when he later illustrates the confidence of a believer who possesses a *heart that has been cleansed* and the *body washed*: "let us approach with a true heart in full assurance of faith, with our hearts sprinkled clean from an evil conscience and our bodies washed with pure water" (Heb 10:22).[17] The testimony of these various New Testament documents gives further evidence that the practice of baptizing new converts into water was normative in the Early Church.

Receiving the Holy Spirit

Although we have already seen substantial evidence of the Holy Spirit functioning as a sealing mark upon early Christians in Chapter 30, it is nevertheless essential for our present study of what conversion looked like to consider the Spirit's role in relation to repentance, belief, and water baptism. We may begin with the words of Jesus' forerunner, John the Baptist, who foretold that the coming Messiah would immerse the repentant with the Holy Spirit: "As for me, I baptize you with water; but one is coming who is mightier than I, and I am not fit to untie the thong of his sandals; he will baptize you with the Holy Spirit and fire" (Luke 3:16). While we may detect hints of John's intended emphasis in this English translation, the Greek makes it clear that the stress is upon the different persons, not the respected baptisms ("*I* baptize you . . . *he* will baptize you"). In other words, John the Baptist is not suggesting that the one coming after him will present a baptism in the Holy Spirit that negates or relativizes baptism in water. That suggestion goes contrary to the testimony of the Early Church. We have seen Jesus himself baptizing, his disciples baptizing, Jesus commissioning his followers to baptize new converts, the practice of baptism in water continued throughout the Book of Acts, and several authors of the New Testament endorsed the practice. Instead, John the Baptist is calling attention to the role of the Messiah in inaugurating the promised restoration of God's people, foretold by the prophets of the Hebrew Bible, demonstrated by the in-breaking of the Holy Spirit. In other words, the gift of the Holy Spirit that all early Christians experienced

---

[17] deSilva, *Perseverance in Gratitude*, 218.

at their conversion did not replace the ritual act of being baptized in water. As we will see, baptism and the gift of the Spirit were paired experiences.

After the ascension of Jesus, the Day of Pentecost marked the climactic moment when the Spirit was given to the Early Church. Prior to ascending into heaven, Jesus informed his followers that they would "be baptized with the Holy Spirit not many days from now" (Acts 1:5). When the Spirit came mightily upon the Early Church, Peter was quick to announce that, in fulfillment of the promises of the prophet Joel, the last days were demonstrably present: "And in the last days it shall be, God declares, that I will pour out my Spirit on all flesh" (Acts 2:17). At the conclusion of Peter's sermon, he summons his audience to repent and be baptized in water in order that they may receive the Holy Spirit as well: And Peter said to them, "Repent and be baptized every one of you in the name of Jesus Christ for the forgiveness of your sins, and you will receive the gift of the Holy Spirit" (Acts 2:38). Accordingly, those who responded appropriately to Peter's preaching received the Holy Spirit after being immersed in water. Henceforth, the Book of Acts portrays all who come to faith as receiving the Holy Spirit, regardless of their race, gender, or age.

Several passages demonstrate a common trend among early Christians who experienced the Holy Spirit at the time of their conversion. When Ananias met Saul after his encounter with Jesus on the Road to Damascus, Saul was filled with the Holy Spirit and baptized in water (Acts 9:17–18). Peter had the privilege of preaching to the first Gentile converts of the Early Church, witnessing the very moment when God gave his hearers the Spirit: "While Peter was still speaking these words, the Holy Spirit fell upon all those who were listening to the message" (Acts 10:44). The testimony put forth at the Jerusalem Council in Acts 15 that God gave the Holy Spirit to Gentiles in the same manner that he gives it to Jewish believers (Acts 15:8) was met with agreement among those present.

A few noteworthy instances offer rare exceptions to the rule within the Book of Acts.[18] One such example occurs at the very first time that the gospel of the kingdom of God was proclaimed to the Samaritans (Acts 8:5–12). Philip was successful at persuading the Samaritans to place their faith in the kingdom of God and the name of Jesus Christ, which was immediately followed by men and women getting baptized in water (Acts 8:12). However, the Samaritans did not receive the Holy Spirit until Peter and John arrived and laid their hands upon the converts. The account indicates that it was at this point that the Samaritan believers received the Spirit: "Then they began laying their hands on them, and they were receiving the Holy Spirit" (Acts 8:17). Another instance of the Holy Spirit being given to converts by the laying on of hands of the apostles appears in Acts 19 where Paul encountered around a dozen of the early followers of John the Baptist all the way up in

---

[18] See the balanced discussion in Keener, *Acts*, 2:1522–27; 3:2820–21.

Ephesus. After Paul told them about Jesus, they were baptized for a second time in the name of the Lord Jesus (Acts 19:4–5). Then, Paul laid his hand upon them, and they received the Holy Spirit (Acts 19:6). These two exceptional cases, being the first time the gospel of the kingdom was preached in Samaria and the time when disciples of John the Baptist heard about Jesus, the promised Messiah, are not normative occurrences. The Early Church did not regard these rare instances when the apostles were called upon to lay hands upon the new believers in order that they may receive the Holy Spirit as the standard practice to be enforced every single time someone accepted the gospel. The regular experience among new converts was that God gave them the Spirit without the need for the apostles to be physically present to place their hands upon those who believed.

Remaining Faithful to the Terms of the New Covenant

Thus far, we have observed that the process of conversion involves repentance, faith in the gospel of the kingdom, immersion in water, and the reception of the Holy Spirit. All four of these elements of initiation into the early Christian movement contribute to the fifth and final aspect of the conversion process, which was living obediently to the terms of the new covenant by faithfully obeying the teachings of Jesus. Those who were initiated into the body of Christ needed to continue in their faith in order to maintain a good standing in the renewed people of God. The terms of the new covenant, naturally, needed to be heeded by those within the covenant agreement, particularly by producing good fruit and performing good works.

The often-radical change of mind that occurred during the process of repentance contributed to the need to live faithfully and produce good works.[19] From the earliest period, John the Baptist, who preached a baptism of repentance, summoned his audiences to prove the legitimacy of their conversion by producing good fruit:

> "Therefore bear fruits in keeping with repentance, and do not begin to say to yourselves, 'We have Abraham for our father,' for I say to you that from these stones God is able to raise up children to Abraham. Indeed the axe is already laid at the root of the trees; so every tree that does not bear good fruit is cut down and thrown into the fire." And the crowds were questioning him, saying, "Then what shall we do?" And he would answer and say to them, "The man who has two tunics is to share with him who has none; and he who has food is to do likewise." And some tax collectors also came to be baptized, and they said to him, "Teacher, what shall we do?" And he said to them, "Collect no more than what you have been ordered to." Some soldiers were questioning him, saying, "And what about us, what shall we do?" And he said to them, "Do not take money

---

[19] Conzelmann, *The Theology of St. Luke*, 99–100.

from anyone by force, or accuse anyone falsely, and be content with your wages." (Luke 3:8–14)

It is clear that John the Baptist was remembered for demanding objective, tangible evidence to prove that a baptized convert's repentance was genuine. Fruit was required "in keeping with repentance" (Luke 3:8). Along similar lines, Christ was remembered as summoning his audiences to repentance and expecting his converts to produce the fruit of good works: "'unless you repent, you will all likewise perish.' And he began telling this parable: 'A man had a fig tree which had been planted in his vineyard; and he came looking for fruit on it and did not find any'" (Luke 13:5-6). We can observe here an example of Jesus telling a parable that encouraged fruitful, good deeds as a direct response to repentance. Even Paul the Apostle recounted his preaching of the gospel that included a call to repent and do works that proved that the repentance was genuine: "[I] kept declaring both to those of Damascus first, and also at Jerusalem and then throughout all the region of Judea, and even to the Gentiles, that they should repent and turn to God, performing deeds appropriate to repentance" (Acts 26:20). When local congregations of Christians are not being faithful to the teachings of Jesus, they are reminded of their responsibilities and summoned again to repent and perform good deeds, such as we can observe in the letter to Ephesus in the Book of Revelation: "repent and do the deeds you did at first" (Rev 2:5).[20] The Early Church believed that true repentance would result in the believer producing good works and godly fruit.

In our previous chapter, we drew attention to the crucial three-fold meaning of "faith" and "believing" as truly referring to trust, loyalty, and obedience. This means that those who believed in Jesus would naturally commit to loyalty to his teachings and obedience to all that he commanded. In Christ's Parable of the Sower, he made it clear that some "believe for a while, and in time of temptation fall away" (Luke 8:13). The ideal believer listens to the gospel of the kingdom with an honest heart, holds it fast, and bears fruit with perseverance (Luke 8:15). Jesus made it abundantly clear to those who believed in him of their responsibility to remain committed to his gospel: "So Jesus was saying to those Jews who had believed him, 'If you continue in my word, then you are truly disciples of mine'" (John 8:31). The wise are those who listen to the teachings of Jesus and obey them (Matt 7:24). When the early Christians called Jesus their Lord, it was expected that they were going to submit to that lordship and obey his commands: "Why do you call me, 'Lord, Lord,' and do not do what I say?" (Luke 6:46). When the narrators of the Gospel accounts reported that those who believed in Jesus *immediately left behind their former life in order to follow him* (e.g., Matt 4:20, 22; 8:22), this portrayal was intended to encourage similar behavior among the readers of these New Testament documents.[21] Believers were committing to a life of obedience to Jesus' teachings.

---

[20] A similar summons to repent and perform good works occurs in Rev 2:14–16, 21–22; 3:3, 19.
[21] France, *Matthew*, 148, 329–31.

We can draw comparable connections between the ritual act of a new convert being immersed in water, demonstrating an awareness among early Christians that those baptized are entering solidarity with the risen Jesus and committing to a sanctified life. Returning to Paul's discussion of baptism in Romans 6, we can see how he associates the resurrection life imparted to Jesus as he was raised from the dead and the new life of the baptized believer who comes out of the water: "Therefore we have been buried with him through baptism into death, so that as Christ was raised from the dead through the glory of the Father, so we too might walk in newness of life" (Rom 6:4). Christ's resurrection life empowers baptized believers, enabling them to walk in newness of life already in the present. In light of this baptismal empowerment, Paul can summon his readers to live faithfully:

> Even so consider yourselves to be dead to sin, but alive to God in Christ Jesus. Therefore do not let sin reign in your mortal body so that you obey its lusts, and do not go on presenting the members of your body to sin as instruments of unrighteousness; but present yourselves to God as those alive from the dead, and your members as instruments of righteousness to God. (Rom 6:11–13)

These four ethical imperatives, the first to appear in Romans, occur as a result of a believer's baptism in water. In other words, Paul is convinced that the ritual act of identifying with the death and resurrection of Jesus through immersion in water functions as the logical starting point for living a faithful life that is free from sin's reign.

Those who have entered into solidarity with the risen Jesus by emerging from the waters of baptism are described as "being raised up with Christ." The Epistle to the Colossians unpacks this much like what we see in Romans: "having been buried with him in baptism, in which you were also raised with him through faith in the powerful working of God, who raised him from the dead" (Col 2:12). The argument in Colossians builds upon the experience of being raised up with Christ through baptism, directing believers to live in a manner that reflects his resurrection life:

> Therefore if you have been raised up with Christ, keep seeking the things above, where Christ is, seated at the right hand of God. Set your mind on the things above, not on the things that are on earth . . . Therefore consider the members of your earthly body as dead to immorality, impurity, passion, evil desire, and greed, which amounts to idolatry. (Col 3:1–2, 5)

Those who have undergone the ritual act of baptism must seek the things of God, while also refusing to associate with the old solidarity that was left behind in the water.[22] Ephesians goes so far as saying that those who have been raised up with Christ, presumably by identifying with Christ through baptism, are now sharing in Christ's enthronement and rule: "and [God] raised us up with him and seated us with him in the

---

[22] Dunn, *Theology of Paul*, 470–71.

heavenly places in Christ Jesus" (Eph 2:6). We will have opportunity to discuss this passage more thoroughly in Chapters 36 and 47, but for now we can observe how early Christian converts shared in the experiences of Christ's resurrection, exaltation, and enthronement to kingship. Naturally, Christians were to live in light of their role as citizens of the kingdom of God, a role that they were, in some sense, already experiencing in the present.

Additionally, since all Christians have received the Holy Spirit, among other things, to empower them to live as God's new creation people in the present, the expectation was for believers to walk faithfully in the Spirit. Since Chapter 31 was dedicated to this topic, we need not repeat its argument here in its entirety. We may, however, review a few key points, such as Paul's expectation that his readers would produce the fruit of the Spirit (Gal 5:22–23) and commit to living obediently by following the Spirit's leading: "If we live by the Spirit, let us also walk by the Spirit" (Gal 5:25). The Spirit thus enabled and empowered the Early Church to walk like Christ and obey his teachings.

On several occasions, the authors of the New Testament make it clear, in no uncertain terms, that converts must continue in the faith as a condition to entering into the kingdom of God when Jesus returns. Members of the new covenant were expected to obey the terms of the agreement, which included fidelity to the words of Jesus and those communicated through his representatives. Note carefully the conditional language that is placed on the salvation of the Christian convert as it relates to remaining and continuing in faithfulness:

> "You will be hated by all because of My name, but it is the one who has endured to the end who will be saved." (Matt 10:22)
>
> "But the one who endures to the end, he will be saved." (Matt 24:13)
>
> "If anyone does not abide in me, he is thrown away as a branch and dries up; and they gather them, and cast them into the fire and they are burned." (John 15:6)
>
> Now I make known to you, brethren, the gospel which I preached to you, which also you received, in which also you stand, by which also you are saved, if you hold fast the word which I preached to you, unless you believed in vain. (1 Cor 15:1-2)
>
> He has now reconciled you in his fleshly body through death, in order to present you before him holy and blameless and beyond reproach—if indeed you continue in the faith firmly established and steadfast, and not moved away from the hope of the gospel that you have heard (Col 1:22-23)
>
> If we endure, we will also reign with him; if we deny him, he also will deny us (2 Tim 2:12)
>
> Christ was faithful as a Son over His house—whose house we are, if we hold fast our confidence and the boast of our hope firm until the end. (Heb 3:6)

> For we have become partakers of Christ, if we hold fast the beginning of our assurance firm until the end (Heb 3:14)
>
> For if we go on sinning willfully after receiving the knowledge of the truth, there no longer remains a sacrifice for sins, but a terrifying expectation of judgment (Heb 10:26-27)

The language that the biblical authors employ in these passages (*enduring, abiding, continuing, holding fast*) strongly exhorts early Christians to obey Jesus and his teachings. Christians are followers of Christ, so they must faithfully follow his words. The bride of Christ needed to remain loyal to her groom. Failure to stay obedient to the terms of the new covenant would result in forfeiture of one's place in the covenant community as well as a negative verdict on the Day of Judgment.

Conclusion

In summary, we have observed that the Early Church portrayed the act of conversion, that is, how converts entered into the community of Christian faith, in terms of five identifiable elements. First, the initiate would undergo repentance, which involves a sincere change of mind and behavior, resulting in genuine transformation. Second, the repentant would believe in the gospel of the kingdom of God, expressing true faith in its promises. Third, the believer would submit to being baptized in water, a ritual act performed by a member of the Christian community. Fourth, the new believer would receive the gift of the Holy Spirit, thereby marking the convert as a child of God and granting the empowerment to live a holy, sanctified life. Finally, the new convert would commit to faithfully obeying the terms of the new covenant by obeying Christ, following his teachings, and continuing to walk in holiness.

In this chapter, we have already seen evidence that several promises to be fulfilled in the age to come were described as having broken into the present in the lives of believers. We noticed that the authors of the New Testament presented the concept of salvation as both something that is future (Matt 24:13) and, in some sense, present (Tit 3:5). Similarly, we briefly drew attention to Ephesians 2:6, which illustrated the future positions of rulership in the kingdom of God as somehow already been experienced among the Early Church. Early Christians were well acquainted with the teachings of Jesus, who portrayed the kingdom of God as both presently available and yet to come, as the promised inheritance. How did Jesus' proclamation of the kingdom of God demonstrably impact how the New Testament writers employed the language of salvation? This is a crucially important topic that we will explore in our next chapter.

36

SALVATION AND THE IN-BREAKING OF THE KINGDOM

The kingdom of God occupied the central focus of Jesus' preaching ministry. He announced the kingdom as gospel, revealed the kingdom in his restorative miracles and exorcisms, and displayed his authority as the anointed king of God's kingdom. We have called attention to how the Gospel of Mark illustrates the first commands of Christ as a summons to repent and believe in the gospel of the kingdom of God (Mark 1:14–15). Jesus' preaching of the kingdom of God was, as we have seen, not simply to remind his listeners of the future promises of restoration, but also to inaugurate God's reign and rule in the present.[1] In other words, the long-anticipated kingdom of God, foretold by the prophets and covenanted to King David's dynasty of sons, has broken into the present in and through Jesus' ministry. The entirety of the New Testament reflects the reality of the age to come spilling over into the present era, with the followers of Christ receiving the primary benefits.

This chapter will examine how the inauguration of the kingdom of God affected the theology and experience of salvation within the Early Church. First, we will explore how the in-breaking of God's kingdom within the ministry of Jesus set the tone for the earliest Christians, particularly through experiencing the rule and reign of God in the present as a taste of the age to come. Second, we will look at how the Early Church's belief in the kingdom of God as both already present and not yet fully consummated affected its descriptions of salvation, redemption, justification, and several other topics. Finally, we will investigate how the promised resurrection from the dead, which is often described as the life of the age to come, also came to be described as both a present and future reality of the disciples. The impact of the kingdom of God breaking into history reoriented how the Early Church understood its own salvation as it looked back at the Messiah's first coming while also longing for his second coming in the future.

The Ministry of Jesus and the Inauguration of the Kingdom of God

No matter which of the four accounts of Jesus' life we read, it is utterly apparent that Jesus' announcement of the gospel of the kingdom and the accompanying restorative miracles dramatically shifted the perception of God's salvific work.[2] Beginning with the

---

[1] Weiss, *Jesus' Proclamation of the Kingdom*, 65–67; Ladd, *The Presence of the Future*, 133.
[2] Ladd, *The Presence of the Future*, 139.

preaching of the kingdom of God, Christ taught two important truths: his faithful disciples will inherit the kingdom in the future, but the kingdom can already be meaningfully experienced in the present.[3] We will devote thorough studies to these two truths in Chapters 46 and 47, but for now, we can briefly sketch out the assurance that those who follow Christ faithfully will enter into that coming kingdom. Jesus taught that his followers *will inherit* the earth (Matt 5:5), they *will inherit* eternal life (Matt 19:29), and they *will inherit* the kingdom when Jesus returns in glory (Matt 25:31–34). This language plainly indicates that the promised inheritance is still in the future for the Early Church. However, Christ also explained that God's kingdom can be experienced in the present whenever his rule and reign are manifested.[4] For example, the kingdom is present among the poor in spirit (Matt 5:3), or as Luke illustrates, among those who are poor (Luke 6:20), since these persons recognize their need for God and *submit to his will*. Jesus taught his disciples that the kingdom would come whenever God's will is accomplished on earth (Matt 6:10). This means that anytime a follower of Christ carries out *the will of God*, God's rule and reign are experienced, and Jesus would often draw positive attention to his disciples performing the will of God in the present (e.g., Matt 12:50; Mark 3:35). The kingdom is experienced when Jesus exorcized the demons (Matt 12:28; Luke 11:20), whenever someone humbled himself like a child (Matt 18:4), and when one forgives his neighbor, just as God has forgiven him (Matt 18:23).[5] Even the repentant tax collectors and sinners were already entering the kingdom, according to Jesus (Matt 21:31). This is what Jesus meant when he announced that the kingdom of God has drawn near (Matt 4:17; Mark 1:15).

We can also see Jesus' language of salvation presented as something that will ultimately be achieved in the future while also being experienced in the present. Matthew sets the tone for the salvific work of Christ at the beginning of his narrative when the angel informs Joseph that the child to be born "will save his people from their sins" (Matt 1:21). As readers continue through Matthew, they come to realize just how the king of God's kingdom ushers forth salvation. On one hand, Jesus clearly taught that his followers needed to remain faithful and persevere to the end in order *to be saved*, that is, in the future (Matt 10:22; 24:13). However, the same verb "to save" regularly appears when Jesus restores, heals, or otherwise rescues those who believe in him. These include the disciples when they are trapped in a boat in the middle of a great storm (Matt 8:25), the hemorrhaging woman (Matt 9:21, 22), and Peter when he was drowning in water (Matt 14:30). Even those who mocked Jesus while he hung on the cross shouted what the readers of Matthew know to in fact be true: "He saved others" (Matt 27:42). This illustration of Jesus performing restorative miracles and feats of rescue further demonstrates how the kingdom of God has broken into the present. Jesus' portrayal of

---

[3] Green, *Salvation*, 104; Ladd, *Crucial Questions About the Kingdom*, 65.
[4] Ladd, *The Presence of the Future*, 130.
[5] Beasley-Murray, *Jesus and the Kingdom of God*, 115–17.

the future inheritance of salvation as something that is already attainable also appears in the other three Gospel accounts.[6] Readers are left with the clear impression that the salvation belonging in the age to come, when God's kingdom is fully consummated on this earth, has spilled over into the present in and through the ministry of Christ.

One telling example of Jesus explaining how his ministry was ushering in God's rule and reign into the present is his explanation of his identity to John the Baptist. It was widely held that the promised Messiah would arrive and defeat evil. John, however, had been imprisoned by those whom most Jews would consider among the evil that the Messiah needed to vanquish. This sure did not feel like the king and God's kingdom had arrived. Therefore, John sent two of his disciples to ask Jesus if he was the Expected One, or whether they should look for someone else, according to Luke 7:19. The response indicates that God's restorative reign and rule were already being experienced by many:

> In that hour, he healed many people of diseases and plagues and evil spirits, and on many who were blind, he bestowed sight. And he answered them, "Go and tell John what you have seen and heard: the blind receive their sight, the lame walk, lepers are cleansed, and the deaf hear, the dead are raised up, the poor have good news preached to them. And blessed is the one who is not offended by me." (Luke 7:21–23)

From the vantage point of John the Baptist, it did not appear as if Jesus was the promised messianic bringer of God's kingdom. However, from Jesus' perspective, the promises of the age to come have indeed broken into the present. In Jesus' response, he quotes a portion of Isaiah 35:5–6 in order to relate to John how the prophetic promises of the renewal of creation, which included the restoration of ailing human beings, were already underway due to his kingdom miracles.[7] Isaiah's prophecy of the eyes of the blind being opened, the deaf hearing, and the lame leaping was coming true in the present. Even the resurrection of the dead, which was meant to be the event that transitioned this present age into the age to come, had already begun with the raising of the widow's son (Luke 7:14).[8] In short, Jesus' clarification to John and his disciples indicates that he was consciously aware that his ministry was contributing to the in-breaking of the kingdom of God into the present and that those who believe and are not offended by Jesus could already experience these promises of restoration.[9]

---

[6] For salvation as that which is attained in the future, see Mark 9:43–47; 10:30; 13:13; Luke 14:14; 18:30; 20:35–36; John 5:28–29; 6:39–40, 44; 12:48. Present references to salvation include Mark 3:4; 5:23; 6:56; 10:52; Luke 7:50; 8:12, 36; 13:23; 19:9; John 3:17; 5:34; 12:47.
[7] Ladd, *The Presence of the Future*, 113.
[8] Hagner, "Gospel, Kingdom, and Resurrection," 119. The Gospel accounts record Jesus raising Jairus' daughter (Matt 9:25; Mark 5:41; Luke 8:54), Lazarus (John 11:43), and the widow's son (Luke 7:14).
[9] Beasley-Murray, *Jesus and the Kingdom of God*, 80–83.

The *Already* and the *Not Yet* in the Theology of the Early Church

Jesus' proclamation of the kingdom of God, his teachings about salvation, and his acknowledgment that his restorative miracles were making the promises of the future kingdom available in the present left a considerable impact on the Early Church.[10] Outside of the four Gospel accounts, the writers of the New Testament continued to portray the key events and promises that defined the age to come as having broken into the present. This theology, known as the inauguration of the kingdom of God or the overlap of the ages, appears several times in the beliefs and teachings of early Christians. Following the lead of Christ himself, the Early Church portrayed the concept of *salvation* as something that is essentially future while also stressing that believers have already been saved in the present.[11] Several texts indicate a widespread awareness that salvation, properly speaking, takes place in the future when Christ's followers attain the resurrection and receive immortality:

> will we be saved through him from the wrath of God. (Rom 5:9)

> For salvation is nearer to us now than when we first believed. (Rom 13:11)

> For God has not destined us for wrath, but for obtaining salvation through our Lord Jesus Christ (1 Thes 5:9)

> so Christ, having been offered once to bear the sins of many, will appear a second time, not to deal with sin, but to save those who are eagerly waiting for him. (Heb 9:28)

> a salvation ready to be revealed in the last time. (1 Pet 1:5)

In addition to these texts, the New Testament authors portrayed the future promises of salvation as having already spilled over into the present in light of what Jesus accomplished in his ministry. Consider how these biblical writers illustrate salvation as a present possession:

> They said, "Believe in the Lord Jesus, and you will be saved, you and your household." (Acts 16:31)

> For in hope we have been saved (Rom 8:24)

> For by grace you have been saved through faith (Eph 2:8)

> [God] who has saved us and called us with a holy calling (2 Tim 1:9)

> baptism now saves you (1 Pet 3:21)

---

[10] Dunn, *Theology of Paul*, 318–19.
[11] Fee, *God's Empowering Presence*, 804.

Within the theology of Paul, we can observe an awareness that the process of salvation is ongoing, particularly in his use of present passive participles to illustrate how believers are currently "being saved" (1 Cor 1:18; 15:2; 2 Cor 2:15). Therefore, a complete picture of the Early Church's teachings on salvation is that it remains a future hope, it has broken into the present, and faithful believers are already experiencing the process of this renewal.[12]

Jesus' preaching of the kingdom of God as both present and future also directly influenced the Early Church's understanding of *redemption*. The concept of redemption, which several Greek nouns and verbs convey with imagery of ransoming, purchasing, or buying someone's freedom, was widely used by the writers of the New Testament. Redemption is illustrated as something yet future, to be attained at the resurrection of the body:

> We ourselves groan within ourselves, waiting eagerly for our adoption as sons, the redemption of our body (Rom 8:23).
>
> And do not grieve the Holy Spirit of God, with which you were marked with a seal for the day of redemption. (Eph 4:30)

The language of redemption and the status of believers as those who have been redeemed also occur as a present reality:

> being justified as a gift by His grace through the redemption which is in Christ Jesus (Rom 3:24)
>
> Christ redeemed us from the curse of the Law (Gal 3:13)
>
> In him we have redemption through his blood (Eph 1:7)

Like salvation, the Early Church characterized redemption as a future hope that has already been inaugurated in the present.[13]

Additionally, we can observe the language of *justification* being transformed by the in-breaking of the kingdom of God.[14] Although we will provide a comprehensive treatment of the Early Church's theology of justification in the following chapter, we can draw attention to its application in a manner relevant to our present study. Paul famously associated justification with the judgment that is to take place on the last day, *on the Day of Judgment*: "for it is not the hearers of the Law who are just before God, but the doers of the Law will be justified" (Rom 2:13). However, it was the conviction of Paul and those in the Early Church that the righteous verdict to be issued on the Day of Judgment has

---

[12] Green, *Salvation*, 129.
[13] Fee, *God's Empowering Presence*, 804.
[14] In the ministry of Jesus, we can already find evidence of justification as both present (Luke 18:14) and future (Matt 12:37).

already been offered in the present, resulting in the justification and the declaration of early Christians as members of the new covenant family of God. Consider these texts that emphasize the reality that believers have already received the justifying verdict:

> For we maintain that a man is justified by faith apart from works of the Law (Rom 3:28)

> Therefore, having been justified by faith, we have peace with God through our Lord Jesus Christ (Rom 5:1)

> Such were some of you; but you were washed, but you were sanctified, but you were justified in the name of the Lord Jesus Christ and in the Spirit of our God. (1 Cor 6:11)

> so that, having been justified by his grace, we might become heirs according to the hope of eternal life. (Tit 3:7)

> You see that a man is justified by works and not by faith alone. (James 2:24)

We will go into further detail on the meaning and importance of justification in the next chapter, but it is evident that its language is employed as something that will take place on the future Day of Judgment, in addition to that verdict being issued already in the present.[15] The early Christians had the inauguration of the kingdom of God to thank for their realization that they had already been declared to be righteous by the cosmic judge.

Closely related to the kingdom of God being something that is already here but not yet fully consummated is the language of *new creation*. The prophets of the Old Testament spoke about an age of renewal where all of the creation of God, not just human beings, would experience restoration and abundant regeneration. The Early Church maintained this hope of the restoration of God's world, linking it to the return of Jesus and the resurrection of the dead:

> "Therefore repent and return, so that your sins may be wiped away, in order that times of refreshing may come from the presence of the Lord; and that He may send Jesus, the Christ appointed for you, whom heaven must receive until the period of restoration of all things about which God spoke by the mouth of His holy prophets from ancient time." (Acts 3:19-21)

> For the creation was subjected to futility, not willingly, but because of Him who subjected it, in hope that the creation itself also will be set free from its slavery to corruption into the freedom of the glory of the children of God. For we know that the whole creation groans and suffers the pains of childbirth together until now. And not only this, but also we ourselves, having the first fruits of the Spirit, even we ourselves groan within ourselves, waiting eagerly for our adoption as sons, the redemption of our body. (Rom 8:20-23)

---

[15] Fee, *God's Empowering Presence*, 804.

The return of Jesus will usher in the long-awaited age of the restoration of God's creation, including faithful human beings. Without question, the "new creation" was part of the future hope, the hope in which creation will be redeemed. Since the worldwide restoration of God's creation has already broken into the present, experienced by believers, we can observe several instances where the language of new creation is a current reality.[16] Consider how the Early Church believed itself to already be part of the new creation that has broken into the present in light of the inaugurated rule and reign of God:

> Therefore, if anyone is in Christ, he is a new creation. The old has passed away; behold, the new has come. (2 Cor 5:17)

> For neither is circumcision anything, nor uncircumcision, but a new creation. (Gal 6:15).

> He has abolished the law with its commandments and ordinances, that he might create in himself one new humanity in place of the two, thus making peace (Eph 2:15)

The illustration of early Christians as God's new creation involves the metaphor of rebirth, which is closely aligned with the language of the *new birth* that often depicts those who have been converted. Therefore, we would do well to include the texts that describe the process of being born again in our survey of new creation passages:

> "Truly, truly, I say to you, unless one is born again he cannot see the kingdom of God." (John 3:3)

> "Truly, truly, I say to you, unless one is born of water and the Spirit, he cannot enter into the kingdom of God." (John 3:5)

> Blessed be the God and Father of our Lord Jesus Christ, who according to His great mercy has caused us to be born again to a living hope through the resurrection of Jesus Christ from the dead (1 Pet 1:3)

> you have been born again, not of perishable seed but of imperishable, through the living and abiding word of God (1 Pet 1:23)

> No one who is born of God practices sin, because His seed abides in him; and he cannot sin, because he is born of God. (1 John 3:9)

> everyone who loves is born of God and knows God. (1 John 4:7)

The widespread use of new creation and new birth imagery for conversion demonstrates the conviction that the promises of the age to come have indeed broken into the present.

Along similar lines is the language of *regeneration*. Although this noun is comparatively rare, appearing only twice in the New Testament, its usage reflects a similar understanding that the kingdom of God and its renewal of God's creation, while

---

[16] Dunn, *Theology of Paul*, 630.

remaining the future hope, is experienced in the present by believers. In Matthew 19:28, Christ taught that his return at the second coming to occupy the throne of David will be a time of "regeneration."[17] The only other instance of this noun appears in a description of believers who have already experienced the regeneration that the Holy Spirit produces among new converts (Tit 3:5). If the kingdom of God is already and not yet, it is no surprise that the concept of regeneration follows the same theological pattern.

We can find evidence that the language surrounding the promised *inheritance* is not yet attained by its heirs, while also experienced in the present by God's faithful people. In Ephesians 1:13-14, the promised Holy Spirit is depicted as the pledge of our inheritance, an inheritance that lies in the future. However, just a few verses earlier, Ephesians remarked that, in Christ, believers have already obtained an inheritance (Eph 1:11). Both truths are balanced without one reality diminishing the other.[18] Similarly, Paul speaks of believers as children of Abraham and heirs according to the promise (Gal 3:29). One of the most explicit promises that Paul describes is that Abraham and his descendants are heirs of the entire world (Rom 4:13), something that has clearly not yet taken place, not least because Abraham is still dead. Nevertheless, Paul's theology still allows him to say twice that, in the present, "all things belong to you" (1 Cor 3:21-22). In light of this evidence, we can include the Christian inheritance among our growing list of promises belonging to the age to come that have been inaugurated among the saved.

The Use of *Resurrection* Language in the Present

Finally, we can explore how the Early Church utilized the concept and language of resurrection in a remarkably similar fashion. Starting with the most obvious point about the future resurrection of the dead and its appearance in the middle of history, we need to look no further than the bodily resurrection of Christ himself. In Chapter 12, we identified how the early Christians came to realize that the time when God would raise the dead and usher in the age to come had broken into the present when he raised Jesus from the grave to immortality. As such, Christ is the first fruits of those who have fallen asleep (1 Cor 15:20), and the rest of the dead would be resurrected at Christ's second coming (1 Cor 15:24). When we examine closely the language of resurrection within the writings of the New Testament, we find a correlating conviction to what happened to Christ on the third day. In particular, resurrection language is quite often metaphorically applied to the process of conversion; that is, when believers come to be saved in the present, they are illustrated as having figuratively come to life. We can trace the use of the metaphor of resurrection to describe conversion to none other than Jesus himself.

---

[17] Weiss, *Jesus' Proclamation of the Kingdom*, 93
[18] Ryken et al., "Inheritance," 421.

Observe the almost casual nature in which Christ illustrates his disciples as having figuratively come to life:

> "this son of mine was dead and has come to life again; he was lost and has been found." (Luke 15:24)
>
> "this brother of yours was dead and has begun to live, and was lost and has been found." (Luke 15:32)
>
> "Truly, truly, I say to you, he who hears my word, and believes Him who sent me, has eternal life, and does not come into judgment, but has passed out of death into life." (John 5:24)

What is interesting is that both Luke and John make it absolutely clear that the resurrection of the dead, the time in which corpses will be raised until immortality, is still a hope in which believers can place their trust (Luke 14:14; 20:35–36; John 5:28–29).[19] Even still, believing in Jesus' gospel and converting to become his disciple is plainly illustrated with the metaphor of resurrection.[20]

Paul the Apostle appears to have continued this teaching of Jesus, portraying those who are in Christ as having already come to life: "Even so consider yourselves to be dead to sin, but alive to God in Christ Jesus" (Rom 6:11). Those who have identified with Christ's resurrection by going through the ritual of baptism are now to reckon their current position in terms of new life, having died and *been made alive in their conversion*. Paul continues his ethical exhortation a few verses later by urging his readers to present themselves as those who have experienced resurrection life already: "present yourselves to God as those alive from the dead" (Rom 6:13). The portrayal of Christians having experienced resurrection life already due to their union with the crucified and risen Jesus also occurs in 2 Corinthians. Note how Paul is keen to relate his own suffering to that which happened to Jesus, while also calling attention to the life of the risen Jesus that is already present among those who are members of Christ's body:

> we are afflicted in every way, but not crushed; perplexed, but not despairing; persecuted, but not forsaken; struck down, but not destroyed; always carrying about in the body the dying of Jesus, so that the life of Jesus also may be manifested in our body. For we who live are constantly being delivered over to death for Jesus' sake, so that the life of Jesus also may be manifested in our mortal flesh. So death works in us, but life in you. (2 Cor 4:8–12)

Paul's theology draws on the overlap of the ages and, in particular, the future resurrection of the dead that is to occur on the last day, which has broken into the middle of history with the raising of Jesus Christ. Those who are in Christ share in these resurrection

---

[19] Nickelsburg, *Resurrection, Immortality, and Eternal Life*, 242–43; Witherington, *John's Wisdom*, 143.
[20] Coloe, *John 1–10*, 149–50.

benefits, having already come to new life at their conversion to Christ. Believers still possess mortal bodies that suffer affliction, persecution, and even death, but they are united to the risen Christ, he whom God has raised unto immortality. The same themes occur in Colossians chapter two, where Paul explicitly outlines how early Christian converts are already sharing in Jesus' resurrection: "having been buried with him in baptism, in which you were also raised up with him through faith in the working of God, who raised him from the dead. When you were dead in your transgressions and the uncircumcision of your flesh, He made you alive together with him" (Col 2:12–13). Paul pictures God not only raising Jesus from the dead, but also raising the faithful with Christ. The contrast between the former life, to which the convert has died, and the present life, which is a resurrection life shared with the risen Jesus, is apparent. Ephesians expresses this theology by portraying believers as not only presently experiencing the resurrection of Christ, but also sharing in his enthronement to rule and reign: "even when we were dead in our transgressions, made us alive together with Christ (by grace you have been saved), and raised us up with Him, and seated us with him in the heavenly places in Christ Jesus" (Eph 2:5–6). This portrayal of salvation includes resurrection language and enthronement language. In light of the in-breaking of the kingdom of God, things that are true concerning the highly exalted Messiah are tangibly felt by the followers of the Messiah. God raised Jesus and set him on the throne at his right hand, so those who are in Christ are illustrated in terms of *a new life and as enthroned rulers*.[21] In other words, believers are, on one hand, presently reigning with Christ, while on the other hand, they seek the day in which they will be physically raised to immortality to truly rule with Christ in the kingdom. Paul's theology allows for both of these to be true at the same time.

We would be remiss if we failed to draw attention to how the phrase *eternal life* appears within the teachings of Jesus as something his followers already possess in the present, while also being placed in the future as the resurrection life that belongs in the coming age. From our initial explorations into the concept of resurrection in Chapter 12, we will recall that the English phrase "eternal life" is more accurately rendered as *the life of the age to come*. This points to the immortality that God will grant to the faithful on the Day of Judgment, particularly by raising the dead (Dan 12:2, 13). Within Jesus' preaching, we find that he was deeply impacted by the language and hope expressed in Daniel 12:2, and Jesus continued to proclaim that the life of the age to come is the promised inheritance.[22] Examples of Christ speaking of eternal life as the future hope include the promise that those who follow him will inherit it *in the age to come* (Mark 10:30; Luke 18:30), that is, *when Jesus returns* (Matt 25:46). Prospective followers inquire of Jesus how they might inherit eternal life, indicating an agreement that it will be given in the future when the faithful will receive their inheritance (Mark 10:17; Luke 10:25; 18:18). Other New Testament authors, particularly Paul and Jude, continue to place eternal life squarely in

---

[21] Lincoln, *Ephesians*, 106–7; Best, *Ephesians*, 221–23.
[22] Ladd, *The Presence of the Future*, 115.

the future (Rom 2:7; 6:22; Jude 1:21). In this regard, the Early Church's view of the life of the age to come mirrored the expectations of many of their Jewish contemporaries, who often spoke about the "world to come" and those who would live in it.

On the other hand, the in-breaking of the kingdom of God affected the language of the life of the age to come. If eternal life primarily referred to immortality granted at the resurrection of the body, then one could understand how early Christian conversion to new life could be illustrated as a present possession of the life of the age to come. When we examine the teachings of Christ, the inaugurator of God's kingdom, we can observe that he often spoke of eternal life as a present possession that a believer already has and experienced:

> For God so loved the world, that he gave his only Son, that whoever believes in him should not perish but have eternal life. (John 3:16)
>
> He who believes in the Son has eternal life; but he who does not obey the Son will not see life, but the wrath of God abides on him (John 3:36)
>
> "Truly, truly, I say to you, he who hears my word, and believes Him who sent me, has eternal life" (John 5:24)
>
> "Truly, truly, I say to you, whoever believes has eternal life." (John 6:47)
>
> "He who eats my flesh and drinks my blood has eternal life" (John 6:54)
>
> "This is eternal life, that they may know You, the only true God, and Jesus Christ whom You have sent." (John 17:3)

The language that Jesus employs in these instances is ambiguous: the life of the age to come is the present possession of his converted believers. This, of course, does not mean that his followers already possess immortality. Instead, it indicates that the kingdom has broken into the present, and in light of this inaugurated rule and reign, resurrection life is available to those who follow Christ.[23] As a good teacher, Jesus often clarified that while his disciples already have eternal life in light of their conversion, Christ will still resurrect them on the last day (John 5:24–29; 6:40, 54). The Early Church experienced a newness of life by converting to Christ, a life that offered a preview into what will be inherited at Christ's second coming to raise the dead and give them new bodies.

Conclusion

In conclusion, we have observed how the Early Church understood the salvific process of conversion after Jesus' inauguration of the kingdom of God. Beginning with the

---

[23] Smith, *Wisdom Christology*, 119–20; Carter, *John: Storyteller, Interpreter, Evangelist*, 100–1; Keener, *John*, 1:329.

ministry of Jesus, we first saw how his preaching of the gospel, restorative miracles, exorcisms, and even his own resurrection from the grave demonstrated how God's rule and reign had drawn near. Christ's ushering in of the kingdom as a reality that his followers experienced affected his use of salvation language, for which he taught that believers are already saved, but the fullness of their salvation still lies in the future. Second, we saw that Jesus' teaching that the kingdom was "already" and "not yet" deeply impacted the beliefs of the Early Church. As such, the authors of the New Testament showed no hesitancy in illustrating several of the promises to be inherited at Christ's return to consummate the kingdom as having already broken into the present. These include *salvation, redemption, justification, new creation, new birth, regeneration,* and even the language of the *inheritance* itself. Finally, we examined how Jesus and, subsequently, the authors of the New Testament, depicted the future resurrection of the dead and the immortal life of the age to come as present experiences for those who have undergone a death and new life in their conversion. For the Early Church, the overwhelming use of the vocabulary describing the promises to be given in the kingdom of God to illustrate Christian converts owes its dependence on Jesus' proclamation that the kingdom of God has broken into the present. The impact of Christ's gospel of the kingdom upon the Early Church cannot be overstated.

One of the pivotal acts that is to take place on the Day of Judgment is the issuing of the verdict to those judged as righteous. This act of justification, as we observed in this chapter, is something that most naturally fits in the context of judgment in the future, but its verdict has been brought forth into the present and granted to those who believe the gospel. How does a believer's righteous status relate to justification in the present and future? Did the early Christians distinguish between their righteousness and God's righteousness? And in what sense did Christ relate to the righteous covenant relationship between the only true God and his believing children? We will thoroughly explore these topics in the next chapter, as they are pivotal to the Early Church's self-understanding of salvation.

37
RIGHTEOUSNESS AND JUSTIFICATION IN THE NEW COVENANT

There are many concepts that the Early Church believed and taught that are fairly simple to grasp. The idea that the one true God is one person, the Father alone, is straightforward. The historical reality that Christ was brought into existence in the womb of his mother, Mary, is uncomplicated. The promise that the faithful people of God will inherit the earth is elementary and crystal clear. However, there are some ideas common among the early Christians that are a bit more complex, requiring the modern reader to possess thorough definitions of such concepts in order to make sense of them. These theological topics include *righteousness* and *justification*. Failing to grasp the crucial meaning and functions of these terms for early Christianity will result in an inability to read several chapters in Paul's epistles with any measure of comprehension. The entire Epistle to the Romans simply cannot be engaged without a clear understanding of these topics. Moreover, readers will be unable to fully appreciate how a believer functions within the new covenant agreement between God and his people.

This chapter will explore the important concepts of righteousness and justification, particularly as they relate to the Early Church's self-understanding of its relationship with the only true God. We will begin by looking at God's own righteousness, and, in the process, contrast it with the righteousness that his covenant people possess. We will also raise the question as to whether Christ's righteous status relates at all to a believer's salvation and position within the new covenant. Second, we will examine the meaning of justification, both in its function within the verdicts issued by the judge on the Day of Judgment as well as its use in the present. Lastly, we will consider what sort of behavior the Early Church expected the righteous people of God to exhibit, asking what happens if a believer decides to no longer live according to the new covenant's terms. The goal of this chapter is to become better acquainted and well-informed on these key soteriological issues, especially as they relate to a believer's position in the renewed people of God.

Defining *the Righteousness of God* and Human *Righteousness*

Beginning with the subject of righteousness, we can observe that the biblical authors ascribe several traits and characteristics to the righteousness that God possesses, while also illustrating the righteousness belonging to God's people in very different ways. The reason for this distinction is that the term "righteousness" regularly refers to the behavior expected between multiple parties,[1] and the most common relationship we find in Scripture is the covenant relationship. Within the covenantal framework, God, of course, is the one who initiates the covenant with another party, and this second party is the recipient of the covenant agreement. Within the Mosaic covenant, this agreement was between Yahweh and the children of Israel. In the new covenant, the agreement is between Yahweh and anyone who responds to the gospel of the kingdom with faith. The distinction between the maker of the covenant and the recipients of the covenantal pact is fairly self-evident.

God's own righteousness, therefore, includes his faithfulness to the covenants he personally initiated.[2] By initiating a covenantal agreement with his people, God is committing to several promises, and God must be faithful to his end of the covenant. Any deeds that God performs within the confines of his covenant with his people are illustrated as "righteous" deeds because they pertain to his obligations stipulated within the covenantal agreement. We highlighted God's faithfulness as a central moral attribute in Chapter 5, and in doing so, we observed several passages that draw attention to God's fidelity to his covenant promises. When the biblical authors praise Yahweh for his faithfulness to the covenant, they portray his commitment by talking about his righteousness:

> Yahweh has made known His salvation; He has revealed His righteousness in the sight of the nations. He has remembered His covenant love (Hebrew: *chesed*) and His faithfulness to the house of Israel; all the ends of the earth have seen the salvation of our God. (Ps 98:2–3)

> But the covenant love (*chesed*) of Yahweh from everlasting to everlasting lasts on those who fear Him, and His righteousness to children's children, to those who keep His covenant and remember His precepts to do them. (Ps 103:17–18)

> "Alas, O Lord, the great and awesome God, who keeps His covenant and lovingkindness for those who love Him and keep His commandments . . . Righteousness belongs to You, O Lord" (Dan 9:4–7)

God's covenantal promises included his oath to Abraham, to whom he committed to blessing the world through Abraham's worldwide family (Gen 12:3). The forgiveness of sins made available to every person through the death of Jesus convinced the Early Church that God had been true to his word that he made to Abraham.

---

[1] Leonhardt-Balzer, "Righteousness in Early Jewish Literature," 807; Seebass and Brown, "Righteousness, Justification," 356–57; Quell and Schrenk, "δίκη κτλ," 195.
[2] Seebass and Brown, "Righteousness, Justification," 363, write, "God's righteousness is essentially his covenant dealings with his people."

In addition to the faithfulness to his covenant promises, God's own righteousness often appeared in secondary contexts where he served as the judge. This illustration appears frequently in the Psalms: "God is a righteous judge" (Ps 7:11); "Judge me, O Yahweh my God, according to Your righteousness" (Ps 35:24)"; "the heavens declare His righteousness, for God Himself is judge" (Ps 50:6). We observed in Chapter 5 that Yahweh, in his role as the righteous judge, performs four key functions (he is impartial, he upholds the law, he vindicates the helpless, and he punishes evil). The righteousness of the judge within the lawcourt setting refers to his behavior as that of a just judge when he carries out these four judicial responsibilities.[3] To speak of the righteousness of the judge is to attribute to him characteristics that clearly set him apart from all other parties involved in the lawcourt, whether it be the plaintiff or the defendant.

The foundational meaning of God's righteousness, which involves his faithfulness to his covenantal promises, combined with the secondary meaning of the righteous judge, produces a third definition of the eschatological judge who will sit for judgment on the last day. If Yahweh was committed to his promises to give the land to his faithful people forever, to definitively establish the kingdom covenanted to David's royal descendant, to vindicate the righteous, and to punish the wicked, then he would need to sit as judge on the Day of Judgment. The biblical authors often portrayed God as the righteous judge who will one day judge righteously:

> He will judge the world in righteousness; He will execute judgment for the peoples with equity. (Ps 9:8)
>
> Before Yahweh, for He is coming, for He is coming to judge the earth. He will judge the world in righteousness and the peoples in His faithfulness. (Ps 96:13)
>
> Before Yahweh, for He is coming to judge the earth; He will judge the world with righteousness and the peoples with equity. (Ps 98:9)
>
> But because of your stubbornness and unrepentant heart you are storing up wrath for yourself in the day of wrath and revelation of the righteous judgment of God, who will render to each person according to his deeds (Rom 2:5–6)

Although there were some clues expressed by the authors of the Old Testament (e.g., Ps 72:1–2; Isa 11:3–4; Jer 23:5), the Early Church confirmed that God had handed over his role as the righteous judge *to Jesus*: "God is now declaring to men that all people everywhere should repent, because He has fixed a day in which He will judge the world in righteousness through a man whom He has appointed, having furnished proof to all men by raising him from the dead" (Acts 17:30–31). In any case, the portrayal of Yahweh as the cosmic judge who will fulfill his covenantal promises, rescue his people, and punish

---

[3] In addition to the texts presented in Chapter 5, God's righteous role as the lawcourt judge is expressed in Deut 32:4; Judg 5:11; 2 Chron 12:16; Ezra 9:15; Pss 7:9–11; 9:4–8; 11:5–7; 89:14; 119:137–138; Isa 5:16; Jer 12:1; Lam 1:18; Dan 9:14; Zeph 3:5; Rev 16:5–7; 19:2.

the wicked is characterized in terms of God judging *in righteousness* and issuing forth his *righteous* judgments.

It should be apparent by this point that God's own righteousness is not a status that he shares with his people. When God righteously initiates and commits to be faithful to his end of covenantal agreements, this righteousness obviously belongs to God alone.[4] When the righteous judge judges between two parties, his role as the enactor of righteous judgments is not something that those present can take upon themselves. Similarly, the one who will stand as the cosmic judge on the Day of Judgment will judge the world in righteousness, but those who are on the receiving end of this judgment do not possess the judge's righteousness that belongs to him as he serves in that role. In other words, God's righteousness is something quite different than the righteousness that his faithful people possess in light of their covenant relationship with him. The righteousness that belongs to God is not imparted, imputed, or otherwise given to Israel or to the Early Church.[5]

Having defined God's own righteousness, we can turn our attention to the righteousness that his people possess. Since we have noted that "righteousness" refers to the behavior expected between multiple parties, we can situate the people of God as "righteous" when they act in accordance with the covenant agreement.[6] The biblical authors understood their righteousness as their covenant status and membership. Naturally, Abraham's belief was reckoned to him as righteousness (Gen 15:6), that is, his membership in the covenant agreement initiated by Yahweh. To be righteous, therefore, one needed to remain faithful to the terms of the covenant that God prescribed.[7] The people of Israel demonstrated their awareness of their need to obey Yahweh's commands, as it directly pertained to their righteous covenant status: "It will be righteousness for us if we are careful to observe all this commandment before Yahweh our God, just as He commanded us" (Deut 6:25). In Psalm 1, the righteous are illustrated as those who delight and meditate on God's instruction (Ps 1:2, 6). To "work righteousness" is to walk with integrity and to speak truthfully from the heart (Ps 15:2). Jesus summoned his listeners to exhibit righteousness greater than that of the scribes and the Pharisees in order to have entrance into the kingdom (Matt 5:20). In order to live in accordance with Jesus' righteous demands, one must listen to and obey his teachings, beginning by responding to his gospel of the kingdom. Paul even made it clear that the "fruit of righteousness" is only available in Jesus Christ, according to Philippians 1:11. Membership in the new covenant, that is,

---

[4] Jewett, *Romans*, 142. Quell and Schrenk, "δίκη κτλ," 203; Wright, *Paul and the Faithfulness of God*, 796.
[5] Wright, "The Letter to the Romans," 403. Jewett, *Romans*, 142, recognizes that God's righteousness is his own "activity in this process of global transformation" rather than being understood as a status of "human righteousness bestowed by God."
[6] Wright, *Justification*, 47, provides a helpful reminder: "The 'relationality' of 'righteousness' does not have to do with 'getting to know someone personally', as 'relationship' implies to most people today, but rather with 'how they are related to one another' . . . in a mixture . . . of covenant and lawcourt."
[7] Sanders, *Paul and Palestinian Judaism*, 544.

righteousness, is given to all who believe: "Christ is the end of the law for righteousness to everyone who believes" (Rom 10:4). When the Early Church spoke about its own righteous status within the covenantal relationship with God, it was not thinking that being righteous was the same as being morally upright.[8] To be righteous was *to live faithfully to the new covenant's terms*. This would produce behavior that could, in a sense, be characterized as moral, but strictly speaking, the "righteous" were those living obediently to Jesus' teachings. These terms (righteousness, righteous, the righteous people) cannot be meaningfully understood apart from God's covenantal agreement with his people.[9]

Another important detail to consider is that the righteous people of God possess that status within the metaphor of the lawcourt. We will recall that Yahweh, the initiator of the covenant, also serves as the righteous judge. Within the typical lawcourt, the judge would listen to the case and decide in favor of one party or the other, and when the judge issues his judgment, the vindicated party is declared to be "righteous." For example, the psalmist prays that Yahweh would act as judge by punishing evil and establishing the righteous party: "O let the evil of the wicked come to an end, but establish the righteous" (Ps 7:9). As a matter of contrast, Yahweh is praised for his willingness to judge in favor of the righteous in need, while also punishing those who are not righteous—the wicked: "For the arms of the wicked will be broken, but Yahweh sustains the righteous" (Ps 37:17). Similarly, "All the horns of the wicked I will cut off, but the horns of the righteous shall be lifted up" (Ps 75:10). These two characterizations of humanity standing in judgment, either as the righteous or as the wicked, was a staple feature in Jesus' teaching about the kingdom of God and how the faithful will enter it on the last day. Consider how the Day of Judgment both identifies and separates the righteous from the wicked:

> So it will be at the end of the age; the angels will come forth and take out the wicked from among the righteous (Matt 13:49)

> But when the Son of Man comes in his glory, and all the angels with him, then he will sit on his glorious throne. All the nations will be gathered before him; and he will separate them from one another, as the shepherd separates the sheep from the goats; and he will put the sheep on his right, and the goats on the left . . . These will go away into eternal punishment, but the righteous into eternal life. (Matt 25:31–33, 46)

> there shall certainly be a resurrection of both the righteous and the wicked. (Acts 24:15)

In this manner, the righteous people of God are those who faithfully live in obedience to the new covenant, anticipate a favorable verdict on the coming Day of Judgment, and are identified in the present as those whom the judge has already declared to be righteous. Paul attributes this process to God's own initiative, which is illustrated in the purpose statement of Romans: "For I am not ashamed of the gospel, for it is the power of God

---

[8] Quell and Schrenk, "δίκη κτλ," 188–91.
[9] Dunn, *Romans 1–8*, 40–41.

for salvation to everyone who believes, to the Jew first and also to the Greek. For in it the righteousness of God is revealed from faith to faith, as it is written, 'But the righteous man shall live by faith'" (Rom 1:16-17). In the preaching of the salvific gospel, God's own righteousness has been revealed, that is, it has been unveiled, allowing his people to see how God has been faithful to his promises. The phrase "from faith to faith" again stresses the covenant relationship, initiated by the faithful God and accepted by a people who live faithfully to its terms.[10] The revelation of God's righteous judgment brings into the present the verdict to be given on the Day of Judgment. If all of this is accomplished in the gospel—the saving message of the kingdom and its crucified and risen king, Jesus— it is reasonable to ask how exactly Jesus fits into the subject of righteousness.

As we have observed several times now, the early Christians regarded their own righteous status as their new covenant membership, and the initiator of the covenant is God, not Jesus. To be sure, Jesus is the mediator of the new covenant (1 Tim 2:5; Heb 8:6; 9:15; 12:24), and Paul is rather explicit that Christ was crucial in being the means through whom God would deal with the sin of Adam and, thus, bring the blessing to the entire world. In Romans 3:21-26, Paul argues that God's own righteousness has been manifested in the present through Jesus' faithful actions that led to his death on the cross.[11] Although God has passed over former sins, his righteousness proves that he is indeed just and the one who justifies those believers whose status rests on Jesus' faithfulness. In other words, Paul has been quite careful to attribute righteousness *to God*, not to Christ, despite Christ's pivotal role in God's plan of redemption. In fact, no passage in the New Testament illustrates the righteousness of the people of God in terms of Christ's righteousness. The lone exception might be found in 2 Corinthians 5:21, but the context suggests otherwise:

> Therefore, we are ambassadors for Christ, as though God were making an appeal through us; we beg you on behalf of Christ, be reconciled to God. He made him who knew no sin to be sin on our behalf, so that we might become the righteousness of God in him. And working together with him, we also urge you not to receive the grace of God in vain (2 Cor 5:20–6:1)

Within this passage, Paul speaks of his own apostolic team of missionaries in the first-person plural ("we") and distinguishes his ministry from his readers ("we beg you"). By following Paul's logic carefully, it is he and his traveling apostolic team of missionaries, not the readers of 2 Corinthians, who "become the righteousness of God" in Christ, that is, they share in God's mission to bring reconciliation to others through the preaching of the gospel. Neither Paul nor the Corinthians become, share in, or are otherwise imputed

---

[10] Longenecker, *Romans*, 178; Jewett, *Romans*, 144; Wright, "The Letter to the Romans," 425.
[11] Romans 3:22 almost certainly points to Jesus' own faithfulness during his ministry, rather than "faith in Christ for all who believe," which would be a redundant double description of believers having faith. See Hays, *The Faith of Jesus Christ*, 156–161; Keck, *Romans*, 104–5; Wright, "The Letter to the Romans," 470–74.

with Christ's righteousness. The passage is still about God's own righteousness—his faithfulness to his covenant promises—that Paul and his team are fortunate enough to participate in bringing to fulfillment.

Defining *Justification*

We have already started to see how justification language is closely intertwined with God's righteousness, so we can pursue the meaning of justification, having laid the groundwork of the covenant and God's role as the righteous judge. We have already drawn attention to the righteousness of the just judge, which is displayed when he vindicates the innocent in court. When the judge finds in favor of one party or another within the lawcourt, that vindicated person is not only declared to be righteous, but they are also *justified*.[12] Justification is the declarative act of the judge to state that someone is in the right: "If there is a dispute between men and they go to court, and the judges decide their case, and they justify the righteous and condemn the wicked" (Deut 25:1).[13] Christ also taught that justification is what the judge will speak on the Day of Judgment: "I tell you, on the day of judgment people will give account for every careless word they speak, for by your words you will be justified" (Matt 12:36–37). In Romans 2:5–16, Paul similarly describes the impartial judgment that will take place "on that day," and, in doing so, he explains how God will justify and judge at that time.[14] So, if justification is the declaration of the judge on the last day to identify those who are God's own righteous people, how did the Early Church come to regard justification as something that has happened in the present?

The most obvious answer to seeing one of God's promises that will take place in the future breaking into the present is to, as we observed in the previous chapter, acknowledge how the age to come has been inaugurated in and through Jesus' proclamation of the kingdom of God.[15] The verdict to be issued on the Day of Judgment is brought forward into the present when a believer places faith in the gospel message. *Present justification* is, therefore, available to those who believe, meaning they are declared to be God's righteous covenant people:

> For we maintain that a man is justified by faith apart from works of the Law. (Rom 3:28)

> Therefore, having been justified by faith, we have peace with God through our Lord Jesus Christ (Rom 5:1)

> nevertheless knowing that a man is not justified by the works of the Law but through the faithfulness of Christ Jesus, even we have believed in Christ Jesus, so that we may be

---

[12] Wright, *Justification*, 70; McConville, *Deuteronomy*, 368.
[13] Tigay, *Deuteronomy*, 230; Christensen, *Deuteronomy 21:10–34:12*, 599
[14] Wright. *Paul and the Faithfulness of God*, 937–38.
[15] Ladd, *Crucial Questions About the Kingdom*, 80.

justified by the faithfulness of Christ and not by the works of the Law; since by the works of the Law no flesh will be justified. (Gal 2:16)

And the Scripture, foreseeing that God would justify the Gentiles by faith, preached the gospel beforehand to Abraham, saying, "In you shall all the nations be blessed." (Gal 3:8)

Therefore the Law has become our tutor to lead us to Christ, so that we may be justified by faith. (Gal 3:24)

The gospel of the kingdom is for everyone who believes, regardless of one's race, ethnicity, or nationality. God justifies, that is, he issues the righteous verdict on those who express faith in the gospel. To be clear, justification does not, strictly speaking, mean to be converted, to be born again, to be saved, or to be sanctified.[16] Justification is what takes place when the judge verbally states that someone is vindicated and righteous, and as such, their sins are forgiven. We can tell who will receive a favorable verdict on the Day of Judgment already in the present.[17] Those who have faith in the gospel, meaning they have made the commitment to trust, loyalty, and obedience, are now counted among God's covenant people.[18] Paul assumes that the faithful promises of God will motivate faithful behavior that lasts the entirety of a believer's life.

Justification by faith in the present, in other words, is not to be to the exclusion of doing good deeds in accordance with the terms of the new covenant. To be sure, Paul contrasts the present act of justification with works of the Law of Moses (Rom 3:28; Gal 2:16), but those are the terms of the old covenant, not the new covenant in which Christians are located.[19] The authors of the New Testament were absolutely adamant that the justifying verdict that the judge will issue on the last day will be based on the entirety of the life of the believer, which takes into account their faithfulness and good works. When Paul describes those who will be justified on the Day of Judgment, he goes to great lengths to illustrate their obedient behavior:

> But because of your stubbornness and unrepentant heart you are storing up wrath for yourself in the day of wrath and revelation of the righteous judgment of God, who will render to each person according to his deeds: to those who by perseverance in doing good seek for glory and honor and immortality, eternal life; but to those who are selfishly ambitious and do not obey the truth, but obey unrighteousness, wrath and indignation. There will be tribulation and distress for every soul of man who does evil, of the Jew first

---

[16] Quell and Schrenk, "δίκη κτλ," 215, argue that, for Paul, the verb *to justify* "does not suggest the infusion of moral qualities."
[17] Seebass and Brown, "Righteousness, Justification," 365.
[18] Wright, *Paul and the Faithfulness of God*, 944, arrives at a similar conclusion: "When Paul speaks about people being 'justified' in the present . . . *the covenant God declares 'in the right', 'within the covenant', all those who hear, believe and obey 'the gospel' of Jesus the Messiah.*"
[19] Dunn, *Galatians*, 136–37. Dunn, *The New Perspective on Paul*, 23, provides an unequivocal definition: "I have no doubt that 'works of the law' refer to what the law requires, the conduct prescribed by the Torah."

and also of the Greek, but glory and honor and peace to everyone who does good, to the Jew first and also to the Greek. For there is no partiality with God. (Rom 2:5–11)

Those who are to receive eternal life, the life of the age to come, on the Day of Judgment, are those who persevere in doing good.[20] These are those who continually seek glory, honor, and immortality. Regardless of one's race, justification will occur on the last day, and the final verdict will be based on a person's good works. James 2:24 argues for much of the same: "You see that a man is justified by works and not by faith alone." Again, when we examine the teachings of Jesus, we find that he set the tone for the Early Church's belief that the judgment that is to take place on the last day will call to account one's deeds:

> Not everyone who says to me, "Lord, Lord," will enter the kingdom of heaven, but he who does the will of My Father who is in heaven will enter. Many will say to me on that day, "Lord, Lord" . . . And then I will declare to them, "I never knew you" (Matt 7:21-23)

> For the Son of Man is going to come in the glory of his Father with his angels, and will then repay every man according to his deeds (Matt 16:27)

> When he returned, after receiving the kingdom, he ordered that these slaves, to whom he had given the money, be called to him so that he might know what business they had done . . . Another came, saying, "Master, here is your mina, which I kept put away in a handkerchief;" . . . He said to him, "By your own words I will judge you, you worthless slave." (Luke 19:15, 20, 22)

> Do not marvel at this; for an hour is coming, in which all who are in the tombs will hear his voice, and will come forth; those who did the good deeds to a resurrection of life, those who committed the evil deeds to a resurrection of judgment. (John 5:28–29)

> See, I am coming soon; my reward is with me, to repay according to everyone's work. (Rev 22:12)

Several other texts indicate that the final justification, which will take place on the Day of Judgment, will take into account the deeds of every person. However, we have examined enough to demonstrate its place among the Early Church's beliefs and teachings.[21]

The Consequences of Rejecting One's Righteous Obligations

This theology of final justification and its verdict that is brought forth into the present, presented to believers as they convert through faith, raises an interesting question about

---

[20] Dunn, *Romans 1–8*, 86, defines this life of faithfulness in terms of "a sustained and deliberate application."
[21] See also Rom 14:10–12; 2 Cor 5:10; Eph 6:9; Col 3:23–25; 2 Thes 1:6–8; 2 Tim 4:14; 1 Pet 1:17; 4:17–18; 2 Pet 2:9; Jude 1:14–15; Rev 2:23; 20:11–13.

how these two events relate. In particular, one might ask what happens if a member of the new covenant, who has been justified by faith, decides to abandon the covenant's terms and walk away. Can someone who possesses righteousness (i.e., covenant status) be removed from the people of God through consistent, unrepentant disobedience? The unfortunate answer to this question that the Early Church would offer is undoubtedly yes, for the righteous people of God must behave appropriately in order to maintain their covenant status. Early Christians only had to look at how Yahweh handled ongoing disobedience in the old covenant to recognize that there were severe consequences for abandoning one's righteous obligations: "Again, when a righteous man turns away from his righteousness and commits iniquity, and I place an obstacle before him, he will die" (Ezek 3:20).[22] God would always be faithful to his end of the covenant agreement, but if the people failed to remain obedient, they would face utter destruction:

> Know therefore that Yahweh God, He is God, the faithful God, who keeps His covenant and His lovingkindness to a thousandth generation with those who love Him and keep His commandments; but repays those who hate Him to their faces, to destroy them (Deut 7:9–10)

> But if your heart turns away and you will not obey, but are drawn away and worship other gods and serve them, I declare to you today that you shall surely perish. (Deut 30:17–18)

> Why do you transgress the commandments of Yahweh and do not prosper? Because you have forsaken Yahweh, He has also forsaken you. (2 Chron 24:20)

> For the upright will live in the land and the blameless will remain in it; but the wicked will be cut off from the land and the treacherous will be uprooted from it. (Prov 2:21–22)

Honoring the terms of the new covenant necessitates faith, commitment, and obedience. In other words, the righteous people in Christ who committed to faith in the gospel and pledged to obey Jesus needed to follow through with those oaths, particularly through prayer, the edification of the believing community, and the leading of the Holy Spirit. Since a believer's conversion involved a symbolic death and a coming to new life, Paul urged them to live appropriately by offering one's entire self to righteous living: "present yourselves to God as those alive from the dead, and your members as instruments of righteousness to God" (Rom 6:13). Those who persisted in sinful behavior were removed from the Christian community, as evidenced by the New Testament authors (Matt 18:17; Rom 16:17; 1 Cor 5:2, 13; 2 Thes 3:6, 14; 1 Tim 1:19–20; Titus 3:10–11).[23] This shunning would include the unrepentant person not being allowed to participate in the sacramental

---

[22] Sanders, *Paul and Palestinian Judaism*, 420, convincingly wrote, "*obedience maintains one's position in the covenant, but it does not earn God's grace as such.* It simply keeps an individual in the group which is the recipient of God's grace."
[23] Schmidt, "Discipline," 216, aptly summarizes the data: "When an individual did not respond to warning(s) or committed a serious offense, it was necessary to effect social isolation . . . In several instances it appears that Paul . . . seems to advocate their final expulsion from the community."

meal, the Lord's Supper (1 Cor 5:11; 2 Thes 3:10). However, *forgiveness was always available* to those who demonstrated sincere repentance: "If your brother sins, rebuke him, and if he repents, forgive him" (Luke 17:3).[24] On the other hand, if a believer persisted in disobedience, without remorse or any desire to repent, then the verdict on the Day of Judgment would certainly be unfavorable: "For if we go on sinning willfully after receiving the knowledge of the truth, there no longer remains a sacrifice for sins, but a terrifying expectation of judgment and the fury of fire which will consume" (Heb 10:26-27).[25]

Conclusion

To recap, we have established thorough and biblical definitions of the complex terms that gave meaning and purpose to God's covenantal relationship with the early Christians: righteousness and justification. First, we observed that the Early Church maintained a clear distinction between God's own righteousness, which conveyed his faithfulness to his covenant promises and his role as the impartial judge, and the righteousness belonging to believers, their covenant status. Within this exploration, we saw how Christ's faithfulness was instrumental to God's plan to deal with sin and bless the world, but a believer's righteous status is something God gives, not Christ. As such, "the righteous" refers to those who are in covenant with Yahweh, and their "righteous deeds" are the obedient works displayed by the righteous as their faithful response to God's gracious initiative. We also look at the concept of justification, the judge's declarative verdict indicating that someone is vindicated and innocent of guilt. Although the Early Church believed that all would stand in judgment on the last day, the inauguration of the kingdom and the overlap of the ages have brought the verdict into the present and granted to those who express faith in the gospel of the kingdom. Those who are justified are marked out, already in the present, to be God's forgiven covenant people. Finally, we noted how the early Christians portrayed the faithful responsibility of the righteous, justified new covenant members to maintain their obedient behavior in order to maintain their good standing in Christ. Repentance and forgiveness were always available to those Christians who sinned, but those who persisted in disobedience were removed from the covenant community and would anticipate an unfavorable judgment on the last day.

Having drawn attention to the highly practical nature of the doctrines associated with soteriology, it is relatively easy to see how living faithfully and in accordance with the leading of the Holy Spirit characterized the daily lives of those within the Early Church. In our following chapter, we will consider some modern applications to this study of salvation.

---

[24] See also John 21:15–17; 2 Cor 2:6–8; 7:10–11; Gal 6:1.
[25] deSilva, *Perseverance and Gratitude*, 346–47; Johnson, *Hebrews*, 261–63; Attridge, *Hebrews*, 292–93.

38
APPLYING SOTERIOLOGY TODAY

When it comes to the study of salvation, the precise nature and definition of the saving gospel message is absolutely imperative to correctly understand by all who claim to be Christians. Our study has thoroughly demonstrated that the Early Church summarized the gospel message that all initiates into the Christian faith were required to understand and believe as "the gospel of the kingdom of God." John the Baptist preached the gospel of the kingdom. Jesus thoroughly preached the gospel of the kingdom. When Jesus sent out the twelve, they preached the gospel of the kingdom. When Jesus commissioned the seventy-two, they also proclaimed the gospel of the kingdom. In the Great Commission, Christ directed his followers to make disciples and to teach them to observe all that he commanded (Matt 28:19–20). Those teachings included the gospel of the kingdom of God, and the evangelism within the Book of Acts confirms continuity with Jesus' definition of the saving message. The gospel of the kingdom was preached in Samaria (Acts 8:12). Barnabas and Paul encouraged the disciples in several cities with the message of the kingdom (Acts 14:21–22). In fact, Paul continued to plant churches, proclaiming Jesus' gospel of the kingdom, and the Book of Acts concludes with Paul teaching the kingdom of God in Rome for a full two years without any opposition (Acts 28:30–31). This overwhelming data concerning the contents of the Early Church's message of salvation is unfortunately at odds with the preaching of the gospel in the twenty-first century. Many churches, pastors, and evangelists have failed to define the gospel as Jesus defined it. In fact, much of the attempted evangelistic preaching in the modern era has absolutely nothing to do with the kingdom of God at all. When you talk to many who claim to be Christian and ask them what they think the kingdom of God is, the answer quite often leaves something to be desired. Most cannot even define the kingdom of God, which demonstrates that *the gospel of the kingdom has been abandoned by a great many of those who identify as followers of Christ*. Let us set a better example by clearly, carefully, and boldly preaching the gospel as Jesus Christ defined it. Let us not water the message down by diminishing the kingdom emphasis within its proclamation. Furthermore, let us continue to preach the gospel of the kingdom in a manner that encourages communities of faith, just as Paul exhorted his churches: "Through many tribulations we must enter the kingdom of God" (Acts 14:22). If others lack the gospel's emphasis on the kingdom, let us gently remind them of what the Early Church believed and taught. In order to make disciples in accordance with the will of Jesus, we must honor his commands and continue to preach his gospel of the kingdom.

Another application relating to our wider study of Soteriology is the conviction of the Early Church that, although believers have been saved, redeemed, and transformed into God's new creation people, the full extent of salvation lies in the future. Yes, it is true that all of the language describing the conversion of sinners into members of the new covenant illustrates that a dramatic and life-changing transformation has already taken place. It is also true, however, that believers have not yet been raised from the dead. They have not yet been given immortality. They have not yet stood before the judge on the Day of Judgment. Most importantly, they have not yet received, tangibly speaking, their promised inheritance. The writers of the New Testament celebrated the salvific conversion of believers who have repented and placed their faith in the gospel of the kingdom. This radical change was not insignificant, nor should it be overlooked. On the other hand, these same authors of the New Testament continued to stress that the hope still lies in the future concerning what has yet to take place. Two things can be true at the same time. Jesus struck a balance between these two realities without favoring one and neglecting the importance of the other. For example, in John chapter five, Christ teaches that whoever hears his gospel and believes in the God who sent Christ already possesses eternal life, and this believer is not coming into judgment, but has instead passed from death unto life (John 5:24). This is a remarkable statement about the realities of belief and conversion. It involves the metaphor of resurrection and the acknowledgment that the life of the age to come is already in the hands of the believer. However, just a few sentences later, Jesus makes it very clear that the process of a believer's redemption has not yet come to completion. In John 5:28–29, he speaks of the real resurrection, that is, the actual raising of dead corpses from the graves: "Do not marvel at this; for an hour is coming, in which all who are in the tombs will hear his voice and will come forth; those who did the good deeds to a resurrection of life, those who committed the evil deeds to a resurrection of judgment." This promised resurrection from the dead, resulting in immortality for the righteous, has clearly not taken place yet. We can find other instances where Jesus speaks of both the present possession of eternal life and the promise of the future resurrection in the same sentence: "For this is the will of my Father, that everyone who beholds the Son and believes in him will have eternal life, and I myself will raise him up on the last day" (John 6:40, see also 6:54). Let us, therefore, seek to attain the better resurrection, the resurrection unto never-ending life. In the process, let us engage in good deeds, just as Jesus described in John 5:29. Let us not wrongly assume that the process of transformation is complete with our conversion, for we were created in Christ Jesus to perform good works (Eph 2:10). May we embrace our status as God's new creation people in the present and live faithfully in accordance with that identity, knowing that the full measure of our transformation is to arrive when Christ returns to reign as king on the earth. Let us never forget that God is not finished with us, and that the resurrection of Jesus anticipates what will happen to all of God's faithful *on the last day*.

As we round out our practical applications of Soteriology, we want to turn our attention to the need to obey Jesus in order to maintain our righteous status within the new covenant. The principle of faithful obedience has been well-documented by this point, but readers may be particularly interested in knowing precisely how to obey. For those who are devoted to Jesus through faith and loyalty, the desire to honor his position as Messiah and respond appropriately to his sacrificial death seems only natural. The authors of the New Testament provide their readers with several ways to engage in the obedient posture that is appropriate for faithfully maintaining one's position in the new covenant. First, the example of Jesus is repeatedly set before readers in a manner that is to be imitated and obeyed. For example, 1 John 2:6 summons believers to walk just as Christ walked. Paul exhorts his readers to have the mind of humility among themselves, an attitude that was also in Christ Jesus (Phil 2:4–5). The Book of Revelation employs the imagery of the faithful following the Lamb wherever he goes (Rev 14:4). Another way in which obedience to Jesus is encouraged is the formation of communities of faith, otherwise known as churches. These gatherings of believers for worship, preaching, prayer, and partaking of the sacraments serve as weekly opportunities to grow in Christ-likeness. Those who follow Jesus are members of his body, and as such, they should fellowship together in church gatherings of like-minded believers. A third way that Christians can remain obedient to Jesus comes from fervent and concentrated prayer. Christ prayed to God that his followers would share a oneness of purpose and mission that he and the Father share (John 17:20–23), a prayer that we can adopt. Similarly, Paul petitioned that the Lord would direct the hearts of his readers in the love of God and in the steadfastness of Christ (2 Thes 3:5). In this prayer, Paul requests that the Thessalonians (and we by extension) would come to imitate Jesus' steadfast endurance, particularly that the imitation would be from the heart. These three examples are practical ways to engage in obedience to Jesus Christ. Let us, therefore, look upon the way that Christ treated others, expressed faith, and preached with boldness, and seek to follow his example. Let us also not forsake the importance of gathering together with others in the body of Christ so that we can be built up and encouraged. Furthermore, let us ask God for help in bringing us into conformity with Christ's mission, while also petitioning to be strengthened in our perseverance so that we can endure like Christ endured. By making intentional choices to live as Christ lived, committing to a community of faith, and praying to be like Jesus, we can live as the obedient people that God has called us to be.

PART SEVEN: ECCLESIOLOGY

39
THE CHURCH AS THE RENEWED PEOPLE OF GOD

It is often stated (correctly) that the church is not the building; it is the people. Although this statement is factually true, people rarely unpack what it means to say that the church refers to a group of people. Who are these people, what defines this distinct group of persons, and how do they relate to the common way in which Jews would distinguish themselves from the nations? Paul presents a helpful clue in 1 Corinthians 10:32, where he portrays three different categories: Jews, Greeks, and the church of God. This indicates that Paul understood the church, the body of Christ, as what we might call a third race that transcends traditional ethnic identification. The *church* is, therefore, a way of speaking about the people of God who find themselves renewed in Christ, without resorting to the ethnicity into which the believer was born.

This chapter will explore how the New Testament authors portrayed the *church* as the renewed people of God rather than the building in which Christians gathered for worship. First, we will look closely at the way in which Jesus redefined the family unit around obedience to his gospel message. Christ's reorganization of the family was picked up by the Early Church, which began describing its converts in terms of brothers, sisters, and children of God the Father. Second, we will examine the various ways in which the apostle Paul illustrates the church of God as the new creation that has already broken into the present. Lastly, we will attempt to discern how the writers of the New Testament depicted the church as the "new Israel" that is clearly distinguished from the nation of Israel. These concepts will help shed some much-needed light on what it means to state that the church is neither Jew nor Greek, slave nor free, or male and female (Gal 3:28).

The Church as the *Renewed Family of God in Christ*

At the core of its meaning, the Greek noun *ekklesia*, commonly rendered in English as "church," refers to an assembly of persons. Early Christians did not invent the word, as the Jews were already employing it in the Greek translation of the Old Testament (the Septuagint) to convey the Hebrew noun for "assembly" (*qahal*) and the verb "to assemble" (also pronounced *qahal*). In the Old Testament, whenever the people of God assembled together, it was clear that all who were present were Israelites, that is, members of the people of Israel. They bore a relation to one another due to their shared heritage and descent from Jacob. However, when we examine the teachings of Jesus, we find several indicators that the family of God is no longer to be defined along ethnic lines of a common ancestry. Instead, Jesus taught that a new family is being formed among those who respond appropriately to his preaching of the gospel of the kingdom of God. Consider how Jesus redefined the meaning of family members in terms of insiders:

> And his mother and his brothers came, and standing outside they sent to him and called him. And a crowd was sitting around him, and they said to him, "Your mother and your brothers are outside, seeking you." And he answered them, "Who are my mother and my brothers?" And looking about at those who sat around him, he said, "Here are my mother and my brothers! For whoever does the will of God, he is my brother and sister and mother." (Mark 3:31–35)

Those who obediently responded to the will of God that was being accomplished in Jesus' ministry were considered the new insider family—those whom Jesus deliberately contrasted with his biological family (his mother and stepsiblings), whom the author identifies twice in this passage as "outsiders."[26] What is striking is the way that the Gospel of Mark immediately transitions to Jesus' famous Parable of the Sower, where he offers another contrast between insiders and outsiders: "To you has been given the secret of the kingdom of God, but for those outside everything is in parables" (Mark 4:11). We can clearly observe that, for Jesus, the insiders are those who understand the kingdom of God, while the outsiders do not possess these crucial insights.[27] In order to be a part of Jesus' redefined family, one must receive, understand, and place one's faith in his gospel of the kingdom of God (Mark 1:14–15). This theme of the renewed family of God is expressed later in the narrative when Jesus talks about how his followers have forsaken their families for his sake and for the sake of the gospel of the kingdom, resulting in a new family:

> "Truly, I say to you, there is no one who has left house or brothers or sisters or mother or father or children or lands, for my sake and for the gospel, who will not receive a hundredfold now in this time, houses and brothers and sisters and mothers and children and lands, with persecutions, and in the age to come eternal life." (Mark 10:29–30)

No doubt, Jesus took his cue from the family of God that was being reorganized around the preaching of the kingdom from John the Baptist, Jesus' forerunner. John, who summoned his audiences to repentance in light of the kingdom that was drawing near (Matt 3:2), sternly warned them against relying on their status as children of Abraham: "And do not presume to say to yourselves, 'We have Abraham as our father,' for I tell you, God is able from these stones to raise up children for Abraham" (Matt 3:9). The breaking in of God's kingdom meant that God's people needed to participate in this restorative rule and reign, particularly by bearing good fruit in keeping with the repentance that comes with accepting the message of the kingdom (Matt 3:8, 10). John's preaching again points to the proclamation of the kingdom of God that transitions a person from

---

[26] Guelich, *Mark 1–8:26*, 181–82, 186; France, *Mark*, 178–79; Wright, *Jesus and the Victory of God*, 237.
[27] Beasley-Murray, *Jesus and the Kingdom of God*, 103–7.

the old solidarity of biological family relations into a new community of faith. This new community, the renewed family of God, is expressed by a commitment to the kingdom of God and its transformative rule and reign that is already being felt by those who demonstrate the fruit of repentance.

As members of this new family of God committed to King Jesus and the gospel of the kingdom, the disciples were already experiencing the renewal of that kingdom in concrete ways.[28] For example, members of this family are to freely offer forgiveness to their brother when he repents of his sins: "If your brother sins, rebuke him, and if he repents, forgive him" (Luke 17:3). If one's brother fails to repent and live in alignment with the ideals of this renewed family, the final step in restoration involves taking the matter before the church—the entire assembly of this new family of believers: "If he refuses to listen to them, tell it to the church. And if he refuses to listen even to the church, let him be to you as a Gentile and a tax collector" (Matt 18:17). Ignoring the pleading of the church to give up one's sin results in being removed from the renewed family of God and being placed in the category of an outsider, as a Gentile or tax collector. Furthermore, Jesus clearly indicated that entrance into the kingdom of God would be granted on the Day of Judgment to those who took care of their fellow brothers and sisters, particularly in the fruit of feeding, welcoming, clothing, and visiting them: "Truly, I say to you, as you did it to one of the least of these my brothers, you did it to me" (Matt 25:40). Even after the resurrection, Jesus instructs the eyewitnesses to inform the disciples of the miracles that just took place, and in the process of conveying these instructions, Jesus describes the disciples as fellow members of his family. One such passage is recounted by Matthew: "Do not be afraid; go and tell my brothers to go to Galilee, and there they will see me" (Matt 28:10). A similar statement is found in the Gospel of John, where Jesus uses familial language and portrays his God and Father as the God and Father of his brethren: "go to my brothers and say to them, 'I am ascending to my Father and your Father, to my God and your God'" (John 20:17).

Jesus' redefinition of the people of God that took place among his kingdom-oriented disciples made a considerable impact on the earliest Christians. This can be observed in the casual use of familial language for the church, demonstrating an awareness and acceptance that the members of the new covenant were the renewed family of God. Consider these examples within the Book of Acts:

> In those days Peter stood up among the brothers (the company of persons was in all about 120) (Acts 1:15)

> "Therefore, brothers, pick out from among you seven men of good repute, full of the Spirit and of wisdom, whom we will appoint to this duty." (Acts 6:3)

---

[28] Osiek and Balch, *Families in the New Testament World*, 123–48; Barton, "Family," 226–29.

So Ananias departed and entered the house. And laying his hands on him he said, "Brother Saul, the Lord Jesus who appeared to you on the road by which you came has sent me so that you may regain your sight and be filled with the Holy Spirit." (Acts 9:17)

But the unbelieving Jews stirred up the Gentiles and poisoned their minds against the brothers. (Acts 14:2)

So, being sent on their way by the church, they passed through both Phoenicia and Samaria, describing in detail the conversion of the Gentiles, and brought great joy to all the brothers. (Acts 15:3)

When we had come to Jerusalem, the brothers received us gladly. (Acts 21:17)

The language of the renewed family is widespread in the letters of Paul, who had an uphill battle convincing his Gentile converts that they had now joined this new community of faith as believing brothers and sisters. In a pastoral attempt to encourage the Thessalonian church that was shaken by persecution and loss of life, Paul and his coauthors illustrated themselves as a gentle nursing mother who cares for her children (1 Thes 2:7). He even uses the imagery of a father exhorting his children: "we were exhorting and encouraging and imploring each one of you as a father would his own children" (1 Thes 2:11). The same imagery appears in Paul's relationship with the Corinthians, particularly in his role as the one who introduced the good news to them: "for in Christ Jesus I became your father through the gospel" (1 Cor 4:15). The exhortation offered to a church comprised of diverse converts directs them to speak to and treat others within the community as one would a fellows family member: "Do not rebuke an older man but encourage him as you would a father, younger men as brothers, older women as mothers, younger women as sisters, in all purity" (1 Tim 5:1–2).

Since the true God is the Father alone, those who are adopted into his family are regarded as sons and daughters. Membership in this renewed family of God is not based on being a natural descendant of Abraham, but rather by having the faith of Abraham, which allows Gentiles to enter the new covenant people of God on equal terms with the Jewish believers.[29] As sons of the Father, all members of this renewed family are counted as heirs of God's promises. Consider the following use of familial language:

For all who are led by the Spirit of God are sons of God. For you did not receive the spirit of slavery to fall back into fear, but you have received the Spirit of adoption as sons, by whom we cry, "Abba! Father!" (Rom 8:14–15)

In return—I speak as to children—open wide your hearts also. (2 Cor 6:13)

for in Christ Jesus you are all children of God through faith. (Gal 3:26)

---

[29] Hays, *Echoes of Scripture*, 96; Wright, *Paul and the Faithfulness of God*, 874, 1022–23.

And if you belong to Christ, then you are Abraham's descendants, heirs according to promise. (Gal 3:29)

And because you are sons, God has sent the Spirit of his son into our hearts, crying, "Abba! Father!" So you are no longer a slave, but a son, and if a son, then an heir through God. (Gal 4:6–7)

Therefore be imitators of God, as beloved children (Eph 5:1)

See what kind of love the Father has given to us, that we should be called children of God; and so we are. (1 John 3:1)

The consistent portrayal of the renewed family of God as *children*, that is, his sons and daughters, not only indicates their new solidarity in the body of Christ, but it also reaffirms the truth that the one true God is the Father alone.

Paul's Theology of the Church of God as *New Creation*

The reorganization of the people of God around faith in the gospel of the kingdom was accompanied by a transformation of these people. Stated differently, those who believed in the message of the kingdom of God experienced that rule and reign in their lives, seeing their identity take on the effects of the powers of the age to come breaking into the present (Heb 6:5). The apostle Paul's theology is saturated with the belief that the ministry, death, resurrection, and exaltation of Jesus inaugurated the kingdom of God, and this belief deeply influenced how Paul illustrated those Christians in his churches. This is first observable in Paul's use of "new creation" to describe those who are in Christ. In Galatians 6:15, Paul describes three racial categories, and in the process, he indicates that the body of Christ is a new third race known as the new creation: "For neither is circumcision anything, nor uncircumcision, but a new creation" (Gal 6:15).[30] In Christ, the former categories of viewing humanity are outdated, since they do not reflect the people defined at their core by the message of the kingdom. Paul repeats this truth when writing to the Corinthians: "Therefore, if anyone is in Christ, he is a new creation. The old has passed away; behold, the new has come" (2 Cor 5:17). While Paul does still anticipate the renewal of creation as a hope to be realized in the future (Rom 8:19–22), he firmly believes that the new creation has already begun among the new covenant people of God—the church that has been transformed by the gospel of the kingdom.

One of the biggest indicators that the new creation has begun in the church is the people's reception of the Holy Spirit. If the future renewal of creation included redeemed, immortal bodies, then having the Spirit already is indicative that the new creation has already broken into the present: "And not only this, but also we ourselves,

---

[30] Hays, "Paul's Letter to the Galatians," 344; Wright, *Paul and the Faithfulness of God*, 1072.

having the first fruits of the Spirit, even we ourselves groan within ourselves, waiting eagerly for our adoption as sons, the redemption of our body" (Rom 8:23). Although Paul and his converts long to be clothed with the future resurrection body, the Holy Spirit has already been given as a pledge by God, beginning the process of new creation (2 Cor 5:4–5). Possession of the Spirit, which is a preview of the full measure of renewal that is to come, should produce in the Church works that reflect the reality of God's redemptive reign in the present. Paul's theology variously illustrates these Spirit-empowered deeds as "the fruit of the Spirit" (Gal 5:22–23), "the fruit of light" (Eph 5:9), and "the fruit of righteousness" (Phil 1:11). Just as the people of God were led by a cloud and pillar of fire in the wilderness trek, Paul argues that the new covenant people of God should similarly follow the leading of the Spirit (Gal 5:16, 18). Those who are being led by the Spirit are rightly identified as the renewed family of God: "For all who are being led by the Spirit of God, these are sons of God" (Rom 8:14). Thus, the gift of the Spirit that one receives at conversion is one of the clearest indicators that the reign and rule of God have broken into the present, experienced by God's new creation people in Christ.

Another key feature of the church functioning as God's new creation is the ongoing act of regeneration and renewal. As citizens of the kingdom of God, the church is not to conform with this present age but is instead to continue in the process of Spirit-led transformation through the renewal of one's thinking: "Do not be conformed to this world, but be transformed by the renewal of your mind" (Rom 12:2). This process of change begins at conversion, where the rare noun "regeneration" appears in one of its two biblical occurrences: "He saved us, not on the basis of deeds which we have done in righteousness, but according to His mercy, by the washing of regeneration and renewing by the Holy Spirit" (Tit 3:5).[31] As such, the promised regeneration of creation that is to take place at Jesus' return (Matt 19:28) has broken into the present, beginning with the reception of the Spirit and continuing in the ongoing renewal of a believer's thinking. New creation, strictly speaking, does not solely reside in the future.

The Church as the *New Israel*

The themes of the renewed family of God and the believer as a new creation in Christ converge in Paul's realization that the church is the new Israel. As surprising as this statement may appear, it does seem to be the best reading of Paul's theology. Beginning with the evidence in Galatians, we can observe Paul contrasting the Jewish identity (circumcision) and Gentile identity (uncircumcision) with the new creation, and having identified this third race of people, he offers peace and mercy upon those who walk by this standard:

---

[31] Weiss, *Jesus' Proclamation of the Kingdom*, 95; Quinn, *Titus*, 221; Towner, *The Letters to Timothy and Titus*, 781–82.

> For neither is circumcision anything, nor uncircumcision, but a new creation. And those who will walk by this rule, peace and mercy be upon them, and upon the Israel of God. (Gal 6:15–16)

In the final verse (Gal 6:16), the translation above gives the impression that Paul is talking about two distinct groups: those who walk by this rule and "the Israel of God." However, most specialists working on Galatians have convincingly argued that the word separating these two groups ("and") possesses a well-known alternative meaning ("even") that would indicate Paul's intent to describe a single group with two complementary descriptions. In other words, Paul would be blessing the new creation with peace and mercy, and then immediately clarifying this group with the new term "Israel of God."[32] By qualifying "Israel" as the Israel *of God*, Paul is giving a new title to the church that distinguishes it from ethnic Israel, which he has already illustrated with the term "circumcision" in the previous verse.[33] The renewed people of God in Christ—the church—are the faithful people God always sought.[34]

Paul revisits this theological truth in an extended argument within Romans. His contention begins by arguing that there are two ways of talking about "Israel": those who descend from Israel and those who can claim the designation without having descended from Israel: "For not all who are descended from Israel belong to Israel" (Rom 9:6). Paul here introduces to the Romans what unfolds to be a lengthy exposition of two different ways of being *Israel*; one defined by ancestry and the other defined by faith in the gospel. This second way of being Israel does not replace the physical descendants of Israel; the two remain distinct in Paul's thought. When he brings the argument to its conclusion, Paul notes how a partial hardening has occurred among the people of Israel due to their unbelief (Rom 11:20), and in the midst of this hardening, believing Gentiles are being grafted into the people of God that is defined by faith: "a partial hardening has come upon Israel, until the fullness of the Gentiles has come in. And in this way all Israel will be saved" (Rom 11:25–26). In this passage, Paul again uses *Israel* in two different ways: one to designate ethnic Israel (who continues in its unbelief in the gospel of the kingdom) and the other to refer to a category of Israel that is not defined along racial lines, but rather by belief ("all Israel"). Since membership in this category of *Israel* is characterized by belief in the gospel, rather than strict ethnicity, it is open to all who believe, namely, the church. As such, Romans 11:26 is similar to Galatians 6:16 in that it portrays the body of Christ—the renewed family of God defined by faith in the gospel—as a new category of *Israel*, without replacing the nation of ethnic Israel as its own category.[35]

---

[32] Sanders, *Paul, the Law, and the Jewish People*, 173–74; Keener, *Galatians* 228–91; Dunn, *Galatians*, 345.
[33] Beale, *Temple*, 277; deSilva, *Galatians*, 510.
[34] Hays, "The Letter to the Galatians," 345–46; Martyn, *Galatians*, 575–77; Wright, *Galatians*, 377.
[35] Wright, "The Letter to the Romans," 688–91; *Paul and the Faithfulness of God*, 1239–52.

We can observe further evidence of Paul's theology of seeing the church as the new Israel in 1 Corinthians, where he argues that when one partakes in a sacrificial meal, there is a genuine ritualistic experience in which those who eat are in fellowship with that very sacrifice. Consider how Paul contrasts the ritual meals of three different groups:

> Is not the cup of blessing which we bless a sharing in the blood of Christ? Is not the bread which we break a sharing in the body of Christ? Since there is one bread, we who are many are one body; for we all partake of the one bread. Look at the nation Israel; are not those who eat the sacrifices sharers in the altar? What do I mean then? That a thing sacrificed to idols is anything, or that an idol is anything? No, but I say that the things which the Gentiles sacrifice, they sacrifice to demons and not to God; and I do not want you to become sharers in demons. (1 Cor 10:16–20)

The three groups Paul describes here are the church, Israel, and the Gentiles. However, when Paul describes "the nation Israel," the Greek phrase that lies behind this English translation (literally "the Israel according to the flesh") offers an important insight into his theology. Since Paul is here qualifying *Israel* as Israel according to the flesh, it suggests that there is another Israel—an Israel according to the promise.[36] As luck would have it, this is exactly what Paul declares elsewhere: "It is not the children of the flesh who are children of God, but the children of the promise are regarded as descendants" (Rom 9:8). All of this again points to Paul having in mind two different categories for Israel: one for the nation of Israel (Israel according to the flesh) and the other for the church (the renewed Israel defined by faith).[37]

Naturally, the Apostle Paul is not the only figure in the New Testament who portrays the church as the renewed Israel. We can already discern the beginning of this concept in the actions of Jesus himself, who began the restoration of Israel by calling twelve disciples (Matt 10:1; Mark 3:14; Luke 6:13), which was surely meant to express the renewal of the twelve tribes of Israel. The Letter of James shows the influence of Jesus' symbolic attempt at reorganizing Israel around himself by opening its correspondence with a description of the Christian community as "the twelve tribes in the Dispersion" (James 1:1). The First Epistle of Peter explicitly characterizes its recipients, who reside in several Gentile regions, with several descriptors formerly belonging to the nation of Israel. The readers of 1 Peter are illustrated as "being built up as a spiritual house for a holy priesthood" (1 Pet 2:5), "a chosen race, a royal priesthood, a holy nation, a people for his own possession" (1 Pet 2:9), which draws upon the description of the Israelites as a treasured possession, a kingdom of priests, and a holy nation in Exodus 19:5–6. The passage is followed by describing the Christians as formerly "not a people, but now you are the people of God" (1 Pet 2:10). This, again, is a citation from the Old Testament,

---

[36] Fee, *The First Epistle to the Corinthians*, 519; Fitzmyer, *First Corinthians*, 392; Thiselton, *The First Epistle to the Corinthians*, 771; Wright, *Paul and the Faithfulness of God*, 1147–48.

[37] Sanders, *Paul, the Law, and the Jewish People*, 172, rightly observes that "Gentiles who enter the people of God do not, after all, in Paul's view, join Israel according to the flesh."

specifically from Hosea 1:9–10, which prophesies about the restoration of *Israel*. We should not miss the point that a promise about Israel's restoration has found its fulfillment *in the church*, among a group of believers in whom the family of God has been renewed.[38]

Conclusion

To summarize, this chapter set out to examine closely how the writers of the New Testament illustrated the church as the restoration of the people of God. Although it is common vocabulary to refer to the building in which Christians gather as a church, the early Christians reserved this language for the body of Christ, that is, for the family of God in Christ. To this effect, we first observed that the church was frequently portrayed in terms of a new family, as brothers and sisters who regard God as their Father. Christ himself began this characterization of his faithful followers as the renewed family, and this theology spread quickly to permeate the language and sense of belonging shared by the earliest Christians. Second, we traced the theology of Paul that depicts this renewed family of God with several other descriptors involving the restoration of the people of God, including *new creation*, as recipients of the *Holy Spirit*, and those who are presently experiencing *regeneration* and *renewal*. Finally, we saw how Paul and other New Testament authors displayed the church as the renewed Israel, often with explicit language, such as "the Israel of God." Following the lead of Christ, who symbolically reorganized the twelve tribes around himself by designating twelve faithful disciples as apostles, the Early Church was thoroughly convinced that its community was the recipient of the many promises of Israel's restoration located in the Old Testament. So, while it is true that "the church is not a building, it is the people," the church is so much more than simply "the people." It is the renewed family of God, in whom the new creation has already begun, bringing fulfillment to God's hope to reorganize his people in and through their faith in the gospel of the kingdom.

We noticed in this chapter's examination of the church that the role of the priesthood was applied to early Christians (Exod 19:5–6; 1 Pet 2:5, 9). In fact, there are several indicators that nearly every aspect of the priesthood has now been handed over to the church, the renewed people of God. In particular, the writers of the New Testament frequently illustrate the body of Christ as the new temple. Why did these biblical authors offer such a portrayal? What purposes did it serve, and why is it relevant to the church's evangelistic mission? We will explore these questions in our next chapter.

---

[38] Boring, *1 Peter*, 98–101, 203–5; Achtemeier, *1 Peter*, 152; Elliott, *I Peter*, 420–21.

40
THE CHURCH AS THE NEW TEMPLE

From the earliest period of God's interaction with his people is the express desire to have the Creator God dwell in the midst of humanity. After creating the heavens and the earth, Yahweh made it a point to walk in the Garden of Eden with Adam and Eve, rather than insisting that humanity be relocated to dwell with him in heaven. After rescuing the Israelites from Egypt, God informs Moses of his intent to have his people construct a sanctuary "so that I may dwell among them," according to Exodus 25:8. In fact, Yahweh plainly admits that he brought them out of the land of Egypt in order that he might dwell among his people (Exod 29:46).[1] The same desire to be in the midst of humanity is repeated during the construction of Solomon's temple (1 Kgs 6:13), which visibly took place when the glory of Yahweh descended in a cloud. Prior to the temple's destruction, Ezekiel prophetically witnessed the presence of Yahweh departing from the temple (Ezek 10:18). When the second temple was built, there were no sightings of the glorious cloud returning to dwell among God's people. In fact, the prophet Malachi offers hope by announcing that "the Lord, whom you seek, will suddenly come to His temple" in Malachi 3:1. Yahweh's deep desire to dwell with his faithful people remains as the Old Testament story comes to a close and the New Testament begins. This story reaches its climax in the temple theology of the early Christians.

This chapter will explore precisely how the Early Church came to be identified as the temple of God, the place in which Yahweh has chosen to dwell. First, we will look at how Jesus' reorganization of the people of God around himself also shifted emphasis away from a physical temple building towards a view that the early Christians were a newly formed temple community. Second, we will look closely at how the writers of the New Testament employed several temple and priestly-related metaphors to the church, that is, to the people with whom God has shared his holy Spirit. Finally, we will examine how the author of the Book of Revelation utilizes its image-filled symbols to illustrate the church as the new temple. By taking stock of the various ways in which the New Testament authors portray the body of Christ as God's temple, we will come to a deeper understanding of the church's mission and purpose. Furthermore, we will gain insight into the self-understanding of the Early Church, which motivated its mission, evangelism, and commitment to holiness.

---

[1] Brueggemann, "The Book of Exodus," 914; Durham, *Exodus*, 397; Johnstone, *Exodus 20–40*, 313.

Jesus and the New Temple Community

When we seek the foundations of a doctrine believed and taught by early Christians, it makes sense to start with a fresh examination of the teachings of Jesus Christ. Fortunately, the four New Testament gospel accounts provide several pieces of data relevant to our study of the church as the new temple dwelling of God. In fact, there are quite a few places where Jesus illustrates his community of kingdom-believing followers as the temple community. For example, when the Pharisees criticized Jesus' disciples for picking and eating some of the heads of grain on the Sabbath, he responded with two references to the temple:

> But he said to them, "Have you not read what David did when he became hungry, he and his companions, how he entered the house of God, and they ate the consecrated bread, which was not lawful for him to eat nor for those with him, but for the priests alone? Or have you not read in the Law, that on the Sabbath the priests in the temple break the Sabbath and are innocent? But I say to you that something greater than the temple is here. (Matt 12:3–6)

As an explanation for what Jesus allowed his followers to do on the seventh day, he noted that King David and his followers were innocent when they partook of the bread that was reserved for priests in the house of God. As the Jewish messiah, the son of David, Jesus seems to be applying the freedom that David and his companions possessed to both him and his companions, the disciples. Furthermore, Jesus draws attention to the daily activities of the priests in the temple that take place on the Sabbath—an activity for which they are not at fault. If Jesus regards his reorganization of the people of God around himself as a new temple community, then it would naturally follow that those who participate in that community are its priests, namely, Jesus' disciples.[2] In this line of thinking, if the priests are able to perform their God-given duties on the Sabbath and be innocent of any commandment–breaking, then the followers of Jesus are likewise innocent of what the Pharisees are accusing them. Jesus then attempts to encourage his opponents to think deeply about the implications of what he is telling them by stating that something greater than the temple is standing right in front of them, that is, Jesus himself, the messianic successor of David, in whom the temple functions are now at work.

Towards the end of Jesus' ministry is the instance when he enters the Jerusalem temple and prophetically cleanses it (Mark 11:15–17). This symbolic act of judgment is immediately followed in the narrative with Jesus conferring the temple's role of mediating God's forgiveness onto his disciples: "Whenever you stand praying, forgive, if you have anything against anyone, so that your Father who is in heaven will also forgive you your transgressions" (Mark 11:25). Within the new covenant that Jesus is inaugurating, his followers are to be the means by which forgiveness is given to others. God is at work in

---

[2] Hagner, *Matthew 1–13*, 329. Nolland, *Matthew*, 484, draws attention to "the 'priestly' ministry of the disciples."

Jesus' temple community, and Jesus' prophetic denunciation of the physical temple in Jerusalem indicates that God is not pleased with how it is functioning. Jesus has been preparing his disciples to carry out the temple's God-given functions and purposes.[3]

Of course, Jesus' reorganization of the people of God around himself as the new temple suggests that Jesus himself plays a crucial role in this transition. We already saw hints of this in Matthew 12:6 ("something greater than the temple is here"), and there are, fortunately, some explicit statements in the Gospel of John. We were introduced to the concept of Wisdom Christology in Chapter 25, and in the process, we briefly examined John 1:14, where God's personified word-wisdom became flesh and lived among us. The Greek verb behind the English translation "lived" (*skenoo*) would be more accurately rendered as the action of *tabernacling* among us. The related noun to this verb—the Greek noun *skene*—refers to a tent, and this noun is often used to describe the tent of meeting in which Yahweh dwelt among his people. In other words, John 1:14 is, among other things, depicting Jesus as the human person in whom God's personified word has dwelt. From the very beginning of the Gospel of John, temple and tabernacle imagery are applied to the human Jesus.[4]

The portrayal of Jesus as the one in whom the new temple is beginning to be revealed reappears in the second chapter of John. In what is the first of many examples of the theme of misunderstanding in the Gospel of John, the narrator clarifies Jesus' attempt at pointing to his body as the new temple:

> "Destroy this temple, and in three days I will raise it up." The Jews then said, "It took forty-six years to build this temple, and will you raise it up in three days?" But he was speaking of the temple of His body. (John 2:19–21)

Consider how the narrative unpacks this typical misunderstanding that occurs several times in John's gospel. First, Jesus makes a key claim pertaining to "this temple." Second, his dialogue partners misunderstand him, typically by interpreting what Jesus said too literally (i.e., the temple in Jerusalem) or by asking a misguided question. The third step, which sometimes but not always occurs after step two, involves a clarification stated by Jesus or, in this case, the narrator (Jesus was speaking about his own body as the temple). The result of the encounter is clear: Jesus speaks of himself as the new temple, and the fact that Jesus made this claim while standing in the Jerusalem temple indicates his intent to draw attention to himself as the new and true temple, one that, unlike the building in Jerusalem, will endure after it is destroyed.

One of the primary functions of the physical temple and its staff of priests was to mediate God's forgiveness to the people. Since Jesus has taken on the role of the

---

[3] Beale and Kim, *God Dwells Among Us*, 150; Dunn, *Jesus Remembered*, 589–90; Marcus, *Mark 8–16*, 796.
[4] Smith, *Wisdom Christology*, 69–71; Beale, *Temple*, 195; Keener, *John*, 1:408–10.

temple, it is no surprise that we find Jesus offering forgiveness of sins to the repentant, apart from the involvement of the Jerusalem priesthood and temple sacrifices.[5] All four gospel writers illustrate Christ as granting forgiveness to others—performing in the process a key temple function in light of the authority that God gave to him (Matt 9:8). As the focal point of the new temple from which the forgiveness of sins can be acquired, the followers of Jesus also shared in this God-given role. Jesus taught his disciples to forgive others just as God has forgiven them: "Forgive us our debts, as we also have forgiven our debtors" (Matt 6:12). Mutual forgiving was to take place between fellow family members in the renewed temple community, as Christ taught his disciples in Matthew 18:21–22. In fact, Jesus explicitly shares with his followers the same Holy Spirit that God gave to him, and in the process, the disciples became equipped and qualified to participate in the forgiveness of sins: "Receive the Holy Spirit. If you forgive the sins of any, their sins have been forgiven them; if you retain the sins of any, they have been retained" (John 20:22–23).

In addition to taking over the Jerusalem temple's role of mediating forgiveness, Jesus performed several miracles that granted purification to those in need. In doing so, Jesus assumes the temple function of enacting cultic rites of purification. On several occasions, Jesus healed persons who were possessed by unclean spirits (Mark 1:23–27; 5:2–13; 7:25–29; 9:25–27), restoring them to wholeness and peace. In addition to announcing the gospel of the kingdom of God, Jesus often performed several miracles that brought the promised reign of God into the present:

> Jesus was going throughout all Galilee, teaching in their synagogues and proclaiming the gospel of the kingdom, and healing every kind of disease and every kind of sickness among the people. The news about him spread throughout all Syria; and they brought to him all who were ill, those suffering with various diseases and pains, demoniacs, epileptics, paralytics; and he healed them. (Matt 4:23–24)

In fact, when Jesus would perform acts involving unclean persons or enter into unclean spaces, it was not Jesus who contaminated impurity, but rather, it was Jesus who granted purification. This included granting healing and wholeness to the hemorrhaging woman (Mark 5:25–34), touching one who has died (Mark 5:41), and healing those who touched the fringe of his cloak (Mark 6:56). For those who were unable to perceive that Jesus was operating as the new temple, it appeared as if Jesus was disregarding ritual purity concerns, particularly in his association with sinners, with whom he would frequently eat and reside in their homes (Luke 5:30; 7:34; 19:7). However, Jesus was the agent of God's restoration, bringing purification to these sinners who repented and believed in his message of the kingdom of God (Luke 15:1–2). As the locus of God's new temple activity, Jesus offered cleansing to the unclean, and he also empowered his disciples to function as members of this new temple community: "Jesus summoned His twelve disciples and gave them

---

[5] Beale and Kim, *God Dwells Among Us*, 74; Beale, *Temple*, 177–78; Dunn, *Jesus Remembered*, 787–88.

authority over unclean spirits, to cast them out, and to heal every kind of disease and every kind of sickness" (Matt 10:1). It should be apparent that the reconstituted temple of God is not a physical structure, but rather within a community of persons in whom God is able to offer forgiveness, purification, and wholeness. It is no wonder that the author of the Epistle to the Hebrews insists that the risen Jesus now serves as the high priest forever (Heb 6:20).

The Early Church's Self-Understanding as God's New Temple

By the time Jesus was taken up into heaven, the Early Church was prepared to continue this ministry as the new temple community. His followers were given an important mandate to proclaim in the name of Jesus the "forgiveness of sins" (Luke 24:47). Furthermore, their mission would begin in Jerusalem, which was the location of the pouring out of the Spirit on the Day of Pentecost. The prophet Joel had prophesied that God would pour forth his Spirit (Joel 2:28), and Peter's inspired sermon declares that this had just taken place in their midst, proving that the last days had begun: "And in the last days it shall be, God declares, that I will pour out my Spirit on all flesh" (Acts 2:17). Having received the Spirit, the Early Church increasingly expressed itself as the renewed temple of God—the place that God has chosen to dwell. Paul observed that the Early Church had already employed architectural language from the Jerusalem temple to describe the apostles in terms of *pillars* in the church: "James and Cephas and John, who were reputed to be pillars" (Gal 2:9). In other words, Paul is acknowledging that the early Christian community was already functioning as the renewed temple community before he encountered the risen Christ.[6]

The letters of Paul helped promote the theology and awareness that the church, the body of Christ, was indeed the new temple dwelling of God. We can observe several instances where Paul's theology of the church as the new temple is plainly illustrated. One example concerns the entire community being depicted as the temple of God due to their possession of the indwelling Holy Spirit:

> Do you not know that you are a temple of God and that the Spirit of God dwells in you? If any man destroys the temple of God, God will destroy him, for the temple of God is holy, and that is what you are. (1 Cor 3:16–17)

While it is not apparent in this English translation, Paul wrote that *you* (second-person plural) are the temple and that the Spirit dwells in *you* (second-person plural). The entire Christian community functions as this new temple, bearing the temple's holiness as a benefit. Furthermore, we can observe that Yahweh's frequently mentioned desire to come

---

[6] Wilckins, "στῦλος," 734–35; Dunn, *Beginning from Jerusalem*, 210; Bruce, *Galatians*, 122–23.

and dwell in the midst of his faithful people finds fulfillment with the Spirit, God's extended presence, dwelling among the new covenant community. It is this acknowledgment of the Early Church's possession of the Spirit that primarily convinces Paul that the Christian community is the dwelling of the promised temple of the Creator God. When Paul attempts to dissuade the Corinthians from visiting the temple prostitutes, he identifies the individual believer as a temple dwelling of the Spirit that ought to result in holy living and the glorification of the true God:

> Shun fornication! Every sin that a person commits is outside the body; but the fornicator sins against the body itself. Or do you not know that your body is a temple of the Holy Spirit within you, which you have from God, and that you are not your own? For you were bought with a price; therefore glorify God in your body. (1 Cor 6:18–20)

As a temple dwelling of the Spirit of God, the early Christians were to behave in accordance with holiness that identified them as the sanctified people in Christ.[7] The same attitude is expressed in Second Corinthians, which preserves another declaration that the church is the temple of God that must distance itself from darkness:

> What agreement has the temple of God with idols? For we are the temple of the living God; as God said, "I will make my dwelling among them and walk among them, and I will be their God, and they shall be my people. Therefore go out from their midst, and be separate from them, says the Lord, and touch no unclean thing; then I will welcome you, and I will be a Father to you, and you shall be sons and daughters to Me, says the Lord Almighty." (2 Cor 6:16–18)

As the temple dwelling of God, the Early Church was to live in a manner that was in alignment with its role as the renewed family of God—the sons and daughters of the Father. Since the reception of the Spirit marks the beginning of the transformative experience of the lives of Christians, the role of serving as God's new temple was, understandably, something into which the community would grow. Consider the language of growth and development as it relates to the Early Church as the temple dwelling of God: "The whole building, being fitted together, is growing into a holy temple in the Lord, in whom you also are being built together into a dwelling of God in the Spirit" (Eph 2:21–22). It is within this early Christian body that God has chosen for his Spirit to dwell.[8]

In the First Epistle of Peter, we can detect further evidence of the Early Church's acceptance of its role as God's temple community. The readers, similar to the message in Ephesians 2:21–22, are "being built up as a spiritual house for a holy priesthood" (1 Pet 2:5). Since the early Christians have assumed the role of the priesthood in this new temple, it naturally follows that they would be offering spiritual sacrifices,

---

[7] Beale, *Temple*, 252; Garland, *1 Corinthians*, 238–39; Sampley, "The First Letter to the Corinthians," 864–65.
[8] Lincoln, *Ephesians*, 158–59; Barth, *Ephesians 1–3*, 273-74; Beale and Kim, *God Dwells Among Us*, 85–86.

rather than animal sacrifices. 1 Peter 2:5 is clear that these spiritual acts of cultic service are directed *to* God, but *through* Jesus Christ. Jesus is the high priest, so the sacrifices are not made to him; they are made to God. Drawing on the illustration of Israel as God's own possession, a kingdom of priests, and a holy nation (Exod 19:5–6), First Peter applies those noteworthy descriptions to the Early Church, noting in the same breath that this new temple community has a mission to declare God's mighty deeds:

> But you are a chosen race, a royal priesthood, a holy nation, God's own people, in order that you may proclaim the mighty acts of him who called you out of darkness into his marvelous light. (1 Pet 2:9)

As newly appointed priests in God's new temple, the early Christians were expected to live holy lives by abstaining from fleshly lusts (1 Pet 2:11) and behaving well among the unbelieving Gentiles (1 Pet 2:12).

This suggests that the Early Church perceived its new role as God's temple, offering spiritual sacrifices, which provides us with the opportunity to examine the use of sacrificial language to illustrate the work of the body of Christ. Paul exhorts the Christians in Rome to offer themselves entirely to God as living sacrifices in Romans 12:1, implying that, under the old covenant, animal sacrifices were to symbolize the giver's full commitment to Yahweh. Paul regarded his humble service and self-emptying acts as a drink offering being poured out upon the sacrifice and offering of the faith belonging to the Philippians (Phil 2:17).[9] When Christians gave sacrificially to others, Paul regarded that generosity as "a fragrant aroma, an acceptable sacrifice, well-pleasing to God" (Phil 4:18). The author of Hebrews similarly praises the sharing and doing good to others as sacrifices pleasing to God (Heb 13:16). Furthermore, praising God with the fruit of one's lips is also portrayed in terms of sacrifices offered by early Christians (Heb 13:15). This data indicates that the Early Church understood its role as the new temple in terms of offering sacrifices in daily life, including worship, serving the needy, and showing love.

The Theology of the New Temple Community in the Book of Revelation

The Book of Revelation is the composition in the New Testament that emphasizes the church's role as the new temple more than any other early Christian writing, which may surprise many. Revelation's rich imagery draws upon the Old Testament in order to illustrate the conquering and faithful body of Christ as holy priests serving in God's new temple. We again see the influence of Exodus 19:5–6 upon the imagery of the early Christians as the beneficiaries of Christ, who has made them into a kingdom and priests in Revelation 1:6; 5:10.[10] The image of the twenty-four elders in Revelation 4:4 has been

---

[9] Beale, *Temple*, 400; Hooker, "The Letter to the Philippians," 513–14; Reumann, *Philippians*, 414–15.
[10] Aune, *Revelation 1–5*, 47–49; Reddish, *Revelation*, 35–36, 112; Beale, *Revelation*, 193–95.

impacted by the twenty-four classes of priests that serve in the temple according to 1 Chronicles 24:7–19.[11] We can be confident that Revelation's twenty-four priestly elders represent faithful Christians because they are characterized as enthroned, wearing white garments, and having crowns upon their heads—all three of which are promises previously offered to *faithful Christians* earlier in the narrative (2:10; 3:5, 11, 21). As priests of God's new temple community, their prayers are likened to bowls of incense (Rev 5:8) that rise up to God's throne, indicating that these prayers of petition function as priestly service that is acceptable to the one seated upon the throne (Rev 8:3–4). The symbolism of the incense that portrays Christian prayer draws upon the altar of incense, which was located in the dwelling place of God (Exod 30:1; 2 Chron 26:16), thereby further highlighting Revelation's portrayal of the Early Church as the new temple.[12]

Revelation employs rich and profound imagery to portray the suffering that early Christian evangelists endured, likening it to the sacrifices made in the temple. Revelation 6:9–11 portrays a vision of the martyrs of the Early Church who were directly persecuted for their preaching of the gospel message:

> I saw under the altar the souls of those who had been slaughtered for the word of God and for the testimony they had given; they cried out with a loud voice, "Sovereign Lord, holy and true, how long will it be before you judge and avenge our blood on the inhabitants of the earth?" They were each given a white robe and told to rest a little longer, until the number would be complete both of their fellow servants and of their brothers and sisters, who were soon to be killed as they themselves had been killed. (Rev 6:9–11)

This vision incorporates several elements of sacrificial temple imagery associated with the early Christian martyrs. First, the deceased are located in proximity to the sacrificial altar. Second, their deaths are illustrated with the verb "to slaughter," which both reflects the language associated with animal sacrifices and also the imagery formerly used to describe Jesus as a sacrificial lamb (Rev 5:6, 9, 12). Third, their sacrifice and prayer longed for their blood to be avenged, highlighting the sacrificial nature of their faithful witness. By associating the evangelistic work of these priestly believers with the images of the altar, slaughter, and blood, there can be no doubt that Revelation contributes to a theology of the Early Church as God's new temple community.[13]

Although we will examine how Revelation brilliantly symbolizes the Early Church with New Jerusalem imagery in Chapter 43, we can take an opportunity now to look at the Christian communities and their portrayal as lampstands. When Jesus appears to John of Patmos, John envisions Jesus in the midst of seven golden lampstands (Rev 1:12–13). We can be confident that these lampstands refer to church communities because Jesus

---

[11] Allen, "The First and Second Books of Chronicles," 441; Beale, *Revelation*, 324; Thompson, *Revelation*, 91.
[12] Beale and Kim, *God Dwells Among Us*, 152; Reddish, *Revelation*, 161–62; Aune, *Revelation 6–16*, 511–15.
[13] See especially Beale, *Temple*, 313–34.

plainly stated as much: "the seven lampstands are the seven churches" (Rev 1:20). Since the lampstand of pure gold, known in Hebrew as a *menorah*, was a standard piece of furniture in the tabernacle dwelling of Yahweh (Exod 25:31–40), we can reasonably conclude that the new temple community of the Early Church possessed a mission that was outward in scope and light-bringing in its evangelistic role.[14] By portraying early Christian communities with the imagery of the tabernacle's lampstand, Revelation continues to stress that the church's mission is deeply characterized by the function of God's dwelling place, namely, to mediate God's redemption, light, and holiness to all creation.

Conclusion

To summarize, this chapter examined several ways in which the Early Church perceived itself as God's new temple community, the place where God dwells in the Spirit. The authors of the New Testament portray a growing awareness, stemming from Jesus' teachings to his earliest followers, that the church, the body of Christ, is the place where God has formed his temple dwelling. We first observed that the community that Jesus formed around himself began to receive the roles and functions formerly belonging to the temple structure in Jerusalem. This was no doubt encouraged because Jesus himself was the human in whom God's tabernacling presence was embodied. Second, we saw that many of the New Testament writings were fully aware that the church was already functioning as the new temple of God. Not only was the body of Christ explicitly illustrated as a temple, but its members were also its pillars, the new priesthood, and the recipients of the Holy Spirit. Finally, we took notice of the special emphases within the Book of Revelation that used images, signs, and symbols to depict the faithful people of God as the new temple community. Since the church was the place where God had chosen to dwell in his Spirit, the body of Christ saw its evangelistic mission as bearing temple functions, namely mediating God's forgiveness and holiness to a world desperately in need of redemption.

In the first century, every religious sect had its own unique set of ritualistic practices, and the Early Church was no exception. The early Christians practiced two rituals that many refer to as sacraments. These are the acts of baptism in water and sharing in a special meal, known as the Lord's Supper. What are these sacraments, why were they important to the Early Church, and what do they tell us about the beliefs of the followers of Christ? We will explore baptism and the Lord's Supper in our next chapter, attempting to provide answers to these essential questions.

---

[14] Brueggemann, "The Book of Exodus," 890; Smith, *Paradoxical Conquering*, 136–38.

41
BAPTISM AND THE LORD'S SUPPER

One of the most common ways to distinguish different religious groups is to organize them by their ritualistic rites and practices. Judaism was fairly recognizable because its adherents practiced physical circumcision, rested on the seventh day, observed kosher food laws, and refused to worship images or idols. Those who participated in the Roman emperor cult made offerings to the Caesars, both living and dead, swore oaths and vows of loyalty, attended festivals that honored the emperor, offered incense, and prayed for his well-being. The Early Church likewise had its own ceremonial rituals, namely the initiation act of immersion in water and a meal of remembrance dedicated to their founder's death. These sacraments, which are known as baptism and the Lord's Supper, were crucially important to the self-identification of early Christians, while drawing influence from Israel's history to give meaning to these rites.

This chapter will examine the Early Church's sacraments of baptism in water and sharing in the Lord's Supper to understand their meaning, function, and significance. Beginning with the practice of baptizing early Christian converts in water, we will look closely at the impact provided by John the Baptist and the teachings of Jesus. Second, we will explore the widespread practice of water baptism in the Early Church and the theology that the New Testament authors attribute to the immersing ritual. Third, we will transition to the sacrament of the Lord's Supper by looking at its formation of meaning within the preaching and deeds of Christ. Lastly, we will investigate the significance of the Lord's Supper as a regular practice in the early Christian communities of faith. By giving attention to these sacramental rituals of the Early Church, we will better understand how its members defined their identity by looking to the past at the ministry of Jesus and also looking forward to the hope of his return.

The Baptism of John the Baptist

As we have typically done in our explorations of the origins of a particular early Christian belief or practice, we start with Jesus. However, when it comes to baptism, we can trace this practice to Jesus' older cousin, John the Baptist. John, who received the nickname "the Baptizer" (typically rendered in English as "the Baptist"), was widely recognized as a Jewish figure who immersed repentant individuals in water for the forgiveness of their sins. As John announced the dawning of God's kingdom, he summoned his audience to prepare for this coming rule and reign by changing their behavior, washing away their sins in the Jordan River, and producing fruit in keeping with that repentance:

> Now in those days John the Baptist came, preaching in the wilderness of Judea, saying, "Repent, for the kingdom of heaven is at hand." . . . Then Jerusalem was going out to him, and all Judea and all the district around the Jordan; and they were being baptized by him in the Jordan River, as they confessed their sins. But when he saw many of the Pharisees and Sadducees coming for baptism, he said to them, "You brood of vipers, who warned you to flee from the wrath to come? Therefore bear fruit in keeping with repentance" (Matt 3:1–2, 5–8)

It is clear from this early reference to the practice of baptism that it involved physically immersing the initiate into a body of water. John didn't sprinkle a handful of water over the heads of the repentant, nor is there evidence that infants placed their faith in the kingdom of God for the remission of sins. The portrayal of John seems clear: he invited those who accepted his message of the dawning kingdom of God, which he further defined as the "wrath to come," to follow through with their repentance by allowing John to physically immerse them in the river.

When we place John in his Jewish and familial context, we can gather some important clues about the significance he attributed to this initiation rite for those who chose to repent upon accepting the claim that the kingdom of God had drawn near. On one hand, John's baptism would have been viewed by many as a challenge to the forgiveness offered by the Jerusalem temple. Within the Jewish practices contemporary with John's ministry, those seeking forgiveness were required to make a pilgrimage to Jerusalem and offer the appropriate sacrifices. What John's baptism offered was forgiveness without having to travel all the way to Jerusalem and provide payment for the sacrificial animals. By removing the distance required for travel and the financial burden of purchasing the animals, it may appear as if John was making God's forgiveness far more accessible.[1] This conclusion, however, overlooks the genuine repentance and fruit of change that John demanded of his listeners, something the temple priests performing the daily sacrifices did not require. John was adamant that those who came to him to be baptized for the forgiveness of their sins must change their ways and demonstrate the fruit of this change.

John's family, particularly his father, Zacharias, the priest (Luke 1:5), made it possible for John to serve in the same role, as temple priests were born into the profession. Since Zacharias was a priest, that role would have been passed on and expected of John. However, it appears that John was supposed to take a Nazarite vow, based on the Angel of the Lord's announcement: "He must never drink wine or strong

---

[1] McGrath, *John of History, Baptist of Faith*, 242; *Christmaker*, 43; Dunn, *Jesus Remembered*, 359.

drink" (Luke 1:15).[2] This sober prohibition was a requirement for those living as a Nazarite (Num 6:3–4).[3] As a Nazarite, John would let the locks of his hair grow long and not allow a razor to cut his hair (Num 6:5), something that is directly at odds with the instructions Moses gave concerning the priests, who were to "not let the hair of your head hang loose" (Lev 10:6). Indeed, according to Ezekiel 44:20, priests "shall surely trim the hair of their heads." This put John in an odd position. Either he was to follow in the footsteps of his father and become a priest, or he was to live in accordance with the announcement of his birth and live as a Nazarite. He could not do both.[4] It appears that John disregarded the expectation of becoming a priest and took the Nazarite vow seriously.[5] We can only speculate that John deliberately made this choice, and by offering an alternative in the form of his baptism to the forgiveness that the Jerusalem temple sought to provide, it looks pretty likely that John took issue with the temple's services.

In any case, the baptism for the forgiveness of sins was one to which Jesus submitted himself, demonstrating his agreement with John's preaching about the kingdom of God and with John himself as a legitimate prophet of God. In other words, by participating in John's baptism, Jesus acknowledged that John's alternative to the forgiveness offered by the Jerusalem temple and its sacrifices was legitimate. In fact, all four gospel accounts make clear that God anointed Jesus with the Holy Spirit at his baptism, further providing validity to John's ministry and preaching (Matt 3:16; Mark 1:10; Luke 3:21–22; John 1:31–34).[6] From that point on, Jesus began performing baptisms in water, presumably baptizing the twelve disciples: "Jesus and his disciples went into the Judean countryside, and he remained there with them and was baptizing" (John 3:22). We even have an indication that Jesus was outpacing the rate at which John was baptizing:

> Now when Jesus learned that the Pharisees had heard that Jesus was making and baptizing more disciples than John (although Jesus himself did not baptize, but only his disciples), he left Judea and departed again for Galilee. (John 4:1–3)

At the conclusion of Jesus' ministry, after God raised him from the dead, Jesus summoned his followers to make disciples, baptize the newly converted, and teach them to observe all that Jesus commanded (Matt 28:19–20). Since Jesus performed baptisms in water and did nothing to redefine this meaning of baptism, the disciples took his instruction in his commission to continue baptizing converts in water. Indeed, this is exactly what the Early Church did, as is observable by several texts in the Book of Acts, where they obeyed Jesus' mandate to immerse the new converts in water. Consider the following texts:

---

[2] McGrath, *Christmaker*, 17.
[3] Dozeman, "The Book of Numbers," 64.
[4] McGrath, *Christmaker*, 22.
[5] McGrath, *John of History, Baptist of Faith*, 226–27.
[6] Dunn, "Spirit," 697; Beasley-Murray, *Baptism in the New Testament*, 55; Larere, *Baptism*, 16.

> And Peter said to them, "Repent and be baptized every one of you in the name of Jesus Christ for the forgiveness of your sins, and you will receive the gift of the Holy Spirit." (Acts 2:38)
>
> But when they believed Philip preaching the good news about the kingdom of God and the name of Jesus Christ, they were being baptized, men and women alike. (Acts 8:12)
>
> As they went along the road they came to some water; and the eunuch said, "Look! Water! What prevents me from being baptized?" . . . And he ordered the chariot to stop; and they both went down into the water, Philip as well as the eunuch, and he baptized him. (Acts 8:36, 38)
>
> "Surely no one can refuse the water for these to be baptized who have received the Holy Spirit just as we did, can he?" And he ordered them to be baptized in the name of Jesus Christ. (Acts 10:47–48)
>
> "Get up, be baptized, and have your sins washed away, calling on his name." (Acts 22:16)

As we can observe, the practice of the early Christians was in accordance with Jesus' own custom of baptizing in water those who repented and believed in the gospel—a custom that Jesus received from John the Baptist.

The Sacrament of Water Baptism in the Early Church

As we observed in Chapter 35, submitting to water baptism was part of the initiation ritual for those who became Christians. The meaning and theological significance that the New Testament authors attributed to the sacrament of baptism represent a serious commitment and a deep devotion to this ritual. The theology of the Apostle Paul demonstrates an awareness of the connection between the baptism that a believer partakes in and the death of Jesus.[7] Consider Paul's discussion of the sacrament in Romans:

> Or do you not know that all of us who have been baptized into Christ Jesus have been baptized into his death? Therefore we have been buried with him through baptism into death, so that as Christ was raised from the dead through the glory of the Father, so we too might walk in newness of life. For if we have become united with him in the likeness of his death, certainly we shall also be in the likeness of his resurrection knowing this, that our old self was crucified with him, in order that our body of sin might be done away with, so that we would no longer be slaves to sin (Rom 6:3–6)

This passage is insightful for several reasons. First, it expresses that submitting to being baptized in water was something that all Christians experienced ("all of us who have been

---

[7] Cullmann, *Baptism in the New Testament*, 14; Larere, *Baptism*, 25; Fitzmyer, *Romans*, 433–35.

baptized"). Second, it offers a helpful illustration of the practice of baptism, where the new convert would be lowered backward into the water to mimic the death of Jesus, who died and was buried. After the convert was horizontally submerged in water, the baptizing attendant would lift them up out of the water, allowing the convert to stand vertically, thereby mimicking the resurrection of Jesus from the dead. Third, Paul indicates that the act of baptism mystically connects the believer with the death of Jesus in a manner that crucifies the old Adam and does away with the sinful body.[8] Similarly, the convert connects with the resurrection of Jesus by committing to now walk in a newness of life, having been freed from the slavery of sin. This suggests that being "baptized into Christ Jesus" is to transition the Christian initiate out of solidarity with Adam and into solidarity with Jesus, the crucified and risen one.

We find similar observations of the meaning and importance of baptism in Galatians, where, in particular, Paul argues that Christian converts are already members of Abraham's promised worldwide family. Note how Paul connects the dots at the conclusion of Galatians chapter three:

> For all of you who were baptized into Christ have clothed yourselves with Christ. There is neither Jew nor Greek, there is neither slave nor free man, there is neither male nor female; for you are all one in Christ Jesus. And if you belong to Christ, then you are Abraham's descendants, heirs according to promise. (Gal 3:27–29)

We again see evidence of an awareness that those who have been immersed in Christian baptism have *entered into* solidarity with Christ and, in the process, *moved away from* their former solidarity with traditional ways of identifying individuals. These former solidarities, which are relativized in Christ, include racial (i.e., ethnic) distinctions, social status differences, and gender hierarchies.[9] Instead, by participating in Christian baptism and transitioning into solidarity with Christ, the convert is now regarded as a descendant of Abraham. The old ways of dividing humanity are part of the old creation, while those who are in Christ are already new creatures (Gal 6:15; 2 Cor 5:17). This status of new creation is made possible by the newness of life that those who are baptized now experience. Furthermore, those who are baptized attain the status of heirs, meaning they will receive the promised land that God covenanted to Abraham and his descendants.

Paul's theology expressed in Galatians 3:27–29 closely parallels his language in 1 Corinthians 12:13, where he notes that those who have been baptized also share in the same Holy Spirit: "For by one Spirit we were all baptized into one body, whether Jews or Greeks, whether slaves or free, and we were all made to drink of one Spirit." Again, Paul observes that those who have been immersed in water have transitioned into the solidarity of the body of Christ despite former racial and social status descriptions. All Christian

---

[8] Wright, "The Letter to the Romans," 539–40; Beasley-Murray, *Baptism in the New Testament*, 136–38.
[9] Beasley-Murray, *Baptism in the New Testament*, 171; Hays, "The Letter to the Galatians," 272–73.

converts experience the same Holy Spirit, despite the recognizable differences between each person and their gifting. To be clear, Paul is not suggesting that ordinary Christian baptism in water has been replaced by a metaphorical "baptism" in the Holy Spirit. Instead, he is remarking that, despite one's former solidarity, every believer has, through the waters of baptism, entered solidarity with Christ, which is the new creation in which each one receives the same Spirit. Paul assumes that the normal conversion experience involves submitting to water baptism and receiving the Holy Spirit, and this assumption, no doubt reinforced by several years of evangelism, is expressed in 1 Corinthians 12:13.

Baptism in water was so commonplace in the Early Church that Paul identified it as the new circumcision, the circumcision of Christ. Observe how Paul contrasts those who have been baptized in Christ with physical circumcision:

> in him you were also circumcised with a circumcision made without hands, in the removal of the body of the flesh by the circumcision of Christ; having been buried with him in baptism, in which you were also raised up with him through faith in the working of God, who raised him from the dead. When you were dead in your transgressions and the uncircumcision of your flesh, He made you alive together with him, having forgiven us all our transgressions, having canceled out the certificate of debt consisting of decrees against us, which was hostile to us; and He has taken it out of the way, having nailed it to the cross. (Col 2:11–14)

In this passage, Paul offers what is effectively a new identity marker to contrast with the designation of those in Judaism, namely "the circumcision."[10] This widespread way of defining the Jewish people is seen, for example, in Romans 3:30; Galatians 2:7; Ephesians 2:11; and Titus 1:10. Paul regards the sacrament of baptism in water as the new marker of God's people, particularly because this experience united the convert in Christ's burial. This again expresses the act of a convert being lowered horizontally into the water to simulate the death of Jesus. By identifying with Jesus' death in the waters of baptism, the initiate has "the body of the flesh" removed, along with having their sins forgiven and being nailed to the cross of Christ. Thus, the sacrament of baptism brought the early Christians into a new, identifiable solidarity by mimicking the death and resurrection of Jesus in the water, resulting in the forgiveness of sins.

Another meaningful passage that connects baptism in water with the resurrection of Jesus appears in 1 Peter. These verses employ the interpretive device of typology to compare God's rescue of the eight persons on the ark through water and the early Christian sacrament of baptism in water that orients the convert in good conscience towards God:

> ... the patience of God kept waiting in the days of Noah, during the construction of the ark, in which a few, that is, eight persons, were brought safely through the water.

---

[10] Dunn, *Beginning from Jerusalem*, 1049; Cullmann, *Baptism in the New Testament*, 56–59.

> Corresponding to that, baptism now saves you—not the removal of dirt from the flesh, but an appeal to God for a good conscience—through the resurrection of Jesus Christ (1 Pet 3:20–21)

By connecting the events of Noah's ark with water baptism with the phrase "Corresponding to that" (which in Greek is the adjective *antitypos* from which we get "antitype"), 1 Peter stresses the salvific nature of the Christian immersion from which the convert partakes. This sacramental immersion ritual is not to be reduced to washing away dirt in a bath; instead, it draws upon Jesus' resurrection and the symbolic act of emerging from the waters of baptism, which connects these two realities. By identifying with the resurrection of Jesus, the baptized convert begins the process of salvation ("baptism now saves you") and makes a genuinely repentant appeal to God, which is made possible by Jesus' victory over death.

Why did the Early Church connect the act of lowering and raising a convert in the act of baptism to the death of Jesus? We may look no further than Jesus' metaphoric uses of the image of baptism to convey his looming experience in which he will be immersed in suffering that leads to death:

> "Are you able to drink the cup that I drink, or to be baptized with the baptism with which I am baptized?" They said to Him, "We are able." And Jesus said to them, "The cup that I drink you shall drink; and you shall be baptized with the baptism with which I am baptized." (Mark 10:38–39)

By relating the cup of suffering to the act of baptism, Jesus anticipates a full, immersive experience that will culminate in his death on the cross. Since Jesus referred to the cup of suffering in Gethsemane (Mark 14:36), we can be confident that he associated his death with the concept of baptism in a manner that was remembered by the Early Church as it unpacked the meaning and significance of the ritualistic sacrament.[11]

The Origins and Meaning of the Lord's Supper

While baptism was a sacrament that the early Christians participated in only once, at the moment of their conversion, the Lord's Supper was celebrated far more frequently. Before we look at the ritualistic practice of sharing in the Lord's Supper, we need to begin by looking at the origins of this meal, which go back to the teachings of Jesus. While it may be tempting to look at the Last Supper, which is recorded in all four New Testament gospels, we can actually find evidence of the ritual earlier in Jesus' ministry. In particular, when Jesus performed the miracle of the feeding of the five thousand with only five loaves of bread and two fish, he did so with words and deeds that remarkably foreshadow the

---

[11] Cullmann, *Baptism in the New Testament*, 19–20; Dunn, *Jesus Remembered*, 803.

elements contained in the Last Supper.[12] Consider how the two events include the same four sequential elements:

> Ordering the people to sit down on the grass, he took the five loaves and the two fish, and looking up toward heaven, he blessed the food, and breaking the loaves he gave them to the disciples, and the disciples gave them to the crowds (Matt 14:19)

> While they were eating, Jesus took some bread, and after a blessing, he broke it and gave it to the disciples, and said, "Take, eat; this is my body." (Matt 26:26)

In both passages, Jesus *took* the bread, *blessed* it, *broke* it for those participating in the meal, and *gave* it to them. Clearly, these two events are related, but why would a miracle story in which thousands are fed be related to the Last Supper? The answer may lie in Jesus' instructions to his disciples, "you give them something to eat." (Matt 14:16). This detail, which is often overshadowed by the miracle that Jesus performed, suggests that the disciples possessed the capacity to participate in this meal, no doubt based on their previous demonstrations of powerful deeds (Matt 10:1, 8). It would appear that the sharing that Jesus intended to take place at the meal was not to involve those who were being fed, but also included the participation of his disciples, who were to share in the miracle itself. This detail no doubt resonated with the disciples during the Last Supper, especially as the meal continued to be observed on a regular basis in early Christian communities after Jesus' resurrection.

When we examine the Last Supper narratives, there does not seem to be an explicit command to continue celebrating the meal after Jesus' death. In other words, the very fact that the Lord's Supper did in fact endure as a regular sacramental meal, despite the absence of Jesus' command to do so, suggests that the Last Supper was deeply impactful upon those who were present. Mark's account indicates that Jesus emphasized his death and the time in which the kingdom of God would be finally consummated:

> While they were eating, he took some bread, and after a blessing he broke it, and gave it to them, and said, "Take it; this is my body." And when he had taken a cup and given thanks, he gave it to them, and they all drank from it. And he said to them, "This is my blood of the covenant, which is poured out for many. Truly I say to you, I will never again drink of the fruit of the vine until that day when I drink it new in the kingdom of God." (Mark 14:22–25)

By breaking the bread and sharing it with his disciples, Jesus described it in terms of his body—the body that was hung on a cross and put to death on the very next day. Similarly, by pouring the wine for his disciples to drink, he likened it to his blood that would be poured out in his death. The two pieces of this highly symbolic meal were clearly intended to orient the thinking of those present towards the death of Jesus. From the perspective

---

[12] France, *Matthew*, 558; Nolland, *Matthew*, 592; Hagner, *Matthew 14–28*, 418.

of the early Christian readers of the New Testament, the death of Jesus was a pivotal event in the past. Jesus, however, was not only interested in directing the attention of those who shared in this meal towards the past, for he also looked forward to that special day in which he would drink the fruit of the vine in God's kingdom.[13] Presumably, the followers of Jesus would also be at the table with Jesus in that kingdom, so the Last Supper would naturally build a hopeful anticipation for an even greater meal to come—a meal shared with Jesus in his Father's kingdom.

The Sacrament of the Lord's Supper in the Early Church

This dual emphasis on the ceremonial meal, which oriented those who shared in it to reflect on the past (when Jesus died) and on the future (when Jesus returns to consummate the kingdom of God), made a considerable impact on those present on the night before Jesus was crucified. In fact, these early Christians continued to reenact this meal that Jesus shared with his disciples on a regular basis. When Paul offers to correct the misuse of the Lord's Supper that was taking place in the church at Corinth, he also highlights the emphasis of reflecting on Jesus' death in the past and looking forward to his return to consummate God's kingdom:

> For I received from the Lord that which I also delivered to you, that the Lord Jesus in the night in which he was betrayed took bread; and when he had given thanks, he broke it and said, "This is my body, which is for you; do this in remembrance of me." In the same way he took the cup also after supper, saying, "This cup is the new covenant in my blood; do this, as often as you drink it, in remembrance of me." For as often as you eat this bread and drink the cup, you proclaim the Lord's death until he comes. (1 Cor 11:23–26)

Paul acknowledges that, as often as the early Christians partake of the Lord's Supper, they underscore both the death of Jesus in the past and the coming of Jesus in the future.[14]

We also learn from Paul's instructions to the Corinthians that the church regularly celebrated the Lord's Supper. Unlike the initiation sacrament of water baptism, which only took place once at the conversion of each Christian, there is evidence that the Early Church routinely partook of this highly symbolic and meaningful meal together. Paul indicates the frequency of this sacramental meal "when you meet together" (1 Cor 11:20), even if the congregation needed correction in how they were performing the sacrament. We also learn that the regular sacrament was indeed a full meal, not small portions. Paul's instructions on the matter, which he received from Jesus himself, included the exhortation to "wait for one another" when they come together to eat

---

[13] Evans, *Mark 8:27–16:20*, 395; Culpepper, *Mark*, 529; Marcus, *Mark 8–16*, 967.
[14] Smith, *From Symposium to Eucharist*, 199; Fitzmyer, *First Corinthians*, 445.

(1 Cor 11:33).[15] The entire body partakes of the same bread, as Paul indicates in 1 Corinthians 10:17. No one present should be left hungry and the drinking should not be in excess (1 Cor 11:21). Jude refers to the practice of sharing in the Lord's Supper as "your love feasts" (Jude 1:12), language indicating the sacrament's celebratory nature.

The Early Church was also convinced that Jesus was intimately present when this sacramental meal took place. In other words, the New Testament authors illustrate this event as a very real sharing, fellowshipping, and communing with the risen Jesus. By partaking of the bread and cup, early Christians understood themselves as abiding in Christ and experiencing the salvific life that he offers:

> So Jesus said to them, "Truly, truly, I say to you, unless you eat the flesh of the Son of Man and drink his blood, you have no life in yourselves. He who eats my flesh and drinks my blood has eternal life, and I will raise him up on the last day. For my flesh is true food, and my blood is true drink. He who eats my flesh and drinks my blood abides in Me, and I in him. As the living Father sent me, and I live because of the Father, so he who eats me, he also will live because of me. This is the bread which came down out of heaven; not as the fathers ate and died; he who eats this bread will live forever." (John 6:53–58)

In this discourse, Jesus promises a present experience of eternal life to those who partake of the flesh and blood symbolized by the Lord's Supper. By sharing in Jesus' body and blood, early Christians understood themselves as sharing in Jesus' God-given life, which in turn heightened the anticipation of the hope of resurrection life on the last day that would result in living forever. Paul employs the Greek noun *koinonia* (literally: a sharing, fellowship, participation) to describe the experience of those celebrating the Lord's Supper: "The cup of blessing that we bless, is it not a sharing in the blood of Christ? The bread that we break, is it not a sharing in the body of Christ?" (1 Cor 10:16).[16] This is why Paul was so adamant that his churches could not attend feasts at pagan temples in which the meals were sacrificed or dedicated to an idol or pagan god:

> I say that the things which the Gentiles sacrifice, they sacrifice to demons and not to God; and I do not want you to become sharers in demons. You cannot drink the cup of the Lord and the cup of demons; you cannot partake of the table of the Lord and the table of demons. (1 Cor 10:20–21)

Those who were in Christ were united to Christ and belonged to him (1 Cor 6:15), and this meant that their behavior mattered, especially regarding these highly religious and ceremonial meals. Instead of eating the bread and drinking the cup in an unworthy manner, Paul encourages his readers to examine themselves with sound judgment (1 Cor 11:27–32). In fact, Christ himself expresses a strong desire that his followers

---

[15] Smith, "Eucharist," 354; *From Symposium to Eucharist*, 192; Thiselton, *The First Epistle to the Corinthians*, 898–99.
[16] See especially Nemes, *Eating Christ's Flesh*, 74–80.

willfully obey his teachings in order that he may come and dine with them in the communion meal: "Behold, I stand at the door and knock; if anyone hears my voice and opens the door, I will come in to him and will dine with him, and he with me" (Rev 3:20). The verb that Jesus uses here appears in other contexts involving the sacramental sharing of the bread and the cup (Luke 22:20; 1 Cor 11:25), demonstrating that he is indeed talking about his desire to fellowship with his followers in the Lord's Supper.[17] Those who failed to take seriously the sanctity surrounding this ritualistic meal would often find themselves under the judgment of God, including being weakened, struck with sickness, or even death (1 Cor 11:30). The writers of the New Testament were deeply concerned with portraying this regular sacramental meal as an intentional time of self-reflection, motivated by all that Jesus accomplished in his death on the cross and the promise of his return to raise the dead and consummate the kingdom of God.

Conclusion

In summary, we have observed that the Early Church observed two special sacraments, each loaded with symbolic meaning that imitated the acts of Jesus Christ. First, we drew attention to John's baptism in water, which set the stage for the practice that became regular in the new covenant, a practice that Jesus continued and taught to his disciples. Second, we saw how the theology and initiation practices of the Early Church emphasized the sacrament of baptism by likening it to the death and resurrection of Jesus, while also associating the sacrament with a demonstrable change in behavior in the life of the new convert. Third, we looked at the ritual meal of the Lord's Supper by observing its origins in the teachings of Jesus, prior to his death. Finally, we examined the regular practice of the Lord's Supper in the meetings of the early Christian communities, as well as the holiness that Jesus and Paul attributed to it, and the need for self-reflection. Christians interested in following the example of the Early Church would do well to continue practicing the sacraments of baptizing new converts in water and regularly sharing in ritualistic communal meals that honor the body and blood of Christ.

As the Early Church began to describe itself as the fulfillment of Judaism and the renewed people of Israel's God, this raised questions about what sort of continuity with Judaism was to be expected among its adherents. Within the people of the new covenant, were the terms of the Mosaic covenant still in effect? Did Jews who converted to faith in Jesus Christ still have to continue to observe the laws of Moses in order to remain in good standing in the Church? What about Gentile converts? Did they have to begin obeying the Jewish laws of Moses after accepting the gospel? We will discuss these questions as they pertain to the role that the Mosaic Law played in the Early Church.

---

[17] Smith, *Paradoxical Conquering*, 109; Beale, *Revelation*, 309.

42

THE CHURCH'S APPROACH TO THE LAW OF MOSES

Two things can be true at the same time. The Early Church was adamant that the Law of Moses, also known as the Torah, was a gift from God. Paul praises the Law as holy, righteous, and good in Romans 7:12. 1 Timothy also acknowledges the goodness of the Torah when applied correctly. Many of the earliest Christians were born Jewish and grew up following the Mosaic commandments as a way of life. The Early Church also recognized that the arrival of the Messiah, the inauguration of the kingdom of God, the cross and resurrection, and the gift of the Spirit marked a significant turning point. In particular, membership in the new covenant that Jesus established was not about being Jewish and adhering to the Jewish works of the Law. Instead, the early Christians were accepted into the renewed family of God by believing in the gospel of the kingdom of God, trusting in Jesus' death and resurrection, and living a Christ-like life empowered by the Spirit that they received at their baptism. In other words, the Early Church affirmed the goodness of the Law of Moses while also regarding *faithfulness* to Christ as what indeed identified a member of God's people in the new covenant.

This chapter will investigate how early Christians navigated the transition from the old covenant (and the Law of Moses, which defined one's membership in that covenant) to the new covenant inaugurated by Christ and his gospel of the kingdom. We will first explore Jesus' positive stance towards the Law of Moses. Second, we will look at how Jesus' God-given role as the authorized interpreter of the Law shifted the emphasis within it, often in ways with which his opponents strongly disagreed. Third, we will give attention to the apostle Paul's theology concerning how the early Christians were not under any obligation to keep the Law of Moses and its distinctive works as they pertain to covenant membership. Fourth, we will examine how the Jewish Paul, having become a Christ follower, regarded his ongoing relationship with the Jewish Law of Moses. Finally, we will note how the ethic of *love empowered by the Spirit* functioned as the fulfillment of all that the Law of Moses required for the Early Church. This chapter aims to clarify the Law of Moses as it pertains to the renewed people of God—the Church.

Christ's Relationship with the Law of Moses

Beginning with Jesus, the mediator of the new covenant, there are certainly times when he spoke well of the laws of Moses. In fact, Jesus incorporated several of them into his teachings. For example, when arguing with the scribes and Pharisees about their traditional interpretations of the Law, Jesus upheld the command to "Honor your father and your mother" (Mark 7:10). In another instance, this time in response to the rich man's question about inheriting eternal life, Jesus endorsed several of the commands of Torah: "Do not murder, do not commit adultery, do not steal, do not bear false witness, do not defraud, honor your father and mother" (Mark 10:19). When a scribe questioned Christ about the greatest commandment, he responded with two:

> "The most important is, 'Hear, O Israel: The Lord our God, the Lord is one. And you shall love the Lord your God with all your heart and with all your soul and with all your mind and with all your strength.' The second is this: 'You shall love your neighbor as yourself.' There is no other commandment greater than these." (Mark 12:29–31)

In fact, when the scribe expressed his agreement with Jesus' summation of the Law of Moses in terms of these two commands from Deuteronomy 6:4–5 and Leviticus 19:18, Jesus offered an encouraging statement, "You are not far from the kingdom of God" (Mark 12:34). In the Sermon on the Mount, Jesus announced that his intention is not to abolish the Law of the Prophets, but instead, he has come to fulfill them (Matt 5:17). In fact, Jesus doubled down on his intention to bring fulfillment to the Law and the Prophets, "For truly I say to you, until heaven and earth pass away, not the smallest letter or stroke shall pass from the Law until all is accomplished" (Matt 5:18). These statements raise an important question, what would this *fulfillment* and *accomplishment* look like?[1]

The Priority of the Inaugurated Kingdom of God

Despite the positive statements and the particular commands of the Torah that Jesus endorsed, he often spoke of his ministry as, in some sense, eclipsing the era of the Law of Moses. For example, Jesus indicated that the inauguration of the kingdom of God through the preaching of John had started something new while at the same time marking off the time of the Law and the Prophets: "The Law and the Prophets were proclaimed until John; since that time the gospel of the kingdom of God has been preached" (Luke 16:16). In other words, the preaching of the gospel of the kingdom of God transitioned the time in which the Law and the Prophets held sway. We have already seen evidence in the previous chapter that demonstrates John's preaching offered a baptism of repentance for the forgiveness of sins—a baptism that accompanied his announcement of the in-breaking kingdom of God. By offering forgiveness through the act of baptism in water, John was demonstrating that the temple in Jerusalem, the priesthood that

---

[1] Witherington, *Matthew*, 127, helpfully states, "Jesus was not abolishing that Law in the sense of declaring it untrue, but by fulfilling it he was making clear that in view of the new eschatological situation, the in-breaking of the Dominion, it was no longer applicable carte blanche but only insofar as Jesus reaffirmed parts of it in his Dominion teaching."

worked there, and their animal sacrifices were being phased out. Jesus continued this trend, urging his disciples to seek God's kingdom first and foremost, along with the associated righteousness (Matt 6:33).

The priority that Jesus gives to his gospel and one's commitment to it can be observed in several statements. James and John, the sons of Zebedee, "left their boat and their father, and followed him" (Matt 4:22), indicating that the call to discipleship in light of the kingdom's inauguration even supersedes honoring one's parents—a command Jesus nevertheless endorses. Similar prioritization of the gospel of the kingdom above the need to honor one's father and mother occurs in Luke 9:60: "Allow the dead to bury their own dead; but as for you, go and proclaim everywhere the kingdom of God." In fact, Jesus redefined the family, mother included, around those who heard the gospel and observed it (Luke 8:21). No wonder some of Jesus' opponents considered him to be a rebellious son.

Naturally, the arrival of Christ, the king of God's dawning kingdom, contributes to the shift in emphasis away from the Law and toward his ministry. The first controversy story in Mark's gospel revolved around Jesus' claim to be the son of man, that is, the christological figure from Daniel 7:13–14 in whom God has invested his privileges and prerogatives. As the highly authorized son of man, Jesus pronounces the forgiveness of sins upon the paralytic, an act that surely was interpreted as taking away the prerogatives of the temple and the priesthood (Mark 2:3–11). However, Jesus was demonstrating that the reign and rule of God were breaking into history in his words and deeds, uniquely positioning him as the locus of God's temple work and the forgiveness God offered therein. Along the same lines, Mark records another controversy story when, after summoning the tax collector Levi to follow him—no doubt with the preaching of the gospel of the kingdom—Jesus dined at his house (Mark 2:14–15). Many tax collectors and sinners, whom Mark informs the reader as "many who followed him" (Mark 2:15), surely gave the impression that Jesus was disregarding the commandments of purity, the regulations of clean and unclean persons, and the kosher food laws. However, those present were no longer sinful persons who were positioned outside of the covenant people of God. They were followers of Christ and his saving message of the kingdom. Moreover, Mark records yet another story involving controversy, this time occurring on the Sabbath as the disciples picked up grain to eat (Mark 2:23). The Pharisees, who were deeply interested in maintaining the sanctity of the Sabbath, even if it meant that Jesus' disciples went hungry, judged their apparent disregard for the Sabbath as unlawful. Jesus defends their actions by noting that David and his companions were innocent when, in their hunger, they took the bread that lawfully belonged to the priests. This example served to encourage the objecting Pharisees to see David and his hungry companions as a type for Jesus, the son of David, and his hungry companions. As the son of David— the promised Jewish messiah, Jesus possessed authority over the temple (2 Sam 7:13). Then, Jesus spoke of the Sabbath itself, how it was instituted *on behalf of man*, not the other way around (Mark 2:27). If the seventh day was installed to offer rest for human beings, that is, those who were created on the sixth day to rule God's creation as kingly image-bearers, then Jesus, the son of man with whom God has shared his kingdom (Dan 7:13–14), likewise possesses lordship over the Sabbath. Once again, Christ and his ministry of the gospel of the kingdom become the focal point of attention that formerly belonged to the laws of Moses.

Jesus' emphasis on his followers devoting themselves as disciples to his kingdom teachings continued to outdo the role formerly belonging to several key commandments of Torah. When Jesus offered an explanation to the parable in which he defined "defilement" as pertaining to things that come forth from the heart and out of a person, he indicated that consuming food no longer defiles:

> He said to them, "Then do you also fail to understand? Do you not see that whatever goes into a person from outside cannot defile, since it enters, not the heart but the stomach, and goes out into the sewer?" (Thus he declared all foods clean.) (Mark 7:18–19)

The narrator, at the conclusion of the statement, makes abundantly clear what can be inferred by Jesus' plain teaching—Jesus authoritatively cleansed all foods, effectively removing the kosher food laws of Leviticus 11 and Deuteronomy 14 from consideration of his followers.[2] It is no surprise that Jesus' command to the seventy that were sent forth to announce the dawning of the kingdom of God included them "eating and drinking whatever" their hosts give to them (Luke 10:7–9).[3] The kingdom of God now has priority over the Jewish food laws.

When it came to physical circumcision, a key commandment that effectively marked out the Jewish people as a distinctive ethnic group (often referred to as "the circumcision"), Jesus apparently did not think that his non-Jewish disciples needed to observe it. In fact, Jesus never demanded that his Gentile converts take upon themselves the commandment of getting physically circumcised. When the Roman centurion, a Gentile, asked Jesus to heal his servant, who was likely also a Gentile, Jesus praised the centurion's faith and looked forward to the day when many Gentiles would dine with Abraham, Isaac, and Jacob in the kingdom of God (Matt 8:5–11; Luke 7:6–9). The sick man was healed from a distance, but the declaration that an uncircumcised Gentile would share table fellowship with the famous Jewish patriarchs truly demonstrated the importance of Jesus' role as the agent of God's redemptive rule and reign. Similar acts of God's salvation are bestowed upon other uncircumcised males, such as those living in the Samaritan city of Sychar (John 4:39–42), the demon-possessed man from the Gentile territory of the Gerasenes (Mark 5:1–20), and the Samaritan leper (Luke 17:11–19), none

---

[2] Räisänen, *Paul & the Law*, 84; Collins, *Mark*, 356; Marcus, *Mark 1–8*, 457; France, *Mark*, 277–79, 291–92.
[3] Nolland, *Luke 9:21–18:34*, 553; Schweizer, *Luke*, 175–76; Morris, *Luke*, 200.

of whom were commanded by Jesus to observe the laws of circumcision. In fact, the topic of circumcision never comes up at all in the teachings of Jesus.[4]

When it comes to the sacrificial system, Jesus taught that the value of human beings and their needs should be prioritized. When Jesus explained the purpose of his ministry was to summon sinners to repentance and faith in the gospel of the kingdom, he told the Pharisees to go and learn the meaning of Hosea 6:6: "I desire compassion, and not sacrifice" (Matt 9:13). The same passage from the prophet Hosea is cited in his defense of the innocence of his hungry disciples picking grain on the Sabbath (Matt 12:7). When a Jewish scribe affirms the oneness of Israel's God, the need to love him with all one's heart, understanding, and strength, in addition to the necessity of loving one's neighbor, he too emphasizes these commands are "much more than all burnt offerings and sacrifices" (Mark 12:33). Jesus determined that this was an intelligent assessment of the Law of Moses (Mark 12:34).

In the Gospel of John, the Law of Moses is frequently illustrated as belonging to the Jews but not to the intended readers of John. Jesus tells his Jewish opponents that Moses gave the law to them (John 7:19). Similarly, Jesus describes the Law as belonging to the Jews. It is "your Law" (John 8:17; 10:34) and "their Law" (John 15:25). The function of the Law of Moses was to anticipate the arrival of the Messiah—something that even Moses wrote about: "We have found him of whom Moses in the Law and also the prophets wrote, Jesus (John 1:45). Importantly, upon his arrival, the people of God were to listen to the commands of Jesus, not Moses. The early Christians were to keep Jesus' commandments (John 14:15, 21; 15:10, 12), since he was the covenant's mediator.

The Early Church and the Law of Moses

After Jesus' resurrection and the pouring out of the Holy Spirit, the Early Church came to understand that God the Father was accepting people into his renewed family who were not adhering to the stipulations contained within the old covenant, as demonstrated by the inclusion of a Gentile named Cornelius (Acts 10:28, 45). This trend was continued in the missionary journeys and in the letter-writing of Paul the Apostle. Paul was absolutely clear that believers were not required to take upon themselves the yoke of the Torah, for they were members of the new covenant in good standing through faith in the gospel and walking by the Holy Spirit. The contrast between membership in God's new covenant and the Mosaic covenant is offered by Paul in 2 Corinthians:

> You are our letter, written in our hearts, known and read by all men; being manifested that you are a letter of Christ, cared for by us, written not with ink but with the Spirit of

---

[4] Wright, *New Testament*, 421.

> the living God, not on tablets of stone but on tablets of human hearts . . . our adequacy is from God, who also made us adequate as servants of a new covenant, not of the letter but of the Spirit; for the letter kills, but the Spirit gives life . . . Therefore having such a hope, we use great boldness in our speech, and are not like Moses, who used to put a veil over his face so that the sons of Israel would not look intently at the end of what was fading away. But their minds were hardened; for until this very day at the reading of the old covenant the same veil remains unlifted, because it is removed in Christ. But to this day whenever Moses is read, a veil lies over their heart; but whenever a person turns to the Lord, the veil is taken away. (2 Cor 3:2–3, 5–6, 12–16)

The Mosaic covenant, defined by the tablets of stone, is clearly something distinguished from the new covenant in which its members possess the Spirit of God.[5]

When Paul established Christian communities in the region of Galatia, he witnessed the believers receiving the Holy Spirit after they believed in the gospel message (Gal 3:2, 5). In possession of the Spirit from God, these Galatian believers possessed a status as sons and daughters of God, that is, members of the renewed people of God. They were not required to observe the distinctive Jewish works of the Law, including physical circumcision, observing special days like the Sabbath and the holy days, and keeping the kosher food laws.[6] However, after Paul left, some Jewish Christians arrived and attempted to compel Paul's converts to adopt the Jewish works of the Law. This is an unacceptable distortion of Paul's apostolic teaching, a radical change of the gospel message itself (Gal 1:6–9). The contrast between being justified (that is, being declared righteous in the covenant family) by practicing the works of the Law on the one hand and being justified by faith is plainly set forth in Galatians 2:

> nevertheless knowing that a man is not justified by the works of the Law but through the faithfulness of Christ Jesus, even we have believed in Christ Jesus, so that we may be justified by the faithfulness of Christ and not by the works of the Law; since by the works of the Law no flesh will be justified. (Gal 2:16)

The distinction that Paul offers between believing in Jesus, the obedient one, and observing the works of the Law is heightened by mentioning these works three times in this passage.[7] Furthermore, Paul draws on Deuteronomy 27:26 to argue that "as many as are of the works of the Law are under a curse; for it is written, 'Cursed is everyone who does not abide by all things written in the book of the Law, to perform them'" (Gal 3:10). In other words, those who observe the Torah of Moses and fail to do so perfectly come under the Torah's own curse. Christ, the king who represents his people, "redeemed us from the curse of the Law, having become a curse for us" (Gal 3:13).[8] Paul goes on to

---

[5] Wright, *Paul and the Faithfulness of God*, 982–83; Dunn, *Theology of Paul*, 147; Harris, *The Second Epistle to the Corinthians*, 271.
[6] de Boer, *Galatians*, 148, helpfully says, "The 'works of the law' apply to any and all deeds required by the law."
[7] Dunn, *The New Perspective on Paul*, 25.
[8] Dunn, *Jesus, Paul, and the Law*, 229.

illustrate how the Law of Moses was a temporary measure in the redemptive purposes of God until Christ arrived and preached faith in the gospel:

> But before faith came, we were kept in custody under the law, being shut up to the faith which was later to be revealed. Therefore the Law has become our tutor to lead us to Christ, so that we may be justified by faith. But now that faith has come, we are no longer under a tutor. (Gal 3:23–25)

This is a monumental admission from Paul, the former Jewish Pharisee. He argues that the Law became our tutor, but now that Christ has arrived, we are no longer under the Law of Moses. A tutor in the ancient world functioned as a nanny of young children until they reached the age of maturity. Paul uses this image of the overseeing tutor to illustrate the period of the people of God under the Law, while also speaking of a time in which these young children reach maturity as sons and daughters, about which he states in the following verse: "for in Christ Jesus you are all children of God through faith" (Gal 3:26). The Law of Moses, according to Paul, served a good, God-given purpose in the past, but now that Christ has arrived, a new era has dawned that is defined by faith (Gal 3:25).[9] The inauguration of the kingdom that Jesus summoned the crowds to believe in and his death and resurrection no doubt influenced Paul's understanding of the lack of relevance of the Laws of Moses in the present.

Paul makes similar arguments in Romans, demonstrating that the Torah comes to its rightful conclusion with Christ, resulting in covenant membership for anyone, Jew or Gentile, who expresses faith: "For Christ is the end of the law for righteousness to everyone who believes" (Rom 10:4). What does Paul mean by "end"? Elsewhere, he declares that "you are not under law" (Rom 6:14), "we are not under law" (Rom 6:15), and "we have been released from the Law" (Rom 7:6). Importantly, the gift of the Spirit plays a crucial role: "the righteous requirement of the Law might be fulfilled in us ... who walk according to the Spirit" (Rom 8:4).[10] The end of the Law—its concluding goal—was achieved with Christ. With the arrival of the Messiah, the Torah has culminated, allowing righteousness for those who believe.[11] Faith in the gospel is what defines the people of God in the new covenant that Jesus inaugurated.

On some occasions, Paul had to fiercely argue against early Christians who wanted to add the observance of the works of the Law to their belief in the gospel of the kingdom. Undergoing physical circumcision, the key outward marker of the Jewish

---

[9] deSilva, *Galatians*, 332–33; de Boer, *Galatians*, 241; Oakes, *Galatians*, 127. Wright, *Galatians*, 238, aptly summarizes Paul's argument: "if you get circumcised, you are going back to the old age, the time of slavery, the temporary regime. You are already an adult: Why put yourself back into the care of the babysitter?"
[10] Räisänen, *Paul & the Law*, 46; Fee, *God's Empowering Presence*, 815.
[11] Jewett, *Romans*, 619–20; Fitzmyer, *Romans*, 584; Wright, "The Letter to the Romans," 655–58.

people, was one of the main works against which Paul contends.[12] Consider the strongly worded denunciations:

> Behold I, Paul, say to you that if you receive circumcision, Christ will be of no benefit to you. (Gal 5:2)
>
> For neither is circumcision anything, nor uncircumcision, but a new creation. (Gal 6:15)
>
> Has anyone been called in uncircumcision? He is not to be circumcised. (1 Cor 7:18)
>
> Abraham received the sign of circumcision as a seal of the righteousness that he had by faith while he was still uncircumcised. The purpose was to make him the father of all who believe without being circumcised, so that righteousness would be counted to them as well (Rom 4:11)
>
> Beware of the dogs, beware of the evil workers, beware of those who mutilate the flesh! (Phil 3:2)

Circumcision, which was formerly the most defining characteristic of Jewish males in the Mosaic covenant, no longer functions that way. In fact, Paul regards baptism in water, which both males and females can partake of, as the new sign of being marked out as God's true people: "you were also circumcised with a circumcision made without hands, in the removal of the body of the flesh by the circumcision of Christ; having been buried with him in baptism" (Col 2:11–12).[13] When it comes to covenant membership in the people of God, physical circumcision no longer cuts it.

Another key identifying marker of Jewish people was the kosher food laws. The kosher food laws, which distinguished the Israelites as a holy people to Yahweh by separating them from unclean Gentiles, no longer divided Jews and Gentiles who believed in the gospel of the kingdom.[14] Following in the footsteps of Jesus, who declared all foods clean (Mark 7:19) and taught his disciples to eat anything set before them (Luke 10:7–8), Paul did not require his churches to observe the food laws of the Torah:

> Now accept the one who is weak in faith, but not for the purpose of passing judgment on his opinions. One person has faith that he may eat all things, but he who is weak eats vegetables only. The one who eats is not to regard with contempt the one who does not eat, and the one who does not eat is not to judge the one who eats, for God has accepted him. (Rom 14:1–3)

---

[12] Ladd, *Theology*, 510; Dunn, *Theology of Paul*, 359. Wright, *Paul and the Faithfulness of God*, 966, notes how Paul "regarded circumcision as irrelevant for Jesus' followers and their identity."

[13] Dunn, *Beginning from Jerusalem*, 651, observes that Paul "must have regarded baptism in the name of Christ as substituting for circumcision—a case of abandoning completely one boundary marker and replacing it with another."

[14] Wright, *Paul and the Faithfulness of God*, 854–55; Dunn, *Theology of Paul*, 356.

> I know and am convinced in the Lord Jesus that nothing is unclean in itself; but to him who thinks anything to be unclean, to him it is unclean. (Rom 14:14)
>
> Do not tear down the work of God for the sake of food. All things indeed are clean (Rom 14:20)
>
> But food will not commend us to God; we are neither the worse if we do not eat, nor the better if we do eat. (1 Cor 8:8)
>
> Eat anything that is sold in the meat market without asking questions for conscience' sake; for the earth is the Lord's, and all it contains. If one of the unbelievers invites you and you want to go, eat anything that is set before you without asking questions for conscience' sake. (1 Cor 10:25–27)
>
> Therefore no one is to act as your judge in regard to food or drink . . . things which are a mere shadow of what is to come; but the substance belongs to Christ. (Col 2:16–17)

Although the food laws of the Torah formerly separated the clean eaters from the unclean (Gentile) eaters, within the new covenant, this rule no longer divides those who have faith.[15] Paul was completely convinced that in the Lord Jesus, nothing is unclean.[16]

In addition to circumcision and the food laws, there was the observance of several special days, most notably the Sabbath, but also the calendar of Jewish holy days prescribed in the Mosaic covenant. Paul did not burden his Gentile converts to Christ with the need to observe these days. In fact, when some attempted to compel his churches to participate in these various weekly, monthly, and annual dates, Paul pushed back with concern.[17] Consider how Paul addresses the topic of the observance of special Jewish days within the confines of the new covenant:

> But now that you have come to know God, or rather to be known by God, how is it that you turn back again to the weak and worthless elemental things, to which you desire to be enslaved all over again? You observe days and months and seasons and years. I fear for you, that perhaps I have labored over you in vain. (Gal 4:9–11)
>
> Now accept the one who is weak in faith, but not for the purpose of passing judgment on his opinions . . . One person regards one day above another, another regards every day alike. Each person must be fully convinced in his own mind. (Rom 14:1, 5)

Paul is quite clear that observing days (sabbaths), months (New Moons), seasons (Jewish feasts), and years (sabbatical or jubilee years) is to practice "weak and worthless" things

---

[15] Dunn, *Beginning from Jerusalem*, 925, concludes Paul's position by stating that he and Gentile believers "now believed that the laws of clean and unclean were no longer relevant to the life of faith."
[16] Longenecker, *Romans*, 1007; Fitzmyer, *Romans*, 696; Ladd, *Theology*, 510.
[17] Regarding Col 2:16–17, Wilson, *Colossians and Philemon*, 218, argues, "The Christian is no longer bound by the regulations of the law of Moses."

(Gal 4:9–10).[18] These Jewish holy days mandated in the old covenant are a shadow of Christ, whose arrival has inaugurated the reign of God and the new covenant (Col 2:16–17).[19] Granted, Paul allows those with a weak conscience, particularly Jewish Christians who grew up observing these days as a regular way of life, to continue doing so without pressuring or compelling those who do not observe. Moreover, when Paul does use the verb "to celebrate a festival" (*eortazo*), he clearly spiritualizes this feast in light of Christ's once-and-for-all sacrifice as the Passover lamb: "For Christ, our Passover lamb, has been sacrificed. Let us therefore celebrate the festival, not with the old leaven, the leaven of malice and evil, but with the unleavened bread of sincerity and truth" (1 Cor 5:7–8). The ministry of Jesus has brought the new covenant into full force, thereby concluding the Mosaic covenant and its obligations.

Paul's Relationship with the Law of Moses

It is all well and good for Paul to instruct his churches to live by the terms of the new covenant (and not those belonging to the old covenant), but how did Paul himself act as a Jewish Christian, raised in the lifestyle of Torah, live in relation to Torah after encountering the risen Christ? Were Jews who converted to Christianity able to continue living the Jewish lifestyle that was reinforced by the Mosaic commandments? Paul offers some helpful answers to these questions as he describes how he interacts with different groups in order to reach them with the gospel message:

> For though I am free with respect to all, I have made myself a slave to all, so that I might win more of them. To the Jews I became as a Jew, in order to win Jews. To those under the law I became as one under the law (though I myself am not under the law) so that I might win those under the law. To those outside the law I became as one outside the law (though I am not free from God's law but am under Christ's law) so that I might win those outside the law. To the weak I became weak, so that I might win the weak. I have become all things to all people, that I might by all means save some. (1 Cor 9:19–22)

This admission is very enlightening, especially as it pertains to Paul, the Jewish Christian, and his relationship with the Torah of Moses. He declares that, despite the freedom he possesses in Christ, he would empty himself of those privileges in order to win others to the gospel. When Paul would speak to Jews, he would "become as a Jew," a phrase suggesting that he understood his default status in Christ as something different. Since Paul has elsewhere stated his convictions that anyone in Christ is a new creation—a distinct category from the traditional binary of circumcised and uncircumcised (2 Cor 5:17; Gal 6:15), we can follow Paul's train of thought with some confidence.

---

[18] Keener, *Galatians*, 194; Dunn, *Galatians*, 227; deSilva, *Galatians*, 365–67; Longenecker, *Galatians*, 182–83.
[19] Arnold, *Colossian*, 540, observes in reference to the festivals, new moons, and Sabbath that "The combination of the three terms is a conventional description of the Jewish festival calendar."

Unpacking what it means to "become as a Jew," Paul writes that he "became as one under the law" while immediately making it clear that he is not under the law (1 Cor 9:20). The Mosaic Law was no longer binding for Paul once he believed the gospel and became a Christ-follower. However, Paul does acknowledge that he follows a different instruction—the instruction of Christ. Quite clearly, the *law of Christ* is something demonstrably different than the *law of Moses*. Paul is under the former, not the latter. The phrase "law of Christ" reappears in Galatians 6:2, where Paul instructs his readers to embody Jesus' example of bearing the burdens of others: "Bear one another's burdens, and in this way you will fulfill the law of Christ." The early Christians were committed to Jesus' teachings and ethical examples as the terms of the new covenant pact with God.

In one of the most detailed autobiographical accounts of Paul's life, the apostle details a marked contrast between his former life in Judaism as a prominent Pharisee. Consider carefully how Paul distinguishes his present outlook from his formative years:

> If anyone else has a mind to put confidence in the flesh, I far more: circumcised the eighth day, of the nation of Israel, of the tribe of Benjamin, a Hebrew of Hebrews; as to the Law, a Pharisee; as to zeal, a persecutor of the church; as to the righteousness which is in the Law, found blameless. But whatever things were gain to me, those things I have counted as loss for the sake of Christ. More than that, I count all things to be loss in view of the surpassing value of knowing Christ Jesus my Lord, for whom I have suffered the loss of all things, and count them but rubbish so that I may gain Christ (Phil 3:4–8)

When Paul looks back on his "flesh," that is, his ethnic identity as a Jew, he has an impressive resume. He was a circumcised Israelite belonging to the only tribe that remained loyal to Judah after Solomon's death. He was a genuine Hebrew, a member of the strictest sect of Judaism, adhering to Torah observance, and exhibited a zeal that mirrored that of famous Jewish figures like Phineas, Elijah, and the Maccabean martyrs.[20] When it came to his covenant status in the Mosaic agreement, he was blameless, but these prestigious privileges have been regarded by Paul as a loss when compared to knowing Christ. In fact, Paul considered being in Christ as having a "surpassing value" compared to his former Jewish accolades—an honor that he now regards as "rubbish" (literally: "dung"). Paul's days of being blamelessly devoted to the law of Moses are behind him.

We have already seen evidence that Paul does not believe that the kosher food laws are binding upon him (Rom 14:14). In the lord Jesus, that is, from the vantage point of being in union with Christ, Paul knows and is convinced "that nothing is unclean of itself." As one who has become a member of the renewed people of God—God's new creation—Paul can confidently say that things like "food will not commend us to God" (1 Cor 8:8), "do we not have the right to eat and drink?" (1 Cor 9:4), and "eat anything that is sold in the meat market" (1 Cor 10:25). Moreover, when Peter was sharing table

---

[20] Dunn, *Beginning from Jerusalem*, 343–46.

fellowship with Gentiles in the Early Church, Paul deemed this as an acceptable practice (Gal 2:12). It was only when Peter vacillated and withdrew from sharing at the table with Gentiles that Paul condemned him as a hypocrite (Gal 2:13). The food laws should never divide the people of God within the new covenant that Christ instituted.

Paul's theology can be witnessed in a key statement concerning reconciliation in Ephesians, where it is explicitly declared in no uncertain terms that Christ abolished the law with its commandments and ordinances:

> But now in Christ Jesus you who once were far off have been brought near by the blood of Christ. For he is our peace; in his flesh he has made both groups into one and has broken down the dividing wall, that is, the hostility between us. He has abolished the law with its commandments and ordinances, that he might create in himself one new humanity in place of the two, thus making peace, and might reconcile both groups to God in one body through the cross, thus putting to death that hostility through it. (Eph 2:13–16)

In this passage, several elements of Paul's teaching, already observable in his earlier letters, are evident. The death of the human Jesus, in his flesh, created a new human race that is distinct from Jews and Gentiles. The Law that formerly divided Jews and Gentiles was brought to nothing. It is no longer binding, having been abolished. The removal of the Mosaic commandments and ordinances provided the opportunity to create the renewed people of God—those who are at peace and reconciled to their Creator.[21]

Love Fulfills the Law of Moses

The abolition of the law of Moses did not result in the Early Church completely disregarding its contents. Early Christians continued to remain monotheists. They refused to lie, steal, murder, or covet. They even repeated the recitation of the *Shema*. Following the lead of Jesus, the Early Church regarded *love* as the act that summed up all that the law of Moses demanded of its followers. Jesus was remembered as summarizing the law in terms of loving Yahweh fully and loving one's neighbor as himself, the two greatest commandments (Mark 12:29–31). In fact, Paul and James continue to reinforce the teachings of Jesus on this matter, namely by pointing to the command in Leviticus 19:18 to love your neighbor as yourself, as that which fulfills what the law demanded:

> The commandments, "You shall not commit adultery; You shall not murder; You shall not steal; You shall not covet"; and any other commandment, are summed up in this word, "Love your neighbor as yourself." Love does no wrong to a neighbor; therefore, love is the fulfilling of the law. (Rom 13:9–10)

---

[21] Cohick, *Ephesians*, 186, observes, "Those laws that separate Jew and gentile are nullified in Christ."

> For the whole law is fulfilled in one word: "You shall love your neighbor as yourself." (Gal 5:14)

> If you really fulfill the royal law according to the Scripture, "You shall love your neighbor as yourself," you are doing well. (James 2:8)

The Early Church continued to reinforce the commandment to show love despite not being under the law of Moses and its covenantal demands. How did the early Christians define and give meaning to this insistence on acting lovingly towards each other? The answer lies in the example provided by Jesus himself: "A new commandment I give to you, that you love one another, even as I have loved you, that you also love one another" (John 13:34). It was Jesus who defined how love was to be shown to one's neighbor. It was his desire to empty himself and take the role of a servant that made an impact on his followers. Believers were summoned to "walk in love, just as Christ also loved you" (Eph 5:2). Likewise, husbands were to "love your wives, as Christ loved the church" (Eph 5:25). Love is the greatest gift because it will endure and never end (1 Cor 13:8).

Conclusion

This chapter has provided an overview of the approaches early Christians adopted regarding the law of Moses. As members of the new covenant, bound to the teachings of Jesus and his apostles, the obligations of the old covenant were no longer binding. We first looked at the positive attitude Jesus took toward the law of Moses. Second, we explored how Jesus' ministry of the kingdom of God breaking into the present marked a new era in the way that God was working with his people, shifting in the process the law of Moses to the past. Third, we took notice of many arguments in which Paul argued that the Early Church was no longer under the law of Moses and that its commandments were not binding upon those who are in Christ. Fourth, we noticed that Paul regarded himself as one of God's new creations—a category distinct from both Jew and Gentile—demonstrating that Paul was no longer under obligation to observe the Mosaic Torah. Finally, we noted how the Early Church followed the lead of Jesus in emphasizing love as the behavior that summed up all that the law of Moses required, while also pointing specifically to Jesus' ethical example as the exact way Christians should demonstrate love toward one another. In doing so, the early Christians fulfilled the law of Christ.

Ephesians 5:25 says, "Christ loved the church and gave himself up for her." In this passage, the Church is personified as the bride of Christ. What relevance did this wedding imagery have to early Christians? How was the bride of Christ to behave as it awaited the second coming of the groom, Jesus himself? We will explore these topics in the next chapter.

43
THE CHURCH AS BRIDE AND NEW JERUSALEM

One of the most notable descriptions of the Early Church that the authors of the New Testament embraced is that it is the bride of Christ. Drawing upon the faithful covenant relationship between God and Israel in the Old Testament, Jesus, the agent of God, now serves in the role of the groom. The bride within the new covenant is, in fact, the Church—the people of God who have embraced Jesus' gospel of the kingdom of God. By portraying the people of God as a bride, the Early Church acknowledged that the very essence of its identity required a faithful and loyal stance towards Christ and his teachings. Infidelity, compromise, and accommodation were not to be found in the bride of Christ.

This chapter examines the significance of the bride role as applied by New Testament writers to the Early Church. First, we will examine in detail how the early Christians viewed themselves as the bride of Christ while also focusing on Christ's role as the faithful groom. Second, we will give attention to the portrayal of the faithful people of God as the heavenly Jerusalem, noting in the process the relevance of illustrating a group of persons with the imagery of a prominent city within the redemptive purposes of God. Finally, we will examine closely how the Book of Revelation combines the images of a bride and the heavenly Jerusalem to encourage its readers to faithfully follow Christ's commands while distancing themselves from a fallen, ungodly culture. This study aims to clarify the Church's role as bride and heavenly Jerusalem while also promoting fidelity to the groom, Jesus Christ.

The Church of God as the *Bride of Christ*

Beginning with the teachings of Jesus, there is evidence that he viewed himself as the groom betrothed to the people of God. All three Synoptic authors record Jesus using the metaphor of a groom within the context of dining with tax collectors and sinners:

> Then the disciples of John came to him, saying, "Why do we and the Pharisees fast, but your disciples do not fast?" And Jesus said to them, "Can the wedding guests mourn as long as the bridegroom is with them? The days will come when the bridegroom is taken away from them, and then they will fast." (Matt 9:14–15)

Jesus' response to this question about fasting seems out of place at first glance. However, once we take note that Jesus is dining in the house of Levi (also known as Matthew), the tax collector who responded appropriately to Jesus' summons to follow him as a disciple (Matt 9:9), the wedding imagery begins to make more sense. In fact, Jesus just previously stated that his mission was to call the sinners, that is, summon them to repent and believe in the gospel of the kingdom (Matt 9:13). We can reasonably conclude that those dining with Jesus did so voluntarily, accepting in the process the call to discipleship and following in the footsteps of Levi.[1]

Returning to the question posed by the disciples of John, why was Jesus feasting with his new converts while others were fasting? Jesus responds by recalling the setting of a wedding, where the groom is present with the invited wedding guests. Naturally, this would be an occasion for celebration, not a mournful fast. When we consider that several Old Testament prophecies likened the restoration of the kingdom and the land promise to a *wedding*, we can discern that Jesus is viewing this celebratory meal with those who have accepted the gospel of the kingdom as a breaking in of that kingdom's restoration:[2]

> Sing, O barren one who did not bear; burst into song and shout, you who have not been in labor! For the children of the desolate woman will be more than the children of her that is married, says Yahweh. Enlarge the site of your tent, and let the curtains of your habitations be stretched out; do not hold back; lengthen your cords and strengthen your stakes. For you will spread out to the right and to the left, and your descendants will possess the nations and will settle the desolate towns. (Isa 54:1–3)

> Therefore, I will now allure her, and bring her into the wilderness, and speak tenderly to her. From there I will give her her vineyards, and make the Valley of Achor a door of hope. There she shall respond as in the days of her youth, as at the time when she came out of the land of Egypt. On that day, says Yahweh, you will call me, "My husband," and no longer will you call me, "My Baal." For I will remove the names of the Baals from her mouth, and they shall be mentioned by name no more. I will make for you a covenant on that day with the wild animals, the birds of the air, and the creeping things of the ground; and I will abolish the bow, the sword, and war from the land; and I will make you lie down in safety. And I will take you for my wife forever; I will take you for my wife in righteousness and in justice, in steadfast love, and in mercy. I will take you for my wife in faithfulness; and you shall know Yahweh. (Hos 2:14–20)

The disciples of the kingdom were already experiencing the wedding promises of the restored kingdom as they reclined at the table with the messianic bringer of God's reign. As such, Jesus presents himself as the groom who is already present at the wedding, a cause for joy and celebration.[3] Although Jesus does give a subtle hint that he will be taken away from them, pointing to his rejection and crucifixion, and that this sudden removal

---

[1] Hagner, *Matthew 1–13*, 238; Williams, "Bride, Bridegroom," 87.
[2] Wright, *Matthew*, 1:101; Ladd, *The Presence of the Future*, 112.
[3] Williams, "Bride, Bridegroom," 88.

from the wedding will be cause for fasting and mourning. In short, the wedding imagery and Jesus' role as the groom, already present at the celebration, indicate that the promise of the restoration of the kingdom of God is already being experienced in Jesus' ministry.[4]

In Matthew 25:1–13, Jesus offers a parable comparing the kingdom to ten virgins who set out to meet the groom. Again, it is clear that the groom refers to Jesus, whose arrival refers to the second coming at a day and hour that no one knows (Matt 25:13), and not even Jesus knows (Matt 24:36). Since the arrival of Jesus consummates the kingdom of God upon the earth, and the parable explicitly illustrates the kingdom with wedding imagery, we can firmly conclude that the groom refers to Christ.[5] It is interesting to note that Matthew preserves an "already but not yet" theology of the groom's wedding, having already recorded Jesus acknowledging that he was in the midst of the wedding guests in Matthew 9:15, while also depicting the future arrival of Jesus to celebrate the wedding feast at his second coming (Matt 25:10).

John the Baptist refers to Jesus as the groom who already is in possession of his bride in John 3:29. The passage states, "He who has the bride is the bridegroom. The friend of the bridegroom, who stands and hears him, rejoices greatly at the bridegroom's voice. For this reason my joy has been fulfilled." John views himself as the best man of the groom, a close friend of Jesus.[6] In context, the bride of Christ likely refers to those disciples whom Jesus baptized (John 3:26). As such, we can confidently identify those who accept Jesus' summons to come unto him collectively as a bride. John the Baptist expresses joy at the coming together of the groom and his bride, which John locates in the ministry of Jesus.[7]

When we turn to the theology of Paul the Apostle, we find several relevant statements concerning the Early Church as the bride of Christ. In 2 Corinthians, Paul portrays his readers collectively as a single bride who is betrothed to Christ, their husband:

> For I am jealous for you with a godly jealousy; for I betrothed you to one husband, so that to Christ I might present you as a pure virgin. But I am afraid that, as the serpent deceived Eve by his craftiness, your minds will be led astray from the simplicity and purity of devotion to Christ. (2 Cor 11:2–3).

When Paul states that "I betrothed *you*" and that he might "present *you*," he uses the second-person plural to refer to the body of Christ, the Early Church, as the virgin bride. His characterization of the bride offers insight into the Church's relationship with Jesus in this wedding metaphor.[8] First, the bride is illustrated as a pure virgin, indicating that

---

[4] Witherington, *Matthew*, 201; Hagner, *Matthew 1–13*, 243.
[5] Hagner, *Matthew 14–28*, 728–30; Culpepper, *Matthew*, 367.
[6] Coloe, *John 1–10*, 103–4.
[7] Keener, *The Gospel of John*, 1:580.
[8] Barrett, *The Second Epistle to the Corinthians*, 272.

the Church is holy and chaste, devoted to Christ in purity. Second, the contrast suggests that refusing to remain faithful and wholly devoted to Christ, even if it involves acts of deception, would put that pure status in jeopardy.[9] Paul's intention, it seems, is to present his readers as a holy and blameless bride, committed and faithful to Jesus and his teachings.

In discussing the role of the law of Moses and the act of water baptism that symbolizes union with the death of Christ, Paul's theology of the Church as the bride reemerges. In Romans 7:4, the apostle argues, "you also were made to die to the Law through the body of Christ, so that you might be joined to another, to him who was raised from the dead, in order that we might bear fruit for God." By once again using the second-person plural *"you,"* Paul depicts the early Christians collectively as a bride that is joined to the one whom God raised from the dead, namely Jesus. The expressly stated purpose of this union with Jesus, the groom, is so that his bride may produce fruitful good works for God.[10]

Another relevant passage appears in Ephesians 5, where instructions are given to husbands and wives. Within these lessons, the marriage between a man and a woman is likened to the relationship that exists between Christ, the groom, and the Church as his bride:

> Husbands, love your wives, as Christ loved the church and gave himself up for her, that he might sanctify her, having cleansed her by the washing of water with the word, so that he might present the church to himself in splendor, without spot or wrinkle or any such thing, that she might be holy and without blemish. (Eph 5:25–27)

Once again, the Early Church is illustrated as the bride of Christ—a bride who is to act faithfully in this covenant relationship. This includes holy living, spotless behavior, and being without blemish in matters of sanctification. The sacrificial death of Jesus cleansed his bride, whom he hopes to present in splendor. The metaphor of the bride necessitates loyalty and submission to Christ, the groom.[11]

When we turn to the Book of Revelation and its symbol-rich imagery, we discover some of the most robust passages portraying the body of Christ as his beautiful bride. Consider the praise sung by the multitude of the redeemed in Revelation 19:

> Then I heard what seemed to be the voice of a great multitude, like the roar of many waters and like the sound of mighty peals of thunder, crying out, "Hallelujah! For the Lord our God the Almighty reigns. Let us rejoice and exult and give him the glory, for the marriage of the Lamb has come, and his Bride has made herself ready; it was granted her to clothe herself with fine linen, bright and pure"—for the fine linen is the righteous

---

[9] Sampley, "The Second Letter to the Corinthians," 148; Martin, *2 Corinthians*, 332–33.
[10] Moo, *Romans*, 417–18; Jewett, *Romans*, 434; Gaventa, *Romans*, 196–98; Dunn, *Romans 1–8*, 362, 368–69.
[11] Cohick, *Ephesians*, 363–64; Lincoln, *Ephesians*, 376–77; Barth, *Ephesians 4–6*, 628–29; Hoehner, *Ephesians*, 758.

deeds of the saints. And the angel said to me, "Write this: Blessed are those who are invited to the marriage supper of the Lamb." And he said to me, "These are the true words of God." (Rev 19:6–9)

There is much to be said about this passage, but focusing on the topic of the Early Church, we can glean several valuable insights. First, we can discern the imagery of clothing that is applied to the bride of Christ, clothing that is explicitly defined for the reader as "the righteous deeds of the saints." The beautiful bride is appropriately clothed with her faithful deeds of the new covenant, her righteous works.[12] Second, the song of praise that the multitude sings acknowledges that the bride has *made herself ready*, indicating a conscious, obedient decision to act righteously.[13] In other words, the Early Church chose to put on the bright and pure clothing as a faithful act of loyalty to her husband. Third, the intended response of Revelation's hymns is for the reader to participate in them, thereby praising and giving glory to the Almighty in light of his rule and reign that the singers are already experiencing.[14] Fourth, the imagery suggests that the marriage of the Lamb has come, and its arrival grants the occasion to bless those who have been invited to the marriage supper. The Greek perfect tense used for the verb "to invite" indicates that the invitation has been offered, and its effects are still experienced in the present. In other words, the readers of Revelation are encouraged to join the hymn of worship and accept the invitation to the marriage supper by putting on the fine linen of obedient and holy works, demonstrating the appropriate posture of a bride who is ready for her groom. Revelation's imagery of the early Christian faithful as the bride of Christ will reemerge later in the narrative, but before we can begin to make sense of that image, we need to become better informed on a related topic.

The Theology of *New Jerusalem* in the Early Church

Returning to the theology of the apostle Paul, we can again observe his depiction of the new covenant people of God as a woman, not unlike his bridal imagery that we have already examined. Particularly in Galatians 4, Paul employs allegory to describe the two covenants—the Mosaic covenant and the new covenant—as distinct women and as different cities of Jerusalem. Consider how Paul allegorizes the two covenants:

> Now this is an allegory: these women are two covenants. One woman, in fact, is Hagar, from Mount Sinai, bearing children for slavery. Now Hagar is Mount Sinai in Arabia and corresponds to the present Jerusalem, for she is in slavery with her children. But the other woman corresponds to the Jerusalem above; she is free, and she is our mother. For it is

---

[12] Koester, *Revelation*, 730, states, "At *present*, Revelation assumes that the bridal garment is woven in the context of a relationship that Jesus the groom has already established with believers."
[13] Blount, *Revelation*, 345; Koester, *Revelation*, 738.
[14] Grabiner, *Revelation's Hymns*, 207.

> written, "Rejoice, you childless one, you who bear no children, burst into song and shout, you who endure no birth pangs; for the children of the desolate woman are more numerous than the children of the one who is married." Now you, my friends, are children of the promise, like Isaac. (Gal 4:24–28)

There is a lot to keep track of when attempting to make sense of Paul's argument here, not least his citation of Isaiah 54:1 (which we have already seen illustrates God's promised restoration as a wedding between a bride and a groom). On one side, Paul positions Hagar as the mother of slavery, who corresponds to the present city of Jerusalem (Gal 4:24–25). On the other side, Paul describes a different woman who resembles a different city. This woman, by virtue of bearing Isaac, is Sarah. She, according to Paul, corresponds to the Jerusalem above, what we might call the heavenly Jerusalem (Gal 4:26).[15] In fact, he argues that she currently functions as the mother figure of the new covenant people of God ("she *is* our mother").[16] In other words, Paul portrays two women as two cities, and he invites his readers to identify with the second woman and city (the heavenly Jerusalem). In doing so, they would position themselves as heirs, according to the promise made to Abraham (Gal 3:29), rather than being enslaved under the old covenant.

Although Paul does intend for his readers to view themselves allegorically as a woman, it is clear that this female figure is not the bride of Christ. However, Paul has identified the new covenant people of God as a city, as the Jerusalem from above.[17] This heavenly Jerusalem is clearly distinguished from the actual city of Jerusalem, which is located in Judea. By illustrating the Early Church as a heavenly city, his use of allegory suggests that he does not intend to interpret the city literally as a physical, tangible place. Rather, the heavenly Jerusalem with which the readers identify is the symbolic and metaphorical counterpart to the capital city of Jerusalem.

The identification of early Christians as a symbolic heavenly Jerusalem appears again in Hebrews chapter twelve. Note carefully how the author argues that his readers have already arrived at this city:

> You have not come to something that can be touched . . . But you have come to Mount Zion and to the city of the living God, the heavenly Jerusalem, and to myriads of angels, to the general assembly and church of the firstborn who are enrolled in heaven, and to God, the Judge of all, and to the spirits of the righteous made perfect, and to Jesus, the mediator of a new covenant, and to the sprinkled blood, which speaks better than the blood of Abel. (Heb 12:18, 22–24)

---

[15] Wright, *Galatians*, 299.
[16] de Boer, *Galatians*, makes the same point: "the Jerusalem above is already making its presence felt on earth over against the present Jerusalem. Not the present Jerusalem, not the church located in that city, is 'our mother,' but rather the Jerusalem above is, the church consisting of Jews and Gentiles free from the law."
[17] Bruce, *Galatians*, 221, similarly argues that the Jerusalem above "is not spatially elevated but is the community of the new covenant."

Similar to Paul's argument in Galatians 4:24–28, the author of Hebrews displays the heavenly Jerusalem as something his readers are already experiencing.[18] Despite not currently residing on or near Mount Zion, these readers "have come" to this city, which is explicitly labeled as the heavenly Jerusalem. Despite their experience of suffering, persecution, and property confiscation as a result of following Christ, the author paints a picture of the reign and rule of God that is already breaking into the present.[19] So, although the readers were reeling from being mistreated for their faith, their outlook should be on their citizenship in the Jerusalem from above, the heavenly city at which they have already arrived, despite being unable to physically touch it (Heb 12:18).[20] This present reality has been made possible by the mediator of the new covenant and his blood, both of which are experiences to which the faithful have also arrived (Heb 12:24).[21] This encouraging image served to motivate the recipients to endure their trials, show gratitude, and continue serving God in reverence and awe (Heb 12:28).

The Bride of Christ is the City of New Jerusalem in the Book of Revelation

With both Paul and the author of Hebrews depicting the heavenly Jerusalem as a symbolic reality that the Early Church is already experiencing in the present, we should not be surprised when it reemerges in the visions of John of Patmos, as recorded in the Book of Revelation. Within this book, the author portrays two opposing cities, which are also described as women, which bears some similarity to Paul's allegorical argument in Galatians chapter four.[22] Consider how John of Patmos introduces these two cities in order to motivate the readers to identify with one of them and wholly reject the other:

> Then one of the seven angels who had the seven bowls came and spoke with me, saying, "Come here, I will show you the judgment of the great harlot who sits on many waters, with whom the kings of the earth committed acts of immorality, and those who dwell on the earth were made drunk with the wine of her immorality." And he carried me away in the Spirit into a wilderness; and I saw a woman sitting on a scarlet beast, full of blasphemous names, having seven heads and ten horns . . . "The woman whom you saw is the great city, which reigns over the kings of the earth." (Rev 17:1–3, 18)

> Then one of the seven angels who had the seven bowls full of the seven last plagues came and spoke with me, saying, "Come here, I will show you the bride, the wife of the Lamb." And he carried me away in the Spirit to a great and high mountain, and showed me the holy city, Jerusalem, coming down out of heaven from God (Rev 21:9–10)

---

[18] Bruce, *Hebrews*, 372.
[19] Beale, *Temple*, 306. Johnson, *Hebrews*, 328, states, "the author solemnly affirms that they have, in principle and in their imagination, if not yet fully with respect to their mortal lives, reached the goal of their pilgrimage."
[20] deSilva, *Perseverance in Gratitude*, 466; Newman, "Jerusalem, Zion, Holy City," 564.
[21] Attridge, *Hebrews*, 376.
[22] Osiek and Balch, *Families in the New Testament World*, 145.

These two introductions to women and cities function as opposite sides of a coin.²³ The first vision portrays an angel telling John, "Come here, I will show you," followed by a description of a woman. This woman is later identified as the great city that reigns over the kings of the earth. When Revelation was written, this city would have been unmistakably recognized as Rome, the city on seven hills (Rev 17:9).²⁴ Once again, we have *a woman who is also a city*, and it is clear, based upon the description of this terrible city, that the ideal readers of Revelation would want absolutely nothing to do with it.

The second vision offers a glimpse at the other side of the coin. The very same angel makes the announcement to John, "Come here, I will show you," followed by yet another description of a woman. This woman is a familiar image to us—the bride of Christ, and she has already been introduced, as we observed in Revelation 19:6–9. Despite being told that he would see the bride (Rev 21:9), John of Patmos was carried away in the Spirit and shown a city (Rev 21:10). What is fascinating about this vision is that the city, identified as the heavenly Jerusalem, is portrayed as *presently descending* from heaven. The language is clear; this is not a future reality, but rather something that can be experienced in the present.²⁵ In this regard, the portrayal of Jerusalem from above as a present reality is precisely what Paul and the author of Hebrews taught. In fact, alert readers of Revelation have already been introduced to the heavenly city of Jerusalem that is currently coming down to earth (Rev 3:12), where the experience of the promised city is interwoven with the Church's behavior in faithfully conquering like Christ.²⁶

What makes the vision in Revelation 21:9–10 so interesting is that it combines the findings we have discovered throughout this chapter, namely, portraying the beautiful bride of Christ, the faithful Church, as a symbolic city.²⁷ This interpretation is strengthened by two important facts. First, the Book of Revelation employs a recurring thematic narrative device known as the "hearing and seeing motif."²⁸ The hearing and seeing motif functions by initially *telling* the reader of Revelation about something. Immediately, the readers are allowed to *see what they were just told*, and what is shown to the readers is intended to unpack and further explain what they were just told. For example, John is told that Jesus is a conquering lion in Revelation 5:5. Immediately, the narrative states "and I saw . . . a Lamb standing, as if slain" in Revelation 5:6. John hears that Jesus is a ferocious lion figure that conquers, but he sees that the way in which Jesus conquers is in the role of a weak, slaughtered lamb. The same hearing and seeing motif appears multiple times in Revelation, so when it occurs in Revelation 21:9–10, readers should be primed to interpret it correctly. In this case, the people of God, identified as a beautiful

---

²³ Bauckham, *The Climax of Prophecy*, 339; Aune, *Revelation 17–22*, 915; Reddish, *Revelation*, 405.
²⁴ Wright, *Revelation*, 154–55; Osborne, *Revelation*, 617; Beale, *Revelation*, 869; Paul, *Revelation*, 284.
²⁵ Mulholland, "Revelation," 590; Caird, *Revelation*, 271.
²⁶ The experience of New Jerusalem (Rev 3:12; 21:2, 10) is enjoyed only by those who conquer (Rev 3:12; 21:7).
²⁷ Storms, *Our God Reigns*, 502.
²⁸ Beale, *Temple*, 366.

bride, are further defined as a perfect city that is presently accessible, since it is currently descending from heaven. Another fact that supports identifying the bride of Christ as a city is the obvious contrast that has been made with the blasphemous woman in Revelation 17:1–3, whom the narrative explicitly labels as a city (Rev 17:18). The same angel introduces both women, uses the same formulaic presentation ("Come here, I will show you"), and leads the reader to equate these women as individual cities. If the terrible woman in Revelation chapter seventeen is identified as a city, then it naturally follows that the readers were to identify the bride of Christ in Revelation twenty-one as a city, as the New Jerusalem.[29]

As the passage unfolds in Revelation 21, the image of the bride of Christ begins to exhibit purpose and meaning. The description of the heavenly city utilizes Revelation's imagery to highlight the role of the bride, the faithful Church.[30] For example, the city is described as a bride who is fully dressed and ready for her groom in Revelation 21:2: "I saw the holy city, the new Jerusalem, coming down out of heaven from God, made ready as a bride adorned for her husband." Just as a bride prepares for the arrival of the groom, the early Christians live faithfully as they await the second coming of Christ, particularly by refusing to compromise with unauthorized worship, idolatry, and accommodation with the fallen Greco-Roman culture.[31] By portraying the gates of the city as never shut (Rev 21:25), the Church should view itself as accepting from every tribe, tongue, people, and nation those who genuinely repent and embrace Jesus' gospel of the kingdom of God.[32] On the other hand, the depiction of unclean things and those practicing abominations or lies being refused entrance into the city (Rev 21:27) motivated the Early Church to refuse to compromise with these sinful behaviors. The beauty of the bride of Christ is maintained by living in holiness, so tolerating sinful, abominable, and dishonest behavior is not appropriate for one made ready for the groom who is coming. Despite the fact that the bride of Christ often suffers harassment, persecution, intimidation, and unfair treatment, the vision of the New Jerusalem depicts a tree of life at its center (Rev 22:2).[33] The leaves of this tree bring "the healing of the nations," reflecting the

---

[29] Storms, *Our God Reigns*, 503, concludes, "the city symbolizes the saints, the people of God. We don't simply live in the new Jerusalem. We *are* the new Jerusalem. This city *is* the church, the Bride of Christ."

[30] Blount, *Revelation*, 385, argues that New Jerusalem is "representing the faithful witnesses as a corporate entity."

[31] Gwyther, "New Jerusalem Versus Babylon," 148, writes, "New Jerusalem represents the faithful followers of Jesus who live contemporaneously with the reception of the text. It is crucial to understand that this reality does not pertain to the remote future, nor is it equivalent to the Christian ἐκκλησίαι of Asia in their entirety. Rather, the portrayal of God's apocalyptic city—New Jerusalem—corresponds with those among the ἐκκλησίαι who have taken a faithful stand against the empire, and only in so far as they maintain that stand."

[32] Gwyther, "New Jerusalem Versus Babylon," 169, observes that these open gates "function to embolden those who wish to enter the city—that is, to come out of Babylon."

[33] Revelation has already prepared its readers for this image of the tree's present accessibility. In Rev 2:7, Christ promises the faithful conquerors access to the tree of life, which is (present tense) in God's Paradise. Moreover, Revelation concludes with an assurance that entrance into the city of New Jerusalem and access to this tree of life are already available to all who are washing (present tense) their robes (Rev 22:14).

Church's mission to bless, forgive, and do good to those who mistreat you.[34] Since the vision of the heavenly Jerusalem is an extension of the reign and rule of God breaking into the present, indicated by the consistent use of present tense of the verb "coming down" (Rev 3:12; 21:2, 9), it is no surprise that the faithful bride of Christ exhibits its restorative features as it offers healing and forgiveness, extending the blessing of Abraham to the nations (Gen 12:3).

Conclusion

This chapter's exploration highlights two key images that early Christians used to define the people of God in Christ: the bride and the heavenly city. We first explored the metaphor of the Church as Christ's beloved bride. In doing so, we noticed that the New Testament authors frequently depicted the bride as a faithfully betrothed woman who lives a holy life, avoids infidelity (whether real or idolatrous), and is clothed in righteous works. Second, we observed how Paul, the author of the Epistle to the Hebrews, and John of Patmos each illustrated the heavenly city—the New Jerusalem—as a present experience of the Early Church. By exploring the topic of New Jerusalem, it became clear that every New Testament reference to this concept indicates that the city is a metaphor for the redeemed people of God's reoriented outlook, with particular emphasis on their membership within the new covenant and the realized eschatology of the kingdom of God. Finally, we examined the imagery in Revelation 21–22, which combines the metaphors of the bride and the heavenly city into a single vision of the faithful Church in all its glory. Drawing on the imagery of the bride of Christ, the Book of Revelation reveals that the Church is to see itself as the holy counterpart to the unholy and ungodly city of Rome—a city also depicted as a woman. Revelation's portrayal of the heavenly Jerusalem, which is also the bride of Christ, encourages followers of Christ to view their commission to bring about the reign of God on earth as it is in heaven as a holy calling that extends God's redemptive healing to the nations. The final blessing in Revelation encourages its readers to wash their bridal robes, which grants them entrance into New Jerusalem and access to the tree of life: "Blessed are those who wash their robes, so that they will have the right to the tree of life and may enter the city by the gates" (Rev 22:14).

What are some of the other essential ways that Ecclesiology, the study of the Church, gives meaning and purpose to the body of Christ? How should the modern, twenty-first-century Church follow in the footsteps of those who lived in the first century? We will explore these questions in the following chapter.

---

[34] Kraybill, *Apocalypse and Allegiance*, 176, is helpful here: "if we understand the arrival of the new Jerusalem to have started already in John's day, and to continue in our own, then the holy city is a symbol of God restoring the world in the present. Someday, when Christ returns, the restoration will be complete."

44
APPLYING ECCLESIOLOGY TODAY

One of the most practical ways to continue the work of the Early Church is to remain committed to the two sacraments: water baptism and the Lord's Supper. Not only do both of these ritual acts serve to remind the communities of faith of the continuing significance of the death and resurrection of Jesus, but they also transform doctrines into visible and tangible displays. Beginning with baptism in water, this initiation rite serves as a public declaration that the convert is moving from one area of solidarity to the new solidarity in Christ. In other words, baptism serves as the visible opportunity to declare to all present that the initiate into the Christian faith is making the conscious and deliberate choice to die to one's former way of living and to identify with the risen Jesus and his newness of life. By going down into the water, the convert unites with Christ's death. By being raised out of the water, the convert similarly unites with the new life that God has given to Jesus. Whether one is converting from an unreligious life or from a different religion, the results are the same; the new Christian is considering the former way of living to be completely and utterly dead to them, choosing instead to live within the sphere of Christ's resurrection. Turning our attention to the Lord's Supper, we have a celebratory meal that recalls Christ's last supper with his disciples on the night that he was betrayed. During this meal, Jesus "gave thanks" (Greek: *eucharisteo*) for the bread and the cup, from which several derive the descriptor "The Eucharist." Like the sacrament of baptism, the Lord's Supper calls to mind the death of Jesus by associating his body with the broken bread and his blood with the cup of wine. While it is certainly true that the body and the blood of Jesus cover the sins of those partaking of the sacramental meal, the death of Jesus also seals the terms of the new covenant in the blood of the one sacrificed. Paul exhorted his readers to recall Jesus' death in the past as well as his future second coming as they commemorate the Lord's Supper: "For as often as you eat this bread and drink the cup, you proclaim the Lord's death until he comes" (1 Cor 11:26). Let us, therefore, continue to practice these important sacraments that the early Christians enacted. Let us not downplay the significance of the sacraments or overlook the deeply motivating effects they have on encouraging those who participate in them to walk in newness of life and to obey the terms of the new covenant. Moreover, let us study Paul's treatments of these Christian rites, beginning in Romans 6 and 1 Corinthians 11, in order that we may better understand how they relate to the wider community of believers. By participating in water baptism and the ceremonial meal of the Lord's Supper, we honor Christ's sacrifice and channel our appreciation for what he did for us into good works and faithful living.

For our second practical application drawn from our study of Ecclesiology, we want to focus on how the Church's identity as the new temple, the dwelling of God, serves to motivate behavior. Many Christians will readily agree that the body of Christ is a temple and that believers are identified as a kingdom of priests. How all of this temple imagery translates into mission and continuing the God-given purpose of his tabernacling presence on earth is less clear. It is one thing to correctly believe that the renewed people of God within the new covenant are a temple community; it is another thing altogether to turn that theological truth into good works. The first thing that the body of Christ should realize is that, because of the gift of the Holy Spirit, the Church functions as the place where people come to meet, encounter, and experience God. Ephesians 2:19–22 is clear: believers *are God's household*, they have been built as *God's new temple*, and they serve, already, as *the dwelling place of God by the Holy Spirit*. When Christians gather together for worship, they don't have to invite God into their presence. God is *already present* through his Spirit. Inviting people to church is an opportunity to encourage others to come and experience the living God who dwells among his redeemed, Christ-following people. The second major way to apply temple theology is to regard the Church as the place where forgiveness takes place. In the Old Testament, God's people regularly gathered in both the tabernacle and the temple to offer sacrifices for atonement. The local priests mediated God's forgiveness to his covenant people. In other words, the temple dwelling of God served as the location where people experienced forgiveness. Christians have inherited the role as priests within the new covenant, so they are the agents of God's forgiveness to others. Therefore, the Church functions as the place where God's mercy and forgiveness are freely given, not earned. Christ taught the Early Church to generously forgive, just as the Father has forgiven them (Matt 6:12). Moreover, Christ also taught that if his followers do not forgive others, God will not forgive them (Matt 6:15). Finally, the mission of the Church is to continue the temple's purpose of proclaiming God's truths to the world. Both Isaiah and Micah prophesied that in the last days, the house of God would attract many people interested in hearing his ways so that they may know how to walk in his paths (Isa 2:2–3; Mic 4:1–2). The inauguration of the kingdom of God has introduced the last days, a reality that was confirmed by the Early Church (Acts 2:17; Heb 1:2; 2 Pet 3:3). As such, Christians understand their mission as fulfilling these prophetic promises. The household of God served as the temple "pillar and support of the truth" (1 Tim 3:15). The Great Commission orients believers to make disciples in the world and teach these new converts to observe Jesus' teachings. Let us, therefore, embody the mission of the temple and commit to sharing the truths of the new covenant with others. Let us embrace the value of forgiveness by offering it freely in the Church. Let us also embrace the presence of the living God through his Spirit, which dwells in our midst when we gather for worship. May we encourage others to experience the only true God and his forgiveness in our communities of faith in fulfillment of the purpose of our identity as the temple.

Our third Ecclesiological application is drawn from the truth that the faithful people of God are illustrated as the bride of Christ, the New Jerusalem. What does it mean to live as a citizen of New Jerusalem? How is John of Patmos using his imagery of a city in Revelation 21:9–22:9 to portray the faithful, conquering Christians? Many readers of the Book of Revelation have simply not had the opportunity to seriously engage with the symbolism John employed to illustrate the holy city as a beautiful bride, which is clearly intended to contrast the unholy city of Fallen Babylon that is also likened to a harlot. If the summons to the seven Asian churches to whom Revelation was originally written included the exhortation to "Come out of her, my people" (Rev 18:4), the intended response requires more of an *ethical separation*, not so much a *change in location*. In other words, the summons to come out of the unholy city does not involve packing a suitcase and relocating. It has to do with a serious change in behavior, and the parallel summons for the readers of Revelation to "enter by the gates into the city" of New Jerusalem by washing their robes (Rev 22:14) confirms this ethical reading. Several times in Revelation, we are told that the city of New Jerusalem is *presently descending* (Rev 3:12; 21:2, 10), indicating that the city is a reality that can be experienced by those who are actively conquering (Rev 3:12; 21:7). Looking closely at the architectural symbolism describing New Jerusalem, we can begin to extract how citizens of this city are to view themselves and function in holiness, that is, as the holy bride of Christ. The city's dimensions, which measure 144,000 stadia based on the twelve edges of the cube that are each 12,000 stadia in length (Rev 21:16), signify a completion of the people of God through its multiples of the number twelve. The nations and the kings of the earth walk by the light of the Lamb (Rev 21:23–25), which again points to a faithful posture of discipleship. The unclean and those who are practicing abominations and lies remain outside of the city (Rev 21:27; 22:15), having not become the conquerors that Christ requires, but the gates will never be closed in hopes that citizens of Fallen Babylon may repent and join New Jerusalem (Rev 21:25). In fact, the light shining out from the city, reflecting the mission of the Church, actively draws people in (Rev 21:24). The tree of life brings healing to the nations, stressing the bride's role in being the people through whom God's redemptive reign and forgiveness are carried out on earth (Rev 22:2). Let us, therefore, serve as "pillars in the temple" of God (Rev 3:12), that is, as foundations of God's temple activity to the world. Let us live in holiness, washing our robes, and refusing to compromise with sin, as is appropriate for the bride adorned for her husband (Rev 21:2, 9). Let us also embrace our citizenship in New Jerusalem by embodying its principles and performing light-bearing good works. Finally, let us serve as the means of healing for the world by speaking truth, forgiving one another, and announcing the gospel of the kingdom that can result in transformative conversion.

PART EIGHT: ESCHATOLOGY

45
OLD TESTAMENT PROMISES OF RESTORATION

It is an interesting exercise to consider the impressions and reflections that one has after reading carefully a body of literature. Having taught several Bible survey courses for over a decade, I have had the privilege of hearing from hundreds of students their immediate reactions to finishing their assigned reading. For those who completed the reading of the entire Old Testament, there was a sense that the literature of the Hebrew Bible left a feeling of longing and anticipation. Readers were often left with the questions of when God would act in history to redeem his people and how he would stay true to his promises. On the other hand, when the same undergraduate students finished reading the New Testament for the first time, I frequently heard about feelings of joy and hope. There was a sense that the Creator had acted in history in and through the human Messiah, and that this accomplishment propelled the hope of the final consummation of the kingdom. Even Peter the Apostle regarded the promises of restoration as sufficient motivation to encourage repentance and obedience to God, according to Acts 3:19-21: "Therefore repent and return, so that your sins may be wiped away, in order that times of refreshing may come from the presence of the Lord; and that He may send Jesus, the Christ appointed for you, whom heaven must receive until the period of restoration of all things about which God spoke by the mouth of His holy prophets from ancient time." In order to understand how the Early Church explained the hope of a new creation that Christ would usher in at his second coming, we need to contend with the Old Testament's message of how God would renew his good creation.[1]

This chapter will highlight the most influential Old Testament promises that deal with the restoration of creation, particularly those that will finally come to pass at the end of the age, when Christ returns to rule and reign. First, we will examine the promises contained within the Abrahamic Covenant, noting how the land promise in particular frequently reoccurs in the narrative of the Hebrew Bible. Second, we will call attention to the promises of the dynasty, throne, and kingdom covenanted to David and his descendants. Third, we will look at some of the prophetic visions (and in some cases, dreams) of the kingdom of God at the height of its consummation. Finally, we will consider how God will renew all creation, including his sinful people and the cursed land, bringing it into a condition of paradise governed by faithful human beings.

---

[1] Gerstenberger, *Theologies in the Old Testament*, 284, provides a helpful reminder: "without the Old Testament the New Testament would be a torso which simply lacked essential elements of theology and ethics."

The Abrahamic Covenant Fulfilled in the Kingdom of God

By this point in our study, the Abrahamic Covenant should be familiar material. We observed in Chapters 5, 15, and 21 that Yahweh summoned Abraham, who was known at the time simply as Abram, to be the faithful human being in whom God would begin to undo the sin of Adam. In Genesis 12:1–3, we have the classic statement of God's assurance to give Abraham the *land*, to provide him with a worldwide family of *descendants*, and to *bless* the world in and through him. As the narrative of the Old Testament continues to unfold, we find numerous occurrences where Yahweh reaffirms these promises to Abraham and to his family. Here is just a sampling of God's reassuring commitment to place faithful human beings in charge of the land:

> Yahweh appeared to Abram and said, "To your descendants I will give this land." (Gen 12:7)

> Yahweh said to Abram, after Lot had separated from him, "Now lift up your eyes and look from the place where you are, northward and southward and eastward and westward; for all the land which you see, I will give it to you and to your descendants forever." (Gen 13:14–15)

> I am Yahweh who brought you out of Ur of the Chaldeans, to give you this land to possess it. (Gen 15:7)

> I will give to you and to your descendants after you, the land of your sojournings, all the land of Canaan, for an everlasting possession; and I will be their God. (Gen 17:8)

> To your descendants I will give this land (Gen 24:7)

After Abraham, Yahweh reaffirmed his covenant promises to Isaac, assuring him that he and his offspring would be heirs of the land: "Sojourn in this land and I will be with you and bless you, for to you and to your descendants I will give all these lands, and I will establish the oath which I swore to your father Abraham" (Gen 26:3). Isaac, in turn, blesses his son Jacob by praying that God's covenantal promises to Abraham would continue through Jacob and his children: "May He also give you the blessing of Abraham, to you and to your descendants with you, that you may possess the land of your sojournings, which God gave to Abraham" (Gen 28:4). Yahweh himself reaffirms this promise directly to Jacob in a dream by committing to not only give the land to Jacob's offspring but also to bless the world through them (Gen 28:13–15). God's promise to make Abraham's family heirs of the land is so sure to come to pass that at one point, he conveys his commitment as if he has *already given it* to Abraham and Isaac: "The land which I gave to Abraham and Isaac, I will give it to you, And I will give the land to your descendants after you" (Gen 35:12).[2] The narrative of the Book of Genesis concludes with Jacob blessing his sons with the promise that they would inherit the land as an

---

[2] Goldingay, *Old Testament Theology*, 1:231.

everlasting possession (Gen 48:4) and with Joseph assuring his brothers that God will bring them into this promised land (Gen 50:24). As the opening book of Scripture, Genesis sets the tone for what is to follow: faithful human beings are destined to inherit the earth and recover the vocation originally promised to Adam.

Throughout the process of God rescuing Israel from Egypt and leading them to the land of Canaan, the Abrahamic promises frequently reappear. Yahweh reaffirms the land promise to Moses prior to the exodus itself: "I will bring you to the land which I swore to give to Abraham, Isaac, and Jacob, and I will give it to you for a possession" (Exod 6:8). When Israel commits a brazen act of disobedience in the golden calf incident, Moses intercedes on behalf of the nation, and in doing so, he recalls God covenantal commitment to Abraham: "Remember Abraham, Isaac, and Israel, Your servants to whom You swore by Yourself, and said to them, 'I will multiply your descendants as the stars of the heavens, and all this land of which I have spoken I will give to your descendants, and they shall inherit it forever'" (Exod 32:13). Upon receiving the land of Canaan, Israel was warned not to commit detestable sins within their lot of inheritance (Deut 24:4); indeed, one of the chief covenant curses for disobedience would involve exile from the land (Deut 28:64). Although the prophets repeatedly warned Israel that committing idolatry and refusing to obey God's commands would result in destruction and exile, there was always a message of hope after punishment that God would fulfill his oaths to Abraham by giving the promised land to his faithful people:

> Then all your people will be righteous; they will possess the land forever (Isa 60:21)

> In those days the house of Judah will walk with the house of Israel, and they will come together from the land of the north to the land that I gave your fathers as an inheritance. (Jer 3:18)

> Then I Myself will gather the remnant of My flock out of all the countries where I have driven them and bring them back to their pasture, and they will be fruitful and multiply. (Jer 23:3)

> For I will take you from the nations, gather you from all the lands and bring you into your own land. (Ezek 36:24)

> But as for you, go your way to the end; then you will enter into rest and rise again for your allotted portion at the end of days (Dan 12:13)

Indeed, even the Psalms show that the Abrahamic land promises were included in the sphere of worship. Of no minor importance is Psalm 37, which emphasizes the inheritance of the land for the righteous in deliberate contrast to the wicked being cut off and destroyed. The psalmist summons his readers to dwell in the land (Ps 37:3), look forward to inheriting the land (Ps 37:9), be humble so that they may inherit the land (Ps 37:11), and wait for Yahweh's blessing so that they can possess the land as their inheritance (Ps 37:22, 34). Those who are heirs are assured that the land will be their possession *forever*: "The righteous will inherit the land and dwell in it forever" (Ps 37:29). When we recall how Adam's image-bearing vocation included his role as a ruler over the land to which he was entrusted, we can see and appreciate how God's faithful people will be put back in charge over God's good world when he raises the dead, enacts judgment, vindicates the faithful, and rewards them according to his commitment to Abraham.

The Davidic Covenant Fulfilled in the Kingdom of God

Of arguably equal importance to the Abrahamic covenant is the Davidic covenant, which we examined in Chapters 5, 21, and 33. Yahweh's commitment, which is recorded in 2 Samuel 7:12–16 and 1 Chronicles 17:11–14, assured King David that his throne in Jerusalem and his kingdom would be ruled by his offspring forever.[3] The history of Israel's kings who descended from David and ruled on the Davidic throne in Jerusalem continued for five centuries until the Babylonians destroyed the temple and exiled most of the Israelites in 587 BC. From that low point in Israel's history, a descendant of David has never ruled as king from Jerusalem. Ezekiel declared that there would be a temporary suspension of the dynasty of rulers until the rightful king arrives: "Remove the turban and take off the crown; this will no longer be the same. Exalt that which is low and abase that which is high. A ruin, a ruin, a ruin, I will make it. This also will be no more until he comes whose right it is, and I will give it to him" (Ezek 21:26–27). This leaves readers of the Old Testament with an important question: How would Yahweh remain faithful to his covenantal promises to David to provide a Davidic offspring to rule and reign over the kingdom forever?

On several occasions, God provided the Hebrew prophets with assurances that he would indeed honor his promises by raising up an anointed ruler who would bring fulfillment to the Davidic covenant. The prophetic testimony concerning this coming Davidic king is substantial:

> There shall come forth a shoot from the stump of Jesse, and a branch from his roots shall bear fruit. And the Spirit of Yahweh shall rest upon him, the Spirit of wisdom and understanding, the Spirit of counsel and might, the Spirit of knowledge and the fear of Yahweh. (Isa 11:1–2)

> A throne will even be established in lovingkindness, and a judge will sit on it in faithfulness in the tent of David; moreover, he will seek justice and be prompt in righteousness. (Isa 16:5)

---

[3] Brueggemann, *Theology of the Old Testament*, 171, observes that from the announcement of the Davidic covenant "the Davidic dynasty becomes an enduring theological datum in Israel's life."

> Behold, the days are coming, declares Yahweh, When I will raise up for David a righteous Branch; and he will reign as king and act wisely and do justice and righteousness in the land. In his days Judah will be saved, and Israel will dwell securely (Jer 23:5–6)
>
> But they shall serve Yahweh their God and David their king, whom I will raise up for them. (Jer 30:9)
>
> In those days and at that time I will cause a righteous Branch of David to spring forth; and he shall execute justice and righteousness on the earth. In those days Judah will be saved and Jerusalem will dwell in safety; and this is the name by which she will be called: Yahweh is our righteousness. For thus says Yahweh, David shall never lack a man to sit on the throne of the house of Israel (Jer 33:15–17)
>
> Then I will set over them one shepherd, My servant David, and he will feed them; he will feed them himself and be their shepherd. And I, Yahweh, will be their God, and My servant David will be prince among them. (Ezek 34:23–24).
>
> My servant David will be king over them, and they will all have one shepherd; and they will walk in My ordinances and keep My statutes and observe them. They will live on the land that I gave to Jacob My servant, in which your fathers lived; and they will live on it, they, and their sons and their sons' sons, forever; and David My servant will be their prince forever. (Ezek 37:24–25)
>
> For the sons of Israel will remain for many days without king or prince, without sacrifice or sacred pillar and without ephod or household idols. Afterward the sons of Israel will return and seek Yahweh their God and David their king; and they will come trembling to Yahweh and to His goodness in the last days. (Hos 3:4–5)
>
> On that day I will raise up the booth of David that is fallen, and repair its breaches, and raise up its ruins, and rebuild it as in the days of old (Amos 9:11)

These prophets emphasize several points concerning Yahweh's intention to fulfill his oaths to David. First, we can observe that this coming anointed king, who was quickly identified in Jewish messianic expectation as the promised Messiah, would indeed be a descendant of David himself. Sometimes, this promised king is spoken of as if he were "David" by the prophets (Jer 30:9; Ezek 34:24; 37:24–25; Hos 3:5). What is meant by this description is that the Davidic descendant will resemble the historical David, who defeated his enemies as a warrior while never succumbing to the sin of idolatry. Second, we observe that, despite the pause in the fulfillment of the Davidic throne and kingdom that the deportation to Babylon caused, the prophets aimed to assure their readers that God would remain true to his commitment at the proper time. This climactic moment of restoration is variously described as the "coming" days (Jer 23:5), "at that time" (Jer 33:15), "in the last days" (Hos 3:5), and "on that day" (Amos 9:11). Finally, when Yahweh acts to raise up a Davidic descendant to sit as king and rule over his kingdom, his reign would never come to an end. Upon being enthroned, the anointed son of David will usher in an era of peace in which the faithful people of God and their children will live in the land forever (Ezek 37:25). The everlasting duration of this reign is further illustrated by Yahweh's insistence that David will never lack a human being to occupy the covenanted Davidic throne (Jer 33:17).[4] These promises created an intense longing for the arrival of the anointed descendant of David who would restore the kingdom to Israel as the coming king and shepherd of God's people.

The inevitable concerns over how and when God would remain faithful to the Davidic covenant bubble up in the Psalms, especially Psalm 89. The psalm begins with an affirmation of Yahweh's commitment to his covenantal promises: "I have made a covenant with My chosen; I have sworn to David My servant, I will establish your seed forever and build up your throne to all generations" (Ps 89:3–4). Further assurances to God's fidelity are recorded in Psalm 89:35–37: "Once I have sworn by My holiness; I will not lie to David. His descendants shall endure forever and his throne as the sun before Me. It shall be established forever like the moon, and the witness in the sky is faithful." From the perspective of the psalmist, however, it appears that God has abandoned his promises to David. The complaint is lengthy and thorough:

> But You have cast off and rejected, You have been full of wrath against Your anointed. You have spurned the covenant of Your servant; You have profaned his crown in the dust. You have broken down all his walls; You have brought his strongholds to ruin. All who pass along the way plunder him; he has become a reproach to his neighbors. You have exalted the right hand of his adversaries; You have made all his enemies rejoice. You also turn back the edge of his sword and have not made him stand in battle. You have made his splendor to cease and cast his throne to the ground. You have shortened the days of his youth; You have covered him with shame. Selah. (Ps 89:38–45)

The psalmist recounts how the line of Davidic kings has suffered the reproach of God's enemies, enemies whom it appears that God has exalted. Not only is the dynasty of royal descendants no longer in power, but the walls and strongholds formerly belonging to the kingdom of Israel are in ruin. Understandably, the psalmist asks God how long will he remain angry at sin: "How long, O Yahweh? Will You hide Yourself forever? Will Your wrath burn like fire?" (Ps 89:46). The psalm comes to its conclusion with a petition that Yahweh would remember the faithfulness that he swore to David and the present mockery that his people suffer (Ps 89:49–50).

The tension between Yahweh's inaction regarding the Davidic covenant and his assurances that he will bring these promises to fruition remains consistent throughout the Old Testament narrative, particularly after the exile and Israel's post-exilic return to the land. Babylon may have been defeated, but the Persians came into power and possessed dominion over the kingdom of Israel and the land promised to Abraham's descendants. After the Persians suffered defeat at the hands of the Greeks, two of the Greek nations

---

[4] Lundbom, *Jeremiah 21–36*, 541; Goldingay, *Old Testament Theology*, 2:492; Kaiser, *Toward an Old Testament Theology*, 230.

(Syria and Egypt) were at odds with each other, with Jerusalem unfortunately positioned between them. Although the Maccabean Revolt led to Israel's independence in the mid-2nd century BC, a Davidic king was not installed as king, which upset many Jews. Inevitably, Israel's independence was cut short when the Romans rose to power and seized control of the land in 63 BC, ending a local Jewish civil war and incorporating the region into the Roman Empire.

Promises of the Kingdom of God in the Book of Daniel

The Old Testament promises of the coming time of restoration often combined elements contained in the Abrahamic and Davidic covenants, most often with the insistence that the inheritance of the land would be the location of the coming kingdom that would endure forever. The hope that God would install faithful human beings over his good earth in order to deal with the curse of sin and the enemies of God motivated many to trust in God's faithfulness to redeem his people, even in times when Israel was under the heel of foreign overlords. The Book of Daniel offers hope that God will rescue his people, usher in the kingdom of God, and place those who have been faithful to him in charge of this coming worldwide dominion. The Book of Daniel also offers much-needed moral guidance to those whose peers are tempted to slide into one of two extreme positions. On the far left are those who compromise by giving up their Judaism in favor of accommodation with the pagan rulers. On the far right are those ripe for violent revolt, planning on taking up the sword against the pagans in order to drive them out of the land and the temple. The consistent message within Daniel, provided by ethical examples of four faithful Israelite boys (Daniel, Hananiah, Mishael, and Azariah), is to neither compromise nor revolt, but instead to remain intensely loyal to God, even if they have to suffer martyrdom. The hope presented in the Book of Daniel is that those who faithfully endure to the end will be *raised from the dead*, *vindicated* by the true God, and *installed in the coming kingdom* that will never pass away.

     In Daniel chapter two, we gain our first glimpse of how the promise of the kingdom of God brings hope to those suffering under the rule of the Gentiles, while also strengthening their resolve to remain faithful, knowing that the God of heaven is in charge and in control of history. Nebuchadnezzar, the king of Babylon, had a dream that only Daniel, a young Israelite, was able to declare and interpret. After God revealed the mystery of the king's dream to Daniel, the young boy proclaimed that Nebuchadnezzar saw a large, awesome statue. This sculpture featured a head made of fine gold, a torso of silver, the belly and thighs of bronze, legs of iron, and feet of an iron and clay mixture. However, this was not the entirety of the king's dream, for there was also a stone that was cut without hands, and this stone fell upon the feet of the statue. The result of this collision was that the entire statue and all its elements became chaff that blew away with the wind, leaving the stone, which formed a large mountain that filled the whole earth.

Fortunately for the readers, Daniel offers an interpretation of this dream, and its conclusion speaks of the hope of the kingdom of God that will never be destroyed. Daniel's God-given interpretation illustrates the statue as four successive kingdoms, beginning with the Babylonian Empire in which King Nebuchadnezzar finds himself: "You are the head of gold" (Dan 2:38). Readers familiar with the well-known history of that region of the world are able to follow Daniel's interpretation and verify the details that he offers. Within the scope of a single sentence, the next two kingdoms are quickly discussed in order to move the narrative quickly to the fourth kingdom: "After you there will arise another kingdom inferior to you, then another third kingdom of bronze, which will rule over all the earth" (Dan 2:39). The Median kingdom and the Persian kingdom best fit these descriptions. The kingdom of Media was pretty small in scope and significance compared to Nebuchadnezzar and his accomplishments as Babylon's king. The third kingdom mentioned, which conquered both Media and Babylon, was the Persian Empire, whose dominion was far-reaching, lasting for two centuries. After offering a single sentence to quickly cover Media and Persia, Daniel provides a lengthy description of the fourth kingdom, the Greek Empire (Dan 2:40–43).[5] The kingdom of Greece is initially depicted in terms of its strength and military might, capable of crushing its opponents. However, the kingdom became divided, so the divided Greek kingdom was partially as strong as iron and partially as brittle as pottery. This aligns with what transpired after the death of the mighty conqueror Alexander the Great, whose dominant empire was divided among his four Greek generals. Jewish history records how two of these Greek generals took control of the regions directly north and south of Judea, placing the Jews in the unfortunate crossfire when these rivals battled one another.

However, the interpretation of the dream concludes on a positive note, with victory for the people of God. Daniel describes how the true God in heaven will establish his kingdom, and, unlike the former kingdoms of Babylon, Media, Persia, and Greece, the kingdom of God will last forever:

> In the days of those kings the God of heaven will set up a kingdom which will never be destroyed, and that kingdom will not be left for another people; it will crush and put an end to all these kingdoms, but it will itself endure forever. Inasmuch as you saw that a stone was cut out of the mountain without hands and that it crushed the iron, the bronze, the clay, the silver and the gold, the great God has made known to the king what will take place in the future; so the dream is true and its interpretation is trustworthy. (Dan 2:44–45)

---

[5] Newsom and Breed, *Daniel*, 80; Collins, *Daniel*, 170; Pace, *Daniel*, 73; Gowan, *Daniel*, 57–58.

It is quite possible that the phrase "the God of heaven will set up a kingdom" is behind the designations *kingdom of God* and *kingdom of heaven* in the New Testament, particularly in the Gospel of Matthew. In any case, Daniel makes it clear to Nebuchadnezzar that the God of heaven is in charge of these pagan kingdoms, allowing them to rise and fall in accordance with his will. The coming kingdom of God will be a worldwide empire that will utterly crush all others. God's kingdom, unlike the four described in the dream, will not be just another kingdom that will be replaced by a more dominant nation to come. On the contrary, when God moves to judge these pagan kingdoms, his dominion will be everlasting. When we examine the stone that utterly demolished the statue in the dream, we find that it was cut from a mountain without human hands, indicating that it was created by God rather than being man-made. Readers of Daniel chapter two were quick to associate the *stone* with the messianic *son of God*, since the words for "stone" (*eben*) and "son" (*ben*) were commonly used as wordplay.[6] As such, the bringer of the kingdom of God would be the son of God, the Davidic king to whom Yahweh has promised to provide a throne and a kingdom forever. The conclusion of Nebuchadnezzar's dream offered a measure of comfort and hope to the readers of Daniel, giving assurance that, despite the seemingly unstoppable nature of whatever kingdom was in power, the true God would remain faithful to his promises. By trusting in the God of heaven, his people would be unlikely to give up their Jewish distinctives in accommodation or to take matters into their own hands through violent revolt and zealotry.

The Restoration of All of God's Creation in the Kingdom of God

The promises of restoration that appear in the Old Testament are not limited to giving humans dominion over the land and placing the Davidic heir on the throne to rule his kingdom forever. When Yahweh moves to restore his creation, this includes all that is wrong, broken, and cursed in the world. Humanity, which was cursed to die and return to the dust at death (Gen 3:17–19), will undergo God's blessing in a manner that allows them to live and function perfectly. Several of the Hebrew prophets look forward to a time in which God will renew his image-bearing human beings. Isaiah foretold of a time when Yahweh would put an end to death, mourning, and the suffering of reproach: "He will swallow up death for all time, and Adonai Yahweh will wipe tears away from all faces, and He will remove the reproach of His people from all the earth; for Yahweh has spoken" (Isa 25:8). Raising the dead and granting immortality to the righteous would certainly bring an end to all dying (Dan 12:2). Not only will God remove death within the new creation, his people will possess no sickness or deformity. Observe how descriptions of renewed human beings are right in the mix of promises to restore the land itself:

---

[6] See Exod 28:9–12; Josh 4:20–22; 1 Kgs 18:31; Matt 3:9; Mark 12:6–10; Luke 3:8.

> The wilderness and the dry land shall be glad; the desert shall rejoice and blossom like the crocus; it shall blossom abundantly and rejoice with joy and singing. The glory of Lebanon shall be given to it, the majesty of Carmel and Sharon. They shall see the glory of Yahweh, the majesty of our God. Strengthen the weak hands, and make firm the feeble knees. Say to those who have an anxious heart, "Be strong; fear not! Behold, your God will come with vengeance, with the recompense of God. He will come and save you." Then the eyes of the blind shall be opened, and the ears of the deaf unstopped; then shall the lame man leap like a deer, and the tongue of the mute sing for joy. For waters break forth in the wilderness, and streams in the desert; the burning sand shall become a pool, and the thirsty ground springs of water; in the haunt of jackals, where they lie down, the grass shall become reeds and rushes. (Isa 35:1–7)

Isaiah foretells a time when the blind will have their sight restored, the deaf will hear, the legs of the lame will be healed, and the mute will burst forth in joyful song. What is important to note is that God's promise to regenerate human beings to live abundantly occurs in the midst of descriptions of the regeneration of barren places on earth. The wilderness, the dry land, the desert, and the burning sands will all be transformed and renewed into locations of flourishing growth. Instead of locations of lifelessness, these regions will become places of water, streams, pools, and springs. When the kingdom of God is finally consummated, *all creation will become new*, not just human beings.

We can also see instances in the prophetic descriptions of the age to come of the animal kingdom coming into harmony and peace. Since the kingdom of God will be a never-ending time of peace and sinlessness, conflict among animals will be nonexistent. Wolves will dwell with lambs, leopards will lie down with young goats, and lions will play nice with both calves and fatlings (Isa 11:6). Moreover, we are told that a little boy will be able to lead these tame animals. Young children will be able to play with a cobra and a viper (Isa 11:8), clearly indicating a reversal of the enmity between human beings and snakes that is described in Genesis 3:15. Ezekiel similarly prophecies of a time when the Davidic kingdom will be fully installed, resulting in a peace that has no place for "harmful beasts of the land" (Ezek 34:25), indeed, the beasts of the earth will no longer prey on the sheep belonging to the Davidic shepherd-king (Ezek 34:28). The prophet Hosea also speaks of a coming day when peace with animals and people will be established: "In that day I will also make a covenant for them with the beasts of the field, the birds of the sky and the creeping things of the ground. And I will abolish the bow, the sword and war from the land, and will make them lie down in safety" (Hos 2:18). Tranquility with the animal kingdom is precisely what one would expect when God once again places all things under the feet of faithful human beings, which includes animals of the field, birds of the heavens, and the fish of the sea, as anticipated in Psalm 8:6–8.

We have already seen glimpses of the worldwide peace that will endure in the kingdom of God, and the Hebrew prophets long for a time when war will be entirely a thing of the past. Both Isaiah and Micah, prophetic figures whose ministries overlapped, spoke about the time to come when all the weapons of battle will be remade into farming equipment, signaling the end of conflict on earth: "they will hammer their swords into plowshares and their spears into pruning hooks" (Isa 2:4; Mic 4:3). The picture of this prophecy of peace is clear that nations will never again take up arms against one another, nor will they even train for battle.[7] Micah includes the line that there will be "no one to make them afraid," allowing each person to sit peacefully under his vine and fig tree (Mic 4:4). Later in the collection of Isaiah's oracles, we find Yahweh's assurance that acts of violence and the destruction of war will completely cease: "Violence will not be heard again in your land, nor devastation or destruction within your borders" (Isa 60:18). Ezekiel speaks of God making a "covenant of peace" when the Davidic Messiah rules his kingdom (Ezek 34:25; 37:26). Micah similarly characterizes the promised shepherd-king as the one who will bring peace in and through his rule (Mic 5:5). Although Zechariah portrays the coming king of Israel with the humble and modest mount of a donkey (Zech 9:9), the king's rule will abolish all chariots, horses of war, and bows: "I will cut off the chariot from Ephraim and the war horse from Jerusalem; and the battle bow shall be cut off, and he shall speak peace to the nations; his rule shall be from sea to sea, and from the River to the ends of the earth" (Zech 9:10). When God set up his kingdom, there will be no one to oppose him.

Finally, we can observe the promises of restoring what Adam and Eve lost in the Paradise of Eden, as several prophetic predictions anticipate the restoration of the tranquil garden on a worldwide scale. In addition to several visions of deserts being renewed into flourishing terrains of green growth (e.g., Isa 35:1–2, 7; 41:18–19; 55:13), we find the language of Eden's restoration. Consider these promises of new creation that recall the Edenic paradise portrayed in Genesis 1–3:

> Indeed, Yahweh will comfort Zion; He will comfort all her waste places. And her wilderness He will make like Eden, and her desert like the garden of Yahweh; joy and gladness will be found in her, thanksgiving and sound of a melody. (Isa 51:3)

> "On the day that I cleanse you from all your iniquities, I will cause the cities to be inhabited, and the waste places will be rebuilt. The desolate land will be cultivated instead of being a desolation in the sight of everyone who passes by." They will say, "This desolate land has become like the Garden of Eden; and the waste, desolate and ruined cities are fortified and inhabited." (Ezek 36:33–35)

> For the day of Yahweh is coming; surely it is near, a day of darkness and gloom, a day of clouds and thick darkness. As the dawn is spread over the mountains, so there is a great and mighty people; there has never been anything like it, nor will there be again after it, to the years of many generations. A fire consumes before them, and behind them a flame burns. The land is like the Garden of Eden before them (Joel 2:1–3)

---

[7] Becking, *Micah*, 162, says, "What has been routine and regular will definitively be abandoned in days to come."

The recurring theme is that on the day God moves in judgment, the day of the Lord, Eden will be restored.[8] The regeneration of God's world will transform wastelands and the desolate places in Paradise on Earth. Similar oracles of the new creation that will accompany the kingdom of God employ the language of a garden that echoes back to the opening chapters of Genesis. For example, Jeremiah prophesied of a time when Yahweh would act to redeem his people, resulting in their livelihood being compared to "a watered garden, and they shall never languish again" (Jer 31:12). Ezekiel's vision of a river that brings growth, life, and an abundance of fish (Ezek 47:7–10) appears to be a restoration of the river that flowed from Eden to water the Garden (Gen 2:10).[9] The prophet also anticipates "all kinds of trees for food," trees with leaves and fruit that will never go bad, but will instead provide food and restoration (Ezek 47:12). Even the mountains will drip with sweet wine and the hills will flow with milk (Joel 3:18; Amos 9:13), further enhancing the new creation's Edenic properties. These promises contributed to the hope of God's faithful people inheriting the land precisely because *the land would resemble the Garden of Eden*.

Conclusion

This chapter has demonstrated that the Old Testament writers set the expectation of a time when God would be true to his promises by redeeming his faithful people and the whole creation. First, we looked at the Abrahamic land promise that Yahweh covenanted to give to the children of Abraham as an inheritance forever. Second, we explored the promises contained within the Davidic covenant, particularly the throne in Jerusalem and the kingdom that would never pass away, both of which rightfully belong to the messianic heir of kings descending from David himself. Third, we looked at the assurance that the God of heaven would bring about his kingdom that would not only last forever but also crush all other opposing kingdoms in a swift act of judgment. Finally, we gave attention to the many ways Yahweh would renew his creation when he ushers in his rule and reign. These promises included the end of death, the complete regeneration of human beings to live without ailments, peace between animals and humans, and the transformation of the land into a new Garden of Eden. When the Early Church announced the gospel of the kingdom of God, this was indeed good news.

Early Christians embraced these Old Testament promises of the restoration of God's good creation and continued to pray for the kingdom to come. In our next chapter, we will examine how the Early Church viewed the kingdom of God, despite having already entered the present, as something that has not yet been fully realized.

---

[8] Wallace, "Eden," 282; Eichrodt, *Theology of the Old Testament*, 1:479–80.
[9] The only New Testament reference to Ezekiel's abundance of fish is in John 21:6–8, which came a result of Jesus' direct involvement, whom the Gospel of John has explicitly portrayed as the new temple in John 2:21.

46
THE FUTURE HOPE OF THE KINGDOM OF GOD

The Early Church inherited several key promises that the Old Testament authors provided for their readers. From the vantage point of the writers of the New Testament, the victory of Christ over the grave that defeated the power of sin and death was celebrated as an event that had already taken place. When the early Christians looked forward, however, there was still a tremendous hope, expectation, and reward that was yet to come. The in-breaking of the kingdom of God and the overlap of the ages indeed provided the experience of the rule and reign of God in the present, but the promises of bodily resurrection, receiving immortality, inheriting the kingdom of God, and living in a world free from sin's curse could only come to fulfillment at the return of Christ.[1] God was not yet finished renewing his creation.[2]

This chapter will set aside for the moment the inauguration of the kingdom in order to examine how the Early Church looked forward to the consummation of God's rule and reign on the earth, an event that would be ushered in at the second coming of Jesus. We will begin our exploration of the early Christian hope with a look at the inheritance promised to the faithful: the land. Second, we will give our attention to the anticipation that Christ would return to rule as king upon the throne that God covenanted to David's royal heir. Third, we will look at the conditions of the consummated kingdom of God that the New Testament authors provide. During this survey, we will draw attention to the continuity that the Early Church found with the promises of restoration that the writers of the Old Testament provided.

The Land as the Christian Inheritance

There are several indicators showing that the preaching of Jesus Christ and his followers reaffirmed the Abrahamic land promises, particularly by illustrating the earth as the inheritance of the faithful people of God. Drawing on the language of Psalm 37 and its repeated emphasis on the righteous as heirs of the land, Jesus plainly stated that his followers would receive the same earthly inheritance: "Blessed are the gentle, for they will inherit the earth" (Matt 5:5).[3] Naturally, the promised inheritance of the land was

---

[1] Green, *Salvation*, 121.
[2] Ladd, *Crucial Questions About the Kingdom*, 66.
[3] Ladd, *Crucial Questions About the Kingdom*, 70–71.

understood to be part of the much larger assurance that believers would inherit the kingdom of God.[4] We can draw attention to the emphasis within the New Testament that displays the kingdom as the *future inheritance* of his faithful disciples:

> Then the King will say to those on his right, "Come, you who are blessed by my Father, inherit the kingdom prepared for you from the foundation of the world." (Matt 25:34)

> Or do you not know that the unrighteous will not inherit the kingdom of God? (1 Cor 6:9)

> Now I say this, brethren, that flesh and blood cannot inherit the kingdom of God; nor does the perishable inherit the imperishable. (1 Cor 15:50)

> I warn you, as I warned you before, that those who do such things will not inherit the kingdom of God. (Gal 5:21)

> For you may be sure of this, that everyone who is sexually immoral or impure, or who is covetous (that is, an idolater), has no inheritance in the kingdom of Christ and God. (Eph 5:5)

Since the kingdom of God is consummated at the end of the age, this promised hope is often illustrated in terms of inheriting *eternal life*, which we have already seen in Chapter 12 as "the life of the age to come" (e.g., Matt 19:29; Luke 10:25; 18:18). The repeated use of the verb "to inherit" in the future tense presented a clear picture of promises that have yet to be attained, which Christ will award at his return.[5]

When Jesus illustrates how his followers will share in his rule and reign upon the earth, he describes the role in terms of being "put in charge of many things" and "having authority" over entire cities. In several places where Christ speaks of his second coming and the time when he will reward those who have remained obedient to him, he describes this reward of inheritance. For example, Jesus asks an important question: "Who then is the faithful and sensible slave whom his master put in charge of his household to give them their food at the proper time?" (Matt 24:45; Luke 12:42). The answer that Christ offers is that it is the slave whom his master finds to be acting faithfully and sensibly when the master arrives, that is, at Christ's return (Matt 24:46). Then, Jesus reaffirms the reward in terms of setting the faithful over his possessions: "Truly I say to you that he will put him in charge of all his possessions" (Matt 24:47; Luke 12:44). The Parable of the Nobleman reflects much of the same promise that Jesus will return to install his obedient followers over many things. Matthew's version of the parable phrases it as follows: "Well done, good and faithful slave. You were faithful with a few things, I will put you in charge of many things" (Matt 25:21, 23). Luke's version of the same parable speaks of the faithful being given charge over cities to rule: "you are to be in authority over ten cities"

---

[4] Weiss, *Jesus' Proclamation of the Kingdom*, 103.
[5] Bauer et al., *Greek-English Lexicon*, 547; Eichler, "Inheritance," 300.

(Luke 19:17); "you are to be over five cities" (Luke 19:19). The Early Church did not simply regard its reward as inheriting the land; they were to be installed as rulers over this land, restoring God's original purpose for humanity to be the faithful image-bearing people through whom he would rule his good creation.

The promise that the faithful people of God would administer God's rule and reign over creation was so foundational to the gospel of the kingdom and the early Christian hope that the apostle Paul could use its truthfulness to promote righteous behavior in his churches. As he attempts to correct the actions of some believers who take others within the body of Christ to court, Paul reminds them that they will one day rule the world:

> Does any one of you, when he has a case against his neighbor, dare to go to law before the unrighteous and not before the saints? Or do you not know that the saints will judge the world? If the world is judged by you, are you not competent to constitute the smallest law courts? Do you not know that we will judge angels? How much more matters of this life? (1 Cor 6:1–3)

Not only will the people of God rule the world when the kingdom of God is finally consummated, but they will even be exalted above the heavenly angels.[6] Paul employs the verb "to judge" in the manner that characterized the earthly rulers presented in the Book of Judges. When Paul routinely asks his rhetorical question, "Do you not know?" he assumes that this truth is common knowledge. His language recalls how Jesus promised that when he returns to take possession of the throne of David, the Twelve would have the distinct privilege of ruling on thrones and judging the twelve tribes of Israel (Matt 19:28; Luke 22:30). Sharing in Christ's rule and reign in the kingdom was the basic hope of the Early Church, and the hope served to motivate the obedience of the faithful.

Paul strongly maintained that the faithful who are in Christ are children of Abraham, and by virtue of being members of Abraham's family, believers will come to possess the land that Yahweh covenanted to Abraham. We may recall our earlier treatment that Paul's theology displayed God's promise to Abraham and his descendants *heirs of the entire world* on the basis of faith, according to Romans 4:13. Paul makes a similar argument in Galatians where he emphatically states that those who belong to Christ are indeed Abraham's seed, and as such, they find themselves as "heirs according to the promise" (Gal 3:29). Since the covenanted promises to Abraham were the land, descendants, and blessing, the language of *heirs* points to the land promise in particular as the inheritance that has been rightfully shared the faithful. Those who converted through the gospel of the kingdom of God were incorporated into the renewed family of God as his children, and Paul was adamant that these children are legitimate heirs of the promised

---

[6] Fee, *The First Epistle to the Corinthians*, 257. Thiselton, *The First Epistle to the Corinthians*, 431, helpfully remarks that "the setting-to-rights of all things includes the non-human creation as well as the world."

inheritance: "if a son, then an heir through God" (Gal 4:7). Since the words "heir," "inheritance," and the verb "to inherit" are semantically related in Greek (just as they are in English), the Early Church would almost instinctively associate its status as heirs with the promised inheritance of the land.

We can find further evidence of the New Testament authors celebrating the promised inheritance of the Early Church in terms of reigning in the age to come. The theology of the faithful ruling in the kingdom of God with Jesus also appears in 2 Timothy 2:12: "If we endure, we will also reign with him."[7] The Book of Revelation speaks of the transformed role of the redeemed in terms of kings and priests who will one day rule on the earth. Note how the promised hope of reigning in Christ's kingdom is contained within this hymn, a hymn that Revelation's readers were to no doubt participate in:

> And they sang a new song, saying, "Worthy are you to take the scroll and to open its seals, for you were slain, and by your blood you ransomed people for God from every tribe and language and people and nation, and you have made them a kingdom and priests to our God, and they shall reign on the earth." (Rev 5:9–10)

This celebratory hymn was anticipated from the introductory greetings of the Book of Revelation, where Christ is illustrated as having already "made us a kingdom, priests to his God and Father" (Rev 1:6). The promise contained within Revelation's visionary oracles concerning the faithful bondservants of God is that their earthly rule will last indefinitely: "they will reign forever and ever" (Rev 22:5). When God's victory over evil is complete, he will once again have faithful human beings ruling over his good creation.

To the surprise of no one, the authors of the New Testament provide several clear indicators that entrance into the kingdom of God remained in the future, specifically at the return of Jesus to consummate his reign.[8] Consider carefully the language portraying the moment when the righteous will enter the kingdom as still to come:

> "For I say to you that unless your righteousness surpasses that of the scribes and Pharisees, you will not enter the kingdom of heaven." (Matt 5:20)

> "Not everyone who says to me, 'Lord, Lord,' will enter the kingdom of heaven, but he who does the will of my Father who is in heaven will enter. Many will say to me on that day, 'Lord, Lord, did we not prophesy in your name, and in your name cast out demons, and in your name perform many miracles?'" (Matt 7:21–22)

> "Truly I say to you, whoever does not receive the kingdom of God like a child will not enter it at all." (Mark 10:15)

---

[7] Towner, *The Letters to Timothy and Titus*, 511, states, "The literal promise of 'ruling with the king' broadens out in the NT to the well-known theme of sharing in Christ's eschatological role of king and judge."
[8] Aune, "Eschatology (Early Christian)," 601; Dunn, *New Testament Theology*, 93.

Joseph of Arimathea came, a prominent member of the Council, who himself was waiting for the kingdom of God (Mark 15:43)

"Jesus, remember me when you come in your kingdom!" (Luke 23:42)

"Through many tribulations we must enter the kingdom of God." (Acts 14:22)

Listen, my beloved brethren: Did not God choose the poor of this world to be rich in faith and heirs of the kingdom which He promised to those who love Him? (James 2:5)

Therefore, brethren, be all the more diligent to make certain about His calling and choosing you; for as long as you practice these things, you will never stumble; for in this way the entrance into the eternal kingdom of our Lord and Savior Jesus Christ will be abundantly supplied to you. (2 Pet 1:10–11)

Although the early Christians were convinced that God's rule and reign had broken into the present, it is clear that the inheritance, possession of the land, and the promised positions of never-ending rulership in the age to come were still in the future. As such, believers longed for Jesus' return, as evidenced in part by the Aramaic phrase "Maranatha" preserved in 1 Corinthians 16:22, which means, "Our lord, come!"

King Jesus and the Promised Throne of David

One of the key events that the Early Church anticipated would take place at Christ's return was that he would finally occupy the throne of David. This chair from which Jesus would rule the kingdom on earth was covenanted by God to David, assuring him that his throne would be established forever. Since the throne of David was geographically located in Jerusalem, the expectation would be that the promised messianic descendant of David would reign as king from Jerusalem. The authors of the New Testament confirm this key detail, often reiterating that Christ will indeed receive the throne that Yahweh promised to David's dynasty of kings. Matthew and Luke, in particular, affirm that Jesus is the promised Davidic Messiah in their genealogies and birth narratives. The Gospel of Matthew begins its biography by plainly informing its readers that Jesus is the son of David (Matt 1:1), making him the rightful heir of the covenanted throne and kingdom that would endure forever. Luke's Gospel records the visitation of the angel Gabriel to Mary and the announcement to her that she will miraculously bear a son who is the long-expected Davidic Messiah:

"And behold, you will conceive in your womb and bear a son, and you shall call his name Jesus. He will be great and will be called the Son of the Most High. And the Lord God will give to him the throne of his father David, and he will reign over the house of Jacob forever, and of his kingdom there will be no end." (Luke 1:31–33)

Several key connections with the Davidic covenant appear in Gabriel's declaration. First, Christ will be called *the Son of the Most High*, which echoes Yahweh's promise to designate the descendant of David with the title "Son of God" (2 Sam 7:14). Second, God will grant to Jesus the promised Davidic throne, the royal chair of the king that would endure forever (2 Sam 7:16). Third, the announcement affirms that Jesus is a legitimate offspring of David ("his father David"), made possible by Mary's betrothal to Joseph, which fulfils the oath that the promised descendants coming forth from David's own loins (2 Sam 7:12).[9] Fourth, as the Davidic king, Christ would possess an unceasing reign over the household of Jacob; indeed, this kingdom would never end. This is precisely the language of the everlasting kingdom that Yahweh assured would be granted to David's royal heir (2 Sam 7:16). From the perspective of the Early Church, the second coming of Jesus would bring fulfillment to the promise that this messianic king would rule from David's throne in Jerusalem and serve as the Most High's human king forever.[10]

Within the ministry of Jesus, we have statements plainly indicating his intention to return and sit upon his throne, that is, the throne of David that rightfully belonged to David's messianic heir. In Matthew 19:28, Christ announced his intent to sit upon the throne of David, while also sharing his rule as king with his disciples: "Truly I say to you, that you who have followed me, in the regeneration when the Son of Man will sit on his glorious throne, you also shall sit upon twelve thrones, judging the twelve tribes of Israel." Speaking of himself as the son of man, Jesus declared that in the coming regeneration of creation—an event that begins at his return—he will take his seat upon his throne. For the early Christians, this event was still to come, as it was self-evident that Christ was not presently ruling from Jerusalem. We can gather from a similar statement where Jesus speaks of his return to occupy the throne of David that this event will coincide with the Day of Judgment.[11] Consider carefully the description that Christ provided of this monumental future event:

> But when the Son of Man comes in his glory, and all the angels with him, then he will sit on his glorious throne. All the nations will be gathered before him; and he will separate them from one another, as the shepherd separates the sheep from the goats; and he will put the sheep on his right, and the goats on the left. Then the king will say to those at his right hand, 'Come, you that are blessed by my Father, inherit the kingdom prepared for you from the foundation of the world (Matt 25:31–34)

Jesus' description of his return as the shepherd-king and judge is pretty straightforward. When he, the son of man, visibly arrives in glory, accompanied by heavenly angels, then this will be the moment when he takes his seat upon his glorious throne. Since this throne is illustrated with the same description that Christ offered earlier in Matthew 19:28, we

---

[9] Bovon, *Luke 1*, 53; Johnson, *Luke*, 37.
[10] Ladd, *The Presence of the Future*, 135.
[11] Beasley-Murray, *Jesus and the Kingdom of God*, 275.

can confidently deduce that the two passages portray one and the same event. Jesus also shifts his own self-description in this passage, referring to himself as the "king" after he takes his seat upon the throne of David (Matt 25:34). Once seated, King Jesus will judge the world, separate the righteous from the wicked, and grant entrance into the kingdom of God for those who behaved appropriately. In other words, Jesus taught that he would have a glorious return to *sit on his throne* and *rule over his kingdom*, both of which belong to him as the heir of the Davidic promises. What Jesus describes here has, obviously, not yet come to pass.

When Jesus triumphantly entered Jerusalem upon a donkey, the crowds acknowledged their belief and conviction that the Messiah, the son of David, would usher in the kingdom of God. Since Jerusalem was the capital city, the arrival of the long-expected Davidic king signaled to many Jewish people that Jesus might take this opportunity to reclaim his rightful throne and begin his rule. Mark tells us that when Jesus entered the city, the crowds went before him and followed behind him, shouting over and over, "Blessed is the coming kingdom of our father David; Hosanna in the highest!" (Mark 11:10). Matthew portrays the cheers highlighting Jesus as the son of David (Matt 21:9), giving an interpretation to how he understood Mark's reference to the kingdom that was still to come. Instead of bringing complete fulfillment to the Davidic covenantal promises, Christ took the role of the Suffering Servant and suffered on the cross. After his resurrection, however, he spent the next six weeks preparing his followers for their missionary work with instruction on the kingdom of God (Acts 1:3). In light of the expectation that the Messiah would arrive in Jerusalem, retake the Davidic throne and establish the kingdom of God, his disciples naturally asked the obvious question: "Lord, is it at this time you are restoring the kingdom to Israel?" (Acts 1:6). Jesus responds to this good and reasonable question by stating that the time of the promised kingdom was fixed by God and was not for everyone else to know: "It is not for you to know times or epochs which the Father has fixed by His own authority" (Acts 1:7). Jesus had previously admitted that even he did not know the day or hour of his second coming (Matt 24:36; Mark 13:32). After answering the disciples' question about the timing of the establishment of the kingdom of God, Christ ascended into heaven, and two angelic messengers reaffirmed the hope of the second coming: "This Jesus, who has been taken up from you into heaven, will come in just the same way as you have watched him go into heaven." (Acts 1:11).[12] With these comforting words, the Early Church set out to preach the gospel of the kingdom to all nations while continually looking forward to Jesus' return to sit on his throne and reign in his kingdom.

After Jesus' ascension into heaven, we find several statements from early Christians expressing their hope in his return to consummate the kingdom of God and bring to fulfillment the renewal of creation. Within the Book of Acts, we find Peter

---

[12] Weiss, *Jesus' Proclamation of the Kingdom*, 83.

summoning his audience to repentance because God will send Christ from heaven to usher in the restorative reign of God: "He may send Jesus, the Christ appointed for you, whom heaven must receive until the period of restoration of all things about which God spoke by the mouth of His holy prophets from ancient time" (Acts 3:21).[13] The writers of the New Testament regularly used the second coming of Christ to strengthen the hope of believers and to motivate faithful behavior. Consider this sampling:

> awaiting eagerly the revelation of our Lord Jesus Christ, who will also confirm you to the end, blameless in the day of our Lord Jesus Christ. (1 Cor 1:7–8)

> For we must all appear before the judgment seat of Christ, so that each one may be recompensed for his deeds in the body, according to what he has done, whether good or bad. (2 Cor 5:10)

> He who began a good work in you will perfect it until the day of Christ Jesus. (Phil 1:6)

> When Christ, who is our life, is revealed, then you also will be revealed with him in glory. (Col 3:4)

> For you yourselves know full well that the day of the Lord will come just like a thief in the night. (1 Thes 5:2)

> I charge you in the presence of God, who gives life to all things, and of Christ Jesus, who testified the good confession before Pontius Pilate, that you keep the commandment without stain or reproach until the appearing of our Lord Jesus Christ (1 Tim 6:13–14)

> I solemnly charge you in the presence of God and of Christ Jesus, who is to judge the living and the dead, and by his appearing and his kingdom (2 Tim 4:1)

> so Christ also, having been offered once to bear the sins of many, will appear a second time for salvation without reference to sin, to those who eagerly await him. (Heb 9:28)

> Therefore be patient, brethren, until the coming of the Lord. (James 5:7)

> when the Chief Shepherd appears, you will receive the unfading crown of glory. (1 Pet 5:4)

> We know that when he appears, we will be like him, because we will see him just as he is. And everyone who has this hope fixed on him purifies himself, just as he is pure. (1 John 3:2–3)

> "Behold, I am coming quickly, and my reward is with me, to render to every man according to what he has done." (Rev 22:12)

---

[13] Walton, *Acts 1–9:42*, 274–76; Fitzmyer, *Acts*, 288–89; Keener, *Acts*, 2:1109–12.

From this unified testimony, we can clearly observe that the Early Church *continually looked forward to the second coming*.[14] There was no hint or suggestion that Jesus had physically returned at any point already, either visibly or invisibly.[15] It was rather self-evident that the resurrection of the dead had yet to take place, the Day of Judgment surely had not commenced, and Christ was not sitting on the throne of David in Jerusalem. Without a doubt, the return of Jesus to consummate the kingdom of God still lay in the future.

How the Early Church Described the Kingdom of God

How did the Early Church conceive of what the kingdom of God in all its glory would look like? In our previous chapter, we saw several visions and prophetic oracles detailing the creation-wide renewal that the kingdom will bring. The writers of the New Testament similarly illustrate the conditions of the rule and reign that Christ will usher in at his second coming. Surely, these details were frequently shared in evangelistic proclamations of the gospel of the kingdom, especially among Gentiles who did not possess a foundation of teaching from the Hebrew Bible that most Jews would naturally have, given their weekly exposure in the synagogue. One of the most vital assurances that the kingdom of God offers is that death will no longer take place within it. We have already seen predictions in Isaiah 25:8 that speak of the time when Yahweh "will swallow up death for all time," and this promise received confirmation in Paul's lengthy treatment on the resurrection in 1 Corinthians chapter fifteen. Two sections of his argument are essential for our consideration:

> For as in Adam all die, so also in Christ all will be made alive. But each in his own order: Christ the first fruits, after that those who are Christ's at his coming, then comes the end, when he hands over the kingdom to the God and Father, when he has abolished all rule and all authority and power. For he must reign until He has put all his enemies under his feet. The last enemy that will be abolished is death. (1 Cor 15:22–26)

> Behold, I tell you a mystery; we will not all sleep, but we will all be changed, in a moment, in the twinkling of an eye, at the last trumpet; for the trumpet will sound, and the dead will be raised imperishable, and we will be changed. For this perishable must put on the imperishable, and this mortal must put on immortality. But when this perishable will have put on the imperishable, and this mortal will have put on immortality, then will come about the saying that is written, "Death is swallowed up in victory. O death, where is your victory? O death, where is your sting?" (1 Cor 15:51–55)

---

[14] Green, *Salvation*, 136.
[15] Ladd, *Theology*, 105, observes that the early Christians did not regard the return of Jesus and the kingdom of God's consummation to have definitively taken place yet: "For Christians of the first three centuries, the Kingdom was altogether eschatological."

In these two parts of Paul's larger argument of the resurrection, he describes the same event twice. In 1 Corinthians 15:22–26, Paul speaks of Jesus' second coming as the climactic time when the dead will be made alive by being raised from their graves. Then, Paul illustrates what takes place next, which he calls "the end" (1 Cor 15:24). This end occurs when Christ has abolished all opposing authorities, *including death itself*, particularly by God putting them under Christ's feet.[16] In the second passage (1 Cor 15:51–55), Paul clarifies for his readers the precise timing of the defeat of death. By quoting Isaiah 25:8 and Hosea 13:14, Paul locates *the final defeat of death at the last trumpet*—the moment when the dead will be raised imperishable and immortal. Having already indicated that the dead will be raised at Christ's second coming, we can observe Paul's insistence that the return of Jesus will usher in a time when death will be permanently defeated, in fulfillment of the Old Testament prophets.[17] The same assurance that there will be no death in God's new creation appears in the description of the new heavens and the new earth in the Book of Revelation. John of Patmos records the loud voice from the throne of God: "He will wipe away every tear from their eyes; and there will no longer be any death; there will no longer be any mourning, or crying, or pain; the first things have passed away" (Rev 21:4).[18] God's victory over death, which will come to full realization at the second coming of Christ, means that there will be no occasion for mourning or crying over someone potentially dying.

Another feature of the kingdom of God that its righteous recipients will enjoy is the renewal of creation. Granting human beings immortality, who were already undergoing transformation as God's new creation (e.g., 2 Cor 5:17; Gal 6:15), is evidence of God's commitment to renew those who were made to rule over his world. Paul speaks of the human longing for the full measure of its redemption, "the redemption of our body" (Rom 8:23). The hope of attaining to an incorruptible body as the final step of God's renewal of his image-bearing humans is placed in the midst of the declaration that all creation will one day be freed and redeemed: "the creation itself also will be set free from its slavery to corruption into the freedom of the glory of the children of God. (Rom 8:20). We can find confirmation of this in Jesus' response to the man crucified alongside him who expressed a desire that Christ might remember him when he comes in his kingdom (Luke 23:42), a request to which Christ responds by assuring him that *he would be in Paradise* (Luke 23:43). For Jesus, the consummated kingdom will look like a restoration of Paradise, the primordial garden illustrated in the opening chapters of Genesis. Second Peter contributes to this description by offering a response to mocking that arose concerning the apparent delay of Jesus' coming (Greek: *parousia*), assuring its

---

[16] Fitzmyer, *First Corinthians*, 572. Hays, *First Corinthians*, 265, observes "The final defeat of Death at the general resurrection will constitute the collapse of all resistance to Christ's power and bring us to the end [*to telos*]."
[17] Blaising et al., *Three Views of the Millennium*, 110–11. Wright, *The Resurrection of the Son of God*, 358, argues that Paul "can pick up a couple of lines from Isaiah and Hosea and turn them into a taunt song against Death. The whole chapter has been, not about coming to terms with Death, but with its defeat."
[18] Roloff, *Revelation*, 236; Storms, *Our God Reigns*, 492–93; Beale, *Revelation*, 1049–50.

readers that the Day of the Lord will indeed come like a thief in the night (2 Pet 3:4, 10). Christ's coming will be accompanied with a fiery judgment that will usher in the new heavens and the new earth: "But according to his promise we are waiting for new heavens and a new earth in which righteousness dwells" (2 Pet 3:13).[19] In other words, the second coming of Jesus will bring with it an entire new creation, inhabited by righteous behavior. Second Peter's description of the new heavens and the new earth echoes the promises in the Book of Revelation, where we find some additional information about this renewed creation. In Revelation 21:1, John witnesses the new heaven and the new earth, and he mentions that "there is no longer any sea." The image-rich symbolism employed by John of Patmos in the Book of Revelation suggests that the absence of sea in the new creation does not refer to the lack of large bodies of water, but rather to the promise that there will be *no more chaotic evil* in the kingdom of God.[20] As such, God's promise, presented a few verses later, "I am making all things new" (Rev 21:5), is a renewal of creation where there is no place for wickedness, sin, or death.

One of the most comforting assurances that Christ and the authors of the New Testament offer about life in the consummated kingdom is that the faithful will be reunited with the people of God who died. The Early Church was firmly convinced that it would see those believers who had died, including the faithful of the Old Testament, at the resurrection, and that their fellowship would last forever in light of the immortality they would receive. Jesus taught that when the kingdom of God is finally established, "many will come from east and west and recline at the table with Abraham, Isaac, and Jacob" (Matt 8:11). This promise presupposes that these three famous patriarchs will be raised from the dead, allowing them to enjoy a banquet with believing Gentiles. Christ made similar promises to his closest followers in Luke 22:30, where he granted that they would "eat and drink at my table in my kingdom." When Paul learned that some of the believers in Thessalonica had unfortunately died, he provided the congregation hope that at Christ's second coming, the dead in Christ would rise first, followed by those who are alive being gathered together by Jesus (1 Thes 4:16–17). As an encouraging conclusion, Paul assured his readers that by this process, "we will always be with the Lord" (1 Thes 4:17), and that these words of hope should be used to comfort those grieving. The author of the Epistle to the Hebrews observes that the dozens of heroes of faith "did not receive what was promised because God had provided something better for us, so that apart from us they would not be made perfect" (Heb 11:39–40). The process of being *made perfect* refers to the resurrection of the body, an event that will happen to all when Jesus returns, allowing the heroes of faith to be united with the faithful readers of Hebrews in the kingdom of God.[21] Finally, true fellowship with God the Father will be

---

[19] Watson, "The Second Letter of Peter," 357.
[20] Bauckham, *Theology*, 53; Beale, *Revelation*, 1041–42; Blount, *Revelation*, 377.
[21] Koester, *Hebrews*, 516, states that "What is 'superior' includes resurrection and the blessings of the new covenant, culminating in eternal life."

made possible when the faithful attain their inheritance on the last day. The Book of Revelation sets forth this promise in order to motivate conquering like Christ: "Those who conquer will inherit these things, and I will be their God and they will be my children" (Rev 21:7). The return of Christ to usher in the kingdom of God upon the earth will provide opportunities to meet, be reunited with, and fully experience God and his faithful people.

Conclusion

In summary, we observed considerable evidence indicating that the Early Church maintained a deep, steadfast hope in the full, future arrival of the kingdom of God, which would accompany Jesus Christ's physical return to earth. First, we observed the content of the reward promised to the early Christians: inheriting the land and reigning over it as rulers. The portrayal of the faithful people of God as heirs of the land contributes to the fulfillment of the Abrahamic covenant, particularly Yahweh's promise to bless the world through Abraham's faithful children, who would in turn take charge of God's world, thereby regaining the position formerly given to Adam. Second, we gave attention to the covenantal promises that God made to King David, which the Early Church anticipated would come to fulfillment at Christ's return. Jesus taught his disciples that he would return, take hold of the throne that rightfully belonged to him, and from it, rule as king of the kingdom of God. Lastly, we examined several truths surrounding the kingdom that Christ was returning to usher in, truths that surely bolstered the hope of early Christians and informed the content of their evangelism. At the second coming of Christ, the enemy of death will be completely defeated, the entire creation will undergo a transformation of regeneration, and there will be a joyful reunion and fellowship with the resurrected saints. These promises of the kingdom of God were plainly and self-evidently still in the future, and there was no hint or suggestion that they had already come to pass.

Although the Early Church continued to anticipate the return of Christ to rule as king over God's world, they nevertheless embraced and celebrated the experience of the reign of God that had already broken into the present. In other words, the realization that the kingdom of God had not yet been fully consummated in no way meant that God's reign was not already being experienced in light of the ministry of Jesus.[22] Two things can be true at the same time, and this includes the Early Church's theology that the kingdom of God was already and not yet. In our next chapter, we will focus on the conviction that the age to come has spilled over into the present age and that those who are in Christ are already enjoying and experiencing the powers of the coming age.

---

[22] Perkins, "The Gospel of Mark," 538.

47
THE PRESENT EXPERIENCE OF THE KINGDOM OF GOD

It should be no surprise at this point in our study that Christ inaugurated the reign and rule of God in his ministry. He spoke about the kingdom in present terms, and he performed restorative miracles that legitimized his proclamation of the kingdom. The Early Church regarded Jesus' resurrection, the event which brought his ministry to a conclusion, as the first fruits of the general resurrection that is to take place on the last day. The gospel of the kingdom of God was the means by which salvation, justification, redemption, and new creation were brought into the present, even when the early Christians maintained that the fullest sense of these key themes was going to be resolved in the future. Christ even spoke of eternal life, the life of the age to come, as a present possession of his faithful followers. The Early Church continued to wait for Jesus' return to consummate God's kingdom on this earth, but it also celebrated the rule and reign of God in the present. Two things can be true at the same time.

This chapter will contribute to the eschatological beliefs of the Early Church by focusing on the present experience of the kingdom of God, which the ministry of Jesus inaugurated. We will begin by looking at how Christ's teachings, miracles, and deeds convinced his followers that the kingdom of God had indeed broken into the present. Second, we will look at the theology of the New Testament authors, including Paul, to observe the impact of the kingdom's inauguration on the earliest Christian communities. Finally, we will look at the imagery in the Book of Revelation to see how it symbolizes the faithful as actively experiencing God's rule as a counter-kingdom to Roman dominance. Our previous chapter's study on the future promises of the kingdom of God is incomplete without fully appreciating how Jesus and his followers expressed the reality that God's rule has broken into the present. The presence of the kingdom of God is often illustrated as *inaugurated eschatology*.[1]

How Jesus Inaugurated the Kingdom of God

We will recall from Chapter 33 that the content of Jesus' evangelistic preaching was not simply the kingdom of God. He preached that the kingdom of God *had drawn near*

---

[1] Dodd, *The Parables of the Kingdom*, 33, preferred the phrase "realized eschatology."

(Matt 4:17; Mark 1:15).[2] In what sense did Jesus' ministry bring the kingdom near? The answer is fairly easy to see, as nearly half of Jesus' teachings, parables, and expositions of the kingdom of God illustrate it as already present.[3] The other half of the evidence positions the full consummation of the kingdom squarely in the future. Regarding the presence of the kingdom, Jesus speaks rather plainly. In the Sermon on the Mount, the very first promise that Christ makes concerns the inaugurated reign of God that already belongs to those who are poor in spirit: "for theirs is the kingdom of heaven" (Matt 5:3). Not only do the Beatitudes begin by speaking of the kingdom in the present tense, but they also end with the very same assurance: "Blessed are those who are persecuted for righteousness' sake, for theirs is the kingdom of heaven" (Matt 5:10). The inheritance of the earth is still the future reward (Matt 5:5), but the reign of God is already experienced by those who are humble and who suffer persecution. Christ again speaks of the presence of the kingdom of God when he contrasts the greatness of John the Baptist with those who are already within its in-breaking rule: "Truly, I say to you, among those born of women there has arisen no one greater than John the Baptist. Yet the one who is least in the kingdom of heaven is greater than he" (Matt 11:11). Jesus follows up this saying by remarking how the inaugurated kingdom is suffering violent attacks in the present, particularly as this reign of God encounters those who are violently opposed to what the bringer of the kingdom has been up to: "From the days of John the Baptist until now the kingdom of heaven suffers violence, and violent men take it by force" (Matt 11:12). Surely the arrest and imprisonment of John the Baptist, the first to summon people to repentance in light of the dawning reign of God, was part of the violence that the in-breaking kingdom had already suffered.[4]

The presence of the kingdom of God is also evident in Jesus' restorative miracles. The writers of the Gospel accounts often portrayed Christ preaching the gospel of the kingdom in lockstep with his healings, indicating that he was not only announcing the reign of God, but he was also proving it by tangibly demonstrating God's restorative rule through the working of miracles (Matt 4:23; 9:35; Luke 8:1–2). We also find Jesus commissioning his disciples to share in the preaching of the reign of God and the enactment of restorative miracles (Matt 10:7–8; Mark 3:14–15; Luke 9:2), which contributed to the inauguration of God's kingdom. Some of the most remarkable miraculous works performed by Jesus and his followers were the casting out of demons, a healing that we can surely classify as an instance of restoration taking place in the present. Christ declared in no uncertain terms that the kingdom of God was present upon the one whom he exorcised demons: "But if I cast out demons by the Spirit of God, then the kingdom of God has come upon you" (Matt 12:28).[5] Luke's version of the same

---

[2] Chilton, *Pure Kingdom*, 60.
[3] Aune, "Eschatology (Early Christian)," 600-1; Dodd, *The Parables of the Kingdom*, 30.
[4] Beasley-Murray, *Jesus and the Kingdom of God*, 91–96.
[5] Ladd, *Crucial Questions About the Kingdom*, 89.

saying, while interpreting the Spirit of God as the finger of God, still emphasizes the presence of God's kingdom when the demons have been cast out: "the kingdom of God has come upon you" (Luke 11:20). Those who were freed from the unclean influences that dominated their bodies would certainly recognize the dawning rule of God over their lives.[6] As Mark describes this new reality, the strong man has been bound (Mark 3:27).[7]

We can also find Jesus describing the new salvific experience of those who have repented and believed in his gospel of the kingdom in terms of the presence of God's rule and reign. One such example is located in Matthew 21:31, where Christ tells those in the temple that "the tax collectors and prostitutes are going into the kingdom of God ahead of you." Jesus' use of the present tense undoubtedly indicated that the repentant are already taking advantage of the reign of God that Jesus' preaching of the kingdom has made available in the present.[8] We can observe a similar contrast between the hypocrites and those who accept Jesus' preaching of the gospel: "But woe to you, scribes and Pharisees, hypocrites! For you lock people out of the kingdom of heaven. For you do not go in yourselves, and when others are going in, you stop them" (Matt 23:13). Jesus' rebuke presupposes that the kingdom can be experienced now. In fact, when pressed about the timing of the kingdom, Jesus drew attention away from observable signs in the future in favor of the rule of God that he himself was already accomplishing right in front of them.[9] Note how Christ stresses the kingdom's presence:

> Now having been questioned by the Pharisees as to when the kingdom of God was coming, he answered them and said, "The kingdom of God is not coming with signs to be observed; nor will they say, 'Look, here it is!' or, 'There it is!' For behold, the kingdom of God is in your midst." (Luke 17:20–21)

Jesus' ministry and preaching of the gospel have plainly brought the kingdom of God near, so those who were looking for God's rule and reign should look no further than the bringer of the kingdom, Jesus the king.[10] Even the disciples understood that the kingdom had been inaugurated, which contributed to the wording of their question, "Who then is the greatest in the kingdom of heaven?" (Matt 18:1), a question that Jesus answers with an affirmation that the reign of God has arrived: "Whoever then humbles himself as this child, he is the greatest in the kingdom of heaven" (Matt 18:4).

It didn't take long in Jesus' ministry for his audience to overlook, ignore, or otherwise misunderstand his intent to inaugurate the kingdom and preview its restoration for those willing to accept it. Thus, he turned to preaching in parables, allowing those who really wanted to understand and had ears to hear to glimpse the core of Jesus'

---

[6] Ladd, *The Presence of the Future*, 139–40; Beasley-Murray, *Jesus and the Kingdom of God*, 75–80.
[7] Beasley-Murray, *Jesus and the Kingdom of God*, 108–9.
[8] Gundry, *Matthew*, 422; Hagner, *Matthew 14–28*, 614; France, *Matthew*, 804–5.
[9] Finnegan, *Kingdom Journey*, 142.
[10] Beasley-Murray, *Jesus and the Kingdom of God*, 97–103.

teachings, while at the same time obscuring his message to those who were indifferent to his summons to discipleship. As such, we possess several recorded parables that speak about the kingdom of God, and many of these comparative stories describe the kingdom of God in a present sense. For example, Jesus compared the kingdom of God in Mark 4:26–29 to one who scatters seed, which produces growth almost immediately, unrecognized by the one who sows. When the crop is ready, it is gathered at the harvest, an image often used to describe the coming day of judgment. However, most of the parable stresses the present growth of the crop, which relates to the kingdom that has already been inaugurated, even though there still exists a future time of harvest.[11] Similarly, Christ told a parable that emphasized how the kingdom is presently hidden and already producing results significant enough to provide enough food for a banquet: "The kingdom of heaven is like leaven, which a woman took and hid in three pecks of flour until it was all leavened" (Matt 13:33).[12] When Jesus provided the Parable of the Tares in the Field and followed it up with an interpretation for his disciples, he illustrates the time of judgment that will occur at the end of the age, and in doing so, Jesus depicts the kingdom as something that is *already present*: "The Son of Man will send forth his angels, and they will gather out of his kingdom all stumbling blocks, and those who commit lawlessness" (Matt 13:41). Other parables plainly illustrate the kingdom in present terms, including the kingdom being compared to one who forgives in light of the forgiveness he has already received (Matt 18:23–35). In Mark 4:30–32, the kingdom is presented as a mustard seed that is already growing into something that will become, surprisingly, a massive tree with large branches. The parables concerning the treasure hidden in a field and the merchant seeing fine pearls both revolve around someone stumbling across something of great value that leads to a radical change of priorities in the present, which closely resembles the act of repentance in light of understanding the preaching of the gospel of the kingdom (Matt 13:44–46).[13] Let us also not forget the resurrection imagery employed twice within the Parable of the Prodigal Son to describe his repentance and incorporation into the family of God: "this son of mine was dead and has come to life again" (Luke 15:24, 32).[14]

The Early Church's Belief in the Inauguration of the Kingdom of God

Cemented by the resurrection of Jesus, his exaltation to sit enthroned at Yahweh's right hand, and the outpouring of the Holy Spirit, the Early Church continued to portray God's reign and rule in present terms. Although there was still a clearly defined hope of the kingdom's final consummation at the return of Jesus, we can find several indicators that

---

[11] Beasley-Murray, *Jesus and the Kingdom of God*, 125–27.
[12] Boring, "The Gospel of Matthew," 309.
[13] Beasley-Murray, *Jesus and the Kingdom of God*, 111–12.
[14] Wright, *The Resurrection of the Son of God*, 437.

early Christians acknowledged the tangible presence of the reign of God, often closely aligned with the experience of the Holy Spirit's empowerment. Here are some examples of the New Testament writers illustrating the kingdom of God as having already broken into the present:

> For the kingdom of God is not food and drink but righteousness and peace and joy in the Holy Spirit. (Rom 14:17)
>
> For the kingdom of God does not consist in words but in power. (1 Cor 4:20)
>
> For He rescued us from the domain of darkness, and transferred us to the kingdom of His beloved Son, in whom we have redemption, the forgiveness of sins. (Col 1:13–14)
>
> Therefore, since we are receiving a kingdom that cannot be shaken, let us give thanks, by which we offer to God an acceptable worship with reverence and awe (Heb 12:28)

The Early Church was convinced that the age to come had broken into the present, and the overlap of the ages meant that the kingdom of God was felt by those who placed their faith in the gospel of the kingdom and joined the renewed family of God.[15] Even conversion was illustrated in terms of having already partaken of the powers of the coming age: "[those who] have tasted the good word of God and the powers of the age to come" (Heb 6:5). Kingdom citizens living in the present age were to undergo a renewal in thinking, or as Paul words it in Romans 12:2, "be transformed by the renewal of your mind."[16]

Although the Early Church believed that Jesus was one day going to return to reign from the covenanted throne of David, it was acknowledged that he is presently enthroned at God's right hand in accordance with Psalm 110:1 ("Yahweh says to my lord: 'Sit at My right hand until I make your enemies a footstool for your feet'"). The language of this psalm points to Christ's exaltation to heaven in order that he may be enthroned at the right hand of God himself, that is, until all enemies have been placed under the feet of Christ. Paul comments on this present reality, and in doing so, he understands Jesus' enthronement at God's right hand in terms of Christ already ruling: "For he must reign until he has put all his enemies under his feet" (1 Cor 15:25).[17] In other words, Christ is already serving in a role as ruler, during which the kingdom of God is experienced by those who are in Christ. In Romans chapter five, Paul contrasts the reign of death that was ushered in by the transgression of Adam with the reign accomplished through the second Adam, Jesus Christ: "For if, because of one man's trespass, death reigned through that one man, much more will those who receive the abundance of grace and the free gift of righteousness reign in life through the one man Jesus Christ" (Rom 5:17). These two

---

[15] Kreitzer, "Kingdom of God/Christ," 524, 526.
[16] Jewett, *Romans*, 733; Longenecker, *Romans*, 924; Dunn, *Romans 8–16*, 713, 717–18.
[17] Wright, *Paul and the Faithfulness of God*, 1106; Dunn, *Theology of Paul*, 244; Beale, *A New Testament Biblical Theology*, 286.

reigns are mentioned again in Romans 5:21, where Paul illustrates righteousness as that which allows grace to reign unto the life of the age to come, eternal life: "as sin reigned in death, grace also might reign through righteousness leading to eternal life through Jesus Christ our Lord." In effect, the obedient act of the man Jesus allowed new covenant status to be made available to all, and all who have been justified *are actively sharing in this present reign and rule* in anticipation of the coming resurrection life, eternal life.[18]

The enthronement in heaven and the present reign of Christ is a victory and experience shared by those in Christ. No passage so clearly illustrates the present sharing of the Early Church with Jesus' inaugurated reign than Ephesians 2:4–6. Note carefully how that which is true of Christ right now is also true of his faithful followers who are united with him:

> But God, being rich in mercy, because of His great love with which He loved us, even when we were dead in our transgressions, made us alive together with Christ (by grace you have been saved), and raised us up with him, and seated us with him in the heavenly places in Christ Jesus (Eph 2:4–6)

This theologically dense reflection of the inauguration of the kingdom of God portrays believers as sharing in Christ's victory in several key ways. First, the act of conversion is illustrated in terms of being made from one's former death due to transgressions. This new life is then taken and associated with God giving life to Jesus, and as such, believers are made alive together with Jesus (Eph 2:5).[19] Second, God's gift of new life is followed up with being raised up from the dead, and since this is what God did to Christ, those who are in union with Christ are also portrayed as being raised up with Christ. Third (and arguably most importantly), God exalted Jesus up to heaven, where Christ took his seat upon a throne at God's right hand. Those united with Christ are likewise depicted as being seated with Christ in the heavenly places. Make no mistake about it, this is some of the most vibrant inaugurated eschatology in the New Testament, where *Christians are illustrated as presently sitting upon thrones and reigning with Christ.*[20] The practical result of already sharing in Christ's rule is that believers would live in accordance with that kingly rule by walking in good works (Eph 2:10).

The Inauguration of the Kingdom of God in the Book of Revelation

When we give our attention to the Book of Revelation and its image-filled symbolism of faithful, conquering Christians, we continue to exhibit the theology that God's reign and

---

[18] Gaventa, *Romans*, 161, 164; Fitzmyer, *Romans*, 422; Jewett, *Romans*, 389; Dunn, *Romans 1-8*, 300.
[19] Wright, *The Resurrection of the Son of God*, 237, helpfully states, "The present state of those in the Messiah is that they have already been 'raised with the Messiah' and seated with him in the heavenly places; what is true of the Messiah in [Ephesians] 1:20–23, in other words, is true of those who are 'in him.'"
[20] Beale, *A New Testament Biblical Theology*, 479, 840; Lincoln, *Ephesians*, 106–7; Best, *Ephesians*, 221–23.

rule have already broken into the present. In an attempt to urge his readers to identify with New Jerusalem while simultaneously distancing themselves from the city of Fallen Babylon, John of Patmos emphasizes his visionary portrayals of the obedient as a counter-kingdom community. Although the faithful can confidently anticipate reigning forever when Christ returns (Rev 22:5), Christ has already reconstituted believers into a kingdom of priests in the present: "he has made us a kingdom, priests to his God and Father" (Rev 1:6).[21] Similarly, those who follow the footsteps of the Lamb will indeed reign upon the earth in the future, but they are already identified as a new kingdom community: "you have made them a kingdom and priests to our God, and they shall reign on the earth" (Rev 5:10).[22] Two things can be true at the same time.

Within the letters to the seven churches contained within Revelation chapters 2–3, we find promised rewards for those who persevere and conquer like Christ, including crowns (Rev 2:10), white garments (Rev 3:4–5), and a throne from which to rule (Rev 3:21). In a fascinating vision, John of Patmos is given a glimpse of a heavenly reality consisting of twenty-four elders who worship the true God. The rhetorical function of this vision is for the readers to identify themselves already in the present with these twenty-four elders who are participating in genuine and pure worship of God the Father, and this portrayal is all the more striking because John observes these elders as already possessing their rewards: "seated on the thrones were twenty-four elders, clothed in white garments, with golden crowns on their heads" (Rev 4:4). The implication of this vision of faithful, conquering believers is clear: although they are destined to reign upon the earth in the consummated kingdom of God, they have already been designated as kings in the present, illustrated with the ruler's attire and seated upon thrones.[23] The Book of Revelation thus reveals the identity of God's people in a manner that should influence their behavior.

Several other passages indicate an awareness that the kingdom of God has not only broken into the present but that the new covenant people of God are already experiencing its presence. When John introduces himself to his readers, he seeks to establish rapport with them by describing himself as one who is sharing in their struggles, their steadfast commitment to endure, and in the kingdom: "I, John, your brother and fellow partaker in the tribulation and kingdom and perseverance which are in Jesus" (Rev 1:9). Later in Revelation, John envisions Satan's expulsion from heaven and his relocation to earth, from which he would persecute the people of God. The triggering events that resulted in the Devil's removal from heaven included the ascension of Christ

---

[21] Mulholland, "Revelation," 424; Reddish, *Revelation*, 35; Koester, *Revelation*, 228. Osborne, Revelation, 66, argues, "It should be understood in an inaugurated sense, referring to Christ's rule now as an anticipation of the future."

[22] Beale, *Revelation*, 363, concludes that "it is apparent that 5:10a speaks of saints already reigning in a present kingdom."

[23] Koester, Revelation, 362–63; Mulholland, "Revelation," 458.

to heaven so that he could share in God's rule (Rev 12:5) and a war in heaven (Rev 12:7). Satan's defeat is then celebrated in terms of the coming of the kingdom of God, which appears to refer to its present inauguration: "Now the salvation, and the power, and the kingdom of our God and the authority of His Christ have come, for the accuser of our brethren has been thrown down, he who accuses them before our God day and night" (Rev 12:10).[24] Believers are given the opportunity to conquer Satan in the following verse, particularly by identifying with the blood of the Lamb, testifying the evangelistic word of the kingdom, and refusing to choose this present life when faced with martyrdom (Rev 12:11). A similar image that combines the reign of God and the faithful behavior of Christ's disciples appears in Revelation 15:2–3. Observe how the symbolism portrays the obedient conquerors and their hymn of worship that praises the active rule and dominion of the one true God:

> And I saw something like a sea of glass mixed with fire, and those who had been victorious over the beast and his image and the number of his name, standing on the sea of glass, holding harps of God. And they sang the song of Moses, the bond-servant of God, and the song of the Lamb, saying, "Great and marvelous are Your works, O Lord God, the Almighty; righteous and true are Your ways, King of the nations!" (Rev 15:2–3)

John of Patmos sees this vision of conquering believers, which gives particular attention to their victory over the beast, his image, and his number. By refusing to compromise with illicit worship and accommodation with the fallen culture, these Christians have proven themselves to conquer, just as the Lamb conquered before them. Their stance resonated with victory echoes. Not only are they standing, but their victory continues (the verb is actually a present participle, "those who are being victorious"). The image of the sea and the song of Moses recall the Israelites' triumph over Pharaoh, the crossing of the Reed Sea, and the exodus from Egypt. Just as the children of Israel sang the song of Moses in the immediate aftermath of their deliverance (Exod 15:1), Revelation portrays these faithful conquerors giving worship to the Almighty, and in doing so, they recognize the reign and rule of God, the "King of the nations." Although the Book of Revelation hopes and looks forward to the time when the kingdoms of the world will become the kingdom of God (Rev 11:15), believers who live as God's kingdom people today can already acknowledge that the Almighty *presently rules* as the king of the nations.[25] The Book of Revelation, in continuity with the New Testament documents written before it, expresses the reign and rule of God as both already inaugurated, but not yet fully consummated. Two things can be true at the same time.

---

[24] Smalley, *Revelation*, 326–27; Beale, *Revelation*, 657–58; Mulholland, "Revelation," 515.
[25] Blount, *Revelation*, 288, helpfully sets this hymn in its immediate political context: "This confession is a direct political contradiction of the claims to global dominion made by Caesar and the empire he oversees."

Conclusion

To summarize, this chapter has demonstrated that the Early Church fully embraced its inaugurated eschatology, the in-breaking of the kingdom of God. While the early Christians continued to look forward to the kingdom's final consummation that was to take place at the second coming, there was no question that God's rule and reign had broken into the present with the ministry of Christ. We first observed that Jesus not only taught that the kingdom of God was *already* and *not yet*, but he also confirmed this two-pronged teaching with his restorative miracles, exorcisms, and even rose from the dead in a definitive sign that the promises of the age to come have been ushered into the present. Second, we saw how the writers of the New Testament followed in the teachings of Christ by illustrating the reign and rule of God as already present and being experienced by the people of God. Half of the passages in the New Testament that speak about the kingdom or the act of reigning and ruling are unambiguously portrayed in the present tense. We even saw evidence of faithful believers sharing in Christ's reign already in the present. Finally, we looked at the symbol-filled Book of Revelation, and we relatively easily discerned that John of Patmos unveiled to his readers the truth that, despite their present suffering, they have already been given an identity as a counter kingdom to Babylon. Although Revelation assures the faithful that they will reign upon the earth, they already participate in God's inaugurated rule when they obediently obey the Lamb, the one who sets the example of a righteous conqueror. To fully appreciate how the Early Church understood and taught the kingdom of God, one must take seriously the undeniable fact that the age to come has spilled over into the present age, ushering in God's rule and reign in a manner that helps equip and give hope to its final consummation on the last day. God's final victory over evil will one day come to fulfillment, but the obedient people of God experience the powers of the age to come already.

Having given adequate attention to the Early Church's doctrine of the future kingdom and its present inauguration, we can direct our attention to looking at the last day itself, the time when Christ will return. The day of Jesus' second coming, which early Christians also described as the "Day of the Lord," has generated a lot of attention among the authors of the New Testament. What will take place on that day? How will we know when it arrives? Will Christ come back secretly, or will his return be visible? Did the Early Church create timetables in order to predict and plot his return on their calendars? How will judgment be handled on that day, and for whom? We will address these key questions in our next chapter.

48
THE SECOND COMING OF CHRIST

If the resurrection of the crucified man, Jesus Christ, was the most crucial event for early Christianity recorded in history, then his second coming will undoubtedly be the most significant and impactful day yet. The Early Church indeed celebrated Christ's victory over the grave, but the final and definitive victory would commence at his return. On that day, the righteous people of God will be raised from the dead, immortalized, rewarded, and installed as image-bearing rulers in the kingdom of God. On the other hand, the wicked will face judgment and their own destruction. God's kingdom will reign forever, establishing peace throughout the entire creation. This hope was absolutely foundational to the Early Church, and it was a significant portion of the teachings of Jesus.

This chapter will focus on the second coming of Christ and the key events surrounding it. We will begin by examining how the Early Church awaited Christ's return from heaven, its visibility, timing, and what sort of events might anticipate his arrival. Second, we will explore how Jesus' second coming was to function as the Day of the Lord, the day on which the living and the dead will be judged. Finally, we will observe how the early Christians expected Christ's return to be the time when they would be rewarded for their faithfulness, in addition to being the opportunity for the wicked to be repaid for their evil deeds. All creation would be held accountable before the judge, which was good news for the people of God, but for those who disobeyed, the anticipation of dreadful judgment.

The Details Surrounding the Second Coming of Jesus

Beginning with Jesus' descent from heaven, the authors of the New Testament portray this coming event as observable, dramatic, and of cosmic scope. This early Christian truth of the distinctly visible nature of Christ's return stemmed from his own teachings. Speaking explicitly of his coming (Greek: *parousia*), Jesus likened it to the flash of lightning: "For just as the lightning comes from the east and flashes even to the west, so will the coming of the Son of Man be" (Matt 24:27).[1] Luke's version of the same saying emphasizes the particular day in which Christ would return: "For as the lightning flashes

---

[1] Nickelsburg, *Resurrection, Immortality, and Eternal Life*, 294; France, *Matthew*, 917; Nolland, *Matthew*, 980.

and lights up the sky from one side to the other, so will the Son of Man be in his day" (Luke 17:24).[2] Rather than being a return that is hidden or obscure, Jesus taught that he will be seen on that momentous day: "And then they will see the Son of Man coming in clouds with great power and glory" (Mark 13:26). After ascending into heaven, the angels plainly indicated to the disciples that Christ would return in the same way that he was taken up, that is, visibly in a cloud (Acts 1:11). Paul also conveyed to his churches that the second coming of Christ would be observable and not hidden. The *parousia* of Jesus Christ would be accompanied by a loud shout, a trumpet call, and the rather obvious event of the dead being raised from their graves (1 Thes 4:16). Paul also illustrates Jesus' return as the arrival of one "in flaming fire" (2 Thes 1:7–8). First John comforts its readers with the assurance that when Jesus returns, the faithful will lay their eyes upon him: "We know that when he appears, we will be like him, because we will see him just as he is" (1 John 3:2). One of the clearest indicators that the second coming will be observed and not obscured appears in Revelation 1:7, where Christ's return is portrayed as an event that every single eye will witness: "Behold, he is coming with the clouds, and every eye will see him, even those who pierced him." The Early Church was adamant that the return of Jesus would not be a secret event; rather, it would be visibly apparent to all.[3]

We have already drawn attention to the early Christian use of the Greek noun *parousia* to describe Christ's physical arrival in Chapter 23. The New Testament authors additionally employ two other terms to illustrate this visible and cosmic event. The first of these is the noun "appearing" (Greek: *epiphania*).[4] It seems rather self-evident that the moment of the *appearing* of Christ would be observable and not invisible. Consider how this noun is used to portray Jesus' second coming:

> And then the lawless one will be revealed, whom the Lord Jesus will destroy with the breath of his mouth, annihilating him by the appearing of his coming. (2 Thes 2:8)

> that you keep the commandment without stain or reproach until the appearing of our Lord Jesus Christ (1 Tim 6:14)

> I solemnly charge you in the presence of God and of Christ Jesus, who is to judge the living and the dead, and by his appearing and his kingdom (2 Tim 4:1)

> Henceforth there is laid up for me the crown of righteousness, which the Lord, the righteous judge, will award to me on that day, and not only to me but also to all who have loved his appearing. (2 Tim 4:8)

In addition to depicting Jesus' return on that day as a visible "appearing," we can also observe the use of the noun "revelation" (Greek: *apokalypsis*) to convey the act of his being revealed. Naturally, if Jesus is being revealed at his second coming, then he is being

---

[2] Weiss, *Jesus' Proclamation of the Kingdom*, 92; Beasley-Murray, *Jesus and the Kingdom of God*, 315–15.
[3] Reese, *The Approaching Advent of Christ*, 145; Ladd, *A Theology of the New Testament*, 203.
[4] Bauer et al., *Greek-English Lexicon*, 385–86.

made visible.⁵ Note how the authors of the New Testament characterize Christ's return in terms of a revelation from heaven:

> awaiting eagerly the revelation of our Lord Jesus Christ, who will also confirm you to the end, blameless in the day of our Lord Jesus Christ. (1 Cor 1:7–8)
>
> when the Lord Jesus is revealed from heaven with his mighty angels (2 Thes 1:7)
>
> the proof of your faith, being more precious than gold which is perishable, even though tested by fire, may be found to result in praise and glory and honor at the revelation of Jesus Christ (1 Pet 1:7)
>
> Therefore, preparing your minds for action, and being sober-minded, set your hope fully on the grace that will be brought to you at the revelation of Jesus Christ. (1 Pet 1:13)
>
> but to the degree that you share the sufferings of Christ, keep on rejoicing, so that also at the revelation of His glory you may rejoice with exultation. (1 Pet 4:13)

By illustrating the Day of the Lord and Christ's return as a *coming*, an *appearing*, and as a *revelation*, the Early Church demonstrates its belief that this cosmic event will be visible and observable to all.

When it came to the timing of Christ's second coming, the Early Church was clear that dating the event was an impossible task. In fact, Jesus plainly taught that the day and the hour of his return was information that was unknown to all, except God the Father himself: "But about that day and hour no one knows, neither the angels of heaven, nor the Son, but only the Father" (Matt 24:36). Mark 13:32 records the very same saying, while Luke made sure to answer the question of the timing of the restoration of Israel with Jesus stating that the Father has fixed this date in his own timing: "It is not for you to know times or epochs which the Father has fixed by His own authority" (Acts 1:7). Christ explained to his followers that no one knows the day of the second coming, not even the brightest and most gifted prophets. The heavenly angels, despite being in the presence of God and, perhaps, being members of the divine council, do not know the day or the hour. Jesus even admitted that he was ignorant of the day.⁶ Had he known it, he surely would have shared this crucial information with the early Christians. However, the teaching of Jesus on this matter is obvious: only God knows, and this information is not for others to know.

Since no one knows, including Jesus himself, when the second coming will take place, those who eagerly anticipated the coming day came to think of it in terms of a *thief in the night*. Of course, the Early Church perceived the second coming in this manner

---

⁵ Bauer et al., *Greek-English Lexicon*, 112.
⁶ France, *Matthew*, 940, rightly rejects attempts at explaining Christ's ignorance in terms of a supposed kenotic christology wherein Christ's omniscience was voluntarily put aside, since this christology belongs "to a much later period of Christian dogmatic development."

precisely because Jesus taught them to do so.[7] We may observe how Christ instructed his disciples to be watchful, since his coming would be like a thief:

> "Therefore, be on the alert, for you do not know which day your Lord is coming. But be sure of this, that if the head of the house had known at what time of the night the thief was coming, he would have been on the alert and would not have allowed his house to be broken into. For this reason, you also must be ready; for the Son of Man is coming at an hour when you do not think he will. (Matt 24:42–44)

The summons to remain vigilant for the unknown day of Christ's return with faithful and obedient lives also appears in Luke 12:39–40, where the illustration of the thief again occurs. Paul indicates that the belief that the unknown day of Jesus' second coming was to be considered as a thief coming in the night was common knowledge: "For you yourselves are fully aware that the day of the Lord will come like a thief in the night" (1 Thes 5:2). Confident that his readers were not living in moral darkness, Paul anticipated that the Day of the Lord would not catch them by surprise: "But you, brethren, are not in darkness, that the day would overtake you like a thief" (1 Thes 5:4).[8] Paul's use of the *thief* imagery shows dependence on the teachings of Jesus. The illustration is also taken up in Second Peter, where the *parousia* of Christ (2 Pet 3:4) is explicitly defined as the Day of the Lord that will come like a thief (2 Pet 3:10). Even in the Book of Revelation, the Lamb continues to describe his second coming in terms of a thief: "I will come like a thief, and you will not know what hour I will come against you" (Rev 3:3); "Behold, I am coming like a thief" (Rev 16:15). Revelation's insistence that Christ is coming at an unknown hour like a thief is noteworthy, as it proves that even after being highly exalted to heaven and receiving the revelation from God (Rev 1:1), he still has not been told when he is coming back. The Early Church, therefore, remained adamant that because only the Father knows the timing of the second coming, the proper response was to stay faithful, morally awake, and obediently vigilant.[9]

What about events that would precede the second coming of Christ? Did the Early Church hold to any beliefs about discernible events that needed to take place in history? In answering these questions, the New Testament writers offer surprisingly little to go on due to their conviction in the truthfulness of Jesus' teaching that only the Father knows the day and the hour. Even so, we can draw attention to two passages that are most relevant to the consideration of events prior to Christ's return. The first passage is the Olivet Discourse, an appropriate teaching from Jesus due to its conclusion that insists that one cannot know the day when he will return (Matt 24:42; Mark 13:33). The Olivet Discourse appears in all three Synoptic gospels, with Matthew and Luke offering clarifications to Mark's rendition. The passage begins with the disciples drawing attention

---

[7] Nickelsburg, *Resurrection, Immortality, and Eternal Life*, 294.
[8] Reese, *The Approaching Advent of Christ*, 168.
[9] Ryken et al., "Thief," 863.

to the temple buildings, to which Jesus responds with a prediction of judgment and destruction: "Truly I say to you, not one stone here will be left upon another, which will not be torn down" (Matt 24:2). This provoked a question from the disciples in an attempt to receive clarification from Jesus: "Tell us, when will these things happen, and what will be the sign of your coming and of the end of the age?" (Matt 24:3). We should carefully note that two different requests are posed in this question, one asking when will the temple buildings be torn down and another desiring to know about the sign of Christ's *parousia*, which will bring the end of the age. Matthew has been careful to separate these two appeals, both in the initial questioning and in Jesus' response. As Jesus describes the destruction of the Jerusalem temple and also his second coming, he offers generalized characteristics of things to take place, such as messianic pretenders, wars, persecution of his followers, many abandoning the faith, and a lack of love. Jesus makes no attempt to set these more general events on any sort of timeline. However, he finally gives an answer to the first request in Matthew 24:36: "Truly I say to you, this generation will not pass away until all these things take place." This answer carefully uses the precise language that the disciples employed in their original question, "when will *these things* happen" (Matt 24:3), that is, the destruction of the temple buildings. Christ's answer is that the temple would be demolished within a generation, that is, within forty years. In the year AD 70, the temple was, in fact, destroyed by the Roman legions during the Jewish War. Readers of the Gospel of Matthew, which was written after the destruction of the temple, would hear Jesus' prediction and immediately recognize that it had already come to pass, a point Matthew clearly wanted to emphasize to his intended audience. As for answering the second request concerning the second coming and the end of the age, Jesus stated that he did not know the day or the hour (Matt 24:36; Mark 13:32).[10] The way that Jesus answered the two requests proves that he clearly distinguished the two events in his mind; the temple buildings would be torn down sometimes within a generation of his prediction, but *he offered absolutely no timetable to his disciples about the day of his second coming*.[11]

The second relevant passage concerning events prior to the return of Christ is located in 2 Thessalonians. Due to a variety of factors, several within the church in Thessalonica had become convinced that the Day of the Lord had already come, resulting in some within the community quitting their jobs. It appears that this particular issue was the very reason Paul decided to compose this epistle. Paul and his apostolic coauthors of the epistle encourage the community of believers not to be caught off guard by the erroneous claim that the *parousia* of Jesus had already arrived:

> Now we request you, brethren, with regard to the coming of our Lord Jesus Christ and our gathering together to him, that you not be quickly shaken from your composure or

---

[10] Boring, "The Gospel of Matthew," 446, rightly notes, "The whole point is to discourage such speculation."
[11] Witherington, *Matthew*, 468, writes, "this text tells us nothing about the timing of these events . . . all such speculating should cease and desist on the basis of the authority of Jesus' own word on the matter."

be disturbed either by a spirit or a message or a letter as if from us, to the effect that the day of the Lord has come. (2 Thes 2:1–2)

In this passage, Paul gently reminds his readers that the second coming (*parousia*) is the moment when all will be gathered to Christ. Furthermore, Paul refers to the return of Jesus as "the Day of the Lord," widely recognized as the day judgment would commence. Since the believers have not been gathered together, nor has the Day of Judgment begun, it is rather self-evident that Christ's return is still in the future. In addition to these obvious and foundational characteristics of Christ's second coming that some of the Thessalonians have overlooked, Paul offers two further events that must take place:

> Let no one in any way deceive you, for it will not come unless the apostasy comes first, and the man of lawlessness is revealed, the son of destruction, who opposes and exalts himself above every so-called god or object of worship, so that he takes his seat in the temple of God, displaying himself as being God. (2 Thes 2:3–4)

According to Paul, Jesus' return that ushers in the Day of the Lord will not occur unless *the apostasy* comes first, in addition to the revelation of a megalomaniacal figure described as *the man of lawlessness*. Unfortunately, Paul does not elaborate on the particular meaning of this apostatizing from the faith. In what way will believers fall away from the faith? Paul does not say. We already observed Jesus mentioning in the Olivet Discourse that many will fall away prior to his return (Matt 24:10), behavior that he attributed more generally in other contexts to giving up the faith due to suffering tribulation or persecution (Matt 13:21; Mark 4:17).

We are in a slightly better position to make sense of Paul's second event that needs to take place before Christ's second coming, which is the revealing of the destructive "man of lawlessness." Paul illustrates this figure as a male who positions himself opposite and above the so-called gods. This arrogant behavior leads him to take his seat in the "temple of God," with the intended result of declaring himself to be a god. Since every other occurrence of this word for "temple" (Greek: *naos*) within Paul's writings refers to the body of Christ, including the statement "For we are the temple of the living God" (2 Cor 6:16), it seems most natural to draw the same conclusion here.[12] If this line of thinking is correct, then there may be an intentional correlation between the apostasy from the faith and this arrogant person's display of himself as a godlike king within the body of Christ. Paul offers a few more clues later in the passage, including the assurance that when Jesus returns, he will destroy the man of lawlessness (2 Thes 2:8), while also offering insight into Satan's empowerment of this wicked figure so that he can perform works of power, signs, and false wonders (2 Thes 2:9). From the perspective of the New Testament authors, there does not seem to be any indication that either of these events have taken place yet. To be sure, however, *Paul offered no timeline, date setting, or any*

---

[12] See especially Beale, *Temple*, 275–81.

other calendar prediction in relation to the apostasy and the revealing of the man of lawlessness.[13] Paul was like every other early Christian who did not know the day or the hour of Christ's return, and he used that uncertainty to encourage his churches to wait eagerly (1 Cor 1:7) and remain awake, alert, and sober (1 Thes 5:6), for he is coming like a thief in the night.

To recap, the authors of the New Testament offered little in the way of discernible events in history that were to occur before Christ could return. Far more attention was given to preparing their readers for the unknown day and hour. The most common metaphor used to describe his return was that of a thief in the night, an illustration that appears in the teachings of Jesus, Paul, Second Peter, and the Book of Revelation. Since only the Father possesses the knowledge of the day when he will send Jesus back to consummate the kingdom, the early Christians did not create timelines, set dates predicting the *parousia*, or engage in any other calendar reworking. Instead, they strove to live faithfully, knowing full well that life was short and that they very well might die before Christ returned. Since the very next moment of their consciousness after death would be at the resurrection, they needed to always be ready through holy living and being obedient to the work Christ had left for them to accomplish.

The Return of Christ and the Day of the Lord

We have already seen several indicators that the second coming of Jesus Christ was believed by the Early Church to be the Day of the Lord. In the Old Testament, discussion surrounding the Day of the Lord primarily pertained to a time of judgment, including a calling to account of God's people. This judgment-filled Day of the Lord reemerges in the New Testament, with the key modification involving Yahweh's sharing his role of the cosmic judge with his agent, the messianic son of God (see Chapters 5 and 24). Since God has handed over the task of judging the world to the human Messiah, the terminology employed by the New Testament writers to express the Day of the Lord included *the day of Christ, the day of Jesus Christ*, and other standard terms (e.g., *in that day* and *the day of wrath*).[14] In order to grasp the full measure of what Jesus will accomplish when he returns from heaven to consummate the kingdom of God upon the earth, we will need to explore precisely how his coming serves as the Day of Judgment.

Beginning with the teachings of Jesus himself, we find several instances where he talks about the Day of Judgment. He identifies "that day" as the time when those who do the will of his Father will enter the kingdom, while those who merely confess Jesus' lordship without obeying will be judged as unworthy to enter (Matt 7:21–23). On multiple

---

[13] Jewett, *The Thessalonian Correspondence*, 191–92.
[14] Reese, *The Approaching Advent of Christ*, 167, 170.

occasions, Christ spoke of the Day of Judgment as the time when those who rejected the proclamation of the gospel of the kingdom would be judged more harshly than some of the most notorious wicked cities in the Old Testament narratives:

> "Whoever does not receive you, nor heed your words, as you go out of that house or that city, shake the dust off your feet. Truly I say to you, it will be more tolerable for the land of Sodom and Gomorrah in the day of judgment than for that city." (Matt 10:14–15)

> "The men of Nineveh will stand up with this generation at the judgment, and will condemn it because they repented at the preaching of Jonah; and behold, something greater than Jonah is here. The Queen of the South will rise up with this generation at the judgment and will condemn it, because she came from the ends of the earth to hear the wisdom of Solomon; and behold, something greater than Solomon is here. (Matt 12:41–42)

> Then he began to denounce the cities in which most of his miracles were done, because they did not repent. "Woe to you, Chorazin! Woe to you, Bethsaida! For if the miracles had occurred in Tyre and Sidon which occurred in you, they would have repented long ago in sackcloth and ashes. Nevertheless I say to you, it will be more tolerable for Tyre and Sidon in the day of judgment than for you. And you, Capernaum, will not be exalted to heaven, will you? You will descend to Hades; for if the miracles had occurred in Sodom which occurred in you, it would have remained to this day. Nevertheless I say to you that it will be more tolerable for the land of Sodom in the day of judgment, than for you." (Matt 11:20–24)

> "But whatever city you enter and they do not receive you, go out into its streets and say, 'Even the dust of your city which clings to our feet we wipe off in protest against you; yet be sure of this, that the kingdom of God has come near.' I say to you, it will be more tolerable in that day for Sodom than for that city." (Luke 10:8–12)

Jesus seems to have warned that those who refuse to respond with repentance will be called to account on the day when the righteous are rewarded with entrance into the kingdom. In John 12:48, Christ refers to this Day of Judgment as *the last day*: "He who rejects me and does not receive my sayings, has one who judges him; the word I spoke is what will judge him at the last day." Jesus also declared that when he returns at his second coming, he will sit on the promised throne of David and commence with judgment (Matt 25:31). All the nations will be gathered before Jesus the judge on that day, and he will separate the sheep from the goats. The righteous "sheep" will inherit the kingdom of God at that time (Matt 25:34, 46), while the unrighteous "goats" will join the Devil and his angels in the punishment of fire (Matt 25:41, 46).[15] The Day of Judgment for both the righteous and the unrighteous commences at Christ's return to rule as king.

---

[15] Hagner, *Matthew 14–28*, 742–43.

Even the parables of Jesus depict the coming Day of Judgment. The theme of judgment, particularly as it relates to how people respond to Jesus' gospel of the kingdom and his summons to repentance, frequently appears in his parables. For example, the Parable of the Tares in the Field is explicitly interpreted by Christ himself for the disciples as illustrating the harvest in terms of the end of the age. This consummation of the age will feature the separation of tares and the good seed. The son of man will send his angels on that day to gather the wicked tares and consign them to the fire that consumes (Matt 13:40–42). As for the righteous sons of the kingdom, they will inherit resurrection bodies and shine brightly in the kingdom of God (Matt 13:43). Another parable, the Parable of the Dragnet, portrays fishermen sorting the good fish from the bad in terms of the judgment that will take place at the end of the age (Matt 13:47–50). This Day of Judgment will consist of the angels separating the wicked from the righteous by throwing them into the fiery furnace. Much more detail is offered in the Parable of the Talents, which illustrates a master leaving to receive a kingdom, and then returning to call to account the behavior of his servants (Matt 25:14–30; Luke 19:11–27). The parable places significant emphasis on the role of judgment that the returning master exercises, particularly as he praises those servants who exhibited faithfulness and severely punishes the unfaithful. Other parables that conclude with a scene of judgment linked with the return of Jesus Christ include the Parables of the Wedding Banquet (Matt 22:2–14), the Faithful and Wise Servant (Matt 24:45–51; Luke 12:42–48), and the Ten Virgins (Matt 25:1–13). As we can see, Christ's insistence that he will return and commence the Day of Judgment extended beyond his ordinary teachings to even include his parables.[16]

Naturally, the foundation that Jesus provided the Early Church concerning the belief that his second coming would be the very Day of Judgment was embraced and reaffirmed in the writings of the New Testament authors. Within the Book of Acts, Luke reports how Paul preached that God has set a day in which he will judge the world through the human Jesus (Acts 17:31). The Apostle Paul supported this doctrine frequently in his own letters, and the evidence is overwhelmingly convincing. Without being exhaustive, here is a sizable sampling of Paul discussing the day of Christ's return as the moment when the judgment will take place, a judgment he hopes will be favorable for his readers:

> But because of your stubbornness and unrepentant heart you are storing up wrath for yourself in the day of wrath and revelation of the righteous judgment of God, who will render to each person according to his deeds . . . on the day when, according to my gospel, God will judge the secrets of men through Christ Jesus. (Rom 2:5–6, 16)

> awaiting eagerly the revelation of our Lord Jesus Christ, who will also confirm you to the end, blameless in the day of our Lord Jesus Christ. (1 Cor 1:7–8)

---

[16] Ladd, *A Theology of the New Testament*, 205–6; Beasley-Murray, *Jesus and the Kingdom of God*, 198–218.

each man's work will become evident; for the day will show it because it is to be revealed with fire, and the fire itself will test the quality of each man's work. (1 Cor 3:13)

so that you may approve the things that are excellent, in order to be sincere and blameless until the day of Christ (Phil 1:10)

holding fast the word of life, so that in the day of Christ I will have reason to glory because I did not run in vain nor toil in vain. (Phil 2:16)

These will pay the penalty of eternal destruction, away from the presence of the Lord and from the glory of his power, when he comes to be glorified in his saints on that day, and to be marveled at among all who have believed (2 Thes 1:9–10)

The theology of Paul consistently portrays the day on which all who will be judged, righteous and unrighteous alike, will be that day that Christ returns.[17] With this in mind, Paul hopes that he may present his converts blameless before the throne of judgment on that day, that is, at Christ's return: "For who is our hope or joy or crown of exultation? Is it not even you, in the presence of our Lord Jesus at his coming? For you are our glory and joy" (1 Thes 2:19–20). Even Paul himself, by conforming to the crucified and risen Jesus, lived in such a way that he may attain to the bodily resurrection unto immortality (Phil 3:11), that he may be made complete and perfect at that time (Phil 3:12), and that he would not be disqualified through a lack of self-control (1 Cor 9:27).

When we examine the rest of the New Testament authors, we find a widespread acceptance that Christ will return and initiate the Day of Judgment. Since this time of calling all to account will include believers, the author of the Epistle to the Hebrews encourages his readers not to abandon their weekly gatherings. Instead, they should meet regularly, encourage, and build one another up "all the more as you see the day drawing near" (Heb 10:25). First Peter exhorts its readers live honorably among the unbelieving Gentiles in hopes that their good works would encourage a change, leading to them giving glory to God on the Day of Judgment, that is, "in the day of visitation" (1 Pet 2:12). First John draws a correlation between believers who faithfully abide in God's love and the confidence they can possess on that day: "By this, love is perfected with us, so that we may have confidence in the day of judgment" (1 John 4:17). Jude even mentions that the judgment that will take place on that great day will include rebellious heavenly angels: "And angels who did not keep their own domain, but abandoned their proper abode, He has kept in eternal bonds under darkness for the judgment of the great day" (Jude 1:6). When the wicked panic and cry out in the Book of Revelation because "the great day of their wrath" (that is, the wrath of God and the Lamb) has come, the question is raised "who is able to stand?" (Rev 6:17). John of Patmos unveils for his reader the answer to this question as he illustrates a great multitude from every nation, tribe, people, and tongue *standing* before the throne and before the Lamb (Rev 7:9). This great multitude is

---

[17] See also 1 Cor 5:5; 2 Cor 1:14; Phil 1:6; 1 Thes 5:2, 4; 2 Thes 2:1–2; 2 Tim 1:12, 18; 4:8.

further characterized as those who "have washed their robes and made them white in the blood of the Lamb" in Revelation 7:14.

The subject of the return of Christ on the Day of Judgment appears frequently in Second Peter.[18] In this epistle, we can see that the unrighteous are kept "under punishment until the day of judgment" (2 Pet 2:9). This day will bring about the consequence of that judgment, namely their annihilation: "the day of judgment and destruction of ungodly men (2 Pet 3:7). Second Peter is clear that the Day of Judgment occurs at the *parousia* of Jesus Christ (2 Pet 3:4), a day that will come like a thief (2 Pet 3:10).[19] Not only will the return of Christ usher in the judgment, it will bring about a cleansing fire over creation in order to usher in the new creation: "But according to his promise we are looking for new heavens and a new earth, in which righteousness dwells" (2 Pet 3:13). The epistle concludes with a fitting benediction in 2 Peter 3:18 that once again draws attention to this highly anticipated day: "To him be the glory, both now and to the day of eternity. Amen."

The Judge of the Living and the Dead

Thus far, we have observed the Early Church's expectation that Jesus would return visibly at an unknown date to usher in the kingdom of God. On this day, judgment would commence, and it appears that all will be called to account, both the righteous and the unrighteous. This judgment was good news for the faithful because it would serve to vindicate them, raise them from the dead, and reward them with immortality and entrance into the kingdom of God. For the wicked, however, Christ's return would hold them accountable for their sinful lives, their ungodly ways, and their mistreatment of God's people. Those who have lived obediently to the one true God would have nothing to fear on the Day of Judgment. In fact, they could anticipate it with joy and confidence. One thing is sure: the *parousia* of Jesus Christ would be the event that rewards each person for their works, and this would necessitate the general resurrection to occur at this time.

When we examine the straightforward teachings of Jesus, we find several instances where he instructed his followers that at his return, everyone would be either rewarded or punished based on their deeds. Consider carefully how Christ portrays the repayment of each person that will take place at his second coming:

> "For the Son of Man is going to come with his angels in the glory of his Father, and then he will repay each person according to what he has done" (Matt 16:27)

---

[18] Watson, "The Second Letter of Peter," 330.
[19] Beale, *A New Testament Biblical Theology*, 155; Bauckham, *Jude, 2 Peter*, 321; Neyrey, *2 Peter, Jude*, 242–43.

> "For whoever is ashamed of me and my words in this adulterous and sinful generation, the Son of Man will also be ashamed of him when he comes in the glory of his Father with the holy angels." (Mark 8:38)

> "Do not marvel at this; for an hour is coming, in which all who are in the tombs will hear his voice, and will come forth; those who did the good deeds to a resurrection of life, those who committed the evil deeds to a resurrection of judgment" (John 5:28–29).

As expected, the rest of the New Testament authors show evidence of following in Jesus' teachings, demonstrating an acceptance that early Christians anticipated the second coming to bring about the judgment of every person. Note the similarity in theology when compared to what Christ himself taught:

> who will render to each person according to his deeds: to those who by perseverance in doing good seek for glory and honor and immortality, eternal life; but to those who are selfishly ambitious and do not obey the truth, but obey unrighteousness, wrath and indignation . . . on the day when, according to my gospel, God will judge the secrets of men through Christ Jesus. (Rom 2:6–8, 16)

> For we will all stand before the judgment seat of God; for it is written, "As I live, says the Lord, every knee shall bow to me, and every tongue shall confess to God." So then each of us will give an account of himself to God. (Rom 14:10–12)

> For we must all appear before the judgment seat of Christ, so that each one may be recompensed for his deeds in the body, according to what he has done, whether good or bad. (2 Cor 5:10)

> knowing that from the Lord you will receive the inheritance as your reward. You are serving the Lord Christ. For the wrongdoer will be paid back for the wrong he has done, and there is no partiality. (Col 3:24–25)

> I solemnly charge you in the presence of God and of Christ Jesus, who is to judge the living and the dead, and by his appearing and his kingdom (2 Tim 4:1)

> But they will have to give an accounting to him who stands ready to judge the living and the dead. (1 Pet 4:5)

> See, the Lord is coming with ten thousands of his holy ones, to execute judgment on all (Jude 1:14–15)

> The nations raged, but your wrath has come, and the time for judging the dead, for rewarding your servants, the prophets and saints and all who fear your name, both small and great, and for destroying those who destroy the earth. (Rev 11:18)

> "See, I am coming soon; my reward is with me, to repay according to everyone's work." (Rev 22:12)

The Early Church was in complete agreement that the righteous would be rewarded on the Day of Judgment, and the wicked would be repaid for their sins on the very same day. In other words, there were no separate days of judgment, one for the righteous and another later for the unrighteous. Instead, Jesus, Paul, and the rest of the New Testament authors consistently portrayed a single Day of Judgment on which the second coming would commence and repay every person. The calling to account that would take place at Christ's *parousia* motivates the early Christians to live faithfully, stay alert, and highly anticipate the kingdom's final consummation. On that day, everything wrong with the world will be made right.

Conclusion

To sum up, the Early Church continued to long for the return of Jesus Christ from heaven to bring to completion what he began during his ministry: to establish the kingdom of God upon the earth. We observed that the early Christians expected Christ's return to be visible, dramatic, and cosmic in its scope, rather than arrive secretly or invisibly. Furthermore, Jesus taught his disciples that the day and hour of his return was information that only the Father possessed. Even Christ did not know when he was returning. This resulted in the Early Church taking the position that believers should be ever vigilant, as Christ's *parousia* would arrive like a thief in the night. The unpredictability of the day of his return meant that his followers did not set any dates, make any predictions, or draw up any timelines to pinpoint when to expect him. Even the few hints of things that would take place prior to the second coming (the destruction of the temple, the apostasy, and the revealing of the man of lawlessness) were never used to triangulate or date when they might expect his return. We also observed how the Early Church, following the teachings of Jesus himself, regarded the second coming as the Day of Judgment. As such, Christ would return to rule as the Messiah over God's kingdom and serve as the judge of the living and the dead. Moreover, this Day of Judgment would require the resurrection of the dead in order to reward the righteous and to sentence the wicked to destruction. The theology of the Early Church was clear that there would only be a single Day of Judgment that would call all to account, the faithful and the unfaithful, the living and the dead. The second coming of Jesus Christ would bring God's victory to its complete fulfillment, resulting in humanity once again ruling over the good creation.

Our study has intentionally left the millennial reign of Christ, which appears only in Revelation chapter twenty, as the concluding area upon which to focus our attention. How have Christian interpreters attempted to explain Revelation's imagery of this thousand-year reign in light of the Old Testament, Jesus' teachings, and the rest of the New Testament? We will explore Christ's millennial reign in our next chapter.

49
THE MILLENNIAL REIGN

Tucked between the longest visionary accounts in the Book of Revelation, namely the portrayal of the city of Fallen Babylon (Rev 17:1–19:10) and the city of New Jerusalem (Rev 21:9–22:9), is John's description of the millennial reign of Christ. Despite the attention that John of Patmos pays to contrasting these two cities, Christians have traditionally devoted considerable attention and study to the contents of Revelation chapter twenty. Since the passage illustrates the reign of Christ that is shared with faithful believers, interpreters interested in the beliefs and doctrines concerning the kingdom of God and the end times have been drawn to uncover its truths. However, as with many of the signs and symbols in the image-rich prophecies contained within the Book of Revelation, the millennial reign has given rise to differing interpretations among careful, God-honoring readers of Scripture.[1] Even Justin Martyr, writing in the middle of the second century AD, acknowledges that not everyone agrees with his reading of Revelation chapter twenty: "But I also informed you," Justin tells his Jewish dialogue partner, Trypho, "that even many of pure and godly mind do not accept it."[2] Justin goes on and lays out his reading of the millennial reign, but he admits that there are other sincere and genuine Christians who remain unconvinced.[3]

This chapter explores Revelation chapter twenty and its depiction of Christ's millennial reign, advancing our broader aim of systematizing the Early Church's theology. To that end, we situate this portrayal within the eschatological framework of the Old Testament, the teachings of Jesus and Paul, and the theology of the Book of Revelation itself—seeking an interpretation that is in continuity, rather than contradicts, the New Testament's unified witness. In essence, we advocate for the *inaugurated millennial* reading, which views the thousand-year period as Christ's present rule and reign, while anticipating his glorious return, the consummation of the kingdom of God upon the earth, his enthronement on David's throne, and the final Day of Judgment. This chapter will also interact with the *premillennial* reading that interprets the symbols and numbers within Revelation chapter twenty literally. Although both views were held by Christians in the

---

[1] Finnegan, *Kingdom Journey*, 174.
[2] Justin Martyr, *Dialogue* 80; Ford, "Millennium," 833; Michaels, "Millennium," 88.
[3] Dodd, "Millennialism," 740. For further reading on the diversity of eschatological views in the second to fourth centuries AD, see Smith, "Unity and Diversity," 7–20.

first to third centuries AD,[4] the *inaugurated millennial* interpretation fits more naturally among the beliefs that Jesus plainly and repeatedly taught the Early Church.

Before examining the image-rich details of Revelation chapter twenty, we should consider the passage as a whole.

> Then I saw an angel coming down from heaven, holding the key of the abyss and a great chain in his hand. And he laid hold of the dragon, the serpent of old, who is the devil and Satan, and bound him for a thousand years; and he threw him into the abyss, and shut it and sealed it over him, so that he would not deceive the nations any longer, until the thousand years were completed; after these things he must be released for a short time. Then I saw thrones, and they sat on them, and judgment was given to them. And I saw the souls of those who had been beheaded because of their testimony of Jesus and because of the word of God, and those who had not worshiped the beast or his image, and had not received the mark on their forehead and on their hand; and they came to life and reigned with Christ for a thousand years. The rest of the dead did not come to life until the thousand years were completed. This is the first resurrection. Blessed and holy is the one who has a part in the first resurrection; over these the second death has no power, but they will be priests of God and of Christ and will reign with Him for a thousand years. When the thousand years are completed, Satan will be released from his prison, and will come out to deceive the nations which are in the four corners of the earth, Gog and Magog, to gather them together for the war; the number of them is like the sand of the seashore. And they came up on the broad plain of the earth and surrounded the camp of the saints and the beloved city, and fire came down from heaven and devoured them. And the devil who deceived them was thrown into the lake of fire and brimstone, where the beast and the false prophet are also; and they will be tormented day and night forever and ever. Then I saw a great white throne and Him who sat upon it, from whose presence earth and heaven fled away, and no place was found for them. And I saw the dead, the great and the small, standing before the throne, and books were opened; and another book was opened, which is the book of life; and the dead were judged from the things which were written in the books, according to their deeds. And the sea gave up the dead which were in it, and death and Hades gave up the dead which were in them; and they were judged, every one of them according to their deeds. Then death and Hades were thrown into the lake of fire. This is the second death, the lake of fire. And if anyone's name was not found written in the book of life, he was thrown into the lake of fire. (Rev 20:1–15)

---

[4] Early proponents of premillennialism include Papias, Justin Martyr, Irenaeus, Tertullian, Commodianus, Victorinus, and Lactantius. Those who held views that were not premillennial include Clement of Rome, the grandsons of Jude, Ignatius (in both his short and middle recensions), Polycarp, Hermas, the authors of *2 Clement*, *Epistula Apostolorum*, and the *Apocalypse of Peter*, Hippolytus, Clement of Alexandria, Origen, Dionysius of Alexandria, and Cyprian. As such, the frequently stated suggestion that premillennial eschatology dominated the early Church is simply not true. The number of Christians in the first four centuries AD who disagree with the premillennial interpretation is more than twice as numerous as the explicit premillennialists.

We can divide this passage into three sections: the first pertains to the binding of Satan, the second describes Jesus Christ's thousand-year reign, and the third illustrates the events immediately following the conclusion of the thousand years.

The Inaugurated Millennial Interpretation of Revelation 20:1–3

We have already seen several indicators in the teachings of Jesus and in the letters of Paul that Christ is sitting at God's right hand until the time when all of his enemies will be placed under his feet (Ps 110:1). Revelation 20:1–15 fits well into this understanding of Christ's exaltation, and it may be fairly described as *inaugurated millenarianism*.[5] At the heart of this reading of the millennial reign is the insistence that the two-stage kingdom believed and taught by the Early Church was first inaugurated in the ministry of Jesus (stage one) and its final consummation will occur on the Day of Judgment, when Christ returns as Messiah and judge (stage two). This interpretation highlights that there remains a single Day of Judgment, which occurs after the millennium comes to an end, and this Day of Judgment coincides with the resurrection of the dead. This resurrection will bring forth everyone from the grave, the righteous and the unrighteous. In the meantime, the faithful readers of Revelation are already sharing in Jesus' inaugurated reign and rule, that is, in the kingdom that has already broken into the present.

Beginning with the first section (Rev 20:1–3), where John illustrates the binding of Satan, the timing of this event requires some discussion. Although it is sometimes claimed by readers that Satan's imprisonment in the abyss occurs at the second coming of Christ, the text says nothing of the sort. In fact, the return of Jesus *is never directly mentioned in Revelation 20:1–15*.[6] On the contrary, by the time the Book of Revelation was written, the Early Church had already expressed the belief that the in-breaking of the kingdom of God results in binding the influence of the strong man.[7] We may recall how Jesus taught that his exorcisms not only proved the inauguration of the kingdom of God, but they also signified a restraining of Satan in the present:

> "But if I cast out demons by the Spirit of God, then the kingdom of God has come upon you. Or how can someone enter a strong man's house and plunder his goods, unless he first binds the strong man? Then indeed he may plunder his house." (Matt 12:28–29)

> "But if I cast out demons by the finger of God, then the kingdom of God has come upon you. When a strong man, fully armed, guards his own house, his possessions are

---

[5] Some have taken to referring to this interpretation as amillennialism. The descriptor "amillennialism" is, unfortunately, often misunderstood as if it were proposing that there is *no millennium at all*. On the contrary, this view insists on the reality of the millennium, namely, that it has already been inaugurated as the reign and rule that believers presently experience in Christ.
[6] Dodd, "Millennium," 739; Smalley, *Revelation*, 503.
[7] Ladd, *The Presence of the Future*, 152.

undisturbed. But when someone stronger than he attacks him and overpowers him, he takes away from him all his armor on which he had relied and distributes his plunder." (Luke 11:20–22)

As such, the presence of the kingdom of God and the binding of Satan were characteristic of Jesus' earthly ministry. Even the verb "to bind" (Greek: *deomai*) used in Jesus' description of the binding of the strong man (Matt 12:29; Mark 3:27) is used in Revelation's portrayal of the binding of Satan (Rev 20:2).[8] Furthermore, we have evidence that the successful preaching of the gospel of the kingdom resulted in a defeat of Satan's authority:

> "Whatever city you enter and they receive you, eat what is set before you; and heal those in it who are sick, and say to them, 'The kingdom of God has come near to you.'" . . . The seventy returned with joy, saying, "Lord, even the demons are subject to us in your name." And he said to them, "I was watching Satan fall from heaven like lightning. Behold, I have given you authority to tread on serpents and scorpions, and over all the power of the enemy, and nothing will injure you." (Luke 10:8-9, 17–19)

Jesus' assessment of the successful ministry of his disciples includes an acknowledgment of Satan's defeat, as evidenced by his fall and a shifting of authority.[9] The cross of Christ also served as a triumphal victory over the Devil. Speaking of being lifted up on a cross, Jesus declared that Satan, the ruler of this world, will be driven out: "Now judgment is upon this world; now the ruler of this world will be cast out. And I, if I am lifted up from the earth, will draw all men to myself" (John 12:31–32). Similar statements of the defeat of Satan due to what Jesus accomplished in his ministry appear in the epistles (Col 2:15; Heb 2:14–15). Notable is Paul's reporting to have heard directly from Jesus that the preaching of the gospel message *to the nations will free them from the influence of Satan*, just as the binding of Satan describes (Rev 20:2): "rescuing you from the Jewish people and from the Gentiles, to whom I am sending you, to open their eyes so that they may turn from darkness to light and from the dominion of Satan to God" (Acts 26:17–18). Even the Book of Revelation teaches that the inauguration of the kingdom has resulted in the throwing down and limiting of Satan's influence (Rev 12:9–10).[10] The faithful may conquer Satan and his deceptive influences by preaching the gospel, identifying with the blood of the Lamb, and enduring steadfast in the face of martyrdom (Rev 12:11).[11] In short, just as the Early Church portrayed the inauguration of God's rule and reign as binding, disarming, and conquering the Devil, Revelation 20:1–3 illustrates the present

---

[8] Beale, *Revelation*, 985; Wright, *Revelation*, 180–81; Myers, *Binding the Strong Man*, 164–67.
[9] Ladd, *The Presence of the Future*, 157.
[10] The Greek text of Revelation 12:9 emphasizes this point by describing how Satan was thrown down "into the earth," perhaps down into the abyss mentioned in Revelation 20:1.
[11] The truth that faithful believers have already conquered the evil one in the present is also expressed in 1 John 2:13, 14. Furthermore, Paul plainly taught that God rescued believers from the domain of darkness, and he has already transferred us into the inaugurated kingdom of his son (Col 1:13).

restriction of the Devil's influence over the nations, keeping them from violently rebelling against God's people in what will amount to the final war (as we will see in Rev 20:7–8).[12]

The Inaugurated Millennial Interpretation of Revelation 20:4–6

The second section (Rev 20:4–6) illustrates the millennial reign proper and those who have come to life in order that they may reign with Christ. Instead of reading into this passage the second coming of Jesus, we may draw again upon the theology of the Early Church, which frequently illustrated the inaugurated reign of God's kingdom in the present in addition to the portrayal of believers as having experienced a coming to life in their conversion. In Chapter 47, we observed numerous indicators that Jesus and his followers believed in and experienced the kingdom of God that had now broken into history. Furthermore, the theology of the Book of Revelation itself has already demonstrated its commitment to the present experience of the kingdom of God (Rev 1:6, 9; 12:10). Readers of Revelation who keep its prophetic mandates have already been reconstituted into kings and priests (Rev 5:10).[13] Revelation 4:4 employs rich imagery of enthroned conquerors. Christ is presently "the ruler of the kings of the earth" (Rev 1:5). We have also seen evidence in Paul's theology that those who have been converted have experienced a coming to life in which they are now sharing in Christ's present reign and rule as enthroned kings:

> But God, being rich in mercy, because of His great love with which He loved us, even when we were dead in our transgressions, made us alive together with Christ (by grace you have been saved), and raised us up with him, and seated us with him in the heavenly places in Christ Jesus (Eph 2:4–6)

There are no compelling reasons to assume that the references to coming to life (Rev 20:4, 5) *must* refer to bodily resurrection. In fact, taking the doctrine of the resurrection of the dead, as presented in both testaments, and dividing it into two resurrections, separated by a millennium of time, *directly contradicts* the biblical authors and Jesus himself. Let us recall how the portrayal of the resurrection of the dead is a single event that encompasses both the righteous and the unrighteous at the same time:

> Many of those who sleep in the dust of the ground will awake, these to everlasting life, but the others to disgrace and everlasting contempt. (Dan 12:2)

> "The men of Nineveh will stand up with this generation at the judgment, and will condemn it because they repented at the preaching of Jonah; and behold, something greater than Jonah is here. The Queen of the South will rise up with this generation at the judgment and will condemn it, because she came from the ends of the earth to hear

---

[12] Beale. *Revelation*, 986; Blaising et al., *Three Views of the Millennium*, 123; Riddlebarger, *Case*, 237–39.
[13] Smalley, *Revelation*, 508; Beale. *Revelation*, 996.

the wisdom of Solomon; and behold, something greater than Solomon is here. (Matt 12:41–42)

"Do not marvel at this; for an hour is coming, in which all who are in the tombs will hear his voice, and will come forth; those who did the good deeds to a resurrection of life, those who committed the evil deeds to a resurrection of judgment." (John 5:28–29)

"having a hope in God, which these men cherish themselves, that there shall certainly be a resurrection of both the righteous and the wicked." (Acts 24:15)

The plain, straightforward reading of these passages portrays one event known as the resurrection of the dead, and this single event will raise the righteous and the unrighteous together.[14] If there is to be one resurrection of the dead, which is to take place when Christ returns at his second coming, then the most natural way to make sense of the illustration of the faithful "coming to life" in Revelation 20:4 is to read it as portraying Christian conversion.[15] The use of resurrection language and metaphors to describe those who repent and believe the gospel of the kingdom has been well-documented already (Chapters 35 & 36). In light of the teachings of Jesus and Paul that existed for decades before the Book of Revelation, it seems far easier to describe the first resurrection as the conversion of believers and the second resurrection that takes place on the Day of Judgment before the white throne as referring to the promised future resurrection of all the dead, rather than to suggest that Revelation chapter twenty is now splitting the single event of the resurrection into two.[16]

When it comes to the length of the inaugurated millennial reign, it is essential not to overlook how numbers function as a whole in the Book of Revelation. Within the book's clearly stated purpose of communicating the revelation of Jesus Christ through the use of signs (Rev 1:1), readers need to ask *how numbers function* as symbols. Seven, for example, is a frequently appearing number in the Book of Revelation that expresses wholeness and completeness.[17] Similarly, the number twelve has a rich biblical history of representing the people of God, beginning with the twelve tribes and finding support in Jesus' reorganization of the people of God through the appointment of twelve apostles.[18] The number four likely represents the universality of creation (e.g., four living creatures, four corners of the earth, four winds).[19] Even periods of 3½ years, variously portrayed as forty-two months or 1,260 days, recall times of intense persecution of the people of God in Israel's history, and as such, these periods of time occur in contexts within the Book

---

[14] Wright, *Revelation*, 176–77.
[15] Smalley, *Revelation*, 508; [15] Johnson, *Triumph of the Lamb*, 293.
[16] Swete, *Apocalypse*, 263; Mulholland, "Revelation," 582–84.
[17] Boring, "Numbers," 298; Josh 6:4–15; 2 Kgs 5:10–14; Ps 12:6; Dan 9:24; Matt 18:22; Rev 5:6.
[18] Boring, "Numbers," 299; Exod 24:4; 28:15–21; Josh 4:12; Matt 19:28; Luke 22:30; Rev 7:4–8; 21:12–14.
[19] Boring, "Numbers," 298. See also Gen 2:10; Isa 11:12.

of Revelation that also characterize limited but difficult times in which the faithful should endure with steadfast obedience.[20]

In light of the regular habit of John of Patmos to employ symbolic numbers with such frequency in his retelling of the revelation he received, it is reasonable to at least ask if the number one thousand might also function symbolically. As it so happens, we can answer this query with relative ease. The number one thousand, particularly in multiples, occurs in the description of the sealed people of God in the numbering of the twelve tribes, which total 144,000 (Rev 7:4–8). Revelation's *hearing and seeing* motif (see Chapter 43) explains these 144,000 in the following verse as "a great multitude which no one could count" (Rev 7:9). Since John's vision explicitly interprets multiples of one thousand as an uncountable multitude, it seems unlikely that one thousand was intended to be identified as a literal, cardinal number.

Furthermore, the dimensions of New Jerusalem, which is depicted as a cube with equal length, width, and height, measure twelve thousand stadia. The sum of the twelve edges of New Jerusalem, naturally, adds up to 144,000 stadia. Once we recall that the city of New Jerusalem is actually a positive description of the beautiful bride of Christ (Rev 21:2, 9–10), then we can again see another way in which the Book of Revelation symbolizes the faithful people of God with the number 144,000.[21] This illustration of the city's (i.e., the bride) dimensions further underscores the symbolic meaning of the number one thousand. In other words, the portrayal of the one-thousand-year reign is likely a symbolic representation of the vastness, completeness, and divinely ordered rule of Christ, a rule that he presently exhibits as a result of the inauguration of the kingdom of God.[22] Since there is no single place outside of the description of the millennium where the Book of Revelation uses the number one thousand (or its multiples) literally, this should caution us against assuming that the millennial reign must be a literal period of time in chapter twenty.[23]

The Inaugurated Millennial Interpretation of Revelation 20:7–15

When we examine the third and final section of the millennium (Rev 20:7–15), Satan is released in order to deceive the nations into rebelling against God's people for *the war*. Three things should be pointed out here. First, it would be rather odd for Satan to drum up a war against immortalized righteous persons, as the premillennial interpretation is

---

[20] The Maccabean Revolt and its fighting against the Syrians lasted 3 ½ years (recorded in Dan 7:25; 9:27; 12:7, 11). During the life of Elijah, Ahab's disobedience led to no rain for 3 ½ years (James 5:17). The Jewish War, which resulted in the temple's destruction, lasted 3 ½ years (fall of AD 66 to spring of AD 70).
[21] Witherington, *Revelation*, 269.
[22] Wright, *Revelation*, 179; Morris, *Revelation*, 229; Smalley, *Revelation*, 502–3; Mulholland, "Revelation," 579.
[23] Even the premillennialist Ladd, *The Revelation of John*, 262, admits that the number 1000 is "an ideal time."

forced to conclude. Why start a war against an unkillable opponent? It makes better sense that this battle occurs at the end of the age, before the people of God receive immortality.

Second, it is difficult to make sense of any sort of armed conflict or war occurring one thousand years into the kingdom of God, especially in light of the recurring promise made by the Hebrew prophets that all weapons of war will be turned into plowshares and pruning hooks (Isa 2:4; Mic 4:3). The prophet Micah was particularly firm in his conviction that nations will *never learn war ever again*: "nation shall not lift up sword against nation, neither shall they learn war any more; but they shall all sit under their own vines and under their own fig trees, and no one shall make them afraid" (Mic 4:3–4). In fact, one of the key promises that the authors of the Old Testament repeatedly emphasized was the establishment of universal peace in the kingdom of God (see Chapter 45). Therefore, it makes better sense to locate Satan's rebellion involving the nations of Gog and Magog as occurring at the end of the age, not within the kingdom of God.

Third, John's characterization of the final battle as "the war" (Rev 20:8) points to a very specific confrontation, not just any random skirmish. Fortunately, John of Patmos has employed this precise phrase ("the war") in previous visions, which fits the book's structure of recapitulating events several times from different visionary vantage points.[24] The first occurrence of the phrase "the war" appears in Revelation 16:14–16, where we find the themes of the great Day of Judgment, the second coming of Jesus like a thief in the night, and the language of Armageddon. The next instance where John employs the phrase "the war" is in Revelation 19:19, which is in the context of Christ's triumphal second coming, a time of judgment poured out on the opposing armies, and the lake of fire.[25] Since these are the only three occurrences in the Book of Revelation where visions describe "the war," it is worth considering whether all three are really illustrating the same event, namely, the same decisive end-times war.[26] If this is the case, then the second coming of Christ, which is not explicitly mentioned in Revelation chapter twenty, would most appropriately occur at this final battle, when the wicked are defeated and the lake of fire appears as a place of judgment. The similarity in the descriptions of these visions, particularly as they report God's judgment upon a large opposing army, is indicative that John of Patmos is referring to one and the same period in history, that is, the time when Christ returns.[27]

---

[24] Blaising et al., *Three Views of the Millennium*, 124–25.
[25] Morris, *Revelation*, 233.
[26] Rowland, "The Book of Revelation," 714; Riddlebarger, *Case*, 250–51; Aune, *Revelation 17–22*, 1079; Smalley, *Revelation*, 512–13; [26] Johnson, *Triumph of the Lamb*, 284–85.
[27] The suggestion that the events at the end of Revelation 19:11–21 occur immediately prior to the events of Revelation 20 is problematic for several reasons. First, this reading suggests that there are two wars (with strikingly similar details), one before the millennium and one after it. Second, it imposes a chronological reading upon John's retelling of his visions, which have been shown to be recapitulatory. Third, this overlooks 1 Corinthians 15:51–55 and Hebrews 12:26–28, passages that point to a single, final victory over death and evil at the time of Christ's return.

If we position the second coming of Christ at this point in the vision, when the fire descends from heaven to consume the wicked army (Rev 20:9), then we are in good company with the beliefs of the Early Church. The expectation that the Messiah would one day come to judge in flaming fire is frequently mentioned in the Gospel accounts and by Paul.[28] Relevant to this inquiry is the description of Christ's fiery second coming in 2 Thessalonians: "Jesus will be revealed from heaven with his mighty angels in flaming fire, dealing out retribution to those who do not know God and to those who do not obey the gospel of our Lord Jesus" (2 Thes 1:7–8). When Jesus returns as judge and king, the enemies of God are destroyed, which is precisely what our exploration of the second coming (and the accompanying Day of the Lord) has led us to expect (see Chapter 48).

What remains is the scene of judgment in Revelation 20:11–15, occupying the largest portion of the chapter on the millennium. Everything that the teachings of Jesus, Paul, and the rest of the authors of the New Testament have indicated points to a single Day of Judgment when all the dead will be raised. John of Patmos portrays here a complementary vision of the judgment, not a contradictory one. Beginning with the description of the throne and the judge sitting upon it, the simplest reading of the symbolism is that it is portraying God as the cosmic judge. While it is true that God has shared the prerogative of judgment with Jesus Christ, this does not mean that God is no longer involved. Even Paul's theology could speak of the Day of Judgment in terms of the *judgment seat of God* (Rom 14:10–12), and in another place he illustrates it as *the judgment seat of Christ* (2 Cor 5:10), and sometimes he *combines the two*: "on the day when, according to my gospel, God will judge the secrets of men through Christ Jesus." (Rom 2:16). These are not separate days of judgment. They are one and the same, carried out by God and enacted in and through his agent, Jesus.[29] Believers would be presented "before our God and Father," that is, in God's presence, at the second coming of Christ (1 Thes 3:13).[30] The single Day of Judgment in John's vision also features an all-encompassing description of the resurrection. At no point is there any indication that only the unrighteous are being raised from their graves. On the contrary, the illustration is that the dead, "the great and the small" (Rev 20:12), refers to every person.[31] This is confirmed by an earlier statement in the Book of Revelation, occurring at the seventh trumpet and the consummation of the kingdom of God:

> Then the seventh angel sounded; and there were loud voices in heaven, saying, "The kingdom of the world has become the kingdom of our Lord and of His Christ; and He will reign forever and ever." . . . "And the nations were enraged, and Your wrath came, and the time came for the dead to be judged, and the time to reward Your bond-servants

---

[28] E.g., Matt 3:10–11; 13:40, 42, 50; 25:41; Luke 3:16–17; 1 Cor 3:13, 15.
[29] Sampley, "The Second Letter to the Corinthians," 87.
[30] Nickelsburg, *Resurrection, Immortality, and Eternal Life*, 307.
[31] Beasley-Murray, *Revelation*, 301; Morris, *Revelation*, 235; Smalley, *Revelation*, 515; Beale. *Revelation*, 1032.

the prophets and the saints and those who fear Your name, the small and the great, and to destroy those who destroy the earth." (Rev 11:15, 18)

This passage describes the consummation of the kingdom of God that takes place at the return of Jesus. All of the regular early Christian teachings concerning the second coming are present: the worldly kingdom becoming the kingdom of God, wrath upon the enemies, the judgment of the dead, the reward of the righteous, and the destruction of the wicked. We should not overlook the key detail that John of Patmos portrays all of these things occurring at a single, given time ("the time came"). There is no thousand-year gap between the rewarding of the righteous and the destruction of the wicked. The judgment of the dead, which self-evidently requires raising them from their graves, occurs at *a single climactic period in time*. Moreover, the phrase "the small and the great" is repeated in reverse in the scene of resurrection in Revelation 20:12, demonstrating that John is illustrating the same event, which occurs at the second coming.[32]

Identifying the resurrection at this great, white throne judgment as the general resurrection of the righteous and the unrighteous is strengthened with the vision's concluding reference to the book of life being consulted (Rev 20:15). Checking the book of life would be a pointless endeavor if the unrighteous were the only ones raised from the dead at this time. John of Patmos describes how the judge will consult this book in the judgment of every single person: "And if anyone's name was not found in the book of life, he was thrown in the lake of fire." The inclusion of this detail makes perfect sense when we see the resurrection of the dead as that which Jesus promised in John 5:28–29; *all in the tombs* will come forth, those who did good deeds to a resurrection unto life eternal, and those who committed evil to judgment.[33] Not only are the wicked cast into destruction, the second death, but even death and the grave are defeated on this Day of Judgment. This aligns with Paul's teaching that when the righteous are raised from the dead, death will then be swallowed up in victory (1 Cor 15:51–55).[34] With death and evil put to rest and the righteous vindicated in resurrection, God's victory has finally arrived, never to be thwarted or threatened again.

One final consideration is that which immediately follows Revelation chapter twenty, namely, the new heavens and the new earth (Rev 21:1). Both premillennialists and inaugurated millennialists agree that the new heavens and new earth are ushered in after the white throne judgment. If the return of Christ occurs at the time of the defeat of Satan and his armies with fire (Rev 20:9), then we possess an interpretation that is in continuity with what is presented in 2 Peter 3:4–13, a passage that describes the *parousia* of Christ (2 Pet 3:4) precisely as the Day of the Lord (2 Pet 3:10) that will be accompanied with the

---

[32] Beale. *Revelation*, 1033; Smalley, *Revelation*, 516; [32] Johnson, *Triumph of the Lamb*, 297.
[33] Keener, *The Gospel of John*, 1:654; observes, "he would one day demonstrate them by raising all from the dead."
[34] Johnson, *Triumph of the Lamb*, 292.

fires of judgment in the heavens and on the earth, resulting in God's promised "new heavens and a new earth" (2 Pet 3:13). In other words, the eschatology of Second Peter portrays the new heavens and new earth being established at Christ's second coming, not a thousand years after his *parousia*. In a further demonstration of continuity, the inaugurated millennial view of Revelation 20:1–21:1 arrives at the same conclusion as the events presented in 2 Peter 3:4–13.[35] There is no need to pit John of Patmos against the clear teachings of Second Peter.

Conclusion

To summarize, the inaugurated millennial reading of Revelation chapter twenty observes the two-stage kingdom in alignment with the theology of the Early Church. Christ brought the reign and rule of God near with his ministry, and his followers participate in this inaugurated kingdom in the present. The millennial period refers to the present reign of Christ, a reign shared with his followers. The description of coming to life at the beginning of the millennium most naturally fits with the frequent portrayal among the New Testament authors of conversion, that is, a dying to one's former manner of life and coming to new life in Christ. The reign of Jesus and his conquering followers in the present binds, disarms, and holds Satan's intent to exterminate the people of God at bay. At the end of the age, there will be one final rebellion, with Satan being allowed to deceive the nations, only to find that their insurrection will be met with the fires of destruction that accompany the Lamb's second coming. The Day of Judgment will commence, and all of the dead will be raised up from their graves. The righteous, having been recorded in the book of life, will inherit everlasting life and reign upon the earth, while the wicked will be annihilated in the second death. The faithful will rule as kings and priests with Christ upon the earth at his second coming, which ushers in the new heavens and the new earth.

Inaugurated millennialists value continuity with the Old Testament, with the teachings of Jesus, with Paul's theology, and especially with the truths already expressed in the narrative of the Book of Revelation. Instead of dividing the Day of Judgment into two different days, this view finds harmony with the Early Church's belief in a single time when all creation will be called to account. Instead of splitting the resurrection of the dead from the grave into two different bodily resurrections, inaugurated millennialism follows the lead of Jesus and Paul, who portray conversion as a coming to life, while also longing for the future bodily resurrection. Rather than interpreting the number one thousand rigidly, this view observes the tendency within the Book of Revelation to employ numbers symbolically. The two stages of the kingdom of God align with what Jesus taught: God's

---

[35] Johnson, *Triumph of the Lamb*, 303.

reign is already present, but is not yet fully realized. Moreover, this reading of the millennium avoids the problems of the premillennial interpretation, which is forced to conclude that rebellion, war, sin, and death continue to exist in the consummated kingdom of God, at least during the first thousand years. Unsurprisingly, there were a large number of early Christians holding views of the end times that are not premillennial.[36]

Our study of eschatology, which encompasses the end and final things, has provided several avenues for considering practical applications. Since every person, including those in the Early Church, will one day stand before the judge, that encounter should motivate how one lives in the present. In our final chapter of this attempt at systematizing the theology of early Christians, we will reflect on how one might apply the doctrines of eschatology.

---

[36] Hill, *Regnum Caelorum*, 75–201.

50
APPLYING ESCHATOLOGY TODAY

Eschatology is one of the most exciting doctrines embraced by the Early Church. Although there certainly is a heightened sense of excitement and hope when thinking about the kingdom of God and the second coming of Christ, there is also an overwhelming feeling of comfort, knowing that the Creator God will be shown to be faithful to his promises. The assurances that God made in his covenants with Abraham and David demonstrate his commitment to not only redeeming his creation, but also to using human beings as the means through whom he will bring about his kingdom on earth as it is in heaven. Yahweh's promises to Abraham included the assurance that humanity would once again *possess the land as their inheritance*, regaining the realm initially delegated to the image-bearing humans in Eden. The second commitment made to Abraham was that he would *bear many descendants*, himself becoming the father of many nations. This promise again echoes back to the first human beings in Genesis, who were instructed to be fruitful, multiply, and fill the earth, which would inevitably produce many image-bearing rulers of the land. Lastly, Yahweh reassured Abraham that it would be through his offspring that *all the families of the earth would be blessed*, thereby cancelling the curse that humanity's disobedience brought upon them. These three Abrahamic promises, covenanted by God to the famous patriarch, will finally be brought to fulfillment at the return of Jesus to consummate his kingdom upon the earth. At that time, the righteous will receive their inheritance over the renewed land; they will possess the capacity to be fruitful and multiply due to their immortality, and there will be no more curse leading to death. These Abrahamic promises are supplemented by the covenantal assurance that Yahweh made with King David, a descendant of Abraham in his own right. Yahweh first assured David that his royal son would build a house for his name. While this promise could point to the Davidic offspring constructing a temple for God, the ambiguity of the noun "house" also points to *a dynasty that would never come to an end*. The second covenantal promise refers to *the throne of David*, the kingly chair in Jerusalem from which his descendants would sit and rule as God's appointed monarchs. Finally, the third Davidic promise ensured that *the Davidic kingdom would last forever*. These closely entwined elements—David's house, throne, and kingdom—would be perpetually established by God himself. The return of Jesus, the immortalized son of David, ensures that God's promises will come to pass. Christ will never die again, ensuring that the dynasty and temple remain forever. His return will result in him sitting enthroned on the seat of David's kingdom, and his kingly rule will have no end. Let us, therefore, give Yahweh praise and glory for his promises. Let us worship this faithful God for his commitment to his covenants with Abraham and David. Finally, let us set our hope upon the triumphal second coming of Jesus, when all these promises will visibly come to pass.

Our second practical application, which is drawn from our larger study of Eschatology, emphasizes how to take these truths and apply them to everyday evangelism. Eschatology, as we have observed, is more than simply developing one's hope about the end of the age and the consummated kingdom of God. It also affects how we share the gospel message. Since the gospel that Jesus preached was the gospel of the kingdom of God, knowing as much as we can about the early Christian hope will only enhance our evangelism. When sharing the message of the kingdom with others, it is helpful to highlight the most exciting features in order to heighten the interest of our listeners. For example, when Jesus returns to enact his rule on earth, there will be worldwide peace that will never come to an end. The prophet Micah prophesied that the nations would hammer their swords into plowshares and their spears into pruning hooks (Mic 4:3). "Nation will not lift up sword against nation, and never again will they train for war," Micah explains. This is good and exciting news, as wars, battles, and fighting continue to occur in our modern times. Jesus will put an end to all hostilities, and there will finally be peace and tranquility when he sits as king over his kingdom. Another promise that will come to pass when Christ returns to consummate the kingdom of God is the defeat of death and all dying. Jesus is presently sitting at the right hand of Yahweh until his enemies are placed under his feet (Ps 110:1). Paul tells us that the last enemy to be abolished is death (1 Cor 15:26), and that death will be swallowed up in victory at the time of the resurrection, that is, when Christ returns (1 Cor 15:52–54). Death, which was part of the curse laid upon sinful humanity in the Garden of Eden, will be eliminated entirely in God's kingdom. As a corollary to the absence of dying in the new creation, the pain, sorrow, and tears shed over those who have been killed will no longer take place. God's people will never again experience the pain caused by tragic and unexpected deaths. In fact, God promises that he will wipe away every tear as he eliminates all mourning, crying, and pain (Rev 21:4). Finally, the return of Jesus will usher in an everlasting era in which no one will be in need of food. Famine, hunger, and malnutrition will be things of the past. Isaiah foresees a time of feasting (Isa 25:6) and Ezekiel describes this coming age as having eliminated all hunger (Ezek 34:29). These truths (never-ending peace, no more death, and the complete end of famine) thoroughly demonstrate the love of God for his people, and they provide the followers of Christ plenty to share with others as they announce the gospel of the kingdom of God. Let us, therefore, draw motivation from these promises as we seek first the kingdom of God and all the great things that will take place within it. Let us not shy away from telling others all that God has in store for his new creation that will be ushered in at the return of Jesus Christ to rule as Messiah on the earth. Let us also seek to build one another up with these powerful truths, especially when we suffer because of war, the death of relatives and friends, or hunger. God's promises are true. They are powerful, and they can keep our eyes on the horizon as we long for the time when everything wrong with this world will be made right. The kingdom of God will fix all of this world's problems, and that is worth celebrating and sharing with others.

In our third and final practical application from our study of Eschatology, I want to focus on the urgent and important need to press on and strive to enter the kingdom of God. Throughout the many missionary journeys of the Apostle Paul, we witnessed his preaching of the kingdom of God to his churches (e.g., Acts 19:8; 20:24–25). His announcement of the kingdom of God continued even during his Roman imprisonment (Acts 28:23, 30–31). What we should not overlook is that Paul spoke about the kingdom both as the content of the saving gospel message and as a motivation for continued faithfulness. In Acts 14:22, we encounter Paul and Barnabas encouraging several churches to continue in the faith, offering the motivating exhortation, "Through many tribulations we must enter the kingdom of God." Believing in the truths of the Early Church is certainly not going to make you popular in this present evil age. Consider how some of the biggest names were treated in the first century. John the Baptist was beheaded, Jesus was crucified, Stephen was stoned to death, and James was killed with the sword. Paul and his traveling companions were regularly imprisoned. For those in the twenty-first century who speak forth and take a stand for the truths that Jesus taught, the persecutions continue in a variety of forms. In some countries, Christians are regularly martyred. In more tolerable nations, the opposition to those who teach the doctrines of the Early Church is more subtle: unenrollment from educational institutions, deplatforming, being labeled a heretic, and even losing one's job. The irony of these forms of persecution is the same today as it was for the early Christians—those enacting the mistreatment would consider themselves religiously conservative. Yet despite all of these forms of harassment and abuse, which are often intended to pressure believers to give up their truths or remain silent, Paul and Barnabas insisted that one must endure to the end. The Christian must continue in the faith. The follower of Jesus must remain committed in order to reach the finish line, which is entrance into the kingdom of God. Despite the consequences in this age, those who embrace the teachings of Jesus cannot give up, cannot recant, and cannot be intimidated into silencing their faithful testimony. We must enter the kingdom of God, *no matter what the world throws at us*. The writers of the New Testament never said it would be easy. They never said that believers will enjoy a life of peace and tranquility upon deciding to follow Christ and become his disciple. We must enter the kingdom of God, despite all the tribulations, persecutions, harassment, slander, and hardships. Let us, therefore, embrace the promises of God that will come to fruition at the return of Jesus to consummate his kingdom upon the earth, using those future promises as motivation to press on and stand firm in our faith. Let us make the commitment to resolutely continue in the faith, maintaining faithfulness in good times and in bad times. Let us also follow the example of Paul and Barnabas, who sought to encourage others to stay the course and weather the storms. Let us pray for the courage to speak, boldness to act, endurance to continue without giving up, and even forgiveness for those who persecute us. In the end, we will find entrance into the kingdom of God, together. In the end, remaining faithful to Jesus will prove itself to be worth the goal: *the life of the age to come.*

Bibliography

Achtemeier, Paul J. *1 Peter: A Commentary.* Hermeneia. Fortress Press, 1996.
Allen, Leslie C. *Ezekiel 20–48.* Word Biblical Commentary. Word Books, 1990.
Allen, Leslie C. "The First and Second Books of Chronicles." In *The New Interpreter's Bible.* 12 vols. Abingdon, 1994–2002.
Allen, Leslie C. *Jeremiah: A Commentary.* Old Testament Library. Westminster John Knox Press, 2008.
Allison, Dale C. Jr. *A Critical and Exegetical Commentary on the Epistle of James.* International Critical Commentary. T & T Clark, 2013.
Allison, Dale C. Jr. *The New Moses: A Matthean Typology.* Fortress Press, 1993.
Alter, Robert. *The Hebrew Bible: A Translation with Commentary.* 3 vols. W. W. Norton & Company, 2019.
Anderson, A. A. *2 Samuel.* Word Biblical Commentary. Word Books, 1989.
Anderson, Bernhard W. *Contours of Old Testament Theology.* Augsburg Fortress Press, 1999.
Anderson, Paul N. "The Having-Sent-Me Father: Aspects of Agency, Encounter, and Irony in the Johannine Father-Son Relationship." *Semeia* 85 (1999): 33–57.
Arnold, Bill T. *Genesis.* New Cambridge Bible Commentary. Cambridge University Press, 2009.
Arnold, Clinton E. *Colossians.* 2nd ed. Word Biblical Commentary. Zondervan Academic, 2025.
Attridge, Harold W. *The Epistle to the Hebrews: A Commentary on the Epistle to the Hebrews.* Hermeneia. Fortress Press, 1989.
Auld, A. Graeme, *1 & II Samuel: A Commentary.* Old Testament Library. Westminster John Knox Press, 2012.
Aune, David E. "Eschatology (Early Christian)." In *Anchor Bible Dictionary*, edited by David Noel Freedman. 6 vols. Doubleday, 1992.
Aune, David E. *Revelation 1–5.* Word Biblical Commentary. Thomas Nelson, 1997.
Aune, David E. *Revelation 6–16.* Word Biblical Commentary. Thomas Nelson, 1998.
Aune, David E. *Revelation 17–22.* Word Biblical Commentary. Thomas Nelson, 1998.
Aune, David E. "Worship, Early Christian." In *Anchor Bible Dictionary*, edited by David Noel Freedman. 6 vols. Doubleday, 1992.
Bacchiocchi, Samuele. *Immortality or Resurrection? A Biblical Study on Human Nature and Destiny.* Remnant Publications, 1998.
Baker, David W. "God, Names of." In *Dictionary of the Old Testament Pentateuch*, edited by T. Desmond Alexander and David W. Baker. IVP Academic, 2003.
Balentine, Samuel E. *Job.* Smyth & Helwys Bible Commentary. Smyth & Helwys, 2006.
Baloian, Bruce. "קצף." In *The New International Dictionary of Old Testament Theology & Exegesis*, edited by Willem A. VanGemeren. 5 vols. Zondervan, 1997.
Barker, Margaret. "The High Priest and the Worship of Jesus." In *The Jewish Roots of Christological Monotheism: Papers from the St. Andrews Conference on the Historical Origins of the Worship of Jesus.* Library of Early Christology. Baylor University Press, 1998.
Barlow, Will. "The Throne Room Problem: Responding to Trinitarian Claims about John 12:41." Presentation at the Unitarian Christian Alliance Conference, Little Rock, AR, October 19, 2024.
Barnett, Paul. *The Second Epistle to the Corinthians.* New International Commentary on the New Testament. Eerdmans, 1997.
Barrett, C. K. *A Commentary on the First Epistle to the Corinthians.* 2nd ed. Black's New Testament Commentaries. A & C Black, 1979.
Barrett, C. K. *Acts 1–14: A Critical and Exegetical Commentary.* International Critical Commentary. T & T Clark. 2006.
Barrett, C. K. "'The Father Is Greater than I' John 14:28: Subordinationist Christology in the New Testament." In *Essays on John*, 19–36. Westminster, 1982.
Barrett, C. K. *The Gospel According to St. John: An Introduction with Commentary and Notes on the Greek Text.* 2nd ed. Westminster Press, 1978.
Barrett, C. K. *The Second Epistle to the Corinthians.* Harper's New Testament Commentaries. Harper & Row, 1973.
Barth, Marcus, and Helmut Blanke. *Colossians: A New Translation with Introduction and Commentary.* Translated by Astrid B. Beck. Anchor Bible. Doubleday, 1994.
Bartlett, David L. "The First Letter of Peter." In *The New Interpreter's Bible.* 12 vols. Abingdon, 1994–2002.
Barton, S. C. "Family." In *Dictionary of Jesus and the Gospels*, edited by Joel B. Green and Scot McKnight. IVP Academic, 1992.

Bassler, Jouette M. *1 Timothy, 2 Timothy, Titus*. Abingdon New Testament Commentaries. Abingdon, 1996.
Bassler, Jouette M. "God (NT)." In *Anchor Bible Dictionary*, edited by David Noel Freedman. 6 vols. Doubleday, 1992.
Bauckham, Richard. *The Climax of Prophecy: Studies on the Book of Revelation*. T & T Clark, 1998.
Bauckham, Richard. "Hades, Hell." In *Anchor Bible Dictionary*, edited by David Noel Freedman. 6 vols. Doubleday, 1992.
Bauckham, Richard. *Jesus and the God of Israel: God Crucified and Other Studies on the New Testament Christology of Divine Identity*. Eerdmans, 2008.
Bauckham, Richard. *Jude, 2 Peter*. Word Biblical Commentary. Word Books, 1983.
Bauckham, Richard. "Life, Death, and the Afterlife in Second Temple Judaism." In *Life in the Face of Death*, edited by Richard N. Longenecker, 80–95. Eerdmans, 1998.
Bauckham, Richard. *The Theology of the Book of Revelation*. New Testament Theology. Cambridge University Press, 1993.
Bauer, David R. "Son of God." In *Dictionary of Jesus and the Gospels*, edited by Joel B. Green and Scot McKnight. IVP Academic, 1992.
Bauer, Walter, Frederick W. Danker, W. F. Arndt, and F. W. Gingrich. *A Greek-English Lexicon of the New Testament and Other Early Christian Literature*. 3rd ed. University of Chicago Press, 2000.
Beale, Gregory K. *The Book of Revelation*. New International Greek Testament Commentary. Eerdmans, 1999.
Beale, Gregory K. *A New Testament Biblical Theology: The Unfolding of the Old Testament in the New*. Baker Academic, 2011.
Beale, Gregory K. *The Temple and the Church's Mission: A Biblical Theology of the Dwelling Place of God*. New Studies in Biblical Theology 17. InterVarsity Press, 2004.
Beale, Gregory K., and Mitchell Kim. *God Dwells Among Us: A Biblical Theology of the Temple*. IVP Academic, 2014.
Beasley-Murray, G. R. *Baptism in the New Testament*. Eerdmans, 1994.
Beasley-Murray, G. R. *Jesus and the Kingdom of God*. Eerdmans, 1987.
Beasley-Murray, G. R. *John*. 2nd ed. Word Biblical Commentary. Thomas Nelson Publishers, 1999.
Beasley-Murray, G. R. *Revelation*. New Century Bible Commentary. Eerdmans, 1983.
Becking, Bob. *Micah: A New Translation with Introduction and Commentary*. Anchor Bible. Yale University Press, 2023.
Beckman, John C. "Pluralis Majestatis: Biblical Hebrew." In *Encyclopedia of Hebrew Language and Linguistics*, edited by Geoffrey Khan. Brill, 2013.
Ben Zvi, Ehud. *Micah*. The Forms of the Old Testament Literature, volume XXIB. Eerdmans, 2000.
Bernard, John. H. *A Critical and Exegetical Commentary on the Gospel according to St. John*. 2 vols. International Critical Commentary. T & T Clark, 1928.
Berkhof, Louis. *Systematic Theology*. Eerdmans, 1949.
Best, Ernest. *Ephesians: A Critical and Exegetical Commentary*. International Critical Commentary. T & T Clark, 2004.
Best, Ernest. *The First and Second Epistles to the Thessalonians*. Black's New Testament Commentaries. Hendrickson, 1986.
Betz, Hans Dieter. *Galatians*. Hermeneia. Fortress Press, 1979.
Beuken, W. "כבש‎." In *Theological Dictionary of the Old Testament*, edited by G. Johannes Botterweck, Helmer Ringgren, and Heinz-Joseph Fabry. 15 vols. Eerdmans, 1974–2006.
Biddle, Mark E. "Flesh in the OT." In *The New Interpreter's Dictionary of the Bible*, edited by K. D. Sakenfeld. 5 vols. Abingdon, 2006–9.
Birch, Bruce C. "The First and Second Books of Samuel." In *The New Interpreter's Bible*. 12 vols. Abingdon, 1994–2002.
Black, David Alan. *Learn to Read New Testament Greek*. 3rd ed. B&H Academic, 2009.
Blaising, Craig A., Kenneth L. Gentry Jr., and Robert B. Strimple. *Three Views of the Millennium and Beyond*, edited by Darrell L. Bock. Counterpoints. Zondervan Publishing House, 1999.
Blenkinsopp, Joseph. *Isaiah 1–39: A New Translation with Introduction and Commentary*. Anchor Bible. Doubleday, 2000.
Blenkinsopp, Joseph. *Isaiah 40–55: A New Translation with Introduction and Commentary*. Anchor Bible. Doubleday, 2002.
Blenkinsopp, Joseph. *Isaiah 56–66: A New Translation with Introduction and Commentary*. Anchor Bible. Doubleday, 2003.
Block, Daniel I. *The Book of Ezekiel: Chapters 1–24*. New International Commentary on the Old Testament. Eerdmans, 1997.
Block, Daniel I. *The Book of Ezekiel: Chapters 25–48*. New International Commentary on the Old Testament. Eerdmans, 1998.
Blomberg, Craig L. and Miriam J. Kamell. *James*. Zondervan Exegetical Commentary on the New Testament. Zondervan, 2008.
Blount, Brian K. *Revelation: A Commentary*. New Testament Library. Westminster John Knox Press, 2009.
Boadt, Lawrence. *Reading the Old Testament: An Introduction*. Paulist Press, 1984.
Bockmuehl, Markus. *The Epistle to the Philippians*. 4th ed. Black's New Testament Commentaries. A & C Black, 1997.

Borgen, Peder. *Bread from Heaven: An Exegetical Study of the Concept of Manna in the Gospel of John and in the Writings of Philo*. Johannine Monograph Series 4. Wipf & Stock, 2017.

Borgen, Peder. "God's Agent in the Fourth Gospel." In *Religions in Antiquity: Festschrift E. Goodenough*, edited by Jacob Neusner. Brill, 1968.

Boring, M. Eugene. *1 Peter*. Abingdon New Testament Commentaries. Abingdon, 1999.

Boring, M. Eugene. "Gospel, Message." In *The New Interpreter's Dictionary of the Bible*, edited by K. D. Sakenfeld. 5 vols. Abingdon, 2006–9.

Boring, M. Eugene. "The Gospel of Matthew." In *The New Interpreter's Bible*. 12 vols. Abingdon, 1994–2002.

Boring, M. Eugene. *Mark: A Commentary*. New Testament Library. Westminster John Knox Press, 2006.

Boring, M. Eugene. *I & II Thessalonians: A Commentary*. New Testament Library. Westminster John Knox Press, 2018.

Boring, M. Eugene. "Numbers, Numbering." In *The New Interpreter's Dictionary of the Bible*, edited by K. D. Sakenfeld. 5 vols. Abingdon, 2006–9.

Boring, M. Eugene. *Revelation*. Interpretation: A Bible Commentary for Teaching and Preaching. John Knox Press, 1989.

Bovon, François. *Luke 2: A Commentary on the Gospel of Luke 9:51–19:27*. Translated by Donald S. Deer. Hermeneia. Fortress Press, 2013.

Bovon, François. *Luke 3: A Commentary on the Gospel of Luke 19:28–24:53*. Translated by James Crouch. Hermeneia. Fortress Press, 2012.

Bowles, Ralph G. "Does Revelation 14:11 Teach Eternal Torment? Examining a Proof-text on Hell." *Evangelical Quarterly* 73, no. 1 (2001): 21–36.

Boxall, Ian. *The Revelation of Saint John*. Black's New Testament Commentary. Hendrickson, 2009.

Boyarin, Daniel. *Border Lines: The Partition of Judaeo-Christianity*. University of Pennsylvania Press, 2004.

Boyd, Gregory A. *God of the Possible: A Biblical Introduction to the Open View of God*. Baker, 2000.

Brant, Jo-Ann A. *John*. Paideia Commentaries. Baker Academic, 2011.

Braun, Roddy. *1 Chronicles*. Word Biblical Commentary. Word Books, 1986.

Bridges, Linda McKinnish. *1 & 2 Thessalonians*. Smyth & Helwys Bible Commentary. Smyth & Helwys, 2008.

Bright, John. *The Authority of the Old Testament*. Grand Rapids: Baker Book House, 1981.

Brown, Colin. "Resurrection." In *The New International Dictionary of New Testament Theology*, edited by Colin Brown. 4 vols. Zondervan, 1986.

Brown, Raymond E. *The Birth of the Messiah: A Commentary on the Infancy Narratives in Matthew and Luke*. Doubleday, 1977.

Brown, Raymond E. *The Death of the Messiah: From Gethsemane to the Grave: A Commentary on the Passion Narratives in the Four Gospels*. 2 vols. Doubleday, 1994.

Brown, Raymond E. *The Epistles of John: A New Translation with Introduction and Commentary*. Anchor Bible. Doubleday, 1982.

Brown, Raymond E. *The Gospel According to John I–XII: A New Translation with Introduction and Commentary*. Anchor Bible. Doubleday, 1979.

Brown, Raymond E. *The Gospel According to John XIII–XXI: A New Translation with Introduction and Commentary*. Anchor Bible. Doubleday, 1979.

Brown, William P. *Ecclesiastes*. Interpretation: A Bible Commentary for Teaching and Preaching. John Knox Press, 2000.

Brown, William P. *The Ethos of the Cosmos: The Genesis of Moral Imagination in the Bible*. Eerdmans, 1999.

Brown, William P. *Obadiah through Malachi*. Westminster Bible Companion. Westminster John Knox Press, 1996.

Broyles, C. C. "Moses." In *Dictionary of Jesus and the Gospels*, edited by Joel B. Green and Scot McKnight. IVP Academic, 1992.

Bruce, F. F. *The Epistle to the Galatians*. New International Greek Testament Commentary. Eerdmans, 1982.

Bruce, F. F. *The Epistle to the Hebrews*. New International Commentary on the New Testament. Eerdmans, 1972.

Bruce, F. F. *The Gospel and Epistles of John*. Eerdmans, 1983.

Bruce, F. F. *Paul: The Apostle of the Heart Set Free*. Eerdmans, 1977.

Brueggemann, Walter. "The Book of Exodus." In *The New Interpreter's Bible*. 12 vols. Abingdon, 1994–2002.

Brueggemann, Walter. *Deuteronomy*. Abingdon Old Testament Commentaries. Abingdon, 2001.

Brueggemann, Walter. *Genesis*. Interpretation: A Bible Commentary for Teaching and Preaching. John Knox Press, 1982.

Brueggemann, Walter. *An Introduction to the Old Testament: The Canon and Christian Imagination*. Westminster John Knox Press, 2003.

Brueggemann, Walter. *Isaiah 1–39*. Westminster Bible Companion. Westminster John Knox Press, 1998.

Brueggemann, Walter. *The Message of the Psalms: A Theological Commentary*. Augsburg, 1984.
Brueggemann, Walter. *Old Testament Theology: An Introduction*. Library of Biblical Theology. Abingdon, 2008.
Brueggemann, Walter. *Theology of the Old Testament: Testimony, Dispute, Advocacy*. Fortress Press, 1997.
Brueggemann, Walter, and Tod Linafelt. *An Introduction to the Old Testament: The Canon and Christian Imagination*. 2nd ed. Westminster John Knox Press, 2012.
Bultmann, Rudolf. "θάνατος κτλ." In *Theological Dictionary of the New Testament*, edited by G. Bromiley. 10 vols. Eerdmans, 1964–74.
Bultmann, Rudolf, and Artur Weiser. "πιστεύω κτλ." In *Theological Dictionary of the New Testament*, edited by G. Bromiley. 10 vols. Eerdmans, 1964–74.
Buswell Jr., James Oliver. *A Systematic Theology of the Christian Religion*. Zondervan, 1962.
Caird, George B. *Paul's Letters from Prison*. Oxford University Press, 1991.
Caird, George B. *The Revelation of St. John the Divine*. Harper's New Testament Commentaries. Harper and Row Publishers, 1966.
Campbell, Anthony F. *2 Samuel*. The Forms of the Old Testament Literature, volume VIII. Eerdmans, 2005.
Campbell, William S. "Covenant and New Covenant." In *Dictionary of Paul and His Letters*, edited by Gerald F. Hawthorne, Ralph P. Martin, and Daniel G. Reid. IVP Academic, 1993.
Capes, David B. "Preexistence." In *Dictionary of the Later New Testament & Its Developments*, edited by Ralph P. Martin and Peter H. Davids. InterVarsity Press, 1997.
Caragounis, J. A. "בן." In *The New International Dictionary of Old Testament Theology & Exegesis*, edited by Willem A. VanGemeren. 5 vols. Zondervan, 1997.
Carroll, Robert P. *Jeremiah: A Commentary*. Old Testament Library. Westminster Press, 1986.
Carson, D. A. *The Gospel According to John*. Pillar New Testament Commentary. Eerdmans, 1991.
Carter, Warren. *John and Empire: Initial Explorations*. T & T Clark, 2008.
Carter, Warren. *John: Storyteller, Interpreter, Evangelist*. Hendrickson Publishers, 2006.
Carter, Warren. *Mark*. Wisdom Commentary. Liturgical Press, 2019.
Carter, Warren. *Matthew: Storyteller, Interpreter, Evangelist*. Rev ed. Hendrickson Publishers, 2008.
Carter, Warren. *What Does Revelation Reveal? Unlocking the Mystery*. Abingdon, 2011.
Cartledge, Tony W. *1 & 2 Samuel*. Smyth & Helwys Bible Commentary. Smyth & Helwys, 2001.
Casurella, Anthony. "Grace." In *Dictionary of the Later New Testament & Its Developments*, edited by Ralph P. Martin and Peter H. Davids. InterVarsity Press, 1997.
Cavallin, Hans Clemens Caesarius. *Life After Death: Paul's Argument for the Resurrection of the Dead in I Cor 15, Part I, An Enquiry into the Jewish Background*. CWK Gleerup, 1974.
Charles, R. H. *The Revelation of St. John: A Critical and Exegetical Commentary*. 2 vols. International Critical Commentary. T & T Clark, 1994.
Charlesworth, James H. "Lady Wisdom and Johannine Christology." In *Light in a Spotless Mirror: Reflections on Wisdom Traditions in Judaism and Early Christianity*, edited by James H. Charlesworth and Michael A. Daise, 92–133. Trinity, 2003.
Childs, Brevard S. *The Book of Exodus: A Critical, Theological Commentary*. Westminster Press, 1976.
Chilton, Bruce. *Pure Kingdom: Jesus' Vision of God*. Studying the Historical Jesus. Eerdmans, 1996.
Christensen, Duane L. *Deuteronomy 1:1–21:9*. 2nd ed. Word Biblical Commentary. Thomas Nelson Publishers, 2001.
Christensen, Duane L. *Deuteronomy 21:10–34:12*. Word Biblical Commentary. Thomas Nelson Publishers, 2002.
Ciampa, Roy E., and Brian S. Rosner. *The First Letter to the Corinthians*. Pillar New Testament Commentary. Eerdmans, 2010.
Clements, Ronald E. "The Book of Deuteronomy." In *The New Interpreter's Bible*. 12 vols. Abingdon, 1994–2002.
Clines, David J. A. *Job 1–20*. Word Biblical Commentary. Word Books, 1989.
Clines, David J. A. *Job 21–37*. Word Biblical Commentary. Word Books, 2006.
Cohick, Lynn H. *The Letter to the Ephesians*. New International Commentary on the New Testament. Eerdmans, 2020.
Coloe, Mary L. *John 1–10*. Wisdom Commentary. Liturgical Press, 2021.
Coloe, Mary L. *John 11–21*. Wisdom Commentary. Liturgical Press, 2021.
Collins, Adela Yarbro. "Son of Man." In *The New Interpreter's Dictionary of the Bible*, edited by K. D. Sakenfeld. 5 vols. Abingdon, 2006–9.
Collins, Adela Yarbro, and John J. Collins, *King and Messiah as Son of God: Divine, Human, and Angelic Messianic Figures in Biblical and Related Literature*. Eerdmans, 2008.

Collins, Clifford J. "שׁלֹח." In *The New International Dictionary of Old Testament Theology & Exegesis*, edited by Willem A. VanGemeren. 5 vols. Zondervan, 1997.

Collins, John J. *The Apocalyptic Imagination: An Introduction to Jewish Apocalyptic Literature*. 3rd ed. Eerdmans, 2016.

Collins, John J. *Daniel*. Hermeneia. Augsburg Fortress Press, 1993.

Collins, Raymond F. *I & II Timothy and Titus: A Commentary*. New Testament Library. Westminster John Knox Press, 2002.

Collins, Raymond F. *Second Corinthians*. Paideia Commentaries. Baker Academic, 2013.

Collins, Raymond F. "Servant of the Lord, The," In *The New Interpreter's Dictionary of the Bible*, edited by K. D. Sakenfeld. 5 vols. Abingdon, 2006–9.

Conzelmann, Hans. *1 Corinthians: A Commentary on the First Epistle to the Corinthians*. Translated by James W. Leitch. Hermeneia. Fortress Press, 1975.

Conzelmann, Hans. *The Theology of St. Luke*. Translated by Geoffrey Buswell. Fortress Press, 1982.

Cotter, David W. *Genesis*. Berit Olam: Studies in Hebrew Narrative & Poetry. Liturgical Press, 2003.

Craddock, Fred B. "The Letter to the Hebrews." In *The New Interpreter's Bible*. 12 vols. Abingdon, 1994–2002.

Craddock, Fred B. *The Pre-existence of Christ in the New Testament*. Abingdon, 1968.

Craigie, Peter C. *Psalms 1–50*. Word Biblical Commentary. Word Books, 1983.

Craigie, Peter C. Page H. Kelley, and Joel F. Drinkard, Jr. *Jeremiah 1–25*. Word Biblical Commentary. Word Books, 1991.

Crenshaw, James L. *Ecclesiastes: A Commentary*. Old Testament Library. Westminster Press, 1987.

Cullmann, Oscar. *Baptism in the New Testament*. The Westminster Press, 1950.

Cullmann, Oscar. *Immortality of the Soul or Resurrection of the Dead? The Writings of the New Testament*. Macmillan, 1964.

Culpepper, R. Alan. *The Gospel and Letters of John*. Interpreting Biblical Texts. Abingdon, 1998.

Culpepper, R. Alan. "The Gospel of Luke." In *The New Interpreter's Bible*. 12 vols. Abingdon, 1994–2002.

Culpepper, R. Alan. *Matthew: A Commentary*. New Testament Library. Westminster John Knox Press, 2021.

Curtis, Edward M. "Image of God (OT)." In *Anchor Bible Dictionary*, edited by David Noel Freedman. 6 vols. Doubleday, 1992.

Darr, Katheryn Pfisterer. "The Book of Ezekiel." In *The New Interpreter's Bible*. 12 vols. Abingdon, 1994–2002.

Davies, G. I. *Exodus 1–18: A Critical and Exegetical Commentary*. International Critical Commentary. 2 vols. T & T Clark, 2020.

Davies, W. D., and Dale C. Allison. *The Gospel According to Saint Matthew*. International Critical Commentary. 3 vols. T & T Clark, 1991–1997.

Davids, Peter H. *The Epistle to James*. New International Greek Testament Commentary. Eerdmans, 1982.

Davidson, Maxwell John. "Angel." In *The New Interpreter's Dictionary of the Bible*, edited by K. D. Sakenfeld. 5 vols. Abingdon, 2006–9.

De Boer, Martinus C. *Galatians: A Commentary*. New Testament Library. Westminster John Knox Press, 2011.

De La Torre, Miquel A., and Albert Hernández. *The Quest for the Historical Satan*. Fortress Press, 2011.

Dearman, J. Andrew. *The Book of Hosea*. New International Commentary on the Old Testament. Eerdmans, 2010.

deClaissé-Walford, Nancy, Rolf A. Jacobson, and Beth LaNeel Tanner. *The Book of Psalms*. New International Commentary on the Old Testament. Eerdmans, 2014.

Dembitz, Lewis N. "Agency, Law of." In *The Jewish Encyclopedia*, edited by Isidore Singer et al. 12 vols. Funk and Wagnalls, 1901–6.

deSilva, David A. *The Letter to the Galatians*. New International Commentary on the New Testament. Eerdmans, 2018.

deSilva, David A. *Perseverance in Gratitude: A Socio-Rhetorical Commentary on the Epistle "to the Hebrews."* Eerdmans, 2000.

Deutsch, Celia M. *Lady Wisdom, Jesus, and the Sages: Metaphor and Social Context in Matthew's Gospel*. Trinity Press, 1996.

Deutsch, Celia M. *Hidden Wisdom and the Easy Yoke: Wisdom, Torah and Discipleship in Matthew 11.25-30*. JSOT Press, 1987.

Di Vito, Robert A. "Anthropology, OT Theological." In *The New Interpreter's Dictionary of the Bible*, edited by K. D. Sakenfeld. 5 vols. Abingdon, 2006–9.

Di Vito, Robert A. "Old Testament Anthropology and the Construction of Personal Identity." *The Catholic Biblical Quarterly* 61, no. 2 (1999): 217–238.

Dibelius, Martin, and Hans Conzelmann. *The Pastoral Epistles: A Commentary*. Translated by Philip Buttolph and Adela Yarbro. Hermeneia. Fortress Press, 1972.

Dodd, Brian J. "Millennium." In *Dictionary of the Later New Testament & Its Developments*, edited by Ralph P. Martin and Peter H. Davids. InterVarsity Press, 1997.

Dodd, C. H. *The Parables of the Kingdom*. Rev ed. Charles Scribner's Sons. 1961.

Donaldson, L. Terrence. "Son of God." In *The New Interpreter's Dictionary of the Bible*, edited by K. D. Sakenfeld. 5 vols. Abingdon, 2006–9.

Donelson, Lewis R. *I & II Peter and Jude: A Commentary*. New Testament Library. Westminster John Knox Press, 2010.

Dozeman, Thomas B. "The Book of Numbers." In *The New Interpreter's Bible*. 12 vols. Abingdon, 1994–2002.

Dozeman, Thomas B. *Exodus*. Eerdmans Critical Commentary. Eerdmans, 2009.

Duke, Rodney K. "Priests, Priesthood." In *Dictionary of the Old Testament Pentateuch*, edited by T. Desmond Alexander and David W. Baker. IVP Academic, 2003.

Dunn, James D. G. *The Acts of the Apostles*. Epworth Commentary. Epworth Press, 1986.

Dunn, James D. G. *Baptism in the Holy Spirit*. Studies in Biblical Theology: Second Series 15. SCM Press, 1974.

Dunn, James D. G. *Beginning from Jerusalem*. Christianity in the Making. Vol 2. Eerdmans, 2009.

Dunn, James D. G. *Christology in the Making: A New Testament Inquiry into the Origins of the Doctrine of the Incarnation*. 2nd ed. Eerdmans, 1989.

Dunn, James D. G. *Did the First Christians Worship Jesus? The New Testament Evidence*. Westminster John Knox Press, 2010.

Dunn, James D. G. *The Epistle to the Galatians*. Black's New Testament Commentary. Hendrickson Publishers, 1993.

Dunn, James D. G. *The Epistles to the Colossians and to Philemon*. The New International Greek Testament Commentary. Eerdmans, 1996.

Dunn, James D. G. "The First and Second Letters to Timothy." In *The New Interpreter's Bible*. 12 vols. Abingdon, 1994–2002.

Dunn, James D. G. "Galatians." In *A Biblical Theology of the Holy Spirit*, edited by Trevor J. Burke and Keith Warrington, 175–86. Cascade Books, 2014.

Dunn, James D. G. *Jesus and the Spirit: A Study of the Religious and Charismatic Experience of Jesus and the First Christians as Reflected in the New Testament*. SCM Press, 1975.

Dunn, James D. G. *Jesus, Paul, and the Law: Studies in Mark and Galatians*. Westminster John Knox Press, 1990.

Dunn, James D. G. *Jesus Remembered*. Christianity in the Making. Vol 1. Eerdmans, 2003.

Dunn, James D. G. "Let John Be John." In *Das Evangelium und die Evangelien*, edited by Peter Stuhlmacher, 309–39. Mohr-Siebeck, 1983.

Dunn, James D. G. *The New Perspective on Paul*. Rev ed. Eerdmans, 2008.

Dunn, James D. G. *New Testament Theology: An Introduction*. Library of Biblical Theology. Abingdon, 2009.

Dunn, James D. G. *Romans 1–8*. Word Biblical Commentary. Thomas Nelson, 1988.

Dunn, James D. G. "Spirit." In *The New International Dictionary of New Testament Theology*, edited by Colin Brown. 4 vols. Zondervan, 1986.

Dunn, James D. G. *The Theology of Paul the Apostle*. Eerdmans, 1998.

Dunn, James D. G. *Unity and Diversity in the New Testament: An Inquiry into the Character of Early Christianity*. 3rd ed. SCM Press, 2006.

Durham, John I. *Exodus*. Word Biblical Commentary. Thomas Nelson Publishers, 1987.

Dyrness, William A. *Themes in Old Testament Theology*. IVP Academic, 1977.

Eichler, Johannes. "Inheritance." In *The New International Dictionary of New Testament Theology*, edited by Colin Brown. 4 vols. Zondervan, 1986.

Eichrodt, Walther. Eichrodt, *Theology of the Old Testament*. 2 vols. Translated by J. A. Baker. Old Testament Library. Westminster Press, 1961–7.

Ellingworth, Paul. *The Epistle to the Hebrews*. New International Greek Testament Commentary. Eerdmans, 1993.

Elliott, John H. *1 Peter: A New Translation with Introduction and Commentary*. Anchor Bible. Yale University Press, 2000.

Epiphanius of Salamis. *The Panarion of Epiphanius of Salamis: Book 1 (Sects 1–46)*. 2nd ed. Translated by Frank Williams. Nag Hammadi & Manichaean Studies 63. Brill, 2009.

Esser, H. "Grace." In *The New International Dictionary of New Testament Theology*, edited by Colin Brown. 4 vols. Zondervan, 1986.

Estes, Daniel J. *Handbook on the Wisdom Books and Psalms*. Baker Academic, 2005.

Evans, Craig A. *Mark 8:27–16:20*. Word Biblical Commentary. Thomas Nelson, 2001.

Fee, Gordon D. *The First Epistle to the Corinthians*. Rev ed. New International Commentary on the New Testament. Eerdmans, 2014.

Fee, Gordon D. *God's Empowering Presence: The Holy Spirit in the Letters of Paul*. Hendrickson Publishers, 2005.

Fee, Gordon D. *Revelation: A New Covenant Commentary*. New Covenant Commentary Series. Cascade Books, 2011.

Finnegan, Sean P. *Kingdom Journey: A Call to Recover the Central Theme of Scripture.* Wipf & Stock, 2023.

Fitzmyer, Joseph A. *First Corinthians: A New Translation with Introduction and Commentary.* Anchor Bible. Yale University Press, 2008.

Fitzmyer, Joseph A. *The Gospel According to Luke I–IX: Introduction, Translation, and Notes.* Anchor Bible. Doubleday, 1981.

Fitzmyer, Joseph A. *The Gospel According to Luke X–XXIV: A New Translation with Introduction and Commentary.* Anchor Bible. Yale University Press, 2005.

Fitzmyer, Joseph A. *Romans: A New Translation with Introduction and Commentary.* Anchor Bible. Doubleday, 1993.

Foerster, Werner. "δαίμων κτλ." In *Theological Dictionary of the New Testament*, edited by G. Bromiley. 10 vols. Eerdmans, 1964–74.

Firth, David G. "Messiah." In *Dictionary of the Old Testament Prophets*, edited by Mark J. Boda and J. Gordon McConville. IVP Academic, 2012.

Ford, J. Massyngbaerde. "Millennium." In *Anchor Bible Dictionary*, edited by David Noel Freedman. 6 vols. Doubleday, 1992.

Fox, Michael V. *Ecclesiastes.* JPS Commentary. Philadelphia, 2004.

Fox, Michael V. *Proverbs 1–9: A New Translation with Introduction and Commentary.* Anchor Bible. Yale University Press, 2000.

France, R. T. *The Gospel of Mark.* New International Greek Testament Commentary. Eerdmans, 2002.

France, R. T. *The Gospel of Matthew.* New International Commentary on the New Testament. Eerdmans, 2007.

Fredericks, Daniel C. "נֶפֶשׁ." In *The New International Dictionary of Old Testament Theology & Exegesis*, edited by Willem A. VanGemeren. 5 vols. Zondervan, 1997.

Fretheim, Terence E. "The Book of Genesis." In *The New Interpreter's Bible.* 12 vols. Abingdon, 1994–2002.

Fretheim, Terence E. "אֱלֹהִים." In *The New International Dictionary of Old Testament Theology & Exegesis*, edited by Willem A. VanGemeren. 5 vols. Zondervan, 1997.

Fretheim, Terence E. "God, OT View of," In *The New Interpreter's Dictionary of the Bible*, edited by K. D. Sakenfeld. 5 vols. Abingdon, 2006–9.

Fretheim, Terence E. "Image of God." In *The New Interpreter's Dictionary of the Bible*, edited by K. D. Sakenfeld. 5 vols. Abingdon, 2006–9.

Fudge, Edward William. *The Fire That Consumes: A Biblical and Historical Study of the Final Punishment.* Verdict Publications, 1982.

Fuller, Reginald H. "The Incarnation in Historical Perspective." *Anglican Theological Review*, Supplementary Series 7 (1976): 57–66.

Furnish, Victor Paul. *II Corinthians: A New Translation with Introduction and Commentary.* Anchor Bible. Yale University Press, 2005.

Garland, David E. *1 Corinthians.* Baker Exegetical Commentary on the New Testament. Baker Academic, 2003.

Gaston, Thomas E. "Does the Gospel of John Have a High Christology?" *Horizons in Biblical Theology* 36 (2014): 129–41.

Gaston, Thomas E. *Dynamic Monarchianism: The Earliest Christology?* 2nd ed. Theophilus, 2023.

Gaventa, Beverly Roberts. *Romans: A Commentary.* New Testament Library. Westminster John Knox Press, 2024.

Gerstenberger, Erhard S. *Leviticus: A Commentary.* Translated by Douglas W. Stott. Old Testament Library. Westminster John Knox Press, 1996.

Gerstenberger, Erhard S. *Theologies in the Old Testament.* Translated by John Bowden. Fortress Press, 2002.

Goldingay, John. *Biblical Theology: The God of the Christian Scriptures.* IVP Academic, 2016.

Goldingay, John. "Covenant, OT and NT." In *The New Interpreter's Dictionary of the Bible*, edited by K. D. Sakenfeld. 5 vols. Abingdon, 2006–9.

Goldingay, John. *Daniel.* Rev ed. Word Biblical Commentary. Word Books, 2019.

Goldingay, John. *Genesis for Everyone: Part One.* Westminster John Knox Press, 2010.

Goldingay, John. *Isaiah 56–66: A Critical and Exegetical Commentary.* International Critical Commentary. T & T Clark, 2025.

Goldingay, John. *Old Testament Theology.* 3 vols. IVP Academic, 2003–9.

Goldingay, John. *Psalms.* 3 vols. Baker Commentary on the Old Testament Wisdom and Psalms. Baker Academic, 2006–8.

Goldingay, John. "Servant of Yahweh." In *Dictionary of the Old Testament Prophets*, edited by Mark J. Boda and J. Gordon McConville. IVP Academic, 2012.

Goldingay, John, and David Payne. *Isaiah 40–55: A Critical and Exegetical Commentary.* International Critical Commentary. 2 vols. T & T Clark, 2014.

Goldingay, John, and Pamela J. Scalise. *Minor Prophets II.* New International Biblical Commentary. Hendrickson Publishers, 2009.

Gordon, Robert P. *1 & II Samuel: A Commentary*. Library of Biblical Interpretation. Regency Reference Library, 1986.
Gorman, Michael J. *Reading Revelation Responsibly: Uncivil Worship and Witness: Following the Lamb into the New Creation*. Cascade Books, 2011.
Gowan, Donald E. *Daniel*. Abingdon Old Testament Commentary. Abingdon, 2001.
Grabiner, Steven. *Revelation's Hymns: Commentary on the Cosmic Conflict*. Library of New Testament Studies. Bloomsbury, 2015.
Graybill, Rhiannon, John Kaltner, and Steven L. McKenzie. *Jonah: A New Translation with Introduction and Commentary*. Anchor Bible. Yale University Press, 2023.
Green, Joel B. *The Gospel of Luke*. New International Commentary on the New Testament. Eerdmans, 1997.
Green, Joel B. *How to Read Prophecy*. InterVarsity Press, 1984.
Green, Joel B. *Salvation*. Understanding Biblical Themes. Chalice Press, 2003.
Green, Joel B. "Soul." In *The New Interpreter's Dictionary of the Bible*, edited by K. D. Sakenfeld. 5 vols. Abingdon, 2006–9.
Greenberg, Moshe. *Ezekiel 21–37: A New Translation with Introduction and Commentary*. Anchor Bible. Yale University Press, 2010.
Grether, Herbert G. "Abaddon." In *Anchor Bible Dictionary*, edited by David Noel Freedman. 6 vols. Doubleday, 1992.
Grogan, G. W. "Conditional Immortality." In *The New International Dictionary of the Christian Church*, edited by J. D. Douglas. Rev. ed. Zondervan, 1978.
Grudem, Wayne A. *Systematic Theology*. 2nd ed. Zondervan Academic, 2020.
Guelich, Robert A. *Mark 1–8:26*. Word Biblical Commentary. Word Books, 1989.
Guhrt, Joachim. "Time." In *The New International Dictionary of New Testament Theology*, edited by Colin Brown. 4 vols. Zondervan, 1986.
Guinan, Michael D. "Davidic Covenant." In *Anchor Bible Dictionary*, edited by David Noel Freedman. 6 vols. Doubleday, 1992.
Gundry, Robert H. *Matthew: A Commentary on His Literary and Theological Art*. Eerdmans, 1983.
Gupta, Nijay K. *Colossians*. Smyth & Helwys Bible Commentary. Smyth & Helwys, 2013.
Guthrie, Shirley C. *Christian Doctrine*. 50th anniversary edition. Westminster John Knox Press, 2018.
Gwyther, Anthony R. "New Jerusalem Versus Babylon: Reading the Book of Revelation as the Text of a Circle of Counter-Imperial Christian Communities in the First Century Roman Empire." PhD diss., Griffith University, 1999.
Habel, Norman C. *The Book of Job: A Commentary*. Old Testament Library. Westminster Press, 1985.
Haenchen, Ernst. *John 1: A Commentary on the Gospel of John, Chapters 1–6*. Translated and edited by Robert W. Funk. Hermeneia. Augsburg Fortress, 1980.
Hagner, Donald A. "Gospel, Kingdom, and Resurrection in the Synoptic Gospels." In *Life in the Face of Death*, edited by Richard N. Longenecker, 99–121. Eerdmans, 1998.
Hagner, Donald A. *Matthew 1–13*. Word Biblical Commentary. Word Books, 1993.
Hagner, Donald A. *Matthew 14–28*. Word Biblical Commentary. Thomas Nelson, 1995.
Hahn, Hans-Cristoph, Colin Brown, and Friedemann Merkel. "Destroy." In *The New International Dictionary of New Testament Theology*, edited by Colin Brown. 4 vols. Zondervan, 1986.
Haight, Roger. *Jesus Symbol of God*. Orbis Books, 2002.
Hamerton-Kelly, Robert G. *Pre-Existence, Wisdom, and the Son of Man: A Study of the Idea of Pre-Existence in the New Testament*. SNTSMS 21. Cambridge University Press, 1973.
Hamilton, Victor P. *The Book of Genesis: Chapters 1–17*. New International Commentary on the Old Testament. Eerdmans, 1990.
Hamilton, Victor P. *The Book of Genesis: Chapters 18–50*. New International Commentary on the Old Testament. Eerdmans, 1995.
Hamilton, Victor P. *Exodus: An Exegetical Commentary*. Baker Academic, 2011.
Hamilton, Victor P. "Satan." In *Anchor Bible Dictionary*, edited by David Noel Freedman. 6 vols. Doubleday, 1992.
Hammer, Paul L. "Inheritance (NT)." In *Anchor Bible Dictionary*, edited by David Noel Freedman. 6 vols. Doubleday, 1992.
Hammer, Raymond. *The Book of Daniel*. Cambridge Bible Commentary on the New English Bible. Cambridge University Press, 1976.
Harder, Günther. "φθείρω κτλ." In *Theological Dictionary of the New Testament*, edited by G. Bromiley. 10 vols. Eerdmans, 1964–74.
Harnack, Adolph. *History of Dogma*. Translated by Neil Buchanan. 7 vols. Dover Publications, 1961.
Harrington, Daniel J. *The Gospel of John*. Sacra Pagina. Liturgical Press, 1998.
Harris, Murray J. *The Second Epistle to the Corinthians*. New International Greek Testament Commentary. Eerdmans, 2013.

Hartley, John E. "Atonement, Day of." In *Dictionary of the Old Testament Pentateuch*, edited by T. Desmond Alexander and David W. Baker. IVP Academic, 2003.
Hartley, John E. *The Book of Job*. New International Commentary on the Old Testament. Eerdmans, 1998.
Hartley, John E. *Leviticus*. Word Biblical Commentary. Thomas Nelson Publishers, 1992.
Hartman, Louis F., and Alexander A. Di Lella. *The Book of Daniel: A New Translation with Notes and Commentary*. Anchor Bible. Doubleday, 1977.
Harvey, Anthony E. "Christ as Agent." In *The Glory of Christ in the New Testament: Studies in Christology in Memory of George Bradford Caird*, edited by L. D. Hurst and N. T. Wright, 239–50. Clarendon, 1987.
Hatch, Sidney. *Daring to Differ: Adventures in Conditional Immortality*. Brief Bible Studies, 1991.
Hawthorne, Gerald F. *Philippians*. Word Biblical Commentary. Word Books, 1983.
Hayes, Elizabeth R. "Justice, Righteousness." In *Dictionary of the Old Testament Prophets*, edited by Mark J. Boda and J. Gordon McConville. IVP Academic, 2012.
Hays, Richard B. *Echoes of Scripture in the Letters of Paul*. Yale University Press, 1989.
Hays, Richard B. *The Faith of Jesus Christ: The Narrative Substructure of Galatians 3:1–4:11*. 2nd ed. Eerdmans, 2002
Hays, Richard B. *First Corinthians*. Interpretation: A Bible Commentary for Teaching and Preaching. John Knox Press, 1989.
Hays, Richard B. "The Letter to the Galatians." In *The New Interpreter's Bible*. 12 vols. Abingdon, 1994–2002.
Hendel, Ronald. *Genesis 1–11: A New Translation with Introduction and Commentary*. Anchor Bible. Yale University Press, 2024.
Hens-Piazza, Gina. *1–2 Kings*. Abingdon Old Testament Commentaries. Abingdon: 2006.
Herrmann, Johannes, and Werner Foerster. "κλῆρος κτλ." In *Theological Dictionary of the New Testament*, edited by G. Bromiley. 10 vols. Eerdmans, 1964–74.
Hill, Andrew E. *Malachi: A New Translation with Introduction and Commentary*. Anchor Bible. Yale University Press, 1998.
Hill, Charles E. *Regnum Caelorum: Patterns of Millennial Thought in Early Christianity*. 2nd ed. Eerdmans, 2001.
Hill, David. *Greek Words and Hebrew Meanings: Studies in the Semantic of Soteriological Terms*. SNTSMS 5. Cambridge University Press, 1967.
Hillers, Delbert R. *Micah: A Commentary on the Book of the Prophet Micah*. Hermeneia. Fortress Press, 1984.
Hodge, Charles. *Systematic Theology: An Introduction to Biblical Doctrine*. 3 vols. Eerdmans, 1952.
Hoehner, Harold W. *Ephesians: An Exegetical Commentary*. Baker Academic, 2002.
Hooker, Morna D. "The Letter to the Philippians." In *The New Interpreter's Bible*. 12 vols. Abingdon, 1994–2002.
Holladay, William L. *Jeremiah 1: A Commentary on the Book of the Prophet Jeremiah Chapters 1–25*. Hermeneia. Fortress Press, 1986.
Holladay, William L. *Jeremiah 2: A Commentary on the Book of the Prophet Jeremiah Chapters 26–52*. Hermeneia. Fortress Press, 1989.
Horn, F. W. "Holy Spirit." In *Anchor Bible Dictionary*, edited by David Noel Freedman. 6 vols. Doubleday, 1992.
Horne, Milton P. *Proverbs–Ecclesiastes*. Smyth & Helwys Bible Commentary. Smyth & Helwys, 2003.
Horsley, Richard A. *1 Corinthians*. Abingdon New Testament Commentaries. Abingdon, 1998.
Hossfeld, Frank-Lothar, and Erich Zenger. *Psalms 2: A Commentary on Psalms 51–100*. Translated by Linda M. Maloney. Hermeneia. Fortress Press, 2005.
Hossfeld, Frank-Lothar, and Erich Zenger. *Psalms 3: A Commentary on Psalms 101–150*. Translated by Linda M. Maloney. Hermeneia. Fortress Press, 2011.
Hossfeld, Frank-Lothar, F. van der Velden, and U. Dahmen. "סלח." In *Theological Dictionary of the Old Testament*, edited by G. Johannes Botterweck, Helmer Ringgren, and Heinz-Joseph Fabry. 15 vols. Eerdmans, 1974–2006.
Houlden, J. L. *The Johannine Epistles*. Harper New Testament Commentary. Harper & Row Publishers, 1973.
Houtman, Cornelis. *Exodus*. Translated by Johan Rebel and Sierd Woudstra. Historical Commentary on the Old Testament. 3 vols. Peeters Publishers, 1993.
Howe, Bonnie G. "Anthropomorphism." In *The New Interpreter's Dictionary of the Bible*, edited by K. D. Sakenfeld. 5 vols. Abingdon, 2006–9.
Hurtado, Larry W. "God." In *Dictionary of Jesus and the Gospels*, edited by Joel B. Green and Scot McKnight. IVP Academic, 1992.
Hurtado, Larry W. *One God, One Lord: Early Christian Devotion and Ancient Jewish Monotheism*. T & T Clark, 2003.
Hurtado, Larry W. "Pre-Existence." In *Dictionary of Paul and His Letters*, edited by Gerald F. Hawthorne, Ralph P. Martin, and Daniel G. Reid. IVP Academic, 1993.
Hurtado, Larry W. "Worship, NT Christian." In *The New Interpreter's Dictionary of the Bible*, edited by K. D. Sakenfeld. 5 vols. Abingdon, 2006–9.

Irons, Charles Lee, Danny Andre Dixon, and Dustin R. Smith. *The Son of God: Three Views of the Identity of Jesus*. Wipf & Stock, 2015.
Japhet, Sara. *I & II Chronicles: A Commentary*. Old Testament Library. Westminster John Knox Press, 1993.
Jeremias, Joachim. "ᾅδης." In *Theological Dictionary of the New Testament*, edited by G. Bromiley. 10 vols. Eerdmans, 1964–74.
Jeremias, Joachim. "γέεννα." In *Theological Dictionary of the New Testament*, edited by G. Bromiley. 10 vols. Eerdmans, 1964–74.
Jeremias, Joachim. *New Testament Theology*. Translated by John Bowden. Charles Scribner's Sons. 1971.
Jewett, Robert. *Romans: A Commentary*. Hermeneia. Fortress Press, 2007.
Jewett, Robert. *The Thessalonian Correspondence: Pauline Rhetoric and Millenarian Piety*. Foundations and Facets. Fortress Press, 1986.
Johnson, Dennis E. *Triumph of the Lamb: A Commentary on Revelation*. R&R Publishing, 2001.
Johnson, Luke Timothy. *The Acts of the Apostles*. Sacra Pagina. The Liturgical Press, 1992.
Johnson, Luke Timothy. *The First and Second Letters to Timothy: A New Translation with Introduction and Commentary*. Anchor Bible. Doubleday, 2001.
Johnson, Luke Timothy. *The Gospel of Luke*. Sacra Pagina. The Liturgical Press, 1991.
Johnson, Luke Timothy. *Hebrews: A Commentary*. New Testament Library. Westminster John Knox Press, 2006.
Johnson, Luke Timothy. *The Letter of James: A New Translation with Introduction and Commentary*. Anchor Bible. Yale University Press, 2005.
Johnston, Philip S. "Afterlife." In *Dictionary of the Old Testament Prophets*, edited by Mark J. Boda and J. Gordon McConville. IVP Academic, 2012.
Johnston, Philip S. "Death and Afterlife." In *Dictionary of the Old Testament Historical Books*, edited by Bill T. Arnold and H. G. M. Williamson. InterVarsity Press, 2005.
Johnston, Philip S. "Sheol." In *The New Interpreter's Dictionary of the Bible*, edited by K. D. Sakenfeld. 5 vols. Abingdon, 2006–9.
Johnstone, William. *Exodus 20–40*. Smyth & Helwys Bible Commentary. Smyth & Helwys, 2014.
Joüon, P., and T. Muraoka. *A Grammar of Biblical Hebrew*. Gregorian and Biblical Press, 2018.
Joyce, Paul M. *Ezekiel: A Commentary*. Library of Hebrew Bible/Old Testament Studies 482. T & T Clark, 2009.
Juce, Esther G. "Wisdom in Matthew: Tripartite Fulfillment." *St. Vladimir's Theological Quarterly* 55, no. 2 (2011): 125–39.
Kaiser, Walter C. Jr. "The Book of Leviticus." In *The New Interpreter's Bible*. 12 vols. Abingdon, 1994–2002.
Kaiser, Walter C. Jr. *Toward an Old Testament Theology*. Academie Books, 1978.
Keating, Daniel A. *Ezekiel*. Catholic Commentary on Sacred Scripture. Baker Academic, 2024.
Keck, Leander E. *Romans*. Abingdon New Testament Commentaries. Abingdon, 2005.
Keener, Craig S. *Acts: An Exegetical Commentary*. 4 vols. Baker Academic, 2012–15.
Keener, Craig S. *Galatians*. New Cambridge Bible Commentary. Cambridge University Press, 2018.
Keener, Craig S. *The Gospel of John: A Commentary*. 2 vols. Hendrickson Publishers, 2010.
Keener, Craig S. *The Gospel of Matthew: A Socio–Rhetorical Commentary*. Eerdmans, 2009.
Keener, Craig S. "Man and Woman." In *Dictionary of Paul and His Letters*, edited by Gerald F. Hawthorne, Ralph P. Martin, and Daniel G. Reid. IVP Academic, 1993.
Kelly, Henry Ansgar. *Satan: A Biography*. Cambridge University Press, 2006.
Keown, Gerald L., Pamela J. Scalise, and Thomas G. Smothers. *Jeremiah 26–52*. Word Biblical Commentary. Word Books, 1995.
Kim, Seyoon, and F. F. Bruce. *1 & 2 Thessalonians*. 2nd ed. Word Biblical Commentary. Zondervan Academic, 2023.
Kirk, J. R. Daniel. *A Man Attested by God: The Human Jesus of the Synoptic Gospels*. Eerdmans, 2016.
Kirk, J. R. Daniel, and Stephen L. Young. "'I Will Set His Hand to the Sea': Psalm 88:26 LXX and the Christology in Mark." *Journal of Biblical Literature* 133, no. 2 (2014): 333–40.
Klein, Ralph W. *1 Chronicles: A Commentary*. Hermeneia. Fortress Press, 2006.
Klein, Ralph W. *1 Samuel*. Word Biblical Commentary. Word Books, 1983.
Kleinknecht, H., F. Baumgärtel, W. Bieder, E. Sjöberg, and E. Schweizer. "πνεῦμα κτλ." In *Theological Dictionary of the New Testament*, edited by G. Bromiley. 10 vols. Eerdmans, 1964–74.
Knight, George W. III. *The Pastoral Epistles*. New International Greek Testament Commentary. Eerdmans, 2013.
Knoppers, Gary N. *I Chronicles 10–29: A New Translation with Introduction and Commentary*. Anchor Bible. Yale University Press, 2004.
Knowles, Michael. *Jeremiah in Matthew's Gospel: The Rejected–Prophet Motif in Matthaean Redaction*. Journal for the Study of the New Testament Supplement Series 68. Sheffield Academic Press, 1993.

Ko, Ming Him. *Leviticus: A Pastoral and Contextual Commentary*. Asia Bible Commentary. Langham Global Library, 2018.
Koester, Craig R. *Hebrews: A New Translation with Introduction and Commentary*. Anchor Bible. Yale University Press, 2001.
Koester, Craig R. *Revelation: A New Translation with Introduction and Commentary*. Anchor Bible. Yale University Press, 2014.
Koester, Craig R. *Symbolism in the Fourth Gospel: Meaning, Mystery, Community*. 2nd ed. Fortress Press, 2003.
Köhler, Ludwig. *Old Testament Theology*. Translated by A. S. Todd. Westminster Press, 1957.
Köhler, Ludwig, Walter Baumgartner, and Johann J. Stamm. *Hebrew and Aramaic Lexicon of the Old Testament*. Translated and edited by Mervyn E. J. Richardson. 4 vols. Brill, 1999.
Kraus, Hans-Joachim. *Theology of the Psalms*. Translated by Keith Crim. Fortress Press, 1992.
Kraybill, J. Nelson. *Apocalypse and Allegiance: Worship, Politics, and Devotion in the Book of Revelation*. Brazos Press, 2010.
Kreitzer, Larry J. "Adam and Christ." In *Dictionary of Paul and His Letters*, edited by Gerald F. Hawthorne, Ralph P. Martin, and Daniel G. Reid. IVP Academic, 1993.
Kreitzer, Larry J. "Kingdom of God/Christ." In *Dictionary of Paul and His Letters*, edited by Gerald F. Hawthorne, Ralph P. Martin, and Daniel G. Reid. IVP Academic, 1993.
Kreitzer, Larry J. "Resurrection." In *Dictionary of Paul and His Letters*, edited by Gerald F. Hawthorne, Ralph P. Martin, and Daniel G. Reid. IVP Academic, 1993.
Krüger, Thomas. *Qoheleth: A Commentary*. Translated by O. C. Dean Jr. Hermeneia. Fortress Press, 2004.
Kuemmerlin-McLean, Joanne K, and David George Reese. "Demons." In *Anchor Bible Dictionary*, edited by David Noel Freedman. 6 vols. Doubleday, 1992.
Ladd, George Eldon. *A Commentary on the Revelation of John*. Eerdmans, 1993.
Ladd, George Eldon. *Crucial Questions About the Kingdom of God*. Eerdmans, 1968.
Ladd, George Eldon. *The Presence of the Future*. Rev ed. Eerdmans, 2002.
Ladd, George Eldon. *The Gospel of the Kingdom: Scriptural Studies in the Kingdom of God*. Eerdmans, 2000.
Ladd, George Eldon. *The Presence of the Future*. Rev ed. Eerdmans, 2002.
Ladd, George Eldon. *A Theology of the New Testament*. Eerdmans, 1975.
Lane, William L. *Hebrews 1–8*. Word Biblical Commentary. Word Books, 1991.
Lane, William L. *Hebrews 9–13*. Word Biblical Commentary. Word Books, 1991.
Larere, Philippe. *Baptism in Water and Baptism in the Spirit: A Biblical, Liturgical, and Theological Exposition*. Translated by Patrick Madigan. The Liturgical Press, 1993.
Lawlor, John J. "Worm." In *The New Interpreter's Dictionary of the Bible*, edited by K. D. Sakenfeld. 5 vols. Abingdon, 2006–9.
Leonhardt-Balzer, Jutta. "Righteousness in Early Jewish Literature." In *The New Interpreter's Dictionary of the Bible*, edited by K. D. Sakenfeld. 5 vols. Abingdon, 2006–9.
Levenson, Jon D. *Resurrection and the Restoration of Israel: The Ultimate Victory of the God of Life*. Yale University Press, 2006.
Levenson, Jon D. *Sinai & Zion: An Entry into the Jewish Bible*. HarperCollins, 1985.
Levine, Baruch A. *Numbers 1–20: A New Translation with Introduction and Commentary*. Anchor Bible. Doubleday, 1993.
Levine, Baruch A. *Numbers 21–36: A New Translation with Introduction and Commentary*. Anchor Bible. Yale University Press, 2009.
Levinthal, Israel Herbert. "The Jewish Law of Agency." *The Jewish Quarterly Review* 13.2 (Oct. 1922): 117–191.
Levison, John R. "Holy Spirit." In *The New Interpreter's Dictionary of the Bible*, edited by K. D. Sakenfeld. 5 vols. Abingdon, 2006–9.
Lieu, Judith M. *I, II, & III John: A Commentary*. New Testament Library. Westminster John Knox Press, 2012.
Lincoln, Andrew T. *Ephesians*. Word Biblical Commentary. Word Books, 1990.
Lincoln, Andrew T. *The Gospel According to Saint John*. Black's New Testament Commentary. Hendrickson Publishers, 2005.
Lincoln, Andrew T. "I am the Resurrection and the Life." In *Life in the Face of Death*, edited by Richard N. Longenecker, 122–44. Eerdmans, 1998.
Lincoln, Andrew T. "The Letter to the Colossians." In *The New Interpreter's Bible*. 12 vols. Abingdon, 1996–2002.
Lindars, Barnabas. *The Gospel of John*. New Century Bible Commentary. Eerdmans, 1981.
Loader, William. "The Central Structure of Johannine Christology." *New Testament Studies* 30, no. 2 (1984): 188–216.
Longenecker, Richard N. *The Epistle to the Romans*. New International Greek Testament Commentary. Eerdmans, 2016.
Longenecker, Richard N. *Galatians*. Word Biblical Commentary. Thomas Nelson Publishers, 1990.
Longman, Tremper III. *The Book of Ecclesiastes*. New International Commentary on the Old Testament. Eerdmans, 1998.
Longman, Tremper III. *Job*. Baker Commentary of the Old Testament Wisdom and Psalms. Baker Academic, 2012.

Longman, Tremper III. "Messiah." In *Dictionary of the Old Testament Wisdom, Poetry & Writings*, edited by Tremper Longman III and Peter Enns. IVP Academic, 2008.
Longman, Tremper III. *Proverbs*. Baker Commentary of the Old Testament Wisdom and Psalms. Baker Academic, 2006.
Lundbom, Jack R. *Jeremiah 21–36: A New Translation with Introduction and Commentary*. Anchor Bible. Doubleday, 2004.
Lundbom, Jack R. *Jeremiah 37–52: A New Translation with Introduction and Commentary*. Anchor Bible. Doubleday, 2004.
Luz, Ulrich. *Matthew 1–7: A Commentary*. Translated by James E. Crouch. Hermeneia. Fortress Press, 2007.
Luz, Ulrich. *Matthew 8–20: A Commentary*. Translated by James E. Crouch. Hermeneia. Fortress Press, 2001.
Luz, Ulrich. *Matthew 21–28: A Commentary*. Translated by James E. Crouch. Hermeneia. Fortress Press, 2005.
Maiberger, P. "פָּרָה." In *Theological Dictionary of the Old Testament*, edited by G. Johannes Botterweck, Helmer Ringgren, and Heinz-Joseph Fabry. 15 vols. Eerdmans, 1974–2006.
Malherbe, Abraham J. *The Letters to the Thessalonians: A New Translation with Introduction and Commentary*. Anchor Bible. Doubleday, 2004.
Marcus, Joel. *The Mystery of the Kingdom of God*. Society of Biblical Literature Dissertation Studies 90. Scholars Press, 1986.
Marcus, Joel. *Mark 1–8: A New Translation with Introduction and Commentary*. Anchor Bible. Doubleday, 2000.
Marshall, I. Howard. *The Gospel of Luke*. New International Greek Testament Commentary. Eerdmans, 1979.
Marshall, I. Howard. *1 and 2 Thessalonians*. New Century Bible Commentary. Eerdmans, 1987.
Marshall, I. Howard. *The Pastoral Epistles*. International Critical Commentary. T & T Clark, 2007.
Marshall, I. Howard. "Son of Man." In *Dictionary of Jesus and the Gospels*, edited by Joel B. Green and Scot McKnight. IVP Academic, 1992.
Martin, Ralph P. *2 Corinthians*. Word Biblical Commentary. Word Books, 1986.
Martin, Ralph P. *James*. Word Biblical Commentary. Word Books, 1988.
Martyn, J. Louis. *Galatians: A New Translation with Introduction and Commentary*. Anchor Bible. Yale University Press, 1997.
Matera, Frank J. *II Corinthians: A Commentary*. New Testament Library. Westminster John Knox Press, 2003.
Matthews, Victor H. "Holy Spirit." In *Anchor Bible Dictionary*, edited by David Noel Freedman. 6 vols. Doubleday, 1992.
Mbuvi, Andrew M. *Jude and 2 Peter*. New Covenant Commentary Series. Cascade Books, 2015.
McCann, Jr., J. Clinton. "The Book of Psalms." In *The New Interpreter's Bible*. 12 vols. Abingdon, 1996–2002.
McCarter, P. Kyle, Jr. *1 Samuel: A New Translation with Introduction and Commentary*. Anchor Bible. Doubleday, 1980.
McConville, J. Gordon. "בְּרִית." In *The New International Dictionary of Old Testament Theology & Exegesis*, edited by Willem A. VanGemeren. 5 vols. Zondervan, 1997.
McConville, J. Gordon. *Deuteronomy*. Apollos Old Testament Commentary. InterVarsity Press, 2002.
McGrath, James F. *Christmaker: A Life of John the Baptist*. Eerdmans, 2024.
McGrath, James F. *John of History, Baptist of Faith: The Quest for the Historical Baptizer*. Eerdmans, 2024.
McGrath, James F. *The Only True God: Early Christian Monotheism in Its Jewish Context*. University of Illinois Press, 2009.
McHugh, John F. *John 1–4: A Critical and Exegetical Commentary*. International Critical Commentary. T & T Clark, 2009.
McIlhone, James P. "Jesus as God's Agent in the Fourth Gospel: Implications for Christology, Ecclesiology, and Mission." *Chicago Studies* 44 (2005): 295–315.
McIntosh, C. A., ed. *One God, Three Persons, Four Views: A Biblical, Theological, and Philosophical Dialogue on the Doctrine of the Trinity*. Cascade Books, 2024.
McKane, William. *Jeremiah 1–25: A Critical and Exegetical Commentary*. International Critical Commentary. T & T Clark, 1986.
McKane, William. *Jeremiah 26–52: A Critical and Exegetical Commentary*. International Critical Commentary. T & T Clark, 2014.
McKinlay, Judith E. *Gendering Wisdom the Host: Biblical Invitations to Eat and Drink*. JSOTSup 216. Sheffield Academic, 1996.
McKnight, Edgar, and Christopher Church. *Hebrews–James*. Smyth & Helwys Bible Commentary. Smyth & Helwys, 2004.
Mendenhall, George E., and Gary A. Herion. "Covenant." In *Anchor Bible Dictionary*, edited by David Noel Freedman. 6 vols. Doubleday, 1992.
Merrill, Eugene H. "Image of God." In *Dictionary of the Old Testament Pentateuch*, edited by T. Desmond Alexander and David W. Baker. IVP Academic, 2003.
Meyer, Paul W. "'The Father': The Presentation of God in the Fourth Gospel." In *Exploring the Gospel of John: In Honor of D. Moody Smith*, edited by R. Alan Culpepper and C. Clifton Black, 255–73. Westminster John Knox Press, 1996.
Meyers, Carol. "Cherubim." In *Anchor Bible Dictionary*, edited by David Noel Freedman. 6 vols. Doubleday, 1992.
Meyers, Carol. *Exodus*. New Cambridge Bible Commentary. Cambridge University Press, 2005.

Meyers, Carol, and Eric Meyers. *Haggai, Zechariah 1–8: A New Translation with Introduction and Commentary.* Anchor Bible. Doubleday, 1987.

Meyers, Carol, and Eric Meyers. *Zechariah 9–14: A New Translation with Introduction and Commentary.* Anchor Bible. Doubleday, 1993.

Meyers, Carol, Toni Craven, and Ross S. Kraemer, eds. *Women in Scripture: A Dictionary of Named and Unnamed Women in the Hebrew Bible, the Apocryphal/Deuterocanonical Books, and the New Testament.* Houghton Mifflin Company, 2000.

Michaels, J. Ramsey. *The Gospel of John.* New International Commentary on the New Testament. Eerdmans, 2010.

Michaels, J. Ramsey. "Millennium." In *The New Interpreter's Dictionary of the Bible*, edited by K. D. Sakenfeld. 5 vols. Abingdon, 2006–9.

Michaels, J. Ramsey. *1 Peter.* Word Biblical Commentary. Word Books, 1988.

Michel, O. "Faith." In *The New International Dictionary of New Testament Theology*, edited by Colin Brown. 4 vols. Zondervan, 1986.

Milgrom, Jacob. *Leviticus 1–16: A New Translation with Introduction and Commentary.* Anchor Bible. Doubleday, 1991.

Milgrom, Jacob. *Leviticus 17–22: A New Translation with Introduction and Commentary.* Anchor Bible. Doubleday, 2008.

Miller, Patrick D. *Deuteronomy.* Interpretation: A Bible Commentary for Teaching and Preaching. John Knox Press, 1990.

Moloney, Francis J. *The Apocalypse of John: A Commentary.* Baker Academic, 2020.

Moloney, Francis J. *The Gospel of John.* Sacra Pagina. The Liturgical Press, 1998.

Montanari, Franco, Ivan Garafalo, and Daniela Manetti. *The Brill Dictionary of Ancient Greek.* Edited by Madeleine Goh and Chad Schroeder. Brill, 2015.

Morris, Leon. *The First and Second Epistles to the Thessalonians.* New International Commentary on the New Testament. Eerdmans, 1979.

Morris, Leon. *Luke: An Introduction and Commentary.* Rev ed. Tyndale New Testament Commentaries. InterVarsity Press, 1997.

Morris, Leon. *Revelation.* Rev ed. Tyndale New Testament Commentaries. Eerdmans, 1999.

Morris, Leon. "Sin, Guilt." In *Dictionary of Paul and His Letters*, edited by Gerald F. Hawthorne, Ralph P. Martin, and Daniel G. Reid. IVP Academic, 1993.

Moulton, James Hope, and Stanley E. Porter. *Moulton's Grammar of New Testament Greek: Volume 1: The Prolegomena.* T & T Clark, 2025.

Mounce, William D. *The Book of Revelation.* Rev ed. New International Commentary on the New Testament. Eerdmans, 1998.

Mounce, William D. *Pastoral Epistles.* Word Biblical Commentary. Thomas Nelson Publishers, 2000.

Mowinckel, Sigmund. *He That Cometh: The Messiah Concept in the Old Testament and Later Judaism.* Translated by G. W. Anderson. Basil Blackwell, 1956.

Mowinckel, Sigmund. *The Psalms in Israel's Worship.* Translated by D. R. Ap-Thomas. Eerdmans, 2004.

Mulholland, M. Robert Jr. "Revelation." In *James, 1–2 Peter, Jude, Revelation.* Cornerstone Biblical Commentary. Tyndale House Publishers, 2011.

Murphy, Roland E. *Ecclesiastes.* Word Biblical Commentary. Word Books, 1992.

Murphy, Roland E. *Proverbs.* Word Biblical Commentary. Thomas Nelson Publishers, 1998.

Murphy-O'Connor, Jerome. *1 Corinthians.* Doubleday Bible Commentary. Doubleday, 1998.

Mussies, Garald. "Languages (Greek)." In *Anchor Bible Dictionary*, edited by David Noel Freedman. 6 vols. Doubleday, 1992.

Myers, Ched. *Binding the Strong Man: A Political Reading of Mark's Story of Jesus.* Orbis Books, 1994.

Nash, Robert Scott. *1 Corinthians.* Smyth & Helwys Bible Commentary. Smyth & Helwys, 2009.

Nelson, Richard D. *Deuteronomy: A Commentary.* Old Testament Library. Westminster John Knox Press, 2002.

Nemes, Steven *Eating Christ's Flesh: A Case for Memorialism.* Cascade Books, 2023.

Nemes, Steven *Trinity & Incarnation: A Post–Catholic Theology.* Cascade Books, 2023.

Neusner, Jacob. *Judaism When Christianity Began: A Survey of Belief and Practice.* Westminster John Knox Press, 2002.

Newman, C. C. "Jerusalem, Zion, Holy City." In *Dictionary of the Later New Testament & Its Developments*, edited by Ralph P. Martin and Peter H. Davids. InterVarsity Press, 1997.

Newsom, Carol A. "The Book of Job." In *The New Interpreter's Bible.* 12 vols. Abingdon, 1994–2002.

Newsom, Carol A., and Brennan W. Breed. *Daniel: A Commentary.* Old Testament Library. Westminster John Knox Press, 2014.

Neyrey, Jerome H. *2 Peter, Jude: A New Translation with Introduction and Commentary.* Anchor Bible. Doubleday, 2004.

Nickelsburg, George W. E. *Resurrection, Immortality, and Eternal Life in Intertestamental Judaism and Early Christianity.* Rev ed. Harvard Theological Studies 36. Harvard University Press, 2006.

Nogalski, James D. *The Book of the Twelve: Micah–Malachi*. Smyth & Helwys Bible Commentary. Smyth & Helwys, 2011.
Noll, Stephen F. "Angels, Heavenly Beings, Angel Christology." In *Dictionary of the Later New Testament & Its Developments*, edited by Ralph P. Martin and Peter H. Davids. InterVarsity Press, 1997.
Nolland, John. *The Gospel of Matthew*. New International Greek Testament Commentary. Eerdmans, 2005.
Nolland, John. *Luke 1–9:20*. Word Biblical Commentary. Word Books, 1989.
Nolland, John. *Luke 9:21–18:34*. Word Biblical Commentary. Thomas Nelson Publishers, 1993.
Nolland, John. *Luke 18:35–24:53*. Word Biblical Commentary. Thomas Nelson Publishers, 1993.
Noth, Martin. *Exodus: A Commentary*. Old Testament Library. SCM Press, 1962.
Novakovic, Lidija. *John 1–10: A Handbook on the Greek Text*. Baylor Handbook on the Greek New Testament. Baylor University Press, 2020.
O'Boyle, Aidan. *Towards a Contemporary Wisdom Christology: Some Catholic Christologies in German, English and French 1965–1995*. Tesi Gregoriana Serie Teologica 98. Gregorian University Press, 2003.
O'Connor, Kathleen M. *Genesis 1–25A*. Smyth & Helwys Bible Commentary. Smyth & Helwys, 2018.
Oakes, Peter. *Galatians*. Paideia Commentaries. Baker Academic, 2015.
Odell, Margaret S. *Ezekiel*. Smyth & Helwys Bible Commentary. Smyth & Helwys, 2005.
Oepke, Albrecht. "ἐγείρω." In *Theological Dictionary of the New Testament*, edited by G. Bromiley. 10 vols. Eerdmans, 1964–74.
Ollenburger, Ben C. "The Book of Zechariah." In *The New Interpreter's Bible*. 12 vols. Abingdon, 1994–2002.
Olson, Dennis T. *Numbers*. Interpretation: A Bible Commentary for Teaching and Preaching. John Knox Press, 1996.
Osborne, Grant. "Resurrection." In *Dictionary of Jesus and the Gospels*, edited by Joel B. Green and Scot McKnight. IVP Academic, 1992.
Osborne, Grant. *Revelation*. Baker Exegetical Commentary on the New Testament. Baker Academic, 2002.
Osiek, Carolyn. *Philippians, Philemon*. Abingdon New Testament Commentaries. Abingdon, 2000.
Osiek, Carolyn, and David L. Balch. *Families in the New Testament World*. Westminster John Knox Press, 1997.
Oswalt, John N. *The Book of Isaiah: Chapters 40–66*. New International Commentary on the Old Testament. Eerdmans, 1998.
Oswalt, John N. "God." In *Dictionary of the Old Testament Prophets*, edited by Mark J. Boda and J. Gordon McConville. IVP Academic, 2012.
Oswalt, John N. "God." In *Dictionary of the Old Testament Wisdom, Poetry & Writings*, edited by Tremper Longman III and Peter Enns. IVP Academic, 2008.
Otzen, Benedikt. "אָבַד." In *Theological Dictionary of the Old Testament*, edited by G. Johannes Botterweck, Helmer Ringgren, and Heinz-Joseph Fabry. 15 vols. Eerdmans, 1974–2006.
Pace, Sharon. *Daniel*. Smyth & Helwys Commentary. Smyth & Helwys, 2008.
Pagels, Elaine. *The Origin of Satan*. Vintage Books, 1996.
Paige, Terence P. "Demons and Exorcism." In *Dictionary of Paul and His Letters*, edited by Gerald F. Hawthorne, Ralph P. Martin, and Daniel G. Reid. IVP Academic, 1993.
Painter, John. *1, 2, and 3 John*. Sacra Pagina. Liturgical Press, 2002.
Parsenios, George L. *First, Second, and Third John*. Paideia Commentaries. Baker Academic, 2014.
Paul, Ian. *Revelation*. Tyndale New Testament Commentaries. IVP Academic, 2018.
Paul, Shalom M. *Isaiah 40–66: Translation and Commentary*. Eerdmans Critical Commentary. Eerdmans, 2012.
Perdue, Leo. *Proverbs*. Interpretation: A Bible Commentary for Teaching and Preaching. John Knox Press, 2000.
Perkins, Pheme. *First Corinthians*. Paideia Commentaries. Baker Academic, 2012.
Perkins, Pheme. "The Gospel of Mark." In *The New Interpreter's Bible*. 12 vols. Abingdon, 1994–2002.
Perriman, Andrew. *In the Form of a God: The Pre-existence of the Exalted Christ in Paul*. Studies in Early Christology 1. Cascade: 2022.
Pervo, Richard I. *Acts: A Commentary*. Hermeneia. Fortress Press, 2009.
Peterson, David G. *The Acts of the Apostles*. Pillar New Testament Commentary. Eerdmans, 2009.
Petersen, David L. *Haggai and Zechariah 1–8: A Commentary*. Old Testament Library. Westminster Press, 1984.
Petersen, David L. "Prophet, Prophecy." In *The New Interpreter's Dictionary of the Bible*, edited by K. D. Sakenfeld. 5 vols. Abingdon, 2006–9.
Pfitzner, Victor C. *Hebrews*. Abingdon New Testament Commentary. Abingdon, 1997.
Pinnock, Clark, Richard Rice, John Sanders, William Hasker, and David Basinger. *The Openness of God: A Biblical Challenge to the Traditional Understanding of God*. InterVarsity Press, 1994.

Pope, Marvin H. *Job: Translated with an Introduction and Notes.* Anchor Bible. Doubleday. 1965.
Prestidge, Warren. *Life, Death and Destiny.* Resurrection Publishing, 1998.
Preuss, H. D. "עוֹלָם." In *Theological Dictionary of the Old Testament,* edited by G. Johannes Botterweck, Helmer Ringgren, and Heinz-Joseph Fabry. 15 vols. Eerdmans, 1974–2006.
Propp, William H. C. *Exodus 1–18: A New Translation with Introduction and Commentary.* Anchor Bible. Doubleday, 1999.
Propp, William H. C. *Exodus 19–40: A New Translation with Introduction and Commentary.* Anchor Bible. Doubleday, 2006.
Quell, Gottfried, and Gottlob Schrenk. "δίκη κτλ." In *Theological Dictionary of the New Testament,* edited by G. Bromiley. 10 vols. Eerdmans, 1964–74.
Quinn, Jerome D. *The Letter to Titus: A New Translation with Notes and Commentary.* Anchor Bible. Doubleday 1990.
Rad, Gerhard von. *Genesis: A Commentary.* Rev ed. Old Testament Library. Westminster Press, 1972.
Rad, Gerhard von. *Old Testament Theology: Volume 1.* Translated by D. G. G. Stalker. Harper & Row, 1962.
Rad, Gerhard von, and Werner Foerster. "διαβάλλω, διάβολος." In *Theological Dictionary of the New Testament,* edited by G. Bromiley. 10 vols. Eerdmans, 1964–74.
Räisänen, Heikki. *Paul & the Law.* Fortress Press, 1986.
Ramelli, Ilaria L. E., and David Konstan. *Terms for Eternity: Aiônios and Aïdios in Classical and Christian Texts.* Perspective on Philosophy and Religious Thought 9. Gorgias Press, 2013.
Reddish, Mitchell G. *Revelation.* Smyth & Helwys Bible Commentary. Smyth & Helwys, 2001.
Reese, Alexander. *The Approaching Advent of Christ.* Grand Rapids International Publications, 1975.
Reid, Barbara E. "Wisdom's Children." *New Theology Review* 15, no. 2 (2002): 46–53.
Reumann, John. *Philippians: A New Translation with Introduction and Commentary.* Anchor Bible. Yale University Press, 2008.
Rhoads, David, Joanna Dewey, and Donald Michie. *Mark as Story: An Introduction to the Narrative of a Gospel.* 2nd ed. Fortress Press, 1999.
Richardson, Alan. *An Introduction to the Theology of the New Testament.* SCM Press, 1958.
Riddlebarger, Kim. *A Case for Amillennialism: Understanding the End Times.* Expanded ed. Baker Books, 2013.
Riesner, Rainer D. "Teacher." In *Dictionary of Jesus and the Gospels,* edited by Joel B. Green and Scot McKnight. IVP Academic, 1992.
Ringe, Sharon H. *Wisdom's Friends: Community and Christology in the Gospel of John.* Westminster John Knox Press, 1999.
Ringgren, Helmer. "אֱלֹהִים." In *Theological Dictionary of the Old Testament,* edited by G. Johannes Botterweck, Helmer Ringgren, and Heinz-Joseph Fabry. 15 vols. Eerdmans, 1974–2006.
Roberts, Jim J. M. *First Isaiah: A Commentary.* Hermeneia. Fortress Press, 2015.
Robinson, John A. T. *The Priority of John.* Edited by J. F. Coakley. Meyer Stone, 1987.
Robinson, John A. T. "The Use of the Fourth Gospel for Christology Today." In *Christ and the Spirit in the New Testament,* edited by Barnabas Lindars and Stephen S. Smalley, 61–78. Cambridge University Press, 1973.
Robinson, John A. T. *Twelve More New Testament Studies.* SCM, 1984.
Roetzel, Calvin J. *2 Corinthians.* Abingdon New Testament Commentaries. Abingdon, 2007.
Roloff, Jürgen. *The Revelation of John: A Continental Commentary.* Translated by John E. Alsup. Fortress Press, 1993.
Rose, Wolter H. "Messiah." In *Dictionary of the Old Testament Pentateuch,* edited by T. Desmond Alexander and David W. Baker. IVP Academic, 2003.
Routledge, Robin. *Old Testament Theology: A Thematic Approach.* IVP Academic, 2008.
Rowland, Christopher C. "The Book of Revelation." In *The New Interpreter's Bible.* 12 vols. Abingdon, 1994–2002.
Rowland, Christopher C. *The Open Heaven: A Study of Apocalyptic in Judaism and Early Christianity.* Crossroad, 1982.
Russell, D. S. *Daniel.* Daily Study Bible. Westminster Press, 1981.
Ryken, Leland, James C. Wilhoit, and Tremper Longman III, eds. *Dictionary of Biblical Imagery.* InterVarsity, 1998.
Sampley, J. Paul. "The First Letter to the Corinthians." In *The New Interpreter's Bible.* 12 vols. Abingdon, 1994–2002.
Sampley, J. Paul. "The Second Letter to the Corinthians." In *The New Interpreter's Bible.* 12 vols. Abingdon, 1994–2002.
Sanders, E. P. *Judaism: Practice & Belief, 63 BCE – 66 CE.* SCM Press, 1994.
Sanders, E. P. *Paul and Palestinian Judaism: A Comparison of Patterns of Religion.* Fortress Press, 1977.
Sanders, E. P. *Paul, the Law, and the Jewish People.* Fortress Press, 1983.
Sarna, Nahum M. *Exodus.* JPS Torah Commentary. Jewish Publication Society, 1991.
Sarna, Nahum M. *Genesis.* JPS Torah Commentary. Jewish Publication Society, 1989.

Sarna, Nahum M. *Understanding Genesis: The World of the Bible in the Light of History*. Schocken Books, 1966.
Sasse, Hermann. "αἰών, αἰώνιος." In *Theological Dictionary of the New Testament*, edited by G. Bromiley. 10 vols. Eerdmans, 1964–74.
Sasse, Hermann. "κοσμέω κτλ." In *Theological Dictionary of the New Testament*, edited by G. Bromiley. 10 vols. Eerdmans, 1964–74.
Sasson, Jack M. *Judges 13–21: A New Translation with Commentary*. Anchor Bible. Yale University Press, 2025.
Schmidt, Thomas E. "Discipline." In *Dictionary of Paul and His Letters*, edited by Gerald F. Hawthorne, Ralph P. Martin, and Daniel G. Reid. IVP Academic, 1993.
Schnabel, Eckhard J. *Acts*. Exegetical Commentary on the New Testament. Zondervan, 2012.
Schnackenburg, Rudolf. *The Gospel According to St. John*. 3 vols. Translated by Kevin Smyth. Crossroad, 1990.
Schneider, J. "God." In *The New International Dictionary of New Testament Theology*, edited by Colin Brown. 4 vols. Zondervan, 1986.
Schuele, Andreas. "Heart." In *The New Interpreter's Dictionary of the Bible*, edited by K. D. Sakenfeld. 5 vols. Abingdon, 2006–9.
Schuller, Eileen M. "The Book of Malachi." In *The New Interpreter's Bible*. 12 vols. Abingdon, 1994–2002.
Schüssler Fiorenza, Elisabeth. *Ephesians*. Wisdom Commentary. Liturgical Press, 2017.
Schüssler Fiorenza, Elisabeth. *Revelation: Vision for a Just World*. Proclamation Commentary. Fortress Press, 1991.
Schweizer, Eduard. *The Good News According to Luke*. Translated by David E. Green. John Knox Press, 1984.
Schweizer, Eduard. "ψυχή." In *Theological Dictionary of the New Testament*, edited by G. Bromiley. 10 vols. Eerdmans, 1964–74.
Scott, J. Julius Jr. "Immortality." In *Dictionary of Paul and His Letters*, edited by Gerald F. Hawthorne, Ralph P. Martin, and Daniel G. Reid. IVP Academic, 1993.
Scott, J. Julius Jr. "Life and Death." In *Dictionary of Paul and His Letters*, edited by Gerald F. Hawthorne, Ralph P. Martin, and Daniel G. Reid. IVP Academic, 1993.
Seebass, H. "Nephesh." In *Theological Dictionary of the Old Testament*, edited by G. Johannes Botterweck, Helmer Ringgren, and Heinz-Josef Fabry. Translated by David E. Green. 15 vols. Eerdmans, 1974–2006.
Seebass, H., and Colin Brown. "Righteousness, Justification." In *The New International Dictionary of New Testament Theology*, edited by Colin Brown. 4 vols. Zondervan, 1986.
Senior, Donald. *Matthew*. Abingdon New Testament Commentary. Abingdon, 1998.
Senior, Donald. *The Passion of Jesus in the Gospel of Matthew*. The Liturgical Press, 1985.
Seow, Choon-Leong. *Daniel*. Westminster Bible Companion. Westminster John Knox Press, 2003.
Seow, Choon-Leong. *Ecclesiastes: A New Translation with Introduction and Commentary*. Anchor Bible. Yale University Press, 1997.
Seow, Choon-Leong. "The First and Second Books of Kings." In *The New Interpreter's Bible*. 12 vols. Abingdon, 1994–2002.
Seow, Choon-Leong. *A Grammar for Biblical Hebrew*. Abingdon, 1987.
Seow, Choon-Leong. *Job 1–21: Interpretation and Commentary*. Illuminations. Eerdmans, 2013.
Shank, Robert. *Elect in the Son: A Study of the Doctrine of Election*. Westcott Publishers, 1970.
Shogren, Gary S. "Mortality and Immortality." In *Dictionary of the Later New Testament & Its Developments*, edited by Ralph P. Martin and Peter H. Davids. InterVarsity Press, 1997.
Simmons, L. M. "The Talmudical Law of Agency." *The Jewish Quarterly Review* 8, no. 4 (1896): 614–631.
Simundson, Daniel J. "The Book of Micah." In *The New Interpreter's Bible*. 12 vols. Abingdon, 1994–2002.
Skelley-Chandler, Stephanie. "Seraph, Seraphs." In *The New Interpreter's Dictionary of the Bible*, edited by K. D. Sakenfeld. 5 vols. Abingdon, 2006–9.
Sleeper, C. Freeman. *James*. Abingdon New Testament Commentaries. Abingdon, 1998.
Smalley, Stephen S. *1, 2, 3 John*. Word Biblical Commentary. Word Books, 1984.
Smalley, Stephen S. *The Revelation of John: A Commentary on the Greek Text of the Apocalypse*. IVP Academic, 2005.
Smith, Abraham. "The First Letter to the Thessalonians." In *The New Interpreter's Bible*. 12 vols. Abingdon, 1994–2002.
Smith, Dennis E. "Eucharist." In *The New Interpreter's Dictionary of the Bible*, edited by K. D. Sakenfeld. 5 vols. Abingdon, 2006–9.
Smith, Dennis E. *From Symposium to Eucharist: The Banquet in the Early Christian World*. Fortress Press, 2003.
Smith, Dustin R. "An Inquiry into the Identity and Meaning of the Devil and Demons." *Journal of Biblical Unitarianism* 1, no. 1 (2014): 43–74.
Smith, Dustin R. "New Testament Portrayals of Wisdom Christology: Meaning, Function, and Purpose." Presentation at the Unitarian Christian Alliance Conference, Little Rock, AR, October 19, 2024.

Smith, Dustin R. *Paradoxical Conquering in the Apocalypse of John.* CreateSpace, 2014.

Smith, Dustin R. "The Plural of Majesty in the Hebrew Bible: Assessing the Extent of Its Pervasiveness and the Implications for Monotheism." Presentation at the Unitarian Christian Alliance Conference, Lawrenceville, OH, October 15, 2022.

Smith, Dustin R. "Taking Philippians 2:6-11 Out of the Vacuum: A Fresh Reading of the Christ-Hymn in Light of the Social-Ethical Argument of Philippians as a Whole." *A Journal from the Radical Reformation* 15, no. 2 (2008): 24–31.

Smith, Dustin R. "Unity and Diversity in Early Church Interpretations of Eschatology." *Journal of Biblical Unitarianism* 2, no. 1 (2015): 7–20.

Smith, Dustin R. "Virginal Conception or Begetting? A Look at the Christology of Matthew 1:18–20." *A Journal from the Radical Reformation* 15, no. 1 (2008): 45–53.

Smith, Dustin R. *Wisdom Christology in the Gospel of John.* Wipf & Stock, 2024.

Smith, Ralph L. *Micah–Malachi.* Word Biblical Commentary. Word Books, 1984.

Smith-Christopher, Daniel L. "The Book of Daniel." In *The New Interpreter's Bible.* 12 vols. Abingdon, 1994–2002.

Soulen, R. Kendall. *The God of Israel and Christian Theology.* Fortress Press, 1996.

Speiser, E. A. *Genesis: Introduction, Translation, and Notes.* Anchor Bible. Doubleday, 1964.

Stein, Robert H. "Last Supper." In *Dictionary of Jesus and the Gospels*, edited by Joel B. Green and Scot McKnight. IVP Academic, 1992.

Stendebach, F. J. "רָגַל." In *Theological Dictionary of the Old Testament*, edited by G. Johannes Botterweck, Helmer Ringgren, and Heinz–Josef Fabry. Translated by David E. Green. 15 vols. Eerdmans, 1974–2006.

Storms, Sam. *Our God Reigns: An Amillennial Commentary of Revelation.* Mentor, 2024.

Strecker, Georg. *The Johannine Letters: A Commentary on 1, 2, and 3 John.* Translated by Linda M. Maloney. Hermeneia. Fortress Press, 1996.

Suggs, M. Jack. *Wisdom, Christology, and Law in Matthew's Gospel.* Harvard University Press, 1970.

Sumney, Jerry L. *Colossians: A Commentary.* New Testament Library. Westminster John Knox Press, 2008.

Sweeney, Marvin A. *I & II Kings: A Commentary.* Old Testament Library. Westminster John Knox Press, 2017.

Swete, Henry Barclay. *The Apocalypse of St. John: The Greek Text With Introduction, Notes, and Indices.* Eerdmans, 1908.

Tannehill, Robert C. *Luke.* Abingdon New Testament Commentary. Abingdon, 1996.

Tate, Marvin E. *Psalms 51–100.* Word Biblical Commentary. Word Books, 1990.

Tengström, S., and Heinz-Joseph Fabry. "רוּחַ." In *Theological Dictionary of the Old Testament*, edited by G. Johannes Botterweck, Helmer Ringgren, and Heinz-Joseph Fabry. 15 vols. Eerdmans, 1974–2006.

Terrien, Samuel. *The Psalms: Strophic Structure and Theological Commentary.* 2 vols. Eerdmans Critical Commentary. Eerdmans, 2003.

Theodoret of Cyrus. *The Questions on the Octateuch.* Vol. 1. Translated by Robert C. Hill. The Library of Early Christianity, volume 1. Catholic University of America Press, 2007.

Thielman, Frank. *The Law and the New Testament: The Question of Continuity.* Crossroad Publishing Company, 1999.

Thiselton, Anthony C. *The First Epistle to the Corinthians.* New International Greek Testament Commentary. Eerdmans, 2000.

Thompson, Henry O. "Yahweh." In *Anchor Bible Dictionary*, edited by David Noel Freedman. 6 vols. Doubleday, 1992.

Thompson, John Arthur. *The Book of Jeremiah.* New International Commentary on the Old Testament. Eerdmans, 1981.

Thompson, Leonard L. *Revelation.* Abingdon New Testament Commentary. Abingdon, 1998.

Thompson, Marianne Meye. *The God of the Gospel of John.* Grand Rapids: Eerdmans, 2001.

Thompson, Marianne Meye. *John: A Commentary.* New Testament Library. Westminster John Knox Press, 2015.

Thompson, Marianne Meye. "John, Gospel of." In *Dictionary of Jesus and the Gospels*, edited by Joel B. Green and Scot McKnight. IVP Academic, 1992.

Thompson, Marianne Meye. *1–3 John.* IVP New Testament Commentary Series. InterVarsity Press, 1992

Thrall, Margaret. *2 Corinthians: A Critical and Exegetical Commentary.* 2 vols. International Critical Commentary. T & T Clark, 2000.

Tigay, Jeffrey H. *Deuteronomy.* JPS Torah Commentary. Jewish Publication Society, 1996.

Tomasino, Anthony. "עוֹלָם." In *The New International Dictionary of Old Testament Theology & Exegesis,* edited by Willem A. VanGemeren. 5 vols. Zondervan, 1997.

Towner, Philip H. *The Letters to Timothy and Titus.* New International Commentary on the New Testament. Eerdmans, 2006.

Towner, W. Sibley. "The Book of Ecclesiastes." In *The New Interpreter's Bible.* 12 vols. Abingdon, 1994–2002.

Towner, W. Sibley. *Daniel.* Interpretation: A Bible Commentary for Teaching and Preaching. John Knox Press, 1984.

Towner, W. Sibley. *Genesis*. Westminster Bible Companion. Westminster John Knox Press, 2001.
Treier, Daniel J. *Proverbs–Ecclesiastes*. Brazos Theological Commentary on the Bible. Brazos Press, 2011.
Tromp, Nicholas J. *Primitive Conceptions of Death and the Nether World in the Old Testament*. Biblica Et Orientalia 21. Pontifical Biblical Institute, 1969.
Tucker, Gene M. "The Book of Isaiah 1–39." In *The New Interpreter's Bible*. 12 vols. Abingdon, 1994–2002.
Tuell, Steven. *Ezekiel*. Baker Books, 2009.
Tuggy, Dale. *What is the Trinity? Thinking about the Father, Son, and Holy Spirit*. CreateSpace, 2017.
Twelftree, Graham H. "Beelzebul." In *The New Interpreter's Dictionary of the Bible*, edited by K. D. Sakenfeld. 5 vols. Abingdon, 2006–9.
Twelftree, Graham H. *Jesus the Exorcist: A Contribution to the Study of the Historical Jesus*. Hendrickson Publishers, 1993.
Twelftree, Graham H. "Temptation of Jesus." In *Dictionary of Jesus and the Gospels*, edited by Joel B. Green and Scot McKnight. IVP Academic, 1992.
Van Pelt, Miles V., and Walter C. Kaiser, Jr. "שָׂעִיר." In *The New International Dictionary of Old Testament Theology & Exegesis*, edited by Willem A. VanGemeren. 5 vols. Zondervan, 1997.
Van Pelt, Miles V., Walter C. Kaiser Jr., and Daniel I. Block. "רוּחַ." In *The New International Dictionary of Old Testament Theology & Exegesis*, edited by Willem A. VanGemeren. 5 vols. Zondervan, 1997.
Vanhoozer, Kevin J. "Systematic Theology." In *Dictionary for Theological Interpretation of the Bible*, edited by Kevin J. Vanhoozer. Baker Academic, 2005.
Vanzant, Michael G. "Dust." In *The New Interpreter's Dictionary of the Bible*, edited by K. D. Sakenfeld. 5 vols. Abingdon, 2006–9.
Verhoef, Pieter A. "Prophecy." In *The New International Dictionary of Old Testament Theology & Exegesis*, edited by Willem A. VanGemeren. 5 vols. Zondervan, 1997.
von Wahlde, Urban C. *The Gospels and Letters of John*. Eerdmans Critical Commentary. 3 vols. Eerdmans, 2010.
Wächer, L. "חתם." In *Theological Dictionary of the Old Testament*, edited by G. Johannes Botterweck, Helmer Ringgren, and Heinz-Joseph Fabry. 15 vols. Eerdmans, 1974–2006.
Wahlen, Clinton. *Jesus and the Impurity of Spirits in the Synoptic Gospels*. Wissenschaftliche Untersuchungen Zum Neuen Testament 2, 185. Mohr Siebeck, 2004.
Wainwright, Elaine M. *Shall We Look for Another? A Feminist Rereading of the Matthean Jesus*. Orbis Books, 1998.
Wallace, Daniel B. *Greek Grammar Beyond the Basics: An Exegetical Syntax of the New Testament*. Zondervan, 1996.
Wallace, Howard N. "Eden, Garden of." In *Anchor Bible Dictionary*, edited by David Noel Freedman. 6 vols. Doubleday, 1992.
Waltke, Bruce K., and Michael P. O'Connor. *An Introduction to Biblical Hebrew Syntax*. Eisenbrauns, 1990.
Walton, John H. *Genesis*. NIV Application Commentary. Zondervan, 2001.
Walton, John H. *Genesis*. Zondervan Illustrated Bible Backgrounds Commentary. Zondervan, 2013.
Walton, John H. *The Lost World of Genesis One: Ancient Cosmology and the Origins Debate*. IVP Academic, 2009.
Walton, John H. "Sons of God, Daughters of Men." In *Dictionary of the Old Testament Pentateuch*, edited by T. Desmond Alexander and David W. Baker. IVP Academic, 2003.
Wanamaker, Charles A. *The Epistles to the Thessalonians*. New International Greek Testament Commentary. Eerdmans, 1990.
Watson, Duane F. "Angels." In *Anchor Bible Dictionary*, edited by David Noel Freedman. 6 vols. Doubleday, 1992.
Watson, Duane F. "Gehenna." In *Anchor Bible Dictionary*, edited by David Noel Freedman. 6 vols. Doubleday, 1992.
Watson, Duane F. "The Letter of Jude." In *The New Interpreter's Bible*. 12 vols. Abingdon, 1994–2002.
Watson, Duane F. "The Second Letter of Peter." In *The New Interpreter's Bible*. 12 vols. Abingdon, 1994–2002.
Watson, Duane F., and Terrance Callan. *First and Second Peter*. Paideia Commentaries. Baker Academic, 2012.
Watts, John D. W. *Isaiah 34–66*. Word Biblical Commentary. Word Books, 1987.
Webb, Barry G. *The Book of Judges*. New International Commentary on the Old Testament. Eerdmans, 2012.
Weeks, Stuart. *Ecclesiastes: A Critical and Exegetical Commentary*. 2 vols. International Critical Commentary. T & T Clark, 2020–22.
Weima, Jeffery A. D. *1–2 Thessalonians*. Baker Exegetical Commentary on the New Testament. Baker Academic, 2014.
Weiss, Johannes. *Jesus' Proclamation of the Kingdom of God*. Translated and edited by Richard Hyde Hiers and David Larrimore Holland. Sigler Press, 1999.
Wenham, Gordon J. *Genesis 1–15*. Word Biblical Commentary. Thomas Nelson, 1987.
Wenham, Gordon J. *Genesis 16–50*. Word Biblical Commentary. Thomas Nelson, 1994.

Westerholm, Stephen. "Grace." In *The New Interpreter's Dictionary of the Bible*, edited by K. D. Sakenfeld. 5 vols. Abingdon, 2006–9.
Westermann, Claus. *Elements of Old Testament Theology*. Translated by Douglas W. Stott. John Knox Press, 1982.
Westermann, Claus. *Genesis 1–11*. Continental Commentary. Translated by John Scullion. Fortress Press, 1994.
Westermann, Claus. *Genesis 12–36*. Continental Commentary. Translated by John Scullion. Fortress Press, 1995.
Wharton, James A. *Job*. Westminster Bible Companion. Westminster John Knox Press, 1999.
Whybray, R. N. *Isaiah 40–66*. New Century Bible Commentary. Eerdmans, 1981.
Wilckins, Ulrich. "στῦλος." In *Theological Dictionary of the New Testament*, edited by G. Bromiley. 10 vols. Eerdmans, 1964–74.
Williams, D. J. "Bride, Bridegroom." In *Dictionary of Jesus and the Gospels*, edited by Joel B. Green and Scot McKnight. IVP Academic, 1992.
Williams, Ronald. *Williams' Hebrew Syntax*. 3rd ed. University of Toronto Press, 2007.
Williams, Sam K. *Galatians*. Abingdon New Testament Commentaries. Abingdon, 1997.
Williamson, H. G. M. *Ezra, Nehemiah*. Word Biblical Commentary. Word, 1985.
Williamson, Paul R. "Covenant." In *Dictionary of the Old Testament Pentateuch*, edited by T. Desmond Alexander and David W. Baker. IVP Academic, 2003.
Wilson, Robert McL. *Colossians and Philemon: A Critical and Exegetical Commentary*. International Critical Commentary. T & T Clark, 2014.
Wilson, Walter T. "Works of Wisdom (Matt 9,9-17; 11,16-19)." *Zeitschrift für die neutestamentliche Wissenschaft* 106, no. 1 (2015): 1–20.
Witherington, Ben, III. *1 and 2 Thessalonians: A Socio–Rhetorical Commentary*. Eerdmans, 2006.
Witherington, Ben, III. *Conflict & Community in Corinth: A Socio-Rhetorical Commentary on 1 and 2 Corinthians*. Eerdmans, 1995.
Witherington, Ben, III. *Jesus the Sage: The Pilgrimage of Wisdom*. Fortress Press, 1994.
Witherington, Ben, III. *John's Wisdom: A Commentary on the Fourth Gospel*. Westminster John Knox Press, 1995.
Witherington, Ben, III. *Matthew*. Smyth & Helwys Bible Commentary. Smyth & Helwys Publishing Inc., 2006.
Witherington, Ben, III. *Revelation*. New Cambridge Bible Commentary. Cambridge, 2009.
Wolff, Hans Walter. *Anthropology of the Old Testament*. Translated by Margaret Kohl. Fortress Press, 1981.
Woods, Edward J. *Deuteronomy: An Introduction and Commentary*. Tyndale Old Testament Commentary. IVP Academic, 2011.
Wray, T. J., and Gregory Mobley. *The Birth of Satan: Tracing the Devil's Biblical Roots*. Palgrave Macmillan, 2005.
Wright, Archie T. "Angels." In *The Eerdmans Dictionary of Early Judaism*, edited by John J. Collins and Daniel C. Harlow. Eerdmans, 2010.
Wright, N. T. *The Climax of the Covenant: Christ and the Law in Pauline Theology*. Fortress Press, 1993.
Wright, N. T. *Colossians and Philemon*. Tyndale New Testament Commentaries. IVP Academic, 2008.
Wright, N. T. *Galatians*. Commentaries for Christian Formation. Eerdmans, 2021.
Wright, N. T. *Jesus and the Victory of God*. Fortress Press, 1996.
Wright, N. T. *Justification: God's Plan and Paul's Vision*. SPCK, 2009.
Wright, N. T. "The Letter to the Romans." In *The New Interpreter's Bible*. 12 vols. Abingdon, 1994–2002.
Wright, N. T. *Matthew for Everyone*. 2 vols. Westminster John Knox Press, 2004.
Wright, N. T. *The New Testament and the People of God*. Fortress Press, 1992.
Wright, N. T. *Paul and the Faithfulness of God*. 2 vols. Fortress Press, 2013.
Wright, N. T. *The Resurrection of the Son of God*. Fortress Press, 2003.
Wright, N.T. *Revelation for Everyone*. Westminster John Knox Press, 2011.
Xeravits, Géza G. "Son of God." In The Eerdmans Dictionary of Early Judaism, edited by John J. Collins and Daniel C. Harlow. Eerdmans, 2010.
Yoder, Christine Roy. *Proverbs*. Abingdon Old Testament Commentary. Nashville, 2009.
Zerwick, Maximilian, and Mary Grosvenor. *A Grammatical Analysis of the Greek New Testament*. 5th ed. Gregorian & Biblical, 2016.
Zimmerli, Walther. *Ezekiel 1: A Commentary on the Book of the Prophet Ezekiel Chapters 1–24*. Translated by Ronald E. Clements. Hermeneia. Fortress Press, 1979.
Zimmerli, Walther. *Ezekiel 2: A Commentary on the Book of the Prophet Ezekiel Chapters 25–48*. Translated by James D. Martin. Hermeneia. Fortress Press, 1983.

Scriptural Index

Genesis
1:1 12, 271, 273
1:2–3 295
1:2–2:4 146
1:3 12, 30, 271
1:4 161
1:5 147
1:6–7 161, 271
1:8 147
1:9 271
1:10 147
1:11 271
1:14 161
1:14–16 271
1:18 161
1:20 271
1:24 271
1:26 79, 80
1:26–27 271
1:26–28 78–79, 83, 85
1:27 54, 68, 79, 85
1:27–28 43, 66, 83
1:28 43, 67, 68, 80, 84, 147, 163, 225
1:31 38, 80, 146
2:2–3 35
2:7 85, 88, 89, 90, 94, 315
2:8 81, 153
2:9 81
2:10 461, 501
2:15 81, 147
2:16 81
2:16–17 148
2:17 150
2:18 151
2:19–20 67, 147
2:21 92
2:22–23 81
2:23 92
3:1 147
3:2 148
3:3 148
3:6 148, 152
3:13–14 149
3:14–15 149
3:15 459
3:16 81, 149
3:16–24 48
3:17 149
3:17–19 43, 60, 458
3:19 89, 91, 97, 149
3:21 149
3:22 81
3:23 81
3:24 58, 81, 153
4:1–4 150
4:3–4 304
4:7 150
4:8 150
5:1 151
5:3 151
5:1–3 82
5:24 151
6:2 151, 152, 154
6:2–4 200, 202, 203
6:4 151, 154
6:5 152
6:6 35
6:6–7 152
6:9 12
6:17 92
7:22 91
9:1 152
9:6 152
9:6–7 82
9:7 83, 152

9:15 92
9:19 153
9:20 153
9:22 153
11:2 153
11:4 153
11:7 154
11:8–9 154
12:1–3 42, 75, 155, 211, 451
12:2 154, 160
12:3 160, 163, 248, 380, 445
12:4 155
12:7 451
13:14–15 451
14:21 94
15:1 211
15:4–6 211
15:6 342, 382
15:7 451
16:7–13 56
16:11 56
17:4–6 211
17:8 451
18:14 31
18:25 47
18:27 90
19:13–15 56
21:17–19 58
21:33 34
24:7 451
25:8 113
25:17 113
26:3 19, 451
26:3–5 212
26:24 21
27:26 218, 304
28:4 451
28:13–15 451
31:11–13 58
32:10 44
32:13 212
32:24–30 58
33:4 304
35:12 451
35:29 113
43:29 40
48:4 452
49:8–10 212, 217, 230
49:29 113
49:33 113
50:1 218
50:24 452

Exodus
1:16 170
2:23–25 52
2:24 43
3:2–6 57
3:6 57
3:7 20
3:7–8 52
3:11 12
3:13 21
3:15 36, 63
4:16 71
4:22 64
4:22–23 235, 303
4:27 304
6:5 52
6:8 43, 452
7:1 71
9:1 12
9:27 20
15:1 305, 481

15:2 11
15:7 63
15:21 305
18:7 304
19:3–8 158
19:5–6 66, 159, 401, 402, 409
20:2–3 159
20:3–5 352
20:5 35
20:12 171
21:6 72
22:8–9 72
22:9 72
22:22–23 49
23:20 57
23:21 57
24:3–4 170
24:3–8 159
24:4 501
24:5–8 172
24:8 170
25:8 161, 403
25:18–22 59
25:31–40 411
28:2–43 161
28:9–12 458
28:15–21 501
29:46 403
30:1 410
31:2–5 312
32:13 43, 452
32:14 32
32:30 65
32:32 65
32:34–33:2 58
33:23 35
34:6 35, 47
34:6–7 39
34:7 47
40:6 161
40:9–10 161
40:34 161

Leviticus
1:4 160
4:1–35 160
4:4 160
4:15 160
4:20 65
4:24 160
4:29 160
4:33 160
5:10 65
6:7 65
7:20 95
8:5–36 160
8:11 161
10:6 414
10:10 160
15:31 162
16:16–22 161
16:24 161
17:7 196
18:6–19 153
19:18 424, 434
19:22 65
21:11 94
23:29 94

Numbers
1:51 161
6:3–4 414
6:5 414
6:6 94
6:22–27 66

6:24–25 40
6:25 35
11:17 295, 312
11:18 35
11:25–26 295
19:13 94
20:16 58
20:24 113
21:6–9 59
22:22 188
22:32 188
23:19 238
24:2–4 295
24:17 122, 213
27:18 295

Deuteronomy
1:30–31 235
4:35 12, 21, 24, 25
4:37–38 52
4:39 13, 21
5:7–9 352
5:16 171
6:4 352
6:4–5 24, 165, 322, 424
6:6–7 24
6:25 382
7:7–8 40
7:9 42, 44
7:9–10 388
7:10 48
8:2 237, 324
8:5 236, 324
9:10 35
10:17 47
10:18 49
12:5 162
12:11 162
12:21 162
12:31 35
14:1 236
14:23 162
16:2 162
16:6 162
16:11 162
18:15 227, 252–254
18:18–19 252, 253
18:19 254
24:4 452
24:7 94
25:1 385
27:26 173, 428
28:1–2 163
28:3 163
28:4 163
28:5–14 164
28:15 48, 164
28:16 164
28:18 164
28:36–41 164
28:63–64 48
28:64 452
30:1–6 165, 173
30:2 165
30:6 175, 323, 327
30:17–18 388
30:19–20 43
31:16 113
32:3 305
32:4 381
32:6 15
32:9 21
32:11 295
32:17 195, 196, 199
32:35 49
32:40 36

530

32:50 113
34:9 312

Joshua
4:12 501
4:20–22 458
6:4–15 501
10:28 95
10:40 91
11:11 91
11:14 91
21:45 44
23:14 98

Judges
2:1 58
3:10 293
5:2–3 305
5:11 381
5:18 95
6:34 294
8:22–23 66
11:29–32 294
13:24 38
14:6 294
14:19 294
15:14 294

Ruth
1:6 21

1 Samuel
2:6 100, 121
2:10 21
2:27 64
9:16 20
10:1 218, 304
10:10 294
10:18 52
11:6 294
11:11 294
16:4 217
16:13 294
17:8–10 236
17:50 236
29:4 188

2 Samuel
3:18 21
4:8 95
6:2 59
7:5 162
7:12 113, 214, 216, 217, 467
7:12–14 228
7:12–16 44, 69, 213, 453
7:13 162, 218, 425
7:14 69, 218, 234, 467
7:16 467
7:22 12
12:1 63
15:5 218
19:22 188
22:6 101
22:11 59
22:51 21
24:10–17 236

1 Kings
2:2 98
2:10 113
3:10 35
5:4 188
6:13 403
6:23–28 59
8:6–7 59
8:11 162
8:11–12 161
8:23 19
11:14 188
11:23 188
11:43 113
12:16 236
14:20 113

14:31 113
15:8 113
15:24 114
16:6 114
16:28 114
18:1 63
18:31 458
22:19 21, 64
22:19–22 306
22:19–23 203
22:40 114
22:50 114

2 Kings
5:10–14 501
8:24 114
10:35 114
13:9 114
13:13 114
13:21 126
14:16 114
14:29 114
15:7 114
15:22 114
15:38 114
16:20 114
19:15 22, 59
20:1–6 33
20:5 33
20:21 114
21:18 114
22:20 112
23:10 136
24:4–11 164
24:6 114

1 Chronicles
13:6 59
16:22 295
17:11 214
17:11–14 44, 69, 453
17:13 69, 234
17:14 214
21:1 188
24:7–19 410
26:16 410
29:20 304
29:23 70

2 Chronicles
9:31 115
10:16 236
11:15 196
12:16 115, 381
14:1 115
15:1 294
16:13 115
19:7 47
20:14 295
21:1 115
24:20 295, 388
34:28 112
36:22 294

Ezra
6:12 21
9:15 381

Nehemiah
9:17 40

Job
1:6 151, 188, 189, 200
1:7 189
1:9 189
1:12 189
2:1 151, 188, 189, 200
2:1–8 189
3:13–17 109
3:13 115
4:17 23, 37
7:8 151
7:9 100
7:21 98, 115

7:24 151
9:8 22
10:8–9 98
10:18–19 109
10:21–22 109
14:1 228
14:12–14 115
14:13–14 100
14:14 121
14:20–21 109
15:14 229
17:14 134
17:16 98, 100
19:25–26 121
21:26 98
24:19–20 134
25:4 229
27:3 90
28:12–13 265
28:20–24 265
28:27–28 265
28:28 267
30:19 98
32:8 90
33:4 90, 295
34:15 93
34:19 47
38:7 151
40:12–13 98
42:17 121

Psalms
1:2 382
1:4 132
1:6 132, 382
2:2 21, 218
2:6 218
2:7 218, 234
2:8 218
2:9 133
2:11 303, 304
2:12 218, 304
3:2 94
3:7 13
4:1 39
6:2 39
6:4–5 94
6:5 101, 110
7:8–9 52
7:9 383
7:9–11 381
7:11 35
7:11–12 50
8:1–9 67–68
8:3–4 68
8:3–6 122
8:4 238
8:5 85
8:6 82
8:6–8 459
8:7–8 68
9:3 39
9:4–6 132
9:4–8 381
9:7 36
9:7–8 50
10:17–18 49
11:4 70
11:5–7 381
12:6 501
13:3 113
15:2 382
16:2 12
16:10 101, 102, 103
18:5 101
18:10 59
18:50 45, 219
19:1 30
22:1 279, 280
22:15 99
25:10 42
26:1 52
26:7–8 162
28:1 110

30:3 101
30:9 99, 110
30:10 39
31:5 42
31:13 151
31:17 110
33:6 30, 271–273
34:16 132
34:21 132
35:24 381
37:2 132
37:3 452
37:9 204, 452
37:9–10 132
37:10 151
37:11 452
37:17 383
37:20 132
37:22 132, 452
37:28 132
37:29 453
37:34 132, 452
37:36 132
38:3 92
39:13 151
41:4 39
41:13 36
42:4 162
43:1–2 52
43:3 63, 301
44:25 99
45:1 69, 305
45:3 69
45:6 72
45:6–7 72, 219, 257
45:7 72
47:7–8 67
48:9–10 162
49:14 101
49:15 101
50:6 381
50:22 133
51:11 297
54:1–4 52
60:7 35
67:1 40
68:5 49
68:18 11
69:28 133
71:22 20
72:1 69
72:1–2 381
72:8 82
72:18 22
75:10 383
76:5–6 110, 115
78:39 92
78:40 35
78:49 63
82:1–4 49
84:4 162
86:3 39
86:13 101
88:3 101
89:1–4 45
89:3–4 219, 455
89:9 69
89:13 69
89:14 69, 381
89:20–21 69
89:24 69
89:26–27 234
89:26–28 45
89:29 219
89:34–37 45
89:35–37 455
89:36 219
89:38–45 455
89:46 455
89:48 101
89:49–50 455
90:2 34
90:3 99
93:1–2 67

94:17 111
95:3 67
95:6 23
95:6–7 37
96:10 67
96:13 381
97:1 67
98:2–3 380
98:6 67
98:9 381
99:1 67
100:3 19
102:26–27 34
103:13 35
103:13–14 90
103:17–18 380
103:19 70
104:1 69
104:24 267, 274
104:29 99
104:30 60, 61, 295, 300
104:35 151
105:15 295
106:37 196
106:37–38 195
107:20 61, 272, 273
109:6 188
109:24 92
110:1 28, 244, 278, 285, 286, 288, 307, 478, 498
110:4 288
111:7 42
111:9 63
115:3 31
115:17 111
116:3 102
119:16 158
119:40 158
119:48 158
119:58 39
119:137–138 381
121:2–4 35
130:7–8 40
132:10–11 45
132:11 219, 226
135:21 11
136:25 92
139:1–4 31–32
139:7 297
140:1–6 52
141:7 100, 102
143:10 301
146:1 11
146:4 91, 99, 111
146:6 42
147:1 11
147:15 61, 272
147:18 61, 272
148:13 22
150:6 90

Proverbs
1:2 268
1:2–4 268
1:8 268
1:12 100
1:19 151
1:20–33 62
1:21 269
1:21–31 268, 269
1:23 62
1:28 265
1:33 266
2:10–13 274
2:21–22 388
3:13 267
3:13–18 269
3:13–24 62
3:15 269
3:16 266
3:17 266, 267
3:18 274
3:19–20 267, 274

4:5 267
4:18 274
5:5 101
7:27 102
8:1–21 269
8:1–36 62
8:7 266
8:19 269
8:22 267
9:22–23 274
8:22–36 269
8:27 274
8:30 274
8:34 266
8:35 266, 274
9:1 269
9:1–5 266
9:1–6 62, 269
9:3 269
9:5 266, 270
9:5–6 266
9:11 266
9:18 100
22:2 37
23:14 101
24:20 133
28:17 94
30:15–16 100
31:10–31 269, 270, 274
31:14 270
31:15 269
31:16 269
31:23 269

Ecclesiastes
3:20 90, 99, 100
9:5 111
9:10 100, 112
12:7 91, 100
12:13–14 47

Isaiah
1:4 20
1:10 64
2:4 460, 503
2:22 90
5:14 100
5:16 381
6:1 21, 66
6:1–8 306
6:2 59
6:3 59
6:6–7 59
6:8 63
6:9–10 354
9:6 72
9:6–7 219
9:8 61, 272, 273
10:1–2 49
11:1 230
11:1–2 453
11:1–5 215, 294
11:2–3 215
11:3–4 381
11:6 459
11:8 459
11:10 228, 230
11:12 501
12:2 11
13:21 196
14:11 134
14:22 64
14:29 59
16:5 45, 453
23:5 45
24:16 20
25:8 458, 470, 471
26:19 104
26:21 50
27:11 23
28:15 102
28:18 102
29:16 37
30:8–9 219

30:9 45
30:27 35
33:10–12 133
33:15–17 219
33:17 67
33:22 67
33:22–24 59
33:15–17 45
33:22 47
34:9–10 140
34:14 196
35:1–2 460
35:1–7 459
35:5–6 369
35:7 460
38:1–5 33
38:18 102, 112
38:19 112
40:6–8 92, 93
40:28 23, 34, 35
41:2 98
41:8 247
41:10 13
41:18–19 460
42:1–2 248
42:1–3 246
42:5 90
42:6–7 246
44:21 247
44:24 22
45:6 21
45:11–12 37
45:21 21
46:9 21
46:9–10 32
48:16 300
49:5 248
49:6 75, 248
49:6–7 246
49:26 93
50:6 249
50:6–10 246
51:3 460
52:2 104
52:13 247, 249
53:3–9 247
53:5 248
53:6 248
53:7–8 249
53:9 249
53:11 21
53:11–12 247
53:12 95, 249
54:1 441
54:1–3 437
55:11 61, 272, 273
55:13 460
57:15 36
60:18 460
60:21 452
63:10 301
63:14–16 324
63:16 15
63:16–17 304
64:8 15
66:1 35, 70
66:15–16 134
66:17 134
66:22 133–134

Jeremiah
1:7 64
1:8 64
2:4 64
2:26 162
2:34 94
3:12 353
3:14 324, 353
3:18 452
3:19 15, 236, 324
5:28–29 49
6:13 162
7:31–32 136
9:12 35

10:12 267, 274
10:16 23
12:1 381
17:5 92
18:7–8 32
19:6 136
23:3 83, 452
23:5 215, 381
23:5–6 84, 454
24:5–7 166
27:5 35
30:9 454
30:18–19 83
31:9 324
31:12 461
31:31–34 166, 175, 178
31:34 170, 172
32:17 31
32:27 93
33:15–17 454
33:17 455
43:6 94
49:2 64
49:10 151
51:15 267, 274
51:39 115
51:57 115

Lamentations
1:18 381
3:4 92
3:21–23 44
5:19 36

Ezekiel
1:4–22 307
1:26 307
1:26–28 21
2:1 238
2:3 238
2:4 64
2:6 238
2:8 238
3:20 388
10:1–22 59
10:18 162, 403
11:17–20 167, 174
11:19–20 322, 323
13:9 35
17:17 94
18:4 94
18:20 94
21:26–27 453
22:6–7 49
22:26 162
28:19 151
31:17 100
34:11–16 70
34:23 236
34:23–24 45, 70, 216, 454
34:25 459, 460
34:28 459
36:10–11 83
36:24 452
36:24–30 167, 174
36:26–27 322, 323
36:28 13, 20
36:33–35 460
37:1–14 150
37:9–12 105
37:11 105
37:13–14 295
37:24 236
37:24–25 84, 216, 454
37:25 455
37:26 83, 460
39:7 20
39:29 298
44:20 414
47:7–10 461
47:12 461

Daniel
1:9 52

1:17 52
2:38 457
2:39 457
2:40–43 457
2:44 334
2:44–45 457
3:24–28 52
4:34 36
6:20–23 52
7:1–14 238
7:13 242, 244
7:13–14 239–241, 254–256, 425, 426
7:14 241
7:15–28 238
7:17–18 52
7:18 239
7:21 239
7:21–22 52
7:22 239
7:24 239
7:25 239, 502
7:25–26 52
7:26 239
7:27 239
9:4–7 380
9:14 381
9:24 501
9:27 502
10:1 201
10:11 56
10:12 201
10:13 59, 201
10:20–21 201
12:2 105, 115, 121–124, 134, 138, 376, 458, 500
12:3 122–123
12:7 36, 502
12:11 502
12:13 113, 122–123, 376, 452

Hosea
1:9–10 402
1:10 236
2:14–20 437
2:18 459
3:4–5 454
3:5 219
6:6 427
8:14 23
11:1 236–237
11:9 20
11:12 42
12:3–4 58
13:14 102, 121, 471

Joel
2:1–3 460
2:12–14 32
2:13 40, 64
2:27 21
2:28 407
2:28–29 316, 322
2:30 317
3:12 50
3:18 461

Amos
1:3 64
9:4 35
9:11 219, 454
9:13 461

Jonah
1:9 13
2:2 106
3:10 33
4:3 95, 151

Micah
3:8 295
3:11 162
4:3 50, 460, 503

4:3–4 503
4:4 460
5:2 70
5:2–4 217
5:4 70, 236, 254
5:5 460
7:20 42

Nahum
1:2–3 50
1:3 35

Habakkuk
1:12 36
2:5 102

Zephaniah
3:5 381
3:15 67
3:20 64

Haggai
1:8 64
2:4 298
2:5 298

Zechariah
3:1 189
3:1–2 189
3:2 189
3:8 217
6:12 218
7:9–12 49
9:9 460
9:10 460
12:8 70, 219, 254
14:9 21, 67

Malachi
2:7 66
2:10 15
3:1 162, 403
3:5 50
3:6 34
4:1 133
4:3 133

Matthew
1:1 210, 211, 221, 222, 466
1:2–6 222
1:3 222
1:5 222
1:6 222
1:16 222
1:18 79, 222
1:19 222
1:20 79, 222
1:21 368
2:14–15 237
2:16 170
3:1–2 333, 413
3:1–6 358
3:2 336, 353, 395
3:5–8 413
3:7–8 334
3:8 395
3:9 395,458
3:10 136, 395
3:10–11 504
3:12 136–138
3:13–17 358
3:16 262, 414
3:17 235
4:1 190, 237
4:2 237
4:3 190, 237
4:5 190
4:6 237
4:8 190
4:10 190
4:11 190, 193
4:17 171, 261, 334, 336, 353, 358, 368, 475

4:20 363
4:21–22 171
4:22 363, 425
4:23 197, 317, 335, 475
4:23–24 406
4:24 197
4:25 356
5:3 368, 475
5:5 204, 368, 462, 475
5:8 172
5:10 475
5:14–16 76
5:17 424
5:18 424
5:20 382, 465
5:22 137
5:28 172
5:29–30 137
5:34–37 177
5:35 35
6:1 15
6:8 32
6:9 15, 304
6:10 368
6:12 406
6:25–32 46
6:33 46, 75, 336, 425
7:13 135
7:19 136
7:21–22 465
7:21–23 387, 489
7:24 363
7:28 170
7:29 171
8:5–11 426
8:10 343
8:11 472
8:16–17 248
8:20 242
8:22 363
8:25 368
8:28–32 197
8:29 204
9:1–3 240
9:2 343
9:2–8 255
9:4 172
9:6 240, 256
9:8 171, 406
9:9 437
9:13 427, 437
9:14–15 436
9:15 438
9:21 368
9:22 343, 356, 368
9:24 119
9:25 369
9:28–29 344
9:29 356
9:34 190
9:35 317, 335, 475
10:1 401, 407, 419
10:7 261, 336
10:7–8 475
10:8 261, 419
10:14–15 490
10:18–20 316
10:20 296, 302
10:22 365, 368
10:28 137
10:30 32
10:39 96
10:40 261
11:1 170
11:2 264
11:11 229, 475
11:12 475
11:18–19 264
11:20 353
11:20–24 490
11:25–27 264, 265
12:3–6 404
12:6 405
12:7 427

12:14–21 248
12:24–29 191
12:28 296, 368, 475
12:28–29 498
12:29 499
12:32 134
12:34 172
12:36–37 385
12:37 371
12:40 106
12:41 353
12:41–42 490, 501
12:42 264
12:50 368
13:15 173
13:19 173, 177, 340
13:21 488
13:23 356
13:24–30 123
13:33 477
13:36–43 51, 123
13:38–39 191, 194
13:40 136–138, 504
13:40–42 491
13:41 477
13:42 504
13:43 123, 491
13:44–46 477
13:47–50 491
13:49 383
13:50 504
13:53 170
13:57 65
14:16 419
14:19 419
14:30 368
14:33 304
15:19–19 172
15:28 356
16:16 234
16:21 38, 47
16:25 96
16:27 93, 241, 387, 493
17:9 128
17:12 242, 243
17:20 344
17:22 243
17:22–23 47
18:1 476
18:4 368, 476
18:10 35
18:17 388, 396
18:21–22 406
18:22 501
18:23 173, 368
18:23–35 50
19:1 170
19:4 23
19:4–6 79
19:26 31
19:28 84, 241, 399, 464, 467, 501
19:29 125, 368, 463
20:18–19 243
20:28 96, 243, 248
21:9 256, 468
21:11 65
21:21–22 344
21:31 368, 476
21:33–43 50
21:37 252
21:42 341
21:43 51
21:44 136
22:1–14 51
22:2 67
22:2–14 491
22:7 51
22:13 51
22:31 128
22:44 28, 286
23:13 476
23:22 35
23:23 346

533

23:33 137
23:34 264
24:2 487
24:3 241, 487
24:10 488
24:13 365, 366, 368
24:14 336
24:27 241, 483
24:36 32, 438, 468, 485, 487
24:37 241
24:39 241
24:42–44 486
24:45 463
24:45–51 491
24:46 463
24:47 463
24:51 136
25:1–13 438, 491
25:10 438
25:13 438
25:14–30 491
25:21 463
25:23 463
25:31 490
25:31–34 138, 241, 368, 383, 467
25:31–46 51
25:34 125, 463, 468, 490
25:35–40 49
25:40 396
25:41 51, 138, 203, 204, 504
25:46 51, 125, 138, 139, 203, 204, 376, 383, 490
26:1–2 170
26:2 242, 243
26:24 243
26:26 419
26:28 170, 172, 237
26:45 243
26:63–64 234
26:64 286
26:67 249
27:30 249
27:37 238, 280
27:40 238, 280
27:42 280, 368
27:43 280
27:46 14, 280
27:50 280
27:52 119
27:61 280
27:62–66 280
28:7 106
28:9 282
28:10 396
28:17 282
28:18 256, 287, 309
28:19-20 7, 262, 336, 358, 414

Mark
1:1 234, 333
1:9–11 235
1:10 262, 414
1:12–13 190
1:14 333
1:14–15 171, 334, 356, 367, 395
1:15 261, 353, 368, 475
1:23–27 406
1:27 171
1:34 198
2:3–11 425
2:8 172
2:10 240, 256
2:14–15 425
2:23 240, 425
2:24 240
2:27 426
2:27–28 241
3:4 96, 369
3:5 172

3:14 401
3:14–15 475
3:22 190
3:27 476, 499
3:31–35 395
3:33–35 171
3:35 368
4:11 354, 395
4:12 354
4:14 340
4:17 488
4:20 356
4:26–29 477
4:30–32 477
5:1–20 426
5:2–13 406
5:23 369
5:25–34 406
5:41 369, 406
6:2 265
6:3 223
6:7 261
6:12 261
6:52 172
6:56 369, 406
7:10 424
7:18–19 426
7:19 430
7:25–29 406
8:17 172
8:29 248
8:31 242, 243, 279
8:31–32 248
8:36 96
8:38 241, 494
9:9 106, 243, 279
9:9–10 128
9:12 243
9:25–27 406
9:31 242, 248, 279
9:43–47 369
9:45 137
10:15 465
10:17 376
10:19 424
10:27 31
10:29–30 395
10:30 123, 134, 369, 376
10:33–34 248
10:34 279
10:38–39 418
10:45 243, 245, 248
10:47–48 223
10:52 356, 369
11:9–10 223
11:10 468
11:15–17 404
11:25 404
11:28 171
12:1–11 50
12:6 252
12:6–10 458
12:9 51, 135
12:10 341
12:28 24
12:29–31 424, 434
12:30 319
12:32 24
12:34 424, 427
12:36 28
12:41–44 49
13:13 369
13:20 94
13:32 32, 468, 485, 487
13:33 486
13:26 484
14:21 243
14:22–25 419
14:24 170
14:36 308, 319, 418
14:55–64 244
15:19 249
15:26 238
15:34 14, 25, 279

15:37 279
15:39 210, 279
15:43 466
15:44–45 280
15:46 280
16:8 282
16:9–20 2

Luke
1:5 413
1:11–20 58
1:13 58
1:15 414
1:18–20 58
1:19 58
1:31–33 466
1:31–35 224
1:35 79, 224, 296
1:37 31
1:46–55 305
1:68–79 305
2:14 305
2:40 265
2:52 265
3:6 93
3:7–8 334
3:8 363, 458
3:8–14 363
3:9 354
3:16 360
3:16–17 504
3:17 137
3:18 334
3:21–22 225, 414
3:22 235, 262
3:23–38 225
3:38 225
4:1–13 190
4:2 237
4:3 237
4:6–7 190
4:9 237
4:13 193
4:14 296
4:18–19 49
4:21 341
4:32 171
4:40–41 198
4:41 234
4:43 171, 259, 261, 335
4:43–5:1 340
5:24 240, 256
5:30 406
5:32 353
5:43 256
6:9 96
6:13 401
6:20 177, 368
6:22 243
6:40 49
6:46 363
7:6–9 426
7:8 171
7:11–15 49
7:14 369
7:19 369
7:21–23 369
7:34 406
7:35 264
7:50 356, 369
8:1 335
8:1–2 475
8:11 340
8:12 173, 177, 369
8:13 363
8:15 173, 356, 363
8:21 425
8:29 200
8:36 369
8:54 369
9:1–2 261, 336
9:2 475
9:11 335
9:22 47, 243

9:24 96
9:26 241
9:59–60 171
9:60 336, 425
10:1–3 261
10:7–8 430
10:7–9 426
10:8–9 499
10:8–12 490
10:9 261, 336
10:13 354
10:16 261
10:17–19 499
10:21–22 264
10:25 125, 376, 463
11:14–26 200
11:15 190
11:20 368, 476
11:20–22 499
11:31 264
11:49 264
12:5 137
12:12 301, 316
12:39–40 486
12:40 241
12:42 463
12:42–48 491
12:44 463
13:3 135, 354
13:5 135, 354
13:5–6 363
13:23 369
14:14 369, 375
14:21 36
15:1–2 406
15:2 354
15:7 354
15:10 354
15:20 35
15:24 375, 477
15:32 36, 375, 477
16:10–12 346
16:16 171, 424
17:3 389, 396
17:4–5 344
17:11–19 426
17:20–21 476
17:24 484
17:27 136
17:28–29 136
17:29–30 137
17:33 96
18:8 241
18:14 371
18:17 356
18:18 125, 376, 463
18:27 31
18:30 123, 134, 369, 376
18:31–32 248
18:32–33 47
19:7 406
19:9 369
19:11–27 51, 491
19:15 387
19:17 464
19:19 464
19:20 387
19:22 51, 387
19:27 51
20:9–18 50
20:13 252
22:20 422
20:34–36 124
20:35–36 369, 375
20:42 28
21:27 242
22:19 172
22:20 170
22:30 464, 472, 501
22:48 243
23:38 238
23:42 466, 471
23:43 471
23:46 91, 280

23:47 280
23:48–49 280
23:53 280
24:13–31 282
24:37 282
24:39 282
24:46 106, 128
24:46–48 262
24:47 354, 407

John
1:1 273
1:1–2 273
1:1–5 270, 271, 273
1:1–18 225, 265
1:2 273
1:3 273
1:4 273
1:5 273
1:14 41, 263, 270, 271, 274, 405
1:17 41
1:31–33 235
1:31–34 414
1:32 262
1:34 235
1:45 427
1:49 234
1:51 245
2:1–5 225
2:3–10 266
2:12 225, 226
2:18–19 260
2:19–21 405
2:21 260, 461
3:3 75, 335, 373
3:5 75, 335, 373
3:13 245
3:14 244, 245
3:15 349
3:16 27, 33, 39, 135, 349, 377
3:17 252, 369
3:18 254
3:22 414
3:26 358,438
3:29 438
3:34 253, 274
3:36 349, 377
4:1–2 358
4:1–3 414
4:19 253
4:23 304, 319
4:24 319
4:34 259
4:39–42 426
5:18 259
5:19 259
5:21 255
5:22 50
5:22–24 255, 259
5:23 252
5:24 349, 375, 377
5:24–29 377
5:25–26 255
5:26 34, 37
5:27 50, 171, 244, 255, 259
5:28–29 104, 106, 124, 369, 375, 387, 494, 501, 505
5:29 349
5:30 50
5:34 369
5:37 35
5:43 253
5:44 22
6:14 65, 253
6:27 244
6:35 266
6:39 124
6:39–40 369
6:40 124, 377
6:42 225

6:44 124, 260, 369
6:51 266
6:53–58 421
6:54 124, 377
7:3–5 226
7:10 226
7:16 274
7:16–18 253
7:19 427
7:34 265
7:40 253
7:41–43 226
7:53–8:11 2
8:16 50, 259
8:17 427
8:28 245, 253
8:31 363
8:38 253
8:41–42 27
8:44 194
10:7 266
10:11 96, 266
10:15 96
10:16 266
10:17–18 47
10:18 171, 260
10:28–29 260
10:29 35
10:30 260
10:30–36 259
10:32 259
10:34 427
11:11–14 116
11:24–25 344
11:24–26 124
11:43 369
11:43–44 116
11:49–50 281
11:51 281
12:13 254
12:17 106
12:23 245
12:25 96
12:31–32 499
12:37–38 248
12:44 252
12:45 252
12:47 369
12:48 254, 369, 490
12:49 259
12:49–50 274
13:3 261
13:16 252
13:18 341
13:20 252, 261
13:31–32 245
13:34 435
13:37 96
14:6 266
14:9 256
14:13 304
14:15 427
14:26 60, 300, 301
14:28 15, 258
15:6 136, 365
15:10 427
15:13 96
15:16 304
15:25 427
15:26 60, 300, 301
16:7 300
16:21 226
16:23 304
17:2 93
17:3 10, 15, 22, 76, 252, 257, 377
17:18 262
17:33 96
18:14 281
18:37 226
19:5 281
19:14 281
19:26–27 225
19:28 281

19:33 281
19:34 281
19:42 281
20:14 282
20:17 14, 15, 27, 257, 261, 396
20:17–18 282
20:19–23 282
20:21 262, 337
20:22–23 406
20:26 282
20:28 257
20:31 210, 226, 234, 356
21:6–8 461
21:14 106
21:15 282
21:15–17 389

Acts
1:3 338, 468
1:5 361
1:6 468
1:7 468, 485
1:8 262, 296, 316, 337, 338
1:9–11 242
1:11 468, 484
1:15 396
2:1–4 316
2:16–17 316
2:17 361, 407
2:17–21 93
2:19 317
2:22–23 275
2:22–24 283
2:23–24 52
2:24 177
2:27 102, 103
2:30 227
2:31 102, 103
2:32–33 285
2:34 28
2:38 354, 358, 361, 415
2:41 359
2:43 317
3:13 14
3:14–15 52
3:15 128
3:19 177, 354
3:19–21 372, 450
3:21 469
3:22 227
3:22–23 177, 254
4:2 128
4:4 357
4:8 316
4:10 106
4:13 316
4:30 317
4:31 317
5:3 301
5:4 301
5:5 91
5:10 91
5:12 317
5:14 357
5:31 28, 285, 354
6:1–6 49
6:3 396
6:8 317
7:30–31 57
7:36 317
7:37 227, 254
7:55–56 286, 307
7:59–60 304
7:60 116
8:4 340
8:5–12 361
8:12 337, 338, 340, 357, 359, 415
8:14 340
8:17 361
8:26–35 249
8:29 301, 316, 325

8:36 415
8:36–39 359
8:38 415
9:17 397
9:17–18 361
9:18 359
10:19 325
10:28 427
10:34–35 48
10:38 296, 317
10:40–41 283
10:42 260
10:44 361
10:44–45 313
10:45 427
10:47–48 415
10:48 313, 359
11:12 325
11:18 355, 359
11:21 357
11:23 41
11:27 65
12:11 56
13:1 65
13:2 316, 325
13:9 316
13:23 227
13:36 116
13:43 41
13:44 341
13:48 357
14:2 397
14:3 317
14:22 338, 346, 466
14:26 41
15:3 397
15:8 361
15:12 317
15:25–26 286
15:32 65
15:40 41
16:6–7 310
16:14–15 359
16:31 370
16:31–32 357
16:33 359
17:3 10, 15, 22, 76
17:11–12 357
17:24–25 34
17:25 19, 90
17:30–31 204, 260, 284, 355, 381
17:31 48, 309, 491
17:32 128
18:8 359
18:27 41
19:4–5 362
19:6 362
19:8 338
19:8–10 340
20:9–10 126
20:17 15
20:21 355
20:24–25 41
20:25 338
20:28 316
20:32 41
21:17 397
22:16 359, 415
23:6 128
24:15 383, 501
24:21 128
26:17–18 499
26:19–20 355
26:20 363
27:23 58
27:25 58
28:23 337, 338
28:28–31 337
28:31 317, 338

Romans
1:1–3 28
1:1–4 227, 229, 284, 338

1:3 93, 267
1:4 128, 286
1:5–6 346
1:7 26, 40
1:9 27
1:16 180, 357
1:16–17 384
1:18 36
1:20 30
1:23 37
1:25 23, 37–38
1:32 138
2:4 355
2:5 355
2:5–6 51, 381, 491
2:5–11 48, 387
2:5–16 385
2:6–8 494
2:7 377
2:11 51
2:13 371
2:16 51, 260, 491, 494, 504
2:29 174, 323
3:1–2 347
3:1–3 181
3:1–4 46
3:3 347
3:5 181
3:9 180, 181
3:10–18 181
3:20 181
3:21–22 46
3:21–26 384
3:22 345, 384
3:23 180
3:24 41, 371
3:26 345
3:28 327, 344, 372, 385, 386
3:29–30 25
3:30 417
4:11 430
4:11–13 343
4:13 374, 464
4:25 183
5:1 372, 385
5:1–2 41, 146
5:5 175
5:6 183
5:8 183
5:9 370
5:10 27
5:12 38, 180, 182
5:12–21 41, 281
5:13–14 182
5:14 281
5:15 184, 282
5:15–19 309
5:17 478
5:19 282
5:20 157, 181
5:21 42, 182, 479
6:3 359
6:3–6 415
6:4 327, 359, 364
6:6 184, 359
6:9 126, 284
6:10 183
6:11 375
6:11–13 364
6:11–14 185
6:13 375, 388
6:14 429
6:15 429
6:17 175, 183
6:20 183
6:22 377
6:23 182
7:6 327, 429
7:7 181
7:9–10 326
7:9–11 182
7:11 183

7:12 326, 423
7:14 183
7:23 183
8:1 179
8:2 178
8:3 184
8:3–4 326
8:3–8 327
8:4 429
8:9–11 309
8:11 129
8:13 325
8:14 301, 324, 399
8:14–15 314, 397
8:15 16
8:16 319
8:19–22 398
8:20 180, 471
8:20–23 372
8:21 183
8:23 316, 319, 371, 399, 471
8:24 370
8:26 319
8:26–27 301, 319
8:29 86
8:34 285, 287
9:6 400
9:8 401
10:1–11 327
10:4 383, 429
10:9 344
10:17 340
11:3 96
11:20 400
11:25–26 400
11:27 175
12:1 305, 409
12:2 399, 478
12:4–5 318
12:6 41, 318
12:17 185
12:21 185
13:8–10 327
13:9–10 434
13:11 370
14:1 431
14:1–3 430
14:5 431
14:10–12 48, 51, 387, 494, 504
14:14 431, 433
14:17 478
14:20 431
15:6 14, 16, 27
15:12 228
15:13 296, 325
15:18–19 296
15:19 317
15:30 325
16:17 388
16:20 194
16:26–27 347
16:27 20

1 Corinthians
1:3 26, 40
1:4–6 41
1:7 286, 489
1:7–8 469, 485, 491
1:9 27, 46
1:18 46, 371
1:24 266
1:30 266
2:4 317
2:4–5 297
2:7–8 267
3:13 492, 504
3:16 299
3:16–17 407
3:17 138
3:21–22 374
3:22–23 258
4:2 347

4:15 397
4:20 478
5:2 388
5:5 492
5:7–8 432
5:10 504
5:11 389
5:13 388
6:1–3 464
6:3 204
6:9 463
6:11 314, 359, 372
6:14 53, 129
6:15 421
6:17 309
6:18–20 408
6:19 299
7:4 439
7:18 430
7:39 117
8:6 15, 38
8:8 431, 433
9:4 433
9:19–22 432
9:27 492
10:4 268
10:6 268
10:11 126, 268
10:16 421
10:16–20 401
10:17 421
10:20–21 199, 421
10:25 433
10:25–27 431
11:3 258
11:7 85
11:17–34 117
11:21 421
11:23–26 420
11:25 174, 422
11:27–32 421
11:30 118, 422
12:11 318
12:12 317
12:13 314, 416
12:18 318
12:28–29 65
12:31 318
13:5 185
13:8 435
14:4 318
14:26 318
14:29–32 65
14:37 65
15:1 357
15:1–2 365
15:2 371
15:3 183
15:6 118, 127
15:7–9 313
15:12 128
15:13 128
15:16–17 130
15:17 344
15:18 118
15:20 106, 118, 127, 374
15:21 309
15:22–26 470, 471
15:23 118, 127
15:24 284, 374
15:25 478
15:27 68
15:28 258
15:29 1
15:42 284, 308
15:42–44 315
15:45 308, 315
15:47 308, 309
15:49 85, 86
15:50 125, 463
15:50–53 93
15:50–54 185
15:51 118
15:51–54 104

15:51–55 470, 471, 503, 505
15:53 284
15:54–55 93
16:22 304, 466

2 Corinthians
1:2 40
1:2–3 26
1:3 14, 27, 286
1:14 492
1:19 234
1:21–22 314
2:6–8 389
2:15 371
3:2–3 428
3:3 301, 323
3:5–6 174, 428
3:12–16 428
3:13–14 174
3:17 298
3:18 86
4:8–12 375
4:14 53, 129
5:4–5 315, 399
5:10 387, 469, 494
5:21 184
5:14 183
5:16 93
5:17 185, 352, 373, 398, 416, 432, 471
5:20–6:1 384
5:21 384
6:13 397
6:16 299, 488
6:18 15, 23
6:16–18 408
7:10–11 389
11:2–3 438
11:3 180
11:13–15 192
11:14 201
11:31 14, 27
12:8–9 304
12:21 355
13:4 38, 53
13:7 185
13:14 320

Galatians
1:3 16
1:3–4 26
1:4 75, 183
1:15–16 27, 41
1:23 338
2:7 417
2:9 407
2:12 434
2:13 434
2:16 345, 386, 428
2:20 184, 238, 345
3:2 428
3:3 313
3:5 297, 428
3:8 173, 386
3:10 173, 181–182, 428
3:13 173, 371, 428
3:14 173
3:16 228
3:19–20 25
3:22 345
3:23–25 429
3:24 386
3:26 397, 429
3:27 359
3:27–29 416
3:28 394
3:29 374, 398, 441, 464
4:4 27, 228, 267
4:6 28, 60, 300, 308, 319, 324
4:6–7 313, 398
4:7 465
4:9–10 432

536

4:9–11 431
4:24–25 441
4:24–28 441, 442
4:26 441
5:2 430
5:5 325
5:14 327, 435
5:16 301, 324, 399
5:18 301, 324, 327, 399
5:19–21 328
5:21 463
5:22 327
5:22–23 318, 324, 328, 347, 365, 399
5:24 325
5:25 321, 325, 365
6:1 325, 389
6:2 433
6:8 136
6:15 61, 352, 373, 398, 416, 430, 432, 471
6:15–16 400

Ephesians
1:3 27
1:7 41, 371
1:11 374
1:13 357
1:13–14 315, 374
1:17 14, 286
1:17–20 28
1:20 285
1:20–21 127
1:20–23 479
1:22 287
2:1 182
2:4–6 479, 500
2:5 41, 182, 479
2:5–6 376
2:6 365, 366
2:8 41, 370
2:10 479
2:11 417
2:13–16 434
2:14 93
2:15 373
2:18 319, 320
2:19 319
2:21–22 408
2:22 299
3:12 345
3:16 297
3:16–17 309
4:5 360
4:6 27, 38
4:13 235
4:18 183
4:22–24 86
4:23–24 184
4:30 301, 315, 371
5:1 398
5:2 435
5:5 463
5:8–9 324
5:9 399
5:14 119
5:25 435
5:25–27 439
6:9 387
6:11–12 194
6:12 200
6:18–19 317

Philippians
1:2 26
1:6 469, 492
1:10 324, 492
1:11 325, 382, 399
1:18 339
1:19 310
1:27 357
1:28 135
2:1 320
2:5 249

2:7 249
2:8 249, 282, 345
2:9 249, 256, 287, 309
2:11 10
2:16 492
2:17 409
3:2 430
3:3 319
3:4–8 433
3:9 345
3:11 492
3:12 492
3:18–19 135
3:20–21 129
4:18 409

Colossians
1:5 357
1:13 499
1:13–14 478
1:14 184, 316
1:15 35, 267
1:15–20 267, 305
1:16 267
1:17 287
1:18 128, 287, 347
1:22–23 365
2:2–3 267
2:5–6 345
2:11–12 430
2:11–14 417
2:12 359, 364
2:12–13 376
2:13 183
2:15 499
2:16–17 431, 432
3:1 286
3:1–2 364
3:3 183
3:4 469
3:5 185, 364
3:9–10 86, 184
3:10 23, 80
3:23 319
3:23–25 387
3:24–25 494

1 Thessalonians
1:1–3 26
1:5 297, 317
1:6 325
1:9-10 16, 28
1:10 128
2:4 36
2:7 397
2:11 397
2:19–20 492
3:13 504
4:13 117
4:13–16 129
4:14 117
4:15 117
4:16 104, 117, 484
4:16–17 472
4:17 1, 117, 472
5:2 469, 486, 492
5:3 138
5:4 486, 492
5:6 489
5:9 370
5:10 117, 183
5:15 185
5:19–20 325
5:23 14, 19
5:23–24 46

2 Thessalonians
1:6–8 260, 387
1:7 485
1:7–8 484, 504
1:7–10 139, 350
1:9–10 492
2:1–2 488, 492
2:3–4 488

2:8 484, 488
2:9 488
2:9–10 192
3:6 388
3:10 389
3:14 388

1 Timothy
1:17 22, 31, 35, 37, 67
1:19–20 388
2:5 303, 309, 384
2:5–6 282
3:11 190
4:1 301
5:1–2 397
5:3–5 49
5:9 1
6:3 185
6:11 347
6:13–14 469
6:14 484
6:15 67
6:16 31, 35, 37

2 Timothy
1:7 297, 325
1:9 41, 370
1:12 492
1:18 492
2:8 229, 338
2:11 129
2:12 365, 465
2:13 347
3:3 190
4:1 469, 484, 494
4:8 484, 492
4:14 387

Titus
1:2 31
1:10 417
2:3 190
3:5 323, 360, 366, 374, 399
3:7 41, 372
3:10–11 388

Philemon
1:3 26

Hebrews
1:2 257
1:3 28, 261, 286, 287
1:4 257
1:8–9 257
1:9 14
1:13 28
1:13–14 203
2:3 176
2:4 297, 317
2:6–8 68
2:8 287
2:14–15 499
2:17 287
3:1 252, 350
3:1–2 176
3:6 176, 365
3:14 366
4:15 287
5:2 38
5:7 93
5:8 351
5:9 176
6:1 355
6:1–2 360
6:2 128
6:5 126, 134, 317, 398, 478
6:18 31
6:20 407
7:14 229, 286, 288
7:16 285, 288
7:18–22 175
7:24 285, 288

7:24–25 126
7:27 288
7:28 288
8:1 28, 286
8:6 175, 384
8:13 175
9:15 175–176, 384
9:28 370, 469
10:10 176
10:12 28, 261, 286
10:17–18 176
10:22 360
10:23 46
10:25 492
10:26–27 137, 366, 389
10:27 52
10:29 301
10:30 301
10:39 96
11:3 30
11:4 350
11:7 350
11:8 350
11:31 350
11:39–40 472
12:1–2 176
12:2 261, 286, 350
12:7 16
12:18 441, 442
12:22–24 441
12:24 175, 384, 442
12:26–28 503
12:28 442, 478
13:5 20
13:15 305, 409
13:16 409

James
1:1 401
1:2–3 348
1:7 348
1:11 135
1:13 20, 31, 34
1:17 16, 34
1:21 177
1:27 49
2:5 177, 466
2:8 435
2:13 52
2:14 351
2:17 177
2:19 25, 199
2:21 351
2:24 351, 372, 387
2:25 351
2:26 91
3:9–10 85
4:5 36
4:7 193
5:7 469
5:9 348
5:12 177
5:17 502
5:20 96

1 Peter
1:2 177, 276
1:3 14, 26, 27, 107, 128, 286, 373
1:5 370
1:7 485
1:9 177
1:10–11 310
1:12 300
1:13 485
1:17 16, 48, 387
1:18–20 275
1:20 276
1:23 373
1:23–25 93
2:5 401, 402, 408, 409
2:9 401, 402, 409
2:10 401
2:12 409, 492

2:21–25 249
2:23 47
3:12 35
3:20–21 418
3:21 360, 370
3:22 286
4:5 494
4:8 318
4:10 318
4:13 485
4:17 52
4:17–18 387
4:19 46
5:4 469
5:10 20

2 Peter
1:8–9 177
1:10–11 466
2:4 202–204
2:5–7 203
2:9 387, 493
2:12 138
3:4 119, 472, 486, 493, 505
3:4–13 505, 506
3:7 135, 137
3:9 33, 36, 355
3:10 472, 486, 493, 505
3:13 472, 493, 506
3:18 41, 493

1 John
2:1–2 177
2:3–6 177
2:13 499
2:14 499
3:1 16, 398
3:2 484
3:2–3 469
3:8 193
3:9 373
3:12 193
3:16 96
3:20 32
3:21–23 28
3:24 298
4:7 373
4:10 28
4:12–13 298
4:17 492
5:9 28
5:10 28
5:11 28
5:19 193
5:20 28

2 John
1:3 16, 26

Jude
1:1 26
1:5 135
1:6 204, 492
1:6–7 202
1:7 138
1:9 59, 194, 201
1:12 421
1:14–15 52, 387, 494
1:20 320
1:21 377
1:25 20, 287, 320

Revelation
1:1 486, 501
1:1–2 339
1:4 34, 59, 203
1:5 107, 177, 287, 339, 500
1:6 14, 16, 409, 465, 480, 500
1:7 484
1:9 339, 500
1:8 23, 37

1:9 480
1:12–13 410
1:18 103, 126, 285
1:20 411
2:5 355, 363
2:7 301, 444
2:8 348
2:10 194, 348, 410, 480
2:11 301
2:13 339
2:14–16 355, 363
2:17 301
2:21–22 355, 363
2:23 387
2:29 301
3:2 14
3:3 355, 363, 486
3:4–5 480
3:5 410
3:6 301
3:11 410
3:12 14, 443, 445
3:13 301
3:14 339
3:19 355, 363
3:20 422
3:21 410, 480
3:22 301
4:1–3 307
4:4 480, 500
4:8 59
4:8–9 37
4:8–11 23, 305
4:10 37
4:11 31, 276
5:5 230, 443
5:6 410, 443, 501
5:6–7 307
5:8 410
5:9 410
5:9–10 465
5:9–12 305
5:10 204, 409, 480, 500
5:13 305
6:8 103
6:9 340
6:9–11 410
6:11 119
6:17 492
7:4–8 501, 502
7:9 492, 502
7:10 305
7:12 305
7:14 178, 493
8:3–4 410
9:20 200
10:6 37
11:3 339
11:7 339
11:8–11 91
11:15 481, 505
11:17 23
11:18 138, 494, 505
12:1–5 230
12:5 481
12:7 481
12:7–8 59, 203
12:8–9 204
12:9 194, 204
12:9–10 499
12:10 481, 500
12:11 96, 481, 499
13:8 177, 276
13:10 348
14:9–11 139
14:11 139, 140
14:12 345
14:13 119
15:2–3 481
15:3 23, 67
15:4 21
15:7 37
16:5–7 381
16:7 23

16:14 200
16:14–16 503
16:15 486
17:1–3 442, 444
17:1–19:10 496
17:6 339
17:8 135
17:9 443
17:18 442, 444
18:2 200
19:1 11
19:1–7 305
19:2 381
19:3 11
19:4 11
19:6 11, 23
19:6–9 440, 443
19:11–21 503
19:15 23
19:19 503
19:20 137
20:1 499
20:1–3 498
20:1–15 497, 498
20:2 194, 499
20:4 340, 500, 501
20:4–6 500
20:5 500
20:7–8 500
20:7–15 502
20:8 503
20:9 504
20:10 137, 139, 140, 204
20:11–13 387
20:11–15 52
20:12 504, 505
20:13 48, 103
20:14 103, 137, 140, 204
20:15 137, 140, 505
21:1 472, 505
21:2 444, 445, 502
21:3 20
21:4 471
21:5 472
21:7 473
21:8 137, 140
21:9 443, 445
21:9–10 442, 502
21:9–22:9 496
21:10 443
21:12–14 501
21:25 444
21:27 444
22:2 444
22:5 465, 480
22:12 387, 469, 494
22:14 444, 445
22:16 231
22:17 301

www.ingramcontent.com/pod-product-compliance
Lightning Source LLC
Chambersburg PA
CBHW060102170426
43198CB00010B/739